W9-DAS-050

THE
NEW
AMERICAN
NATION
1775–1820

*A Twelve-Volume
Collection of Articles
on the Development
of the Early American
Republic*

Edited by

PETER S. ONUF
UNIVERSITY OF VIRGINIA

A GARLAND SERIES

THE NEW AMERICAN NATION
1775–1820

Volume

2

★

PATRIOTS, REDCOATS, AND LOYALISTS

Edited with an
Introduction by

PETER S. ONUF

GARLAND PUBLISHING, INC.
NEW YORK & LONDON
1991

Introduction © 1991 by Peter S. Onuf

Library of Congress Cataloging-in-Publication Data

Patriots, redcoats, and loyalists / edited with an introduction by Peter S. Onuf.
    p.   cm. — (New American nation, 1776–1815 ; v. 2)
    Includes bibliographical references.
    ISBN 0-8153-0437-4 (alk. paper) : $49.99
    1. United States—History—Revolution, 1775–1783. I. Onuf, Peter S. II. Series.
    E. 164.N45   1991 vol. 2
    [E208]
    973s—dc20   91-15282
    [973.3]   CIP

Printed on acid-free, 250-year-life paper.
Manufactured in the United States of America

THE NEW AMERICAN NATION, 1775–1820

EDITOR'S INTRODUCTION

This series includes a representative selection of the most interesting and influential journal articles on revolutionary and early national America. My goal is to introduce readers to the wide range of topics that now engage scholarly attention. The essays in these volumes show that the revolutionary era was an extraordinarily complex "moment" when the broad outlines of national history first emerged. Yet if the "common cause" brought Americans together, it also drove them apart: the Revolution, historians agree, was as much a civil war as a war of national liberation. And, given the distinctive colonial histories of the original members of the American Union, it is not surprising that the war had profoundly different effects in different parts of the country. This series has been designed to reveal the multiplicity of these experiences in a period of radical political and social change.

Most of the essays collected here were first published within the last twenty years. This series therefore does *not* recapitulate the development of the historiography of the Revolution. Many of the questions asked by earlier generations of scholars now seem misconceived and simplistic. Constitutional historians wanted to know if the Patriots had legitimate grounds to revolt: was the Revolution "legal"? Economic historians sought to assess the costs of the navigation system for American farmers and merchants and to identify the interest groups that promoted resistance. Comparative historians wondered how "revolutionary" the Revolution really was. By and large, the best recent work has ignored these classic questions. Contemporary scholarship instead draws its inspiration from other sources, most notable of which is the far-ranging reconception and reconstruction of prerevolutionary America by a brilliant generation of colonial historians.

Bernard Bailyn's *Ideological Origins of the American Revolution* (1967) was a landmark in the new historical writing on colonial politics. As his title suggests, Bailyn was less interested in constitutional and legal arguments as such than in the "ideology" or political language that shaped colonists' perception of and responses to British imperial policy. Bailyn's great contribution was to focus attention on colonial political culture; disciples and critics alike followed his lead as they explored the impact—and limits—of "republicanism" in specific colonial settings. Meanwhile, the social historians who had played a leading role in the transformation of colonial historiography were extending their work into the late colonial period and were increasingly interested in the questions of value, meaning, and behavior that were raised by the new political history. The resulting convergence points to some of the unifying themes in recent work on the revolutionary period presented in this series.

A thorough grounding in the new scholarship on colonial British America is the best introduction to the history and historiography of the Revolution. These volumes therefore can be seen as a complement and extension of Peter Charles Hoffer's eighteen-volume set, *Early American History*, published by Garland in 1987. Hoffer's collection includes numerous important essays essential for understanding developments in independent America. Indeed, only a generation ago—when the Revolution generally was defined in terms of its colonial origins—it would have been hard to justify a separate series on the "new American nation." But exciting recent work—for instance, on wartime mobilization and social change, or on the Americanization of republican ideology during the great era of state making and constitution writing—has opened up new vistas. Historians now generally agree that the revolutionary period saw far-reaching and profound changes, that is, a "great transformation," toward a more recognizably modern America. If the connections between this transformation and the actual unfolding of events often remain elusive, the historiographical quest for the larger meaning of the war and its aftermath has yielded impressive results.

To an important extent, the revitalization of scholarship on revolutionary and early national America is a tribute to the efforts and expertise of scholars working in other professional disciplines. Students of early American literature have made key contributions to the history of rhetoric, ideology, and culture; political scientists and legal scholars have brought new clarity and sophistication to the study of political and constitutional thought and practice in the founding period. Kermit L. Hall's superb Garland series, *United States Constitutional and Legal History* (20 volumes, 1985), is another fine resource for students and scholars interested in the founding. The sampling of recent work in various disciplines offered in these volumes gives a sense of the interpretative possibilities of a crucial period in American history that is now getting the kind of attention it has long deserved.

Peter S. Onuf

INTRODUCTION

Recent work on the impact of the war on society has provided a new and illuminating context for the study of military history. John Shy, the leading exponent of the new military history, has shown that the Patriot militia played a crucial political role during the war, despite their notorious shortcomings in battle. Local mobilization efforts brought the war home to ordinary Americans, forcing them to make their own declarations of independence—or of continuing fealty to King George III.

The ideal of the citizen-soldier encouraged widespread popular participation in the war effort. It also, however, raised fundamental questions about the status of a professional army in republican society. A profound ambivalence about "standing armies," which republican ideologues saw as the instruments of despotic power, guaranteed that the Continental Army would never adequately be supported and that the national war effort always would be at risk. Building on Richard H. Kohn's seminal work on civil–military relations (*The Eagle and the Sword*, 1975), recent historians have explored the implications of this fundamental problem for the Revolutionary War years. Charles Royster's *A Revolutionary People at War* (1979) is the leading study both of popular attitudes toward the Continental Army and of the development of a professional ethos in the army itself; in *To Starve the Army at Pleasure*, Wayne Carp provides an excellent account of Congress's chronic failure to support the war effort.

The great strength of the new war-and-society studies is that they emphasize the importance of popular attitudes as well as practical problems of support and supply. The question of loyalties merges with the study of ideological transformation that now dominates the historiography on the origins of the war. The new military history also promises to illuminate the limits of revolutionary mobilization. Many of the essays in this volume examine the broader struggle for the hearts and minds of the American people, which helped determine the outcome of the military conflict.

John Adams estimated that one-third of the population was Patriot, another third, Loyalist, and the remainder, neutral. Early Loyalist historiography revolved around the question of numbers: the consensus is that Adams exaggerated Loyalist strength. Recently, however, writers have emphasized the contingency of loyalties and therefore the futility of counting heads. The persuasiveness of Patriot appeals depended on rapidly changing circumstances, most notably on the success of grass-roots mobilization and the location of the opposing armies. Loyalists, as William Nelson showed in his elegant short study *The American Tory*, were often located at the margins of colonial society or in elite groups with powerful ties to the motherland. But these margins were by no means fixed, and no simple formula can explain the distribution of support or opposition to the Patriot cause.

British policymakers and commanders sought military victory in order to prepare the way for postwar reconstruction and the reestablishment of civil authority. They generally understood that the exercise of unlimited force—the total devastation of the American countryside—would have subverted these war aims. But the imperatives of conducting a limited war, and badly exaggerated assessments of the extent of popular royalism, virtually guaranteed British failure. There are many useful survey histories of the war, notably Piers Mackesy's *War for America* (1964), which delineate the strategic and political constraints of making war. Works by Ira Gruber and Paul Smith offer particularly valuable accounts of the ultimately disastrous confusion of political goals and military means in the British war effort.

The essays in this volume provide a series of case studies on the contest for loyalties and the conduct of the war. They remind us of the importance of individual choices for the history of great public events. The political and ideological transformations that figure so centrally in our understanding of the Revolutionary era only took effect when individual Americans acted on them—or resisted their implications. Certainly, as studies of mobilization make clear, the contexts of social and political action are crucially important: it is in these contexts that the deeper and compelling logic of Patriot—or Loyalist—appeals becomes manifest. But principled commitments, such as those of many common soldiers held as prisoners by the British, as well as the failure of "sunshine patriots" to live up to their own rhetoric, cannot simply or finally be explained by the calculus of interest or of force.

Peter S. Onuf

ADDITIONAL READING

E. Wayne Carp. *To Starve the Army at Pleasure: Continental Army Administration and American Political Culture, 1775-1783*. Chapel Hill: University of North Carolina Press, 1984.

Robert M. Calhoon. *The Loyalist Perception and Other Essays.* Columbia: University of South Carolina Press, 1989.

Ira D. Gruber. *The Howe Brothers and the American Revolution.* New York: Atheneum, 1972.

Don Higginbotham. *War and Society in Revolutionary America: The Wider Dimension of Conflict.* Columbia: University of South Carolina Press, 1988.

Richard H. Kohn. *The Eagle and the Sword: The Federalists and the Creation of the Military Establishment in America, 1783–1802.* New York: Free Press, 1975.

Piers Mackesy. *The War for America, 1775–1783.* Cambridge: Harvard University Press, 1964.

William H. Nelson. *The American Tory.* Oxford: Clarendon Press, 1961.

Charles Royster. *A Revolutionary People at War: The Continental Army and the American Character, 1775-1783.* Chapel Hill: University of North Carolina Press, 1979.

John Shy. *A People Numerous and Armed: Reflections on the Military Struggle for American Independence.* New York: Oxford University Press, 1976.

———. *Toward Lexington: The Role of the British Army in the Coming of the American Revolution.* Princeton, NJ: Princeton University Press, 1965.

Paul H. Smith. *Loyalists and Redcoats: A Study in British Revolutionary Policy.* Chapel Hill: University of North Carolina Press, 1964.

CONTENTS

Volume 2—Patriots, Redcoats, and Loyalists

Heard Robertson, "The Second British Occupation of Augusta, 1780–1781," *Georgia Historical Quarterly*, 1974, 58:422–446.

Charles Royster, "'The Nature of Treason': Revolutionary Virtue and American Reactions to Benedict Arnold," *William and Mary Quarterly*, 1979, 36(2) (Third Series)163–193.

Henry J. Young, "Treason and its Punishment in Revolutionary Pennsylvania," *Pennsylvania Magazine of History and Biography*, 1966, 90(3):287–313.

James Donald Anderson, "Thomas Wharton, Exile in Virginia, 1777–1778," *Virginia Magazine of History and Biography*, 1981, 89(4):425–447.

Jacob E. Cooke, "Tench Coxe: Tory Merchant," *Pennsylvania Magazine of History and Biography*, 1972, 96(1):48–88.

Edward H. Tebbenhoff, "The Associated Loyalists: An Aspect of Militant Loyalism," *New York Historical Society Quarterly*, 1979, 63(2):115–144.

Joseph J. Casino, "Elizabethtown 1782: The Prisoner-of-War Negotiations and the Pawns of War," *New Jersey History*, 1984, 102(1–2):1–35.

Robert Ernst, "A Tory-eye View of the Evacuation of New York," *New York History*, 1983, 64(4):376–394.

ACKNOWLEDGMENTS

Volume 2—Patriots, Redcoats, and Loyalists

Robert Middlekauff, "Why Men Fought in the American Revolution," *Huntington Library Quarterly*, 1980, 43(2):135–148. Reprinted with the permission of the Huntington Library. Courtesy of Yale University Sterling Memorial Library.

John E. Ferling, "'Oh That I Was A Soldier': John Adams and the Anguish of War," *American Quarterly*, 1984, 36(2):258–275. Reprinted with the permission of the author, and the American Studies Association as publisher. Courtesy of Yale University Sterling Memorial Library.

Jesse Lemisch, "LISTENING TO THE 'INARTICULATE': William Widger's Dream and the Loyalties of American Revolutionary Seamen in British Prisons," *Journal of Social History,* 1969, 3(1):1–29. Reprinted with the permission of the Carnegie Mellon University. Courtesy of Yale University Sterling Memorial Library.

John K. Alexander, "Forton Prison During the American Revolution: A Case Study of British Prisoner of War Policy and the American Prisoner Response to That Policy," *Essex Institute Historical Collections*, 1967, 103(4): 365–389. Reprinted with the permission of the Essex Institute, Salem, Massachusetts. Courtesy of the Essex Institute.

Piers Mackesy, "British Strategy in the War of American Independence," *Yale Review*, 1963, 52(4):539–557. First published in the *Yale Review*, copyright Yale University. Courtesy of the *Yale Review.*

William B. Willcox, "British Strategy in America, 1778," *Journal of Modern History*, 1947, 19(2):97–121. Reprinted with the permission of the University of Chicago Press. Courtesy of Yale University Sterling Memorial University.

Stephen Conway, "To Subdue America: British Army Officers and the Conduct of the Revolutionary War," *William and Mary Quarterly*, 1986, 43(3) (Third Series):381–407. Originally appeared in the *William and Mary Quarterly*. Courtesy of Yale University Sterling Memorial Library.

Neil L. York, "Pennsylvania Rifle: Revolutionary Weapon in A Conventional War?" *Pennsylvania Magazine of History and Biography,* 1979, 103(3):302–324. Reprinted with the permission of the Historical Society of Pennsylvania. Courtesy of Yale University Sterling Memorial Library.

Ira D. Gruber, "Lord Howe and Lord George Germain: British Politics and the Winning of American Independence," *William and Mary Quarterly*, 1965, 22(2) (Third Series):225–243. Originally appeared in the *William and Mary Quarterly*. Courtesy of Yale University Sterling Memorial Library.

William L. Calderhead, "British Naval Failure at Long Island: A Lost Opportunity in the American Revolution," *New York History*, 1976, 57:321–338. Reprinted with the permission of the New York State Historical Association. Courtesy of Yale University Sterling Memorial Library.

Paul David Nelson, "Guy Carleton versus Benedict Arnold: The Campaign of 1776 in Canada and on Lake Champlain," *New York History*, 1976, 57:339–366. Reprinted with the permission of the New York State Historical Association. Courtesy of Yale University Sterling Memorial Library.

Hugh F. Rankin, "Cowpens: Prelude to Yorktown," *North Carolina Historical Review*, 1954, 31:336–369. Reprinted with the permission of the *North Carolina Historical Review*. Courtesy of the *North Carolina Historical Review*.

Heard Robertson, "The Second British Occupation of Augusta, 1780–1781," *Georgia Historical Quarterly*, 1974, 58:422–446. Reprinted with the permission of the Georgia Historical Society. Courtesy of the *Georgia Historical Quarterly*.

Charles Royster, "'The Nature of Treason': Revolutionary Virtue and American Reactions to Benedict Arnold," *William and Mary Quarterly*, 1979, 36(2) (Third Series):163–193. Originally appeared in the *William and Mary Quarterly*. Courtesy of Yale University Sterling Memorial Library.

Henry J. Young, "Treason and its Punishment in Revolutionary Pennsylvania," *Pennsylvania Magazine of History and Biography*, 1966, 90(3):287–313. Reprinted with the permission of the Historical Society of Pennsylvania. Courtesy of Yale University Sterling Memorial Library.

James Donald Anderson, "Thomas Wharton, Exile in Virginia, 1777–1778," *Virginia Magazine of History and Biography*, 1981, 89(4):425–447. Reprinted with the permission of the Virginia Historical Society. Courtesy of Yale University Sterling Memorial Library.

Jacob E. Cooke, "Tench Coxe: Tory Merchant," *Pennsylvania Magazine of History and Biography*, 1972, 96(1):48–88. Reprinted with the permission of the Historical Society of Pennsylvania. Courtesy of Yale University Sterling Memorial Library.

Edward H. Tebbenhoff, "The Associated Loyalists: An Aspect of Militant Loyalism," *New York Historical Society Quarterly*, 1979, 63(2):115–144. Reprinted with the permission of the New York Historical Society. Courtesy of Yale University Sterling Memorial Library.

Joseph J. Casino, "Elizabethtown 1782: The Prisoner-of-War Negotiations and the Pawns of War," *New Jersey History*, 1984, 102(1-2):1–35. Reprinted with the permission of the New Jersey Historical Society. Courtesy of Yale University Sterling Memorial Library.

Robert Ernst, "A Tory-eye View of the Evacuation of New York," *New York History*, 1983, 64(4):376–394. Reprinted with the permission of the New York State Historical Association. Courtesy of Yale University Sterling Memorial Library.

Why Men Fought in the American Revolution

By ROBERT MIDDLEKAUFF

IN THE BATTLE OF EUTAW SPRINGS, South Carolina, the last major action of the Revolutionary War before Cornwallis surrendered at Yorktown, over 500 Americans were killed and wounded. Nathanael Greene had led some 2200 men into the Springs; his casualties thus equaled almost one fourth of his army. More men would die in battles in the next two years, and others would suffer terrible wounds. Although the statistics are notoriously unreliable, they show that the Revolution killed a higher percentage of those who served on the American side than any war in our history, always excepting the Civil War.[1]

Why did these men—those who survived and those who died—fight? Why did they hold their ground, endure the strain of battle, with men dying about them and danger to themselves so obvious? Undoubtedly the reasons varied from battle to battle, but just as undoubtedly there was some experience common to all these battles—and fairly uniform reasons for the actions of the men who fought despite their deepest impulses, which must have been to run from the field in order to escape the danger.

Some men did run, throwing down their muskets and packs in order to speed their flight. American units broke in large actions and small, at Brooklyn, Kip's Bay, White Plains, Brandywine, Germantown, Camden, and Hobkirk's Hill, to cite the most important instances. Yet many men did not break and run even in the disasters to American arms. They held their ground until they were killed, and they fought tenaciously while pulling back.

In most actions the Continentals, the regulars, fought more bravely than the militia. We need to know why these men fought and why the American regulars performed better than the militia. The answers surely will help us to understand the Revolution, especially if we can discover whether what made men fight reflected what they believed—and felt—about the Revolution.

Several explanations of the willingness to fight and die, if necessary, may be dismissed at once. One is that soldiers on both sides fought out of fear of their officers, fearing them more than they did battle. Frederick the Great had described this condition as ideal, but it did not exist in ideal or

---

[1] *The Toll of Independence: Engagements and Battle Casualties of the American Revolution,* ed. Howard H. Peckham (Chicago, 1974), p. 90 for Eutaw Springs, pp. 132-133 for the comparison of the Revolution and the Civil War.

1

practice in either the American or British army. The British soldier usually possessed a more professional spirit than the American, an attitude compounded from confidence in his skill and pride in belonging to an old established institution. British regiments carried proud names— the Royal Welsh Fusiliers, the Black Watch, the King's Own—whose officers usually behaved extraordinarily bravely in battle and expected their men to follow their examples. British officers disciplined their men more harshly than American officers did and generally trained them more effectively in the movements of battle. But neither they nor American officers instilled the fear that Frederick found so desirable. Spirit, bravery, a reliance on the bayonet were all expected of professional soldiers, but professionals acted out of pride—not fear of their officers.

Still, coercion and force were never absent from the life of either army. There were, however, limits on their use and their effectiveness. The fear of flogging might prevent a soldier from deserting from camp, but it could not guarantee that he would remain steady under fire. Fear of ridicule may have aided in keeping some troops in place, however. Eighteenth-century infantry went into combat in fairly close lines and officers could keep an eye on many of their men. If the formation was tight enough officers might strike laggards and even order "skulkers," Washington's term for those who turned tail, shot down.[2] Just before the move to Dorchester Heights in March 1776, the word went out that any American who ran from the action would be "fired down upon the spot."[3] The troops themselves approved of this threat, according to one of the chaplains.

Washington repeated the threat just before the Battle of Brooklyn later that year, though he seems not to have posted men behind the lines to carry it out. Daniel Morgan urged Nathanael Greene to place sharp-shooters behind the militia, and Greene may have done so at Guilford Court House. No one thought that an entire army could be held in place against its will, and these threats to shoot soldiers who retired without orders were never widely issued.[4]

A tactic that surely would have appealed to many soldiers would have been to send them into battle drunk. Undoubtedly some—on both sides— did enter combat with their senses deadened by rum. Both armies commonly issued an additional ration of rum on the eve of some extraordinary action—a long, difficult march, for example, or a battle, were

[2] *The Writings of George Washington*, ed. John C. Fitzpatrick (Washington, D.C., 1931-44), V, 480.

[3] Jeanette D. Black and William G. Roelker, *A Rhode Island Chaplain in the Revolution: Letters of Ebenezer David to Nicholas Brown, 1775-1778* (Providence, R.I., 1949), p. 13.

[4] *Writings of Washington*, V, 479-480; Christopher Ward, *The War of the Revolution* (New York, 1952), II, 786.

two of the usual reasons. A common order on such occasions ran: "The troops should have an extraordinary allowance of rum," usually a gill, four ounces of unknown alcoholic content, which if taken down at the propitious moment might dull fears and summon courage. At Camden no supply of rum existed; Gates or his staff substituted molasses to no good effect, according to Otho Williams. The British fought brilliantly at Guilford Court House unaided by anything stronger than their own large spirits. In most actions soldiers went into battle with very little more than themselves and their comrades to lean upon.[5]

Belief in the Holy Spirit surely sustained some in the American army, perhaps more than in the enemy's. There are a good many references to the divine or to Providence in the letters and diaries of ordinary soldiers. Often, however, these expressions are in the form of thanks to the Lord for permitting these soldiers to survive. There is little that suggests soldiers believed that faith rendered them invulnerable to the enemy's bullets. Many did consider the glorious cause to be sacred; their war, as the ministers who sent them off to kill never tired of reminding them, was just and providential.[6]

Others clearly saw more immediate advantages in the fight: the plunder of the enemy's dead. At Monmouth Court House, where Clinton withdrew after dark leaving the field strewn with British corpses, the plundering carried American soldiers into the houses of civilians who had fled to save themselves. The soldiers' actions were so blatant and so unrestrained that Washington ordered their packs searched. And at Eutaw Springs, the Americans virtually gave up victory to the opportunity of ransacking British tents. Some died in their greed, shot down by an enemy given time to regroup while his camp was torn apart by men looking for something to carry off. But even these men probably fought for something besides plunder. When it beckoned they collapsed, but it had not drawn them to the field; nor had it kept them there in a savage struggle.[7]

Inspired leadership helped soldiers face death, but they sometimes fought bravely even when their leaders let them down. Yet officers' courage and the example of officers throwing off wounds to remain in the fight undoubtedly helped their men stick. Charles Stedman remarked on Captain Maitland, who at Guilford Court House was hit, dropped behind

[5]Otho Williams, "A Narrative of the Campaign of 1780," in William Johnson, *Sketches of the Life and Correspondence of Nathanael Greene* (Charleston, S.C., 1822), I, 494; "A British Orderly Book, 1780-1781," ed. A. R. Newsome, *North Carolina Historical Review*, 9 (1932), 289.

[6]For typical references to Providence see Herbert T. Wade and Robert A. Lively, *This Glorious Cause: The Adventures of Two Company Officers in Washington's Army* (Princeton, N.J., 1958).

[7]Orderly Book, June 12-July 13, 1778, Benjamin Fishbourne et al., Huntington Library MS BR96.

3

for a few minutes to get his wound dressed, then returned to the battle.[8] Cornwallis obviously filled Sergeant Lamb with pride, struggling forward to press into the struggle after his horse was killed.[9] Washington's presence meant much at Princeton, though his exposure to enemy fire may also have made his troops uneasy. His quiet exhortation as he passed among the men who were about to assault Trenton—"Soldiers, keep by your officers"—remained in the mind of a Connecticut soldier until he died fifty years later.[10] There was only one Washington, one Cornwallis, and their influence on men in battle, few of whom could have seen them, was of course slight. Junior and noncommissioned officers carried the burden of tactical direction; they had to show their troops what must be done and somehow persuade, cajole, or force them to do it. The praise ordinary soldiers lavished on sergeants and junior officers suggests that these leaders played important parts in their troops' willingness to fight. Still, important as it was, their part does not really explain why men fought.

In suggesting this conclusion about military leadership, I do not wish to be understood as agreeing with Tolstoy's scornful verdict on generals—that despite all their plans and orders they do not affect the results of battles at all. Tolstoy did not reserve all his scorn for generals—historians are also derided in *War and Peace* for finding a rational order in battles where only chaos existed. "The activity of a commander in chief does not at all resemble the activity we imagine to ourselves when we sit at ease in our studies examing some campaign on the map, with a certain number of troops on this and that side in a certain known locality, and begin our plans from some given moment. A commander in chief is never dealing with the beginning of any event—the position from which we always contemplate it. The commander in chief is always in the midst of a series of shifting events and so he never can at any moment consider the whole import of an event that is occurring."[11]

The full import of battle will as surely escape historians as participants. But we have to begin somewhere in trying to explain why men fought rather than ran from revolutionary battlefields. The battlefield may indeed be the place to begin, since we have dismissed leadership, fear of officers, religious belief, the power of drink, and other possible explanations of why men fought and died.

[8]Charles Stedman, *The History of the Origin, Progress, and Termination of the American War* (Dublin, 1794), II, 38.

[9]Roger Lamb, *An Original and Authentic Journal of Occurrences during the Late American War* (Dublin, 1809), p. 362.

[10]William S. Powell, "A Connecticut Soldier under Washington: Elisha Bostwick's Memoirs of the First Years of the Revolution," *William and Mary Quarterly* (hereafter *WMQ*), 3rd Ser., 6 (1949), 102.

[11]*War and Peace*. Bk. XI, Ch. ii.

ENGRAVING BY G. C. FINDEN AFTER A. CHAPPEL SHOWING WASHINGTON IN EXPOSED POSITION URGING ON HIS TROOPS AT PRINCETON, FROM EXTRA-ILLUSTRATED EDITION OF LOSSING'S *PICTORIAL FIELD-BOOK OF THE AMERICAN REVOLUTION.*

The eighteenth-century battlefield was, compared to that of the twentieth, an intimate theater, especially intimate in the engagements of the Revolution, which were usually small even by the standards of the day. The killing range of the musket—eighty to one hundred yards—enforced intimacy, as did the reliance on the bayonet and the general ineffectiveness of artillery. Soldiers had to come to close quarters to kill; this fact reduced the mystery of battle, though perhaps not its terrors. But at least the battlefield lost some of its impersonality. In fact, in contrast to twentieth-century combat, in which the enemy usually remains unseen and the source of incoming fire unknown, in eighteenth-century battles the foe could be seen and sometimes even touched. Seeing one's enemy may have aroused a singular intensity of feeling uncommon in modern battles. The assault with the bayonet—the most desired objective of infantry tactics—seems indeed to have evoked an emotional climax. Before it occurred tension and anxiety built up as the troops marched from their column into a line of attack. The purpose of their movements was well understood by themselves and their enemies, who must have watched with feelings of dread and fascination. When the order came sending them forward, rage, even madness, replaced the attacker's anxiety, while terror and desperation sometimes filled those receiving the charge.[12] Surely it is revealing that the Americans who ran from battle did so most often at the moment they understood that their enemy had started forward with the bayonet. This happened to several units at Brandywine and to the militia at Camden and Guilford Court House. The loneliness, the sense of isolation reported by modern soldiers, was probably missing at such moments. All was clear—especially that glittering line of advancing steel.

Whether this awful clarity was harder to bear than losing sight of the enemy is problematical. American troops ran at Germantown after grappling with the British and then finding the field of battle covered by fog. At that time groping blindly, they and their enemy struggled over ground resembling a scene of modern combat. The enemy was hidden at a critical moment, and American fears were generated by not knowing what was happening—or about to happen. They could not see the enemy, and they could not see one another, an especially important fact. For, as S. L. A. Marshall, the twentieth-century military historian, has suggested in his book *Men against Fire,* what sustains men in the extraordinary circumstances of battle may be their relationships with their comrades.[13]

These men found that sustaining such relationships was possible in the intimacy of the American battlefield—and not just because the limited

---

[12]See Samuel Webb to Silas Deane, Cambridge, July 11, 1775, in Massachusetts Historical Society *Proceedings,* 1875-76 (Boston, 1876), p. 83.

[13]*Men against Fire* (New York, 1947). See especially Ch. x.

140

6

arena robbed battle of some of its mystery. More importantly it permitted the troops to give one another moral or psychological support. The enemy could be seen, but so could one's comrades; they could be seen and communicated with.

Eighteenth-century infantry tactics called for men to move and fire from tight formations which permitted them to talk and to give one another information—and reassurance and comfort. If properly done, marching and firing found infantrymen compressed into files in which their shoulders touched. In battle physical contact with one's comrades on either side must have helped men control their fears. Firing the musket from three compact lines, the English practice, also involved physical contact. The men of the front rank crouched on their right knees; the men of the center rank placed their left feet inside the right feet of the front; the rear rank did the same thing behind the center. This stance was called—in a revealing term—"locking." The very density of this formation sometimes aroused criticism from officers who complained that it led to inaccurate fire. The front rank, conscious of the closeness of the center, might fire too low; the rear rank tended to "throw" its shots into the air, as firing too high was called; only the center rank took careful aim, according to the critics. Whatever the truth of these charges about accuracy of fire, men in these dense formations compiled a fine record of holding their ground. And it is worth noting that the inaccuracy of men in the rear rank bespoke their concern for their fellows in front of them.[14]

British and American soldiers in the Revolution often spoke of fighting with "spirit" and "behaving well" under fire. Sometimes these phrases referred to daring exploits under great danger, but more often they seem to have meant holding together, giving one another support, reforming the lines when they were broken or fell into disorder, disorder such as overtook the Americans at Greenspring, Virginia, early in July 1781 when Cornwallis lured Anthony Wayne into crossing the James with a heavily outnumbered force. Wayne saw his mistake and decided to make the best of it, not by a hasty retreat from the ambush, but by attacking. The odds against the Americans were formidable, but as an ordinary soldier who was there saw it, the inspired conduct of the infantry saved them—"our troops behaved well, fighting with great spirit and bravery. The infantry were oft broke; but just as oft rallied and formed at a word."[15]

14 Eighteenth-century tactics are discussed with discernment by R. R. Palmer in Edward M. Earle, *Makers of Modern Strategy* (Princeton, N.J., 1941); William B. Willcox, *Portrait of a General: Sir Henry Clinton in the War of Independence* (New York, 1964); Franklin and Mary Wickwire, *Cornwallis: The American Adventure* (Boston, 1970). For "locking" and other aspects of firing and marching see Humphrey Bland, *An Abstract of Military Discipline* (Boston, 1747); Edward Harvey, *The Manual Exercise as Ordered by His Majesty in 1764* (Boston, 1774); Timothy Pickering, *An Easy Plan of Discipline for a Militia* (Salem, 1775).

15 *The Diary of Josia Atkins* (New York, 1975), p. 38.

These troops had been spread out when the British surprised them, but they formed as quickly as possible. Here was a test of men's spirits, a test they passed in part because of their disciplined formation. In contrast at Camden, where the militia collapsed as soon as the battle began, an open alignment may have contributed to their fear. Gates placed the Virginians on the far left apparently expecting them to cover more ground than their numbers allowed. At any rate they went into the battle in a single line with at least five feet between each man and the next, a distance which intensified a feeling of isolation in the heat and noise of the firing. And to make such feelings worse, these men were especially exposed, stretched out at one end of the line with no supporters behind them.[16]

Troops in tight lines consciously reassured one another in several ways. British troops usually talked and cheered—"huzzaing" whether standing their ground, running forward, or firing. The Americans may have done less talking and cheering, though there is evidence that they learned to imitate the enemy. Giving a cheer at the end of a successful engagement was standard practice. The British cheered at Lexington and then marched off to be shot down on the road running from Concord. The Americans shouted their joy at Harlem Heights, an understandable action and one which for most of 1776 they rarely had opportunity to perform.[17]

The most deplorable failures to stand and fight usually occurred among the American militia. Yet there were militia companies that performed with great success, remaining whole units under the most deadly volleys. The New England companies at Bunker Hill held out under a fire that veteran British officers compared to the worst they had experienced in Europe. Lord Rawdon remarked on how unusual it was for defenders to stick to their posts even after the assaulting troops had entered the ditch around a redoubt.[18] The New Englanders did it. They also held steady at Princeton—"They were the first who regularly formed" and stood up under the balls "which whistled their thousand different notes around our heads," according to Charles Willson Peale, whose Philadelphia militia also proved their steadiness.[19]

What was different about these companies? Why did they fight when others around them ran? The answer may lie in the relationships among

[16]The *Virginia Gazette*, Sept. 6, 1780, contains an account of the extended disposition on the left. Ward, II, 722-730, provides a fine study of the battle, as does Wickwire, pp. 149-165.

[17]Tench Tilghman to his father, Sept. 19, 1776, in *Memoir of Lieut. Col. Tench Tilghman* (Albany, 1876), p. 139.

[18]Francis Rawdon to the earl of Huntington, June 20, 1775, Hastings Papers, Huntington Library.

[19]Charles Willson Peale Diary, Jan. 3, 1777, Huntington Library.

their men. Men in the New England companies, in the Philadelphia militia, and in the other units that held together, were neighbors. They knew one another; they had something to prove to one another; they had their "honor" to protect. Their active service in the Revolution may have been short, but they had been together in one way or another for a fairly long time—for several years, in most cases. Their companies, after all, had been formed from towns and villages. Some clearly had known one another all their lives.[20]

Elsewhere, especially in the thinly settled southern colonies, companies were usually composed of men—farmers, farmers' sons, farm laborers, artisans, and new immigrants—who did not know one another. They were, to use a term much used in a later war, companies of "stragglers" without common attachments, with almost no knowledge of their fellows. For them, even bunched tightly in line, the battlefield was an empty, lonely place. Absence of personal bonds and their own parochialism, coupled to inadequate training and imperfect discipline, often led to disintegration under fire.[21]

According to conventional wisdom, the nearer the American militia were to home the better they fought, fighting for their homes and no one else's. Proximity to home, however, may have been a distraction which weakened resolve; for the irony of going into battle and perhaps to their deaths when home and safety lay close down the road could not have escaped many. Almost every senior American general commented on the propensity of the militia to desert—and if they were not deserting they seemed perpetually in transit between home and camp, usually without authorization.

Paradoxically, of all the Americans who fought, the militiamen best exemplified in themselves and in their behavior the ideals and purposes of the Revolution. They had enjoyed independence, or at least personal liberty, long before it was proclaimed in the Declaration. They instinctively felt their equality with others and in many places insisted upon demonstrating it by choosing their own officers. Their sense of their liberty permitted, even compelled, them to serve only for short enlistments, to leave camp when they liked, to scorn the orders of others—and especially those orders to fight when they preferred to flee. Their integration into their society drove them to resist military discipline; and their

---

[20] For a fine study of a Massachusetts town and its militia see Robert A. Gross, *The Minutemen and Their World* (New York, 1976); for a general view of the colonial militia, John Shy, "A New Look at the Colonial Militia," *WMQ*, 3rd Ser. 20 (1963), 175-185. is outstanding.

[21] The conclusions in this paragraph were suggested by Edward C. Papenfuse and Gregory A. Stiverson, "General Smallwood's Recruits: The Peacetime Career of the Revolutionary War Private," *WMQ*, 3rd Ser., 30 (1973), 117-132. The Nathanael Greene Papers in the Huntington Library contain materials which tend to confirm these impressions.

9

ethos of personal freedom stimulated hatred of the machine that served as the model for the army. They were not pieces of machine, and they would serve it only reluctantly and skeptically. At their best—at Cowpens, for example—they fought well; at their worst, at Camden, they fought not at all. There they were, as Greene said, "ungovernable."[22] What was lacking in the militia was a set of professional standards, requirements and rules which might regulate their conduct in battle. What was lacking was professional pride. Coming and going to camp as they liked, shooting their guns for the pleasure of the sound, the militia annoyed the Continentals, who soon learned that most of them could not be trusted.

The British regulars were at the opposite pole. They had been pulled out of society, carefully segregated from it, tightly disciplined, and highly trained. Their values were the values of the army, for the most part, no more and no less. The officers, to be sure, were in certain respects very different from the men. They embodied the style and standards of gentlemen who believed in service to their king and who fought for honor and glory.

With these ideals and a mission of service to the king defining their calling, British officers held themselves as aloof as possible from the peculiar horrors of war. Not that they did not fight; they sought combat and danger, but by the conventions which shaped their understanding of battle they insulated themselves as much as possible from the ghastly business of killing and dying. Thus the results of battle might be long lists of dead and wounded, but the results were also "honourable and glorious," as Charles Stedman described Guilford Court House, or reflected "dishonour upon British arms," as he described Cowpens. Actions and gunfire were "smart" and "brisk" and sometimes "hot," and occasionally a "difficult piece of work." They might also be described lightly—Harlem Heights was "this silly business" to Lord Rawdon. To their men, British officers spoke a clean, no-nonsense language. Howe's terse "look to your bayonets" summed up a tough professional's expectations.[23]

For all the distance between British officers and men, they gave remarkable support to one another in battle. They usually deployed carefully, keeping up their spirits with drum and fife. They talked and shouted and cheered, and coming on with their bayonets at the ready "huzzaing," or coming on "firing and huzzaing" they must have sustained a sense of shared experience. Their ranks might be thinned by an American volley, but on they came, exhorting one another to "push

---

[22]Greene to Gov. Reed, Mar. 18, 1781, Nathanael Greene Papers, Huntington Library. On Feb. 3, 1781, Greene wrote Gov. Nash that 20,000 militia would not provide 500 effective troops, the way they "come and go."

[23]Stedman, II, 382, 360; Rawdon to the earl of Huntington, Aug. 3, 1775, Sept. 23, 1776.

144

10

on! push on!'' as at Bunker Hill and the battles that followed.[24] Although terrible losses naturally dispirited them, they almost always maintained the integrity of their regiments as fighting units, and when they were defeated, or nearly so as at Guilford Court House, they recovered their pride and fought well thereafter. And there was no hint at Yorktown that the ranks wanted to surrender, even though they had suffered dreadfully.

The Continentals, the American regulars, lacked the polish of their British counterparts but, at least from Monmouth on, they showed a steadiness under fire almost as impressive as their enemy's. And they demonstrated a brave endurance: defeated, they retired, pulled themselves together, and came back to try again.

These qualities—patience and endurance—endeared them to many. For example, John Laurens, on Washington's staff in 1778, wanted desperately to command them. In what amounted to a plea for command, Laurens wrote: ''I would cherish those dear, ragged Continentals, whose patience will be the admiration of future ages, and glory in bleeding with them.''[25] This statement was all the more extraordinary coming from Laurens, a South Carolinian aristocrat. The soldiers he admired were anything but aristocratic. As the war dragged on, they came more and more from the poor and the propertyless. Most probably entered the army as substitutes for men who had rather pay than serve, or as the recipients of bounties and the promise of land. In time some, perhaps many, assimilated the ideals of the Revolution. As Baron Steuben observed in training them, they differed from European troops in at least one regard: they wanted to know why they were told to do certain things. Unlike European soldiers who did what they were told, the Continentals asked why.[26]

Continental officers aped the style of their British counterparts. They aspired to gentility and often, failing to achieve it, betrayed their anxiety by an excessive concern for their honor. Not surprisingly, like their British peers, they also used the vocabularies of gentlemen in describing battle.

Their troops, innocent of such polish, spoke with words from their immediate experience of physical combat. They found few euphemisms for the horrors of battle. Thus Private David How, September 1776, in New York noted in his diary: ''Isaac Fowls had his head shot off with a cannon ball this morning.'' And Sergeant Thomas McCarty reported an engagement between a British foraging party and American infantry near New Brunswick in February 1777: ''We attacked the body, and bullets

[24] Rawdon to the earl of Huntington, June 20, 1775.

[25] To his father, Mar. 9, 1778, in *The Army Correspondence of Colonel John Laurens* (New York, 1897), p. 136.

[26] *Rebels and Redcoats*, ed. George F. Sheer and Hugh F. Rankin (New York, 1957), p. 354.

11

flew like hail. We stayed about 15 minutes and then retreated with loss.'' After the battle inspection of the field revealed that the British had killed the American wounded—"The men that was wounded in the thigh or leg, they dashed out their brains with their muskets and run them through with their bayonets, made them like sieves. This was barbarity to the utmost.'' The pain of seeing his comrades mutilated by shot and shell at White Plains remained with Elisha Bostwick, a Connecticut soldier, all his life: A cannon ball "cut down Lt. Youngs Platoon which was next to that of mine[;] the ball first took off the head of Smith, a Stout heavy man and dashed it open, then took Taylor across the Bowels, it then Struck Sergeant Garret of our Company on the hip [and] took off the point of the hip bone[.] Smith and Taylor were left on the spot. Sergeant Garret was carried but died the Same day now to think, oh! what a sight that was to see within a distance of six rods those men with their legs and arms and guns and packs all in a heap[.]''[27]

The Continentals occupied the psychological and moral ground somewhere between the militia and the British professionals. From 1777 on their enlistments were for three years or the duration of the war. This long service allowed them to learn more of their craft and to become seasoned. That does not mean that on the battlefield they lost their fear. Experience in combat almost never leaves one indifferent to danger, unless after prolonged and extreme fatigue one comes to consider oneself already dead. Seasoned troops simply learn to deal with their fear more effectively than raw troops do, in part because they have come to realize that everyone feels it and that they can rely on their fellows.

By winter 1779-1780, the Continentals were beginning to believe that they had no one save themselves to lean on. Their soldierly qualifications so widely admired in America—their "habit of subordination,''[28] their patience under fatigue, their ability to stand sufferings and privations of every kind may in fact have led to a bitter resignation that saw them through a good deal of fighting. At Morristown during this winter, they felt abandoned in their cold and hunger. They knew that food and clothing existed in America to keep them healthy and comfortable, and yet little of either came to the army. Understandably their dissatisfaction increased as they realized that once again suffering had been left to them. Dissatisfaction in these months slowly turned into a feeling of martyrdom. They felt themselves to be martyrs to the "glorious cause.'' They would

---

[27] *Diary of David How* (Morrisania, N.Y., 1885), p. 28; "The Revolutionary War Journal of Sergeant Thomas McCarty,'' ed. Jared C. Lobdell, *Proceedings of the New Jersey Historical Society,* 80 (1964), 45; Bostwick, 101.

[28] Laurens to his father, Jan. 14, 1779, *Army Correspondence,* p. 108

146

12

on! push on!'' as at Bunker Hill and the battles that followed.[24] Although terrible losses naturally dispirited them, they almost always maintained the integrity of their regiments as fighting units, and when they were defeated, or nearly so as at Guilford Court House, they recovered their pride and fought well thereafter. And there was no hint at Yorktown that the ranks wanted to surrender, even though they had suffered dreadfully.

The Continentals, the American regulars, lacked the polish of their British counterparts but, at least from Monmouth on, they showed a steadiness under fire almost as impressive as their enemy's. And they demonstrated a brave endurance: defeated, they retired, pulled themselves together, and came back to try again.

These qualities—patience and endurance—endeared them to many. For example, John Laurens, on Washington's staff in 1778, wanted desperately to command them. In what amounted to a plea for command, Laurens wrote: ''I would cherish those dear, ragged Continentals, whose patience will be the admiration of future ages, and glory in bleeding with them.''[25] This statement was all the more extraordinary coming from Laurens, a South Carolinian aristocrat. The soldiers he admired were anything but aristocratic. As the war dragged on, they came more and more from the poor and the propertyless. Most probably entered the army as substitutes for men who had rather pay than serve, or as the recipients of bounties and the promise of land. In time some, perhaps many, assimilated the ideals of the Revolution. As Baron Steuben observed in training them, they differed from European troops in at least one regard: they wanted to know why they were told to do certain things. Unlike European soldiers who did what they were told, the Continentals asked why.[26]

Continental officers aped the style of their British counterparts. They aspired to gentility and often, failing to achieve it, betrayed their anxiety by an excessive concern for their honor. Not surprisingly, like their British peers, they also used the vocabularies of gentlemen in describing battle.

Their troops, innocent of such polish, spoke with words from their immediate experience of physical combat. They found few euphemisms for the horrors of battle. Thus Private David How, September 1776, in New York noted in his diary: ''Isaac Fowls had his head shot off with a cannon ball this morning.'' And Sergeant Thomas McCarty reported an engagement between a British foraging party and American infantry near New Brunswick in February 1777: ''We attacked the body, and bullets

---

[24] Rawdon to the earl of Huntington, June 20, 1775.

[25] To his father, Mar. 9, 1778, in *The Army Correspondence of Colonel John Laurens* (New York, 1897), p. 136.

[26] *Rebels and Redcoats*, ed. George F. Sheer and Hugh F. Rankin (New York, 1957), p. 354.

145

13

flew like hail. We stayed about 15 minutes and then retreated with loss.'' After the battle inspection of the field revealed that the British had killed the American wounded—"The men that was wounded in the thigh or leg, they dashed out their brains with their muskets and run them through with their bayonets, made them like sieves. This was barbarity to the utmost." The pain of seeing his comrades mutilated by shot and shell at White Plains remained with Elisha Bostwick, a Connecticut soldier, all his life: A cannon ball "cut down Lt. Youngs Platoon which was next to that of mine[;] the ball first took off the head of Smith, a Stout heavy man and dashed it open, then took Taylor across the Bowels, it then Struck Sergeant Garret of our Company on the hip [and] took off the point of the hip bone[.] Smith and Taylor were left on the spot. Sergeant Garret was carried but died the Same day now to think, oh! what a sight that was to see within a distance of six rods those men with their legs and arms and guns and packs all in a heap[.]"[27]

The Continentals occupied the psychological and moral ground somewhere between the militia and the British professionals. From 1777 on their enlistments were for three years or the duration of the war. This long service allowed them to learn more of their craft and to become seasoned. That does not mean that on the battlefield they lost their fear. Experience in combat almost never leaves one indifferent to danger, unless after prolonged and extreme fatigue one comes to consider oneself already dead. Seasoned troops simply learn to deal with their fear more effectively than raw troops do, in part because they have come to realize that everyone feels it and that they can rely on their fellows.

By winter 1779-1780, the Continentals were beginning to believe that they had no one save themselves to lean on. Their soldierly qualifications so widely admired in America—their "habit of subordination,"[28] their patience under fatigue, their ability to stand sufferings and privations of every kind may in fact have led to a bitter resignation that saw them through a good deal of fighting. At Morristown during this winter, they felt abandoned in their cold and hunger. They knew that food and clothing existed in America to keep them healthy and comfortable, and yet little of either came to the army. Understandably their dissatisfaction increased as they realized that once again suffering had been left to them. Dissatisfaction in these months slowly turned into a feeling of martyrdom. They felt themselves to be martyrs to the "glorious cause." They would

[27] Diary of David How (Morrisania, N.Y., 1885), p. 28; "The Revolutionary War Journal of Sergeant Thomas McCarty," ed. Jared C. Lobdell, Proceedings of the New Jersey Historical Society, 80 (1964), 45; Bostwick, 101.

[28] Laurens to his father, Jan. 14, 1779, Army Correspondence, p. 108

14

fulfill the ideals of the Revolution and see things through to independence because the civilian population would not.[29]

Thus the Continentals in the last four years of the active war, though less articulate and less independent than the militia, assimilated one part of the "cause" more fully. They had advanced further in making American purposes in the Revolution their own. They had in their sense of isolation and neglect probably come to be more nationalistic than the militia—though surely no more American.

Although these sources of the Continentals' feeling seem curious, they served to reinforce the tough professional ethic these men also came to absorb. Set apart from the militia by the length of their service, by their officers' esteem for them, and by their own contempt for part-time soldiers, the Continentals slowly developed resilience and pride. Their country might ignore them in camp, might allow their bellies to shrivel and their backs to freeze, might allow them to wear rags, but in battle they would not be ignored. And in battle they would support one another in the knowledge that their own moral and professional resources remained sure.

The meaning of these complex attitudes is not what it seems to be. At first sight the performance of militia and Continentals seems to suggest that the great principles of the Revolution made little difference on the battlefield. Or if principles did make a difference, say especially to the militia saturated with natural rights and a deep and persistent distrust of standing armies, they served not to strengthen the will to combat but to disable it. And the Continentals, recruited increasingly from the poor and dispossessed, apparently fought better as they came to resemble their professional and apolitical enemy, the British infantry.

These conclusions are in part askew. To be sure, there is truth—and paradox—in the fact that some Americans' commitments to revolutionary principles made them unreliable on the battlefield. Still, their devotion to their principles helped bring them there. George Washington, their commander-in-chief, never tired of reminding them that their cause arrayed free men against mercenaries. They were fighting for the "blessings of liberty," he told them in 1776, and should they not acquit themselves like men, slavery would replace their freedom.[30] The challenge to behave like men was not an empty one. Courage, honor, gallantry in the service of liberty, all those words calculated to bring a blush of embarrassment to jaded twentieth-century men, defined manhood for the

[29]S. Sidney Bradford, "Hunger Menaces the Revolution, December 1779-January 1780," *Maryland Historical Magazine*, 61 (1966), 5-23; *Correspondence and Journals of Samuel Blachley Webb*, ed. W. C. Ford (New York, 1893), II, 231-232.

[30]*Writings of Washington*, V, 479.

147

15

eighteenth century. In battle those words gained an extraordinary resonance as they were embodied in the actions of brave men. Indeed it is likely that many Americans who developed a narrow professional spirit found battle broadly educative, forcing them to consider the purposes of their professional skill.

On one level those purposes had to be understood as having a remarkable importance if men were to fight—and die. For battle forced American soldiers into a situation which nothing in their usual experience had prepared them for. They were to kill other men in the expectation that even if they did they might be killed themselves. However defined, especially by a Revolution in the name of life, liberty, and the pursuit of happiness, this situation was unnatural.

On another level, one which, perhaps, made the strain of battle endurable, the situation of American soldiers, though unusual, was not really foreign to them. For what battle presented in stark form was one of the classic problems free men face: choosing between the rival claims of public responsibility and private wishes, or in eighteenth-century terms choosing between virtue—devotion to the public trust—and personal liberty. In battle, virtue demanded that men give up their liberties and perhaps even their lives for others. Each time they fought they had in effect to weigh the claims of society and liberty. Should they fight or run? They knew that the choice might mean life or death. For those American soldiers who were servants, apprentices, poor men substituting for men with money to hire them, the choice might not have seemed to involve moral decision. After all they had never enjoyed much personal liberty. But not even in that contrivance of eighteenth-century authoritarianism in which they now found themselves, the professional army, could they avoid a moral decision. Compressed into dense formations, they were reminded by their nearness to their comrades that they too had an opportunity to uphold virtue. By standing firm they served their fellows and honor; by running, they served only themselves.

Thus battle tested the inner qualities of men, tried their souls, as Thomas Paine said. Many men died in the test that battle made of their spirits. Some soldiers called this trial cruel; others called it "glorious." Perhaps this difference in perception suggests how difficult it was in the Revolution to be both a soldier and an American. Nor has it ever been easy since.

16

"OH THAT I WAS A SOLDIER": JOHN ADAMS AND THE ANGUISH OF WAR

JOHN E. FERLING

West Georgia College

NO POPULAR PERCEPTION OF THE AMERICAN REVOLUTION HAS BEEN SO PERVASIVE as the imagery of the "Spirit of '76." It evokes the notion of noble sacrifice, of virtuous ordinary citizens abandoning their daily pursuits in order to seize their weapons and fight a despotic foe. Indeed, when hostilities with Great Britain erupted in 1775 a "Rage Militaire" swept across the colonies. Manuals explaining martial techniques poured off the presses and citizens rushed to hone their skills in military exercises. Young boys and old men took up arms, some in the local militia, others in the Continental Army.[1] Among those choosing to bear arms were many who had been activists in the protracted political controversy with the parent state. Philip Schuyler and John Sullivan left the Continental Congress to serve as officers under another former congressman, George Washington. Other members of Congress, such as John Dickinson and Patrick Henry, went on to serve in their colony's trainband units. Some radicals—like Philadelphia's Joseph Reed, who joined Washington's staff, and Quartermaster General Thomas Mifflin—relinquished lucrative positions in order to further the war effort.

Of course, not all able-bodied men became warriors. One who did not was John Adams. Not that he did not wish to bear arms. He yearned to wear a uniform, to march off to battle. Yet he never became a soldier.

In fact, the War for Independence was not the only armed conflict that Adams encountered. The French and Indian War began when he was twenty-one years old. He also wished to soldier in that struggle, but he never served. During his presidency, moreover, the Quasi-War with France occurred, once again confronting him with the anguish and strain of a likely state of war.

Adams's experience provides a unique opportunity to study the stresses faced by

---

[1]Charles Royster, *A Revolutionary People at War: The Continental Army and American Character* (Chapel Hill: Univ. of North Carolina Press, 1979), 25–53. On the imagery of the "Spirit of '76" see: Michael Kammen, *A Season of Youth: The American Revolution and the Historical Imagination* (New York: Knopf, 1978), 186–259.

18

a noncombatant in several early American wartime milieus. In addition, the emotional dilemma that he endured by not soldiering has not been scrutinized previously, yet it helped to shape his conduct and even the policies he would pursue during his presidency.

*　*　*

In 1756 John Adams was a Latin schoolmaster in Worcester, a village about fifty miles west of Boston. He was not a happy young man at that moment. He disliked his teaching job, although he saw it as a temporary calling, a means to earn money so that he might study the law. That was the year the French and Indian War began, and when military recruiters swarmed over Worcester, Adams too was caught up in the general fervor for hostilities. "I longed more ardently to be a Soldier than I ever did to be a Lawyer," he later admitted. His health was good. He never had been in "higher Spirits in my Life," he said, adding that "my mind and Body are in a very easy situation, tortu[red] with no Pain." He eagerly turned out to watch the drills of the British troops that paused in Worcester, and he hardly disagreed with a close friend who admitted to a longing to soldier, for he looked upon these redcoats as his superiors.[2]

Yet Adams did not enlist. His failure to soldier troubled him, even prompting him once to confess ruefully that he was the first member of his family "who has *degenerated* from the virtues of the house so far as not to have been an officer in the militia. . . ." His only wartime service was confined to carrying a military dispatch from Worcester to Newport, Rhode Island. The round-trip journey that he undertook was one of only about one hundred miles; it was over a relatively busy thoroughfare, and it was about five hundred miles from the nearest war zone. Yet he believed his mission had been so arduous as to have harmed his health, and shortly thereafter he did fall ill. Visits to several physicians resulted in only partial relief, and he continued to suffer from gastro-intestinal pains until he returned home to Braintree, whereupon his "excellent Father . . . by his tender" care succeeded where so many physicians had failed.[3]

Adams's behavior during the early stages of this war suggest that he was

[2]L. H. Butterfield et. al., eds., *The Earliest Diary of John Adams* (Cambridge: Harvard Univ. Press, 1966), 91; Adams to Richard Cranch, 2 Sept. 1755 and 29 Aug. 1756, in Robert J. Taylor et. al., eds., *Papers of John Adams* (Cambridge: Harvard Univ. Press, 1977–), I, 3, 15; Adams to Abigail Adams, 13 Feb. 1776, in L. H. Butterfield et. al., eds., *Adams Family Correspondence* (Cambridge: Harvard Univ. Press, 1963–), I, 347; L. H. Butterfield, ed., *Diary and Autobiography of John Adams*, 4 vols. (New York: Atheneum, 1964), I, 110; III, 266–67. Hereafter the following abbreviations will be used when citing the above works: Taylor, *PJA*; Butterfield, *AFC*; and Butterfield, *DAJA*. In addition, the abbreviations "JA" and "AA" will be used to denote John Adams and Abigail Adams in citations of their correspondence.

[3]Butterfield, *DAJA*, III, 267–69; Peter Shaw, *The Character of John Adams* (Chapel Hill, Univ. of North Carolina Press, 1976), 46–47. In his memoirs Adams recollected that he had applied for a captain's commission during this war, but there is no evidence to support such a claim. See Butterfield, *DAJA*, III, 267, 267n. Emphasis added to the word "degenerated."

19

profoundly distressed by his failure to soldier, to the point even that his illness—the symptoms of which bear a striking resemblance to ills that would chronically occur later in moments of great tension—was, in all likelihood, due more to emotional stress than to physiological origins.[4] Yet why was he so distraught? The war erupted during a difficult period for Adams. Just twenty-one years old in 1756, he was in the throes of a protracted struggle for self-identification. He had reached the point in the life cycle when, according to Erik Erikson, "each youth must forge for himself some central perspective and direction . . . out of [the] effective remnants of childhood and the hopes of anticipated adulthood."[5]

No reader of the diary that John Adams kept as a young adult could fail to notice that he was troubled by deep-seated feelings of inadequacy and worthlessness. He was the son of a successful, locally preeminent father, one who was assertive and exacting in the demands he made on his son. That young John was troubled by a sense of inferiority was not an uncharacteristic legacy for a child raised in such an environment.[6] Deacon John Adams, John's father, comes to us as a shadowy figure, almost all we know of him reposing in the brief accounts left by his son. Evidently he had risen from humble beginnings to a lofty position in Braintree, Massachusetts. Not only had he attained a comfortable economic position, his material good fortune had resulted in social fulfillment. He was elected to be an officer in the local militia, and, as his title suggests, he was a leader in the hamlet's Congregational Church. The Deacon expected no less of his son, or—what is even more important—so John believed, for that is the impression he conveyed in his autobiography.[7]

The earliest clash with his father that Adams mentioned in his memoirs came over his schooling. Deacon Adams dictated that his son attend school, where he was expected to do well enough to earn admission to Harvard College. Even then displaying feelings of inadequacy, John admitted his anxiety at being "sett down for a fool" before his classmates, and he pleaded with his father to be permitted to quit school. When his father refused, young John rebelled. He played the truant, his marks were poor, and he frequently implored his father to let him become a simple farmer. Yet always the Deacon's response was the same: "you must go to

[4]Butterfield, *DAJA*, II, 6; JA to AA, 9 Oct. 1781, in Butterfield, *AFC*, IV, 224; III, 143–44n; Shaw, *Character of Adams*, 186–90; Page Smith, *John Adams*, 2 vols. (New York: Doubleday, 1962), I, 70–71.

[5]Erik H. Erikson, *Young Man Luther: A Study in Psychoanalysis and History* (New York: W. W. Norton, 1958), 14, 43.

[6]Sigmund Freud, *New Introductory Lectures on Psychology* (New York: W. W. Norton, 1964), 81–95; Freud, *The Problem of Anxiety* (New York: W. W. Norton, 1936), 42–52, 69–92; Freud, *An Outline of Psychoanalysis* (New York: W. W. Norton, 1940), 1–21; Freud, *Inhibitions, Symptoms, and Anxiety*, in James Strachey, ed., *The Standard Edition of the Complete Psychological Works of Sigmund Freud*, 24 vols. (London: Hogarth, 1953–1976), XX, 132–67; Henry P. Laughlin, *The Neuroses* (Washington: Butterworth, 1967), 1–51; Helen B. Lewis, *Shame and Guilt in Neurosis* (New York: International Univ. Press, 1971), 18–61.

[7]Butterfield, *DAJA*, III, 256, 276, 261; "Genealogical Notes," in Taylor, *PJA*, I, 351–52; Smith, *Adams*, I, 7–8; Charles Francis Adams, *Three Episodes in Massachusetts History*, 2 vols. (Boston, 1892), I, 714–15.

school." When John eventually completed his preparatory training and passed the entrance examination for college, he acknowledged that he was gratified principally because "my Parents [were] very happy."[8]

Upon graduation from Harvard, John's choice of a career produced still more inner turmoil. He wished to pursue the law, although his father wanted him to become a Congregational minister. Adams agonized over the matter for two years, choosing first one profession, then the other. The Deacon loathed attorneys, seeing them as motivated solely by vulgar, selfish interests, thinking all counselors would sacrifice the public welfare to satisfy their own ambitions. His view of lawyers, moreover, probably reflected the outlook of most residents of mid-eighteenth-century Massachusetts.[9] Thus, young John's choice of the legal field not only represented still another rebellion against his father's wishes, but it also could hardly help but raise doubts in his mind about his own motives in pursuing such a scorned undertaking.

Privately John admitted that he found a legal career enticing largely because what he most craved was renown and material success. Otherwise, he feared, he would "live and die an ignorant, obscure fellow." Yet he was unable to justify such feelings, knowing that they conflicted with the views both of his father and of society. He feared that his ambition was "mean and base," and he referred to his "Love of Fame" as his "cardinal Vice and cardinal Folly." His anxiety evinced itself in self-loathing: he questioned his abilities, he vilified his behavior. He denounced his "Self Conceit" and his "unsociable disposition," censured his laziness and proclivity for daydreaming, reproached himself for the time he wasted in idle amusements, and generally thought of himself as "dull" and witless. Nevertheless, after much agonizing he did become an apprentice law student. He was "not without Apprehensions" concerning his choice, he told a friend, but he rationalized his decision by suggesting that the law could never be a means for his attainment of power and notability. Besides, as an attorney he would "be able to do more good to his fellow man . . . than in any other calling." He was more honest with himself. If "conscience disapproves" of one's actions, he noted, the "loudest applauses . . . are of little Value."[10]

Another problem troubled Adams, too. Virtually all the men in Braintree were engaged in hard physical labor, mostly as yeomen. His father, whom he characterized as a man of "Industry and Enterprize," was both a farmer and a shoemaker, and both his younger brothers were trained for a lifetime of farming. His agrarian

---

[8]Butterfield, *DAJA*, III, 257–59; Shaw, *Character of Adams*, 5.
[9]Butterfield, *DAJA*, III, 263; John Murrin, "The Legal Transformation: The Bench and Bar of Eighteenth Century Massachusetts," in Stanley N. Katz, ed., *Colonial America: Essays in Political and Social Development*, 3d ed. (Boston: Knopf, 1983), 547, 555–58. In an early essay Adams created a fictional father who expressed views that undoubtedly were similar to those of the Deacon. He had this character say: "Let me warn you against that Ambition, which I have observed in Men of [the legal] Profession. Too many Lawyers will sacrifice all to their own Advancement." See "Clarendon to Pym, 1766," Taylor, *PJA*, I, 161–62.
[10]Butterfield, *DAJA*, I, 7–8, 10, 12–14, 21–22, 24–25, 37, 73; III, 263; JA to Charles Cushing, 1 April 1756, Taylor, *PJA*, I, 12–13.

21

society, moreover, lauded hard work, as every churchgoer soon discovered after listening to repeated sermons on the topic. The work performed by lawyers was very different, of course. It was desk work, soft work. The physical demands made on attorneys were similar to those imposed on clergymen, and young Adams was explicit in equating the latter profession with banality and inefficacy. Many ministers seemed to him to be "effeminate" and "unmanly" sorts. He must have worried about lawyers as well, for he even equated their pursuits with valitudinarianism. He was never "so happy as among the Creek Thatch," he later remembered, a reference to his infrequent days of hard labor as a youth on his father's farm; even after his retirement from the presidency he seemed to apologize for never having acquired the skills of a farmer. In his memoirs, moreover, he took pains to depict his youth as "normal," a time given to the pleasures of physical pursuits—to fishing and hunting, swimming and wrestling—until the sedentary world of schooling was imposed upon him.[11]

Yet this problem was linked to another. If Adams's society praised the hard worker, it absolutely exalted and ennobled another member of the culture: the soldier. No region rivaled New England in its glorification of its fighting men. Warriors had played a crucial role in the establishment of Anglo-American hegemony in New England. Almost every generation from the beginning of English colonization to Adams's time had experienced war with the Native Americans or the French; unlike Europe, where warfare continued to be waged by professional armies, the colonists had relied on the citizen-soldier, the militiaman, and the volunteer in their struggles. In this environment of episodic life-and-death struggles, the soldier came to be venerated. Articulate spokesmen for society, especially the clergy, repeatedly glorified the alleged virtues of warriors. Soldiering was depicted as an act of "true manliness and grandeur," as a "just, honorable" pursuit. In the popular mind warriors soon were thought to be strong, vigorous, tenacious, and masculine; the opposite qualities—indolence and effeminacy, in particular—were attributed to cowardly soldiers and, by implication, to those who refused to bear arms. Not surprisingly, as Philip Greven has noted, this often bellicose society socialized its young males with a strident manliness, urging little boys to manifest presumed masculine traits that were identical to those virtues prized in soldiers. Nor was it surprising in such an environment that soldiers became society's heroes. Warriors were the subject of heroic narratives and of poetic elegies, accounts that stressed the bravery, fortitude, and the physical prowess and agility of contemporary soldiers as well as those who had fought in earlier generations. Monuments were erected to these heroes, and hamlets were named in their honor.[12]

[11]Butterfield, *DAJA*, III, 256–57, 262–63; Shaw, *Character of Adams*, 273.

[12]Oliver Peabody, *An Essay to revive and encourage Military Exercises*. . . . (Boston, 1732), 16, 18–19; Thomas Prentice, *A Sermon Preached at Charlestown, on a General Thanksgiving for the Reduction of Cape-Breton* (Boston, 1745), 29; William McClenachan, *The Christian Warrior: A Sermon*. . . . (Boston, 1745), 7–8; John E. Ferling, *A Wilderness of Miseries: War and Warriors in Early America* (Westport, Conn.: Greenwood Press, 1980), 57–92; John E. Ferling, "The New England Soldier: A Study in Changing Perceptions," *American Quarterly*, 33 (1981), 26–45; Philip Greven, *The Protestant Temperament: Patterns of Child-Rearing, Religious Experience, and the Self in Early America* (New York: Knopf, 1971), 246–47, 284–85, 322.

22

Living in such a milieu, Adams found these war years to be discomforting. Already vexed by feelings of inadequacy, uncertain of his motives, troubled by his sedentary life style, he believed that he wanted to soldier, for he saw such conduct as active, virtuous, and heroic. His was an inner conflict, so great, in fact, that at times he seems to have been almost overwhelmed by self-doubt and anxiety, though he never actually grew dysfunctional. The healthy personality will weather a crisis such as this, employing various strategies until it has mastered its environment; ultimately it will emerge with an enhanced sense of inner unity.[13] Adams succeeded because he contrived a strategy for the extirpation of his inner pain, though not before his personal actions had manifested his emotional turmoil.

Adams adopted a two-fold strategy. He convinced himself that he had made a sacrifice. His horseback ride to deliver a military message was an act of courage, he came to believe, an arduous journey that no one else would undertake, and one that he believed had provoked a dangerous illness. He was "cured" only when his father sanctioned his behavior through his benevolent solace. In addition, he virtually succeeded in convincing himself of the merits of his intellectual endeavors. Men of learning, he told himself, could exhibit "manly and noble" virtues in civilian pursuits; because of their contributions to society, such men should be esteemed even above soldiers. He adopted as his creed Ovid's admonition to a soldier, a statement he quoted in one of his earliest essays:

> You have strength without intelligence; I have concern for the future./ You are able to fight. You are outstanding only in body; I am outstanding in intellect./ My mind is superior to my hand. All my force is in my mind.[14]

His strategies evidently succeeded, for his diary—kept almost daily for the duration of the war—gave no further indication of anxiety arising from his civilian status.

* * *

Adams was packing his belongings in preparation for the trip to the Second Continental Congress when news reached Braintree of the colonists' clash with British regulars at Lexington and Concord. He was seized by a need to visit the scene of the shootings, and he immediately rode to these villages. When he returned home that evening he collapsed. Another great personal crisis had engulfed him, for although he characterized his symptoms as "allarming," his subsequent descriptions of his condition strongly suggest that he again had fallen ill from emotional stress.[15]

[13]Erik H. Erikson, "Identity and the Life Cycle," *Psychological Issues*, 1 (Nov. 1959), 51, 95, 122–28; Erikson, *Childhood and Society*, 2d ed. (New York: W. W. Norton, 1963), 188–94; Erikson, *Young Man Luther*, 100–01.
[14][John Adams], "On Political Faction, Man's Nature, and the Law," in Taylor, *PJA*, 1, 88, 90n.
[15]Butterfield, *DAJA*, III, 314.

23

Adams was too ill to depart for Philadelphia with the other congressional delegates from Massachusetts. His wife nursed and comforted him, however, and within a few days he was able to set out. Yet he had not come to grips with the source of his affliction. Soon the customary somatic distresses that accompanied his personal trials reappeared. In letters home he variously described himself as "miserable," "not well," "wornout," "completely miserable," "quite infirm," "very bad," and as "low in spirits and weak in health." In addition to these woes, he was distressed by "Fidgets, Fidlings, and Irritabilities." He complained of an inability to sleep, and he feared that he was going blind.[16]

What plagued Adams? He attributed his illnesses and fatigue to his work load. No one could doubt that he devoted an inordinate amount of time to his congressional duties, often working sixteen to eighteen hours a day. Still, his exertions were not unprecedented, for he always had been something of an overworker. The urgency of the times, moreover, were sufficient to test the mettle of any politician, and he knew full well the personal hazards he risked by serving a colony in a state of rebellion. Yet he had served actively from April 1774 to April 1775—including his service at the First Congress—without undue stress. What was different after April 19, 1775, of course, was that the Anglo-American troubles had passed from the peaceful stage to the point of violent resistance. It was not coincidental that Adams collapsed following his trek to Lexington and Concord.

Adams exhibited no qualms over the violent nature of the colonial revolt, however. He simply did not question the propriety of this war. By early in 1775 he believed hostilities were inevitable. He convinced himself of Britain's ineffable corruption and of the existence of a ministerial plot to extirpate American liberties, and he concluded that the colonists must resist the parent state. At the First Congress he had even become exasperated with those whose fear of war led them to a conciliatory posture, those who "shudder at the prospect of blood." He depicted the colonial protest as a "great christian as well as moral duty and virtue," and he wrote home to exhort the citizenry to arm themselves and to train for the coming clash. He even came to believe that the war might be beneficial. He conjectured that the conflict might purify America. Perhaps, he said, the travail would be a "Furnace of Affliction [that] may refine" the colonists. When the war did begin he saw it as a popular struggle, what he termed a *"people's war,"* for which he felt no real responsibility.[17]

---

[16]JA to AA, 29 May, 2, 6, 10, 23 June, 12 July, and 26 Sept. 1775, Butterfield, *AFC*, I, 207, 208, 212, 213, 226, 243, 285; JA to James Warren, 21 May, 27 June, 23 July 1775, Taylor, *PJA*, III, 11, 49, 87.

[17]JA to AA, 7 Oct. 1774, 2 May, 7 July 1775; 16 March 1776, Butterfield, *AFC*, I, 165, 192, 241; II, 176; Butterfield, *DAJA*, III, 324, 328; JA to James Burgh, 28 Dec. 1774, Taylor, *PJA*, II, 206; JA to Mercy Warren, 3 Jan. 1775, ibid., II, 210; "Letters of Novanglus," ibid., II, 232, 255, 267, 284; "To a Friend in London," 21 Jan. 1775, ibid., II, 216; JA to James Warren, 15 March 1775, ibid., II, 405; JA to William Tudor, 29 Sept. 1774, in Edmund C. Burnett, ed., *Letters of Members of the Continental Congress*, 8 vols. (Washington: GPO, 1921–1936), I, 60. Adams's views on the clash with Great Britain were quite within the mainstream of colonial thought after 1773. See Bernard Bailyn, *The Ideological Origins of the American Revolution* (Cambridge: Harvard Univ. Press, 1967).

24

It was far less easy, however, for Adams to resolve the problem of his own wartime service. He longed—or he thought he did—to soldier, yet he was unable to make the leap from legislator to warrior. It was a vexatious problem for him, one that tormented him off and on for nearly two years, anguishing him in a manner that corresponded to the torments he had experienced during the French and Indian War.

Once again he was besieged by feelings of worthlessness, exacerbated in this instance by the knowledge that he was in little danger in Philadelphia, while at home his family was in great peril. Before the end of 1775 his wife and children fell ill, the victims of epidemics of smallpox and dysentery that swept over Braintree, spreading like a dark stain from the rival army camps to the civilian sector; moreover, his brother Elihu, a captain in the militia, died that summer of a camp disease, and his mother-in-law also perished in the epidemic.[18]

In the atmosphere of spirited service and sacrifice that swept over America in 1775, Adams once again began to speak of soldiering. "Oh that I·was a Soldier!—I will be," he pledged.[19] Yet that longing aroused another deep inner conflict within Adams, producing an anxiety that arose from feelings of guilt. During the French and Indian War, Adams, still a young man, had been troubled because he had not soldiered. In the War for Independence he knew that no one seriously expected him—now over forty years of age—to soldier. The problems he evinced after 1775, thus, were of a different origin than those he had confronted twenty years before. He now harbored wishes that he believed he should not have embraced. He was burdened by an unresolved conflict over his motives for wishing to bear arms.

Adams saw himself as a tender, merciful, benign man. Although hardly a pacifist, he looked upon violent behavior with circumspection and reservations. To recommend that a man respond to violence with an act of force was "the sentiment of a Brute," he had written; he equated bellicose actions with the "Fowl upon the Dung Hill that . . . instantly . . . prepares for Combat" over the slightest provocation. Even self-defense, he believed, should not extend beyond doing what was absolutely essential for self-preservation. Obviously one should attempt to ward off an attacker, but "a blow received is no sufficient provocation for fifty times so severe a blow, in return." He knew that many—especially the "lowest and most despised Sort of Soldiers"—would label such behavior as cowardly, although "it would be thought the truest *bravery* . . . by the greatest philosophers and legislators."[20]

Yet Adams did not harbor feelings of malice toward soldiers. Almost alone among men, he believed, soldiers and statesmen shared the unique opportunity to "refine" the character of their peoples. He was drawn to George Washington because he believed his "modest and virtuous . . . amiable, generous and brave"

[18]AA to JA, 10 Aug., 8, 16, 25 Sept. 1775; Butterfield, *AFC*, I, 272, 276–80, 284.

[19]JA to AA, 29 May 1775, ibid., I, 207.

[20]"U to *Boston Gazette*, 1 Aug., 5 Sept. 1763, Taylor, *PJA*, I, 75, 85, 87; [John Adams], "An Essay on Man's Lust for Power. . . .," ibid., I, 82–83; "Humphrey Ploughjogger" to the *Boston Evening Post*, 20 June 1763, ibid., I, 65; AA to JA, 22 Oct. 1775, Butterfield, *AFC*, I, 311; Butterfield, *DAJA*, III, 320.

25

qualities afforded him the chance to become such a soldier; General Charles Lee's "Zeal for the Rights of Humanity" afforded him a similar opportunity, and, in his view, Nathanael Greene and Henry Knox also brought the proper qualities to the command post. He would have preferred a society in which great statesmen were lionized above great soldiers, but he knew of no such place. The soldier always will "Wear the Lawrells," whereas the statesman will toil in oblivion.[21] The Anglo-American war was barely six months old before striking proof of his observation was available. Dr. Joseph Warren, the Boston physician-agitator who was killed on Bunker Hill, and General Richard Montgomery, who perished in the assault on Quebec, became the first great heroes of this war; meanwhile, before he ever led an army in battle in 1775, Washington had become the most revered living American.

Deep down Adams knew that this was precisely why he longed to soldier. He realized that he was deeply moved by the glamor of bearing arms and by the veneration so often heaped upon the soldier. Yet he was equally certain that he could not reconcile such behavior with his notion of virtue. All his life, he believed, he had steeled himself against "selfish and avaricious" conduct, striving always to act for reasons other than "Interest and Money." "Nothing has ever given me, more Mortification, than a suspicion . . . that I was actuated by private Views," he commented in the summer of 1776, reiterating that he was content to opt for insignificance and to leave to others "all the Honours and Offices this World has to bestow."[22] Yet unmistakeably he wished to soldier, and that desire triggered an anxiety alert, a distressed state that he was compelled to bear until he resolved his ambivalence.

During the early years of the war Adams's spirits seemed to vacillate as the intensity of the fighting ebbed and flowed. His collapse in April 1775 was followed by several weeks of near hysterical behavior (characterized by his manifold physical ills). After the colonists' superlative showing at Bunker Hill, and the protracted hiatus in the fighting that followed, his anxiety waned and he enjoyed good health. Yet when he learned of Montgomery's death and the failure of the Canadian invasion, his doubts and guilt resurfaced. On March 1, 1776, he noted in his diary that a "martial Spirit has seized all the Colonies." His next entry was curiously philosophical: "Resentment is a Passion, implemented by Nature. . . . Injury is the Object which excites it. . . . A Man may have the Faculty of concealing his Resentment, or suppressing it, but he must and ought to feel it. . . ." With his "Nerves tremulous," as he put it, his health sank to even lower depths in mid-summer as the British prepared to invade New York.[23]

[21]JA to AA, 17 June 1775, Butterfield, *AFC*, I, 215; JA to General Charles Lee, 13 Oct. 1775, Taylor, *PJA*, III, 202; JA to Jonathan Mason, Jr., 18 July 1776, ibid., IV, 391; Shaw, *Character of Adams*, 90.

[22]JA to AA, 23 June, 7 July, 7 Oct. 1775; 18 Aug. 1776, Butterfield, *AFC*, I, 226, 242, 295; II, 99–100.

[23]JA to AA, 26 Sept. 1775, Butterfield, *AFC*, I, 285; Butterfield, *DAJA*, II, 235–36; JA to James Warren, 27 July 1776, Taylor, *PJA*, IV, 413–14.

At first he declared that the "Pride and Pomp of War . . . have no Charms for me," but later he described the military regimen as "Sublime" and "Beautiful." During the next several months he mused at the presumed joy of shooting redcoats, and he spoke of his "ambition to be engaged in more active, gay, and *dangerous* Scenes." He talked of leaving Congress to accept a commission in the Massachusetts militia; he was determined to share in the "Laurells [that] will be reaped by our officers," he said. Adams spoke of his desire to "march too upon some . . . Emergency in Rank and File." When the British invaded Pennsylvania in 1777 he postured his indignity at Congress's abandonment of Philadelphia, suggesting that he had "a strong Inclination" to stay and "meet them in the Field." Roman senators, he asserted angrily, had not fled when attacked by the Gauls.[24]

"We must all be soldiers," Adams proclaimed, adding that it was desirable for every man to be obliged to fight, to face the stark alternatives of conquering or of dying. "Every body must and will and shall be a soldier," he again exclaimed, and he added that he was reading military manuals in preparation for bearing arms. He would serve however his country demanded, go "wherever she shall order me . . . without dismay." However, when Congress asked him to undertake a somewhat risky mission to Canada in 1776, he declined on the ground that his command of French was inadequate, a curious excuse in light of his subsequent diplomatic missions to France. Nor did he ever witness a battle during the war, something that many of his colleagues in Congress experienced either as observers or as combatants. He came close to the war only three times. One was the occasion of his visit to Lexington and Concord, whereupon he fell ill. A second instance came in September 1776 when, accompanied by Benjamin Franklin and Edward Rutledge, he went behind British lines under a flag of truce to negotiate with Admiral Richard Howe; unlike his companions, Adams was shaken by the experience, fearing that he might be kidnapped by the redcoats. Finally, he visited an army hospital early in 1777; he found the grim sights that confronted him too much to bear, falling into what he called the most melancholy mood he had ever experienced.[25]

Adams claimed that he would have entered the army had he come from the middle or southern states, but New England had an abundance of qualified officers. Usually, though, he attributed his failure to bear arms to age and infirmity: "I am too old, and too much worn, with Fatigue of Study in my youth," he

[24]JA to AA, 13 Feb. 1776, 19, 24 Aug. 1777, Butterfield, *AFC*, I, 347; II, 319, 327; JA to General Nathanael Greene, 22 June 1776, *Microfilm Edition of the Adams Papers* (Boston: Massachusetts Historical Society, 1954–1959), Reel 89; JA to Gen. Thomas Mifflin, 15 Aug. 1776, ibid.; JA to Gen. Samuel Parsons, 19 Aug. 1776, ibid.; JA to AA, 7 May 1775, Charles Francis Adams, ed., *Familiar Letters of John Adams to his Wife Abigail Adams During the Revolution* (Boston, 1876), 53–54; JA to Samuel Cooper, 30 May 1776, Taylor, *PJA*, IV, 221. Hereafter the *Microfilm Edition of Adams Papers* will be cited as *Adams Papers*.

[25]JA to Cooper, 30 May 1776, Taylor, *PJA*, IV, 221; JA to AA, 29 May 1775; 18 Feb. 1776; 13 April 1777, Butterfield, *AFC*, I, 207, 349; II, 209; Butterfield, *DAJA*, II, 272–73; III, 417–21.

27

complained. His "treacherous shattered Constitution," he remarked, negated his desire to soldier.[26]

His excuses were not sufficient to convince himself. Unable to resolve the quandary, Adams first spoke of retiring from politics, then he again fell ill. He was "weary, thoroughly weary;" he was "not a little concerned about [his] Health." He added that his ailments had given him reason to fear an "irreparable Injury to my Constitution."[27] Yet his maladies did not incapacitate him. Indeed, they were part of the tortuous strategy by which he resolved his ambivalence toward fighting.

Beginning in 1776 he assumed a Herculean task: more than any other congressman, Adams undertook the legislative management of the war. As the first head of the Board of War and Ordnance, he was what a biographer has described as a "kind of *de facto* Secretary of War." Another scholar suggested that because of his tireless attention to military matters, Adams became a "war department" unto himself, while still another historian wrote that in supervising the war he worked like a "galley slave bent on his oar."[28] In fact, Adams was pursuing a purging process not too dissimilar from the one that had succeeded during his French and Indian War crisis. In this instance he needed to convince himself that he suffered no less as a congressman than did soldiers, and he had to believe in the merits of his congressional work. He began by mildly criticizing some of his colleagues who left Congress to soldier. He went on to claim that the "Fatigues of War are much less destructive to Health than the painfull, laborious Attention to Debates and to Writing." He convinced himself that the "Army is the Place for Health—the Congress the Place for Sickness." He complained of his crushing work load and of the "solitary, gloomy, and disconsolate Hours" he was compelled to keep. His routine, he said, left him no time for "Pleasure . . . and . . . no opportunity to meddle with Books. . . ." "I am a lonely, forlorn Creature," he cried. He had sacrificed his law practice for the sake of public service, he said, with the result that now he was a man of "desperate fortune" faced with "Ruin."[29]

He thought his sacrifices as a "soldier" had been unlimited. He had traversed "an ordeal Path, among red hot Ploughshares," he once remarked. He had compromised his health "beyond Prudence, and safety," he told a friend. "I, poor Creature," he wrote his wife, am "worn out with scribbling, for my Bread and my Liberty." His service, he added, was a crushing burden. "The Business I have had upon my mind has been as great and important as can be entrusted to [one] Man,

[26]JA to Mason, 18 July 1776, Taylor, *PJA*, IV, 391; JA to Samuel Chase, 14 June 1776, ibid., IV, 313; JA to AA, 13 Feb. 1776, Butterfield, *AFC*, I, 347; JA to Parsons, 19 Aug. 1776, Butterfield, *DAJA*, III, 448.

[27]JA to Warren, 27 July 1776, Taylor, *PJA*, IV, 414; JA to AA, 11 July 1776, Butterfield, *AFC*, II, 44.

[28]Smith, *Adams*, I, 289; Shaw, *Character of Adams*, 101; Gilbert Chinard, *Honest John Adams* (Boston: Little, Brown, 1933), 109–10.

[29]JA to AA, 13 Feb., 28 April, 22 May, 11 July 1776; 17 Feb., 2 Sept., 26 July 1777; 12 May 1780, Butterfield, *AFC*, I, 347, 399, 412–13; II, 44, 163, 336, 289; III, 342; JA to James Warren, 26 Sept 1775; 27 July 1776, Taylor, *PJA*, III, 170; IV, 414; JA to Mercy Warren, 25 Nov. 1775, ibid., III, 318.

and the Difficulty and Intricacy of it is prodigious;'' he cried. For the sake of his country he had renounced "My Ease, my domestic Happiness, my rural Pleasures, my Little Property, my personal Liberty, my Reputation, my Life." "What have I not hazarded?" Soon he saw himself as a soldier, one who was "running dayly Risques of my Life." "Poor, Unhappy I,'' he dolefully concluded.[30]

Like a soldier at the front lines Adams longed for the serenity of his home in Braintree. He yearned for the rural life, for an escape from the "Smoke and Noise" of the city. He ached at the abandonment of his family; in the summer of 1776 he considered for the first time moving his wife and children to Philadelphia, an option he had previously refused to consider, though during the entirety of the previous year his family had lived on the doorstep of the British army. He did not bring them south, however, and he spent the balance of his congressional years isolated from them. He was ill and terribly homesick, he wrote, but he vowed not to "leave the *Field* untill the Campaign is ended." Adopting a military metaphor, he proclaimed "I cannot excuse myself from these duties, and I must march forward until it comes my turn to fall." If the war ever ended, he said, again seizing upon the fittest rhetorical flourish, he planned to "retreat like Cincinnatus to my plough."[31]

Adams ultimately was called on to join Franklin in Paris as part of the United States diplomatic service, and he experienced two hazardous trans-Atlantic crossings. During the first voyage, a winter crossing in 1777, his ship was fired on by a British vessel, and for a few hours Adams faced the terrifying prospect of falling into the hands of the enemy; only a fortuitous storm saved him. The second voyage, still another difficult winter crossing from America, ended in Spain in 1779; then Adams and his party were compelled to make an arduous six-week journey via horse and mule from El Ferrol to France, a trek in mid-winter across some of western Europe's most rugged terrain. The dangers he faced and the sacrifices he made—both the real and the imagined perils—resolved his quandary. Moreover, he had become certain that his service was unselfish and in the real interests of the public and of the Republic. "Ambition in a Republic," he had concluded, "is a great Virtue, for it is nothing more than a Desire to Serve the Public, to promote the Happiness of the People. Thus, Ambition is but another name for public Virtue, and public Spirit."[32]

[30]JA to James Warren, 25 June 1774; 26 Sept. 1775; 27 July 1776, Taylor, *PJA*, II, 100; III, 170; IV, 414; JA to Mercy Warren, 25 Nov. 1775, ibid., III, 318; JA to Gen. Daniel Roberdeau, 24 Dec. 1777, *Adams Papers*, Reel 89; JA to James Lovell, 24 Dec. 1777, ibid.; JA to Benjamin Rush, 8 Feb. 1778, ibid.; JA to AA, 23 June, 24 July 1775; 19 March, 28 April, 22 May, 11 July 1776; 17 Feb., 26 July, 2 Sept. 1777; 12 May 1780, Butterfield, *AFC*, I, 226, 255, 363, 399, 412–13; II, 44, 131, 163, 289, 336; III, 342.

[31]JA to AA, 28 April, 16 July 1776; 16 March, 4 Aug. 1777; 23 Sept. 1778, Butterfield, *AFC*, I, 399; II, 50, 176, 299; III, 91; JA to Benjamin Highborn, 29 May 1776, Taylor, *PJA*, IV, 417; JA to James Warren, 16 March 1780, in *Warren-Adams Letters: Being Chiefly a Correspondence Among John Adams, Samuel Adams, and James Warren*, 2 vols., Massachusetts Historical Society, *Collections* (Boston, 1925), II, 129–30.

[32]Butterfield, *DAJA*, II, 276–92, 400–34; JA to ?, 27 April 1777, *Adams Papers*, Reel 91.

29

On the eve of his first voyage he still spoke of soldiering in tones that revealed his feelings of guilt. Afterwards there was no evidence of anxiety aroused by the civilian role he chose to play in this war. He had found inner peace by convincing himself that he was as much a soldier as the man in the trenches, and he was satisfied of the virtuousness of his actions. As he put it, he had to "study Politicks and War that my sons may have liberty to study Mathematics and Philosophy. . . ." Ultimately, he even was truly able to believe what he had told a friend at the beginning of the conflict: "Wearing a Uniform . . . is not all. . . . Politicks are the Science of human Happiness and War the Act of Securing it.""

* * *

The five years after 1783 was perhaps the happiest, most tranquil period that Adams had experienced since the early 1760s, a time when he had been a newly married, rising young attorney. Adams spent these years on diplomatic missions at Auteuil, a suburb of Paris, then in London as the United States Minister. With independence secured the times suddenly must have seemed placid by contrast to those busy, sometimes desperate, years of the Revolution, and Adams gave every appearance of being happy and at ease in this new environment. Abigail lived with him much of the time, a considerable departure from their almost constant separation during the decade after 1774. As Peter Shaw has observed, moreover, the two seemed to grow closer than they had been in years, even rekindling the concupiscence of their courtship period. The source of frequent blandishments and daily deference, an exalted elder statesman and venerated patriot, his earlier identity problems seemed to have been reconciled, and by most accounts he appears to have been a man at ease with himself. In fact, as Shaw has noted, in the two paintings for which Adams sat in the 1780s, his was a demeanor that conveyed a "genuine serenity," a "sense of vindication" that his actions had been noble and virtuous. "

When Adams returned to the United States in 1788 he was surprised by the fuss made over him. Later that year he was elected to the new office of vice president, the only post he would have taken, he remarked, since he regarded all other federal offices—except the presidency, of course—as "beneath him." Powerless and frequently neglected, or so he thought, he was not terribly happy during the eight years in which he occupied this post. Yet in 1796, when Washington announced his intention to retire, Adams's life suddenly changed. That autumn enough presidential electors shared his view that he was the "heir apparent" to Washington to select him to be the nation's second chief executive."

"JA to AA, 12 May 1780, Butterfield, *AFC*, III, 342; JA to Tudor, 14 Nov. 1775, Taylor, *PJA*, III, 296. On Adams's awareness of the hazards he faced in making the Atlantic crossing, see JA to Elbridge Gerry, 23 Dec. 1777, *Adams Papers*, Reel 89.

"Shaw, *Character of Adams*, 187, 192.

"AA to Granddaughter AA, 16 July 1798, Caroline de Windt, ed., *Journal and Correspondence of Miss Adams, Daughter of John Adams, Second President of the United States*, 2 vols. (New York, 1841), II, 89; Smith, *Adams*, II, 880.

30

John Adams undoubtedly hoped for a serene, pacific presidency. He did not get his wish, however. He had no sooner taken office in 1797 than news arrived of French maritime violations against America's neutral vessels, depredations arising from French hostility to the recently ratified Jay Treaty with Great Britain. President Adams recommended a two-fold response to these assaults: he strengthened America's military capabilities, and, in an act of conciliation, he dispatched a team of commissioners to negotiate a settlement. The commissioners, however, were insulted by secret agents of the French government, negotiations were aborted, and war fever gripped some circles—notably, in Adams's own Federalist Party.

War seemed inevitable, and at times Adams appeared to be the most vocal exponent of a bellicose policy. Yet, with the country poised on the brink of war, President Adams suddenly demurred. He convened the Congress, but instead of asking for a declaration of war as many expected, he announced the nomination of a minister plenipotentiary to the French Republic. Within a few months the crisis abated. Nevertheless, the Federalist Party was rent by his decision to negotiate, and in the elections of 1800 the Party tottered and Adams was defeated in his bid for reelection.

Adams's behavior in this episode—known as the Quasi-War Crisis—baffled many contemporaries, and it has been the source of persistent controversy among scholars.* However, if his actions are seen in light of his two previous war-related anxiety attacks, much of the mystery of his conduct disappears.

Adams had come to the presidency certain that the nation required peace. He believed that another war so soon after the long War for Independence might destroy the gains of the Revolution, perhaps even resulting in the breakup of the fragile union. A state of war, he warned, would provoke the creation of a "many bellied Monster of an Army to tyrannize over Us," it would shackle the nation with a pernicious debt, and it would "totally dissadjust [sic] our present Government, and accelerate the Advent of Monarchy and Aristocracy by at least fifty Years."[37] Earlier in the decade great excitement had been generated by the disruption of

---

*Historical assessments of Adams's role in the Quasi-War Crisis have fallen into two broad categories. One school insists that Adams acted primarily with the national interest in mind, and without regard to the political consequences his action might entail. For this view, see Smith, *Adams*, II, 1002, 1029-30; Alexander De Conde, *The Quasi-War: The Politics and Diplomacy of the Undeclared War with France, 1797-1801* (New York: Scribner's, 1966); Ralph Adams Brown, *The Presidency of John Adams* (Lawrence: Univ. Press of Kansas, 1975); John R. Howe, *The Changing Political Thought of John Adams* (Princeton: Princeton Univ. Press, 1966); William Stinchcombe, "The Diplomacy of the WXYZ Affair," *William and Mary Quarterly*, 34 (1977), 590-617. A second school has argued that Adams acted primarily because of personal considerations and that his conduct throughout the crisis was self-serving. Initially, they argue, the President believed that bellicose conduct would result in positive political benefits; by 1799, however, Adams perceived a swing in public opinion, and his artful and seemingly impulsive manner thereafter can be explained only as his desperate attempt to retrieve the political gains that had been jeopardized by the war hawks in his party. For this argument, see Stephen G. Kurtz, *The Presidency of John Adams: The Collapse of Federalism, 1795-1800* (Philadelphia: Univ. of Pennsylvania Press, 1957); Manning J. Dauer, *The Adams Federalists* (Baltimore, Johns Hopkins Univ. Press, 1953).

[37]Chinard, *Honest John Adams*, 262-79; Howe, *Changing Political Thought of Adams*, 194-205.

31

American maritime activities by the Algerine pirates, but Adams, then the vice president, had urged President Washington to pursue a pacific policy. He also had deplored the warmongering during the Jay Treaty crisis, and he had assured his wife, Abigail, that if the country went to war "it shall not be my fault." In that crisis he had suggested that a foreign conflict would be dishonest—he called it "knavish." In fact, throughout his vice presidency he called for a "humane and pacific foreign policy," stressing the need to avoid "hazardous and expansive and bloody experiments." When the crisis with France commenced in the final days of the Washington administration, Adams censured as "anarchical warriors" those who urged hostilities. After his election to the presidency he maintained that he bore no prejudice against France. He wished for peace, he insisted, and he promised to "make no aggressions" on either Britain or France. His Inaugural Address was so moderate, in fact, that some Federalists privately denounced it as a "temporizing" statement, and soon even Talleyrand, the Directory's Foreign Minister, professed that Adams seemed to be more conciliatory than his predecessor.[38]

From the outset of the Quasi-War Crisis Adams privately resisted those who urged immediate conflict, asserting that if "forced into war" it would be against his "Inclination and Judgment." In the spring of 1798 he took precautionary measures, and he sought to strengthen American forces by augmenting the fleet and by creating a new national army. Yet he did not want war. For the first time he even spoke of soldiers in less than complimentary terms, and he advised some college students against enlisting in the new army. He also warned the citizenry not to be "dazzled" by martial splendors. Adams additionally denigrated those who clamored for war. He called them the "worst Ennemies" of the Republic. At one point he acknowledged that the conduct of France might have justified a declaration of war, but he added quickly that while a conflict "might be just, [it] may not always be necessary. I have it much at heart to settle all disputes with France," he added.[39]

While Adams certainly was convinced of the efficacy of his stance, his resolve may only have been strengthened by the knowledge that Alexander Hamilton, a man who personified so much that he detested, was perhaps the most vocal proponent of a belligerent course. President Adams regarded Hamilton as "proud"

[38]Shaw, *Character of Adams*, 202; Smith, *Adams*, II, 853, 858, 889, 903; James D. Richardson, ed., *A Compilation of the Messages of the Papers of the Presidents*, 20 vols. (New York: Bureau of National Literature, 1897–1917), I, 263; JA to James Lloyd, 29 March 1815, in Charles Francis Adams, ed., *The Works of John Adams, Second President of the United States: With a Life of the Author*, 10 vols. (Boston, 1850–1856), X, 148; JA to AA, 18 Dec. 1796, *Adams Papers*, Reel 382; Albert Hall Bowman, *The Struggle for Neutrality: Franco-American Diplomacy During the Federalist Era* (Knoxville: Univ. of Tennessee Press, 1974), 299; Stinchcombe, "Diplomacy of the WXYZ Affair," 596.

[39]JA to the Morris County (New Jersey) Grand Jury, 3 April 1799, *Adams Papers*, Reel 394; JA to the Boston Marine Society, 7 Sept. 1798, ibid., Reel 391; Adams to the Dutchess County (New York) Grand Jury, 22 Sept. 1798, ibid.; and JA to the Officers and Soldiers of the Chester (Pennsylvania) Light Infantry Company, 17 Sept. 1798, ibid.; JA to the New Jersey Legislature, 26 Feb. 1799, ibid., Reel 393; Smith, *Adams*, II, 964; JA to Henry Knox, 20 March 1797, Adams, *Works*, VIII, 535. Emphasis added.

and "conceited," an intriguer, a power-hungry, duplicitous scamp, and even as lascivious and oversexed, the sort "with as debauched Morals as old [Benjamin] Franklin. . . ." Moreover, he believed Hamilton was moved solely by selfish pursuits. For instance, when Congress created the new army to meet the emergency, Adams immediately came under pressure from a well-orchestrated campaign to name Hamilton as its commander. He saw Hamilton behind the "intrigue"; he believed he was meant to be "the dupe of it." The president instead selected Washington to command the army, but when the retired hero insisted on Hamilton as his second-in-command, Adams could only accede to his wishes. Thereafter, Adams viewed Hamilton's warmongering as a ploy by which to fulfill his own narrow ends.[40]

If Adams primarily expressed temperate feelings in private, the nation heard and saw the president assume a quite different posture. His public rhetoric took on a considerably more obdurate and bellicose edge. "Let us have war," he said at one point. He told a correspondent that the "finger of destiny writes on the wall the word: War." The public heard him speak frequently on behalf of strengthening the armed forces, and it heard him castigate those who "cant about peace" and those "who snivel for it." War, he said, "is . . . less dreadful than iniquity or deserved disgrace." He was disgusted, he claimed, by the "babyish and *womanly* blubbering" of those who wished to avoid hostilities. Fear, he charged, had ignominiously put "petticoats" on those who called for peace. "America is not SCARED"; it would resist France with "manly determination," he reiterated. He even began to appear in public wearing a full military uniform with a sword strapped to his side.[41]

While contemporaries saw his conduct as inexplicably vacillating, contradictory, and irresolute, the president's behavior was, in fact, not unlike that which he had exhibited in earlier trials. While he publicly blustered and postured, speaking in martial tones and wearing military regalia, he was tormented privately by self-doubts. Ultimately, too, he experienced a recurrence of those ills that had accompanied his earlier crises. A rash and itch appeared; he was troubled by headaches, and he wrote Abigail that he lived in agony.[42] He spoke of his "torments," and he quipped that if "Robespierre were to cut off my Head I should not feel half the Pain that I suffer every Hour." He complained that he looked forty years older than when he took office. He lost weight, and Abigail mentioned that she had never seen him appear to be so pale. He wrote his wife of his afflictions, but he cautioned her to tell no one lest "I should lose all my character for firmness. . . . Indeed I sometimes suspect I deserve a character for peevishness rather than firmness." Soon, as he

[40]JA to AA, 9 Jan. 1797, *Adams Papers*, Reel 383; JA to James McHenry, 29 Aug. 1798, Adams, *Works*, VII, 588; Smith, *Adams*, II, 908, 984; Jacob E. Cooke, *Alexander Hamilton* (New York, 1982), 183, 187.

[41]De Conde, *Quasi-War*, 81; Smith, *Adams*, II, 999, 1004–06; JA to Knox, 30 March 1797, Adams, *Works*, VIII, 535; JA to Wolcott, 27 Oct. 1797, ibid., VIII, 559; JA to the Inhabitants of Providence, 30 April 1797, ibid., IX, 185; JA to John Quincy Adams, 21 March 1797, ibid., VIII, 537. Emphasis added.

[42]JA to AA, 15 Nov., 14 Dec. 1799, *Adams Papers*, Reel 392.

33

frequently did in such instances, Adams slid into an emotional malaise. He acknowledged his "state of depression, agitation, and anxiety," and in the summer of 1799 he even recognized his symptoms as identical to those that had occurred in earlier times of stress."[43] He fled the capital for his farm in Massachusetts, seeking solace there with his family. During these months extensive gaps appear in his normally voluminous correspondence, an indication of his lassitude. He grew more querulous than ever. At times he was so irascible that Abigail thought it unwise even to permit him to see state letters. He acted the perfect curmudgeon, snapping irritably at his family and the hired help. He avoided and insulted old acquaintances, treating several persons in a contemptible and uncivil manner. For the first time in nearly twenty years he spoke of retirement. In private he talked of quitting the presidency, and he told his family that it was time "to bid farewell to Politicks." He began to pity himself once again. "What have I ever enjoyed? All my Enjoyments have been on the farm." His fear of impending doom also resurfaced, and he told his wife that he doubted whether he could physically survive the next two years in office."[44]

Adams was dedicated to peace, for he believed that a war with France might be ruinous for the new nation. He also realized that to steer the United States clear of conflict required that he resist a war fever that burned within his countrymen. The easier choice would have been to take the country to war, and he was sorely tempted by that course. Those temptations produced difficulties for Adams not unlike those that had tormented him during the early years of the War for Independence. Once again he was beset by anxiety for harboring wishes that he believed he should not have entertained. He knew that war might be politically expedient, that his fame and power might be enhanced by a popular conflict. At times in 1798 it seemed that the temptations were too great, that war would be his choice. At one point he even complained to his wife that war already should have been declared; Abigail, closer than anyone to his innermost thoughts, expected war and began to stockpile commodities that would disappear when the struggle commenced. The president told the students of Princeton College that there was "no means of averting the storm," and on another occasion he wrote: "To me there appears no alternative between actual hostilities on our part and national ruin." Adams told a British diplomat that he expected America to fight the French for a year or two, then to be joined by Great Britain either as an ally or a co-belligerent. James Madison even charged that Adams alone was responsible for the war atmosphere. a sentiment echoed by George Logan, a Philadelphia Quaker leader, and by Timothy Pickering. the Secretary of State."[45]

[43]JA to AA, 4, 8, 9 Feb., 17 Dec. 1799, ibid., Reels 393 and 392; Shaw, *Character of Adams*, 263.
[44]JA to AA, 9, 22 Feb., 3 April 1799, *Adams Papers*, Reels 393 and 384; Lynne Withey, *Dearest Friend: A Life of Abigail Adams* (New York: Free Press, 1981), 259; JA to McHenry, 29 Aug; 1798, Adams, *Works*, VIII, 588; Smith, *Adams*, II, 966, 982, 987; Shaw, *Character of Adams*, 257–58.
[45]Smith, *Adams*, II, 953–55; Kurtz, *Presidency of Adams*, 300, 290–91; De Conde, *Quasi-War*, 80, 406n; Janet Whitney, *Abigail Adams* (Boston: Little, Brown, 1948), 280.

34

Yet as easy as the war path might have been to take, Adams knew full well that to choose such a course would be to surrender to ambition and self-interest, to sacrifice what he believed was the nation's best interest to his own monumental selfishness. That hardly resolved his anxieties, however. His old fear of being seen as a weakling—this time for having pursued peace—resurfaced. Hence, he attired himself as a soldier and spoke in a strident, pugnacious manner. Those strategies served as crutches to assist him through the crisis. Meanwhile, his sense of manliness was reinforced by his pending assumption of the responsibilities as commander-in-chief of the new army that he had fathered; in fact, John Quincy Adams later wrote that his father's ardor for war began to abate the very moment the army was created.[46]

While he redeployed many of the strategies that had succeeded in earlier quandaries, Adams took pains to assure that the door to negotiations remained open. Out of a dedication to peace, he carefully, consciously, resisted a widespread belligerent temperment on the part of the public; finally, late in 1799, having atoned for his forbidden desires, satisfied that his intent was "honourable" and "just and righteous," Adams proceeded to act as he always had longed to act. He sought peace by dispatching a minister plenipotentiary to France. In his mind he had acted selflessly. In fact, he later wrote, he had acted with the knowledge that "I was signing my own death warrant as a public man. . . . But I thought my duty to my country ought to prevail over every personal . . . consideration." He had acted—he could only have acted—when he believed that his decision had been made in the "strictest purity."[47]

[46]John Quincy Adams and Charles Francis Adams, *The Life of John Adams*, 2 vols. (Philadelphia, 1871), II, 280.

[47]AA to Mary Cranch, 30 Dec. 1799, in Stewart Mitchell, ed., *New Letters of Abigail Adams* (Boston: Little, Brown, 1947), 224–25; De Conde, *Quasi-War*, 441n; JA to Mercy Warren, 19 Aug. 1807, in Charles Francis Adams, ed., "Correspondence between John Adams and Mercy Warren," Massachusetts Historical Society, *Collections*, 5th Ser., 4 (1883), 470–72.

35

JESSE LEMISCH

LISTENING TO
THE "INARTICULATE"

William Widger's Dream and the Loyalties of American Revolutionary Seamen in British Prisons

"Of kings and gentlemen," wrote W. E. B. Du Bois, "we have the record ad nause[a]m and in stupid detail. . . ."[1] But of "the common run of human beings," he went on, "and particularly of the half or wholly submerged working group, the world has saved all too little of authentic record and tried to forget or ignore even the little saved." "Who built the seven towers of Thebes?" echoed Bertolt Brecht, "The books are filled with names of kings."[2] Such appeals for what might be called a history of the inarticulate have come not only from the left, nor have they necessarily been populist in intent. A century ago, looking at history with somewhat different sympathies, Frederick Law Olmsted, a self-proclaimed "honest growler," spoke as much to the question of validity as to that of humanity:

Men of literary taste . . . are always apt to overlook the working-classes, and to confine the records they make of their own times, in a great degree, to the habits and fortunes of their own associates, or to those of people of superior rank to themselves, of whose sayings and doings their vanity, as well as their curiosity, leads them to most carefully inform themselves. The dumb masses have often been so lost in this shadow of egotism, that, in later days, it has been impossible to

JESSE LEMISCH is in the department of history of Roosevelt University. An earlier version of this paper was read in a session on "Writing the History of the Inarticulate" at the American Historical Association meetings, New York City, December 1968.

[1] For this and the following, see Du Bois' preface to Herbert Aptheker, ed., *A Documentary History of the Negro People in the United States* (New York, 1951), p. v.

[2] *Selected Poems*, trans. H. R. Hays (New York, 1947), pp. 108-109.

discern the very real influence their character and condition has had on the fortune and fate of nations.[3]

Should the character and condition of the "dumb masses" play a minor role in historiography? *Must* they? The answer to the first question, at least, seems clear: the most conservative standards of evidence and proof require that historiography include a history of the inarticulate. No generalization has much meaning until we have actually examined the constituent parts of the entity about which we are generalizing. No contention about the people on the bottom of a society—neither that they are rebellious nor docile, neither that they defer to an authority whose legitimacy they accept nor that they curse an authority which they deem illegitimate, neither that they are noble nor that they are base—no such contention even approaches being proved until we have in fact attempted a history of the inarticulate. Consensus, in order to demonstrate its validity, must confront the conservative rocks of evidence and sail safely through them, as must any generalization which claims to describe a society on the basis of research on only a part of that society.[4]

---

[3] *A Journey in the Seabord Slave States, with Remarks on Their Economy* (New York, 1861), pp. 214-215, quoted in Stephan Thernstrom, *Poverty and Progress: Social Mobility in a Nineteenth-Century City* (Cambridge, Mass., 1964), p. 1. For Olmsted's self-description, see p. ix of *Journey*.

[4] For further remarks on inaccuracies in the historiography of early America due to elitism, see my "The American Revolution Seen From the Bottom Up," in Barton J. Bernstein, ed., *Towards A New Past: Dissenting Essays in American History* (New York, 1968), pp. 3-45. Cf. Michael Rogin, "Progressivism and the California Electorate," *Journal of American History*, LV (Sept. 1968), 298: "conclusions that progressivism was not a movement of 'the people' can hardly be sustained until the behavior of the people is actually examined."
Similar comments may be made concerning the use of the concept of ideological hegemony. Deriving the term from Antonio Gramsci, a Marxist theoretician who was especially concerned with the role of intellectuals in twentieth-century Italian politics, Eugene D. Genovese defines ideological hegemony as "the seemingly spontaneous loyalty that a ruling class evokes from the masses through its cultural position and its ability to promote its own world view as the general will" ("Marxian Interpretations of the Slave South," in Bernstein, ed., *Towards a New Past*, p. 123). Genovese correctly contends that an understanding of "class struggle . . . presupposes a specific historical analysis of the constituent classes" (p. 98), but he draws conclusions about the hegemony of the slaveholders with very little examination of "the masses," who, he contends, accepted that hegemony (pp. 90-125; see also his *The Political Economy of Slavery: Studies in the Economy and Society of the Slave South* [New York, 1965]). Genovese's work has produced rich results for our understanding of the slaveholders, but it tells us less about the "loyalty" or otherwise of the nonslaveholders; one does not need to contend that the latter were in open, or even furtive, rebellion to note that there remain enormous complexities which prevent a definition of "to rule" as synony-

Can we write a history of the inarticulate? It was, in part, to answer that question that I undertook my study of merchant seamen in early America. That study began in dissatisfaction with the role assigned to this group in the secondary literature of the American Revolution.[5] In that literature, seamen appear with great frequency, battling over impressment and rioting in the streets of colonial cities. But although the accounts suggest that seamen acted consistently against British authority, when historians narrate such events it seems to me that they generally evade their central task—explanation.[6] In the absence of other explanations, it frequently appears that Jack Tar rioted because he is and always has been boisterous and irresponsible, the willing victim of alcoholic fantasies, seeking merely to blow off steam. Or at best the seamen rioted because they were manipulated by certain ill-defined groups.

Even accepting a large role for the accidental and the irrational in human affairs, it seems to me that the job of the historian as social scientist is to limit as much as possible the area within which explanation must rely upon such factors. Manipulation exists and irrationality exists, and the historian must acknowledge them when he finds them. But the historian who would make his discipline a more rigorous one should have as his *working assumption* that human actions are generally purposeful and are related to some system of values as well as needs; given that assumption, it is inadequate for him to "explain" the recurrent conduct of large groups of men who seem to act consistently in accord with certain values by making those groups simply the puppets of their social superiors or the victims of alcohol.

In order to explain the seamen's conduct, I found that I would have to ask of them some of the same kinds of questions which intellectual historians generally ask of an elite: questions concerning loy-

mous with "to evoke loyalty." The existence of hegemonic mechanisms does not demonstrate the existence of hegemony. This important area needs fuller exploration. (See also my "New Left Elitism," *Radical America,* I [Sept.-Oct. 1967], 43-53; and my "Communication," *American Historical Review* [in press]).

[5] For a partial summary of this research, see my "Jack Tar in the Streets: Merchant Seamen in the Politics of Revolutionary America," *William and Mary Quarterly,* 3d Ser., XXV (July 1968), 371-407. Except where otherwise noted, this is the source for the following statements about seamen and historiography.

[6] For some notable exceptions, see Carl Bridenbaugh, *Cities in Revolt: Urban Life in America, 1743-1776* (New York, 1955), pp. 114-117, 305-312; Richard B. Morris, *Government and Labor in Early America* (New York, 1946), pp. 188-193, 225-278; and Oliver M. Dickerson, *The Navigation Acts and the American Revolution* (Philadelphia, 1951), pp. 218-219.

alties and beliefs, all examined within a context which assumed that Jack Tar, like Thomas Jefferson, had ideas and perhaps something which might be called an ideology. On the track of these ideas, I found that actions which might in themselves appear inexplicable made more sense when causality was explored: the historian decides in advance that Jack Tar is a rebel without cause when he neglects to look for cause. The rioting of the pre-Revolutionary decades, for instance, makes more sense when seen against the background of an ancient and bloody tradition of violent resistance to British authority; impressment, commented a Pennsylvania Revolutionary leader, had produced "an estrangement of the Affections of the People from the Authority" of the British, which had led in turn, "by an easy Progression . . . to open Opposition . . . and Bloodshed."[7]

I found inadequacies in the approach to the Revolution—primarily from the top down—generally taken by historians. *Of course,* British officials—insensitive as they were to grievances of the victims of the policies which they administered—could find no better explanation than manipulation for the conduct of the seamen. *Of course,* Admiralty records distorted the realities of impressment, leading those who based their research on such sources to see impressment in the context of a manning problem rather than in the context of deprivation of personal liberty.

The struggle to get inside Jack Tar's head suggested the notion of what might be called an "experimental history." One way of evaluating the contention that a crowd is manipulated is to ask, what would the crowd do in the absence of those alleged to be its manipulators? The social psychologist might devise such a condition, but the historian has no choice but to accept the data provided by the past. As it happens, in the New York Stamp Act riots of 1765, precisely such a condition existed: witnesses who are in conflict on other matters agree that at one point whatever leaders the crowd had had lost control.[8] At this point, eschewing plunder, the crowd (including some four to five hundred seamen) marched some distance in a new direction and in orderly fashion to attack the logical political target. What is of interest to us here is not that in this

---

[7] Joseph Reed, President of Pa., quoted in my "Jack Tar in the Streets," p. 395.

[8] See my unpubl. diss. (Yale, 1962), "Jack Tar vs. John Bull: The Role of New York's Seamen in Precipitating the Revolution," pp. 88-91.

particular instance a crowd demonstrably had political thoughts of its own but rather that if one attempts to devise conditions under which one might evaluate the thought and conduct of crowds, one may find a historical situation which approximates these conditions.[9]

The notion of an "experimental history" seems crucial for a history of the inarticulate. Given the absence of a laboratory and the impossibility of controlling conditions experimentally, one must sensitize oneself to seek such conditions in the existing data. In effect, the historian of the inarticulate must train himself to think as if he were an experimental social psychologist; he must try to devise experiments for testing various contentions; then he must look to history and do his best to find a "natural experiment"—a situation in which such an experiment was in fact acted out.[10]

∾

One night in 1781—which is some sixty thousand nights ago—American seaman William Widger, who was nobody,[11] dreamt this

---

[9] Cf. Merle Curti's criticism of historians for their reluctance "to try to adapt experimental logic to situations where actual experimentation is impossible" (rev. of C. Vann Woodward, ed., *The Comparative Approach to American History* [New York, 1968] in *Journal of American History*, LV [Sept. 1968], 373). Historians are of course limited to what psychologists call "natural experiments"; their predictions are made *a posteriori*, and the experiment cannot be rerun under other conditions to determine whether the variable focused upon is in fact the decisive one.

[10] Such training might fruitfully begin with study of the imaginative and rigorous experiments on obedience and defiance devised by Stanley Milgram. See his "Behavioral Study of Obedience," *Journal of Abnormal and Social Psychology*, LXVII (1963), 371-378; "Issues in the Study of Obedience: A Reply to Baumrind," *American Psychologist*, XIX (Nov. 1964), 848-852; "Some Conditions of Obedience and Disobedience to Authority," *Human Relations*, XVIII (1965), 57-76; and "Liberating Effects of Group Pressure," *Journal of Personality and Social Psychology*, I (Feb. 1965), 127-134. Milgram's experiments were called to my attention by Prof. Naomi Weisstein of the Dept. of Psychology, Loyola Univ., Chicago. Weisstein briefly discusses Milgram's work and other experiments with broad implications for the writing of history (especially work by R. Rosenthal and by S. Schachter and J.E. Singer) in "Kinder, Küche, Kirche as Scientific Law: Psychology Constructs the Female," a paper presented at the meeting of The American Studies Association, Univ. of California, Davis, Oct. 1968 (revised version forthcoming in *Psychology Today*).

[11] Widger (1748-1823) was a Marblehead privateersman captured in the brig *Phoenix*, Feb. 12, 1779, and committed to Mill Prison, May 10, 1779. After the war Widger became master of the brig *Increase*. For his dream, see "Diary of William Widger of Marblehead, Kept at Mill Prison, England, 1781," *Essex Institute Historical Collections* (Salem, Mass.), LXXIII-LXXIV (1937-38), 347 (hereafter cited as *EIHC*). Concerning Widger, see "Diary," *ibid.*, LXXXIII, 311-312; *Boston Gazette, and the Country Journal*, July 1, 1782; Benjamin J.

dream as sentries marched around his Revolutionary War prison:

Last night I Dreamed I was in Marblehead and See [saw] Sylvester Stevens[.][12] after discourseing with him about his Giting home I said to him tis Damd hard now I have Got so near home and Cant git their. . . . he asked me What the Matter was[;] I sayes Why you See I am this Side of the weay and the Souldiers Standing Sentrey over by Mr. Roundays house. . . . I Left him and Went a Little further & met Georg Tucker down by the eand of Bowden's Lain wheir he Stouped and Shock hands with me and Said he Was Glad to See me[;] he Said my Wife was Just Deliver'd a Boy. . . . I Started at that and Said it was a dam'd Lye it was imposable for I had been Gone tow [two] years and leatter [later] and it was inposable. . . . I Left him in a Great pashan and I was Going Down towards Nickes cove I met my Mother and Stopt and talked with hur[.] She asked me wheir [whether] I was not a Going home to see my wife[.] I told hur no I was dam'd if ever I desired to See hir a Gain[.] She Said the Child was a honest begotten Child and it was Got before I went to See and it was mine[.] I Said it was inposable for the Child to be Mine for I had been Gone Mour then two years and it was Inpousable[.] I told hur I was a dam'd foule to Coum home but I Could go back in the Brig I came in. . . . She pursuaded upon me to go home but . . . I was in Such a pashan I Swore I would Never See hur a Gain. . . . She intreated me to go home but I Swore I would not and it was no use to ask me[;] but before I was don talking With hur a bout it I awaked.

What did you, who are somebody, dream last night—or a thousand nights ago? This is not an argument for dream analysis. It simply says that even the most fragile and evanescent sort of historical evidence can be retrieved if we will only look for it. The naval prisons of the American Revolution are an especially rewarding place to look for evidence for the history of the inarticulate. A rich concentration of sources from conflicting points of view enables us to look into the mind of the common seaman; here, we can begin to say meaningful things about what significance the Revolution had for at least some of the inarticulate.

During the Revolution, captured American seamen found themselves imprisoned up and down the Atlantic coast and offshore,[13]

Lindsey, *Old Marblehead Sea Captains and the Ships in Which They Sailed* (Marblehead, 1915), p. 131; Thurlow S. Widger, "The Widger Family" (n.d.; typescript at Essex Institute), pp. 4, 9-13. I am indebted to Dorothy M. Potter, Librarian at the Essex Institute, for help in securing biographical information about Widger.

[12] One of Widger's shipmates; Stevens escaped from Mill Prison (*Boston Gazette, and the Country Journal*, July 1, 1782).

[13] For New York, see the numerous citations in the following pages.

and at various places in the British Isles.[14] The three major prisons for captured seamen were a fleet around the prison ship *Jersey* at New York and, in England, Mill and Forton prisons on land at Plymouth and Portsmouth. During the war these three prison complexes held upwards of ten thousand and perhaps as many as twenty or thirty thousand captured American seamen.[15]

For Norfolk, see "Biographical Memoir of Commodore [Richard] Dale," *The Port Folio*, VIII, ser. 3 (June 1814), 500.

For Rhode Island: John K. Alexander, ed., "Jonathan Carpenter and the American Revolution: The Journal of an American Naval Prisoner of War and Vermont Indian Fighter," *Vermont History*, XXXVI (Spring 1968), 78-79; Charles Collins to Benjamin Franklin, July 8, 1779, in Franklin Papers (American Philosophical Society), XV, 26; "Diary of George Thompson of Newburyport, Kept at Forton Prison, England, 1777-1781," *EIHC*, LXXVI (July 1940), 222.

Quebec: "Reminiscences of the Revolution: Prison Letters and Sea Journal of Caleb Foot," *EIHC*, XXVI (March 1889), 105-108.

Halifax: Commissioners of Sick and Hurt Seamen (hereafter abbreviated as CSHS) to Admiralty, Feb. 25, 1777, Jan. 5, 1778, Sept. 17, 1779, Public Record Office, Admiralty 98/11/86, 153-154, 12/176-179; Admiralty to CSHS, Aug. 1, 1777, Jan. 14, 1778, Sept. 8, 1779, March 15, 1782, National Maritime Museum, Greenwich, Adm/M/404, 405; [Boston] *Independent Chronicle and the Universal Advertiser*, Feb. 5, 1778; John Blatchford, *Narrative of the Life & Captivity. . .* (New London, 1778), pp. 3-6.

St. John's: *Salem* [Mass.] *Gazette*, Oct. 17, 1782.

West Indies: Admiralty to CSHS, July 3, Dec. 7, 1780, Sept. 15, 1781, Sept. 3, 1782, Adm/M/404, 405; Account of George Ralls, Nov. 7, 1778, New-York Historical Society; Secretary of State to Admiralty, Dec. 5, 1781, Adm/1/4146.

14 For Mill and Forton Prisons, see numerous citations in the following pages. Smaller numbers of Americans were kept, usually temporarily, at such places as Kinsale, Kilkenny, and the Cove of Cork in Ireland, at Edinburgh, at Liverpool, Deal, at the Nore, off Chatham, at Bristol, Pembroke, Shrewsbury, Falmouth, Weymouth, and Yarmouth. Mention of these is scattered throughout the correspondence between the Admiralty and the CSHS. (Admiralty to CSHS, 1777-83, National Maritime Museum, Greenwich, Adm/M/404-405; CSHS to Admiralty, 1777-83, Public Record Office, London, Adm 98/11-14). A fuller description of these prisons and more specific citations will appear in my full-length study, "Jack Tar in the Darbies: American Seamen in British Prisons during the Revolution," to be completed shortly.

15 For almost complete figures for Mill (1296 American prisoners) and Forton (1200) see John Howard, *The State of the Prisons in England and Wales . . .* (4th ed.; London, 1792), pp. 185, 187. *Jersey's* logs list a total of 7773 (Adm 51/493 and Adm 51/4228). But more than twenty ships held captured seamen at New York during the war, and although *Jersey* was the major prison ship, others, such as *Good Hope*, held more than three hundred at one time (*New Hampshire Gazette*, Feb 9, 1779), and *Jersey* did not receive her first prisoners until June, 1779. Thus it is likely that the total for New York will be more than doubled when figures are found for the other prison ships. In addition, the figure for *Jersey* alone is low because there are two gaps in the logs (Nov. 21, 1777–Aug. 2, 1778, and Dec. 25, 1780–Feb. 14, 1781) one of them during the period of *Jersey's* service as a prison ship, and because, as will be seen below, those who kept *Jersey's* logs were far from faithful record keepers. Mill and Forton were set up early in 1777 explicitly for Americans captured at sea: Admiralty to CSHS, March 13, April 19, 1777, Adm/M/404; Commis-

These prisons, in many ways different, had this in common: here thousands of American common seamen were imprisoned, most of them under atrocious conditions, segregated from their officers, and with little hope of release but much opportunity to defect. They were confronted with the necessity to make decisions which they themselves perceived as tests of their loyalty to one another and to the new nation. Those decisions were expressed in specific acts which can be measured quantitatively. These preconditions, then, make our laboratory: here we find solid data concerning the conduct of common seamen; in addition, the sources enable us to move beyond conduct into consciousness. William Widger's dream suggests how deeply into consciousness—some would say beyond—we can dig. In the prisons we can observe the society which the men construct on their own, how they govern themselves, their culture, their values, their ethos, and their ideology.

A situation *in certain ways* similar, that of Americans in prisoner-of-war camps in North Korea in the early 1950's, seemed not only to military men, but also to psychiatrists, psychologists, sociologists, and journalists, a basis for a sometimes critical re-examination of the American as *civilian*.[16] Conduct in prison, they said, could be explained in terms of "diverse aspects of our culture,"[17] and thus that conduct in turn illuminated American culture, character, and

sioners' Memorandum, March 14, 1777, Adm 98/11/87-88; CSHS to Admiralty, Dec. 15, 1777, Adm 98/11/149; Commissioners' Minute, April 22, 1777, Adm 99/49. The New York prison ships primarily held soldiers after the Battle of Long Island, e.g., Jabez Fitch, *A Narrative of the Treatment with which the American Prisoners were Used, Who Were Taken by the British and Hessian Troops on Long Island. . .* [publ. as *Prison Ship Martyr, Captain Jabez Fitch: His Diary in Facsimile*] (New York, 1903). But by the end of 1777 and for the rest of the war the prison ships were reserved for seamen, while soldiers and their officers were kept on land: Albert G. Greene, ed., *Recollections of the Jersey Prison-Ship: Taken and Prepared for Publication from the Original Manuscript of the late Captain Thomas Dring, of Providence, R.I., One of the Prisoners* (New York, 1961 [1st ed.: Providence, 1829]), p. 50; Danske Dandridge, ed., *American Prisoners of the Revolution* (Charlottesville, 1911), p. 405; [New York] *Royal Gazette*, Jan. 15, 1779.

16 The content of that re-examination varied greatly; for conflicting interpretations, together with summaries of the views of others, see Eugene Kinkead, *In Every War But One* (New York, 1959) and Albert D. Biderman, *March to Calumny: The Story of American POW's in the Korean War* (New York, 1963).

17 The phrase appears in Kinkead, p. 18. According to Biderman, "Kinkead's book is misleading with regard to the strengths as well as the weaknesses that may be characteristically American" (p. 45). Biderman sees among the prisoners in Korea "a noteworthy display of group organization and discipline (although not always the traditional Army variety of organization or one that can easily be perceived by the more traditionalistic Army officers. . . .)"; he finds the roots of certain kinds of prisoner resistance in characteristics and "generalized dispositions" which are "peculiarly" or "distinctively" American (pp. 43-45 and passim).

values. (Dr. Spock himself reconsidered permissiveness.)[18] Although it is tempting to draw conclusions about comparative strengths of national loyalties in the eighteenth and twentieth centuries from an examination of the two sets of prisoners, that is not what is intended here. (In any case, conditions were too dissimilar for facile comparisons of the two groups.) Korea is introduced here solely as a *methodological* analogue, that is, a recent instance in which scholars in various disciplines felt that an examination of a war-prisoner situation could reveal something of the culture and values of the men. Like Korea, the British prisons of the American Revolution offer a ready-made laboratory for the examination of the degree and quality of national and group loyalty. In the British prisons we can study the estrangement of American popular affection from British authority and the process by which Americans came to see a new authority as legitimate.

Jersey and the other prison ships at New York were places of crowding, filth, disease, and death.[19] Contemporaries estimated that close to 12,000 died there during the war.[20] Interestingly—and not

---

[18] "Are We Bringing Up Our Children Too 'Soft' For The Stern Realities They Must Face?" *Ladies' Home Journal*, Sept. 1960, 20-25, discussed in Betty Friedan, *The Feminine Mystique* (New York, 1963), pp. 373-374. Both Spock and Friedan accepted Kinkead uncritically.

[19] Ample documentation for this contention may be found in the various sources cited in this article. For reasons of space, I am here giving only brief attention to physical conditions in the prisons and prison ships, while focusing instead on the conduct of the men.

[20] The figure usually offered is 11,644; although it was generally offered for *Jersey* alone, it was probably intended as a total for all the twenty or so prison ships at New York, of which *Jersey* was the best known. See *Connecticut Gazette*, April 25, 1783; *Pennsylvania Packet*, April 29, 1783; *New York Packet, and the General Advertiser* [Fishkill], May 8, 1783; David Ramsay, *The History of the American Revolution* (Philadephia, 1789), II, 285; Dring, pp. 4-5; Thomas Andros, *The Old Jersey Captive; or, A Narrative of the Captivity of Thomas Andros, (Now Pastor of the Church in Berkley,) on Board the Old Jersey Prison Ship at New York, 1781* (Boston, 1833), p. 8. (For a lower estimate, see Henry Steele Commager and Richard B. Morris, eds., *The Spirit of 'Seventy-Six: The Story of the American Revolution as Told by Participants* [2 vols.; New York, 1958], II, 854).
Since we do not know how the figure was derived, we must distrust it. But British prison officials who were in New York after the war had ample opportunity to deny it and never did: (James Lenox Banks, *David Sproat and Naval Prisoners in the War of the Revolution* [New York, 1909], p. 107 [cf. p. 22], Charles I. Bushnell, ed., *The Adventures of Christopher Hawkins . . . first Printed from the original Manuscript. Written by Himself* [New York, 1864], p. 263). Conservative projections on the basis of known daily death rates derived from sources cited in this article produce a total over 11,000. (Almost one third of one captured crew was dead within seven weeks—Henry Onderdonk, Jr., *Revolutionary Incidents of Suffolk and Kings Counties; with an Account of the Battle of Long Island, and the British Prisons and Prison-Ships at New-York*

unpredictably—the historian who relied only on *Jersey*'s logs and other official sources would be left almost totally unaware of the realities which led Henry Steele Commager and Richard B. Morris to describe the prison ships as the Revolution's Andersonville.[21]

A few prisoners had the misfortune to spend time both in *Jersey* and in one of the old buildings used as prisons at Plymouth and Portsmouth in England; they invariably concluded that *Jersey* was worse.[22] Part of the difference between *Jersey* and the English prisons is simply the difference between imprisonment ashore and imprisonment in a ship. Another major element of difference offers sharp testimony to the cruelty of civil war. In occupied New York, the prisoners' fellow Americans could hardly bring themselves to acknowledge their presence and their troubles;[23] in England, however, people at all levels of society poured out charity, aid, and comfort, some of it open, some of it underground. "Why, Lard,

---

[New York, 1849], p. 240). There may be support for a large projection in the most substantial sort of evidence: actual remains, uncovered over the years; see I. N. P. Stokes, *The Iconography of Manhattan Island, 1498-1909* (New York, 1895-1928), V, 1398, 1493; Henry R. Stiles, ed., *Account of the Interment of the Remains of American Patriots who Perished on Board the Prison Ships during the American Revolution* (New York, 1865), p. 10; and Prison Ship Martyrs' Monument Assoc., *Secretary's Report of the Obsequies of the Prison Ship Martyrs at Plymouth Church, Brooklyn, New York, June 16, 1900* (New York, 1901), p. 17; cf. Dring, pp. 60, 146.

21 II, 854. One captain stopped recording deaths in *Jersey*'s log after six weeks, and the others never started; see entries for Feb. 20, March 4, April 3, 5, 1781, Adm 51/4228, and see logs, *ibid., passim,* and Adm 51/493. The only disease mentioned anywhere in the logs is smallpox, and that is mentioned only once (June 5, 1782). See also my "Jack Tar in the Streets," p. 402n. (Conversely, relying solely on accounts by prisoners would also be misleading; for some criticism of these sources, see·nn.24, 45 below.)

22 E.g., "Journal of William Russell," in Ralph D. Paine, ed., *The Ships and Sailors of Old Salem: The Record of a Brilliant Era of American Achievement* (New York, 1909), p. 169. The Continental Congress agreed; see Worthington Chauncey Ford, ed., *Journals of the Continental Congress, 1774-1789* (Washington, 1904-37), XXII, 245-246. See also Dring, pp. 79-80.

Both Mill and Forton had held French and Spanish prisoners during the Seven Years War, although neither had been designed for that purpose (Admiralty to CSHS, March 13 and April 19, 1777, Adm/M/404; CSHS to Admiralty, Nov. 22, 1780, Adm 98/13/137). Forton had been built as a hospital for sick and wounded seamen at the beginning of the century and was still referred to in Admiralty correspondence early in the war as "Forton Hospital" (John S. Barnes, ed., *Fanning's Narrative: Being the Memoirs of Nathaniel Fanning, an Officer of the Revolutionary Navy* [New York, 1912], p. 9; Admiralty to CSHS, March 13, 1777, Adm/M/404). At least one of the buildings at Mill dated back to Queen Anne's time (Andrew Sherburne, *Memoirs of Andrew Sherburne: A Pensioner of the Navy of the Revolution* [2nd ed.; Providence, 1831], p. 84).

23 For some possible minor exceptions, see Dring, pp. 74-78, and Onderdonk, p. 248.

neighbour," observed a surprised Sunday gawker at Forton, the Americans "be white paple; they taulk jest as us do, by my troth."[24] Englishmen filled the prisoners' charity boxes, raised several thousand pounds for them in meetings throughout England, supported them on the floor of Parliament, and finally helped them to escape and concealed them.[25]

Although never so bad as *Jersey*, the English prisons, too, had their share of bad food,[26] overcrowding, and bad health,[27] brutal

[24] Fanning, p. 11. Although in this instance contemporary evidence almost precisely confirms Fanning's report (cf. Charles Herbert, *A Relic of the Revolution* [Boston, 1847], pp. 19-20), most reminiscences of dialogue must of course be taken with a grain of salt. (Fanning seems to have written the section of his *Narrative* dealing with his imprisonment before and/or during 1801, although he "compiled" and "copied" it from his "old journal" [pp. i, 123n.; 124].) While most of the sources on which this article is based are contemporary, a few are later reminiscences. The latter must be used with caution—just as we would use the memoirs of a Benjamin Franklin, or a Henry Adams, or old former slaves. In each case we should, as Edward P. Thompson advises, hold sanctimoniousness up to "a Satanic light and read backwards"; our sources must be "critically fumigated" (*The Making of the English Working Class* [New York, 1964], p. 58, 493). At the same time, we must be certain that we are not—as so often seems to be the case—applying critical standards which vary by race or class, so that the reminiscences of an aged Franklin seem acceptable as sources, while the reminiscences of aged former slaves are dismissed. (Consider also the tendency of historians of slavery to accept plantation records while largely ignoring the rich materials contained in the Federal Writers' Project's Slave Narrative Collection.) Such sources as the latter are complex and difficult to use; rather than ignoring them, we would do better to develop methodologies for distinguishing what is genuine in them from what is later superimposition. For such an attempt, see Jesse Lemisch, J. Gordon Melton, and John R. Cory, "A Methodology of Gospel Scholarship Applied to the History of the 'Inarticulate'" (in preparation).

[25] Olive Anderson, "The Treatment of Prisoners of War in Britain during the American War of Independence," *Bulletin of the Institute of Historical Research*, XXVIII (1955), 81; John K. Alexander, "Forton Prison during the American Revolution: A Case Study of British Prisoner of War Policy and the American Response to that Policy," *EIHC*, CIII (Oct. 1967), 378-379; Herbert, p. 85-89; Petition of two hundred prisoners to the Lords in Parliament, June, 1781, Adm/M/405; Admiralty to CSHS, Dec. 11, 1777, Adm/M/404; "Journal of Samuel Cutler," *New-England Historical and Genealogical Register*, XXXII (Jan.-Oct., 1878), 187; *Annual Register for 1778* (London, 1779), pp. 78-79. The Americans were somewhat more effective in getting help to their countrymen in England than to those imprisoned in America; see, e.g., CSHS to Admiralty, Jan. 2, 1778, Adm 98/11/152. For English help to American escapees, see n.65 below.

[26] Widger, "Diary," LXXIII, pp. 316, 320; Herbert, pp. 60, 75, 140; Ralls Account, New-York Historical Society; Cutler, p. 396; "Humanitas" to Admiralty, Aug. 29, 1777, encl. in Admiralty to CSHS, Sept. 3, 1777, Adm/M/404; "A Yankee Privateersman in Prison in England, 1777-79 [Journal of Timothy Connor]," *New-England Historical and Genealogical Register*, XXX-XXXIII (1876-79), XXX, 352. (Connor's authorship is uncertain; see William R. Cutter to Librarian of State Dept., Jan. 31, 1893, with the original manuscript in the Library of Congress, Manuscript Div., U.S. Navy, Accession 748.)

[27] CSHS to Admiralty, July 23, 1779, Feb. 11, 1783, Adm 98/12/106-107, 14/301; Carpenter, p. 83.

guards, and harsh punishment.[28] To the prisoners, the agent who ran the prison was "the old crab," "arbitary cruel & inhuman," "as full of Spite as an Infernal fiend could bee," "divested of every humane feeling."[29] When a friendly peer visiting Mill Prison was told that the agent was a "dirty fellow," he replied: "Government keeps dirty fellows, to do their dirty Work."[30] But although the Commissioners of Sick and Hurt Seamen did not succeed in securing prisoners from "every evil of captivity, but captivity itself," the story of Mill and Forton is less a story of physical deprivation than is *Jersey*.[31] This provides us with a valuable comparison, enabling us more nearly to test the quality of the men's response to captivity itself rather than simply to physical deprivation.

There is no ambiguity about the meaning of *Jersey*: by any standard it is undoubtedly a tale of atrocity. Despite Samuel Eliot Morison's exhortation that we not "stir up" the "unpleasant subject of the treatment of American naval prisoners,"[32] there would seem to be important reasons to do so. If history contains horrors, the attempt to forget them is likely to lead to the necessity to relive them. But in noting that the American Revolution was, among other

---

[28] Widger, "Diary," LXXIII, 335; Thompson, "Diary," p. 227; Connor, XXXII, 165.

[29] Fanning, p. 10; Ralls Account, New-York Historical Society; Widger, "Diary," LXXIV, 37; *Pennsylvania Journal*, Sept. 22, 1781.

[30] Russell, p. 164. One historian who failed to find anything "recriminatory or vindictive" in the correspondence between the Admiralty and the CSHS offered this as evidence of "tolerance and good sense" in official attitudes toward the prisoners (Eunice H. Turner, "American Prisoners of War in Great Britain, 1777-1783," *Mariners' Mirror*, XLV [Aug. 1959], 200). This proves nothing of the sort and suggests the reverse: consensus among administrators should be an ominous sign for those who study the administrated. Olive Anderson—who defends prisoner policy in England as "strikingly enlightened" and dismisses harsher versions as originated by "propagandists" and perpetuated by "race-tradition"— nonetheless moves away from Turner's formalism and closer to the truth of actual decision-making when she notes that the Admiralty "rarely had enough time, knowledge or interest to take an independent line. Normally therefore they merely authorized or implemented the commissioners' proposals. . ." (pp. 65, 82, 83).

[31] The Commissioners, Sept., 1779, quoted in Anderson, 72. According to figures derived from official sources, 4.57 percent of the prisoners in Mill and Forton died (Howard, pp. 185, 187, 191). Such figures seem to be confirmed by an American source (*Boston Gazette, and the Country Journal*, June 24, July 1, 8, 1782) whose 3.5 percent figure for deaths in Mill alone almost precisely duplicates the British source. I am indebted to John K. Alexander, a graduate student at the Univ. of Chicago, for the latter figure and for other valuable assistance in many areas, especially in connection with my research on the English prisons. (For figures for Forton, see Alexander, "Forton Prison," pp. 380, 380n.)

[32] *John Paul Jones: A Sailor's Biography* (Boston, 1959), pp. 165-166. (Morison did not want to provide "fuel for American Anglophobes. . . .")

things, a cruel war, we do so not only out of motives of humanity, but because we want to know the truth of the matter. Was the American Revolution different from others—say, the French Revolution? Certainly it was. Was the American Revolution peculiar in that it was primarily legalistic and not so bloody? The facts of life and death in the prison ships do not jibe with that picture; America, too, was born in bloodshed. In any case, we will never have an accurate answer so long as we study the legalisms and avoid the bloodshed.

But our aim goes beyond the telling of atrocities: our interest is in the thought and conduct of the men. In order to understand that thought and conduct, we must consider the ways in which prisoners could regain their freedom. For much of the war, exchange as prisoners of war seemed hopeless. First of all, they were *not* prisoners of war; they were rebels, candidates for hanging,[33] detained under a suspension of *habeas corpus*.[34] If informal exchanges took place, formal cartels were repeatedly delayed. We cannot explore here the intricacies of exchange policies on both sides and the tortuous discussions of the matter. It should be noted that if legal status was an obstacle to exchange on the British side, American governments were also sometimes dilatory and uninterested. In America, Washington instructed the commissary-general of prisoners "absolutely to reject every overture for exchanging" captured privateersmen, who were civilians and therefore not "proper subjects of military capture."[35] Washington took little interest in the exchange of naval prisoners in general,[36] and the civilians in the prison ships at New York were at the bottom of the heap, their fate essentially in the hands of their friends, relatives, home towns. Washington's policy stressed instead palliation of conditions in the ships, and the logic of the policy was stated most bluntly by Secretary of War Benjamin Lincoln: ". . . to reconcile them as much as possible to the miseries of a loathsome confinement until they can be exchanged—and to

---

[33] Until March 25, 1782 (22 Geo. III, c. 10). See, e.g., Benjamin Franklin to John Adams, April 21, 1782, Adams Mss. Trust, Mass. Historical Society.

[34] 17 Geo. III, c. 9 ("North's Act").

[35] Washington to John Beatty, Aug. 19, 1779, John C. Fitzpatrick, ed., *The Writings of George Washington from the Original Manuscript Sources, 1745-1799* (Washington, 1931-44), XVI, 131.

[36] Washington to Major General William Heath, June 29, 1780, *Writings,* XIX, 93; Washington to Mrs. Theodosia Prevost, May 19, 1779, *Writings,* XV, 105: Washington to Board of War, June 16, 1780, *Writings,* XIX, 17.

prevent them—from an idea that they are neglected, engaging in the service of Britain. . . ."[37]

In France, Franklin devoted more energy to trying to arrange exchanges. The British—and sometimes the French—presented obstacles.[38] The British told the prisoners that the Americans were responsible for delays.[39] In common with some officials in America, Franklin thought that the British deliberately delayed exchanges in order to influence the prisoners to go into the British navy, and there is evidence from the prisoners that, regardless of the cause, delays were often so used by recruiting officers.[40] "Where to lay the blame I'm at a loss," wrote one prisoner from Mill.[41] "If Job himself was here," wrote another, "his patience would be worn out."[42] Hopes for exchange fluctuated, many became cynical, and finally concluded, "them hopes are gone. . . ," "Out of all hopes."[43]

"There is nothing but death or entering into the British service before me," wrote a prisoner from *Jersey*.[44] The narrow limits of the choices available to captured seamen forced them to consider the alternative.[45] There was no confusion in the prisoners' minds

---

[37] Banks, pp. 99-100.

[38] See, e.g., American Commissioners to Stormont, April 3, 1777, *London Chronicle*, Nov. 6, 1777; Benjamin Franklin to Wuibert, Lund, McKellar and other prisoners at Forton, Oct. 20, 1778, Library of Congress (copy); Benjamin Franklin to David Hartley, Jan. 25, 1779, Library of Congress (transcript); Alexander, "Forton Prison," p. 385.

[39] This produced some poignant letters from prisoners to Franklin, e.g., Jacob Smith to Benjamin Franklin, Jan. 24, 1783, Franklin Papers, XXVII, 47, APS; two hundred eighty American Prisoners at Forton to Benjamin Franklin, Feb. 3, 7, 1780, Historical Society of Pa.; Samuel Harris to Benjamin Franklin, June 12, 1781, Bache Collection, APS.

[40] Franklin to David Hartley, March 21, 1779, Library of Congress (letterbook copy); Franklin to S[amuel] Huntington, March 4, 1780, National Archives; Connor, XXXII, 281; *New-York Gazette; and the Weekly Mercury*, Feb. 12, 1781; Banks, pp. 79, 88-89; Dandridge, ed., *American Prisoners*, p. 403.

[41] Russell, p. 134.

[42] Herbert, p. 219.

[43] Herbert, pp. 78, 135, 164; Connor, XXXI, 20, 213, 286, XXXII, 280, 283; Thomas Smith, "Letter," *EIHC*, XLI (April 1905), 227.

[44] Onderdonk, p. 238.

[45] Some had no choice in the matter. Impressment of captured seamen in the early stages of the war brought complaint from Jefferson in the Declaration of Independence (Carl L. Becker, *The Declaration of Independence: A Study in the History of Political Ideas* [New York, 1958], p. 190). For other information concerning impressment, both before and after captives' arrival in prison, see, e.g., Admiralty to Vice-Admiral Graves, Sept. 9, 1775, Adm 2/550; Graves to Admiralty, Nov. 10, 20, 1775, Adm 1/485; John Fisher to Admiralty, Dec. 5, 1781, Adm 1/4146; *New-Jersey Gazette*, May 9, 1781; Hawkins, pp. 31-32; and George Little *et al.* to Benjamin Franklin, Aug. 25, 1781, Franklin Papers, LX,

about the meaning of enlistment: it constituted a clear act of disloyalty, what we call "defection"—as did they. "What an honour to walk his majestey['s] Quarter deck," roared a recent captive who refused.[46] To prisoners, to join meant, in their words, to be "seduced," to "desert their country's cause."[47] They called those who refused to defect the "brave Americans," "true sons of America."[48] A seaman delivering a speech to his fellow prisoners in *Jersey* congratulated them for their refusal to be bribed into deserting "the banners of our country."[49] Defectors were coerced, "hooted at and abused,"[50] and prisoners solemnly swore to remain loyal to their country.[51]

Service in the British navy meant "fighting against the liberties of their country" to Americans in Paris and back home.[52] For our purposes it is more significant, and historiographically useful,

16, APS; Ebenezer Fox, *The Adventures of Ebenezer Fox in the Revolutionary War* (Boston, 1847), pp. 93-94. At another point (p. 136), Fox, whose reminiscences are cast in the form of somewhat sanctimonious grandfather stories, acknowledges drawing upon Ramsay, William Gordon's *History of the Rise, Progress, and Establishment of the Independence of the United States of America* (London, 1788), and Charles Botta's *History of the War of Independence of the United States of America*, trans. George Alexander Otis (New Haven, 1840-41). He does not acknowledge that in sections dealing with *Jersey*, he often borrows and adapts from Dring (cf., e.g., Fox, pp. 100 ff., and Dring, pp. 23 ff.; Fox, p. 114, Dring, p. 38). Although his memory of certain events which occurred while he was in *Jersey* is thus strongly assisted by Dring, most of what Fox says is clearly his own.

There is also plagiarism in some of the diaries and journals of the English prisons. See Alexander's "'American Privateersmen in the Mill Prison during 1777-1782': An Evaluation," *EIHC*, CII (Oct. 1966), pp. 322-326; cf. Howard Lewis Applegate, "American Privateersmen in the Mill Prison during 1777-1782," *EIHC*, XCVII (Oct. 1961), 303-320; Alexander, "Forton Prison," p. 366n., and "Jonathan Haskins' Mill Prison 'Diary': Can it Be Accepted at Face Value?" *New England Quarterly*, XL (Dec. 1967), 561-564. In each such case, it is only the identity of the author, not the authenticity of the information provided, which is in question. Wherever I have found plagiarism, I have attempted to use the more reliable of the two sources.

[46] Robert Wilden Neeser, ed., *Letters and Papers Relating to the Cruises of Gustavus Conyngham, a Captain of the Continental Navy, 1777-1779* (New York, 1915), p. 161.

[47] Andros, p. 18; Dring, p. 71; Russell, p. 127.

[48] Herbert, pp. 156, 177.

[49] Dring, p. 93.

[50] Henry B. Dawson, ed., *Recollections of the Jersey Prison-Ship: From the Original Manuscripts of Captain Thomas Dring* (Morrisania, N.Y., 1865), p. 187. See also, e.g., Sir Thomas Pye to Admiralty, May 30, 1781, in Admiralty to CSHS, June 5, 1781, Adm/M/405.

[51] Herbert, p. 202.

[52] American Commissioners to Lord North, Dec. 12, 1777, Library of Congress; Russell, 94-95. See also Franklin's remarks at the Constitutional Convention, quoted in my "Jack Tar in the Streets," p. 404.

that the prisoners *themselves* saw it that way. The act of enlistment may mean different things to those who are actually faced with the choice and to those who only consider it from afar. And even among the prisoners, defection had many individual causes and consequences, some of them in conflict. Regardless of the diverse and individual significances of defection, we can say that the men in the prisons had a set of beliefs, an ethos concerning defection. In that ethos, refusal to defect was seen as loyalty to the Revolution, defection as disloyalty. The adherence of the prisoners to this belief establishes one of the major preconditions for our natural experiment studying the seamen's loyalties under pressure.

The laboratory is by no means perfect. Many enlisted, or were impressed, between the time of their capture and their arrival at prison.[53] Once in prison, some enlisted because various coercions seemed to them strong enough to remove the voluntary quality of the decision, and some doubtless enlisted because they genuinely believed that that course would increase their opportunities for escape.[54] But most of the factors which make the prisons a less than ideal laboratory tend to mislead us in a conservative direction; that is, we know that defection was, if anything, a maximal measure of disloyalty; a few may have defected despite a high degree of loyalty to the American cause. Finally, an important positive feature of the prisons as laboratory is that the men were quartered separately from their captains; the officers demanded separation, protested to the British when they felt that separation was inadequate and tried to arrange it themselves.[55] In most cases our

---

[53] For one instance in which 25 out of a crew of 100 entered in the ship which captured them, see Connor, XXXI, 284, and Alexander, "Forton Prison," p. 368. (For some indication of the coercive circumstances under which this took place, see Fanning, pp. 2-4.) It should be noted that capturing vessels, including this one, were also the scene of resistance and escape attempts on the way in (see Fanning, 2-5). For some other instances of resistance, escape and refusal to defect between capture and imprisonment, see Carpenter, p. 79; CSHS to Admiralty, Dec. 29, 1780, Adm 98/13/166; Marion S. Coan, ed., "A Revolutionary Prison Diary: The Journal of Dr. Jonathan Haskins," *New England Quarterly*, XVII (June-Oct. 1944), 295; Cutler, p. 187; Hawkins, p. 63; and Fox, pp. 93-94. For what appears to be the commitment of almost an entire 120-man crew to Mill Prison some five months after capture and after much pressure to defect and shunting about from ship to ship, see Herbert, pp. 17-44, 258; *Boston Gazette, and the Country Journal*, June 24, 1782; and Haskins, p. 295. At present, no meaningful quantitative statements on the relative frequency of defection as opposed to escape *before* imprisonment can be made. For quantitative statements on these matters *after* imprisonment, see below.

[54] Fox, pp. 146-147, 149, 167 ff., 209; Blatchford, p. 22; Anderson, p. 71.

[55] For the separate quartering of men and officers in both prison ships and

52

sources allow us to distinguish between seamen and captains and to be reasonably certain that we are describing the activities of common seamen.

Thus with no apparent way out, the men were offered a choice. If the conditions under which the choice was made are not so clean as they would be were we constructing an experimental situation to study the choice, interpretations of the Korean prisoner-of-war experience suggest that this is nonetheless a fruitful site for the study of the loyalties of the inarticulate in the American Revolution.

∾

To an extraordinary degree, captured American seamen remained Americans. In the prisons our measure of loyalty can approach precision. For *Jersey*, a generous estimate indicates that, with death more likely than exchange, for every one hundred men who arrived in the ship, only eight chose to defect.[56] Similarly, in Mill and Forton, the overall defection rate was between seven and eight percent,[57] and of the defectors it is possible that fifty percent were what the prisoners called "Old Countrymen,"[58] born in the British Isles. Thus, while birthplace clearly did make a difference, the similarity of conduct under the immensely different conditions of Mill

---

prisons ashore, see, e.g., Cutler, pp. 395, 396; Herbert, p. 92; CSHS to Admiralty, Jan. 14, 30, 1778, Adm 98/11/154-55, 164-165; Fanning, pp. 14, 15; Russell, p. 171; Dring, pp. xiv-xv, 25, 39-40. Insofar as the British were responsible ιor the separation, there is some indication that they did it because they felt that quartering officers and men together operated to inhibit defection by the men (*New-York Gazette; and the Weekly Mercury*, Feb. 12, 1781). See also, Conyngham, p. 171. For American officers' demands and arrangements for separation, see Dring, p. 25, and CSHS to Admiralty, Jan. 30, 1778, Adm 98/11/164-166. For a related complaint by Congress, see *Journals*, XX, 622.

56 *Jersey*'s logs (Adm 51/493 and 51/4228) record no one entering before May 17, 1781. This presumably reflects a failure to keep records on the matter rather than an absence of defection. After that date, the tally is regular and probably reliable. Between May 17, 1781, and April 7, 1783, the log describes 487 men as "entered," "volunteered," or "enlisted" (a few in services other than the navy). The figure may be generous, since some of these were doubtless impressed. During the same period, 5995 men are listed as arriving.

57 See my "Jack Tar in the Streets," p. 403n., where British and American sources are in close agreement. Cf. Alexander, "Forton Prison," p. 384, where an American prisoner in Forton offers information indicating a defection rate in *Forton alone* of 5.7 percent (in the period June 14, 1777–July 2, 1779).

58 Anderson (p. 72n.) says that "a high proportion" of the defectors were "old countrymen." For some descriptions of defections by "old countrymen" see Connor, XXXI, 288, and Herbert, pp. 63, 107, 155 (where one group of 30 defectors is described as "chiefly old countrymen"). Of 64 defectors in Herbert, 243-257, 32 were from England, Scotland, or Ireland. See also n.103 below.

53

and Forton on the one hand and *Jersey* on the other suggests that the degree of physical deprivation was not relevant: the men's conduct seems to have been rooted more in who they were, and what their loyalities were, than in the material circumstances of their imprisonment.

Men escaped more often than they defected—perhaps three or four times as often: almost eight hundred escaped from Mill and Forton.[59] What did escape mean to the prisoners? It was a serious matter, involving great and sometimes mortal risks both for those going out and those remaining inside. Those attempting escape from *Jersey* might be shot in the act[60] or flogged in punishment.[61] In the English prisons, failure meant forty days on half allowance in the Black Hole and a plunge to the bottom of the exchange list.[62]

---

[59] In Mill and Forton, over-all escape figures are between 17.4 percent (derived from *Boston Gazette,* May 24–July 8, 1782) and 30.0 percent (derived from Adm 98/11-14; Howard, pp. 185, 187). The disparity may be partially explained by the fact that British figures are based simply on reports of escapees —many of whom were later retaken, and of whom many tried again—while the American figures are totals of escapees *not retaken.* Thus the higher figure is an approximate measure of the prisoners' *intent,* the lower figure a measure of their *success.* In Forton alone, Adm 98/11-14 gives a figure of 44.7 percent, while an American prisoner gives a figure of 27.0 percent (for 1777-79) (Connor, XXXIII, 36-39).

Jersey's log is almost totally silent on the matter of escapes, mentioning only two attempts (March 7, 1781, and Feb. 3, 1782, Adm 51/493 and 51/4228). Numerous references to escapes in other sources cited in this paper indicate that the captains simply did not record escapes. On the other hand, the log does list frequent repairs of ports broken open by prisoners presumably escaping or planning to do so. For repair of ports, see logs, Oct. 9, 1780, Oct. 11, 1781, May 15, 16, June 5, 12-14, Oct. 31, and Nov. 11, 1782. Several of these entries explicitly describe the repairs as necessary in order to prevent escapes. For prisoners' descriptions of such destruction as a necessary preliminary to escape, see, e.g., Hawkins, p. 78; Onderdonk, p. 236. Fox (p. 131) describes the apparent escape of 200 men in a three-month period (cf. Hawkins, p. 72) during which time the log lists a maximum of 68 defections (log of *Jersey,* March–May, 1782). This suggests a ratio of escape to defection of approximately 3 to 1. None of the figures offered above include escapes between the time of capture and arrival in prison.

[60] For *Jersey,* see, e.g., Andros, p. 23; Hawkins, p. 74; Dring, pp. 110-112. Even those trying to flee a shipboard fire could expect to be shot (*New-York Gazette; and the Weekly Mercury,* Feb. 12, 1781). In Mill and Forton, at least in the early part of the war, the guards did not have orders to fire at escaping prisoners (Alexander, "'American Privateersmen,'" 336-337, and "Forton Prison," p. 381). There is indication that these orders were later revised, or that there was a difference between orders and actual execution (Herbert, p. 150; Widger, "Diary," LXXIV, 152; Russell, p. 159).

[61] *New-York Gazette; and the Weekly Mercury,* Feb. 12, 1781.

[62] Herbert, p. 54; Thompson, "Diary," p. 238; CSHS to Admiralty, June 26, 1778, Jan. 5, 1779, Oct. 31, 1781, Adm 98/11/206, 398-400, 13/493-495; Benjamin Golden to Benjamin Franklin, Dec. 2, 1781, Franklin Papers, XXIII, 94, APS; Ralls Account, New-York Historical Society.

Getting out of *Jersey* still meant a perilous swim to the shore and the possibility of recapture once ashore.[63] In England, where a large reward was offered for escaped Americans, men whom the prisoners called "five pounders"—"peasants, who were always lurking about" and who "would sell their fathers"—beat the bushes with dogs and clubs;[64] some of them had probably been tipped off by guards with whom they were in collusion.[65]

If most prisoners displayed a great deal of courage and ingenuity in their escape attempts, some were merely in collusion with guards, turnkeys, or civilians, splitting the five pound reward, sometimes after a night and a day of sex and liquor in a civilian's home on the outside.[66] Joyrides such as these suggest some of the complexities involved in generalizing about what escape meant to prisoners.[67] We can note, however, that for the majority who were serious about it, escape meant a rejection of the most available alternative way of leaving prison: defection. Just as defection implied disloyalty, escape implied loyalty; we have evaluated the loyalties of twentieth-century prisoners in this way,[68] just as Washington did when he commended escaped seamen as he would have praised brave and loyal soldiers.[69] "We committed treason through his [Majesty's]

[63] See, e.g., Hawkins, pp. 73-75, 82-87; log of *Jersey*, March 7, 1781, Adm 51/4228; Onderdonk, pp. 236-237; [N.Y.] *Royal Gazette*, Dec. 8, 1781.

[64] Connor, XXX, 347, XXXI, 19, XXXII, 165; Fanning, p. 10; Haskins, p. 299.

[65] CSHS to Admiralty, Oct. 27, 1779, Nov. 14, 1780, Adm 98/12/240-241, 13/133-134; Admiralty to CSHS, April 29, 1782, Adm/M/405. Prisoners also received a great deal of help from a kind of underground railway in which British clergymen played a major role: Thompson, "Diary," pp. 232-233, 241-242; John Thornton to American Commissioners, Memorandum, Jan. 5-8, 1778, Harvard College Library; Philip Hancock to American Commissioners, Aug. 2, 1778, Franklin Papers, L(i), 45, APS; G. Williams to Benjamin Franklin, Oct. 2, 1778, Franklin Papers, XII, 5; Cutler, p. 397.

[66] Luke Matthewman, "Narrative," *Magazine of American History*, II (March 1878), p. 182; Admiralty to CSHS, Oct. 17, 1781, Adm/M/405, Justices of Peace of Fareham to Admiralty, Sept. 29, 1779, in Admiralty to CSHS, Oct. 15, 1779, Adm/M/404, Major General Smith to Secretary at War, Feb. 14, 1782, in Admiralty to CSHS, March 2, 1782, Adm/M/405; CSHS to Admiralty, Nov. 22, 1780, April 12, 1782, Adm 98/13/139, 14/141.

[67] But we can say that collusive escapes were *in addition* to such totals as the 27 percent for *successful* escapes (see n.59 above), since those in collusion with guards were returned to prison.

[68] In Korea, "not one of our men escaped from a permanent enemy prison camp and successfully made his way back to our lines" (Kinkead, pp. 16-17. For a strong qualification of this statement and disagreement about its implications, see Biderman, pp. 84-90 and *passim*.) One of the results of the Korean experience was the promulgation by President Eisenhower in 1955 of a new Code of Conduct for the Armed Forces. Article III included a pledge that, if captured, "I will make every effort to escape and aid others to escape" (Biderman, p. 279).

[69] Dring, p. 180.

earth," was the way one captive described his escape.[70] A seaman laughed as prisoners made it past "the grand Lobster guard";[71] others mocked defection by using the pretense of enlisting as a mask for organized escape.[72] "Kiss my arse!" signaled an escapee, once out of *Jersey*'s firing range.[73] "Do you know that it is a great crime to break one of His Majesty's locks?" asked a prison commander;[74] "I told him that I did not regard His Majesty nor his locks. What I was after was my liberty."

Underlying escape was organization and cooperation. Not only those escaping but also many of those staying behind were direct participants in escape attempts. There were tools to be gotten and concealed, locks to be picked, bars to be broken, holes to be cut or dug, dirt to be hidden.[75] Plans for the escape had to be agreed upon, contingency plans had to be made in case detection took place, signals had to be devised, and arrangements made for rendezvous. The decision had to be made that the time had come to put the plan into execution. During the escape itself, guards had to be deceived or overwhelmed, prisoners had to be assisted out through holes or broken ports. The one hundred and nine men who escaped from Mill one night in December 1778 after a month's digging had previously drawn lots to decide the order of egress, and two men checked them off a list as they entered the hole.[76] None of these decisions and plans made themselves; a historical record which presents us with *faits accomplis*, decisions made and carried out, should invite us to look beyond, into the process leading to these decisions, and to recognize that these actions could not have been taken without serious thought, much discussion, and mutual trust.

The cooperation behind escapes is one facet of the larger story of prisoner organization and self-government. What follows, although only a sampling of the material available, is intended to

---

70 Conyngham, p. 194.
71 Carpenter, p. 83.
72 Fox, pp. 124-125.
73 Fox, pp. 129-130.
74 For this and the following, see Foot, p. 107.
75 For some of the cooperative actions described here and below, see Hawkins, pp. 78-83, Dring, pp. 109-110; Fox, pp. 116, 119-120, 124; Onderdonk, p. 236; Matthewman, p. 182; Herbert, p. 52; and CSHS to Admiralty, July 24, 1781, Adm 98/13/413-414.
76 CSHS to Admiralty, Jan. 5, 15, 1779, Adm 98/11/398-401, 411-412: Herbert, pp. 203-207.

suggest that exploration of the specifics of the prisoners' self-government and even their culture is feasible.[77] First of all, just as prison officials posted a list of regulations to let the prisoners know, as the officials put it, "what behaviour is expected on their Part,"[78] there was a parallel but in many senses more inclusive structure erected by the prisoners themselves, who, as one put it, "adventured to form themselves into a republic, framed a constitution and enacted wholesome laws, with suitable penalties."[79] Early in the war, prisoners created "a code of By-Laws . . . , for their own regulation and government. . . ."[80] These codes, or "Articles," had a quite literal existence; written copies existed, and they were posted and read aloud periodically.[81] These rules, and the behavior which *they* sanctioned, competed with the official rules for the prisoners' respect.

Legislation by prisoners ranged from health to morality to political conduct. There were rules requiring "personal cleanliness . . . , as far as . . . practicable" and forbidding smoking, "blackguarding," drunkenness and theft.[82] "Due observance of the Sabbath . . ." was honored in the breach.[83] Consider this, and consider prisoners petitioning for a clergyman,[84] and the shame of one at being over-

---

[77] My "Jack Tar in the Darbies" will give fuller attention to these matters. For some model studies dealing with the politics and culture of lower-class groups in different environments, see, e.g., Thompson, *Making of the English Working Class,* and several excellent studies by Herbert G. Gutman (e.g., "The Worker's Search for Power: Labor in the Gilded Age," in H. Wayne Morgan, ed., *The Gilded Age: A Reappraisal* [Syracuse, 1963], pp. 38-68, and "Protestantism and the American Labor Movement: The Christian Spirit in the Gilded Age," *American Historical Review,* LXXII [Oct. 1966], 74-101). The stance and methodology of Black historiography are also rich with models and implications for the rewriting of white history "from the bottom up." See, e.g., communications by Anna Mary Wells, Vincent Harding, and Mike Thelwell, *N.Y. Rev. of Books,* Nov. 7, 1968; and John Henrik Clarke, ed., *William Styron's Nat Turner: Ten Black Writers Respond* (Boston, 1968).

[78] For the rules, see Thompson, "Diary," pp. 238-240. CSHS to Admiralty, Jan. 28, 1778, Adm 98/11/162, notes that the rules were first posted Nov. 30, 1777. Cf. Herbert, p. 82, and Howard, pp. 473-474.

[79] Sherburne, p. 83.

[80] Dring, p. 84. Cf. Herbert, pp. 145-146; Sherburne, p. 85. There is no evidence of such a written code at Forton, although there is ample evidence of organized self-government, e.g., CSHS to Admiralty, Jan. 27, 1779, Adm 98/11/442-444.

[81] Dring, p. 86, 91-94; Herbert, pp. 145-146, 148; Sherburne, p. 85.

[82] Dring, p. 85; Herbert, pp. 68, 145; Widger, "Diary," LXXIV, 144; Russell, p. 155; Sherburne, p. 83.

[83] Dring, pp. 85, 89; Andros, pp. 18-19, and n.86 below.

[84] Widger, "Diary," LXXIV, 142.

heard praying "like a minister,"[85] and consider another, complaining, "It is a great grievance to be . . . debarred from hearing the gospel preached on the Lord's day. . . ."[86] In such evidence as this, and more like it, there hangs a tale, not yet told, of the real meanings of religion in early America. (And other untold tales, of Franklinian virtues among the inarticulate, are to be found in men fretting over their shipmates' "blaspheming their Maker continually,"[87] and others, keeping accounts of whittled ladles sold to visitors at a shilling apiece,[88] and others, struggling toward literacy through diligent study, leaving prison captains-to-be.)[89]

Survival requires that any group living together make rules on such matters as hygiene. But just as prisoner legislation in more political areas—to be examined shortly—expresses an active rather than a passive response to their situation, so some of their rules for moral conduct indicate that their culture is not fully explicable simply in terms of the minimal necessities for group survival. "No giant like man should be allowed to tyranize over, or abuse another who was no way his equal in strength."[90] "No prisoner, when liberated, could remove his chest."[91] Many distributed other property before escape or exchange[92] or, afterwards, tried to will money left in the prison agent's hands to other prisoners.[93] Loyalties to town and crew flourished,[94] and communal institutions established by the captors—such as the mess—were imbued by the captives with a deeper meaning than the British intended.[95]

"A secret, . . . revealed to the guard, was death."[96] Committees were formed to deal with informers; trials were held, sentences handed down, punishments carried out.[97] In *Jersey,* a prohibition

---

[85] Sherburne, p. 99.

[86] Herbert, p. 78.

[87] Haskins, p. 425.

[88] Cutler, pp. 187, 306; Herbert, pp. 45-46.

[89] Fanning, pp. 15, 15n.; Sherburne, p. 83-84. Some of the Franklinian virtues suggest an individualistic strain amidst what seems a predominantly collectivist ethos. Disobedience by prisoners to prisoner-made rules and norms constitutes another significant area of deviation (see n.103 below).

[90] Andros, p. 18.

[91] Dring, p. 129.

[92] Dring, p. 129; Hawkins, p. 81.

[93] CSHS to Admiralty, May 6, 1779, Adm 98/12/9-10.

[94] E.g., Sherburne, p. 82-83; Herbert, p. 161.

[95] Thompson, "Diary," p. 240; Dring, pp. 33-34, 81-82; Fox, pp. 115-120; Herbert, p. 67; Sherburne, pp. 85-86.

[96] Andros, p. 17.

[97] Thompson, "Diary," pp. 225, 226; Andros, pp. 17-18; Herbert, p. 116;

of defection may have been written into the by-laws.[98] An anti-defection agreement carrying harsh penalties was posted in Forton,[99] and in Mill over one hundred signed this paper:

> We, whose names are hereunto subscribed, do, of our own free and voluntary consent, agree firmly with each other, and hereby solemnly swear, that we are fully determined to stand, and so remain as long as we live, true and loyal to our Congress, our country, our wives, children and friends, and never to petition to enter on board any of His Britannic Majesty's ships or vessels, or into any of his services whatsoever.[100]

Those prisoners who sought to defect did so only "very slyly."[101] Even Old Countrymen, complained a British admiral, "dare not make known their Intentions," lest they be exposed, like the defecting Americans, "to the Resentment of the other Prisoners, who threaten the lives of those who offer to serve in the Navy. . . ."[102]

It is clear that some prisoners stayed only under compulsion, disobeying many of the prisoner-made rules described above, and undergoing harsh punishments at the hands of other prisoners. What stands out in the prisons is not that there was disunity but that, in this hostile environment, there was sufficient unity to maintain effective self-government. There were various forms of organization: there were votes and lotteries, and other arrangements, to assure the equitable distribution of food and clothing; there were committees for trial and punishment and committees of correspondence which drew up, read aloud, and circulated for signatures petitions and remonstrances, addressed to Franklin, to Washington, to the House of Lords, to "Friends and Fellow Countrymen in America." Hundreds signed these documents, protesting prison conditions, seeking to publicize their situation on the outside and to bring about exchange or amelioration. Beneath the guns and

---

Hawkins, pp. 69-71; CSHS to Admiralty, Jan. 27, 1779, Nov. 12, 1781, Adm 98/11/442-444, 13/503-505.

[98] See Andros, pp. 17-18, where prisoners' refusal to defect is described in the context of an enumeration and discussion of the prisoners' rules; also, see Dring, pp. 91-94, where a shipboard orator, using the rules as the "text of . . . his discourse," praised his fellow prisoners for not defecting.

[99] Thompson, "Diary," p. 225.

[100] Herbert (p. 202) contends that more supported the document than signed it.

[101] Herbert, p. 183.

[102] Sir Thos. Pye to Admiralty, May 30, 1781, in Admiralty to CSHS, June 5, 1781, Adm/M/405.

bayonets of the British the prisoners maintained a legal structure which in many ways directly contradicted the official structure.[103]

When Captain Thomas Dring sat down in 1824 to recall his experiences as a twenty-three year old imprisoned in *Jersey* in 1782, he found it "an astonishing fact" that the prisoners had obeyed the by-laws so long and so well.[104] The prisoners were "so numerous" and, thought the old captain—by now a leading citizen of Providence—they were "of that class . . . who are not easily controlled, and usually not the most ardent supporters of good order." And yet, men so prone to disorder as Dring supposed them to be had paid what he called "a willing submission" to the rules. They mutually supported their own good order and reserved for themselves the right to decide when British authority deserved obedience and when they would reject it as unjust and therefore unworthy of obedience: ". . . if any man misbehaves and deserves punishment, we will deliver him up, or punish him ourselves, rather than he should go unpunished; but rather than see a man chastised unjustly, we will do our utmost for his rescue."[105] In this way they attempted to overrule British authority, through demonstration and direct action, based always on what Edward Thompson has called

---

[103] Defection and informing were of course major forms of disobedience to prisoner government. In the English prisons, in regard to defection as well as other matters, we often find that the division is between Americans and Old Countrymen: "The Americans unanimously hang together, and endeavor to keep peace in prison, but if the [Old Countrymen] were stronger than . . . [the Americans] we should have a hell upon earth" (Herbert, p. 119). For committees, trials, and punishments for theft, see Widger, "Diary," LXXIV, 144; Sherburne, pp. 83, 85; Herbert, pp. 68, 145-146; and Dring, pp. 85-86. For forms of distribution of food and clothing, see, in addition to the mess, Herbert, pp. 166 (voting), and Russell, p. 157 (lottery). For petitions and remonstrances, see Committee of Prisoners in *Jersey* to "Friends and Fellow Countrymen in America," [N.Y.] *Royal Gazette*, June 12, 1782; Petition signed by 100 prisoners in *Jersey*, Aug. 15, 1782, Banks, p. 101; 280 American Prisoners in Forton Prison to Benjamin Franklin, Feb. 7, 1780, Historical Society of Pa.; Herbert, p. 62 (petition read aloud in prison yard); CSHS to Admiralty, Sept. 8, 1777, Adm 98/11/132; To the House of Lords from "upwards of two hundred American Prisoners . . . in Mill Prison . . . in behalf of themselves and others, their countrymen and Fellow Captives," June, 1781, encl. in Admiralty to CSHS, June 23, 1781, Adm/M/405; and CSHS to Admiralty, Oct. 4, 1782, Adm 98/14/254.

[104] For this and the following, see Dring, pp. iii-iv, 84-85.

[105] Herbert, p. 184; see also pp. 78, 174.

[106] P. 68. For such action, see, e.g., Widger, "Diary," LXXIII, 335, LXXIV, 41; J. How to Major General Mocher, Feb. 23, 1782, in Admiralty to CSHS, March 16, 1782, Adm/M/405; Russell, p. 162; Connor, XXX, 352, XXXI, 213 ("Our provisions not being good we condemned them. . . ."); Dring, ed. Dawson, p. 179; CSHS to Admiralty, Oct. 28, 1782, Adm 98/14/262.

"some legitimising notion of right."[106] They had withdrawn their loyalties from the British and had given legitimacy to their own prison government, a government deriving its just powers from the consent of the governed.

If the government of the prisoners was legitimate, that was not only because it was the prisoners' own but also because it was *American*. They were quite articulate in their nationalism. We have already seen how they viewed the decision concerning defection in the context of national loyalty. In addition, from the very beginning, they expressed contempt for what they perceived as the merely pretended legalisms by which the British attempted to define them as rebels, pirates, and traitors. "D[am]n his Majesty & his pardon too . . . what murder or treason have we done Prey [?]"[107] They damned the King and tried and punished those who damned the Continental Congress.[108] They delivered fiery patriotic speeches and held contemptuous dialogues with their captors.[109] They sang defiant and exultant songs, of the Stamp Act and the Boston Tea Party, and Bunker Hill, along with songs of lamentation by English widows and generals on the harshness of the war in America, longing for peace. Their songs wished "bad luck to the King and Queen/ And all the Royal family . . . ,"

> Success unto America likewise to Washington
> Here is a health unto America that scorns to be
> control'd.[110]

---

107 Carpenter, pp. 83-84. See also Mary Barney, ed., *A Biographical Memoir of the Late Commodore Joshua Barney: From Autobiographical Notes and Journals* (Boston, 1832), p. 88; Herbert, pp. 34, 44; and Haskins, p. 433. The challenge to the legitimacy of the prisoners' commitment was in many senses a just one; see CSHS to Admiralty, May 17, 1780, Adm 98/12/456 for an attempt by the Commissioners to have some Americans sent to Mill "although we are aware they possibly cannot be legally committed to Prison for want of Evidence. . . ." And of course North's Act, under which they were committed, came under fire for its suspension of *habeas corpus* (*Annual Register for 1777* [London, 1778], pp. 53-66; *The Works of the Right Honorable Edmund Burke* [rev. ed.; Boston, 1866], II, 193).

108 Haskins, p. 305.

109 Dring, pp. 89-95; Carpenter, p. 84.

110 Prisoners' songs are a rich source for the patriotic as well as other aspects of the seamen's lives. See, e.g., Hawkins, pp. 63-64; Carpenter, p. 86. The songs quoted above are part of a manuscript from Forton Prison in the Library of Congress, containing more than fifty songs. Most songs are given a specific date (in 1778); there is a journal entry and several notations such as "Success to the Honourable Continental Congress. . . ." George Carey of the Dept. of English, Univ. of Maryland, is at work on a monograph on these "Songs of Jack Tar in the Darbies." I am grateful to him for the use of his transcript and a xerox of the songs and for some useful advice.

There were frequent patriotic demonstrations and celebrations of American victories: American flags and thirteen cheers for the French King's birthday; cheers to commemorate the defeat of Burgoyne; huzzas for the French, for the Spanish, and for the Dutch; for the capture of Cornwallis, American flags in hatbands, a parade around the prison yard, and, at night, an illumination: ". . . generale Respect agreable to the present ability of the prison."[111] And, on the Fourth of July: stars and stripes, cheers and songs, and, for some, bayonets and death. On their cockades they wrote, "INDEPENDENCE" and "LIBERTY OR DEATH." Seeing what was on their heads, but never really knowing what was on their minds, the prison keeper doubled the guard.[112]

∼

Unquestionably, the seamen were nationalists. That is not, however, a mark of distinctiveness. Indeed, their nationalism might be seen as a measure of the extent to which they shared in the consensus and did not conceive of their interests as distinctive;[113] they rallied strongly to the support of a government which was not theirs.[114]

To say, simply, that the seamen were nationalists says nothing about the *content* of their nationalism—what it was they thought they were being loyal to when they were loyal to "America," the values which they fastened to their nationalism and expressed through it.

The prisoners articulated a collectivist ethical code. Their government was egalitarian, and in their culture and conduct they showed a high degree of awareness of themselves as a group and loyalty to that group. There is a distinctive flavor about this

---

111 Connor, XXXII, 72; Herbert, p. 175; Russell, 131; Widger, "Diary," LXXIV, 43-44, 156-157; Sherburne, pp 88-89; Benjamin Golden to Benjamin Franklin, Dec. 2, 1781, Franklin Papers, XXIII, 94, APS.

112 Herbert, pp. 141-142; Russell, pp. 129; Widger, "Diary," LXXIV, 30; Dring, pp. 97-105.

113 Ironically, one way in which the seamen moved in the direction of a distinctive definition of their own interests was on those few occasions when they tempered their nationalism with rage over what they saw as their country's desertion of them and threatened in turn to desert their country unless Washington and others made stronger efforts to exchange them. See [N.Y.] *Royal Gazette*, June 12, 1782, and n.44 above.

114 See, e.g., my "Jack Tar in the Streets," pp. 378-380, 387-388, 404.

egalitarianism and collectivism, seeming to set the seamen's values apart from the individualism and hierarchism[115] of the leaders of the Revolution. But does this constitute politics? The line between politics and what has been called "pre-politics"[116] is uneven and unclear, and no law of nature nor of man dictates that the one become the other, that potentiality become actuality. Although ethical code and group conduct would seem to have both implications and potentialities for politics, they are probably closer to "pre-politics" than to politics. What of constitution-making, laws, trials, petitions, committees, votes, and the rest of the structure of self-government in the prisons? This seems more nearly to be politics, especially when we note that the seamen self-consciously connected them with the ideals of the larger struggle; they governed themselves in accord with abstract notions of liberty, justice, and right, and they associated these notions with the birth of a new and better nation. Their nationalism clearly had political dimensions.

If the seamen had politics, that does not mean that they had class politics in the prisons. "Class happens," writes Edward Thompson, "when some men, as a result of common experiences . . . , feel and articulate the identity of their interests as between themselves, and as against other men whose interests are different from . . . theirs."[117] This describes what happened in the prisons, but with the vital qualification that it happened in the *nationalist* sense.[118] If *class* happened, it would be more likely to occur after the war, when independence *per se* was no longer the predominant issue and the seamen were able to test against the new realities the ideals for which they had fought.

---

[115] Although the term itself is rarely applied to the political thought and conduct of the Revolution's leaders, it seems to fit the descriptions offered by recent analysts: see, e.g., studies by Roy N. Lokken, J.R. Pole, and Richard Buel, Jr., cited in my "American Revolution Seen from the Bottom Up," pp. 34-35.

[116] "*Pre-political* people . . . have not yet found, or [have] only begun to find, a specific language in which to express their aspirations about the world" (E. J. Hobsbawm, *Primitive Rebels: Studies in Archaic Forms of Social Movement in the 19th and 20th Centuries* [New York, 1965], p. 2; see *passim* for a working out of the definition in more specific terms).

[117] P. 9.

[118] I am indebted to Christopher Z. Hobson for insights into the relations between class and nationalist consciousness; see his unpubl. M.A. thesis (Univ. of Chicago, 1969), "Economic Discontent, Ghana 1951-66: A Study in the Class Dynamics of Third-World Nationalist Movements," especially chap. V. See also Staughton Lynd, *Class Conflict, Slavery, and the United States Constitution: Ten Essays* (Indianapolis, 1967), pp. 13-14.

The decision of the inarticulate to give their loyalties to one side or another in war has been a matter of fundamental importance in history, a decision with enormous political meaning. In the Revolution, men like William Widger chose the American side. William Widger was somebody; he had individuality, dignity, and values of his own. He expressed those values, in part, in his nationalism, and he and his fellow prisoners held to their nationalism with a strength which cannot be explained by manipulation. The nationalism of the seamen was as authentic as the nationalism of a Jefferson, an Adams, or a Franklin; in this sense, the Revolution happened from the bottom up as well as from the top down.

ᴄᴛᴏ

We know what William Widger dreamt sixty thousand nights ago.[119] If we can find William Widger's dream in the published *Historical Collections* of the Essex Institute; if we can find, in Yale's Franklin Collection, rich and poignant letters from seamen which even convey, through their spelling, something of the sound of the spoken language;[120] if Philip Freneau, the man who came to be called "The Poet of the American Revolution," shared some of the experiences of "The British Prison Ship" and wrote of them;[121] if the seamen themselves left us ample materials which invite us to examine their politics, their loyalties, and their culture; if sources such as these and others exist, from which it is possible to construct laboratories in which the inarticulate can be heard—then is it not time that we put "inarticulate" in quotation marks and begin to see

---

[119] For some other dreams and fever fantasies, see Russell, pp. 152-153, and Sherburne, pp. 93-94, 99-100.

[120] In addition to letters cited above from Americans in English prisons, many Americans—some of whom had been captured by the French as English—wrote Franklin from French prisons, begging his assistance, e.g., Jonathan Atkin to Benjamin Franklin, Nov. 10, 1778, Franklin Papers, LX, 3, APS; William Gardner to Benjamin Franklin, March 21, 1779, Franklin Papers, XIII, 215; and James Mathews to Benjamin Franklin, Oct. 19, 1782, Historical Society of Pa. All of the correspondence to and from Franklin cited in this article was originally examined in photocopy form at the Franklin Collection at Yale (citations are given to original repositories). I am grateful to Leonard W. Labaree and to Helen C. Boatfield in connection with these items and for innumerable other kindnesses over many years.

[121] Fred Lewis Pattee, ed., *The Poems of Philip Freneau, Poet of the American Revolution* (3 vols.; Princeton, 1902-07), II, 18-39, and Freneau's *Some Account of the Capture of the Ship "Aurora"* (New York, 1899).

the term more as a judgment on the failure of historians than as a description of historiographical reality?[122]

---

[122] Not considered in this paper are certain ideological barriers to writing a history of the "inarticulate." Prominent among these is pluralism, aptly described by Michael Paul Rogin (*The Intellectuals and McCarthy: The Radical Specter* [Cambridge, 1967], p. 282), as "not . . . the product of science but . . . a liberal American venture into conservative political theory." Pluralism is an explicitly elitist doctrine; it praises the distribution of power among elites, and in so doing it justifies the exclusion from political power of the "illegitimate." Thus Daniel Bell writes, "Democratic politics means bargaining between *legitimate* groups and the search for consensus" ("Passion and Politics in America," *Encounter,* VI [Jan. 1956], p. 61; emphasis added). Just as pluralism as political philosophy justified the exclusion of the "illegitimate," pluralism as historiography justified the exclusion of the past "illegitimate," which is to say the "inarticulate." Thus we have seen the past too uncritically through the eyes of such men as Olmsted's "Men of literary taste" and too little through eyes defined by pluralists as illegitimate. (See my rev. of Bernard Bailyn, *The Origins of American Politics* [New York, 1968], in *New Republic,* May 25, 1968, pp. 25-28, and also my study in progress, "Anti-Communism as a Goal of Recent American Historiography.")

Comments on Books Received

Free But Not Equal: The Midwest and the Negro During the Civil War. By V. JACQUE VOEGELI. (Chicago: University of Chicago Press, 1968. vii + 215 pp. $5.95)

Long accustomed to self-righteous condemnation of Dixie's racial mores, non-Southerners have been recently called upon to adjust their focus. Phrases such as "white backlash" suggest that white racism may be more widespread than we previously have been willing to acknowledge. V. Jacque Voegeli's study shows that Negro inferiority was the credo of nearly all Midwesterners, from abolitionists to Copperheads. Civil War and emancipation did little to shake this credo or to foster a commitment to equality. Emancipation itself was widely opposed; its advocates justified it solely by military necessity and hoped that the end of Southern slavery would drain the North of its few blacks. The Midwest offered no welcome to freedmen: restrictions on franchise, education, and property ownership were eased only slightly during the period. Voegeli has enhanced our awareness of the depth of American race prejudice and its power to limit our political and social choices. —*Michael W. Homel,* University of Chicago

FORTON PRISON DURING
THE AMERICAN REVOLUTION:
A CASE STUDY OF BRITISH PRISONER OF WAR POLICY
AND THE AMERICAN PRISONER RESPONSE TO THAT
POLICY

By JOHN K. ALEXANDER

TWO STRIKINGLY DIVERGENT VIEWS exist on the British treatment of American naval prisoners confined in England during the American Revolution. American historians have tended to see the British policy as "not generally humanitarian;" prison officials are usually pictured as "arbitrary," "heartless," and "cruel."[1] On the other hand, British historians normally argue that given eighteenth century prison standards, British policy was "strikingly enlightened."[2] This divergence is probably caused more by the availability of sources than by national prejudice.[3] American historians primarily employ American documents, especially prisoner diaries and journals. Conversely, British historians lean most heavily upon official British records. Both groups often become prisoners of their sources' logical bias. Only by combining prisoner accounts and official American records with official British records can we hope to obtain a balanced picture of British prison policy and the effect of prison life on Americans. These different, and often antagonistic sources have been utilized in this attempt to examine Forton Prison,[4] one of the two large camps in England used to

1. Howard L. Applegate, "American Privateersmen in the Mill Prison During 1777-1782," Essex Institute *Historical Collections,* XCVII (October, 1961), 305 and Charles Paullin, *The Navy of the American Revolution* (Chicago, 1906), p. 268. See also Ralph D. Paine, *Ships and Sailors of Old Salem,* (New York, 1909); Gardner W. Allen, *A Naval History of the American Revolution* (2 vols.; Boston, 1913); Danske Dandridge, *American Prisoners of the Revolution* (Charlottesville, Virginia, 1911).

2. Olive Anderson, "The Treatment of Prisoners of War in Britain During the American War of Independence," *Bulletin of the Institute of Historical Research,* XXVII (1955), 83. See also Eunice H. Turner, "American Prisoners of War in Great Britain 1777-1783," *The Mariner's Mirror,* XLV (August, 1959), 200-206; Francis Abell, *Prisoners of War in Britain 1756 to 1815; a Record of Their Lives, Their Romance, and Their Sufferings* (London, 1914).

3. See *e.g.* Dandridge, pp. 138, 192.

4. There are weaknesses in the prison journals that must be noted. There were Americans confined in Forton from June 1777 to at least March 1783. The only prisoner account I could find that covers the period after October 1780 is one letter dealing primarily with escapes.

365

67

confine American naval prisoners.[5]

In evaluating the Forton experience, it is important to remember that prisoners taken at sea often spent long periods in custody before entering a land prison. It was in men-of-war such as the *Terrible* and the *Andromeda* that future Forton men began their lives as prisoners. Once in Forton the Commission of Sick and Hurt Seamen[6] visited the prisoners, listened to their grievances, for-

Only two sources were available for the year 1780 and they are both scimpy. However, for the period June 1777 to Fall 1779 there are five separate accounts that, taken together, cover the period quite well. For the period after October 1780 I have essentially had to rely on official British and American records.

Also, Jonathan Carpenter (see n. 10) and Timothy Connor (see n. 11) were involved in a plagiarism. Although the plagiarism is obvious, the thief is not. Connor's records show that both men were at Forton; each kept a diary before entering the prison. Carpenter's diary is much shorter, much less detailed and has far fewer entries than does the Connor journal; whereas Connor usually made almost daily entries, Carpenter averaged only about two entries per month. However, for one six month period, Connor wrote nothing while Carpenter continued to write at his normal pace. It may be significant that while Carpenter put only two entries in his diary during his first two weeks at Forton, as soon as the plagiarism started, he made three entries in a week. My guess is that Carpenter is the borrower. Actually, for this study, the identity of the plagiarist is not that important since, at worst, the two sources can be accepted as one legitimate source. In the few cases where I wanted to cite material involved in the plagiarism, I have cited Connor. All citations from Carpenter refer to material that is not found in Connor.

5. From June 13, 1777 to November 6, 1782 Forton held a total of 1200 American prisoners. Mill, the other principal camp, held 1296 Americans from May 27, 1777 to August 1, 1782. (See John Howard, *The State of the Prisons* [4th ed.; London: J. Johnson, C. Dilly, and T. Cadell, 1792], pp. 185, 187.) There were many smaller temporary prisons in England. The prison at Kinsale, Ireland occasionally held large numbers of Americans, but Forton and Mill were the chief areas of confinement. For a discussion of Mill see Applegate (n. 1) who must, however, be compared with John K. Alexander, " 'American Privateersmen in the Mill Prison During 1777-1782': An Evaluation," Essex Institute *Historical Collections,* CII (October, 1966).

6. This government commission was in charge of directing all the prisons that held American seamen. The CSHS was directly responsible to the Admiralty. Entry Books, containing the Commission's letters to the Secretary of the Admiralty, are preserved in the Public Record Office, Ad(miralty) 98, books 11 to 14. I have not been able to examine this source in its entirety. Dr. L. Jesse Lemisch of the University of Chicago kindly allowed me to use his photostatic copies of parts of the Admiralty 98 records. The selection contains a broad sampling of the items that deal with American prisoners of war. Original letters and records of the Lords of the Admiralty dealing exclusively with American prisoners, contained in two volumes, are preserved at the National Maritime Museum. The volume for 1777-1780 is designated as Ad/M/404; the volume for 1781-1783 is designated as Ad/M/405. Unless otherwise noted, all correspondence in these volumes was sent by the Admiralty to the CSHS.

warded petitions of complaints, and generally watched out for their welfare.[7] However, there were no Commissioners on the men-of-war. This enhanced the possibility of ill treatment. The situation was even more difficult because Americans were legally traitors and pirates, not prisoners of war.[8] To all of this must be added the British navy's crying need for seamen. The experience of Nathaniel Fanning points up how some British captains attempted to intimidate and pressure prisoners into joining the King's navy. After "pretty unanimously" saying they would not defect and serve the King, Fanning and his fellow captives were told: "You are a set of rebels, and it is more than probable that you will all be hanged on our arrival in Portsmouth." Immediately thereafter the Americans' sea bags were stolen from them. Threats and pilfering continued. British seamen remarked: "D[am]n my eyes shipmate, but you have got a d[am]n fine coat there—fine hat— fine shoe buckles. . . . Come, come! ship mates, these fine things will only be a plague to you [in the ship's hold]." To which, according to Fanning, a midshipman added: "That is right lads, strip the d[amne]d rebels, and give each of them a frock and trousers, those will be good enough for them to be hanged in!" Even as the prisoners were about to disembark at Portsmouth, they were told: "There is she [the *Princess Amelia*] on board of which you are to be hanged."[9] Such treatment surely enhanced the possibility of defection.

The experience of others parallels that of Fanning. Captured in American waters, Jonathan Carpenter and his mates were "put in irons and crowded Down betwizt Decks, half Starved like Poor devils." After spending time on a prison ship in Rhode Island harbor, Carpenter was sent to England. Once at Portsmouth he

7. See *e.g.*, 98/11/93-94, 134-35, 137-38; letters of September 17, 1777, December 6, 1777, and CSHS to Ad. of November 12, 1777 in Ad/M/404.

8. 17 Geo. III, c. 9 passed in March 1777, said Americans taken in arms on the seas were guilty of "piracy" and were to be committed to prison as criminals for "the crime of high treason." This act was continued each season until the prisoners were designated as prisoners of war in March 1782 by 22 Geo. III, c. 10. (See 18 Geo. III, c. 1; 19 Geo. III, c. 1; 20 Geo. III, c. 2; 21 Geo. III, c. 2; 22 Geo. III, c. 1.)

9. Nathaniel Fanning, *Memoirs of . . . an American Naval Officer*, edited by John S. Barnes (New York, 1912), pp. 2, 3, 8. This account was probably written about 1805. Fanning hated the British government, loved the dramatic, and, at times, suffered from a poor memory. His bolder comments must be viewed with reserve.

69

was shifted from guard ship to guard ship to "make me enter on board a Kings ship."[10]

Timothy Connor writes that on the *Terrible* American prisoners received only "three-quarters of [prisoner?] allowance." He declared that although the prisoners were forced to do heavy work, "we almost starved. . . . Sometimes we had nothing but burgout and peas without salt, butter or meat; only what we begged from some of the sailors, as it happened there were some of our own countrymen on board." This entire treatment clearly seems to have been designed to make defection appear to be the best way— possibly the only way—to survive. And it worked. Connor later wrote that in one instance twenty-five American privateersmen out of a crew of one hundred were reported to have entered on the man-of-war that captured them. And the report seems well founded. The privateersman in question, the *Angelica,* carried ninety-eight men of whom only sixty-four were sent to Forton. Allowing for the possible detention of some men for questioning or medical care, the entry rate probably was at least twenty-five percent.[11]

The treatment of prisoners on men-of-war was not always so harsh. The captain of the *Terrible* served the rebel officers "a dinner, with a bottle of wine and some beer to drink" when the ship arrived in Portsmouth.[12] Still, although the evidence is not as full as one would like, it seems quite possible that American naval prisoners were more abused before they arrived at Forton than they were in the prison itself.[13] As Caleb Foot said, leaving a British ship and going to Forton "was like coming out of Hell and going into Paradise." When Carpenter learned that he was to be transferred from a guard ship to Forton, he too "rejoiced at an Opportunity to go to Prison."[14]

10. Jonathan Carpenter MS in the Vermont Historical Library, pp. 44-45. The page references are to Carpenter's numbering. In this and the other prisoner sources, I shall not clutter the text with notations of improper spelling and grammar.

11. Timothy Connor, "Journal," edited by William Cutler, *The New England Historical and Genealogical Register,* XXX (1876), 174-77, 343-52; XXXI (1877), 18-20, 212-13, 282-88; XXXII (1878), 70-73, 165-68, 281-86; XXXIII (1879), 36-41. (Page references will be given without notation of volume unless references to overlapping pages are made.) For the above, see pp. 177 and 284 (XXXI).

12. *Ibid.,* p. 343.

13. See petition of Stephen Hall dated November 21, 1780 in Ad/M/404 and petition of American prisoners dated June 26, 1782 in Ad/M/405.

14. Caleb Foot, "Reminiscences of the Revolution," edited by Caleb Foote, Essex Institute *Historical Collections,* XXVI (March, 1889), 110.

70

Once the American seamen arrived at Portsmouth, they were "examined [,] tryed & committed [to Forton] . . . as Rebels & Pirates."[15] As a result of the examination, each man was issued a warrant charging him with treason.[16] However if Fanning's experience was typical, the examination conducted by the Admiralty's representatives must have been reassuring. Fanning explained:

> These commissioners treated us with no abusive language; no imperious or domineering threats; on the contrary, they assured us we should be kindly used as prisoners of war; that as it appeared to them that we had been robbed of our wearing apparel, we should be furnished in a few days with each a decent suit at the King's expense.[17]

From the examination the prisoners were marched "under heavy guard" to Forton Prison which was located approximately one mile from Gosport and two miles from Portsmouth.[18] As noted, from June 13, 1777—when the first American seamen entered Forton—until November 1782, a total of 1200 Americans took that march.[19] During 1777-1779 Forton's American population averaged about 200 to 250; from 1779 the average was closer to 350. After mid-1782 the prison population declined steadily due to exchanges. Only rarely were there more than 400 Americans in the prison at any one time.[20]

In the early stages of the war, Forton prison consisted of "two large spacious buildings" with an ample airing ground in between them.[21] By 1778 the prisoners were separated so that "under offi-

---

This source consists mainly of letters written while Foot was in Forton; Carpenter, MS, p. 46.

15. Carpenter, MS, p. 46.

16. See also Connor, p. 343 and George Thompson, "Diary," Essex Institute *Historical Collections*, LXXVI (July, 1940), 222.

17. Fanning, p. 9. The examiners probably did not use the phrase "prisoners of war."

18. Connor, pp. 175, 175n.

19. I have no way of establishing how many Americans were in Forton from November 1782 until the final release date in mid-1783. Once France and Spain entered the war these nations' men were also confined at Forton. The foreign prisoners were kept in a separate prison and not allowed to mingle with the Americans.

20. See letter of July 7, 1781 in Ad/M/405; 98/11/130, 148, 339; 98/13/379; 98/14/240, 301; William Widger, "Mill Prison Diary," Essex Institute *Historical Collections*, LXXIII (1937), 326, 340 and LXXIV (1938), 40, 143.

21. Fanning, p. 9 and Connor, p. 175n. Fanning describes an additional airing ground of "about three quarters of an acre of level ground" and the CSHS (98/11/87) noted that Forton was "capable of containing 2158 men with a sufficient airing ground for that number."

71

cers [and] sailors" occupied one building while the officers of "somewhat higher grades" occupied the other building. During the first year prisoners were at Forton, a shed was erected in the middle of the airing ground which was "open on all sides to admit the free circulation of air; under which were seats for our [*i.e.,* prisoner] accommodation when the weather was hot and sultry."[22] No arrangement for separate hospital facilities was made when the prisons were being readied to hold Americans. But the original plan of sending the sick to Haslar Hospital was abandoned in mid-1777 and a separate hospital capable of holding one-eighth the total number of prisoners was erected.[23] The prison area was surrounded by eight feet high pickets driven into the ground about two inches apart.[24]

The prisoners were notified of their rights and duties by twelve regulations that were posted in the prison yard. The rules dealt far more with punishments than with rights. Only two kinds of punishments were authorized: (1) "Closer Confinement" and (2) reduction in food allowance.[25] Closer confinement meant being put in what the prisoners called the black hole which was "a very small room [with] neither bed nor bedding to lie on, but the soft side of a good plank."[26] A man in the black hole received only half the regular food allowance.[27] A prisoner could be put in

22. Fanning, p. 9. The CSHS in November 1777 had requested the shed to be erected "as many ill consequences in point of Health, would be apprehended if the Prisoners by having no shelter to walk under in bad winter weather, were obliged to continue for any length of time both day and night in their Lodging Wards." (98/11/137; see also letter of December 6, 1777 in Ad/M/404.)

23. 98/11/88, 94, 135-37.

24. Fanning, pp. 9-10.

25. Thompson, pp. 238-40 and 98/11/162. As the war continued two other kinds of punishment were authorized. In January 1779 the Admiralty decreed that anyone who tried to escape would be put at the bottom of the exchange list. (See Thompson, p. 225 and letter of January 6, 1779 in Ad/M/404.) In February 1779 the Admiralty granted the CSHS request to have the authority to put the "most refractory" prisoners into irons as was done in common gaols. (See letter of February 16, 1779 in Ad/M/404.) There is, however, no record in any of the sources that a prisoner was put in irons.

26. This description is a combination of two comments by Connor, pp. 345, 347.

27. Thompson, pp. 238-40. There is some question as to what half allowance meant. Fanning, with his usual exuberance, says the men got only bread and water; Foot says the ration in the hole for a week was two pounds of beef and one pint of peas; Connor says the daily fare was "six ounces of beef, half a pound of bread, [and] one pint of small beer." Connor's list does constitute half allowance and is probably the most accurate. (See Fanning, p. 13; Foot, p. 100; Connor, p. 344.) For a discussion of the full food allowance see below, pp. 375-376.

the hole for not obeying the agent, for trying "to Raise any discontent or Mutiny among the prisoners," or for causing "any disturbance" in the prison.[28] A forty-day stay in the black hole awaited those who were captured trying to escape.[29] Prisoners could also be placed on half allowance for whatever time it took to replace government property they had "willfully" destroyed.[30]

The actual punishments inflicted were, for the day, not overly harsh. For being drunk and striking the prison doctor and cook, a prisoner was merely put in the black hole for twenty-two days. When the prisoners destroyed the prison's lock they paid for it and received no further punishment. There was one instance—but only one—of corporal punishment being given. A prisoner received twelve lashes for stealing a set of "silver knee-buckles."[31] It is especially significant that when escapee Edward Manning was captured by a press gang, Connor said of him: "I do not expect to see him again, as they are in great want of men." But Manning was returned to prison. And when other escapees were taken by press gangs they too were returned to prison.[32] This practice is surprising. England did need seamen and the press gang was a well-established institution. The Commission and the Admiralty could easily have winked at the rules and let the press gang have any escapee they could catch.[33] Surely such a policy would have reduced escape attempts. That the British officials did not condone such action undercuts the argument of excessive punishments.

It is hard to obtain a clear picture of how the Americans felt about their captors. Most prisoners did not like the agent Newsham. For Fanning, he was the "old crab," an "ill natured" man who dealt in "cruelty and revenge."[34] Connor reported that at least once Newsham forced new prisoners to "deliver up their

28. Thompson, pp. 238-40. The time spent for these offenses was "as the case may deserve."
29. Ibid., p. 238 and see also Connor, pp. 344-45.
30. Thompson, p. 240.
31. Connor, pp. 18, 20, 71, 73.
32. Ibid., pp. 165, 349, 351; 98/13/120, 166; letter of November 1, 1780 in Ad/M/404; letters of August 30 and September 2, 1782 in Ad/M/405.
33. There is one case, but again only one, of pressed men not being returned. See letter of October 18, 1780 in Ad/M/404.
34. Fanning, p. 9. The adjective "most" is my impression from reading the prisoners' accounts; no other prisoner, however, spoke of Newsham so hatefully. See also Carpenter MS, pp. 49, 51-52; Foot, 97; 98/12/44.

73

money by point of the bayonet." Before a large assembly of prisoners who were taunting him, Newsham cried out: "[It is] Tiburn or Execution-Dock which you Deserve." One prisoner asserted that when the Commissioner came "to Rigtifey our Grivences . . . non of us Culd get an Opportunity to Speek to him on account of the Agent [Newsham,] the Doctor and the Clerk Keppet Close by His Side."[35] However Newsham did forward some of the prisoners' complaints to the Commission.[36]

The prisoners' relations with the turnkeys and with some guards seems to have been, at times, less than hostile. Turnkeys informed the prisoners of the latest gossip about exchanges. One turnkey made a bet with the prisoners that an exchange was imminent. On one occasion the officers of the guard "let [twenty-four men] out of the blak hole by Intersection." A prison clerk, probably for a price, even arranged for one prisoner to slip out of prison and spend a few hours with a woman and a bottle of spirits.[37]

There are, however, examples of friction. Two days of tension followed an insult written to a guard who was harassing prisoners who were trying to buy beer. A prisoner and a turnkey exchanged blows at least once. One prisoner was "wounded" by an officer of the guard whom the prisoner had, according to Newsham, "insulted and imitated." Another prisoner struck the prison doctor and cook, but he did so "being a little in liquor." Foot saw the guards as "bloody thieves often insulting us by words and deeds." Surely the prisoners were not too pleased with guards who stopped escape attempts after taking bribes to let the prisoners escape.[38]

Unquestionably there was one group of guards the prisoners detested—and apparently with good reason. In March 1779, a corporal of the guard shot and killed John Whright. Fanning claims that the captain of the guard was burning the prisoners' shirts that had been hung out to dry; when the prisoners tried to take them down he had his guards fire, killing Whright and wounding several others. An inquest held that the death was an

35. Connor, p. 345; Carpenter MS, p. 52; Thompson, p. 226.
36. 98/11/132.
37. Connor, pp. 212, 351-52; Fanning, p. 11; Thompson, p. 223; letter of September 17, 1777 in Ad/M/404; disposition of John Long dated September 29, 1781 in Ad/M/405.
38. Connor, pp. 18, 20, 71; Foot, p. 110; Thompson, pp. 224, 225; letter of April 3, 1782 in Ad/M/405.

accident. The prisoners disagreed. Thompson asserted that the "villian" corporal had "tretened the prisoners before." Foot proclaimed it "cruel murder." Fanning says the turnkeys told him that the guards had planned the killing.[39] This is, however, the only incident of its kind reported by either the prisoners or the British officials. If this killing was murder, it was a singular event. Since the guard units at Forton were changed regularly,[40] the hatred of the "villian" corporal and his fellows probably did not extend to the officer who helped prisoners get out of the black hole. It seems likely that some prison officers and some guards were hated, some liked.[41]

The daily schedule of the prisoners is also hard to firmly establish. Fanning seems to imply that the prisoners were normally allowed to be in the yard throughout the daytime hours. Connor's only direct reference states that on weekdays the prisoners were kept in their buildings "till the sun was half an hour high." The Commission ordered the prisoners to be kept in the airing ground as much as possible during the daylight hours. The rules of the prison said that from nine to two the prisoners had the right to attend "an open market by the Gate."[42] During good weather the prisoners probably did spend most of the day in the yard.

Apart from planning and executing escapes,[43] the prisoners occupied themselves in numerous pursuits. Many were constant letter writers and, of course, several kept diaries and journals.[44] In the officers' prison, where two French prisoners were confined, many Americans learned French.[45] In the other building there were "regular schools" which taught reading, writing, arithmetic, and navigation. Fanning suggests that so many first learned to read and write in Forton that their confinement "was a most fortunate

39. Fanning, pp. 11-12; Foot, p. 110; Thompson, p. 227; Carpenter MS, p. 50. Fanning's narrative contains the only detailed account of this incident.

40. See n. 86 below.

41. This judgment is partly based on my study of Mill Prison. See Alexander, (n. 5) pp. 333-34.

42. Fanning, pp. 13, 20; Connor, p. 344; Thompson, p. 239; 98/11/-138. On the use of the market see Carpenter MS, p. 50 and Connor p. 71.

43. See below pp. 381-384.

44. On letter writing see especially Foot, passim; Thompson, passim; Carpenter MS, p. 50.

45. Fanning, pp. 14-15. I cannot account for this exception to the rule of separation of French and American prisoners. Possibly the two men were Americans with a French background.

circumstance in the whole course of their lives."[46] Although none of the prisoner accounts tells of Fourth of July celebrations,[47] the prisoners did often compose and sing patriotic songs. When the French prisoners were noisily celebrating their King's birthday in 1778, the Americans, with their "continental jack flying," joined in the festivities. For Christmas of the same year Connor noted "a merry Christmas eve with the mass." Connor probably was not unique in having his own private celebrations. He wrote: "This day I enter into the twenty-eight year of my age; it was attended with one p.o.g. [i.e., drunk] as much as I could afford." The British officials provided water and tubs for washing clothes and encouraged the prisoners to keep themselves clean. They also decreed that the prisoners were "by turns to sweep and clane the prison, and the prison yard." Brooms and scrapers were provided for this work.[48]

The prisoners spent considerable time following the news of the day. They were probably as well informed as the general English populace. The prisoners seemed to have little trouble getting newspapers; they even sent people to Gosport and Portsmouth to get them. The men were allowed to send and receive letters although the Agent was supposed to examine all letters coming or going. This was hardly a hindrance since the prisoners continually received and sent letters through friends who came to visit them. The men even got mail from France written by men who had escaped from Forton.[49] Once Newsham intercepted a letter sent from Mill to a Forton prisoner. After inspecting it, the Admiralty ordered the letter to be delivered. Newsham was not always this strict. Without Admiralty authorization, he allowed a statement written by Benjamin Franklin to be read to the prisoners.[50]

46. Fanning maintained: "Many of these have since been advanced to the rank of masters of vessels: otherwise had they never seen Forton prison, they never would have been more than sailors." See *ibid.*, p. 15.

47. *Cf.* Mill Prison celebrations as discussed in Applegate, p. 314 and Alexander, p. 323.

48. Connor, pp. 40, 72, (XXXII) 283 and Thompson, p. 239.

49. Connor, pp. 18-20, 72, 166, 281, (XXXI) 285, 345, 347, 350; Thompson, p. 239; Carpenter MS, pp. 48, 50, 53; Foot, p. 97; Widger, LXXIII, 40, 143 and LXXIV, 346.

50. Letters of August 27 and October 22, 1778 in Ad/M/404. Newsham was severely reprimanded by the Admiralty, who decreed that all such statements should not be read without Admiralty authorization.

The prisoners also received news directly. British visitors, especially the Reverend Wren and Mr. Duckett, who distributed subscription monies, saw the prisoners regularly. These friends passed on the latest news. With new prisoners coming into the prison, the men had yet another source of information.[51] There was apparently no British conspiracy to manage the news that the prisoners received. If such an attempt was made, it failed miserably.

Naturally the prisoners were concerned with their supply of food. The British acknowledged this concern by allowing the prisoners to choose two of their number, who could be replaced at the prisoners' will, to inspect the weighing, preparing, and issuing of food. These men were to see that the food was "good in Quality" and met the posted specifications of seven quarts of beer, seven pounds of bread, four and one-half pounds of beef, two pints of peas, and either four ounces of butter or six ounces of cheese per man, per week.[52] If the prisoners believed they were not being properly victualed, they could write a protest to the agent who was "to Redress it as soon as possible." If the agent did not rectify the situation, the prisoners could write to the Commission for help. But this rule could cut both ways. If the prisoners' complaints were "unjust," they could be "put upon half Allowance and in Closer Confinement, as the Case May deserve."[53] This system had one vital flaw. The agent influenced the dispensation of contracts to feed the prisoners.[54] If Newsham colluded to have bad or short weight rations supplied, he would not have been anxious to so inform the Commission; and given the tradition of corruption in victualing the Royal Navy, it would have been remarkable if some corruption had not been practiced at Forton.[55] The important question is not that there were irregularities, but rather how extensive they were.

The prisoners made surprisingly few references to the food

51. Connor, *passim* and see below, pp. 378-379, on subscriptions.
52. Prisoners of war got ten and one-half instead of seven pounds of bread a week. See Thompson, pp. 239-40; 98/11/93-94, 162; letter of April 30, 1777 in Ad/M/404.
53. Thompson, p. 240.
54. See *e.g.*, "Humanitas" to the Ad., April 29, 1777 in Ad/M/404.
55. See *e.g.*, Daniel Baugh, *British Naval Administration in the Age of Walpole* (Princeton, 1965), pp. 403-405, 424-26, 447-51 and John J. Keevill *et al.*, *Medicine and the Navy: 1200-1900* (4 vols.; Edinburgh, 1957-1963), III, 83-85.

situation. Fanning, probably with his usual exaggeration, said the "small pittance of provisions" left him "part of the time half starved," which forced him to pick up or beg bones to satisfy his hunger.[56] Thompson maintained that the prisoners' meat was boiled into a broth that was "nothing but Clare water." However, Connor, who kept the most detailed diary, made only three references to receiving "stinking beef" or other bad provisions. In one case all the prisoners threw the bad beef "into the cook's window, and left and went without any." When the meat was bad again the next day, Newsham ordered cheese to be issued in its place. On the third occasion cheese was again substituted for poor beef.[57]

British friends of the prisoners charged that the prison agents viewed their offices "only as lucrative jobs, which were created merely for their emolument." Through a "natural cruelty" and by defrauding the prisoners, the agents allegedly reduced the prisoners to great "penury and distress."[58] When the eminent prison reformer, John Howard, visited the prison in 1782 he found that "all" of the six-pound loaves of bread "wanted some ounces of weight." But he also pointed out that "gentlemen concerned for the American prisoners . . . had obliged the contractors to be *more careful* in discharging their duty." Howard clearly implies that the Americans were supplied with better food than the French prisoners received.[59]

Lack of clothing was a real problem for many of the Americans when they entered Forton. The thievery practiced on the ships that had captured them was a primary cause of the clothing problem. Throughout the summer months, when good weather prevailed, nothing was done to alleviate this situation.[60] Finally in November 1777 the Commission asked the Admiralty to eradicate the "great want of cloathing and of Shoes and Stockings amongst many of the prisoners." In December the Admiralty directed the

56. Where the bones in the yard came from is not made clear. Fanning also says that an inquiry by "the proper authority" proved that the prisoners were being served bread that contained powdered glass. No other source, either prisoner or official, refers to such an occurrence. The powdered glass was, one would guess, a product of Fanning's desire to make Americans hate the British government. See Fanning, pp. 11, 17-18.

57. Thompson, p. 241 and Connor, pp. 213, 343, 352.

58. *Annual Register* for 1778 (London, 1779), pp. 78-79.

59. Howard, p. 187. It is possible, although I think wrong, to interpret Howard's comment as saying that no one showed concern for how victualing contracts were fulfilled.

60. Foot, p. 95.

Commission to provide shoes and clothing "from time to time" as "may be proper for Persons under their circumstances." However if prisoners sold their clothing, they were not to receive replacement articles. [61]

An inspection was to be held each month to determine what articles the prisoners needed. The Commission claims that they continued to carry out these monthly inspections.[62] In late December 1777 the prisoners at Mill Prison were provided with shoes and clothing. The situation at Forton is less clear. Fanning says no clothing was ever provided. Connor notes that clothing inspections were held in May and June of 1778, but these are his only references to being inspected. The prisoners could buy clothing at the open market, but this hardly qualifies as provided clothing.[63] The British did provide clothes, although not as regularly as the official accounts imply.[64]

The clothing problem was greatly complicated after March 25, 1782 when the Americans were made prisoners of war. By established practice, the articles needed by prisoners of war were paid for by the prisoners' own government. The Commission continually asked the Admiralty if the prisoners were to be supplied with clothing. The Admiralty did not resolve the question. In consequence, lacking American assistance, the prisoners' clothing situation deteriorated quickly. In September 1782 the Commission noted that the prisoners needed all different kinds of clothing. In the same month, the prisoners sent a memorial stressing their need for shoes. Soon the Commissioners were pleading with the Admiralty either to have an American representative supply prisoner needs or to send all the Americans away.[65]

The housing at the prison was quite adequate. The officers' quarters were especially "spacious." The men were provided with hammocks, a coverlet, a straw bed, and a straw pillow. But if Fanning's description is accurate, the quality left something to be desired. He maintained that the beds and pillows "were full of

61. Each prisoner was to have a cap, a jacket, a waistcoat, a pair of breeches, two shirts, two pairs of stockings, and a pair of shoes all of the same quality provided to the Royal Navy. See 98/11/371 and letter of December 6, 1777 in Ad/M/404.

62. 98/11/371 and Alexander, pp. 331-32.

63. Fanning, p. 9; Connor, pp. 20, 352; Thompson, pp. 224, 239.

64. See 98/11/170 and 98/13/507.

65. 98/14/251, 254, 301; 22 Geo. III, c. 10.

knits and *lice.*"[66] At least where American officers were concerned, the British paid some attention to making life reasonably comfortable. The separation of officers and common seamen was done at the American officers' own request. The common seamen merely had a fireplace to warm themselves at "alternately;" the officers, far fewer in number, were provided with a separate fireplace in their own apartment. The officers also were provided with a covered night tub that was to be emptied every morning.[67] For the officers in Forton, life was certainly more comfortable than it was for the common seaman.[68]

The question of how adequately the necessities of life were provided can not be separated from that of the assistance the prisoners received from: (1) the subscription and local charity, (2) the American government, especially through Benjamin Franklin's efforts, and (3) friends and escaped prisoners.[69] The most important aid the prisoners received came from the subscription. On December 25, 1777 Connor wrote "now the people begin to use humanity throughout England. . . . There are subscription books opened in many parts of England for our relief." He was right. A meeting of Middlesex justices raised £3815, 17s. 6d. for "cloathing and other necessaries." In Cornhill £800 was subscribed "in less than an hour." And in other parts of the country similar subscriptions were held to aid Americans in Forton and Mill.[70] The prisoners began to receive subscription money in January 1778. The Reverend Wren and Mr. Duckett, who administered the fund in the Forton area, continued to provide money until at least June 1779. A second subscription fund, taken up in 1779, continued to provide some assistance into 1781 although the amount of money the prisoners received continually decreased. Officers normally received twice the amount the regular seamen did. Carpenter, a common seaman, notes that from

66. Fanning, pp. 9, 16 and Thompson, p. 240.
67. 98/11/155, 164-66.
68. For example, none of the eleven men who died in Forton while Connor was there were officers. See Connor, pp. 36-39.
69. The aid received from friends was not a significant part of the total aid received. See *e.g.*, Connor, pp. 345, 347; Thompson, p. 223; Foot, pp. 97-98; Fanning, p. 22.
70. Connor, p. 347; *Annual Register* for 1777 (London, 1778), p. 216; *Annual Register* for 1778, p. 162. I could not determine the total amount of the subscription fund. Fanning (p. 18) said the total fund amounted to eight to ten thousand pounds; this is probably an overestimation.

February 19, 1778 to June 25, 1779, he received £3, 2s. 3d. This amounts to about 1s. 2d. a week. From mid-1779, the average was probably closer to 6d. per man per week.[71] In addition to delivering the subscription monies, Wren and Duckett occasionally provided clothing for some men. Fanning reported that when the subscription monies were exhausted, Wren "used to go round the neighbourhood to beg clothes and money for us."[72]

The subscription fund was augmented by American aid. As early as October 1777, Franklin had written to his friend David Hartley, M.P., asking him to distribute among the needy prisoners two to three hundred pounds. In December 1778, through Franklin's efforts, the Forton prisoners received fifty-six pounds of tobacco. They were also promised, in the name of the American Congress, one hundred great coats. Franklin's representative, Mr. Thornton, also expressed his desire to "occasionally" provide meat for the officers and to glaze the officers' windows. When the subscription was ending, Franklin made arrangements to send the prisoners 6d. a week. But Thomas Digges, who was entrusted with the monies Franklin sent, embezzled all but thirty of four hundred and ninety-five pounds sterling sent to him.[73]

With the aid the prisoners received until at least 1781, they were able to buy extra food and clothing. Due to this aid, the prisoners probably lacked little in the way of basic necessities during all of 1778. As Fanning remarked, while the subscription lasted, "I made out to live pretty comfortable."[74] The British government cannot be credited with the outside aid the prisoners received. At the same time, the government did not try to stop such aid.[75] If the British government was "inhuman" and "barbarious" as Franklin claimed, it should have tried to stop this outside aid.[76]

Probably the best index of how adequately the prisoners were

71. See Applegate, p. 313; Connor, pp. 280-84 passim, 348; Carpenter MS, p. 49.

72. Fanning, p. 19 and Thompson, p. 222.

73. 98/11/152; Edward Hale, Franklin In France (Boston, 1887), pp. 200-201; Benjamin Franklin. Writings, edited by Albert Smyth (10 vols.; New York, 1905-1907), VII, 71 and VIII, 109, 231-32, 413.

74. Fanning, p. 10.

75. The Admiralty's first response to a proposed subscription was to stop it, but they changed their minds within a week. See letters of December 11 and December 15 in Ad/M/404.

76. See Franklin, Writings, VII, 68-72.

81

provided the necessities of life is the death rate among prisoners.[77] Howard notes that from June 1777 to November 1782, 69 Americans died in Forton. That is, only 5.75 percent of the total American prisoner population died. This figure seems accurate. Connor's record of 415 prisoners in Forton from June 1777 to July 1779 lists only eleven prisoner deaths. This is a death rate of only 2.65 percent.[78] Other prisoners' accounts substantiate this low death rate. In February 1779 Carpenter recorded: "We are very healthy in this place. Since the first Prisoners were committed which is almost 2 Years." Foot never hesitated to paint a dark picture, but in all his letters dated from April 1779 to April 1780 he said that he and his friends were in good health.[79] This impressive health record is *prima facie* evidence that the prisoners' basic needs were not, to any extensive degree, willfully neglected.[80]

This record can be accounted for in part by the Commission's enlightened attitude toward smallpox. When smallpox appeared among prisoners, the Commission ordered that the men be innoculated if they requested it.[81] The Commission also showed great concern for cleanliness. The prisoners were provided with wash tubs and ordered to keep their clothing and persons clean. At periodic times, there were general cleanings and smokings to disinfect the prison. However, the record could have been better. Howard noted that when he visited the prison in 1782, the hospital wards "were not clean."[82]

77. Due to the small numbers involved, the death rate will be expressed in percentages rather than the normal demographic form.

78. Howard, p. 187 and Connor, pp. 36-39.

79. Carpenter MS, p. 49 and Foot, *passim.*

80. As Anderson noted (p. 69), unlike the Americans, the French and Spanish "were normally not prisoners for long." Still, at Forton the French death rate was 1.5 and the Spanish rate of 5.5 almost reached the American death rate. The rate was kept as high as it was for three principal reasons. Some prisoners probably died of wounds they received. No matter how many health precautions were taken, large numbers of men living in a small area for long periods of time enhanced the chance that outbreaks of fevers and smallpox might have epidemic proportions. Most important, from 1780 to 1785 there were ague epidemics throughout England and the influenza epidemic of 1782 was extremely deadly. The 1782 scourge especially took its toll in prisons. These epidemics probably account for the final American death rate of 5.75 which is far higher than the rate of 2.65 for the period 1777-1779. See 98/14/215-16; Charles Creighton *et al.,* *A History of Epidemics in Britain* (2d ed., 2 vols.; New York, 1965), II, 362-70; Howard, pp. 185, 187.

81. 98/11/118; Carpenter MS, pp. 49-50; letter of July 12, 1777 in Ad/M/404.

82. Thompson, p. 239; Carpenter MS, p. 51; Howard, p. 187; 92/12/3.

Throughout the war the Commission paid special attention to matters of health. Before Forton was even opened, provision was made for hiring an assistant surgeon "whose duty will be once a day to examine and report to the [Haslar Hospital] Physician & Surgeon who of the Prisoners may be Sick." When, in April 1777, it was decided to keep the sick at Forton, rather than sending them to Haslar, a pharmacist was added to the Forton staff. When a new prison hospital building was erected, care was taken to place it away from the other prison buildings. The shed constructed in the airing ground was viewed as a health measure. The Commission also took pains to see that prisoners were not lodged too closely. When a "sudden infectious sickness" stuck the Forton and Mill prisons in the summer of 1782, the Commission called in extra physicians to attend to the prisoners.[83]

As one reads the prisoners' thoughts, it is quite clear that their greatest concern was not food, clothing, or medicine. The one thread that runs most consistently through their accounts is the burning desire to regain their freedom. It is not surprising that the prisoners' chief activity was planning and executing escapes.[84] The Commissioners realized that Forton, originally designed as a hospital complex, was not a good site for a prison. Throughout the war they stressed the fact that escapes could be prevented only by "the proper disposition and vigilance of the guard."[85] The guards at Forton were militia units, sometimes composed of "invalids." These groups were rotated regularly, probably about every month. At first, ten guards were employed, but soon the number was increased to thirty; by July 1778, the guard numbered two officers and sixty men.[86] The need for an increase in guards is possibly related to the fact that the guards did not, at first, have orders to fire at escaping prisoners. It is not clear if such orders were ever issued. For at least part of 1777 no such orders existed and the frequency of escape attempts indicates that orders to fire may never have been issued.[87]

83. Fanning, pp. 9, 16; 98/11/88, 94, 135-37, 150-51 and 98/14/215-16; letter of December 6, 1777 in Ad/M/404.
84. See below, pp. 382-383.
85. See e.g., 98/11/116, 218-19, 260; 98/12/240-43; 98/13/140-41.
86. Connor, pp. 70, 168, 281, (XXXI) 285; 98/11/96, 140.
87. 98/11/117, 398; letters of July 10, 1777 and November 3, 1778 in Ad/M/404. Olive Anderson states that the prison guards "had no orders to fire on American prisoners who attempted to escape." However she does not note upon what information she bases this comment and she

Not all escape efforts were undertaken to gain freedom. In July 1777, the Admiralty made the mistake of establishing a £5 reward for the return of Americans who had escaped.[88] This reward helped thwart escapes by bringing into existence civilian "five pounders." These people, who "were always lurking about," hunted down Americans who tried to escape.[89] But there were also American five pounders. They were

> one or many, who agree with some one of the [British] boors, on such a night they will be out and come to his house, which they do, and spend the night and perhaps the next day drinking, &c.; he then brings them to the Commissary, and receives five pounds for each, half of which goes to the prisoners.[90]

Prison guards were occasionally brought into this scheme and the reward would be split three ways.[91] The Commissioners repeatedly told the Admiralty that the number of escapes and recaptures left "no doubt that it is done by collusion [to] share the reward."[92] The prisoners had found a way to augment the subscription.[93]

Of course there were constant attempts to really escape.[94] The Commissioner's records list 536 men as having escaped from Forton between June 1777 and April 1782. A good many of these men were recaptured. Also men who escaped more than once were listed each time they escaped.[95] Connor's detailed list says that 112 out of 415 Americans in Forton fled the prison. Since Connor would have known if a man was recaptured, the 112 figure probably represents the number who were not retaken. If

---

does not indicate if this was the situation throughout the war. See her "American Escapes from British Naval Prisons During the War of Independence," *Mariner's Mirror*, XLI (1955), p. 238.

88. Letter of July 10, 1777 in Ad/M/404. The regular reward for capturing prisoners of war was 10s.

89. Fanning, p. 10 and Connor, p. 347.

90. Luke Matthewman, "Narrative," *Magazine of American History*, II (March, 1878), 182.

91. At times the collusion was merely between guards and civilian five pounders. See *e.g.*, 98/13/133-34, 136-41, 148.

92. See *e.g.* 98/11/141; Justices of Peace to Ad., October 15, 1779 in Ad/M/404; and n. 85 above.

93. It is impossible to determine how much money prisoners made this way. The fund dried up only after April 29, 1782 (Ad/M/405) when the reward was lowered to 10s.

94. Several prisoners tried to escape from men-of-war and from other prisons before they got to Forton. See Foot, pp. 105-107; Fanning, pp. 3-5; Matthewman, p. 181.

95. Compiled from 98/11-14 *passim*.

this is so, the escape rate, at least for the 1777-1779 period, was almost twenty-seven percent.[96]

The escape methods used by the prisoners were varied and often imaginative. The men constantly tried to dig their way to freedom. They "jumped" the pickets, bored through building walls and floors, and once "made a bold push, and broke open the door." The prisoners broke out of the cook's room, the hospital, the storeroom, the French prison yard, and even the black hole. One resourceful seaman tried to escape through the privy-house.[97] However the prisoners—and the Commission—agreed that the easiest way to escape was, as one prisoner said, "by Force of half a Guinea."[98] Guards were continually being bribed. Although they often accepted bribes and then foiled the escape, a man with money had the best chance of escaping to France.[99] Once the men got away from the prison, they had a special friend waiting, for the Reverend Wren mixed a little treason with his humanity. Wren gave escapees clothing and information on how to get to London and from there to France. In France, Franklin provided money and helped the former prisoners get back to America.[100]

The Americans in Forton were very concerned lest informers thwart escapes. The desire to stop prisoner information led them to organize a form of government. Believing that one of the prisoners, a man named Rodgers, was an informer, a Committee in the Affair of Rodgers passed sentence on him of one hundred stripes. To protect Rodgers, Newsham put him in the hospital. The Committee was not so easily stopped. The Commission reported to the Admiralty that four Americans "dragged. . .

96. Connor, pp. 36-39. Fanning (p. 15) claims that 138 out of a total of 367 prisoners escaped in a period of twelve months. This would be an escape rate of slightly less than thirty-eight percent. However, there is no indication of how Fanning arrived at these figures.

97. Connor, pp. 19, 73, 166, 280, 281, (XXXII) 284, 287-88, 343, 344, 345, 348; Carpenter MS, pp. 47, 50; Thompson, pp. 224-26; Fanning, pp. 13-14; Matthewman, pp. 181-82.

98. Nathaniel Harrington, "Letter," *The New England Historical and Genealogical Register*, LIC (July, 1897), 322; [?] to Ad., July 28, 1778 in Ad/M/404.

99. *Ibid.;* Thompson, pp. 224, 225; Foot, pp. 97-98, 100-101; Thomas Smith, "Letter," Essex Institute *Historical Collections*, XLI (April, 1905), 227.

100. Harrington, p. 323; Matthewman, p. 182; Thompson, pp. 232-33; ed. Francis Wharton *Revolutionary Diplomatic Correspondence* (6 vols.; Washington: Government Printing Office, 1889), II, 391, 434, 725; CSHS to [?], August 18, 1781 in Ad/M/405.

Rodgers [out] and beat him in a cruel manner to the endangering [of] his Life if he had not been rescued by the Guard."[101]

The American seamen could always escape by volunteering to enter the King's navy. Very few men chose to use this option. And some who entered probably did so to be able to escape more easily.[102] Connor's records—which are probably the most accurate[103]—list twenty-three men as having entered in a year and a half. This entered rate of 5.7 percent is only about one-fifth the escape rate. There are two major reasons for this low entry ratio. Given the pressure usually applied at the time of capture, those most likely to enter probably did so on the British men-of-war. Once in Forton, after a man had volunteered to enter, he had to wait for a pardon to be issued before he could leave the prison. During this period, the volunteers were, as the British Admiral Sir Pye noted, "exposed to the Resentment of the other Prisoners who treatened the Lives of those who offer to serve in the Navy,

101. Thompson, p. 225 and 98/11/442-44.
102. See *e.g., Annual Register* for 1778, p. 78 and John Blatchford, *Narrative of the Life and Captivity of John Blatchford* (New London, 1788), p. 22 as microfilmed in the American Cultural Series, Item 29 in Reel 21. These examples of entering to be able to escape do not specifically relate to men from Forton. However, it seems likely that some Forton prisoners used the same tactics.
103. Admiralty records for the same period list thirty-six prisoners pardoned to enter the King's service. In four cases a man was pardoned twice and one of the men was subsequently exchanged. Thus the actual total of pardoned men is thirty-one But not all of these entered. On December 9, 1778, pardons were issued to twenty Forton prisoners. Of this number, four refused to go when called for; two were Frenchmen, and one had escaped. A comparison of Connor's list with the list of December 9 reveals that fifteen of the twenty did eventually enter. Thus, fifteen Americans actually entered whereas the official records list twenty entered. This brings the official total down to only three more than Connor's total. Connor's figure is more accurate because he knew who escaped and who refused to go after having volunteered. For the whole course of the war, the total number of men the official records list as entering is 136. (This figure is a gross one that does not take note of the corrections made above.) Assuming Connor's entered percentage held true for the whole war, the Admiralty figures should be reduced by about thirty-six per cent, yielding an entered figure of approximately eighty-seven. If the Admiralty figures' degree of error noted above was constant, the total should be reduced by twenty-eight per cent yielding an entered figure of about ninety-eight. If the uncorrected official record of 129 entered by November, 1782 is compared with Howard's total population of 1200, the entry per cent is slightly less than eleven per cent. Corrected by the projected Admiralty error figure of twenty-eight per cent, this entered figure is lowered to 7.8 per cent. The actual entered figure is probably somewhere between Connor's 5.7 per cent and the corrected Admiralty figure of 7.8 per cent. See Ad/M/404-405, *passim;* 98/11/381-82; Connor, pp. 36-39.

and prevent many from entering."[104] Pye was right; intimidation was practiced. For example, on January 21, 1779, the "officers and Seamen and others" signed an agreement that anyone who volunteered to enter a British ship was to receive thirty-nine stripes and have an ear cut off. This agreement—another example of prisoner government—was posted and, of course, immediately torn down by the prison officials. As Pye said, many "natives of Great Britain and Ireland, who wish[ed] to serve" the King, found it wiser to stay in Forton rather than incur the other prisoners' wrath.[105]

If a man could not escape and was not willing to enter, he could always hope to be exchanged. But the question of exchange was a thorny one. Franklin wrote to Hartley that an exchange "would be for the good of Mankind [by showing] that *Nations* should maintain honourably with each other, tho' engag'd in War."[106] Franklin's use of the word "nations" is very important. If Britain established a regular cartel with America, it would be a tacit admission that America was a sovereign nation. This was out of the question. Because of this legal problem, all dealings between Franklin and the British government were carried on informally with Hartley being the intermediary. Although Franklin's first request for an exchange was summarily rebuffed, by the spring of 1778 the Admiralty was willing to arrange an informal exchange.[107] The arrangements dragged on for almost a full year which prompted Franklin to complain that "the Delays have been of Design, to give more Opportunity of seducing the Men by Promises and Hardships to seek their Liberty in engaging against their Country."[108] Franklin was mistaken. The long delay was apparently caused by bureaucratic red tape. Franklin was not able to have the French Ministry issue the necessary ship passport until September 1778; the final list of British captives did not reach the Admiralty until late October.[109] The Admiralty then had to

104. Pye to Ad., May 30, 1781 in Ad/M/405; and see p. 368 above.
105. *Ibid.* and Thompson, p. 225. There is no record of such sentences being carried out. On June 5, 1781 (Ad/M/405) the Admiralty granted Pye's request that prisoners be allowed to leave Forton as soon as they agreed to enter. Pardons were then issued after the man had entered.
106. Franklin, *Writings*, VII, 193. Italics added.
107. Hale (n. 73), pp. 194, 203.
108. Franklin, *Writings*, VII, 267.
109. *Ibid.*, pp. 174, 188; 98/11/337-41, 379; letter of October 22, 1778 in Ad/M/404.

have the King pardon the Americans. When the King issued the pardons in December, he decreed that the exchange was to be made "with as little delay as possible." The first prisoners to be exchanged left from Mill. When writing to the Mill agent, the Admiralty directed him to carry out the exchange "as expeditiously as may be."[110] By late 1779 the Admiralty was saying: "It would be a great accommodation to the Service if all the American prisoners could be sent away at this time."[111] The British government seemingly wanted to be free of the American prisoners almost as much as the prisoners wanted to be free. This is not surprising. Collusion five pounders were increasing all the time. The total cost of prison maintenance was high, the American defection rate low. Although the Commission and the Admiralty did not, in their correspondence, speculate on the possibilities of entries, they must have realized that the number of men likely to enter would not be worth the cost incurred by purposefully delaying exchange. In addition, the buildings at Forton were needed for the care of sick marines. Clearly the luxury of keeping men in prison in hopes that they would defect was a luxury the Admiralty could not afford.[112] Although the Admiralty did not try to delay exchanges, officers in charge of getting Americans to defect used the delays to try to get the men to enter. These naval officers were not above telling the men "there will be no exchange, so as to get the more." However, these lies were not very effective.[113]

In June 1779 the first Forton prisoners to be exchanged, 119 of them, sailed for France. Because there were few British prisoners of war in France, no further exchanges took place until February 1780.[114] After that date, the exchange lapsed again due to Franklin's not having any British prisoners to exchange.[115] Exchanges became easier to conduct after March 1782 when Parliament made Americans prisoners of war. In April, the Ad-

110. Letters of December 12, 1778 and February 12, 1779 in Ad/M/-404.
111. Letter of November 11, 1779 in Ad/M/404.
112. 98/11/396-401 and 98/12/263-64.
113. Connor, p. 281.
114. 98/12/262-63, 276, 360-62 and Wharton, III, 522.
115. Franklin resented the fact that he was not given credit for the British seamen freed by American privateersmen. He also maintained that the British denied him credit for 500 British prisoners he turned over to the French. See Wharton, III, 522, 608-609, 745 and cf. letter of February 9, 1780 in Ad/M/404.

miralty ordered all American prisoners to be sent to North America where they were to be exchanged.[116] The American prisoners captured after the spring of 1782 were kept in prison until their numbers warranted sending an exchange ship. Finally on March 3, 1783, the Admiralty ordered all American prisoners to be sent to France.[117]

Life in Forton was a constant test of the American's mental strength. It was easy to become discouraged. Caleb Foot stated clearly and fairly fully the factors that could destroy a prisoner's moral. In 1780 he wrote to his wife:

> My welfare . . . is very poor at present for here we lie in prison, in a languishing condition and upon very short allowance, surrounded by tyrants, and with no expectation of being redeemed [by exchange] at present, for we seem to be cast out, and forsaken by our country, and no one to grant us any relief in our distress; and many of our noble countrymen are sick and languishing for the want of things to support nature in this low estate of health; and many of them have gave to the shades of darkness. Some others have entered on board his majesty's ships, to get clothes to cover their nakedness, which is to the shame of America. . . . Many of my countrymen that had money have made their escape, and I should have done the same if I had money or friends; but for the want thereof I must lie in prison till the wars are over and not have the pleasure to receive one letter from home.[118]

Although Foot is exaggerating about the prisoners "languishing,"[119] he does point up the elements that affected morale. Food, clothing, news from home, the state of health, treatment by the guards, the entry rate, and the prospect of leaving Forton were the key determinants of morale. Probably the most significant factor was the hope of leaving, especially by exchange. The prisoners'

116. The British displayed real concern for these prisoners' welfare. Each man was to get up to 20s. worth of slops; the transports going to America were to carry adequate medical supplies and a doctor; the men were to be delivered to either the Delaware River area or to Boston as was "most suitable to their convenience." See 98/14/171, 176-177, 182-83 and letters of April 11 and May 11, 1782 in Ad/M/405.

117. Letter of March 3, 1783 in Ad/M/405. This is the last reference to prisoners in Forton that I am acquainted with.

118. Foot, pp. 97-98.

119. After saying how sick the prisoners were, Foot, closed by saying "all the prisoners that belong to Salem are in good health at present." Cf. also his statements with those he made on pp. 95-97.

89

accounts constantly speculate on the possibility of exchange. Connor's journal shows the normal thought pattern. "No news of ships being come yet to carry us home, and we begin to grow in dispair." "Mr. Wrenn and Mr. Duckett . . . assured us that our exchange was every day expected, which kept us in high spirits." For about two weeks the entries continue, "in great hopes;" "we still remain in high spirits;" "in great hopes yet." But then, "we have heard no news [of exchange] as yet" and finally, "no news of our exchange. Out of all hopes once more."[120] And the pattern repeats itself.[121]

This is not to say the prisoners passively accepted their lot, far from it. They had ways of keeping their spirits up. Most prisoners consciously identified their suffering with America's struggle for independence. Fellow prisoners, both in Forton and Mill, were "my dear countrymen." Potential turncoats were to be intimidated and severely punished. The King was openly damned. When Newsham said America would be subdued, the prisoners retorted: "Over power & Subdue America—ah thats the least of my concern. You have not done it yet nor won't till the D[evil]ls blind." Once exchanged, prisoners would sing:

> In Support of the thirteen states
> For which we indured Captivity
> The Motto now that cures all fates
> For me is Death or Liberty
>
> . . . .
>
> And let's be resolute and brave
> O se how just our cause appears
> For Independence we will have
> If we fight for it fifth Years.[122]

When they broke the prison lock, stole the prison keys, fought with the guards, flew their "continental Jack," regulated conduct by committees, and escaped, I believe these seamen felt they were helping to create a nation of freemen.[123]

---

120. Connor, pp. 167, 168, 280, 350.

121. Ibid., pp. 283-84 (XXXII). See also Carpenter MS, pp. 46-54 passim; Foot, 97, 99-100; Fanning, pp. 19-20; Jonathan Haskins, "Diary," ed. Marion Coan, New England Quarterly, XVII (1944), 434.

122. Foot, pp. 97, 99-100; Carpenter MS, pp. 51-52, 55; pp. 383-385 above.

123. Connor, pp. 71-73, (XXXII) 286, 288 and Gentleman's Magazine for 1778 (London, 1778), p. 332. For some this enthusiasm for America may have been merely a defense mechanism to stave off depression. But to totally dismiss such enthusiasm as merely a defense mechanism would be wrong.

Are the British to be indicted for their treatment of American prisoners in Forton? Was Foot exaggerating when he called Forton a "Valley of Destruction" and a "place of murder"?[124] The killing of John Whright, which Foot was referring to, probably was murder. Still, that is the only instance of such an atrocity. More important, the total number of men who died in Forton was surprisingly low. Given such a low death rate, how "bloody" could the guards have been? How poorly clothed and how poorly fed could the prisoners have been?

The definitive analysis of the British treatment of American prisoners is still to be written. The treatment on British men-of-war appears to have been quite harsh and should be investigated further. Mill Prison has not been as fully examined as it should be. The smaller prisons in England and the large camp at Kinsale, Ireland, must also be studied. Fortunately some very good work is being done on British naval prisons in North America.[125] The information obtained from such studies will have to be combined with work on how American soldiers were treated. But while the overall picture is not yet clear, this much is sure: Forton was no Andersonville.

124. Foot, p. 111.
125. Dr. L. Jesse Lemisch has graciously allowed me to examine his extensive manuscript on the prison ships of New York. He convincingly demonstrates that living conditions on the prison ships were intolerable and murderous. He notes that the few men who were unlucky enough to be on both the prison ships and in Forton or Mill prisons all agreed that the prison ships were far more deadly. The picture drawn of the prison ships is one of "calculated inhumanity" designed to force men to enter the Royal Navy. Certainly life on the *Jersey* and life in Forton were two vastly different things.

BRITISH STRATEGY IN THE WAR OF AMERICAN INDEPENDENCE

By PIERS MACKESY

IN the first century of American history-writing it seems to have been a necessary part of the national creed that the War of Independence was won primarily by the tactical prowess of the rebels on the field of battle; and though interest in the war has widened and deepened, there are places where the old legend still holds on tenaciously. One of those places is the battlefields themselves, and the legend is preserved in cast iron along the roads of the eastern seaboard. There is a particularly striking example in New Jersey on the site of the successful rearguard action which General Clinton fought at Monmouth Court House during his withdrawal from Philadelphia in 1778. There, with twelve miles of baggage to protect, and Washington close on his heels, he turned and launched a local counterstroke which enabled him to disengage in the night and make his way without further danger to Sandy Hook. Yet the historical marker by the roadside characterizes the battle in a succinct and confident phrase as An Important American Victory.

Now the truth of course is that in so far as the war was won on the battlefield it was won by the attrition of British resources and the avoidance of decisive defeat—to which the British commanders greatly contributed. The decisive factors in the American success were strategic. Obviously in a sense this is true of all wars; yet there can have been few in which ultimate victory was gained to the accompaniment of so consistent a record of defeat in the field. As one British staff officer wrote admiringly of General Greene, "the more he is beaten, the farther he advances in the end. He has been indefatigable in collecting troops, and leading them to be defeated." I can think of only one important tactical defeat of British troops in the field, the

93

battle of the Cowpens in January 1781; and had it not been for the misconduct of Colonel Rahl and the miscalculations of Burgoyne, the same would have been true of the Germans. This fact accounts for the bitterness of the British and Hessian troops who surrendered at Yorktown. They had fought the rebels for five years, and their superior training and discipline had told in their favor on countless battlefields; and they felt that if history was on the side of the men who carried the muskets, they would not now be piling their arms and colors. When they heard their bands playing "The World Turned Upside Down," these men did not look into the future or realize the long-term repercussions of the American victory throughout the world. Their own world was their regiments, and they knew the words of the tune the bands were playing:

> If ponies rode men, and if grass ate the cows,
> And cats should be chased into holes by the mouse . . .
> If summer were spring and the other way round,
> Then all the world would be upside down.

All this is now common ground. The causes of the British failure were political and strategic; they were failures of a negative kind through most of the war, since except on rare occasions the British held the strategic initiative, yet failed to win a decision; failures of a positive kind when they suffered their two great strategic disasters at Saratoga and Yorktown. Yet the history of the British conduct of the war still remains unwritten. This is partly because the war was lost, and it is painful to dwell on defeat; partly because George III and his Ministers were vilified by domestic enemies, whose accusations, perpetuated in the *Parliamentary Debates,* form the most accessible source of information. There one may read the half-informed and wholly disingenuous criticisms of the opposition, and the misleading and partial replies of Ministers. These, supplemented by the *Annual Register* and memoirs like Horace Walpole's, dominated the entire history of this period for many generations. They are riddled with lies, special pleading, and gossip. Though the political history of the reign has been rewritten from better sources, the major decisions of the war have still to be reassessed.

From the very beginning of the war a few people maintained that the cause was hopeless: and hindsight has strengthened and extended their argument. The Americans, it now runs, were numerous, skilled in handling weapons, and defending a country of limitless space and limited resources: they had no cities whose loss would be fatal to the political, moral, or industrial foundations of their military effort; they were free to refuse battle except on favorable terms, and to retreat into fastnesses where the British could not follow or attack them. When the maritime powers of Europe intervened in the struggle, the argument continues, its futility became all too evident. The British Army was now drawn into defensive commitments throughout the globe which made it impossible to reinforce or even keep up the strength of the force in America, while the navy faced odds which meant that it could no longer guarantee the Atlantic supply-line or the army's lateral communications on the American coast. Only the blindness and folly of the King and his immediate advisers, particularly Lord George Germain, forced England to continue the struggle.

So runs the indictment, delivered from the godlike pinnacles of after-knowledge. But I have spent some time looking at British documents on the conduct of the war, and have tried to look at it from a point where the view is more constricted—let us say from the middle of St. James's Square in London—and with the help of the eyes of two men whom it has only recently become respectable to consult: King George III and Lord George Germain.

Now it is possible to argue that the political objectives of the war were so ill-conceived that the success or failure of the strategy is a matter of indifference: that if America had been reconquered it would have done England no good in the long run anyway, and that it was more important to withdraw from the struggle by an act of political discretion than to wage it against heavy odds in a spirit of military optimism. To this argument there was one reply which was absolutely conclusive if it was true. It was used with much vividness of expression by the King and many other people, but I will put it in the words

95

which Germain used after Yorktown: "we can never continue to exist as a great and powerful nation, after we have lost or renounced the sovereignty of the American colonies."

Now we, being wise after the event, know that this idea was wrong. But to reject it before 1783 was to reject the whole system of economic beliefs which had shaped the British Empire. Statesmen are not built in that mould; and there are enough examples in our own day of policy firmly based on fossilized assumptions to make an Englishman at least somewhat wary of condemning George III and those who shared his beliefs. And they were not all simple souls like the King. When the cause was lost and it was becoming apparent that trade with America did not depend on political sovereignty, a sophisticated mind like Lord Sheffield's could still fight for the Navigation System as the foundation of power on which wealth must ultimately be rooted. And there was another strategic argument which is worth considering: that in time of future war a hostile America would wreck the British homeward-bound West Indian trade and make the West Indies untenable. It is true that in the War of 1812 British trade was not much inconvenienced, but in fact the danger was never fully tested. If America had intervened when Britain's European enemies had powerful navies intact and British resources were already at full stretch, American warships and American bases might have achieved very different results.

But even supposing that the loss of America would be disastrous, the administrative difficulties of the task facing the Ministry were appalling. Setting aside the naval effort, the British government committed itself in the course of the war to transporting, reinforcing, and supplying between fifty and sixty thousand troops in the Western Atlantic between Newfoundland and Tobago. The initial effort of lifting the army which was to fight the campaign of 1776 in Canada and around New York completely swamped the country's shipping resources. Had it not been for the determination of Germain and the support of the King, the Admiralty and Navy Board would have thrown in their hand and declared it to be impossible. It was certainly, as Lord Sandwich declared, unprecedented. Contemporaries, including Sir William Howe, acknowledged the greatness of the achievement, for which the credit lay principally with Germain; and in our own day Walter Millis has written that it is entitled to the respect of modern staff officers and logisticians.

It had been assumed at the outset that the army would quickly recover a sufficient depth of country in America to supply most of its own needs in the way of provisions, fodder, and fuel. But this hope was constantly disappointed in the coming years, and Germain found himself responsible for seeing that fifty thousand troops were fully supplied across three thousand miles of ocean. This he achieved, with the cordial help of the Treasury and at the cost of a good deal of friction. The maintenance of the armies abroad in the last year of the war was to require 120,000 tons of shipping, composed of ships of between 250 and 400 tons. The whole effort across the ocean was unparalleled in the history of the world, and it was successful. A good deal has sometimes been made of the pressure of these supply problems on the commanders in the field, but any excuse was good enough to shift responsibility for failure onto the home government, and the difficulties of the Atlantic pipeline made relatively little difference to the course of operations on land. The pressure was felt most in a different quarter; for the continuing financial burden of the operation fell heavily on Lord North, as head of the Treasury and Exchequer, and it probably did more to depress his spirits and undermine his resolution than did the operational problems of the war.

The course of operations was nevertheless influenced by a problem which might be described as administrative, and in a disastrous manner. The selection of theatre commanders had always been a difficult task: difficult not only because political and social pressures sometimes pushed bad candidates forward, but also because of the genuine impossibility of foretelling how an officer would measure up to the command of a theatre of war when the only evidence available related to his record in peacetime or as a subordinate on the battlefield. The Elder Pitt had fired two commanders on the main front in America in the course of two years; and the problem in the American Rebellion

97

was yet more difficult. In the first place the commanders' task was infinitely more complicated and diffuse, calling for a rare combination of tactical and strategic ability with statesmanship; and in the second place the intense political warfare at home constantly handicapped the government in its choice of commanders and inhibited them from removing failures.

At the very outset the American theatre was saddled with three fairly junior generals who were sent out to give some much-needed military help to General Gage. For that purpose skill in training troops and handling them in the field was most needed; and Howe, Burgoyne, and Clinton all had good reputations. But much more was needed in a commander-in-chief who had to deal with the intensely complicated strategic and political situation in the rebel colonies; and all these men in turn found themselves handling problems that were too big for them. Howe conveniently resigned when he had failed; but Clinton held the command for four years in which he gave ample reasons for removing him. But the political situation when he took over was becoming so tricky that it was very difficult to do so. Generals and admirals who thought they had a grievance mostly had seats in Parliament, where they found eager support from the political enemies of the Ministry. After the naval storms which centered on the Keppel affair, and the return from America of Howe, Burgoyne, and Carleton, it was very difficult indeed to remove the well-connected Clinton, and the Ministry was saddled with him for the rest of its existence. The only soldier who emerged who might have had the stature for the American command was Carleton, who fell out with Germain in 1777; but though Germain handled him unwisely and probably with a degree of personal rancor, I am inclined to believe that Carleton gave some grounds for criticism by his operations in Canada in 1776, and responded to it with an intemperate violence which was difficult to overlook.

The operational consequences of inadequate commanders are all too obvious. They meant lost tactical opportunities, apathetic direction in the theatre, and the muffling of the strategic designs laid down by the Ministry. Less obvious perhaps was the dearth of advice on which the government could rely, and of constructive plans from the men who were in the best position to put them forward. For the campaign of 1777 Howe sent home no less than three separate plans, but provided no general reasoning about how the war should be won. The Ministry accepted his proposals, and indeed the final one reached them so late that they were presented with a *fait accompli* and had to accept it, relying on Howe's common sense to relate his own movements to the general plan which included Burgoyne's advance from Canada. Clinton was worse than Howe. His psychology has recently been explored in an interesting experiment by Professor Willcox of the University of Michigan and a psychologist colleague, and the facts are certainly curious enough to make him a profitable subject for study: on occasion a bold tactician, a bold memorialist on paper when he was a subordinate, but in supreme command reduced to a kind of paralysis, incapable of decision and execution, withdrawing himself from his army, and throwing his energies into violent quarrels with his naval colleagues and the Ministry. Germain and the Cabinet attempted to supply the general planning of which he was apparently incapable; and in return they received endless complaints of interference and appeals to be left alone, but never any counterproposals of Clinton's own, and seldom any action. It is worth contrasting Clinton with the Duke of Wellington, who laid the foundation of his Peninsular victories with a lucid memorandum to the Cabinet on the strategic situation of Portugal, and from this proceeded by rational and systematic steps to develop his strategy as the war progressed. I think it is true to say that in the whole course of his command Clinton never put forward a clear appreciation of his task or any rational suggestions for advancing it.

It was of course difficult in the extreme to form a reliable intelligence appreciation. There was little understanding of the political situation and attitudes of the rebels, and their fighting qualities were difficult to assess, for those who knew the Americans best in 1775 respected them the least. Nor was the government free to use every means known to warfare. British hands were tied by considerations of policy and sentiment. This truth has not always been recognized, but when one considers the usages of eighteenth-century war and the methods employed by occupying armies throughout history against insurgent populations, one realizes that the army behaved with a moderation which may have been to its detriment. I do not mean to suggest that rebels taken in arms should have been treated as traitors, which, as Carleton once had cause to remind Washington, could only lead to mutual massacre; but the strict usages of war could have been enforced with a rigor which might have considerably reduced the rebels' already somewhat qualified enthusiasm for the military life. It is possible to speculate, as Major Mackenzie did, on the consequences of a tougher policy about giving quarter. At the attack on Fort Washington, for instance, the American commander rejected the preliminary summons, and considerable casualties were inflicted on the Hessians when they stormed the outworks. Howe would have been perfectly entitled to let them storm the inner defenses, and the Germans would have made a considerable butchery in the crowded enclosure. It is at least conceivable that Washington would thereafter have found it even more difficult to gather an army, and that garrisons like those of the Delaware forts in 1778 might have been more hesitant about standing an assault in the future. Again, if warnings had been issued that partisans not in uniform would be executed out of hand, and a few examples had been made, it is possible that the population as a whole would have lost some of its taste for killing couriers and annoying the army's communications. This of course is an uncertain presumption: it did not work for the French in Spain, but the Americans were mostly members of a prosperous farming and mercantile community, and suffered neither from the poverty nor the fanaticism of the Spaniards. And again, if the coastal towns had been systematically ravaged as Marlborough ravaged Bavaria, instead of being spasmodically and half-heartedly raided, the rebels' privateers and merchant shipping would have been hard hit and their importing of supplies and munitions seriously impeded.

But from all this the British recoiled. Nor was it wholly a matter of political calculation, though that played its part. Conscience as well as policy was at work. "Here pity interposes," wrote General Phillips, "and we cannot forget that when we strike we wound a brother." When General Tryon burned the village of New Haven in 1779 he thought it necessary to send a sort of apologia to his commander-in-chief for his action; and when Clinton himself was presented with a loyalist proposal to kidnap Washington he turned it down because the proposers were evidently determined to kill the American commander if they could not bring him off alive. I am not aware that this objection was ever raised when Colonel Keyes went into the western desert to collect the scalp of General Rommel. Even the King, in spite of his constant insistence that the British must strike hard, never forgot the distinction between subjects and enemies: "Notes of triumph would not have been proper," he wrote after Howe's Long Island victory, "when the successes are against subjects not a foreign foe." And when a foreign officer proposed to raise a body of troops on an avowed principle of plunder he dismissed it as "very diverting . . . very curious, when intended to serve against the colonies."

To turn from the difficulties of planning to the plans themselves, I think it is pretty plain that until Saratoga at least, organized resistance in the colonies could have been broken; and though disorganized resistance by guerrilla bands would have been impossible to suppress with regular forces over so vast an area, Germain was one of many who believed that once the Continental Army was destroyed and Congress dispersed, the policing could be done by loyalist militias with no more than a stiffening of regulars. This belief was held by colonial governors and officials as well as by statesmen in London. The assumption behind it was that the rebellion was the work of a highly organized and determined minority. At one time it would have been difficult to find historians on either side of the Atlantic who would have admitted such a possibility for a moment, but today there would be more hesitation in rejecting it. It is now clear at any rate that the loyalists did indeed form a high percentage of the population, though since the local machinery of government and coercion had been seized by the rebels before conservative opinion was formed or countermeasures organized, it was exceedingly difficult for the loyalists to organize an opposition or resistance and in the longer run even to maintain their courage. And here too the twentieth century has something to teach us. It is too easily assumed by exiles and officials that a population which is not constructively in favor of rebels is positively against them. Furthermore, it is very difficult to take military action against a rebel nucleus without inconveniencing and antagonizing the population as a whole and giving the movement a general cohesion it may have lacked. Both these things happened in the American Revolution. Armies, for instance, could not operate without requisitioning, a procedure known by that name when Washington did it and by the name of plunder when it was done by Howe.

Thus the difficulties of mobilizing loyalist support was certainly considerable; but Germain's views on strategy at the outset were as least as sound as those of the school which advocated purely external pressure on the colonies by blockade, coastal attacks, and Indian raiding. The reasoning of the maritime school was that England could maintain only small forces beyond the Atlantic in proportion to the size of the country, and could not replace her casualties: therefore British casualties were more telling than rebel ones, and a series of winning battles which did not lead to a decision would destroy the army and mean ultimate defeat, while a single serious reverse might destroy the moral asset of superior discipline and training. Therefore, said this school of thought, the war should be conducted with the minimum of risk to the British troops: their commitments should be limited to the defense of bases for the fleet, and to coastal raiding.

This maritime policy might have made life intolerable for the colonists: it was not likely to make them love the mother country more, or pave the way to an enduring political settlement. Germain's view was different: "one decisive blow on land" was essential, then loyal support could be rallied while the navy commanded the rebel coasts. Before one condemns this policy one must ask oneself the question: "What would have happened if Howe had destroyed the rebel army around New York in 1776 and reached Philadelphia?" I believe the whole course of the rebellion would have been changed. To support the policy there was the memory of American jealousies and failures in the Seven Years' War, which encouraged the hope that the colonies would fall apart if a decisive defeat were inflicted on their troops. And there was the international scene to be considered. France was certain to try to exploit Britain's embarrassments, and the sooner the whole dispute was settled by victory the better. The great effort mounted in 1776 was in a sense a gamble on quick results to forestall and discourage the French.

On how to apply the force which was being collected there was general agreement from the beginning. It was the Hudson Valley plan—the plan which led two years later to Saratoga. New England is the heart of the rebellion, so ran the argument; isolate her, and the rest of the colonies will come to their senses. Isolate her, therefore, by striking north from New York and south from Lake Champlain to seize control of the crossings of the Hudson. Then the army in Canada can be used in an offensive role. Afterwards New England may be invaded on a broad front from the rear, in conjunction with a force from Rhode Island. This plan was put forward in the autumn of 1775 not only by Gage, the returning commander-in-chief, but also by Howe and Burgoyne, who came to grief over it two years later. Its execution got off to a slow start in 1776 because Howe had been unable to evacuate Boston before the winter, while in Canada Carleton had been driven back to Quebec and had to reconquer the country in order to reach his intended starting point on Lake Champlain. The offensive was resumed in 1777.

This is not the place to go into the arguments over the responsibility for Saratoga. I will say no more than this: both Howe and Burgoyne had endorsed the general outlines of the plan; Howe was fully aware of the general plan when to the astonishment of all he sailed away from New York to the Chesapeake; and Burgoyne had served in Canada throughout 1776, so that when he virtually wrote his own instructions over Germain's signature he was in a better position than most people to assess the difficulties of his enterprise. The decisions that led to his misfortune were operational ones taken by himself; and his claim that he was rigidly bound by his instructions to persevere in face of the certain destruction of his army has no more substance than Howe's contrary claim that he was left without orders and in ignorance of the general plan. The only avoidable error on the part of Germain and the Ministry was the choice of Burgoyne to lead the northern force.

The disaster at Saratoga of course was the end of the Hudson plan, and the intervention of France a few months later followed by that of Spain and Holland altered the framework of the American War entirely. But before I go on to consider the implications of the intervention of the European maritime powers, I will carry the story of American strategy through to its conclusion. By "American strategy" I mean the master plan for bringing the colonies back into the Empire. The changing situation modified but did not alter the fundamental assumptions on which Germain's strategy was based. The first year after Saratoga was spent in contracting and redeploying the army to meet the requirements of the wider war against France: Philadelphia was abandoned in order to reinforce the West Indies and Florida. But the forward policy in America was resumed at the beginning of 1779 with a new directive from Germain. It was framed in consultation with North and Amherst and with the advice, not merely of "sycophantic refugees" as was alleged, but with the help of Lord Carlisle and William Eden, the newly returned Peace Commissioners, which in the circumstances was perhaps the best advice available. The plan had military support; and if Clinton disliked it he let his case go by default.

The new directive recognized the improbability that Washington could now be forced to a decisive battle, though this was still regarded as the most hopeful method of winning the war, and the fact that there were no strategic or political objectives in the colonies whose seizure could of itself lead to the collapse of the rebellion. If Clinton could not bring Washington to action, he was to contain the Continental Army with his main force, and make it possible for detachments to recover and protect individual provinces till a loyalist militia could be organized and an assembly could meet. That is to say, instead of a single decisive campaign, there was to be piecemeal recovery and re-integration of individual provinces behind the umbrella of the main army.

Clinton had difficulties and shortages to contend with, but he did as little as possible to give the scheme a fair trial. He always opposed the restoration of civil government, even in New York. Nothing whatever was accomplished in 1779, and the first offensive was mounted in South Carolina in the spring of 1780. Georgia had been recovered by a small force at the end of 1778; and the American Department had great faith in the policy of attacking from the southern end of the rebellion, where the colonies were believed to be especially vulnerable through their dependence on importing their means of existence and their large slave populations. At first all went well. The rebel southern army surrendered in Charleston, and by the middle of the summer the entire province of South Carolina seemed to have been pacified. But as soon as a guerrilla leader appeared in the field the rebellion flared up again, and a ferocious civil war broke out between loyalist and rebel militias. It was a struggle in which the balance of terror favored the rebels, since Cornwallis's aim was to conciliate and pacify, and that of the rebels was to stoke the flames of hatred. In due course nevertheless Cornwallis's mobile columns should have been able to suppress the trouble; but now a detachment of American regulars under Gates approached from the north, gathering the rebel militia around it as it advanced. Cornwallis dealt with that force at Camden, but he came to the conclusion that he could not protect and pacify South Carolina unless he overran the rebel strongholds further north. This conclusion drew him into the great advance across North Carolina which realized the fears of those who had predicted from the beginning that the British Army would be ruined by a series of winning battles, and it eventually led Cornwallis empty-handed and with depleted ranks to the Jamestown Peninsula in the Chesapeake.

Did Cornwallis's misfortune justify the original predictions of disaster? Only in a limited and special sense. It is true that the numberless militia played a decisive part in frustrating the British hopes; but the element which first necessitated Corn-

105

wallis's offensive and then enabled the militia to hold together and resist it was the continued existence of a force of American regular troops. The nature of the problem was described a few months afterwards on the other flank of the theatre by General Haldimand, the commander-in-chief in Canada:

It is not the number of troops Mr. Washington can spare from his army that is to be apprehended, it is the multitude of militia and men in arms ready to turn out at an hour's notice at the shew of a single Regiment of Continental Troops. . . .

As the great nineteenth-century student of war Jomini pointed out in connection with the Spanish guerrilla effort against Napoleon, it was the presence in the theatre of war of an intact force of regulars which made it possible for the irregulars to operate with real effect, by forcing the French occupying troops to concentrate and give up their hold on the countryside. This was the main achievement of the Continental troops in the southern colonies. Their presence in North Carolina encouraged the militia to prevent the loyalists from joining Cornwallis, to sever the communications between Cornwallis's main force of regulars concentrated to the northward and his outlying detachments of militia, and thus to lay the foundations of Ferguson's defeat at King's Mountain in a battle between militias. They enabled them too to play their part in regular battle, to inflict casualties on Cornwallis's irreplaceable regulars, to defeat Tarleton at the Cowpens, and to force on Cornwallis the Pyrrhic victory of Guilford.

In other words, as Germain had appreciated, it was essential to the plan of piecemeal pacification and resettlement that Washington's regular forces should be effectively contained and prevented from intervening. Much more could have been done in this direction by a more active policy on the part of Clinton and the northern wing of the army based on New York. An earlier and stronger diversion in Virginia might have made a great difference. More effective and perhaps decisive in itself would have been the seizure of the forts guarding the Highlands of the Hudson, which Benedict Arnold maintained could be stormed. For one brief moment while Burgoyne was being sur-

106

rounded at Saratoga, the forts were actually in British hands, and were abandoned only because Howe's removal to the Chesapeake had stripped New York of troops. Later Clinton was undoubtedly handicapped by shortages of men; and though his own character contributed most to the prevailing inertia at New York, a stronger force might have made him happier about the security of his base and encouraged him to be more venturesome. More troops, however, were out of the question, owing to the pressure which the European powers were exerting against the West Indies and the British Isles themselves.

So far I have tried to suggest that British military policy in America had at least a rational basis. I now want for a moment to consider the American struggle in the context of the wider war against France, Spain, and Holland. England had allowed herself to slip into the situation which her statesmen had always dreaded, a war against the maritime powers of Europe with no Continental allies to impose a check on France's freedom to devote her resources to naval warfare. Now these maritime powers held colonial bases from which they could and indeed intended to strike the most damaging blows against the British colonies and economy. The American colonies had been permanently settled, creating a new race which was producing its own political and social traditions, which had a somewhat imponderable economic value to the mother country, and whose sentiments were rapidly drifting away from sympathy with the British people. The case of the colonies which the French now threatened was entirely different. In the West Indies and India the settlers did not form complete social and economic units capable of exercising political choice: they were planter or trader societies exploiting alien populations. The loss of British sovereignty here would not mean independence: it would mean the transfer of their wealth to a supplanting power and a European rival; and the wealth at stake was immense. India was so distant that it was only slowly pulled into the war, and began to exert a strategic pull on British resources from about 1780; but the West Indies exerted their full pressure from the moment France's intentions

107

became clear. The reinforcements drawn from America in 1778 to defend the Lesser Antilles was the beginning of a struggle which contracted the scale of effort in America and drew in all the additional resources which became available as the war went on. It was announced at the time that the main effort was now directed against France, and an attempt was made by means of the Carlisle Mission to reach a settlement with the Americans. That of course failed. When Spain entered the war the evacuation of America was ruled out once more. The depressed and indeterminate Lord North murmured something about the objects of the American War not being worth the cost of obtaining them, to which the King replied that this was "only weighing such events in the scale of a tradesman behind his counter." King George and Lord George Germain were agreed that the loss of the American colonies would mean the loss of the sugar islands, and that therefore England must play for the whole stakes.

This may seem unwise, but there were several grounds for hoping that England might eventually prevail. In the first place one or two victories at sea would have altered the balance completely and given England the strategic initiative. France would have been unable to deploy her military power beyond the seas; and England, after sweeping up as many of the French and Spanish islands in the Caribbean as she thought necessary to her security and prosperity, would have been free to concentrate her military resources in America. With another ten thousand men and the assured command of American waters, even Clinton should have been able to destroy or paralyze Washington's army and enable Cornwallis to consolidate his hold in the south.

The naval victories were not achieved, though there was no inherent reason why they should not have been. A stronger hope, however, was that if the country could keep afloat it would win a war of attrition through its longer purse and the disunity of its enemies. Germain and the King intended to hasten the process and at the same time provide the best defense of England's Caribbean colonies by taking the offensive wherever it was possible. One aspect of this was the succession of small but potentially damaging blows which Germain mounted against the Spanish possessions in Central America, attacks which were intended both to protect Jamaica and to push Spain into making a separate peace without the bribe of Gibraltar. Another aspect of Germain's offensive spirit was his constant effort to mount offensives against the French islands in the Lesser Antilles. But success depended on assembling enough troops to take the islands and, more important, on collecting enough ships to win the command of West Indian waters. He was frustrated in this by the departmental opposition of the two armed services: that is to say, by Lord Amherst and Lord Sandwich.

The British Isles were in some danger of invasion, and while the commander-in-chief of the army resisted the dispatch of troops from the home forces, Sandwich at the Admiralty insisted on retaining a fleet in the English Channel strong enough to challenge the enemy if they attempted to seize the command of the water and pass an army across it. The Admiralty has always had a tendency to be riveted by the fear of invasion and consequently to overinsure in home waters. The effect of this is a strategic paralysis: the sacrifice of the initiative to the enemy. To this line of thinking Germain and the King were strongly opposed. A tame defensive war, said Germain, would be fatal. He and King George believed that it would be disastrous for England to insist on an impenetrable shield of warships: the country must be willing to resist a landing on the beaches with her troops, so that enough ships could be spared to to gain the initiative in overseas theatres, and especially the vital Caribbean. There was at least some naval support for this view. The officer who later became Lord Barham wrote a powerful memorandum in the autumn of 1779 in favor of taking the offensive in the West Indies as the only way of defending the British sugar islands; and before the end of the war he came to the conclusion that too much had been sacrificed to an overstrong Channel fleet—a fleet which in no circumstances could be made strong enough to give battle to the combined fleets of France and Spain if they made a really determined attempt at invasion, yet was nevertheless stronger than was necessary for the purpose of

109

impeding the movement of invasion craft from the French coast. If bolder use had been made of the fleet to obtain a strategic surprise in the West Indies, the shape of things in the western Atlantic might have been very different.

But though Germain's hope of winning the local initiative in the western Atlantic was disappointed, there still seemed a real likelihood by 1781 that the enemy alliance would crack from within. The Americans were at the end of their tether, the French officers at Rhode Island were appalled by what they saw of the political and military condition of the rebellion, and the French government was making provisions for pulling its forces out of America at the end of the campaign. In the diplomatic sphere a mediation was being floated by Austria and Russia, and France's need of peace to mend her financial troubles was so great that Vergennes was prepared if necessary to lead the Americans up the garden path to a peace conference and desert them. Spain had given him a bad fright in the previous year by engaging in separate peace talks with England, and in order to keep Madrid in the war French naval resources were being drawn increasingly into the pursuit of such purely Spanish objects as Gibraltar, Minorca, and Jamaica. So confident was the British Cabinet in June 1781 that the tide was flowing in its favor that it actually rejected the Austro-Russian mediation on the grounds that it could admit no discussion by other powers of the American colonies' future. In the light of what followed this was a mistake, but it must be remembered that they were playing for high stakes, and I believe their calculations had a fair chance of being justified. As late as October 1781 Germain was looking forward to a campaign in the Chesapeake-Delaware area, and warning Haldimand in Canada to make the most of Ethan Allen's secessionism in Vermont. At the very moment when he wrote, French siege guns were battering the new earthworks in Cornwallis's position at Yorktown.

Yorktown changed everything. It was the result of a strategic surprise at sea which completely upset the calculations of states-

110

men. The British admirals in the West Indies had assumed that their opponent de Grasse would send a large part of his fleet home to Europe at the end of the summer to convoy the trade and refit in their home yards, and thought they were safe in frittering away their own strength for convoys and refitting. De Grasse's orders told him to do exactly what the British assumed —to send home ten sail of the line to Europe—but he ignored them. On receiving appeals to save the desperate situation in Virginia he let his merchant shipping wait for their convoy, and took his whole fleet to the Chesapeake: about 27 sail of the line instead of 17. He thus prevented the relief of Cornwallis, and the army besieged in Yorktown was forced to surrender.

The 7000 troops lost at Yorktown seem trifling in numbers. They would have been very difficult to replace in the circumstances of the war and at that distance from home, but even without them a desultory pressure could have been kept up on the coasts and estuaries of the American colonies. This was what Germain would have done till the tide of fortune changed; but Yorktown produced a consequence which ruled it out. The country gentlemen in Parliament despaired of bringing the American struggle to a successful conclusion, and there was a revolt in the House of Commons against the policy of coercing America. Germain was thrown overboard, but the Ministry failed to stay afloat. In March 1782 a new government came into power, dedicated to abandoning America and ending the war. But while the negotiations dragged on the operations of war were taking a turn which raised a question about the future. While the American theatre was reduced to total stalemate, Rodney won a victory at the Saints which turned the tide in the Caribbean, and Lord Howe relieved Gibraltar under the eyes of the main fleets of France and Spain. When the negotiations were concluded at the turn of the year Vergennes was as desperate for peace as Lord Shelburne himself. Half the members of Shelburne's Cabinet were in favor of continuing the struggle; and it may well be that with a little more perseverance the country would have won a very different settlement at the end of another twelve months.

THE JOURNAL OF
MODERN HISTORY

Volume XIX   JUNE 1947   *Number 2*

BRITISH STRATEGY IN AMERICA, 1778

WILLIAM B. WILLCOX

THE War of American Independence, on the British side, was punctuated by lost opportunities. The Americans usually derived lasting advantages from their victories and sometimes from their defeats, but for their opponents even the most sensational triumphs were ephemeral. The successful defense of Boston was followed by its evacuation; Howe's gains in 1776 were canceled within a year by Burgoyne's surrender; Rhode Island was held against heavy odds in 1778 only to be abandoned fourteen months later; the southern campaign opened brilliantly, with the triumphs at Charleston and Camden, and ended with the final disaster at Yorktown. Success in battle, offensive or defensive, contributed little to strengthening the basic position of the British. The explanation is partly in factors beyond their control which curtailed their freedom of action, partly in the strategic ideas of their government and field commanders.

Both the factors and the ideas are thrown into sharp relief by the events of 1778. The campaigning of that year was, on the surface, indecisive. The new Franco-American alliance failed to produce any tangible gain for the allies.

While the British turned to the defensive with great success, it brought them no nearer to victory. They had their first experience of the danger from France, and it might have been fatal if luck had not helped to extricate them. By autumn the war appeared to be still in its usual condition of stalemate.

Under the surface, however, the whole strategic framework had been altered. In the first phase of the struggle, from Lexington through Saratoga, the British had had certain limits within which they could operate. They had seldom been more than hazily aware of these, and they had paid dearly for overstepping them—as witness the loss of Burgoyne. Then came French intervention, which changed their limits drastically. Could they change their thinking in the light of previous failure and present emergency, revise their premises, and evaluate realistically the types of warfare now open to them? If they could, they might still hold their own. If they could not, they would have to depend on the misfortunes and blundering of the enemy. The initial measure of their reaction is their plans for 1778. That campaign was crucial, because it set the pattern of things to come.

The pattern can be understood only in

97

relation to what had already happened. Before judgment can be passed on the strategy of the British after France intervened, two things must be done: first, outline their strategic possibilities in the preceding period and the use to which they had put them—their background of experience; second, determine how the spread of the war affected those possibilities and whether it created any new ones. Such a survey, if it is in terms which the contestants would have understood, is a necessary prelude to assessing the competence of the British high command as it showed itself in action in the campaign of 1778.

During the first phase of the Revolution the colonies might have been reduced by either of two methods, on the one hand a naval war and on the other what may be called a "territorial" war. The two were sometimes hard to distinguish, but the fundamental difference was obvious: one stressed the role of the navy, the other that of the army. Each had its advantages and drawbacks, which had been amply demonstrated by three seasons of campaigning.

The aim of a naval war was to protect British commerce and to choke off American. The fleet, based on the enemy's coast, attacked his privateers, blockaded his ports, and destroyed his shipping and dock facilities by periodic raids; the army, operating as a marine corps, garrisoned the base or bases for the fleet and furnished the troops for raids. This form of warfare had advantages of two sorts. On the political side it exerted pressure gradually, cumulatively, and—for the majority of the people affected—inconspicuously. It could therefore be waged simultaneously with attempts at negotiation, whereas active land campaigning would have embittered the struggle. On the military side the ad-

vantage was security. No harm could come to a fleet which the Americans were powerless to reach; the troops, whether in garrison or on raids, were almost equally safe because of their mobility. The British could establish, supply, and reinforce a base by sea more rapidly than the enemy could concentrate against it by land; and if necessary, they could evacuate it without losing more than prestige. Hence a naval war appealed to the cautious strategist. Its only drawback was that it imposed dispersion of force: the more effectively the navy was to operate, the more widely scattered its bases must be and the greater the consequent risk to each. This risk was negligible in the first phase of the Revolution, but it was a major factor after France intervened.

The aim of a territorial war was not the complete occupation of the colonies, for which the British lacked both the manpower and the supplies. The most that they could hope for was to occupy a single key area—a wedge to break the rebellion into segments. The navy could then cut communication between the segments, and they were not expected to survive independently. Furthermore, if the area had navigable waterways, the fleet could guard the army's supply lines. This was a major consideration. The British base was the sea, and the troops, in the face of a hostile population, depended on contact with the sea; whenever the contact was broken, they could not hold together long enough to win a campaign. Hence they were tethered by their supply lines to the coast. They could not expect to win the war on the battlefield; the Americans, with the countryside itself for their base, could normally avoid a decisive battle by retiring beyond range of pursuit. The only chance of imposing such an action on the enemy was to drive the wedge of British power systematically inland, blow by blow, until Washington was forced into a final engagement and defeated. The rebellion would then be stripped of its army and split apart.

An offensive of this nature was far more dangerous than a naval war, if only because of logistics. For the same reason it put a premium on winning and maintaining the support of the Loyalists. From them the British rarely obtained effective front-line soldiers; "these provincials, if not sustained by regular troops, are not to be trusted."[1] But when they were so sustained, provincials were invaluable for overawing the countryside, keeping open communications, and freeing the regulars for combat. As the area of occupation was extended, the pressure on supply lines and the need of winning local supporters increased. The need and the difficulties of meeting it were drawbacks which inhered in this type of strategy. But they were counterbalanced by the great advantage that a territorial war, unlike a naval, offered a relatively quick decision.

Haste was not a determining factor at the start of hostilities. For the first two years the government hoped for a political settlement; military operations, in consequence, were confined to a naval war and supplementary land campaigns. These operations were too small in scale to affect more than a fraction of the enemy coast line. The British abandoned Boston before taking New York; they seized Rhode Island only at the end of 1776 and Philadelphia the following year; at this period they never seriously molested the trade of the Chesapeake or the Carolinas. They lacked the resources, if

not the will, for a full-scale effort to strangle colonial commerce.

The effort which they made was inconclusive. After two years of it the threat of foreign intervention was growing; the British needed a quick decision, and they embarked on a territorial war. Their first problem was where the wedge could be driven to split the rebellion in half. Geography suggested one of the two areas into which the navy could penetrate deeply, either the line of the Hudson and Lake Champlain or the coastal belt between the Chesapeake and the Alleghenies. They chose the first in 1777, because it was then at the center of the war; four years later, when the focus had shifted southward, they chose the second. In consequence the two disasters to British armies occurred, respectively, on the shores of the Hudson and of the Chesapeake.

Canada and New York were the logical points of departure for a double-pronged offensive to cut off New England from the central colonies. But the British threw logic to the winds. They combined a territorial war, based on Canada, with an extension of the naval war on the rebel coast. Instead of making a major drive northward toward Albany, to join with Burgoyne's expedition, the bulk of the force at New York sailed to capture Philadelphia. This move sacrificed the strategic prerequisite, command of the Hudson, without which Burgoyne was doomed. By the time he reached the river, his supply line to Canada had snapped; he could neither go on, retreat, nor stay where he was. His surrender emphasized the complete dependence of inland operations on logistics.

This was the British background of experience at the beginning of 1778. They had tried the two types of strategy open to them. Naval war had not been pushed

[1] [Lieutenant-General Sir Henry Clinton to General Benjamin Carpenter,] Jan. 18, 1778, Sir Henry Clinton papers, Clements Library, University of Michigan (cited hereafter as "CP"). I have modernized spelling and punctuation throughout.

to the limits of the possible and had failed to bring them victory; their attempt at territorial war had disregarded those limits and had brought them disaster. They were left with only three posts in the area of rebellion: Philadelphia, which denied the Delaware to American shipping; Rhode Island, which did the same for Narragansett Bay; and New York, the main naval base, which closed the Hudson and enabled the fleet to curb privateering on the Jersey coast and in Long Island Sound. The three garrisons contained a total of some twenty-five thousand men, and the naval squadron consisted of six ships of the line and three 50's. So much for the British position and force; it remains to consider how the intervention of France affected their prospects.

The most momentous effect was to expose them to enemy sea power. They had known before how to meet such a danger; during the Seven Years' War they had succeeded, to a large degree, in thwarting hostile operations overseas by containing the French fleet in European waters. If they could do so again, their own squadrons, while decreased in size, might still patrol the American coast almost unchallenged. Their prospects in the colonies would be little changed by renewing the old duel with France—but only on condition that they fought the duel in the old way.

That way was abandoned, apparently without thought of the consequences. The Royal Navy was weaker, both absolutely and relatively, than it had been in 1763, and the government decided that it could not close the Atlantic to the enemy. This decision was a major strategic liability for the British during the rest of the war. They felt its ill effects from the Indian Ocean to the Caribbean and nowhere more forcefully than in the North American theater. Why, then, was the decision made? A conclusive answer is impossible unless more evidence comes to light; that which is available is only suggestive.

The minister chiefly responsible was the first lord of the admiralty, the Earl of Sandwich. For months he had been making plans for the expected war with France, but there is no sign that he considered the possibility of blockade. When he was later called to account for this omission in the house of lords, he tried to evade the question by producing a variety of red herrings. But the opposition realized the significance of what had happened and was not to be put off. His arguments were torn to shreds by a distinguished admiral, the Earl of Bristol, and Sandwich was silenced if not enlightened.[2] This evidence is too fragmentary and negative to justify a conclusion. But it suggests that a naval policy of the utmost moment was put forward by the

[2] The importance of allowing the French access to the Atlantic is emphasized by Alfred T. MAHAN, *The influence of sea power upon history, 1660–1783* (24th ed.; Boston, 1914), pp. 524–30. Sandwich's plans for a naval war with France are outlined in his memorandum to Lord North in December 1777 (G. R. BARNES and J. H. OWEN [eds.], *The private papers of John, earl of Sandwich, first lord of the admiralty, 1771–1782* [4 vols.; [London], 1932–38; "Publications of the Navy Records Society," Vols. LXIX, LXXI, LXXV, and LXXVIII] [cited hereafter as *"Sandwich papers"*], I, 332–35). The debate in the house of lords was held on May 25, 1778; Sandwich spoke in answer to the arguments of the Duke of Richmond and was answered in turn by Bristol. The opposition was attacking simultaneously in the house of commons. See [William COBBETT], *The parliamentary history of England, from the earliest period to the year 1803* (36 vols.; London, 1806–20), XIX (for 1777–78) (cited hereafter as *"Parl. hist."*), 1146–51, 1153–58, and 1161–75; Mrs. Paget TOYNBEE (ed.), *The letters of Horace Walpole, fourth earl of Orford* (16 vols.; Oxford, 1903–5), X, 254; and A. F. STEUART (ed.), *The last journals of Horace Walpole during the reign of George III from 1771–1783* (2 vols.; New York and London, 1910), II, 178–79. If there is other evidence on this crucial point, I should be grateful to hear of it.

admiralty and accepted by the cabinet without proper weighing—perhaps even without awareness—of its strategic implications. Those implications began to be obvious before the struggle with France was four months old.

They appeared first in North America, where the whole character of the war was changed by the decision of the government. British fleets and armies operated thereafter under a Damoclean sword. The most that the admiralty could do, once a French squadron was known to be at sea, was to have it followed in equivalent strength to its probable destination. This was at best a hazardous defense. What constituted equivalent strength? How could the destination be foretold for certain? Would the British covering squadron arrive in time? Such uncertainties were henceforth among the chief worries of the high command, and with good reason. They undermined the premises on which British strategy had rested.

The dangers of naval war were vastly increased. Dispersion was only as safe as the dispersed elements, which were now jeopardized by French sea power. If the British ever lost command of American coastal waters, even temporarily, their garrisons would be exposed to reduction in detail. Territorial war was equally dangerous for them. They had already experienced the difficulty of maintaining supply lines between a field army and its base, but they had had little trouble in supplying the base itself from Great Britain. Hereafter they would never be secure. A French fleet might isolate an army, if it depended on water-borne communications, or might cut off supplies from overseas by blockading the port of entry. In either case enemy sea power would knock the props from under a land campaign.

Both methods of warfare, in summary, would be hazardous whenever the British lost naval superiority on the American coast. Their expedient of detaching squadrons from the home fleet could not, in the nature of things, maintain continuous superiority, and they actually lost it at least once in every campaign from 1778 until the end of the war. Their choice of strategies, therefore, was a choice of risks. In a naval war they risked the loss of a base, in a territorial war the loss of a field army. The first danger was demonstrated for them in the summer of 1778; the second came true in the autumn of 1781. During those three years they were gambling against strategic odds, which they might have calculated at the beginning.

If the risks outweighed the probable gains, why did they continue the struggle? Common sense suggested abandoning the American war and concentrating on the French. This course appealed to a number of Englishmen, regardless of their attitude toward the colonies. "Declare them independent," urged the young British minister to Prussia, "and add the independence of all French and Spanish colonies and islands. In order to support this step, let our fleets and armies evacuate North America, fall upon Santa Domingo, Martinique, Cuba, and force a free trade in the Gulf of Mexico. The straight road to the gold and silver mines, the sugar islands, and the revolt of the Spanish settlements, these will be the consequence of this vigourous measure. Our Presbyterian colonies will be more than compensated for."[3]

[3] H[ugh] E[lliot] to William Eden, Mar. 28, 1778, Benjamin F. STEVENS (ed.), *Facsimiles of manuscripts in European archives relating to America, 1773–1783* (25 vols.; London, 1889–98), Vol. IV, No. 410. Strikingly similar ideas were expressed in an anonymous memorandum sent to Lord George Germain, the secretary of state for the colonies, on

Such drastic action, it may be argued, was the logical alternative to containing French sea power in Europe. Containing it would have isolated the American war from the French. Once the two were strategically fused, the British had little prospect of regaining their colonies until they had vanquished the House of Bourbon—and they had never yet defeated France singlehanded, let alone France and Spain. The featherweight hope was overbalanced by the sure disadvantage of continuing the fight in America. It would drain their resources for no military purpose, not even that of diversion; a far larger proportion of British than of French strength would be diverted. For France the rebellion was an extremely useful side show. For Britain, plunged into a global war, it was a liability which needed liquidating.

King George himself was quick to grasp this reasoning up to a point. When he became convinced that France would intervene and that Spain would follow suit, he suggested turning the bulk of British troops from North America against the French and Spanish West Indies. "If we are to be carrying on a land war against the rebels and against those two powers, it must be feeble in all parts and consequently unsuccessful."[4]

His argument was sound, but it stopped short of the logical conclusion. A withdrawal from America would not be strategically effective unless it were complete, and it could not be complete unless peace were signed. Otherwise the Americans would in all probability not stop fighting, because they had too great an interest in acquiring Canada; the British would therefore have to keep substantial garrisons on the St. Lawrence and in Nova Scotia. Peace was conceivable, by the spring of 1778, on only one condition: that the British acknowledge the independence of the United States. This concession was the key to their military problem. If they rejected independence, they would have to reject with it the plan of withdrawing their forces, on a scale sufficient to affect the war elsewhere, and reconcile themselves to being "feeble in all parts and consequently unsuccessful."

Independence was an impossible solution for political rather than military reasons. There is some indication that Lord North saw the need for it.[5] But he was in no position to say so. The idea was opposed by members of his cabinet and by leaders in the opposition, and the king himself was the final obstacle. For all his awareness of the military factors, King George would not consider independence. His ministers therefore had no choice about continuing the hazardous American war, although they realized that it would have to be with reduced force. Their recourse was to expedients, in negotiating and campaigning, by which they hoped to bridge the gap between political and strategic necessity. The resultant scheme, formulated as French intervention became more probable, was a paradox. On the one hand, the government offered the colonies everything short of indepencence; on the other, it adopted a plan of campaign which stultified the offer.

The olive branch was held out to the rebels by a commission, authorized by parliament in February 1778, to treat

___

March 2, 1778 (Germain papers [Clements Library], Vol. VII). The opposition in the house of commons argued at times on the same lines, but less cogently (*Parl. hist.*, XIX, 943-44 and 949-50).

4 John W. FORTESCUE, *The correspondence of King George the Third from 1760 to December 1783* (6 vols.; London, 1927-28), IV, 36.

5 See A[lexander] W[edderburn] to Eden, Apr. 1, 1778], STEVENS, Vol. IV, No. 426.

for the repeal of all obnoxious acts, the pardon of offenders, and the suspension of hostilities. The commissioners named were the Earl of Carlisle, William Eden, George Johnstone, and the commanders-in-chief of the army and navy in North America; the commission thus fused civil and military authority in a single effort at reconciliation.[6] But the chance of success was slim. Just after Saratoga had revealed the weakness of Britain's land power, just when France was preparing to neutralize Britain's naval power, to offer to repeal statutes and pardon offenders was to offer too little too late. This fact was apparent in Downing Street, and it is not surprising that Eden complained of "the coolness with which this business has been from the first treated by the cabinet."[7]

Meanwhile the government was slowly making military preparations and designs. The danger from France had been felt in naval circles for at least a year.[8] It had been obvious to the cabinet since January, when the British ambassador to Versailles had urged his government to open hostilities whenever the moment was propitious.[9] But the cabinet, anxious to postpone the breach, had avoided provocative moves. Despite the pleadings of Sandwich, the fleet was not put on a war

footing until after March 13, when the French disclosed in London their treaty of amity with the United States.[10] By then the navy was dangerously far behind in the race of mobilization.

A plan of campaign for North America had been completed a few days before. It took into account the probability of French intervention, but it showed little strategic acumen. Lord Amherst had insisted that resuming the offensive on land would require thirty to forty thousand additional men, an impossible number, and that a naval war was therefore the only course; Sandwich had argued that the fleet should no longer dance attendance on the army but that the troops should be used to guard naval bases and help in coastal raids.[11] Such views prevailed, and the idea of territorial war in the northern colonies was rejected out-of-hand.

The plan adopted did not envisage any withdrawal of force. The instructions dispatched in early March by Lord George Germain, the secretary of state for the colonies, held out hope of substantial reinforcements during the summer. But they were to be used to strengthen the two widely separated flanks of the British position, on the one hand, Canada, Nova Scotia, and Newfoundland; on the other, the Floridas. As for the center, Germain dwelt on two possibilities which might end the war. One, of which he was patently skeptical, was that Washington could soon be brought to a decisive action and defeated. The other, in which he professed to believe, was that the Americans would accept the terms offered by the commission. If neither possibility materialized, the New England coast was to be harried

[6] For a full account of the genesis of the commission and its work and intrigues in America see Carl VAN DOREN, *Secret history of the American Revolution* (New York, 1941), chaps. iii and iv. The naval commander-in-chief, Lord Howe, resigned from the commission but remained co-operative (STEVENS, Vol. V, No. 500, and Vol. XI, Nos. 1099 and 1100).

[7] Eden to Lord North, Mar. 30, 1778, STEVENS, Vol. IV, No. 411. Horace Walpole had more pungent comments on the futility of the commission (TOYNBEE, X, 190–92, 193, and 197).

[8] See my article, "Admiral Rodney warns of invasion, 1776–1777," *American Mercury*, IV (1944), 193–98.

[9] Lord Stormont to Lord Weymouth, Jan. 21, 1778, STEVENS, Vol. XXI, No. 1846.

[10] *Sandwich papers*, I, 333–35, 342–43, 349–52, and 363; and II, 4.

[11] FORTESCUE, IV, 15 and 21.

by raids from the two major bases at Halifax and New York. Philadelphia might have to be abandoned in order to obtain the necessary raiding force, even though its loss, as Germain euphemistically put it, "may be productive of some ill consequences." When the season for forays ended in the autumn, the next step would be an attack on the southern colonies, supported by diversions in Maryland and Virginia.[12]

This plan was a collection of strategic fossils, unrelated to the situation which had evolved from Burgoyne's disaster and the growing hostility of France. The skeletons of old ideas were jumbled together—large garrisons for two areas, posts for a raiding war in a third, diversionary operations in a fourth, and conquest in a fifth. The scheme involved almost a maximum dispersion of force. It therefore placed maximum emphasis on naval superiority, just when that superiority was being undermined by the bustle in the dockyards of Toulon and Brest.

The government was simultaneously giving thought to improving the one advantage which the British were sure of in the impending naval war in American waters. The French had no adequate facilities short of the West Indies for refitting their damaged ships; they could consequently operate in the northern theater only in brief summer campaigns. The British were in a better way as long as they possessed New York, but even

its facilities were far from satisfactory. If its dockyards were improved to the level of those at Halifax, or if a base were established farther south where ships and troops could operate throughout the winter, the whole British position would be strengthened. In early March, therefore, a commissioner of the navy was ordered to America to create a proper dockyard at New York, Rhode Island, or wherever he and the naval commander-in-chief thought fit.[13] The project appears to have been shelved, however, in the turmoil of the next few weeks. If the commissioner ever reached America, his work was negligible. The New York yards were not noticeably improved, despite the reiterated complaints of the naval commandant.[14] No other base was established. The British were never able, in consequence, to improve their advantage of position.

The French defiance of March 13 produced a rush of new plans in London. The one which gained most rapid acceptance was for an attack on the coveted French West Indian island of St. Lucia. If forces could be dispatched quickly and

[12] Germain to Clinton, Mar. 8, 1778, HISTORICAL MANUSCRIPTS COMMISSION, *Report on the manuscripts of Mrs. Stopford-Sackville, of Drayton House, Northamptonshire* (2 vols.; London, 1904–10) (cited hereafter as *"Stopford-Sackville MSS"*), II, 95–97. See also Germain to Sir William Howe and Howe's gloomy response, *ibid.*, pp. 93–94 and 107–8. The difficulties in raising troops and the expedients resorted to by the government at this time are summarized in Robert BEATSON, *Naval and military memoirs of Great Britain, from 1727 to 1783* (2d ed., 6 vols.; London, 1804), IV, 292–93; and STEUART, II, 89–90.

[13] Germain to Sir William Howe, Mar. 12, 1778, Germain letter-book (Germain papers), appen.; see also Roland G. USHER, Jr., "The civil administration of the British navy during the American Revolution" (unpublished thesis, University of Michigan Library), pp. 405–6 and 409–12. The plan, recommended by Sandwich, had been opposed in admiralty circles on the ground that "your possession of those places is to the last degree precarious" (Robert Gregson to Lord Shelburne, Jan. 15, 1778, Shelburne papers [Clements Library], Vol. CXLVI, No. 121). Gregson's argument assumes that a war can be won by the policy of nothing risked, nothing lost—a policy which had more place than it deserved in British strategy.

[14] See, e.g., Rear-Admiral James Gambier to Clinton, Nov. 13, 1778, CP; and Gambier to Sandwich, Sept. 22, 1778, *Sandwich papers*, II, 315. The shortcomings of the New York dockyards subsequently played an important part in the Yorktown campaign (see my article, "The British road to Yorktown: a study in divided command," *American historical review*, LII [1946], 32–33).

secretly from North America, that enemy base might be seized before it was reinforced. The matter was discussed and agreed upon by the cabinet on the 14th, and preparations were set afoot.[15] War with France was an old game with conventional moves. The West Indies were a far more important part of the board than North America, and a blow at St. Lucia was in the best tradition of the Seven Years' War.

This design forced a change of plan in the American theater. Once a strong detachment sailed from there to the Caribbean, the remaining force would be insufficient to guard even the three bases at Philadelphia, New York, and Newport, let alone to raid the New England coast. "It is a joke," the king immediately concluded, "to think of keeping Pennsylvania."[16] Alarmists suggested that the fleet should retire to Halifax, but Amherst pointed out that this would permit the Americans to attack the West Indies by sea. He urged the immediate evacuation of Philadelphia; if the commission's terms were rejected, New York and Newport should be abandoned, too, and the bulk of the army turned against the French islands.[17]

Amherst's views were accepted in substance by the cabinet on the 18th. It was decided to split the army in Pennsylvania: three thousand men should go to the Floridas, the rest to New York; if the commission failed and the Americans threatened "to drive the troops into the sea," New York in turn might have to be evacuated.[18] The decision was sent to

America on the 21st, in a dispatch from Germain and in instructions from the king. The dispatch expressed the hope that New York might be held "to give dignity and effect to the commissioners' negotiations."[19] The instructions were less optimistic. Five thousand men were to be embarked at once for St. Lucia, three thousand for St. Augustine and Pensacola. Philadelphia was to be evacuated by sea. New York, if seriously threatened, would have to be given up also, but in that case it was hoped that Rhode Island could be retained (an absurd idea, since Newport could never be supplied from Nova Scotia). If worst came to worst, the army was to be withdrawn to Halifax and such detachments as could be spared sent on to the defense of Canada.[20] These instructions meant that the government, ten days after France had declared itself, was already envisaging the loss of the thirteen colonies.

The evacuation of New York was made contingent on either one of two factors, the failure of the commission or the danger of an overwhelming enemy offensive. It must have been apparent in London that these factors were closely interrelated. If congress and the people were disposed to treat, the American army was unlikely to have the will or the means to overwhelm a major post. The safety of New York thus depended on the success of the negotiations. But the

[15] *Sandwich papers*, I, 361–65. For the background of the plan see *ibid.*, pp. 325–26 and 357–58; and FORTESCUE, IV, 46.

[16] The king to North, Mar. 23 [should be 13?], 1778, FORTESCUE, IV, 74.

[17] *Ibid.*, pp. 64–65.

[18] *Sandwich papers*, I, 364.

[19] STEVENS, Vol. XI, No. 1068.

[20] *Ibid.*, No. 1069. See also John W. FORTESCUE, *History of the British Army* (13 vols. in 20; London, 1899–1930), III, 252–53. The author rightly emphasizes the dependence of Rhode Island on New York, but he is mistaken in assuming (pp. 251 and 259) that the post at Newport was a complete strategic liability. It gave the British many advantages, as they found to their cost soon after they evacuated it in 1779 (see my article, "Rhode Island in British strategy, 1780–1781," *Journal of modern history*, XVII [1945], 304–31).

last hope of success was removed by the mandatory part of the instructions—the order to evacuate Philadelphia. Great Britain had only as much bargaining power as it had prestige, and both were sinking rapidly. Retreat from the capital of the rebellion was a final confession of impotence, which foredoomed the work of the commissioners before they began. Their hopes were sacrificed, Lord Carlisle complained when he heard the news, to "an attack upon an insignificant West India island in the most unfit season of the year."[21] St. Lucia was scarcely insignificant, but neither was Philadelphia.

Official planning had reached a low ebb. The government was making overtures at the same time that it was insuring their rejection. It was hoping to hunt out American shipping, when at any moment its own squadrons might become quarries for the French. It was contemplating, as a last resort, the evacuation of everything between Nova Scotia and Florida; yet it was ignoring the one condition—the independence of the United States—which might convert that loss into a strategic asset. Such confusion of thought suggests that there may have been a commensurate division of counsel in London.

An open division appeared within a few weeks, caused by the development of the first naval crisis of the war. The British ambassador to Versailles had sent warning in February that the French Mediterranean squadron, under the Comte d'Estaing, would soon make for the Atlantic; the purpose was then thought to be a junction with the main fleet at Brest.[22] The ministry did nothing,

even after war had become inevitable, because the navy was in no state to act.[23] There was lengthy discussion of whether the enemy squadron could be intercepted at the Straits of Gibraltar; the king and North hoped that it could be, but Sandwich and the commander of the home fleet, Admiral Keppel, insisted that the requisite detachment could not be spared.[24] Professional opinion was almost sure to prevail. This meant that the Channel squadron would be kept intact and supine while the French decided whether to concentrate against it or to strike elsewhere—that the British, in short, would lose the initiative at the start.

The enemy actually had no intention of joining forces at Brest. Estaing's quarry was on the American coast. He sailed from Toulon on April 13; less than ten days later, while he was still in the Mediterranean, a report of his true destination was received in London. North was virtually convinced by this intelligence, and Germain was emphatic that help must be sent to New York immediately.[25] Sandwich and Keppel, however,

[23] It has frequently been assumed that the order to evacuate Philadelphia was caused by the danger from Estaing (MAHAN in *The influence of sea power*, p. 359, and in William L. CLOWES [ed.], *The Royal Navy: a history from the earliest times to the present* [7 vols.; London, 1897–1903], III, 397; Sydney G. FISHER, *The struggle for American independence* [2 vols.; Philadelphia and London, 1908], II, 165; Louis GOTTSCHALK, *Lafayette joins the American army* [Chicago, 1937], p. 237). Lord Howe had been warned in general terms, months before, that there was a naval menace from France (William M. JAMES, *The British navy in adversity: a study of the War of American Independence* [New York, 1926], p. 95). The specific threat of Estaing, however, was not recognized in London until weeks after the instructions of March 21 had gone out, and it therefore played no part in the evacuation.

[24] *Sandwich papers*, II, 22–23; FORTESCUE, *Correspondence*, IV, 112–13 and 119–20.

[25] *Sandwich papers*, II, 33–36 and 38–39; FORTESCUE, *Correspondence*, IV, 122.

[21] I.e., in the hurricane season (STEVENS, Vol. I, No. 101, p. 14). For further complaints by Carlisle and the other commissioners see *ibid.*, Vol. I, No. 74, Vol. V, Nos. 496, 500, and 501, and Vol. XI, No. 1109; also *Stopford-Sackville MSS*, II, 115–16.

[22] Feb. 20, 1778, *Sandwich papers*, I, 343–44.

were hesitant and dared not risk the move. They now feared that Estaing was feinting, to draw off a British squadron to America, and that his real design was to join with the Spanish fleet at Cadiz for a surprise attack on the British Isles.[26] Spain appeared to be maintaining neutrality—as it did, in fact, for another year—but they felt that they could not trust appearances. They were faced with the question which beset British ministers and admirals throughout the rest of the war: where was the enemy going? Until that was known beyond doubt, sending a detachment in pursuit might jeopardize the safety of Great Britain. The navy had lost the initiative not only in home waters but everywhere. It now had to dance to the tune which the French were calling.

By May 4 Germain assumed that the question was finally settled. He drafted his first word to New York of the danger which impended: Estaing had sailed with eleven ships of the line and one 50, and Halifax was his probable objective; a rescue force of thirteen of the line, under Vice-admiral John Byron, would leave Spithead within a day or two.[27] This vital dispatch had to go by packet boat, because in all the home fleet there was not a frigate to spare "if the fate of the nation depended on it."[28] The West Indies packet, the "Grantham," was diverted

to Philadelphia for the purpose, and duplicate dispatches were sent by the regular New York packet. The two left together on the 11th, but the latter was captured en route. The "Grantham" got through, fortunately not to Philadelphia. She ran into Estaing's squadron, eluded his frigates after a two-day chase, and on June 29 encountered the British fleet, which had just evacuated Philadelphia. Her vital news reached New York on July 1, a week before the French made the Delaware.[29] Meanwhile the consoling part of the dispatch—Byron's immediate departure—had been falsified by developments in England.

The squadron could not leave Spithead when expected. The ships, despite the long forewarning, had been outfitted only for service in European waters, and increasing their supplies for the American voyage took precious days.[30] During that interval their destination was changed, on the advice of Commodore Sir Samuel Hood, from Halifax to New York.[31] This gain, however, was more than offset by the decision, taken on May 13, to countermand Byron's sailing until the situation grew clearer.[32] A frigate had been sent to Gibraltar in mid-April to observe Estaing when he passed through the Straits. She and another frigate followed

[26] Sandwich papers, II, 47–54. For Keppel's influence over the king and the disagreements in the cabinet during this crisis see STEVENS, Vol. V, No. 513.

[27] Germain to Clinton, May 4, 1778, CP. The dispatch opened with another warning: the Americans threatened Canada, which Clinton was to reinforce with whatever troops he thought necessary. Lord George apparently ignored the flagrant inconsistency between this order and the French naval threat. For details of Estaing's actual force see below, n. 78.

[28] Sandwich to Germain, May 2, 1778, Stopford-Sackville MSS, II, 140.

[29] STEVENS, Vol. V, No. 508; an undated memorandum filed at the end of 1778, Germain papers, Vol. VIII; Clinton's three-volume manuscript history among his papers, "An historical detail of seven years campaigns in North America from 1775 to 1782," etc. (cited hereafter as "Historical detail"), I, 118–19; CLOWES, III, 398. BEATSON's account (IV, 331) is inaccurate in details.

[30] FORTESCUE, Correspondence, IV, 132–33.

[31] Sandwich papers, II, 56; FORTESCUE, Correspondence, IV, 137 and 143–44.

[32] Sandwich papers, II, 58 and n. Estaing was known to have American pilots with him, and by the 17th even Keppel was convinced that his most tempting objective was the British force in America (ibid., p. 64).

him into the Atlantic, until there was no doubt of his destination, and then raced for England; they arrived, respectively, on June 2 and 3. At last the government had proof positive, and on the 9th Byron put to sea.[33] By then the French had an advantage in time which nothing could redress.

The welter of conflicting information and changing plans in London had its repercussions across the Atlantic. But it did not, as it might have done, lose the war in one disastrous campaign. The hesitations of the ministry were largely offset by the good luck and good management of the theater commanders and by the halfheartedness of the French. While Byron's squadron was marking time at Portsmouth, the strategic focus was shifting to New York. The shift was fortunate for the British cause.

It happened to coincide with a change in the army command. Sir William Howe had tendered his resignation immediately after Saratoga, and the king had accepted it when he learned the full extent of that disaster. The logical successor was Howe's second-in-command, Sir Henry Clinton. As the only British general who had won any success in action during the previous campaign, Clinton was popular in England.[34] But his character provided strong reasons against his appointment.

Sir Henry was querulous to a degree. He was at loggerheads, sooner or later, with almost every general and admiral with whom he had to work in America; and he periodically attempted to resign. His experience with Howe was no exception; by the beginning of 1778 he was en-

deavoring to return home on leave to secure his release from an intolerable position. "There are no steps I will not take, *ever so serious*, to avoid service under a man I neither esteem as an officer or a man; nor will I be any ways connected with him."[35] Years of such recrimination had made a reputation for Clinton, even in a carping age, and the thought of promoting him aroused misgivings in high quarters. "It is certainly not desirable, if it can be avoided," Lord North wrote the king in January, "to employ any general who declares himself unwilling to continue in his command and complains of slights and ill treatment."[36]

But who else was there? The veteran Lord Amherst declined. Lord Cornwallis had come to England on leave, and the crisis was too urgent to wait on his return. North's doubts were overridden, as they often were. Three weeks after he had expressed them, Germain sent the dispatch informing Clinton of his promotion.[37]

Sir Henry was dreading the honor. This crisis of his career momentarily revealed his character, and it is worth observing; it was one of the determinants of what the British did and did not do in North America for the next three years. What he said is revealing only at second glance. He wished that the armies, if Howe had to go, might be divided into three commands under three mutually

[33] *Ibid.*, pp. 8–9.

[34] But he was scarcely called to the chief command, as a flatterer assured him, by "the universal voice of the people" (Charles Mellish to Clinton, Mar. 2, 1778, CP).

[35] Clinton to Major Duncan Drummond, Jan. 9, 1778, *ibid.* I have italicized French phrases, but other italics are in the original throughout. Drummond, in London, was working through Clinton's kinsman, the Duke of Newcastle, to put pressure on North and the king. The duke threatened that Sir Henry would come home even if he were made commander-in-chief. See Drummond to Clinton, with enclosures and Clinton's endorsement, Jan. 10, and the letters between Newcastle and North, Mar. 3 and 4, 1778, *ibid.*

[36] FORTESCUE, *Correspondence*, IV, 10.

[37] Germain to Clinton, Feb. 4, 1778, CP.

124

independent generals, himself among them; on that basis he was willing to serve anywhere, even "(God forbid!)" in Florida. But his hope was that Sir William and his brother would stay, no matter what he thought of the former. "I cannot conceive it possible that government can be so unwise [as] to take the command from these people. If they have made mistakes, they best know how to remedy [them]. They best know what can and ought to be done, and *à plus fort*[e] *raison* how to do it. This command cannot, therefore, fall upon my shoulders."[38]

He felt, in other words, that his shoulders were not strong enough. The feeling suggests that his prickly self-esteem and his belittling of his colleagues concealed, as hypercriticism so often does, a strain of moral timidity. He was certainly anxious, at least in the mood of that moment, to avoid the impending responsibility—so anxious that he preferred the absurdity of a trisected command, with even Florida for his province.

Anxiety is understandable in any man called, at such a juncture, to command the king's forces in America, and Clinton's should not be overemphasized. He apparently took his promotion without a mumur when it came, and his planning showed both energy and independence. He may have been timid at the core, but he knew his business; he was effective whenever he had the prerequisites he needed, sufficient time and force. He rarely had enough of either, and he was too methodical to make up for the lack by improvising. Cornwallis, beside him, seems like a virtuoso—and Cornwallis is famous for a climactic defeat. Clinton preserved the army carefully and ingloriously in the face of recurrent dangers.

This demanded competence, of a sort which is illustrated in his first few months of command.

Those months were made perilous by the French fleet. Crisis at sea was chiefly the concern of his fellow-commander-in-chief, Richard Howe, at that time a viscount and vice-admiral. Lord Howe was on the verge of following his younger brother into retirement. But he remained until his successor arrived at the end of the campaign, and his character left an impress on it. If Clinton was an artisan in his profession, Howe was an artist. He used whatever means came to hand to reach a necessary end, where Sir Henry tailored the end to fit his means. Howe did not court danger, like Cornwallis; but he met it, when thrust upon him, with equal energy. He stands out as one of the few, with Hughes, Hood, and Rodney, who preserved the standards of naval proficiency in the dark days between Hawke and St. Vincent.

Howe was about to face a problem which would have given pause to the hardiest. But meanwhile he and Clinton were going about their business ignorant of what was impending. Sir Henry arrived in Philadelphia on May 8, and the following day he received the instructions of March 8 and 21.[39] The latter took precedence; he began to carry them out, though with scant enthusiasm. "Those who framed them, I am to suppose, saw all the consequences that would attend them—saw I should no longer be able to keep up appearance of offense in this country, so necessary to assist the operation of the commission; saw I should *probably* finally be reduced to retire to Halifax. My instructions are *positive;* I cannot misunderstand them, nor dare I disobey them. I am directed to evacuate Philadelphia. My fate is hard: forced to

<hr/>

[38] Clinton to unknown, Mar. 31, 1778. Sir Henry received the notification of his appointment on April 14 ("Historical detail," I, 99).

[39] *Ibid.*

125

an apparent retreat with such an army is mortifying."[40]

Clinton dared not disobey the spirit of his orders, but he took liberties with their letter. In the first place he decided not to send the St. Lucia expedition from Philadelphia, as instructed, but to wait until he had concentrated his forces at New York; his reason was that the fleet was not at the moment in position to provide the requisite convoy. In the second place he rejected the idea of evacuating Philadelphia by sea; there were enough transports for only a fraction of the army, and he determined to take his whole force overland rather than divide it.[41] He subsequently had reason to congratulate himself on both decisions. They kept the army safe ashore at the moment when the enemy fleet arrived.

The march through the Jersies toward New York began on June 18. The two American forces with which Sir Henry had to deal were Washington's, advancing from Valley Forge to threaten his rear, and that with which Major General Gates had been watching New York. Clinton dreamed originally of turning his retreat into an offensive by striking north, between the divided enemy, toward the highlands of the Hudson.[42] But the dream faded as soon as he was in the field. The great size of his baggage train —which was twelve miles long—dictated the easiest possible route. The train made an obstacle out of the Raritan River, and he determined to bear south of it toward

Sandy Hook for a junction with the fleet.[43] This decision had an additional purpose. "Though the principle of my march was unquestionably retreat, I wished to avoid every appearance of a precipitate one. . . . . I had hopes that Mr. Washington might possibly be induced to commit himself at some distance from the strong grounds of Princeton, along which he had hitherto marched."[44]

Washington obliged. At Monmouth Court House he attacked Clinton's rear, which was guarding the baggage train. Sir Henry seems to have hoped at the time that this would be the decisive action envisaged in the instructions of March 8, but he subsequently persuaded himself that such a battle could never have been fought in the terrain around Monmouth.[45] The engagement, although it was bitterly contested, had little strategic result. The British retreat continued as planned, until the army made contact with Hood's squadron at the Hook. The troops were conveyed in transports to New York, and the ferrying was completed by July 5.

It was not a moment too soon. Six days before, on June 29, Howe had received from England his first intimation of the French approach. But he could do

[40] Clinton memorandum, dated May 1778 and filed at the end of that month, CP. On June 18, according to Eden, Sir Henry's feelings were still "roused beyond his powers to govern them" (STEVENS, Vol. V, No. 500).

[41] Clinton to Germain, May 23 and June 5-13, STEVENS, Vol. XI, Nos. 1084 and 1093.

[42] [Clinton to Major-General Daniel Jones, commanding at New York,] undated and filed at the end of June 1778, CP.

[43] Clinton to Germain, July 5, 1778, STEVENS, Vol. XI, No. 1114. The implication is that Sir Henry changed his plans en route. If so, he was extremely lucky that word of the change got through to the fleet. His communications with it and with New York, during the march, were hazardous to a degree (see Clinton to Howe, June 29, 1778, CP, and the letter cited in n. 42).

[44] "Historical detail," I, 105-6; see also H. H. PECKHAM (ed.), "Sir Henry Clinton's review of Simcoe's *Journal*," *William and Mary College quarterly historical magazine*, XXI (2d ser., 1941), 364.

[45] In a letter written soon afterward he blamed the inconclusive result on the heat, and in his history he blamed it primarily on terrain; compare [Clinton to Eden,] July 3, 1778, CP, with "Historical detail," I, 106.

little except wait. Extricating the army from its exposed position left him scant time for his own preparations, and there were few which he could make until he knew when and where the enemy would strike. The tension of waiting lasted until July 7, when he heard that the French had been sighted two days before off the coast of Virginia. "This event," as he guardedly put it to Clinton, "involves other considerations for the rule of my conduct."[46] The naval war in American waters was beginning.

British frigates dogged the enemy. On the evening of the 9th Estaing was off the Jersey coast; on the morning of the 10th he was reported off the Hook.[47] From there he had two possible moves: a frontal attack on New York harbor, to coincide with a land assault by Washington's army; or a move against Rhode Island, again in conjunction with American troops. The British were forced wholly onto the defensive, and they had the problem of guarding against these two threats simultaneously.

The first one aroused no misgivings in the navy. Howe disposed his outnumbered squadron inside the Hook, where the fire of the ships would be most effective if the enemy tried to cross the bar. He earnestly hoped that they would risk it. "These people seem to affect an attempt to enter the port. . . . . If they really shall prosecute such an attack here, I think it a most fortunate circumstance in our state. We should succeed at no time if we can fail on such an occasion."[48]

The British position, however, had one weakness. Sandy Hook was at that time an island, some four miles long, and it was not garrisoned. If the French landed

and mounted batteries, they could force Howe from his anchorage. In that case, as he put it, the whole Royal Navy could not save New York.[49] On the 13th he asked Clinton for howitzers, presumably to be set up on the island; two days later Sir Henry prepared to occupy it, and by the 19th it was held and fortified by a respectable force equipped with artillery.[50] The defense was so thorough that the French, in the opinion of Howe's second-in-command, "must lose their ships if they should attempt the harbour."[51]

Meanwhile the danger to Rhode Island had not been neglected. The Americans, under Major General John Sullivan, had been threatening that post since March, and in late May they had begun to concentrate their forces on the mainland. The British commander, Major-General Sir Robert Pigot, had countered by vigorous raids against their supply depots.[52] His superiors at New York suspected what was in the wind as soon as the French appeared; one of Howe's initial aims at the Hook was that "of engaging the French admiral's attention, that the reinforcement may get to Rhode Island."[53] The only route still open was the Sound, and Howe feared that the Americans might close that at any moment by mounting coastal bat-

---

[46] Howe to Clinton, July 8, 1778, CP.

[47] *Idem* to *idem*, [July 10, 1778,] *ibid.*

[48] *Idem* to *idem*, July 11, [1778], *ibid.*

[49] The remark was quoted in Cornwallis to Clinton, [July 17, 1778,] *ibid.* Howe subsequently repeated his comment, somewhat ambiguously, in the house of commons (*Parl. hist.*, XX [for 1778–80], 340).

[50] Howe to Clinton, July 13, Charles O'Hara [to Clinton], July 15, and [Clinton to Howe, July 19,] 1778, CP; and "Historical detail," I, 118.

[51] Rear-Admiral James Gambier to Sandwich, July 21, 1778, *Sandwich papers*, II, 306–7. For a detailed account of Howe's dispositions see CLOWES, III, 399–401; and JAMES, pp. 98–100.

[52] Sir William Howe to Clinton, Mar. 17, and Pigot to Clinton, May 27 and 30, 1778, CP; FORTESCUE, *British Army*, III, 257–58; and BEATSON, IV, 315–20.

[53] Howe to Clinton, [July 10, 1778,] CP.

127

teries east of New York. But Clinton acted promptly, and five battalions got through to Newport.[54]

The French had sacrificed by delay what they had gained by surprise. They might, on the one hand, have been able to force a way into New York harbor within a day or two of their arrival; once the Hook was fortified, the chance was virtually gone.[55] They might, on the other hand, have sailed for Rhode Island soon after reaching New York; a prompt blockade of Narragansett Bay would have been more effective than coastal batteries in cutting off reinforcements from Pigot. But Estaing, torn between the hope of attacking New York and the fear that his larger ships drew too much water to pass the bar, wasted precious days in waiting for pilots who could solve his dilemma.[56] By the time they had persuaded him that the attempt was hopeless, he had lost his best moment for attacking Rhode Island.

The British were also torn between a hope and a fear. The hope was that Byron would come. The French would then be in desperate straits, caught between the two British squadrons and with no port of refuge nearer than Boston. "I never in my life longed to see the finest of women," wrote Rear-Admiral Gambier, "more than I do to see Admiral Byron."[57] The fear was that a fleet of

victualers, expected from Cork, would come instead of Byron. It would almost surely blunder into the French squadron and be dispersed or captured; the garrison of New York, already on short rations, could then be starved into surrender. The prospects were succinctly put by William Eden. "If Byron arrives before the monsieurs depart, I hope that Messrs. d'Estaing and Bougainville[58] will shortly afterwards dine with me as prisoners of war. If he should not arrive, and if we cannot beat them without waiting for him, I must in some capacity dine with them, for I shall not have any means of dining elsewhere."[59]

On the 21st Clinton heard that the long-awaited attack on New York was imminent.[60] On the following day the French, favored by wind and tide, made as if to attempt the bar. Then suddenly they changed course and disappeared to the southward. They never returned. New York was saved, and the first phase of the campaign was over.

But the enemy still had naval superiority and therefore the initiative. The British dared not move in force to the defense of Rhode Island—the most likely French objective—for fear of unguarding New York. The strategic dilemma was like that of three months before, when the fear of exposing the British Isles had kept Byron's ships idle at Portsmouth.

[54] *Idem* to *idem*, July 11, [1778,] *ibid.*; and "Historical detail," I, 118.

[55] Sir Henry took the initial danger more seriously than the navy did (C[linton to his sisters], Aug. 1, and to unknown, Sept. 21, 1778, CP).

[56] Louis Édouard CHEVALIER, *Histoire de la marine française pendant la guerre de l'indépendance américaine* (Paris, 1877), pp. 111–12; and JAMES, pp. 100–101.

[57] Gambier to Sandwich, July 12, 1778, *Sandwich papers*, II, 303. Howe was more prosaic; he sent a dispatch boat to Halifax in an unsuccessful attempt to make contact with Byron (Howe to Clinton, July 12 and 26, 1778, CP; and BEATSON, IV, 338–39).

[58] Louis Antoine de Bougainville, the famous explorer, who was at this time captain of the "Guerrier," 74.

[59] STEVENS, Vol. V, No. 504. The victualing fleet had actually sailed at the end of May with orders to go to Philadelphia—two months after the instructions had gone out to evacuate that city! The fleet escaped from the Delaware by chance and reached New York in September (*ibid.*, No. 519, and Vol. XI, No. 1154).

[60] John Campbell to Clinton, July 21, 1778, CP; and Gambier to Sandwich of the same date, *Sandwich papers*, II, 306. On the feasibility of forcing the passage see MAHAN, pp. 360–61; and CLOWES, III, 401–2.

128

The problem before Clinton and Howe was smaller in scale but even more complicated, because of the orders for the Florida and St. Lucia expeditions. If Estaing had by any chance quitted the coast entirely, the cabinet would not condone further delay in sending the detachments southward. If he were still in the offing, the dispatch of eight thousand men might be fatal; either they would be intercepted and destroyed en route, or the enemy would return for another assault on New York or Newport. Uncertainty again paralyzed British planning.

Eden, who fancied himself as a strategist, urged a bold solution. The naval crisis nullified all orders from London, he argued, and Clinton was no longer "wrapped up in a napkin by the slovenly instructions of the 21st March."[61] The French had shifted the focus of the war from the West Indies to North America, and a British victory at New York would now be decisive.[62] If only Howe and Clinton would forget St. Lucia and keep their forces intact until Byron arrived, the British might recover the colonies and secure the West Indies at one stroke. The alternative—to carry out the orders of March 21—"must be fatal both to the honour and interests of our country."[63]

This argument had much to be said for it. But Eden's enthusiasm touched no spark from his fellow-commissioners. Lord Carlisle, his junior by four years, reprimanded him in fatherly fashion: orders were orders, and it was improper for anyone to recommend disobedience who would not have to bear the consequences.[64] Clinton was equally unmoved.

The thought of his coming weakness depressed him beyond the point where he could plan boldly for using his current strength. "You have but one army. 'Tis a good one; it has never been affronted. You may want it. You ought to have kept it together, nursed it, cherished it. By the present arrangement I wish one half of it may not be under ground by Christmas, and the rest reduced to an ignominious flight to avoid still greater disgrace."[65]

New York would soon be left with only twelve thousand men, Sir Henry wrote Germain on the 27th, and its defense in the best conditions required a minimum of fifteen thousand. Without it Rhode Island would be blockaded in short order, as soon as the Americans occupied Long Island and controlled the Sound. Both posts were therefore untenable; he expected to evacuate them before the end of September and to fall back on Halifax.[66] This was no mood for winning a war or even for a last-ditch defense. The pessimism of the March instructions seemed about to come home to roost in London.

Clinton's dispatch was no more than written, however, before its gloom was dissipated by the need for immediate action. Howe received news the same evening that the French squadron had been sighted on a northeasterly course, obviously bound for Rhode Island. An improvement in the weather the next day convinced him that Newport would be attacked on the 29th at latest, and he

[61] Eden to Clinton, July 5; see also *idem* to *idem*, July 1, 1778, CP.

[62] Eden minute, July 29, 1778, STEVENS, Vol. V, No. 508.

[63] Eden to Clinton, July 29, 1778, CP.

[64] STEVENS, Vol. V, No. 509.

[65] [Clinton to the Duke of Newcastle,] July 27, [1778,] CP.

[66] STEVENS, Vol. XI, No. 1123. This dispatch, received in September, aroused consternation in the government (see Germain to William Knox, his secretary, Sept. 14, and North to Knox, Sept. 20, 1778, HISTORICAL MANUSCRIPTS COMMISSION, *Report on manuscripts in various collections* [8 vols.; London, 1901–13], VI, 150–51).

asked Clinton to confer on their course of action.[67] But a course was hard to determine while one burning question remained unanswered. "Where is Byron? Sure he is not tacked to a fleet of merchant ships? If he is ———!"[68] Until that question was settled, Clinton could do little more than write letters. He warned Pigot to be in hourly expectation of the French fleet, if it had not already arrived, and of a strong detachment from Washington's army; "let us know by the return of the messenger what is your state, hopes, fears, how long you can hold out."[69]

On the 30th came the first sign of Byron. One of his ships, the "Cornwall," 74, turned up at New York; she had lost touch with the squadron in a gale on the 3d, but she brought the welcome news that New York, not Halifax, was the appointed rendezvous.[70] By the 31st another ship of the line and two 50's had arrived from elsewhere.[71] With these reinforcements Howe felt that at last he could attempt the relief of Newport. He refused Clinton's offer of troops, presumably because the risk was so grave that he dared not encumber himself with

transports. Foul wind delayed him at the Hook until August 6, and on the 9th he arrived off Narragansett Bay.[72] It was the second crucial moment of the campaign.

Pigot had had ample warning and a small reinforcement, and he had made good use of both. By the middle of July he had fortified Goat and Conanicut islands as well as Rhode Island itself; his only complaint was a shortage of supplies.[73] On the morning of the 29th the French fleet arrived. That was the moment, as Estaing realized, for a joint assault by sea and land. But Sullivan's forces were not yet fully prepared, and the golden opportunity passed.[74]

Pigot watched and waited. On the 30th two French ships of the line passed through Narragansett Passage and anchored off the north end of Conanicut; one of them was hulled by the British batteries. On August 3 the French landed on Conanicut unopposed, since the defenders had already withdrawn to Rhode Island. On the 5th the two ships drew nearer to Newport harbor, and the British burned four of their precious frigates to keep them out of enemy hands. The same evening Pigot, convinced that the main squadron would soon force Rhode Island Passage, withdrew from the northern part of the island to the lines outside Newport. Seamen from the destroyed frigates were pressed into service to man

---

[67] Howe to Clinton, Nos. 1 and 2 of July 28, 1778, CP.

[68] [Clinton to his sisters,] Aug. 1, 1778, *ibid.*

[69] Clinton [to Pigot], July 29, 1778, *ibid.*

[70] Howe to Clinton, July 30, 1778, *ibid.* BEATSON is puzzled to account for the change in rendezvous from Halifax to New York (IV, 330, 339, and 340 and n.). The change, as already mentioned, was suggested by Hood and adopted by the government weeks before Byron sailed. It was not known in New York until the "Cornwall" arrived, however, because it had been made in London after the "Grantham" had left with the most recent dispatches, those of May 4.

[71] The "Raisonnable," 64, and the "Centurion," 50, had been ordered to New York from the Halifax squadron; the "Renown," 50, had arrived from the West Indies on the 25th (Howe to Clinton, July 26, 1778, CP; "Historical detail," I, 120; STEVENS, Vol. I, No. 101; and CLOWES, III, 404).

[72] "Historical detail," I, 120; where the date of Howe's arrival is mistakenly given as the 8th; CLOWES, III, 404–5; and JAMES, pp. 102–4.

[73] Pigot to Clinton, July 17, 1778, CP.

[74] Georges LACOUR-GAYET, *La marine militaire de la France sous le règne de Louis XVI* (Paris, 1905), p. 163. Major General Nathaniel Greene, although he was one of the most enthusiastic advocates of the attack on Rhode Island, had urged Sullivan to delay until his full force was collected (George W. GREENE, *The life of Nathaniel Greene, major-general in the army of the Revolution* [3 vols.; New York, 1871], II, 100).

the batteries (as they were three years later at Yorktown), and transports were sunk between Rose and Rhode islands to obstruct the narrow entrance to the harbor.[75] Pigot still did not know whether Clinton intended him to make a last-ditch defense. But he was now committed to one, no matter what the French did; the sacrifice of transports immobilized him until more could be sent from New York.[76] "He writes perfectly cool and quiet," headquarters concluded, "and does not seem to be under the least apprehension."[77] He had nothing to apprehend except surrender, for the fate of the campaign was no longer in his hands.

On the 8th Estaing's squadron, which had been at anchor three miles off the harbor mouth, weighed and came into Rhode Island Passage. On the morning of the 9th Sullivan's troops landed on the northern end of Rhode Island. Almost immediately afterward the sails of a fleet appeared over the southern horizon. In the nick of time Lord Howe was coming to the rescue.

What he could do was highly problematical. He had eight ships of the line and five 50's, as against his adversary's eleven of the line and one 50. Estaing was slightly superior in number of guns and greatly so in weight of metal.[78] The British crews

were veterans, on the other hand, most of whom had campaigned in American waters for several years, and their commander was one of the most resourceful officers in the service. The French were less than four months out of Toulon, and few of them had any experience of fleet maneuvers under fire; their commander was a landsman who was far from being, in Suffren's phrase, "aussi marin que brave." The French, in summary, were favored by the tangibles of fire power, the British by the intangibles of experience. Only the test of battle would determine where the advantage lay.

Howe was unwilling to risk the test unless conditions favored him. The wind was blowing into the bay, as usual at that season, so that he had the weather gauge and hence the tactical initiative. He refused to take it, presumably because assaulting the French in the close quarters of their anchorage would sacrifice his advantage in maneuver. He cast anchor himself, convinced that he was powerless to help Pigot.[79] At that point fortune took a hand. During the night the wind veered to the north; Estaing at once came out, as Grasse later came out of the Chesapeake, to settle the campaign by a naval battle. Howe took off, and the antagonists jockeyed for position for a day and a half; then they were stopped by a storm. "Had we been in action when the gale came on, ... one half of both fleets, at least, would have gone to the bottom. This might have answered well enough to save Rhode Island, ... but it would have been poor sport for us *in* the water."[80] When the wind abated, on the

[75] Pigot to Clinton, July 31—Aug. 1, Aug. 2, 3, and 31, 1778, CP. This account differs somewhat, particularly in dates, from the descriptions given by JAMES (p. 102) and Mahan (in CLOWES, III, 402-3).

[76] Pigot to Clinton, Aug. 16, 1778, CP.

[77] [Clinton to Howe, Aug. 6, 1778,] *ibid.*

[78] The British had one 74, seven 64's, and five 50's; the French had two 80's, six 74's, three 64's, and one 50. For further details see CLOWES, III, 406, n. 1; and LACOUR-GAYET, pp. 629-30. George Johnstone, the commissioner, subsequently tried to prove to the house of commons that Howe's fleet had been equal in force to the enemy (*Parl. hist.*, XX, 350-53). The absurdity of Johnstone's argument was proved by his own experience three years later (see my article, "The battle of Porto Praya, 1781," *American Neptune*, V [1945], 74 and n. 28).

[79] JAMES, p. 104; and BEATSON, IV, 345. Howe's attitude contrasted with the confidence rife in London and in his own fleet, for which see FORTESCUE, *Correspondence*, IV, 194 and 195; *Sandwich papers*, II, 311-12; and STEVENS, Vol. I, No. 86.

[80] [Commodore] J[ohn] E[lliot to Eden], Aug. 18, 1778, STEVENS, Vol. V, No. 515. See also CLOWES,

13th, the two squadrons were scattered, damaged, and in no state to seek each other. Howe made for the Hook to refit, and Estaing turned again toward Narragansett Bay.

Those were anxious days at New York. Clinton was preparing artillery, transports, and victualers for the relief of Pigot and was hoping for a convoy. Gambier, the naval commandant in Howe's absence, was playing with the idea of sending some frigates through the Sound to attack the small force left behind by Estaing when he put to sea. But these schemes were subsidiary to the problem of locating Howe. He was said to be off the Hook in a dismasted frigate. Not far from her the hulk of a twodecker was visible through the storm; she looked like a French 74, but no one could get near enough to be sure. Gambier finally became so alarmed that he sent out virtually everything that would float to search for the British ships and assist them to port.[81]

On the evening of the 17th Howe at last appeared, and his captains began to straggle in the next day. They dared not anchor outside the bar, even when their ships had only minor damage, because they did not know where or in what condition the French might be.[82] In New York it was strongly suspected that the enemy was returning to Rhode Island.[83]

Hence the ships had to be refitted without a moment's delay. The dockyards apparently performed miracles, for by the 22d—a mere four days—Howe was ready to sail a second time to the rescue of Pigot.

Meanwhile, on the 20th, Estaing reappeared in Narragansett Bay. This was a hard blow to the beleaguered garrison, which was hoping for a different flag. "The sight of Lord Howe," Pigot wrote to Clinton on the 21st, "would have given us much pleasure. . . . . This is the twelfth day since the British fleet left us. Our anxiety was great, and we flattered ourselves much that they would be successful. We are impatient to hear of them [and we] should likewise be happy to hear from your excellency."[84]

Impatience is understandable. The Americans had attacked in force on the 14th, and their pressure had steadily increased. On the 16th Pigot had inquired whether Clinton planned to help him and had first mentioned the possibility of surrender. By the 21st Sullivan was reported to have nineteen thousand men on the island (a fantastic exaggeration); the French fleet lay off the harbor, and there was still no word from New York.[85]

But Clinton was far from idle. Fifteen transports were ready in the Sound and two at New York, enough to carry more than three thousand men.[86] Everything depended on accurate intelligence of the French designs. Estaing had been reported off the Delaware on the 15th, and

III, 403 and 405–10; LACOUR-GAYET, pp. 165–69; and GOTTSCHALK, pp. 249–51.

[81] James Pattison to Clinton and Lord Rawdon to Clinton, Aug. 16, Gambier to Clinton, Nos. 2 and 3 of Aug. 16 and Nos. 1 and 2 of Aug. 17, and [Clinton to Gambier,] Aug. 17, 1778, CP.

[82] STEVENS, Vol. V, No. 515. A large French squadron was actually south of the Hook. Admiral Byron, making for New York with the remnants of his fleet, had a brush with the enemy on the morning of the 18th and promptly made off for Halifax, where he arrived on the 26th (BEATSON, IV, 340–41).

[83] Gambier to Clinton, No. 4 of Aug. 17, 1778, CP.

[84] Pigot to Clinton, Aug. 21, 1778, ibid. This message was carried through the French fleet by a daring naval lieutenant in a whaleboat (BEATSON, IV, 353–55).

[85] Pigot to Clinton, Aug. 16, 21, and 31, and Sir James Wallace to Major-General Tryon, Aug. 21, 1778, CP. The American forces were, in fact, only three thousand regulars and five thousand militia (GREENE, II, 123).

[86] Gambier to Clinton, Aug. 21, 1778, CP.

definite word was received on the 22d that he was bound for Rhode Island; Howe expected him to remain there until Pigot surrendered.[87] Sir Henry suggested, as he had before, that the admiral should take the transports with him, but Howe again preferred to be unencumbered. The final arrangement was that the troops should go through the Sound as far as New London; if no word was received there from the fleet, they would return to Huntington Bay or Whitestone. Meanwhile Howe would reconnoiter Estaing's position and form a plan on the spot.[88]

Pigot's dispatch of the 21st, with its exaggerated report of the attacking force, reached New York on the 24th. Howe at once moved his squadron over the bar, but he still could not sail because his ships were undermanned. The next day he received news that changed the whole picture: the French had left Rhode Island. He therefore assured Clinton that the troops could safely go whenever they were ready. He himself was off to Boston, which was the enemy's most probable destination.[89]

When Estaing returned to Rhode Island, he never intended to stay. His renewing the blockade was a British fear and an American hope, but for him it involved prohibitive risk. Ever since his visit to the Hook, a month before, he had known that Byron's ships were on their way from England; he now knew that at least one of them had arrived. His orders

from the king were specific: if the squadron was likely to be outnumbered, it must make for Boston.[90] Common sense dictated the same course. The French ships needed immediate repair; otherwise they would be no match for Howe, let alone for him and Byron. The Americans urged that Providence had better facilities for refitting than Boston.[91] But this begged the question. The fleet was useful at Rhode Island, not at Providence; its function was to shield the attacking army from British naval power, and it was no longer in condition to perform that function. If it withdrew, the attack would collapse. But if it did not withdraw, it might be destroyed and the army with it. Estaing, therefore, was inflexible. He offered to stay only long enough to cover the retreat of Sullivan's forces to the mainland. When this offer was refused, he sailed for Boston on the 22d.[92]

His departure freed Clinton's hands. Word from Howe that the coast was clear reached Sir Henry at Flushing on the 27th, and an enclosure from Pigot added the information that the Americans were still on Rhode Island in force. Four thousand men were promptly embarked in transports which Gambier had somehow managed to collect.[93] Clinton's design was to seize Bristol Neck, on the mainland north of the island, thereby "possessing myself of all their batteries,

[87] Howe to Clinton, Aug. 22, 1778, *ibid.*

[88] Clinton to Howe, Aug. 21, and Howe to commanding officer of the troops embarking at Long Island, Aug. 24, 1778, *ibid.* This arrangement was reproduced in detail, two years later, in Clinton's and Arbuthnot's design against the French position at Newport (WILLCOX, "Rhode Island in British strategy," *loc. cit.*, pp. 310–11).

[89] Howe to Clinton, No. 1 of Aug. 24, and Aug. 25, 1778, CP. The accounts in BEATSON (IV, 355) and in JAMES (p. 107) are inaccurate in details.

[90] LACOUR-GAYET, pp. 159 and 169.

[91] GOTTSCHALK, pp. 251 and 254.

[92] For the bitterness between the French and Americans caused by this "desertion" see GREENE, II, 120–25; and GOTTSCHALK, pp. 251–69.

[93] "Historical detail," I, 120–21; and STEVENS, Vol. XI, No. 1152. Outfitting Howe's fleet and Clinton's expedition had denuded New York of men and ships, to the point where Gambier considered hoisting his flag in a storeship (Gambier to Clinton, Nos. 2 and 3 of Aug. 27, Cornwallis to Clinton, Aug. 28, and Gambier to Clinton, Sept. 1, 1778, CP; and *Sandwich papers*, II, 308–10).

stores, boats, etc., and reducing General Sullivan to something like the Saratoga business, and with very few troops destroy all that was at Providence."[94] The opportunity was alluring.

The wind defeated it. For days the transports were delayed in their passage through the Sound, while Washington warned Sullivan and the Americans began their retreat. Pigot's forces pressed them, with more vigor than success, and were repulsed in a sharp engagement on the 29th. Sullivan's withdrawal was not seriously interrupted; it continued into the early morning of the 30th, when the last of his troops crossed to the mainland. Only a few hours later Clinton arrived. His design had failed by the narrowest margin.

Pigot had known since the 27th that help was coming.[95] Sir Henry subsequently criticized him for pressing the Americans so hard that they were hurried out of the trap being set for them.[96] The criticism is ill grounded. Sullivan knew of the impending danger, and bringing him to action was as likely to impede as to accelerate his retreat. Howe's conduct is more open to question than Pigot's. When the admiral left New York, he knew that Narragansett Bay was clear of the French. He arrived off Boston on August 30, and he must therefore have passed Rhode Island while the Americans were still on it. If he had been less intent on finding Estaing, he might have recognized another quarry nearer to hand. His fleet could presumably have trapped Sullivan's army on the island and held it there until Clinton arrived. Instead the admiral stuck to his course, which brought him off Boston three days

behind the enemy fleet.[97] For his purpose those days might as well have been months.

The British failure to intercept the enemy virtually ended the campaign. Clinton returned to New York, while a detachment carried out a raid on New Bedford and Martha's Vineyard in early September. Howe endeavored to reach Rhode Island but was blown back to New York; he made over the command to Gambier, in the absence of Byron, and prepared to sail for home.[98] Clinton urged him to use the squadron, in conjunction with an army of six thousand, for a *coup de main* against Boston. The admiral refused on two gounds—that failure would bring ridicule on him and that he had resigned the command and could not resume it; "he also talked of private pique [with] ministers."[99] The fighting mood of the summer had apparently given way to depression, and he felt that America would have to be abandoned.[100] He left on the 22d; four days later Byron at last arrived. Clinton pressed his scheme on the new commander and offered to use the force destined for St. Lucia.[101] But Byron was no more enthusiastic than Howe had been, and nothing came of the idea.

During October the detachments for

[94] Clinton to unknown, Sept. 21, 1778, CP.

[95] Pigot to Clinton, Aug. 31, 1778, *ibid.*

[96] Clinton to unknown, Sept. 21, 1778, *ibid.*

[97] Howe to Clinton, Sept. 11, 1778, *ibid.*; STEVENS, Vol. V, No. 522 (where the three days are condensed to twelve hours); and CHEVALIER, p. 118.

[98] Howe to Clinton, Sept. 11 and 12, 1778, CP.

[99] Undated memorandum in Clinton's hand, filed in Vol. "Clinton I," *ibid.* Howe's anger with the ministry found expression after he returned to England (see *Parl. hist.*, XX, 340–41).

[100] STEVENS, Vol. V, No. 519.

[101] The date of Howe's departure, usually given as the 25th, is established by Gambier to Clinton, No. 1 of Sept. 23, 1778, CP. For Sir Henry's proposition to Byron see Clinton [to Lord Rawdon?], Sept. 29, 1778, *ibid.*; and STEVENS, Vol. I, No. 101, pp. 23–24. The scheme was not to blockade the French, as FISHER asserts (II, 216), but to destroy them by a combined operation.

the southern colonies and the St. Lucia expedition were preparing at New York. The latter finally sailed on November 4; the same day Estaing, eluding Byron's blockade, slipped out of Boston and made for the West Indies. For five weeks the British expedition sailed on a parallel course with the French squadron, and at any moment the vulnerable convoy might have been destroyed by an encounter with the ships of the line. That disaster was averted by the accident that the two forces never sighted each other, and on December 10 the troopships joined the West Indies fleet. St. Lucia was invested at once, before Estaing could come to its relief, and was captured by the narrowest margin of time.[102] Thus the attack planned in London in March was executed in the Caribbean nine months later.

Clinton had provided the wherewithal for it, at a heavy price. The detachments had reduced his force by ten thousand men, and he was left with between thirteen and fourteen thousand fit for duty; more than half of them were Germans. This meant, in his opinion, that nothing could be expected of the next campaign. "To see such an army dissolved—and I fear to such little purpose—is heartbreaking."[103] He was convinced that Great Britain could no longer afford him reinforcements, and he accordingly requested permission to resign.[104]

The request grew from his pessimism about the prospect for British arms. He recognized the fact that Estaing's failures had created an opportunity; he doubted, with good reason, that it could be utilized. The Americans "are tired of the war and a little jealous of their chiefs since the French alliance and failure of their attempts to assist them. One more vigourous campaign, *tout sera dit.*" Vigor, however, would require an additional thirty thousand men to conquer the only area where conquest would be decisive, the Hudson and Connecticut valleys. If such a force was out of the question (and he must have known that it was), coastal raids were a poor substitute. " 'Tis a doubt with me," he continued, "whether that sort of war is worthy of a great nation, nor is it certain at this period . . . . that it would succeed." He preferred withdrawal from the area of revolt; Canada, Nova Scotia, and the Floridas might serve as foci for an Indian war on the frontiers.[105] Why such warfare should be more worthy of a great nation than raiding, or more successful, he failed to say.

The military prospects seemed far brighter to Germain in London than to Clinton in New York. Lord George may have been whistling to keep up his courage, but his tune was cheerful. He virtually forbade Clinton to evacuate New York: Canada might be reinforced, if necessary, by the troops from Rhode Island. The Americans were doubtless despondent over the outcome of Estaing's "botched enterprise," and the authority of congress must have been proportionately weakened; soon the mass of the people would show a willingness to

---

[102] *Sandwich papers*, II, 333-36; CLOWES, III, 427-32; and FORTESCUE, *British Army*, III, 265-72.

[103] Clinton [to William Keppel and others], Oct. 10, [1778,] CP. See also "Historical detail," I, 123-25.

[104] Clinton to Germain, Oct. 8, 1778, STEVENS, Vol. XI, No. 1175. This request, carried again by Drummond, was rejected despite the best efforts of the Duke of Newcastle. Clinton was fobbed off with compliments, vague promises of reinforcement, and assurances that he was unfettered by his instructions (Drummond to Clinton, Dec. 5 and 17, and Germain to Clinton, Dec. 3, 1778, CP).

[105] Clinton memorandum, Sept. 4, 1778, CP. He considered seven thousand a sufficient reinforcement if the French could be contained in Europe (Clinton to General Carpenter, Sept. 21; see also [Clinton to Newcastle,] Nov. 26, [1778,] *ibid.*, and STEVENS, Vol. I, No. 97).

negotiate.[106] Willingness should be precipitated by military pressure. If Spain remained neutral, reinforcements might be spared for a full-scale offensive in 1779. Otherwise the colonists would have to be worn down by raids, which would probably end the war if they were carried out "with spirit and humanity."[107]

The impact of French sea power had deepened Clinton's pessimism, but it seems to have taught nothing to Germain and his naval colleagues. The record of the campaign was before them, to prove how basically the war had changed since March. There is no indication that they reviewed that record with a critical eye. They certainly did not draw lessons from it, although it was as suggestive then as it is today. A summary of what had happened speaks for itself.

The government decided to evacuate Philadelphia, largely for the sake of capturing St. Lucia. Clinton was ordered on March 21 to make the evacuation by sea and to send the West Indies and Florida expeditions from the Delaware, although French naval preparations had been a matter of concern since January. Estaing's destination was suspected in London in late April, but the caution of the admiralty allowed him to sail unopposed into the Atlantic three weeks later. No warning was sent to America until May 11, and no countermeasures were taken at home until Byron sailed on June 9. In consequence the French fleet appeared on the coast long before help was in prospect. Its appearance almost cost the British New York, came within an ace of costing them Rhode Island, and postponed the sailing of the St. Lucia expedition for nearly four months.

This is the record; to what does it

point? To the truism, for one thing, that no strategic design is sounder than the methods of implementing it. In view of the political and economic importance of the West Indies, the attack on St. Lucia had much to commend it; the evacuation of Philadelphia, just when the commissioners arrived, may or may not have been a fair price to pay. In any case the method of attacking one and abandoning the other was highly dangerous; it involved committing to the ocean simultaneously almost the whole of the king's forces in North America. This danger became obvious when Estaing's purpose was suspected in London. If he could not have been stopped, Clinton and Howe could at least have been warned in time.[108] But weeks passed before word was sent them, and it arrived too late to be of use. By May the slipshod methods of the government had made likely the defeat of its planning.

Defeat was averted by two factors. One was the caliber of the British field commanders: if Pigot had been less resourceful, or if a man like Gambier had been in the place of Howe, the errors of the ministry might have borne disastrous fruit. The other was a series of lucky accidents: Clinton's fortuitous decision to march overland to New York with his whole force; the draft of Estaing's largest ships, which dissuaded him from attempting the bar when he first reached the Hook; the storm which shattered his fleet off Rhode Island; the chance that he missed the British transports on the way to the West Indies in November. Resourceful commanders and good luck are useful adjuncts of strategy, but they cannot redeem an unsound design.

[106] Germain to Clinton, Sept. 25, 1778, CP.

[107] Idem to idem, Nov. 4, 1778, ibid.; the substance of this letter is repeated in STEVENS, Vol. XII, No. 1206.

[108] The failure to send warning caused great indignation among the British officers in America (BEATSON, IV, 336–37).

The campaign was unsound in conception as well as in implementation. The government failed to take into account the requirements for the kind of war which it planned to wage in America. Those requirements were a fleet and a base of operations, each strong enough to defend itself against attack. The strength of the fleet could have been maintained, once Estaing had sailed, either by stopping him at Gibraltar or by detaching Byron immediately; the rejection of both courses as too dangerous indicated a flaw in the original design. A more obvious shortcoming of that design was the lack of emphasis on New York. Its possession was prerequisite for a naval war; yet the government shelved a project for improving its yards and ordered its garrison cut almost in half. A good argument could have been made for abandoning the whole area or, alternatively, for holding New York—and Rhode Island if possible—in sufficient strength to harry the New England coast with impunity. It is hard to defend a strategy which fell between these alternatives. The two posts were to be held, at least pending the outcome of negotiations, but held in grossly inadequate strength. The results were that the work of the commissioners was stultified, the posts reduced to a desperate defensive, and the St. Lucia expedition almost frustrated. The importance of the American theater had become subordinate to that of the West Indian, but the two areas were interdependent. Bad planning for the one jeopardized success in the other.

The conclusion is inescapable. The thinking of the British high command, in the crisis of 1778, showed no change commensurate with the drastic change in the military problem. The decision to revert to a naval war was based on considerations of the moment, such as the vulnerability of St. Lucia, and was not a fundamental revision of policy. Much as revision was needed, it was never made; British planning remained extempore. For that reason it was easily reversed again at the end of 1779, when everything was staked on a territorial war in the southern colonies.

War, like politics, is an art of the possible, and the British never gave systematic study to their possibilities in America. Instead they trusted unduly to improvisation and luck. Both stood them in good stead during the campaign of 1778. But their good fortune was dangerous; they pressed it thereafter until it ran out at Yorktown. Cornwallis' position there was similar, on a larger scale, to Pigot's at Newport three years before, and the similarity was not accidental. During those years the strategic framework of the war and the British methods of waging it remained essentially unaltered— and essentially unrelated. In the disparity between them lay the seeds of disaster.

UNIVERSITY OF MICHIGAN

To Subdue America:
British Army Officers and the
Conduct of the Revolutionary War

Stephen Conway

IN an important sense, the American Revolutionary War was markedly different from the wars fought in Europe earlier in the eighteenth century. In those conflicts monarchs, statesmen, and generals saw their armies as the protagonists and their peoples as playing only a secondary role. Although civilians were obliged to contribute materially by providing money and other vital supplies, their attitudes seldom counted for much in the reckonings of the men who planned and conducted operations.[1] In America, by contrast, the military strategists had little choice but to pay closer attention to popular feeling. Democratic practices had accustomed Americans to a say in their government, and they were an armed people, with long-established militia organizations that enhanced their capacity to participate directly on one side or the other. These distinctive features of American life ensured that the war was less a struggle for territory on the European model than a contest for the political allegiance of the people.

Sir William Howe and Sir Henry Clinton, the British commanders in chief for most of the period of hostilities, were acutely aware of this unconventional dimension of the conflict. Clinton, indeed, wrote of the need "to gain the hearts & subdue the minds of America."[2] But the views of these commanders, although they will be discussed below, are not the

Dr. Conway is editor of the *Correspondence of Jeremy Bentham* for the Collected Works of Jeremy Bentham, University College London. Acknowledgments: I wish to thank the owners and custodians of the manuscript collections that I cite, or from which I quote, particularly His Grace the Duke of Grafton (Grafton Papers); His Grace the Duke of Northumberland (Percy Papers); Viscount Barrington (Barrington Papers); Baron Hotham (Hotham Papers); Dr. J. L. Campbell of Canna (Campbell of Inverneil Papers); Mr. S. W. Fraser (Spencer Stanhope Papers); and Mr. Oliver Russell (Macpherson Grant Papers). I am also indebted to Dr. Joseph S. Tiedemann of Loyola Marymount University, who kindly supplied an advance copy of his article on Queens County, New York, which appeared in the January 1986 issue of the *William and Mary Quarterly*.

[1] See Carl von Clausewitz, *On War*, ed. and trans. Michael Howard and Peter Paret (Princeton, N.J., 1976), 590-591 (Bk. VIII, Ch. iii), and Michael Howard, *War in European History* (Oxford, 1976), 72-73.

[2] Memo. of conversation, Feb. 7, 1776, Clinton Papers, William L. Clements Library, Ann Arbor, Mich.

main concern here. Attention will be focused on the opinions of their subordinates, the officers entrusted with the execution of the policies and plans of the commanders in chief. Many of these officers seem also to have been aware that the role of the people made the struggle in America different, but they were far from agreed on how this special kind of war should be waged. Two conflicting sets of attitudes stand out as particularly interesting—the conciliatory and the hard-line. Officers who recommended or practiced restraint did so, in some instances, for moral reasons associated with the humanitarian values of the Enlightenment or from an older sense of chivalry. Others were primarily motivated by more immediately practical considerations. They believed that mild treatment would pay political dividends. They sought to win goodwill in order to facilitate military victory and, perhaps more important, to make that victory lasting and worthwhile. "Hard-liners," on the other hand, advocated a tough approach, usually intended to bludgeon the colonists into submission. This article analyzes these contrasting attitudes and assesses their influence on the British army's conduct of the war.

Although conciliationist and hard-line arguments that will be discussed here emerge from the sources with sufficient frequency to suggest that they were not peculiar to the persons expressing them, they are inevitably drawn from the views of a fairly small sample of officers. To calculate the number of officers who served in America during the war is by no means easy, but between 3,500 and 4,000 seems a reasonable estimate.[3] Examination of the surviving letters, journals, diaries, and other relevant papers yields little or nothing for the great majority. In most cases, in fact, no more is known of an officer than his name as it appears in the extensive but usually impersonal and unilluminating official records. Even those who left written memorials to their participation in the war, or about whom it is possible to gather indirect information, frequently confined their comments to other matters: sometimes plain and uncritical narratives of military operations or discussion of duties, more commonly weather observations, family business, gossip, complaints about high prices, appeals for money, and, perhaps above all, promotion prospects. Of the 170 or so officers for whom I have some evidence, only about half can be said to have expressed views of any kind on how the war should be fought.

Several of these officers cannot be accommodated in the division between conciliationists and hard-liners. From the beginning of the struggle at least a few seem to have believed that *any* attempt to use the army to subdue America was highly unlikely to succeed. Some favored

[3] Precision is impossible. This estimate is based on the presence in the 13 colonies, at one time or another, of 58 regular regiments of foot, 2 of cavalry, and detachments from the foot guards, marines, artillery, and engineers. I have used the full establishment strengths as multipliers (though not every officer in each corps actually served in America) and have added a figure for new officers per year for each unit's service period to take account of turnover of personnel (though many new officers in fact came from other regiments already in America).

withdrawal of the troops and, like Secretary at War William Wildman, viscount Barrington, pinned their hopes on maritime pressure. A naval blockade, according to Capt. George Harris of the Fifth Foot, was "the only possible way of distressing them, as we can cut off every intercourse with other nations and by that means bring them to reason, at a much smaller expense than it can possibly be effected by land."[4] As the conflict dragged on, the number of officers who despaired of success through military coercion almost certainly increased. After Saratoga, Edmund Stevens of the Coldstream Guards argued that unless the troops were vastly reinforced, it would be best to abandon hopes of an armed solution and try negotiation instead.[5]

It should also be noted that officers who can confidently be categorized as hard-liners or conciliators were perfectly capable of changing their minds. Take Capt. Patrick Ferguson of the Seventieth Foot. In August 1778 he advised the laying waste of large tracts of Connecticut, sparing only "the houses (but not the Crop or moveables) of known Loyalists."[6] He could hardly have been unaware that this would lead to great distress for colonists not deeply committed to the Revolutionaries. Yet only two months later, Ferguson was explaining to Clinton that during his own raid on the coast of New Jersey he had been careful to ensure that "no manner of Insult or Injury has been offered to the peaceable Inhabitants, nor even such as without taking a Lead have been made from the Tyranny or Influence of their Rulers [the Revolutionary authorities] to forget their Allegiance." Indeed, rather than destroy the houses of Quakers that had been used by the patriot forces to store their baggage, Ferguson decided that the "Injury to be thereby done to the Enemy would not compensate for the sufferings of these innocent People."[7] Ferguson, it must be acknowledged, was particularly flexible, willing to adjust his ideas rapidly to meet what he saw as the needs of the moment. Nevertheless, many of his colleagues similarly changed their minds in ways that suggest that the dividing line between the two attitudes should be envisaged as a permeable membrane rather than an impenetrable barrier.

These caveats and qualifications registered, we should consider the attitudes of the commanders in chief. The significance of the views of their subordinates becomes apparent only when it is recognized that they were

[4] Stephen Rumbold Lushington, *The Life and Services of General Lord Harris* . . . (London, 1840), 58-59.
[5] Stevens to [Charles Manners, marquis of Granby], Dec. 13, 1777, in *The Manuscripts of His Grace the Duke of Rutland* . . . , III (Historical Manuscripts Commission, *Fourteenth Report, Appendix, Part I* [London, 1894]), 12.
[6] Hugh F. Rankin [ed.], "An Officer Out of His Time: Correspondence of Major Patrick Ferguson, 1779-1780," in Howard H. Peckham, ed., *Sources of American Independence: Selected Manuscripts from the Collections of the William L. Clements Library,* II (Chicago, 1978), 308.
[7] Ferguson to Clinton, Oct. 10, 15, 1778, C.O. 5/96, 177, 179, Public Record Office.

141

to a great extent determined by the approach of Howe and Clinton.[8] In general terms the commanders' stance can be characterized as moderate and restrained. At the start of the war, surrounded by hostile New Englanders, Howe was reported to be willing to employ the most extreme methods,[9] but away from besieged Boston, and before he became disillusioned in Philadelphia, he was convinced that mild treatment of civilians was essential if the British were to gain worthwhile victory. This conviction helps to account for his determination to curb his soldiers' theft and unauthorized destruction of property. Other officers—and politicians in Britain—sometimes claimed that he had not done enough in this respect, and his reluctance to carry out the threat of extreme punishment has been interpreted as a sign of an equivocal attitude toward plundering. Eventually, however, he ordered several soldiers who had been caught stealing from the local people to be executed without trial.[10] His pardoning of some offenders, moreover, was not due to any wish to condone their irregularities but accorded with normal judicial practice, which required only a few examples to be made to deter others, rather than the punishment of every malefactor.[11] On a number of occasions Howe showed himself ahead of his subordinates in wanting harsh penalties applied. When three soldiers of the Twenty-second Foot were sentenced to be flogged for stealing sheep in Rhode Island, he disapproved highly of the officers who had "adjudged the delinquents to

[8] What follows is not intended as a comprehensive assessment of the thinking of Howe and Clinton, let alone of British strategy in general. For a fuller picture many good studies are available. I have found especially valuable Ira D. Gruber, *The Howe Brothers and the American Revolution* (Chapel Hill, N.C., 1972), and "Britain's Southern Strategy," in W. Robert Higgins, ed., *The Revolutionary War in the South: Power, Conflict, and Leadership* (Durham, N.C., 1979), 205-238; William B. Willcox, *Portrait of a General: Sir Henry Clinton in the War of Independence* (New York, 1964); Piers Mackesy, *The War for America, 1775-1783* (London, 1964); Paul H. Smith, *Loyalists and Redcoats: A Study in British Revolutionary Policy* (Chapel Hill, N.C., 1964); R. Arthur Bowler, *Logistics and the Failure of the British Army in America, 1775-1783* (Princeton, N.J., 1975); and John Shy, "The Military Conflict Considered as a Revolutionary War," in *A People Numerous and Armed: Reflections on the Military Struggle for American Independence* (New York, 1976), 193-224, and "British Strategy for Pacifying the Southern Colonies, 1778-1781," in Jeffrey J. Crow and Larry E. Tise, eds., *The Southern Experience in the American Revolution* (Chapel Hill, N.C., 1978), 155-173.

[9] "1775 & 1776 Decr & Jany. Conversations with Sir W. H. relative to the Southern Expedition," Clinton Papers.

[10] See entries of Sept. 9, 15, 1777, Great Britain Orderly Book, 1776-1778, Clements Lib. For Howe's earlier threats see entries of Sept. 6, Oct. 31, 1776, Aug. 27, 1777, *ibid.*, and P.R.O. 30/55/107, 143, P.R.O.

[11] For Howe's belief in selective punishment see his letter to William Legge, earl of Dartmouth, Jan. 22, 1776, C.O. 5/93, 60. For the use of pardons in England see Douglas Hay, "Property, Authority and the Criminal Law," in Douglas Hay *et al.*, *Albion's Fatal Tree: Crime and Society in Eighteenth-Century England* (New York, 1975), 40-49.

receive Corporal punishment for a Crime deemed Capital by law."[12] Similarly, in Pennsylvania, he announced his dissatisfaction when a private of the Forty-third Foot was acquitted of the charge of plundering.[13]

Howe's wish to combat such crimes undoubtedly sprang from a variety of motives. Contemporary writers deprecated the ill-usage of civilians in warfare, and a letter from Howe to George Washington of July 16, 1776, indicates that he wanted to fight in a fashion appropriate to the humanitarian mood of the age.[14] There were also, of course, sound military reasons for acting against plundering and vandalism: they squandered resources that might have benefited the army; resulted in the loss of soldiers through death, injury, or capture by the enemy; and, if unchecked, could all too easily bring about a general erosion of discipline.[15] All the same, it is clear that, for Howe, political considerations were often as important as moral and military ones. He criticized or prohibited plundering specifically on the ground that it was likely to estrange loyal or potentially friendly Americans. His message to the troops—at least in the Middle Colonies— was that they came as liberators, not as conquerors.[16]

Clinton's commitment to conciliatory methods was less explicit but just as sincere. Although he had always been more skeptical than Howe about the strength of the loyalists—and was therefore not so demoralized when they consistently failed to come foward in the anticipated numbers—he accepted that they had a crucial role to play in British strategy and saw part of his task as encouraging the "friends to government" and securing the waverers.[17] On the whole, he believed that leniency and moderation were the best means to achieve these ends. Like Howe, he made strenuous efforts to minimize plundering, and for much the same reasons—because he recognized that anything less was not only militarily unwise and morally reprehensible but also likely to be politically damaging. It is significant that he ordered the body of a trooper of the Seventeenth Light Dragoons

[12] [Allen French, ed.], *Diary of Frederick Mackenzie: Giving a Daily Narrative of His Military Service as an Officer of the Regiment of Royal Welch Fusiliers during the Years 1775-1781 in Massachusetts, Rhode Island, and New York*, I (Cambridge, Mass., 1930), 251, hereafter cited as *Mackenzie Diary*.

[13] Entry of Sept. 2, 1777, Great Britain Orderly Book, 1776-1778; W.O. 71/84, 197-200, P.R.O.

[14] P.R.O. 30/55/3, 229(1). For the opinions of contemporary writers see Jean-Jacques Rousseau, *Du Contrat Social* (Geneva, 1762), Bk. I, Ch. iv; Emmerich de Vattel, *Le Droit des Gens* (Neuchatel, 1758), Bk. III, Ch. viii, ss. 145-147.

[15] See entries of Feb. 1, Sept. 15, 1777, Great Britain Orderly Book, 1776-1778; Journals of Capt. John Peebles, Cuninghame of Thorntoun Papers, G.D. 21/492/9, 3, Scottish Record Office, Edinburgh; "Proposed Reformations for the American Army" (that is, the British army in America), n.d., Germain papers, Vol. 17, Clements Lib.

[16] Entries of June 29, Nov. 21, 1776, Sept. 15, 1777, Great Britain Orderly Book, 1776-1778; *The Kemble Papers* (New-York Historical Society, *Collections*, XVI [New York, 1884]), I, 473, hereafter cited as *Kemble Papers*; Gruber, *Howe Brothers*, 145-146.

[17] Willcox, *Portrait of a General*, 493-494.

143

who had been killed while robbing an inhabitant's house to be hung on a gibbet for all to see, both as a warning to the soldiers and to impress on civilians the army's disapproval of such thefts.[18]

True, in Boston—long before he became commander in chief—Clinton had toyed with the idea of using coastal raids to bring the Americans to terms, which hardly suggests a conciliatory disposition.[19] But that was in Boston, where the frustrations and humiliations of the siege convinced almost every officer that such a course was necessary. After Clinton assumed responsibility for running the war, he did occasionally explore the possibility again, pondering whether raids would overawe the people. On reflection, however, he seems to have banished these speculations to the back of his mind. It appears that he canvassed the opinions of his advisors on this subject only once, and then halfheartedly.[20] The incursions actually carried out on his instructions never formed part of a concerted policy of destruction and waste; in fact, Clinton went out of his way to repudiate the notion of a "War of devastation."[21] The raids were ad hoc responses to military problems of the moment. The descent on Virginia in May 1779, for example, was designed principally as a diversion in favor of British forces in South Carolina.[22] Other raids were intended to destroy American privateering bases or provoke Washington's army to offer battle.[23] Moreover, Clinton had no wish to see civilians suffer during these attacks. His orders for a projected raid on Philadelphia in 1781 directed that the greatest care be taken that "the peaceable Inhabitants are not on any Account molested in Person or Property,"[24] revealing both his humanitarian distaste for a war of severity and his political belief, even at this late stage, that this was the best way to win friends to the royal cause.

This belief appears to have motivated Howe and Clinton for most of the conflict. Sometimes they were forced to let more pressing considerations override it, but in general they sought to minimize the distresses of noncombatants. That this approach was condemned by officers calling for a more gloves-off pursuit of the war is scarcely surprising. More so is the criticism voiced by those who favored leniency and restraint. Their complaint was not that Howe and Clinton were too soft on civilians but, on the contrary, that the commanders' unwillingness to go far enough

[18] W.O. 71/90, 410-416; Order Book, II, 63-64, Clinton Papers, Vol. 266.

[19] Clinton to Henry Pelham Clinton, duke of Newcastle, Dec. 3, 1775, Newcastle of Clumber MSS, NeC 2385b, Nottingham University Library, Nottingham, Eng.

[20] Clinton to Newcastle, Sept. 21, 1778, *ibid.*, NeC 2614; William H. W. Sabine, ed., *Historical Memoirs from 26 August 1778 to 12 November 1783 of William Smith* ... (New York, 1971), 396.

[21] Willcox, *Portrait of a General*, 251; Clinton to Newcastle, Sept. 21, 1778, Newcastle of Clumber MSS, NeC 2614.

[22] "Instructions for Major General Mathew," Apr. 29, 1779, Clinton Papers.

[23] Ferguson to Clinton, Oct. 10, 1778, C.O. 5/96, 176; Henry Clinton, *The American Rebellion: Sir Henry Clinton's Narrative of His Campaigns, 1775-1782*, ed. William B. Willcox (New Haven, Conn., 1954), 130.

[24] Clinton to Maj. Gen. James Robertson, [June 1781], Clinton Papers.

down the conciliationist road gave serious offense even to loyal colonists and made it impossible to have the desired impact on American opinion generally.

When officers who expressed conciliatory views are examined as a group, certain characteristic attitudes and objectives stand out. Without exception, they strongly opposed plundering and associated indiscipline. Of course, many officers who cannot accurately be described as conciliators also condemned such crimes. They did so for the military and moral reasons already stated; indeed, with regard to the latter it is worth noting that "shameful" was a common epithet applied to plundering.[25] But while these considerations actuated some, the advocates of a conciliatory approach condemned pillage mainly because, like Howe and Clinton, they felt that such indiscipline would make it much more difficult to secure civilian goodwill.

This conciliationist thinking can be glimpsed in the journal of Maj. Stephen Kemble of the Royal Americans, the deputy adjutant general and a native of New Jersey, who consistently denounced the irregularities of the troops in New York and, on November 2, 1776, ruefully recorded, "no wonder if the Country People refuse to join us."[26] Maj. Gen. James Robertson's conviction that predation had to be checked can be more thoroughly documented. In orders he appealed to the better natures of his men, stressing that most Americans were loyal and deserved "all the blessings that attend British liberty."[27] In correspondence Robertson lamented the willingness of many of his colleagues to condone the pillaging he so condemned. "Those who formerly wishd our approach," he wrote to Lt. Gen. Jeffrey, Lord Amherst on January 7, 1777, "And would with Joy have seen Us triumph Over the rebels, will now Arm to defend their All from Undistinguished plunder."[28] Writing to his father about the same time, the Honorable Charles Stuart, major of the Forty-third Foot, struck the same note. The excesses of the troops had become a serious problem, he believed, because Howe had failed to carry out his threats of summary execution of plunderers. As a result, indiscipline was "persuading to enmity those minds already undecided, and inducing our very Friends to fly to the opposite party for protection."[29] Brig. Gen. Francis

[25] See, for instance, "The Diary of Lieutenant John Barker," *Journal of the Society for Army Historical Research*, VII (1928), 101; Peebles's Journal, Cuninghame of Thorntoun Papers, G.D. 21/492/7, 17; entry of June 21, Seventh Foot Orderly Book 1778 (copy), Historical Society of Pennsylvania, Philadelphia; entry of June 17, Fortieth Foot Orderly Book, 1777, George Washington Papers, Ser. 6B, Vol. I, Library of Congress.

[26] *Kemble Papers*, I, 96.

[27] *Mackenzie Diary*, I, 56.

[28] Amherst Papers, U 1350 079/14, Kent Archives Office, Maidstone. See also Robertson to Amherst, Nov. 9, 1776, *ibid.*, U 1350 079/13.

[29] Stuart to John Stuart, earl of Bute, Feb. 4, 1777, in E. Stuart-Wortley, ed., *A Prime Minister and His Son* . . . (London, 1925), 99. This was, of course, before Howe authorized the summary execution of a number of plunderers in Sept. 1777.

McLean, in charge of the army contingent on the Penobscot expedition of 1779, was equally convinced that the British could aspire to hold the allegiance of significant numbers of colonists only if the troops behaved themselves. Shortly after landing at the Penobscot River, McLean issued a proclamation assuring the inhabitants that his soldiers would refrain from plundering. He then worked diligently during the following months to keep his word, informing Clinton that not the least injury had been offered to any of the settlers.[30] Lt. Col. Archibald Campbell of the Seventy-first Foot, who led the force that captured Savannah in December 1778, thought and acted in much the same fashion. While his men were still on board ship he explained that they had come to relieve and protect "His Majesty's Loyal Inhabitants . . . who have long withstood the Savage Oppression of Congress" and accordingly gave strict instructions against plundering.[31] When the town fell, Campbell took great pains to preserve it from the ravages of the troops, and as his small force moved deeper into Georgia he continued to be attentive to the regularity of the soldiers, placing safeguards even on the property of known Revolutionaries.[32]

There was more to a lenient and restrained approach, however, than a determination to minimize indiscipline. Conciliatory officers were often just as concerned to ensure that the army's legitimate demands on the population caused the least possible offense. Lt. Gen. Hugh, Earl Percy showed himself particularly attuned to the sensitivities of the residents of Rhode Island. When he discovered that in the area under his jurisdiction there were some 1,400 tons of hay, most of which Howe wanted for his forces, Percy told the commander in chief that "it is absolutely necessary to leave at least 800 Ton for the Stock of the Inhabitants, without which, they must be reduced to the greatest State of Misery."[33] In Percy's case it is possible to argue that a sense of noblesse oblige was more important than an awareness of the political advantage that could flow from such considerate treatment. The aristocratic Percy perhaps saw the civilians under his protection in the same light as he saw the soldiers under his command or, indeed, the tenants who were to depend upon his will when he inherited his father's estates: they were all objects of his paternalistic care.[34] This said, Percy's later comments on the harshness of his successor at Rhode Island suggest that his motives were mixed and that he was acting

[30] McLean to Clinton, June 26, 1779, P.R.O. 30/55/17, 2088(2); McLean to Clinton, Aug. 23, 1779, P.R.O. 30/55/18, 2214(6).
[31] "Journal of an Expedition against the Rebels of Georgia," 20-23, Campbell of Inverneil Papers, Isle of Canna, Scotland.
[32] Ibid., 46, 54, 98; "Memoirs of an Invalid," 158, Amherst Papers, U 1350 Z9 A; "History of Europe," The Annual Register . . . 1779 (London, 1802), 35.
[33] Percy to Howe, Feb. 9, 1777, Percy Papers, Vol. XLIX, pt. A, 13, Alnwick Castle, Northumberland. See also Bowler, Logistics, 69, 79.
[34] It was characteristic that after Bunker Hill he sent home at his own expense the widows of the men of his regiment killed in the battle, and arranged for the women to be given a further sum of money once they arrived in Britain. See Dictionary of National Biography, s.v. "Percy, Hugh." Percy appears to have been acutely aware of his aristocratic status. Howe wrote to Maj. Gen. James Grant on

in some part from a desire to gain positive political benefit from his mild approach.[35]

Major General Robertson, whose origins were decidedly more humble[36] and whose political ideas were more clearly stated, displayed much the same concern in New York. His reputation of having been a corrupt and selfish man, who profited from all manner of peculation, some of which detrimentally affected the inhabitants, is largely based on the vitriolic portrait penned by the loyalist judge Thomas Jones. Jones's view seems to have been colored by anti-Scots prejudice, disapproval of Robertson's lechery, and outrage at his apparent sympathy for the New York Presbyterians, Jones's particular bête noir.[37] There is hardly any doubt that Robertson did make money by dubious means, but little evidence to corroborate Jones's accusations that he milked the local people as well as the British government. Robertson's public and private writings disclose his keen attention to American opinion. When he ordered the people of Kings and Queens counties, Long Island, to supply the troops with ready-made fascines, he was typically careful to arrange with leading citizens the quota to be expected from each township, so "that this burthen might be light by being equally born by all."[38] Similar sensitivity can be seen in Brigadier General McLean's approach to the gathering of supplies at Penobscot. On August 23, 1779, he proudly told Clinton that "not an Article [has] been taken by the Navy or Army since our arrival, without payment."[39] In this connection the conduct of Maj. Robert McLeroth of the Sixty-fourth Foot, another officer well known for his commitment to conciliatory methods, is also worthy of mention. Retiring after a skirmish in South Carolina with the patriot leader Francis Marion, McLeroth not only left a surgeon to attend the wounded, which was normal practice, but gave money to the tavern keeper with whom they were lodged to ensure that subsisting the injured would not bring financial disadvantage to the civilians involved.[40]

Mar. 18, 1777: "Ld. Percy going home disgusted—The story is long & will keep untill we meet, but he thinks I have not treated him according to his rank as an Offr. & *Heir apparent to the Dukedom of Northumberland*" (Macpherson Grant Papers, bundle 252, Ballindalloch Castle, Banffshire, Scotland). See also Bowler, *Logistics*, 27n, 69-70.

[35] Percy to Clinton, Sept. 4, 1777, Clinton Papers.

[36] Although in May 1781 his daughter married John Henderson, a Scottish M.P. and heir to a baronetcy, Robertson's origins appear to have been lowly. He was born in Newbigging, Fife, and is thought to have started his military career as a common soldier.

[37] Thomas Jones, *History of New York during the Revolutionary War, and of the Leading Events in the Other Colonies at That Period*, ed. Edward Floyd De Lancey (New York, 1879), I, 162-164, II, 2-3, 166n, 190.

[38] Robertson to William Axtell and Archibald Hamilton, July 5, 1780, Henderson of Fordell Muniments, G.D. 172, box 46, bundle Ra/6, S.R.O.

[39] McLean to Clinton, Aug. 23, 1779, P.R.O. 30/55/18, 2214(6).

[40] See Hugh F. Rankin, *Francis Marion: The Swamp Fox* (New York, 1973), 125, 134. For McLeroth's reputation see Edward McCrady, *The History of South Carolina in the Revolution, 1780-1783* (New York, 1902), 102.

147

Conciliators also opposed indiscriminate destruction of private property as likely to lessen British chances of success in the vital contest for American hearts and minds.[41] Robertson questioned the wisdom of Maj. Gen. the Honorable John Vaughan's incendiary attack on Esopus, New York, arguing that it had done little to advance the British cause. He accepted that the destruction of some kinds of property was militarily imperative. "Mills, Stores & Shipping that could have been usefull to the Enemy" he declared legitimate targets. On the other hand, "burning houses that add value to a Country wch might have been for the King's use gives the people a notion that we despair of possessing it & therefore leads them to despair of our protection & to court the Enemys favor."[42] Officers who thought like this were disturbed by the prospect of greater use of such methods. In September 1778 Charles Stuart disapprovingly reported to his father the policy of destruction urged by the unsuccessful and resentful peace commissioners under Frederick Howard, earl of Carlisle. Stuart made plain his dislike of their recommendations in a manner that reveals his dissatisfaction with the way in which the British had already behaved. "We have no occasion to try whether acts of severity will cause the people to submit," he wrote, for the ill conduct of the army in the previous campaign had "planted an irrecoverable hatred wherever we went."[43] An unknown officer who sent a paper to Amherst "on some Improvements Proposed . . . to be made in the Plan of the American War" was equally critical of the rationale of the hard-liners. By supposing that the colonists, if sufficiently intimidated, would "rise up against the Congress and force them to make the Concessions which we require," the proponents of severity, he argued, were deceiving themselves. Rather, he claimed, "so far as the People of America are galled and distressed, they will impute their Sufferings to the hands that inflict them, not to those who have drawn such Sufferings upon their Country. They will impute them to the immediate, not to the remote cause of them, and direct their Animosity accordingly."[44]

Some officers, anxious to supplement their appeals for restraint and moderation with a more positive approach, called for the restoration of civilian control in certain pacified areas. Although Howe and Clinton opposed a return to civil government in New York on the grounds that it would make requisitioning more difficult and might result in provisions

[41] Other officers took a similar line but for different reasons. Capt. Frederick Mackenzie of the Royal Welch Fusiliers was deeply unhappy about plans for widespread destruction of housing in Rhode Island in 1778, not because he was worried about the immediate impact on American opinion, but because he feared for the army's honor and reputation in more general terms. See *Mackenzie Diary*, II, 329.

[42] Robertson to Amherst, Oct. 27, 1777, Amherst Papers, U 1350 079/19.

[43] Stuart to Bute, Sept. 16, 1778, in Stuart-Wortley, ed., *Prime Minister and Son*, 132.

[44] W.O. 34/110, 145.

reaching patriot hands,[45] several of their subordinates were convinced that a bold initiative would reap sufficient rewards to justify the risks. They contended that restoration, by demonstrating that the army was not merely trying to impose an authoritarian regime reliant on its bayonets, would undermine Revolutionary assertions that the British intended to enslave America. Robertson, although he disapproved of a full return to civilian rule in New York when Clinton finally consented to this after Yorktown,[46] argued strongly for restoration earlier in the war. In October 1777 he told Amherst that a civil administration would have created "an example of happiness that wou'd have been the envy of all those who are suffering the miseries of Anarchy" under the Revolutionaries.[47] Archibald Campbell, sent to Georgia with a civil governor's commission in his pocket, employed the same argument. He had no real wish to be governor but was totally committed to a rapid installation of civilian control. A "Proper Governour" and the "Re:establishment of Legal Government," he wrote on January 19, 1779, "whilst the minds of the People in the neighbouring Provinces are worn out by persecutions, extortions, apprehensions; must operate more powerfully than twenty thousand troops."[48]

A set of related assumptions underpinned the thinking of many who favored a conciliatory line. The first was that there existed a significant body of determined American loyalists: hence Robertson's desire to "Support the good Subjects Against the bad."[49] The second was that most Americans were potentially or fundamentally loyal even if they had been deceived by the conspiratorial band of Revolutionary leaders who now exercised a tyrannical hold over them: hence frequent references to the way in which the people had been duped and to the oppressive government under which those outside the British lines were living.[50] From these two assumptions a third followed by way of conclusion—that the fidelity of the loyal could be maintained, and the allegiance of the "deluded" regained, only if the army acted with consideration toward the colonists generally and demonstrated the benefits of British rule in the particular areas it occupied. This belief was perhaps best articulated—as so often— by Robertson. He has been accused of being chiefly concerned to avoid offending the Revolutionaries in order to protect his substantial New York property from confiscation,[51] but his correspondence with his

[45] Memorandum Book, 12-13, 51-52, Andrew Elliot Papers, box 7, New York State Library, Albany, N.Y.

[46] Robertson to Amherst, Mar. 22, 1782, Amherst Papers, U 1350 079/23.

[47] Robertson to Amherst, Oct. 27, 1777, ibid., U 1350 079/19.

[48] Campbell to [William Eden], Jan. 19, 1779, Additional MSS 34416, fol. 246, British Library.

[49] Robertson to Amherst, Nov. 9, 1776, Amherst Papers, U 1350 079/13.

[50] For instance, Stuart to Bute, July 9, 1776, in Stuart-Wortley, ed., Prime Minister and Son, 82.

[51] Jones, History, ed. De Lancey, II, 402-404; L.F.S. Upton, The Loyal Whig: William Smith of New York and Quebec (Toronto, 1969), 123.

daughter strongly suggests that he sincerely believed that his endeavors to "keep or Create friends to the King" were the "best way to win a Country."[52] In a letter of September 15, 1780, he summed up his position in distinctly utilitarian language. Having described Lt. Gen. Charles, Earl Cornwallis's spectacular victory at Camden, South Carolina, he told his daughter: "but force does not Alter inclinations. It is by Showing people that they may be happy And by Contrasting their present State, [with] taxes, pressings, oppression, All the ills both of Anarchy and tyranny, of high prices And want of Money, with the ease and Security the people Under the Kings protection enjoy, that I build the hope of Alluring them rebels to return to their duty, As sure As Men Seek happyness and fly from Misery, this will happen."[53]

Turning from the conciliators to the hard-liners, we find very different ideas on how the war should be conducted. When the supporters of severity urged a harsh approach, they meant, above all, much greater destruction of private property. Such officers were dubbed by a New Jersey loyalist as "fire and sword men,"[54] and the following sample of extracts from their letters testifies to the appropriateness of this description: "the only way of terminating this Affair [is] to Carry devastation and terror on the Point of your Sword"; "nothing but the Bayonet & Torch will ever Bring this Country['s] People to reason"; "Nothing will secure these People but Fire & Sword."[55] The hard-liners treated as heroes those officers who led destructive raids on American settlements, particularly Vaughan, the commander of the force that burned Esopus.[56] Vaughan and his ilk were praised not just for what they had done but because their actions seemed to point the way to what the hard-liners most wanted—the elevation of the use of the torch into the very concerted policy that Clinton rejected. We can see this in the comments of Maj. Sir James Murray of the King's Own Regiment, a participant in the attack on New Bedford in September 1778: "we have been a little employed of late in burning and destroying and we are in hopes that the fashion may take root."[57] We see it also in Maj. Gen. James Grant's pointed criticism of

[52] Robertson to Anne Loudoun Robertson, Mar. 21, 1778, Henderson of Fordell Muniments, G.D. 172, box 46, bundle Ra/2.

[53] Ibid., Ra/10. See also Parliamentary Register, XII (1779), 278: "I always considered the great object of the war to be the regaining the people, and to do this by letting them see we were their friends."

[54] Charles W. Parker, "Shipley: The Country Seat of a Jersey Loyalist," New Jersey Historical Society, Proceedings, N.S., XVI (1931), 127.

[55] Capt. Thomas Davis to Amherst, July 19, 1778, W.O. 34/111, 71; Capt. Patrick Campbell to Alexander Campbell, July 8, 1778, Campbell of Barcaldine Muniments, G.D. 170/1711/17, S.R.O.; Lt. Col. Banastre Tarleton to Cornwallis, Nov. 8, 1780, P.R.O. 30/11/4, 63.

[56] Parker, "Shipley," N.J. Hist. Soc., Procs., N.S., XVI (1931), 127.

[57] Murray to Mrs. Elizabeth Smyth, Oct. 24, 1778, in Eric Robson, ed., Letters from America, 1773-1780 ... (New York [1951]), 61.

Clinton for failing to use incendiary methods in New Jersey after the British evacuation of Philadelphia,[58] and, perhaps most thoroughly, in the remarks of Col. Charles O'Hara of the Coldstream Guards, who argued in a letter to his old colleague Sir Charles Thompson that the scene of operations should be moved to the "most inveterate" of the rebel provinces, where "Fire & Sword, should Ruin & desolate the remotest corners of them."[59]

Faith in the effectiveness of destruction united the hard-liners, but their letters and papers also disclose other recommended ingredients of a war of severity. A number of officers favored the uninhibited employment of Indians, whose mode of warfare made them especially feared on the frontier. In besieged Boston, Maj. Francis Bushill Sill of the Sixty-third Foot reacted with gruesome delight to news that several Revolutionary soldiers had been scalped by Indians after a skirmish: "I am glad to find they have begun for they are like fox-hounds [and] Require blooding."[60] Major General Grant was more restrained when he wrote of the work of Indians reported to be acting on the orders of the British commander at Detroit. Even so, his satisfaction was obvious. The three scalps taken would do more good, he announced, "than if we had killed a hundred of them."[61]

Some officers believed that allowing the troops to take what they wanted from the people was integral to the effective conduct of the war. Lt. the Honorable Richard Fitzpatrick of the First Foot Guards was certain that most of his colleagues thought this way. On July 5, 1777, he informed his brother that they saw severity as the only means of winning the war and that, "declaring every where these sentiments," they were "fomenting if not encouraging all kinds of pillage, plunder, & barbarity."[62] Fitzpatrick, however, is hardly an ideal witness. He was a firm opponent of the war and was inclined to portray in an unflattering light the vast majority of his fellow officers who did not share his views. He failed to recognize that offenses against civilians were condoned for many other reasons: because officers stood to gain by them,[63] because officers were too insouciant or unprofessional to counter them,[64] or because even those who wanted to

[58] Grant to [Richard Rigby?], Oct. 12, 1778, Letterbook, 1776-1778, Macpherson Grant Papers, bundle 772.

[59] O'Hara to Thompson, Sept. 20, 1778, Hotham Papers, DD HO 4/19, Brynmor Jones Library, University of Hull, Hull, Eng.

[60] Sill to John Spencer, Sept. 29, 1775, Spencer Stanhope of Cannon Hall Muniments, 60542/10, Sheffield Central Library.

[61] Grant to Rigby, May 12, 1776, Letterbook, 1775-1776, Macpherson Grant Papers, bundle 2.

[62] Fitzpatrick to John Fitzpatrick, earl of Upper Ossory, July 5, 1777, Miscellaneous MSS, Lib. Cong.

[63] See allegations to this effect in W.O. 71/89, 437-444, and memo. of conversation with Maj. Balfour, Jan. 13, 1777, Robinson Papers, Lucas Collection, L 29/214, Bedfordshire Record Office, Bedford.

[64] For example, Maj. Gen. William Tryon to Clinton, Nov. 3, 1777, Clinton Papers, and entry of Aug. 30, 1781, Eightieth Foot Orderly Book, Boston Public

protect the people felt that soldiers should be permitted a certain latitude as compensation for the hardships of military life.[65] Furthermore, Fitzpatrick either ignored or was unaware of the determined opposition of several hard-liners to plundering and similar irregularities. Major General Grant condemned the excesses of the Hessian auxiliaries, as did Charles O'Hara, who also took pains to check marauding by the forces under his command in North Carolina in 1781.[66] Likewise, Maj. Gen. William Tryon, a consistent advocate of fire and sword, was keen to keep his men on a short leash.[67] We can surmise that for such officers the military disadvantages of allowing undisciplined behavior were of paramount importance. Their fear of losing control of their men—"Nothing destroys their discipline and takes off those Qualities which constitute the Soldier so effectually," one contemporary wrote of the effect of plundering on the plunderers[68]—probably outweighed their desire to give the war a sharper cutting edge. They fervently believed in the efficacy of organized and directed destruction and seizure but were unwilling to countenance a free-for-all that might endanger their own position.

Still, even if Fitzpatrick exaggerated and oversimplified, his criticism was not entirely misdirected. There were hard-liners prepared to loosen the reins for political purposes. Capt. Francis, Lord Rawdon of the Sixty-third Foot, writing from New York in September 1776, contended that "we should (whenever we get further into the country) give free liberty to the soldiers to ravage at will," so that the Americans—"these infatuated wretches"—"may feel what a calamity war is." Although Rawdon later exerted himself to maintain discipline among the troops he commanded in the South, it is significant that a month before penning the passage just quoted he displayed a complete unwillingness to take seriously the rapes committed by soldiers camped on Staten Island. On that occasion he merely commented that the victims were "so little accustomed to these vigorous methods that they don't bear them with the proper resigna-

---

Library, Boston, Mass. See also the frequency with which it was found necessary to order commanders of corps to read the rolls regularly to keep track of their men: entries of July 5, Aug. 23, 24, Nov. 11, Dec. 5, 19, 1776, June 14, Sept. 23, 1777, Great Britain Orderly Book, 1776-1778, and Mil. Doc. 1037, 63-64, Royal Artillery Institution, Woolwich.

[65] Cuninghame of Thorntoun Papers, G.D. 21/492/13, 3; Rankin [ed.], "Officer Out of His Time," in Peckham, ed., *Sources of American Independence*, 336-337.

[66] Grant to Rigby, Sept. 24, 1776, Letterbook, 1775-1777, Macpherson Grant Papers, bundle 2; O'Hara to Thompson, Sept. 20, 1778, Hotham Papers, DD HO 4/19; A. R. Newsome, ed., "A British Orderly Book, 1780-1781," *North Carolina Historical Review*, IX (1932), 378-379.

[67] Memo. of Tryon-Clinton conversation, Feb. 1776, Clinton Papers; Tryon to Clinton, Nov. 3, 1777, *ibid.;* King's American Regt. Orderly Book, Sept. 11, 1777, Clements Lib.; Edward H. Tatum, Jr., ed., *The American Journal of Ambrose Serle, Secretary to Lord Howe, 1776-1778* (San Marino, Calif., 1940), 176.

[68] "Proposed Reformations for the American Army," Germain Papers, Vol. 17.

tion."[69] Lt. Col. Banastre Tarleton of the British Legion was similarly reluctant to suppress the indiscipline of his men when this affected the inhabitants. Although he denied knowledge of criminal acts perpetrated by his troops when these were brought to his notice by Cornwallis,[70] his corps acquired great notoriety as a result of its excesses in the backcountry of South Carolina. Given Tarleton's almost continual presence with the Legion, it is difficult to accept that he was unaware of these offenses.[71]

Supporters of draconian measures also pressed for a more uninhibited approach in the collection of supplies. Tarleton, pouring scorn on conciliators and urging less sensitivity in requisitioning, observed that "Coolness Apathy & Civil Law will never supply Hussars with Horses."[72] Major General Grant went farther, arguing that American towns should be "laid under Contribution for Cattle, Sheep and other Articles of Provision for the Subsistance of the Troops."[73] "Contribution" was in fact an accepted system for securing essentials for the maintenance of armies in wartime, even if in European conflicts towns were generally obliged to part with money rather than livestock and other foodstuffs.' But Emmerich de Vattel, the leading author on public law of the period, was anxious to stress that, while enforced contributions were legitimate, moderation was essential, together with careful attention to the ability of an area to meet the demands made on it.[74] Grant appears to have been thinking along rather different lines. Indeed, his coupling of contribution with the burning of coastal settlements makes it hard to avoid the conclusion that he was looking for a return to *Kontribution* in the style of Wallenstein, the utter ruthlessness of which had helped to create the general European wish never to repeat the horrors of the Thirty Years' War.[75]

Why, then, were officers prepared to call for such severe methods? Hardly surprisingly, advocacy of a hard line was often partly a capitulation to instinctive reactions rather than wholly the product of a reasoned

---

[69] Rawdon to Francis Hastings, earl of Huntingdon, Aug. 5, Sept. 23, 1776, in Francis Bickley, ed., *Report on the Manuscripts of the Late Reginald Rawdon Hastings, Esq., of the Manor House, Ashby de la Zouch*, III (Historical Manuscripts Commission, *Twentieth Report* [London, 1934]), 185, 179, hereafter cited as *Hastings MSS*.

[70] Tarleton to Cornwallis, Dec. 26, 1780, P.R.O. 30/11/4, 404.

[71] Lt. Col. Nesbitt Balfour to Cornwallis, June 12, 1780, P.R.O. 30/11/2, 140. See also Tarleton to Cornwallis, Aug. 5, 1780, P.R.O. 30/11/63, 20.

[72] Tarleton to Capt. John André, Feb. 19, 1779, Clinton Papers.

[73] Grant to Lt. Gen. Edward Harvey, Aug. 10, 1775, Letterbook, 1775-1777, Macpherson Grant Papers, bundle 2.

[74] Vattel, *Le Droit des Gens*, Bk. III, Ch. x, s. 165. Myron P. Gutmann notes that from the end of the seventeenth century contribution was better organized and less onerous for civilians than it had been earlier (*War and Rural Life in the Early Modern Low Countries* [Princeton, N.J., 1980], 62-64).

[75] Martin van Creveld, *Supplying War: Logistics from Wallenstein to Patton* (Cambridge, 1977), 8-9; F. Redlich, "Contributions in the Thirty Years' War," *Economic History Review*, 2d Ser., XII (1959), 254.

analysis of the requirements of the kind of war being waged in America. A form of class hatred appears to have affected some. There is ample evidence that many officers held the colonists in low regard: "a scape Gallows race, the genuine progeny of their worthy Ancestors from Newgate and the Old Baily," was the scathing judgment of Capt. Patrick Campbell of the Seventy-first Foot, at any rate before he married Sally Pearsall of New York. Whether such hostility to Americans in general satisfactorily explains Campbell's preference for "the Bayonet & Torch" and "the rod" is uncertain,[76] but others made perfectly obvious the correlation between their view of the colonists and their predilection for rigorous measures. For Capt. William Glanville Evelyn of the King's Own Regiment, who described Americans as "upstart vagabonds, the dregs and scorn of the human species," laying waste the country "and almost extirpating the present rebellious race" were prerequisite to a restoration of British dominion.[77]

Closely connected with antipathy to the colonists was a deep aversion to rebellion. Discipline and hierarchy were bound to appeal to men whose very lives might depend upon their maintenance. Some officers, it is true, were not always amenable to discipline from above, for those who were gentlemen first and soldiers second were often reluctant to be seen as mere tools of arbitrary superiors.[78] But this independence of spirit was strictly confined to their relationship with other officers and gentlemen: few were willing to tolerate even the smallest manifestation of the same spirit in the rank and file. The dreadful specter of insubordination, even of mutiny, can therefore be presumed to have influenced the attitude of the officers toward the colonists. At the same time, their attitude was probably based on more general considerations. It almost certainly sprang from a strong feeling that civil insurgency was "unnatural"—the adjective commonly used by officers in this connection.[79] This reflected the traditional notion that rebellion was a sin against the ordained dispensation, a belief founded in classical antiquity and Christian scripture, given detailed and learned expression in works such as Grotius's influential *De Jure Belli ac*

---

[76] Campbell to Duncan Campbell of Glenure, Feb. 10, 1777, Campbell of Barcaldine Muniments, G.D. 170/1176/10/1; Campbell to Alexander Campbell, July 8, 1777, *ibid.*, G.D. 170/1711/17.

[77] Evelyn to Rev. Dr. William Evelyn, Feb. 18, 1775, and to Mrs. Frances Leveson Gower, Aug. 19, 1775, in G. D. Scull, ed., *Memoir and Letters of Captain W. Glanville Evelyn . . .* (Oxford, 1879), 51, 65.

[78] Alan J. Guy, *Oeconomy and Discipline: Officership and Administration in the British Army, 1714-63* (Manchester, 1985), 37-42; Geoffrey Best, *War and Society in Revolutionary Europe, 1770-1870* (London, 1982), 129-130. For indications of this attitude in the American war see Maj. William Dansey to Lt. Col. John Yorke, Mar. 27, 1782, in "The Letters of Captain William Dansey," *The Iron Duke*, XXVIII (1952), 103, and Maj. James Wemyss to André, Apr. 22, 1780, Clinton Papers.

[79] See, for example, Sir James Murray to Mrs. Elizabeth Smyth, Mar. 5, 1778, in Robson, ed., *Letters from America*, 52.

Pacis,[80] and only partly qualified for Englishmen by the events of the Revolution of 1688-1689. In some quarters attitudes had changed. Vattel, for instance, in *Le Droit des Gens*, rejected the argument "that the laws are not made for rebels, for whom no punishment can be too severe," and counseled moderation, especially if insurgents were sufficiently numerous to oblige the sovereign to wage formal war.[81] Vattel's "laws of war" were, however, only a combination of recorded practice and wishful thinking, and even if some military men were prepared to accept something like them to regulate behavior toward enemy soldiers and noncombatants, they were disinclined to respond to appeals for the application of such restraints during a rebellion that they considered far from justified. Much as William Augustus, duke of Cumberland, whom Vattel praised for humanity to the French at Dettingen, thought it perfectly legitimate to treat the rebellious Highlanders with the utmost severity in the '45 uprising,[82] so, thirty years later, many British officers believed it quite proper to suspend any limitations on their conduct in dealing with the rebellious Americans. Capt. the Honorable William Leslie of the Seventeenth Foot revealed this almost en passant in the midst of an account of the war in New Jersey, which he sent to his mother on Christmas Day 1776. He explained that the "Desolation that this unhappy Country has suffered must distress every feeling heart" but added that "the Inhabitants deserve it as much as any set of people who ever rebelled against their Sovereign."[83]

A passionate desire for vengeance seems to have motivated a number of officers. Those who had seen friends and colleagues wounded or killed could readily be persuaded that extreme measures were justified as retribution. "The Numbers of fine young men from fifteen to five and twenty with loss of limbs &c. hurts me beyond conception," wrote Maj. John Bowater of the Marines, "And I every day curse Columbus and all the discoverers of this Diabolical Country, which no Earthly Compensation can put me in Charity with."[84] Casualties incurred by the army at Boston in 1775 appear to have helped turn Major Sill into the sanguinary supporter of scalping we met earlier. Before he left Ireland, Sill was opposed to the government's coercion of the colonists and wanted to treat them "with Lenity and endeavour to soften the miseries of a Civil War as

---

[80] Hugo Grotius, *De Jure Belli ac Pacis Libri Tres* . . . (Paris, 1625), Bk. I, Ch. iv.

[81] Vattel, *Le Droit des Gens*, Bk. III, Ch. xviii, s. 287. See also Martin J. Clancey, "Rules of Land Warfare during the War of the American Revolution," *World Polity*, II (1960), 210-211.

[82] Vattel, *Le Droit des Gens*, Bk. III, Ch. viii, s. 158; W. A. Speck, *The Butcher: The Duke of Cumberland and the Suppression of the 45* (Oxford, 1981), 125-126, 143, 164, 170.

[83] Leslie to Wilhelmena Leslie, countess of Leven and Melville, Dec. 25, 1776, Leven and Melville Muniments, G.D. 26/9/513, S.R.O.

[84] Bowater to Basil Fielding, earl of Denbigh, Nov. 17, 1777, in Marion Balderston and David Syrett, eds., *The Lost War: Letters from British Officers during the American Revolution* (New York, 1975), 147.

much as lays in my power." But the bloody events of Bunker Hill profoundly affected him ("the Shocking Carnage that day will never be erased out of my mind 'till the day of my Death"), and the following September he was bitterly recanting his sympathy for the colonists and arguing that "nothing can have an effectual Lasting possession of this noble Continent but harsh absolute and severe Methods."[85]

Nor was it just heavy losses in set-piece battles that could provoke these sentiments. The guerrilla fighting that took place on the periphery of and between conventional operations seems also to have been influential; indeed, the emotions it engendered were probably more likely to push officers toward a hard-line stance. Experience of constant harassment in New Jersey in the winter of 1776-77 certainly wrought a change in the attitude of Lt. Col. Enoch Markham of the Forty-sixth Foot. At first he wrote to his brother expressing sincere regret at the distress of the people and the terrible scenes of destruction in the country, but a few weeks of exhausting duty against partisan attacks changed his tune. Having described the hardships suffered by his men—"They had small parties skulking about us"; "The whole regiment was jaded to death"—Markham went on to criticize British humanity toward the Americans and by implication to urge a tougher approach for the future.[86]

Frustration played a part as well. As the war lengthened and the prospect of victory dimmed, the number and vehemence of the hard-liners increased. By July 1777 Lt. Col. Thomas Sterling of the Forty-second Foot was "heartily tired" of the war, "as I can see no end in the manner we go on." He feared it would become a fifty-year struggle "if we do not adopt severe measures."[87] American success at Saratoga won many converts to this view. Writing in January 1778, Maj. Samuel Holland of the Guides and Pioneers explained "that desolation is the onlay remady left to bring them to their Reasons,—Tho' I must Confess that I mention it with horror, as no boddy has been more against Plundering & Destruction than I have been, as long as there were any hopes of milder recources."[88] Later that year, anticipating the failure of the peace commissioners under the earl of Carlisle, Capt. Francis Downman of the Royal Artillery was similarly disposed to see widespread destruction as the only answer. If the Revolutionaries were to reject the "fair proposals" offered, which he thought provided everything they could want short of Independence, then "the country I hope will be laid waste from stem to stern."[89]

[85] Sill to Spencer, Mar. 2, July 6, Sept. 29, 1775, Spencer Stanhope of Cannon Hall Muniments, 60542/6, 8, 10.

[86] Markham to William Markham, Dec. 17, 1776, letter-journal, Dec. 1776–Jan. 1777, in Clements Markham, *Markham Memorials* ..., I (London, 1913), 177, 178-180.

[87] Sterling to Sir William Sterling of Ardoch, June 25–July 3, 1777, Abercairny Muniments, G.D. 24/1/458, S.R.O.

[88] Holland to Lt. Gen. Frederick Haldimand, Jan. 31, 1778, Additional MSS 21732, fol. 10.

[89] F. A. Whinyates, ed., *The Services of Lieut.-Colonel Francis Downman* ... (Woolwich, 1898), 86.

Hatred, fear, anger, and frustration all help to account for a predilection for severity, but any temptation to provide an explanation exclusively, or even primarily, in these terms should be resisted. The comments of several officers that leniency was really cruelty, since it was interpreted as a sign of British weakness and therefore served only to prolong the struggle,[90] indicate a calculating as well as an emotional dimension to hardline attitudes. Indeed, some advocates of severity clearly based their arguments on perceptions of the disposition of the Americans and their likely reaction to a concerted policy of harshness in the same manner as conciliators based their ideas on assumptions about the nature of the rebellion and of colonial responses to mild treatment.

The starting point for such hard-liners was a deep skepticism toward assertions that there were large numbers of genuine loyalists. Col. the Honorable William Harcourt of the Sixteenth Light Dragoons spoke for many of his colleagues when he told his father that "we are almost without a friend (I mean upon principle) on this side of the Atlantic."[91] But if most supporters of severity agreed with this assessment, their opinions varied as to the true complexion of the colonists. Some, such as O'Hara, came to believe that the vast majority were irreconcilable rebels and that worthwhile victory was therefore impossible. Propelled by this defeatism into considering the postwar world, O'Hara argued for harsh measures as a means of weakening the new states and reducing their capacity to pursue their enmity toward Britain.[92] More hard-liners, however, were optimistic; they saw harshness as the way to victory—a belief, incidentally, to which O'Hara himself had subscribed in an earlier, more hopeful mood.[93] Like the conciliators, they thought that most colonists were recoverable. All but a few, in their view, were either totally devoid of principles, and therefore uncommitted, or at heart lukewarm loyalists, fearful of the patriots but inclined to an accommodation with the mother country.[94] Where these hard-liners differed from the supporters of leniency, of

[90] For instance, Capt. William Sutherland to Dugald Gilchrist, May 30, 1777, Gilchrist of Ospisdale Muniments, G.D. 153, box 1, bundle 4, S.R.O.; Patrick Campbell to Alexander Campbell, July 8, 1778, Campbell of Barcaldine Muniments, G.D. 170/1711/17; James Grant to Anthony Chamier, Aug. 11, 1775, Letterbook, 1775-1777, Macpherson Grant Papers, bundle 2.

[91] Harcourt to Simon Harcourt, Earl Harcourt, May 31, 1777, in Edward William Harcourt, ed., *The Harcourt Papers*, XI (Oxford [1880]), 213. See also Grant to Harvey, June 7, 1777, Letterbook, 1776-1778, Macpherson Grant Papers, bundle 772, and O'Hara to Augustus Henry Fitzroy, duke of Grafton, Nov. 15, 1780, Grafton Papers, Ac. 423/196, West Suffolk Record Office, Bury St. Edmunds.

[92] O'Hara to Grafton, Nov. 1, 1780, Grafton Papers, Ac. 423/190. See also Stuart-Wortley, ed., *Prime Minister and Son*, 132.

[93] O'Hara to Thompson, Sept. 20, 1778, Hotham Papers, DD HO 4/19.

[94] See Capt. the Hon. Charles Cochrane to [Andrew Stuart], Oct. 19, 1777, Stuart-Stevenson Papers, MS 5375, fol. 38, National Library of Scotland, Edinburgh; *Mackenzie Diary*, I, 298; and Bowater to Denbigh, June 5, 11, 1777, in Balderston and Syrett, eds., *Lost War*, 131.

course, was in their judgment of how Americans could be brought to abandon the Revolutionary leadership and return to the British connection. While officers of a conciliatory turn of mind thought that they could be wooed back to their proper allegiance, for the fire-and-sword men who believed them redeemable, intimidation was the key. Since most Americans lacked firm principles, their argument ran, they were prone to fall in behind the side that demonstrated the greater muscle. To counter the fear created by the oppressive grip of the Revolutionary authorities, it was therefore necessary to impress them with British power and frighten them into forcing their leaders to give way. This was the reasoning so roundly condemned by the anonymous author of the paper sent to Amherst, and there is no reason to doubt that he had heard it expressed by hard-line colleagues.

Most officers, unfortunately, were less inclined to record their assumptions than their recommendations, but this intimidatory logic occasionally emerges from the sources in unmistakable form. We can see it in a letter written by Major General Tryon after his devastating raid on Connecticut in July 1779. He reported to Clinton that the dominance of the Revolutionaries rested on "the general Dread of their Tyranny and the arts practiced to inspire a Credulous Multitude with a presumptuous Confidence in our forbearance." He continued: "I confess myself in the Sentiments of those, who apprehend no Mischief . . . from the Irritation of a Few in the Rebellion, if a general Terror and Despondency can be awakened among a People already divided."[95] The same kind of assessment appears in the diary of Capt. Frederick Mackenzie. On June 9, 1778, this diligent and experienced officer devoted considerable space to explaining his conversion to a harsh approach. "The great body of the people are desirous of a reconciliation," he wrote. "Very few parts of America know, as yet, what the horrors of War are, and if their houses, farms, and other property was destroyed and laid waste, their resentment would turn upon Congress, and their numerous other rulers." Only when the colonists became more frightened of the British army than they were of the Revolutionary authorities, he argued, could Britain hope to bring the struggle to a successful conclusion.[96]

We shall now consider the influence of conciliatory and hard-line attitudes on the actual conduct of the war. In all conflicts, officers have the power to shape significantly the image their army presents. They can advance or frustrate the intentions of headquarters. In America, the commanders in chief faced special difficulties in this respect, for they had to contend not only with distance and poor communications as limitations on their control, but also with the independent-mindedness of some of

[95] Tryon to Clinton, July 20, 1779, C.O. 5/98, 122, in William S. Powell, ed., *The Correspondence of William Tryon and Other Selected Papers*, II (Raleigh, N.C., 1981), 867.
[96] *Mackenzie Diary*, I, 298-299.

their subordinates. The nature of the struggle ensured a considerable degree of local autonomy, and the reluctance of certain officers to see themselves as bound by central directions meant that, in the absence of other inhibitions, they would almost inevitably grasp the chance to translate rhetoric into reality. In the War for Independence, it seems to have been the hard-liners who took the greatest advantage of such opportunities, even to the point where their activities undermined the generally conciliatory approach of Howe and Clinton, thus creating an impression that the British were willing to use methods that these commanders opposed.

This is not to say that the men of mild and moderate views were totally without influence. Several of their number held detached commands and were able to put their ideas into practice. In Georgia, Lt. Col. Archibald Campbell was in control for the first few crucial months after the fall of Savannah; at Penobscot, Brigadier General McLean; in parts of South Carolina, Major McLeroth; in Rhode Island, Earl Percy. All these officers experienced some success in winning over the local people. Campbell, who wrote in January 1779 of his "hope of being the first officer to take a stripe and star from the rebel flag of Congress," was able to record in the following month that some 1,100 Georgians had joined the loyalist militia and pledged allegiance to the king.[97] News of McLean's sensitive handling of the settlers at Penobscot led him to be described by the Hessian major Carl Baurmeister as "probably the first Briton who understands the art of winning the confidence of the inhabitants."[98] In South Carolina, McLeroth was similarly praised by a fellow officer for the "great service" he had rendered by his "mild and equitable behaviour to the Inhabitants."[99] Percy was so popular in Rhode Island that his return to England in June 1777 was reported to have been sincerely regretted by large numbers of residents.[100]

Yet the achievements of these conciliators were only ephemeral. Their patient work was undone, the goodwill they engendered rapidly evaporated, when they were replaced by officers with radically different views. In Rhode Island, for instance, the mood of civilians soon changed. Percy's successor, Maj. Gen. Richard Prescott, was captured in his nightshirt by Revolutionary raiders, an unfortunate circumstance that Percy, with a certain mischievous satisfaction, put down to the unwillingness of the local

[97] Campbell to the earl of Carlisle, Jan. 18, 1779, in *The Manuscripts of the Earl of Carlisle, preserved at Castle Howard* (Historical Manuscripts Commission, *Fifteenth Report, Appendix, Part VI* [London, 1897]), 413-414; "Journal of an Expedition," 103, Campbell of Inverneil Papers.

[98] Bernard A. Uhlendorf, trans., *Revolution in America: Confidential Letters and Journals 1776-1784 of Adjutant General Major Baurmeister of the Hessian Forces* (New Brunswick, N.J., 1957), 313.

[99] Rawdon to Cornwallis, Sept. 4, 1777, Clinton Papers.

[100] Robert Boucher Nickolls to Huntingdon, June 9, 1777, in *Hastings MSS*, III, 192; "Address of the inhabitants of Newport," May 3, 1777, C.O. 5/94, 416-419.

people to provide any warning, which itself he attributed to Prescott's treating them "with rather too much Severity."[101] At Penobscot the situation was similarly transformed with McLean's departure. His successors were arbitrary and thoughtless in their dealings with the people, with the consequence that residents pressed for a speedy restoration of civilian government.[102] In Georgia the story was much the same. Campbell handed over command to the hard-bitten Swiss soldier of fortune Maj. Gen. Augustine Prevost and his brother Lt. Col. Jacques Marc Prevost, neither of whom made any great effort to endear themselves to the inhabitants. When it suited them, they overlooked serious plundering, and Augustine Prevost made obvious his total lack of concern for civilians who had failed to serve alongside his troops during the Franco-American siege of Savannah.[103] In South Carolina promotion removed McLeroth from the scene in December 1780; his going left the people exposed to far less considerate treatment.[104]

Major General Robertson, in a position of authority in New York for many years, first as commandant of the city, then as royal governor of the province, was no more able to make a lasting impact. Installed as governor in 1780, he was widely expected to secure the return of civil administration, a step he had long recommended; yet although he continued to advocate such a restoration, he failed to bring it about. This failure has been explained by his wish to protect the army from a flood of prosecutions for theft and fraud, and his assertions of commitment to the principle of restoration have been dismissed as hypocritical,[105] but personal factors were perhaps more important. He was already elderly when appointed governor, and by the autumn of 1781 perceptive observers noted that he had become inconsistent and inclined to dotage.[106] His thinking seems to have been further debilitated by the death of his beloved daughter.[107] Even before this stage, however, he was becoming lukewarm about restoration, probably due to the influence of Andrew Elliot, the collector of customs and superintendent of police at New York, who was convinced

[101] Percy to Clinton, Sept. 4, 1777, Clinton Papers.

[102] John Calef to Germain, Sept. 10, 1780, "Intelligence from Penobscot January 15th. 1782," John Calef Papers, Miscellaneous MSS (bound), Clements Lib.

[103] Enclosures in Sir James Wright to Germain, May 20, 1780, C.O. 5/665, 262-263, 266; Augustine Prevost to Germain, Nov. 1, 1779, C.O. 5/182, 182. For Augustine Prevost's closer attention to discipline on another occasion see entry of July 6, 1779, British Army Siege of Savannah Orderly Book, Lib. Cong.

[104] See Rankin, *Francis Marion*, 134.

[105] See Jones, *History*, ed. De Lancey, II, 164-165, 402. Upton suggests that both Robertson and Chief Justice Smith prevaricated because neither wanted to be condemned by the Revolutionaries for allowing civilian courts to pass sentence of death on patriots (*Loyal Whig*, 124).

[106] Sabine, ed., *Smith Memoirs*, 461; *Mackenzie Diary*, II, 537, 676.

[107] Sabine, ed., *Smith Memoirs*, 503. See also Robertson to Haldimand, Aug. 26, 1782, Additional MSS 21734, fol. 536.

that a return to civil government would be disastrous.[108] According to Chief Justice William Smith, Elliot's rival for Robertson's ear, Elliot undermined Robertson's commitment not only by the force and persistence of his arguments but also by encouraging the declining old general's belief that he would succeed Clinton and therefore could not afford to alienate the army by placing it under civilian restraint.[109] Whatever the reasons, it seems safe to conclude that Robertson was unfit to carry into execution the ideas he had so eloquently presented earlier in the war.

The difficulties Robertson encountered in trying to combat indiscipline among the troops owed much less to his own weakness. He made vigorous efforts to prevent plunder, and, at first, as a brigade commander and New York commandant, he had some success, just as Percy, McLean, Campbell, and McLeroth did with their own small forces.[110] But when it came to imposing order on larger and scattered bodies of troops, not always under his watchful eye, Robertson met with the same problems as the much-criticized commanders in chief. Despite his endeavors, the British army in the New York area committed all manner of offenses against the inhabitants. Fences were pulled up in contravention of repeated injunctions against this practice, houses were plundered, produce was stolen, and civilians were beaten, raped, even murdered.[111] Nor was Robertson able to make tolerable the army's unavoidable demands on the local people. His hope that supplies and services would be obtained fairly and in an unburdensome manner seems often to have been frustrated by the arbitrary and grasping behavior of those who acquired the provisions, timber, and transport.[112]

Robertson's failure to curb the irregularity of the troops and the impositions of personnel of the ancillary services points to a crucial problem for the supporters of restraint. Quite simply, there were not enough of them, particularly in the lower reaches of the army's hierar-

[108] Memorandum Book, 8-9, 51-52, 55-56, Andrew Elliot Papers, box 7.

[109] Sabine, ed., *Smith Memoirs*, xiv, 294, 304.

[110] Robertson to Amherst, Nov. 9, 1776, Amherst Papers, U 1350 079/13; Capt. Francis Hutcheson to Haldimand, Feb. 16, 1777, Additional MSS 21680, fol. 175; *Parliamentary Register*, XIII (1779), 278-279.

[111] Joseph S. Tiedemann, "Patriots by Default: Queens County, New York, and the British Army, 1776-1783," *William and Mary Quarterly*, 3d Ser., XLIII (1986), 35-63; entries of Aug. 22, 23, 24, 31, Sept. 4, 6, 1776, Great Britain Orderly Book, 1776-1778; Tatum, ed., *Serle Journal*, 77, 86-87; William Kelby, *Orderly Book of the Three Battalions of Loyalists Commanded by Brigadier-General Oliver De Lancey* (Baltimore, 1972), *passim*; W.O. 71/82, 405-425; W.O. 71/86, 177-180, 200-206; W.O. 71/88, 330-350, 362-372, 393-398; W.O. 71/90, 377-383, 410-416; W.O. 71/92, 1-34, 227-234, 411-419; W.O. 71/93, 185-195; W.O. 71/94, 297-302.

[112] Jones; *History*, ed. De Lancey, I, 320-321, 330-331, 336-338; John McAlpine, *Genuine Narratives, and Concise Memoirs . . . of J. McAlpine* (London, 1788), 50-58; A.O. 12/110, 8-9, P.R.O.

chy.[113] There were, to be sure, officers in subordinate positions within the main forces, with little or no chance to impress as commanders of separate detachments, who were inclined to conciliatory methods. Charles Stuart was certainly one. Lt. Col. Henry Hope of the Forty-fourth Foot was probably another; Robertson praised him for having made the British grenadiers "less feared by our friends."[114] There was also Capt. Sir George Osborne of the Third Foot Guards, an officer who criticized the Hessians' plundering and, in Pennsylvania, took steps to return to their owners goods stolen by drunken members of his corps.[115] But these men stand out; there is no indication that most of their colleagues thought as they did. There were, it must be said, occasional converts to moderation, such as Lord Rawdon. The fire-eating young captain of 1776 had become an altogether more mellow officer by 1780. As a lieutenant colonel operating in the Waxhaws district of South Carolina, he did his utmost to win over the Scotch-Irish there by treating them with "particular kindness & Lenity" and by maintaining strict discipline among his troops.[116] For the most part, however, as we have seen, the conversions were in the opposite direction.

Conciliatory attitudes were most widespread in 1776, when British military success and the apparent loyalty of New Yorkers persuaded a number of officers to favor generosity. Frederick Mackenzie and John Bowater, who were both to urge destruction later in the war, in 1776 lauded Howe for his humanity.[117] Even at this stage, however, there were doubters—"Too great an Indulgence for their past behaviour" was the stern verdict of Capt. William Bamford of the Fortieth Foot in December 1776 on the magnanimity of the commander in chief toward the people of New Jersey[118]—and setbacks, first at Trenton and Princeton, then more dramatically at Saratoga, caused the number of vocal supporters of severity to grow. In December 1777 it was reported that Major General Vaughan of Esopus fame was "the cock of the Ball" at New York, the majority of officers being "fire and sword men."[119] The events of 1778

[113] Not many subalterns expressed views that can safely be classified as hard-line or conciliatory. A few showed some sympathy for the people, without clearly emerging as committed to a lenient approach for political reasons. See, for example, the journal of Lt. William Digby of the Fifty-third Foot (Additional MSS 32413, fol. 64). Most seem to have been more concerned with promotion and pay.

[114] Robertson to Amherst, Nov. 12, 1780, Henderson of Fordell Muniments, Letterbook, 1780-1783, G.D. 172, Vol. Rv.

[115] Osborne to Germain, Oct. 29, 1776, C.O. 5/93, 501; Osborne to Barrington, Dec. 20, 1776, Barrington Papers, H.A. 174/1026/6a(4), East Suffolk Record Office, Ipswich; W.O. 71/84, 262-263.

[116] Rawdon to John Rawdon, earl of Moira, Aug. 20, 1780, Miscellaneous MSS, Lib. Cong.; Rawdon to Cornwallis, Dec. 5, 1780, Clinton Papers.

[117] *Mackenzie Diary*, I, 111; Bowater to Denbigh, Nov. 5, 1776, in Balderston and Syrett, eds., *Lost War*, 103.

[118] "Bamford's Diary," *Maryland Historical Magazine*, XXVIII (1933), 20.

[119] Parker, "Shipley," N.J. Hist. Soc., *Procs.*, N.S., XVI (1931), 127. See also ——— to William Eden, n.d. (early 1778?), Additional MSS 34415, fol. 2.

further augmented the ranks of the hard-liners, and by November 1779 surgeon Robert Roberts felt able to claim that everyone "whose honesty would suffer him to be open to reason, has long been convinced that lenity was not even a palliative for the Fever of Rebellion"[120]—an exaggeration, unquestionably, but another sign of the numerical superiority enjoyed by the votaries of severity.

But did this numerical superiority lead to preponderant influence? At first glance it appears not. The commanders in chief did not succumb to the many siren voices calling for the widespread use of the torch. The army pursued no concerted policy of destruction comparable to the ravaging of the Palatinate on the instructions of the marquis de Louvois in 1688-1689 or the devastation of Bavaria by the duke of Marlborough and Prince Eugene in 1704. Nor was America laid under contribution in the style suggested by Major General Grant. Contributions were exacted at Martha's Vineyard in September 1778 by Maj. Gen. Charles Grey,[121] but this seems to have been the only occasion when the army turned to this method of sustaining itself, and then as a result of necessity, not official predilection for contribution as a system.

If we focus on the war as actually fought, however, rather than on its conduct as ordained by Howe and Clinton, a different picture comes into view. The numerical superiority of the hard-liners meant that many localities were subjected to small-scale versions of the general policy of harshness that they advocated—probably many more than experienced the benevolent attentions of conciliatory officers. Even some of the areas that were the targets of authorized destructive raids were treated far more severely than Clinton intended, because officers like Tryon saw fit to exceed the spirit if not the letter of their orders.[122] Elsewhere the country was ravaged without any kind of high-ranking authorization. When the British made an exploratory advance into New Jersey in July 1780, Springfield was burned "against the positive orders of the commanding officers" because junior officers, if the reaction of Lt. George Mathew of the Coldstream Guards is representative, were unwilling to keep their men from setting fire to houses "from which the rebels had fired on them."[123] On other occasions, officers in charge of smaller detachments operating far from headquarters took it upon themselves to employ a policy of destruction. The South Carolina backcountry was unlucky enough to be the scene of a number of such local initiatives. Tarleton appears to have dealt particularly harshly with much of this area, while from Cheraw district Maj. James Wemyss of the Sixty-third Foot reported

---

[120] Roberts to Thompson, Nov. 8, 1779, Hotham Papers, DD HO 4/20.

[121] See Henry Cabot Lodge, ed., *André's Journal: An Authentic Record of the Movements and Engagements of the British Army in America from June 1777 to November 1778 . . .* , II (Boston, 1903), 36.

[122] "Hints for C. Loyd," Nov. 9, 1779, Clinton Papers; Clinton, *American Rebellion*, ed. Willcox, 131; Sabine, ed., *Smith Memoirs*, 167.

[123] "Mathew's Narrative," *Historical Magazine*, I (1857), 105.

that he had burned about fifty houses and plantations in order to enforce obedience.[124]

From the British perspective, then, the hard-liners often exercised a significant influence at the local level, an influence that can be fairly described as subversive of the designs of the commanders in chief and the conciliatory officers beneath them. But how did matters appear from the American perspective? This is not the place to analyze in any detail colonial responses to the British army. Nonetheless, in a struggle in which the allegiance of the Americans was held to be vital, what they themselves perceived to be the dominant strain in the army's thought and practice is obviously important. Did they believe that they were treated in a moderate and mild fashion or with severity? It could be argued that the message conveyed to them was confusing in the extreme. After all, severity and leniency were used in different areas at different times, though neither was given a full trial. Any contemporary trying to summarize the British approach would therefore have been justified in finding it studded with contradictions. These contradictions seem to have left Americans largely unaffected, however, for most of them appear to have seen the British policy as straightforward and unambiguous. Staunch loyalists might complain that they were neglected and slighted while Revolutionaries were treated with unnecessary generosity,[125] but patriotically inclined, neutral, undecided, and uncommitted opinion tended to view the British as inordinately harsh.

Of course it was not always the activities of self-proclaimed hard-liners that made Americans think this way. The decisions of the commanders in chief sometimes gave serious offense, as when Howe, in accordance with customary wartime practice, ordered houses immediately outside the British lines at Philadelphia to be leveled to deprive the patriot forces of cover.[126] Americans were also roused by actions of careless or bullying officers whose views on the way in which the war should be fought are unknown—officers such as Lt. Lord William Murray of the Forty-second Foot, whom Phebe Pemberton accused of treating her tenants with "barbirous unbecoming behaviyour, very unworthy of a British Nobleman and Officer," and Ens. George Stewart of the Eighty-second, who ordered his men to break into John Somendike's New York storehouse and dump

---

[124] Wemyss to Cornwallis, Sept. 20, 1780, P.R.O. 30/11/64, 92. For similar activities elsewhere see Tarleton to Clinton, July 2, 1779, C.O. 5/98, 128; Maj. William Gardner to Augustine Prevost, Feb. 4, 1779, P.R.O. 30/55/15.

[125] For instance, Rev. Samuel Seabury to Dr. Myles Cooper, Feb. 9, Nov. 15, 1777, Fettercairn Papers, box 75, Natl. Lib. Scotland, and "Journal of Rev. Joshua Wingate Weeks, Loyalist Rector of St. Michael's Church, Marblehead, 1778-1779," *Essex Institute Historical Collections*, LII (1916), 10.

[126] "The Diary of Robert Morton," *Pennsylvania Magazine of History and Biography*, I (1877), 30; Thomas Parke to James Pemberton, Dec. 3, 1777, Pemberton Papers, Vol. XXXI, 50, Hist. Soc. Pa.

his merchandise into the street to make room for the regimental baggage.[127]

But if the hard-liners were not solely responsible for making the British appear committed to severity, without their activities it is difficult to conceive that this impression could have been conveyed so forcefully to so many Americans. By their very nature, the burning of homes and laying waste of farms made a deeper, more lasting impact than all the kindness and consideration displayed by conciliatory officers. Taking South Carolina as an illustration, the actions of Tarleton and Wemyss can be said to have overshadowed the efforts of McLeroth, who was made to appear as an admirable exception rather than an example of British moderation and leniency. The patriot press, which enjoyed unchallenged access to Americans outside the areas held by the British, naturally enhanced the notoriety of the hard-liners by providing a regular diet of tales of destruction, insult, and injury experienced at the hands of the king's troops. It was largely owing to the severity of hard-liners, whether reported in the newspapers, passed on orally, or personally suffered, that the army was styled by Americans as a set of men who "mark their own way with ruin and devastation," as "merciless Tyrants," "barbarians," and "our Cruel Enemies."[128] John Lucas of Maryland, writing to his brother-in-law after the war had finished, expressed a lament that can stand as an epitaph to the failure of both the commanders in chief and the conciliatory officers to impose their ideas on the army as a whole. "I cou'd never have believed," he announced with barely diminished outrage, "that Old England wou'd have descended to such a mean, barbarous way of carrying on a war."[129]

[127] Phebe Pemberton to Murray, Feb. 14, 1778, Pemberton Papers, XXXI, 122; Capt. Edward Williams to Somendike, Sept. 2, 1779, to Stewart, Sept. 2, 1779, Mil. Doc. 963, II, 31-32, Royal Artillery Inst.

[128] Quoting from Cornelia Bell to Andrew Bell, Jan. 30, 1777, in J. Lawrence Boggs, "The Cornelia (Bell) Paterson Letters," N.J. Hist. Soc., Procs., XV (1930), 511; Lt. Samuel Tirrell to Garrett Minor, Sept. 30, 1781, Garrett Minor Papers, Lib. Cong.; Elizabeth Ambler to Mildred Dudley, n.d., Elizabeth Jacquelin (Ambler) Carrington Papers, Lib. Cong.; Evert Byvanck to John Byvanck and Garret Abeel, Jan. 28, 1777, Byvanck Papers, New York State Lib.

[129] Lucas to Ferdinand Huddleston, Nov. 7, 1783, Huddleston of Sawston Correspondence, 488/C2/L21, Cambridgeshire Record Office, Cambridge.

Pennsylvania Rifle: Revolutionary Weapon in A Conventional War?

AT THE beginning of the War for Independence, leading Americans confidently expected the Pennsylvania rifle to help them secure a swift victory. This firearm, perfected well over a decade before the Revolution, was to become, temporarily at least, a source of fierce national pride; many assumed it would give the American soldier a ready-made advantage over his musket-toting British counterpart. The Pennsylvania rifle, with its peculiar characteristics adapted to and evolved from the frontier experience, stood then and continues to stand as a monument to colonial ingenuity. As one writer penned effusively, the rifle "was the truest kind of American invention, the certain product of an American culture."[1]

Popularizers of the rifle have been numerous and vocal. They paint a picture of colonial riflemen—rough-hewn giants of the primordial forest—marching forth to vanquish the minions of George III in more or less the same manner they furthered the course of westward empire. What riflemen did in the woodlands to advance civilization they did on the seaboard to ward off defeat from behind, or so the story goes.

However, filiopietistic notions about the rifle have been shattered, the myth of its pervasive significance all but dispelled. Still, there is a mystique associated with the rifle, perhaps because it is so often thought of in connection with native American genius. True, the rifle did not play as important a role as its protagonists once claimed. Nevertheless, it had a potential almost untapped during the war.

---

1 Roger Burlingame, *March of the Iron Men* (New York, 1938), 121, who is echoed in John A. Kouwenhoven, *Made in America* (New York, 1948), 17–18. Like statements can be found in William J. Heller, "The Gunmakers of Old Northampton," *Pennsylvania German Society Publications*, XVII (1908), 6; Harry P. Davis, *A Forgotten Heritage* (Huntington, W. Va., 1941), 82–93.

302

Though by no means a superweapon, it could have been used more effectively. That it was not is a commentary on the social nature of invention and technological innovation, for a new weapon is of limited value unless there is a new doctrine to go along with it, and an industrial sector capable of producing it. A combination of factors, from military conservatism and industrial incapacity to an inability to see how the rifle could and should be improved, militated against its use. The rifle's peculiar wartime career can be traced to attitudinal and institutional restraints on technology in general and invention in particular in preindustrial America. Attitudinally, since American political and military leaders were unaccustomed to viewing invention as part of a larger technological and social hierarchy, they did not know how the rifle could best be used, or if its use would prove more disruptive than productive. Institutionally, the rebellious colonies lacked the managerial experience with large-scale production and centralized bureaucracy necessary to build a munitions industry from scratch. The rifle, then, serves as a fine example of the technological limitations of preindustrial America.

The superiority of rifled gun barrels had first been discovered in the late fifteenth or early sixteenth centuries by gunsmiths in central Europe. Whether by accident or experiment they found that a gun barrel scored with spiraling lands (high points) and grooves (depressions) was much more accurate than a smoothbore weapon. Spinning motion imparted to a bullet made it fly truer, cutting down on loss of velocity and propensity to windage.[2] Rifles consequently spread from the forests of Germany to other parts of Europe, as hunters preferred this more accurate weapon.[3]

---

2 Robert Held, *The Age of Firearms* (New York, 1957), 138. In 1635 the first patent for rifling was granted in England; see James F. Severn, "The Rifled Bore, Its Development and Early Employment," *The American Rifleman*, CX (March 1962), 30. Benjamin Robins was probably the first Englishman to make extensive experiments with rifled pieces, however. For his report to the Royal Society of July 2, 1747, in which he predicted the rifle would revolutionize warfare, see James Wilson, ed., *The Mathematical Tracts of the Late Benjamin Robins* (London, 1761), I, 328-341.

3 Greased patches were not widely used in Europe until later because many subscribed to the "retarding and resisting" theory of rifling, which postulated that improved velocity and range came from the friction and compression generated when the ball was mashed down by a mallet. Held, *Age of Firearms*, 139; Henry J. Kauffman, *The Pennsylvania-Kentucky Rifle* (Harrisburg, 1960), 2.

167

Militarily, however, rifles saw little use in Europe until well after the American Revolution. Prior to the Napoleonic wars, rifles were used primarily by irregulars and light infantry—such as German *jaegers*—to shield columns of musket- and bayonet-equipped regulars. European military dogma emphasized "brute strength and cold steel," thereby relegating the sniping warfare of riflemen to a secondary status.[4]

German immigrants first introduced rifles to the American colonies around 1700. Rifle production, in fact, began as a Pennsylvania monopoly, but by 1750 rifles were common in frontier communities along the length of the Alleghenies. Just prior to the Revolution shops had spread to Baltimore, Maryland; Alexandria, Cumberland, Winchester and Richmond, Virginia; Camden, South Carolina; Salisbury and Augusta, Georgia; and a few Pennsylvania gunsmiths reportedly migrated to western New York.[5]

The rifle went through a metamorphosis in colonial America, and differed strikingly from its European forebear. A few years after importation it became obvious a number of changes were desirable if not absolutely necessary to adapt the rifle to American conditions. Thus, colonial gunsmiths made basic alterations in rifle construction, leading to a distinctively American archetype peculiarly suited to American life.

Backwoodsmen complained that the short and heavy rifles used in central Europe, weighing close to twenty pounds, were incompatible with their needs. And since most hunted out of necessity, not love of sport, they wanted an even more accurate weapon. Gunsmiths accordingly lengthened the barrel to increase accuracy. In addition, they reduced the caliber and exterior barrel dimensions

4 J. F. C. Fuller, *British Light Infantry in the Eighteenth Century* (London, 1925), 46–70 *passim*.

5 Felix Reichmann, "The Pennsylvania Rifle: A Social Interpretation of Changing Military Techniques," *Pennsylvania Magazine of History and Biography*, LXIX (1945), 314; Carlton O. Wittlinger, "The Small Arms Industry in Lancaster County, 1710–1840," *Pennsylvania History*, XXIV (1957), 121–136; John C. Dillin, *The Kentucky Rifle* (Washington, 1924); Horace Kephart, "The Rifle in Colonial Times," *Magazine of History*, XXIV (1890), 79–81; Kauffman, *Pennsylvania-Kentucky Rifle*, 8–31; Francis Jordan, *The Life of William Henry* (Lancaster, 1910), 3–55 *passim*; Charles W. Sawyer, *Firearms in American History* (Boston, 1910), 153–157; Townsend Whelen, *The American Rifle* (New York, 1918), 6; Harold L. Peterson, *Arms and Armor in Colonial America* (Harrisburg, 1956), 155.

to cut down on weight. Hunters who traveled long distances on foot for extended periods appreciated this last modification in particular. Greased patch and hickory ramrod totally eclipsed mallet and iron ramrod because the patch-wrapped bullet took less time to load and helped guard against the accumulation of fouled powder in the barrel. Quick repetition of fire was indispensable for hunting, but was even more essential for the hit-and-run tactics of Indian warfare, and such warfare was a frontier fact of life. Colonial riflemakers also made dozens of minor alterations, from casting thicker trigger guards to selecting choice native hardwoods like curly maple and cherry for gunstocks.

These improvements enhanced the rifle's growing reputation as a precision firearm. It outstripped the smoothbore musket in accuracy and sophistication of design. Yet the musket was by far the most commonly used weapon during the American Revolution and for several decades after. On first observation this seems inexplicable. Muskets were accurate up to a range of eighty yards. Rifles, on the other hand, were deadly at thrice that distance. Muskets generally had a larger bore, but what the rifle surrendered in knockdown power it more than made up for in ease of carrying.

Pound for pound, a rifle was more efficient. Still, the musket had three advantages. First, it could use coarser powder; because cleaning fouled powder out of a grooved barrel was difficult, riflemen chose their powder carefully. Second, most rifles were made according to the users' specifications, not a uniform design. Riflemen consequently prepared their own cartridges, usually on the spot. Muskets were more "standardized"—the term is applied loosely here—hence musket-carrying soldiers often fired prepared cartridges. And they could ordinarily load more quickly since they did not have to worry about a snug fit. Third, and perhaps most important, muskets generally came complete with bayonets while rifles did not. Though uneven powder quality could only be eliminated with improved production, standardizing rifles and equipping them with bayonets posed technological obstacles no greater than those posed by musket production. But as will be seen, problems associated with introducing rifles into the American army derived as much from mental as from physical obstacles.

Despite their drawbacks, muskets were admirably suited to the

169

volley fire tactics of the day. After two or three exchanges of gunfire, European military thinkers believed bayonets should decide the ultimate fate of battle, so their manual of arms dealt only superficially with the proper aiming and firing of muskets. Many tacticians viewed muskets as merely convenient handles for bayonets. European footsoldiers were accordingly trained to fight in a solid line arrayed in an open field, ready at any moment for the tide-turning thrust of "cold steel." The individualistic type of warfare practiced by irregulars in Europe and riflemen in America "did not fit into the eighteenth century European pattern, and European habits died hard."[6]

In a war where the enemy preferred to follow traditional precepts, backwoods riflemen were confronted by their antithesis. Riflemen fought a mobile style of war, putting a premium on expert shooting—not massed volley fire, concealment, not open field formation, and quick movement, not the measured cadence of a linear assault. American rifles lacked bayonets, since bayonets represented a different martial philosophy, a philosophy of limited worth in the forest. Rifles could easily be adapted to take bayonets, but that did not mean the rifleman's performance against the British would improve correspondingly. Differences in fighting techniques went much deeper, as musket and rifle symbolized antipodal approaches to war. The American rifle had evolved from a different set of demands, a different mode of life. During the Revolution frontier riflemen faced something alien to their understanding; adjusting to the situation unnerved many and proved impossible for others.

Neither the riflemen nor their admirers knew this at the outset of the war; realization came only with time. Thus, when need arose for volunteers to assist the New Englanders laying siege to Boston, Patriot leaders turned to the riflemen. George Washington thought they would make excellent soldiers. Remembering his experiences with Braddock and the limitations of regulars in forest warfare, he looked to independent-minded riflemen, expecting them to form the core of a Continental Army. Numerous congressional delegates shared Washington's faith. Richard Henry Lee boasted that Fin-

---

6 Eric Robson, "The Armed Forces and the Art of War," *The New Cambridge Modern History*, VII (Cambridge, England, 1957), 174.

castle County and five other western Virginia counties could raise 1,000 riflemen each, all of whom could hit an orange from 200 yards.[7] John Hancock had not yet met a rifleman, but the guarantees of Pennsylvania, Maryland, and Virginia leaders made him their champion. "They are the finest marksmen in the world," he exclaimed, "they do execution of their Rifle Guns at an amazing distance."[8]

Consequently, on June 14, 1775, Congress resolved that "six companies of expert riflemen, be immediately raised in Pennsylvania, two in Maryland, and two in Virginia."[9] Counties along the Susquehanna River in Pennsylvania seemed to be overrun with eager volunteers, so Congress amended that state's quota from six to eight companies, those eight companies to be formed into an independent Pennsylvania Rifle Regiment. Even then Lancaster County had too many volunteers, so it organized two companies. Congress gave its assent, and the rifle regiment went from eight companies to nine.[10] Meanwhile Virginia and Maryland had no difficulty in bringing their four companies to strength; volunteers were swarming in as they had in Pennsylvania. The Virginians in particular were reputed to be fierce warriors, many having seen action in Lord Dunmore's War. In all, over 1,250 riflemen marched to Boston when Congress had originally called for slightly less than 1,000.

Congress made certain the companies were outfitted in grand style, allocating $15,000 for the Pennsylvania Rifle Regiment's expenses. At Reading and other towns along the route to Massachusetts the men received new rifles, knapsacks, blankets and canteens. Marylanders and Virginians enjoyed the same treatment.[11]

Riflemen caused a stir in each town they passed through. A Baltimore resident reported that Daniel Morgan's company of Virginians

---

[7] James C. Ballagh, ed., *The Letters of Richard Henry Lee* (New York, 1970), I, 130–131.

[8] Edmund C. Burnett, ed., *The Letters of the Members of the Continental Congress* (Washington, 1921–1936), I, 134.

[9] Worthington C. Ford, ed., *The Journals of the Continental Congress, 1774–1789* (Washington, 1904–1937), II, 89.

[10] *Ibid.*, II, 104, 173.

[11] "The Journal of Aaron Wright," *Boston Evening Transcript*, Apr. 11, 1862, p. 1; Thompson's itemized expenses in Peter Force, ed., *American Archives*, 4th series (Washington 1837–1853), 1045–1046; Daniel Morgan's in Ford, ed., *Journals*, III, 267, 319–320, 329, 370.

looked "truly martial, their spirits amazingly elated, breathing nothing but a desire . . . to engage the enemies of American liberty."[12] The *Boston Gazette* noted the arrival of the riflemen in August, describing them as "an excellent Body of Troops . . . heartily disposed to prosecute, with the utmost Vigour, the Noble Cause in which they are engaged."[13] And the speed with which the companies made their trek boosted their reputation, the Pennsylvanians from Cumberland County covering 441 miles in twenty-six days.[14]

Rifleman attire astounded New Englanders. Most wore buckskin breeches, some with belts of wampum tied around the top. Almost all had on wool or linen hunting shirts, ranging from ash-colored to deep brown or dark grey. A few sported mocassins ornately decorated with porcupine quills. Tomahawk, hunting knife, soft felt hat, powder horn and bullet pouch completed their garb.[15] Washington would have preferred that the whole army be so attired, not only because of lightness and natural camouflage, but also because it would help remove "those Provincial distinctions which lead to Jealousy and Dissatisfaction." Besides, the British would fear everyone so dressed as a deadly marksman.[16]

At Washington's behest the riflemen displayed their sharpshooting skills at Cambridge, as they had at various points along their line of march. They purportedly gave an extraordinary show of accuracy with their weapons, hitting a mark from 200 yards—some doing this while on the "quick advance." Others struck targets seven inches in diameter from a range of 250 yards.[17] Leaving their audience agape,

12 *Virginia Gazette* (Purdie), Aug. 19, 1775.

13 *Boston Gazette and Country Journal*, Aug. 14, 1775.

14 George Morison, "Journal of the Expedition to Quebec," in Kenneth Rogers, ed., *March to Quebec* (Garden City, 1938), 506–508; flattering pieces on the riflemen are in Horace Kephart, "The Birth of the American Army," *Harper's Monthly Magazine*, XCVIII (May 1899), 961–970; William W. Edwards, "Morgan and His Riflemen," *William and Mary Quarterly*, 2nd series, XXIII (1914), 73–106; also see Henry J. Young, "The Spirit of 1775," *John and Mary's Journal*, no. 1 (March 1975).

15 John Joseph Henry, *Account of Arnold's Campaign Against Quebec* (Albany, 1877), 11; James Thacher, *Military Journal* (Hartford, 1862), 31; James Graham, *Life of Daniel Morgan* (New York, 1858), 63.

16 John C. Fitzpatrick, ed., *The Writings of George Washington* (Washington, 1932–1945), III, 325, 404, 415; V, 336; and II, 229, for Washington's feelings in 1758.

17 Thacher, *Military Journal*, 31; earlier demonstration by a Virginia company in Force, ed., *American Archives*, 4th series, III, 2; "Diary of John Harrower, 1773-1776," *American Historical Review*, VI (1900), 100.

they bivouacked in a special area, and were exempted from routine duties. Washington, it would appear, wanted to put his model soldiers on display.

Initially, riflemen caused a furor within the British lines, British sentries not being accustomed to their deadly sniping. Catching their opponents napping, nefarious "rebel" sharpshooters picked off the careless and unwary by long-range shots or in twilight sorties. Patriot newspapers gleefully followed their exploits.[18] The propaganda value of the rifle aside, however, British soldiers in general adjusted to their menace and stayed safely out of sight behind breastworks. It did not take long for some American officers to discover that their great expectations were ill-founded, both as a result of rifleman temperament and the state of affairs at Boston.

Riflemen proved to be a mixed bag. Camp life was dull, forays and skirmishes with the British infrequent and even less consequential. With their highly touted weapons practically neutralized by siege tactics, some enlisted personnel grew bored and sullen. Their tempestuous dispositions vexed Washington and his staff, causing admiration in August to give way to criticism in October. Raucous and unlettered frontiersmen ignored military protocol, and their pretentiousness caused resentment. After a mob of Pennsylvanians broke a companion out of the Prospect Hill guardhouse, observers gave vent to their disgust. A New Englander characterized riflemen as "mutinous" and "vicious"; General Charles Lee "damned them and wished them all in Boston"; while Washington "said he wished they had never come."[19] Benjamin Thompson, later Count

---

[18] *New York Journal,* Aug. 17, 1775; Caleb Haskell, "Diary at the Siege of Boston and on the March to Quebec," in Roberts, ed., *March to Quebec,* 467, 468–472; Fitzpatrick, ed., *Writings of Washington,* III, 393–394; IV, 84; William Heath, *Memoirs* (Boston, 1798), 18; Frank Moore, ed., *The Diary of the American Revolution* (Hartford, 1876), 119–120.

[19] Prospect Hill incident in Henry S. Commager and Richard B. Morris, eds., *The Spirit of Seventy-Six* (New York, 1967), 156–157; Fitzpatrick, ed., *Writings of Washington,* III, 490–491. Derisive comments are in the Adams Papers, Massachusetts Historical Society microfilm: Artemus Ward to John Adams, Oct. 30, 1775, I, 92 (reel 345); John Thomas to John Adams, Oct. 24, 1775, I, 10 (reel 345); Samuel Osgood to John Adams, Oct. 25, 1775, I, 103 (reel 345). Adding substance to the charges, see the list of deserters from the rifle companies in the George Washington Papers, Library of Congress microfilm, series 4, entry of Oct. 23, 1775 (reel 34). And it would seem that not all of the riflemen were truly marksmen, as some were weeded out and sent home. Fitzpatrick, ed., *Writings of Washington,* III, 490; and muster rolls in Force, ed., *American Archives,* 4th series, III, 253–254; IV, 491–492.

Rumford, scoffed "of all useless sets of men that ever encumbered an army, surely the boasted riflemen are . . . the most so."[20] Indeed, riflemen had done little to warrant the confidence many, especially the disappointed Washington, had in them.

Yet Washington realized, if somewhat belatedly, that Boston was not the best place to test the rifle's effectiveness, for light infantry tactics based on mobility could not be used there. Even though disappointed in the behavior of some enlisted men in the rifle companies, he kept his faith in their weapon. Accordingly, on January 1, 1776, the Pennsylvania Rifle Regiment was redesignated the First Regiment of the Army of the United Colonies, reflecting Washington's desire to mold his army around the riflemen. And that same month Congress directed Pennsylvania to raise five new Continental regiments, specifying that each regiment have one company of riflemen.[21] Both Washington and Congress wanted riflemen to comprise a significant portion of the "national" army. Apparently they still hoped to capitalize on the rifle's inherent superiorities.

Congress recognized that sending more than 1,200 riflemen to Boston merely skimmed the surface of a vast reservoir. Riflemen appeared in abundance in the Continental and militia levies assembled in 1775 and 1776 from New York to Georgia. Pennsylvania, for example, raised an additional 1,000 riflemen for state service in March 1776.[22] In short, there were many more rifles available, and many more riflemen under arms, than is normally appreciated.

Yet it cannot be assumed that because there were more riflemen in the Continental Army and state militia than is commonly conceded, the rifle's significance has been likewise slighted. The mediocre record of Continental riflemen at Boston has been noted. Three of those rifle companies later went on the Quebec expedition. Instead of filling their enemy with dread, most of the riflemen were taken prisoner. Because they fought along narrow streets in a drizzling downpour, they held no noticeable advantage over their opponents. On the contrary, faster loading, less temperamental

---

20 Commager and Morris, eds., *Spirit of Seventy-Six*, 155.

21 Ford, ed., *Journals*, IV, 29. The regiment's title changed to the First Regiment of the Pennsylvania Line in July 1776, when a state numbering system was adopted.

22 Force, ed., *American Archives*, 4th series, V, 677, 681, 1225; William Henry Egle, ed., *Pennsylvania in the War of the Revolution* (Harrisburg, 1890), I, 263.

muskets equipped with bayonets were better for house-to-house fighting. The edge riflemen might have enjoyed if the battle had been fought in the open was negated once they passed within the city walls. Rather than exploiting their weapon's superiorities, they became victims of its inadequacies. Rifles had to be employed more imaginatively to be effective, otherwise all of the patriots would have been better off with muskets and bayonets.

Continental riflemen in South Carolina compiled a slightly better record than their counterparts further north. When Sir Henry Clinton made his bid to take Charleston in June 1776, South Carolina riflemen acquitted themselves well. Indeed, Charles Lee, commanding at Charleston, showed that the source of his irritation in Boston had been riflemen, not their rifles. He counted heavily on this weapon because "the enemy entertain a most fortunate apprehension of American riflemen."[23] They did not have much of a chance to prove their mettle, but they did prevent an amphibious assault from turning the flank of Fort Sullivan.[24]

Interestingly enough, militia in Virginia and North Carolina made the first significant use of the rifle. In December 1775, Virginia riflemen turned out with other Virginia troops to maul a combined British and Loyalist force at Great Bridge. Three months later North Carolina riflemen trounced a column of Loyalists at the battle of Moore's Creek Bridge.[25] At both engagements the Patriots picked the site of battle, fought from concealment, left themselves an easy line of retreat, and, because their opponents had to approach along a narrow front, their accurate fire held sway. The Virginians and North Carolinians maximized the rifle's advantages and avoided a situation where its lack of a bayonet and slowness of loading would be factors.

Until the raising of a special corps under Daniel Morgan in 1777, Continental riflemen rarely had such opportunities. And while

[23] Jared Sparks, ed., *Correspondence of the American Revolution* (Freeport, 1970), II, 501–502.

[24] Edward McCrady, *The History of South Carolina in the Revolution* (New York, 1969), I, 152–153.

[25] Great Bridge in Force, ed., *American Archives*, 4th series, IV, 501–502; William Gordon, *The History of the Rise, Progress and Establishment of the Independence of the United States* (London, 1788), II, 111–113; Moore's Creek Bridge in Gordon, *History*, II, 209.

Morgan's contingent is often pointed to as the high-water mark for riflemen during the war, rifles were already being phased out several months earlier. In terms of numbers, there were never more riflemen in the Army than in the summer of 1776. The New York campaign would be the last time riflemen comprised a substantial portion of the Army. Washington had perhaps 2,000 riflemen at New York. Present were some New York militia riflemen, the original Pennsylvania Rifle Regiment (less two companies taken at Quebec), a new (though incomplete) regiment of Virginians and Marylanders, two Pennsylvania state rifle regiments, plus rifle companies in each Pennsylvania and Virginia line regiment. Washington, having forgiven the sins of the riflemen at Boston, would have liked to have had more. At his request Congress induced the original Pennsylvania riflemen—"a valuable and brave body of men"—to re-enlist for a bounty.[26] Washington and Congress, then, still intended to keep riflemen a significant part of the Continental Army. Considering the way those riflemen were used, one might wonder why.

American commanders on Long Island, for example, did not use them effectively. Riflemen accounted for fully one-third of the 2,800 front-line troops stationed there in August 1776, but they were split into small groups. When General William Howe seized the initiative and a British and Hessian column outflanked the American defenses, riflemen and their musket-carrying companions fled or were taken. Most riflemen had no chance to capitalize on their superior range because of the unexpectedness of the British move.[27] One participant noted that German *jaegers*, like American riflemen, did not have bayonets. But unlike Americans, *jaegers* were skilled in linear as well as irregular tactics.[28] Psychologically unprepared to deal with bayonet-wielding regulars, numerous riflemen simply broke and ran. German mercenaries therefore dismissed

26 Fitzpatrick, ed., *Writings of Washington*, IV, 501–502. The original Pennsylvania Rifle Regiment (now the First Regiment of the Pennsylvania Line) was severely understrength, however—see Force, ed., *American Archives*, 5th series, I, 331–332. Attempts to raise new companies in Ford, ed., *Journals*, V, 473; understrength character of the Virginia-Maryland regiment in Fitzpatrick, ed., *Writings of Washington*, V, 202, 216; Burnett, ed., *Letters*, I, 518.

27 Henry Johnston, *The Campaign of 1776 Around New York and Brooklyn* (Brooklyn, 1878), 64–65; Force, ed., *American Archives*, 5th series, I, 1213–1214; Commager and Morris, eds., *Spirit of Seventy-Six*, 433–440.

28 Johnston, *Campaign*, part 2 (documents), 50.

them as contemptible. "Riflemen were mostly spitted to the trees with bayonets," jeered a Hessian officer, "these frightful people deserve more pity than fear."[29] A British officer later wrote that his comrades went out "rebel hunting" at night. Before unlucky riflemen could reload after their first shot they were "run through . . . as a rifleman is not entitled to any quarter."[30] Whatever mystique had been formerly associated with their prowess had rapidly worn off.

Admittedly, riflemen fared somewhat better on Manhattan Island than they had on Long Island, winning a few minor skirmishes.[31] Skirmishes, however, did not alter the course of the campaign. Washington abandoned Manhattan, moved up to White Plains, crossed into New Jersey and ultimately retreated into Pennsylvania. The Maryland and Virginia rifle regiment did not make the trip. It fell captive to the British, along with the rest of the garrison left isolated at Fort Washington by the main army's withdrawal. The dogged resistance of those riflemen turned out to be one of the few bright spots during the siege of Fort Washington. They fought in open order in hilly terrain north of the fort, inflicting frightening casualties among their attackers by a sniping fire. But because the Hudson was on their flank they could not withdraw and they eventually laid down their arms.[32] Tactically, they fought as was their wont; strategically, the British dictated the terms of battle.

Washington ended 1776 with the tattered remnants of an army. His victory at Trenton and fortunate escape through Princeton left him mulling over his prospects for the coming year. Of the 2,000 or so riflemen in the army six months earlier, less than a quarter remained. A growing number of officers agitated for their elimination altogether. Peter Muhlenberg, colonel of a Pennsylvania line regiment, requested that the men in his command be uniformly armed

29 Edward J. Lowell, *The Hessians* (Port Washington, 1965), 65–66.

30 Moore, ed., *Diary of the American Revolution*, 349–350.

31 Riflemen skirmishes at Harlem Heights in Commager and Morris, eds., *Spirit of Seventy-Six*, 470–471; Johnston, *Campaign*, part 2 (documents), 86–87; Johnston, *The Battle of Harlem Heights* (New York, 1970), 54–55; Fitzpatrick, ed., *Writings of Washington*, VI, 146, 179; Throg's Neck in Christopher Ward, *The War of the Revolution* (New York, 1952), I, 255; Heath, *Memoirs*, 59–60; Mamaroneck in Lowell, *The Hessians*, 75–76.

32 Alexander Graydon, *Memoirs of His Own Times* (New York, 1969), 192–202; John W. Fortescue, *A History of the British Army* (London, 1899–1920), III, 191–193.

with muskets.[33] Anthony Wayne complained "I don't like rifles— I would rather face an Enemy with a good Musket and Bayonet without ammunition." If Wayne had his way he would see "Rifles Intirely laid Aside."[34] The Board of War hesitated to accept any new rifle companies. If enough muskets had been available, it "would speedily reduce the number of rifles" and replace them with muskets, "as they are more easily kept in order, can be fired oftener, and have the advantage of bayonets." Washington joined the Board of War and his subordinate officers in favoring a substitution of muskets for rifles in line regiments.[35]

Riflemen, in a sense, became scapegoats for defects in the American Army in general. Most American soldiers, not just riflemen, could not match British regulars. For both military and political reasons the Continental Army had not fought a truly "revolutionary" war. Whether or not Washington and Congress had ever intended to is debatable. If not, then their reliance on riflemen seems to have been based on the misconception that bayonetless rifles and backwoodsmen unappreciative of linear tactics could be all things to all people. As time wore on the army became more conservative in form and function. Thus, in the winter of 1777–1778, esteem for the rifle reached its nadir. That winter spent at Valley Forge witnessed significant changes in the American Army. Rifles had steadily fallen in reputation since the halcyon days of 1775, but wholesale disavowal of those weapons came only with the teachings of General Baron Wilhelm von Steuben.

Von Steuben sought to professionalize an amateurish army. The wide variety of weapons in American regiments—muskets, rifles, carbines, and fowling pieces—dismayed him. He corrected that by eliminating everything but bayonet-equipped muskets, insofar as

---

[33] Muhlenberg to Washington, Feb. 23, 1777, Washington Papers, series 4 (reel 40); also see John W. Wright, "The Rifle in the American Revolution," *American Historical Review*, XXIX (1924), 293–299.

[34] Wayne to the Board of War, June 3, 1777, Anthony Wayne Papers, III, 89, Historical Society of Pennsylvania.

[35] Force, ed., *American Archives*, 5th series, II, 1247; Wayne to Richard Peters, Feb. 8, 1778, Wayne Papers, IV, 78. Also see the letter of Col. William Thompson of South Carolina requesting that most of his rifles be replaced with muskets in Burnett, ed., *Letters*, II, 452.

stocks on hand would allow. He taught the manual of arms, platoon volley fire, and proper use of the bayonet.[36]

The "new" American army emerging in the spring of 1778 was an army built around von Steuben's staid European principles. He deserves credit for transforming "rag, tag and bobtail" into a cohesive, disciplined fighting force. Yet his improvements entailed a rejection of most facets of native American warfare, a retrogression to "tried and true" fundamentals of eighteenth-century European warfare.

Von Steuben merely formalized an already present tendency. Prior to 1778 American military leaders had not implemented a systematic approach to war. A smattering of English, French, and German textbook procedures had been meshed with dicta of frontier warfare to produce soldiers comfortable with neither. Inclusion of riflemen in the Continental Army in 1775 and 1776 reflected Washington's desire to integrate the best aspects of frontier warfare into his battlefield tactics. Integration failed, however. Washington had men adept at linear tactics or irregular tactics, but few proficient at both. Riflemen were the least prepared to face the British, not because they did not know how to fight, but because they only knew how to fight in one particular fashion. Those most inclined to use rifles were also the least inclined to fight British regulars on the latter's terms. When faced with a crumbling army, American leaders understandably fell back on European techniques instead of experimenting with something new. In 1778 Charles Lee proposed an alternative to the von Steuben plan, but by then the trend could not be reversed.[37]

A new approach would have required a more eclectic borrowing from European and American military experience. Back in 1757, New England pastor Gad Hitchcock proposed just such a mixture. Hitchcock stressed that the well-trained colonial ought to be adept at both European and Indian warfare. He should "not be unacquainted with the Methods of War that are practised by the

---

36 John M. Palmer, *General Von Steuben* (New Haven, 1937), 140, 151–157; enthusiastic reception of von Steuben's modifications noted in Timothy Pickering to Congress, Papers of the Continental Congress, National Archives microfilm, Item 147, III, 143 (reel 158).

37 Lee in the Lee Papers, *Collections of the New-York Historical Society*, II (1872), 383–389.

Enemy"; he should be able to "fight skillfully, either in the Wilderness or the field."[38] Though addressing himself to prospective militiamen in the French and Indian War, Hitchcock might have offered the same advice in 1775. Hitchcock recommended putting the colonial soldier on a par with his foe, be he Indian or European. The rifle would have given an added dimension. A bayonet-equipped rifle would have held the upper hand, its users fighting at long range whenever possible, but able to deal with the British their way if necessary.

Daniel Morgan's special rifle corps was the closest the Continental Army came to filling Hitchcock's prescription. In June 1777, Washington authorized Morgan to assemble a light infantry regiment of 500 riflemen.[39] The hulking Virginian scoured the ranks and selected men primarily from Pennsylvania and his home state. (Considering the difficulty Morgan had in finding rifles, the new regiment probably stripped the main army of them.) Morgan's Rifle Corps was treated as an elite body, as indeed it was. Some of the men in the regiment had marched with the original rifle companies to Boston in 1775, and had since been seasoned by experience. Though none had modified their guns to take bayonets, they were not as prone to panic. Henry Knox, in fact, valued the regiment as the most "respectable body of Continental troops that were ever in America."[40]

In August Washington detached the Rifle Corps and sent it to assist the northern army under General Horatio Gates, informing Governor Clinton of New York that Morgan's men were the "pick of the army." He asked Israel Putnam to exaggerate the number of men with Morgan, hoping Indians serving with Burgoyne, on his way down the Hudson, would lose heart and go home.[41]

---

[38] Gad Hitchcock, *Sermon* (Boston, 1757), 12. For the conventional, nonrevolutionary character of the war see John Shy's essays "American Strategy: Charles Lee and the Radical Alternative," and "The Military Conflict Considered as a Revolutionary War," both reprinted in his *A People Numerous and Armed* (New York, 1976), 132-162, 193-224.

[39] Fitzpatrick, ed., *Writings of Washington*, VIII, 156, 236-237, 246; flattering assessment of Morgan's unit in Henry Carrington, *Battles of the American Revolution, 1775-1781* (New York, 1877), 61-62.

[40] Commager and Morris, eds., *Spirit of Seventy-Six*, 537.

[41] Fitzpatrick, ed., *Writings of Washington*, IX, 70-71, 78, 82, 102.

At the battles of Freeman's Farm on September 19 and Bemis Heights on October 7, when Burgoyne tried desperately to turn Gates's flank, riflemen distinguished themselves again and again. Morgan and his regiment fought from concealment, letting loose a withering fire in both engagements. Burgoyne later confessed in testimony before the House of Commons that the riflemen slew an inordinate number of his officers, and caused dozens of Indians and Loyalist militia to desert.[42] William Digby of the Shropshire Regiment observed that at Freeman's Farm all but one of the officers in his regiment fell to the riflemen.[43] At Bemis Heights, a British sergeant lamented, "the riflemen from trees effected the death of numbers," including General Simon Fraser.[44]

Morgan's men bested light infantry, grenadiers, and *jaegers*, the cream of Burgoyne's army. Yet they did not fight alone. They had been reinforced by veteran units armed with muskets and bayonets. If not for their support the riflemen would have been driven from the field at least once during the fighting at Freeman's Farm. Thus Morgan's men may have been the catalyst bringing success in the Saratoga campaign, but they did not win it singlehandedly. After all, they constituted a small portion of Gates's 11,000-man army. And despite the lessons of two years of war, their guns could not take bayonets. Either riflemen refused to modify their weapons, fearing they would have to fight in close order, or Washington and his staff did not see how rifles could have been made more complete.

Morgan returned to the main Army a conquering hero. But, like the Army in general, his corps was decimated by the severe winter of 1777–1778 and several sharp actions with the British over that period. Finally, in July 1778, Washington sent a portion of the regiment west for frontier duty and disbanded the remainder, ordering the men to return to their old units. This not only ended

---

42 John Burgoyne, *A State of the Expedition From Canada* (London, 1780), 30, 102, 121–122. For commentaries on Morgan's unit and riflemen in general, see Don Higginbotham, *Daniel Morgan* (Chapel Hill, 1961), 16–77; John S. Pancake, *1777: The Year of the Hangman* (University, Ala., 1977), 82–83, 146–187.

43 Commager and Morris, eds., *Spirit of Seventy-Six*, 580; also see James Wilkinson, *Memoirs of My Own Times* (Philadelphia, 1816), I, 243–247.

44 Roger Lamb, *Memoirs of His Own Life* (Dublin, 1811), 199; also Thacher, *Military Journal*, 101–102; Charles Stedman, *The History of the Origin, Progress and Termination of the American War* (New York, 1969), I, 336–344.

the chapter on Morgan's contingent, it for all intents and purposes closed the book on the rifle in the Continental Army.[45] The irony of this was that it occurred less than a year after Morgan's Saratoga triumph.

Yet the days of Morgan's regiment had been numbered from the beginning. A special light infantry corps equipped with muskets and bayonets had been organized in July 1778. It would have been assembled earlier if trained men and adequate supplies had been available. Washington ordered each line battalion to organize a light infantry company, the individual companies in each battalion to combine as an independent regiment during campaigns.[46] In other words, Washington essentially reinstituted the system he had pushed for in 1775, except that he replaced riflemen with units armed and trained to fight in the same manner as regular line troops. Considering the tactics of the Continental Army by 1778, that seemed the logical decision. Washington overcame the handicap of having two types of soldiers—riflemen and musket-equipped regulars—in the same army. It was his formal announcement that the Continental Army was more European than American.

Disappearance from the Continental Army did not mean rifles were no longer used in the war. In the South, Continental riflemen were being phased out in favor of musket-armed regulars by 1777, as in the main army under Washington, but many of those men ended up in the partisan corps of Andrew Pickens, Francis Marion, and Thomas Sumter.

Southern militia, in fact, made the best long-term use of the rifle. Battle lines and full-scale engagements were few and far between, and the rifle finally came into its own. Riflemen won several victories. A small company of Virginians stunned Banastre Tarleton at

---

45 Fitzpatrick, ed., *Writings of Washington*, XII, 140, 200, 214, 284, 406; XIII, 110; XIV, 43; XVII, 85. The corps was not officially disbanded until Nov. 7, 1779, when the riflemen returned from western New York. The rifles were stored with the Commissary of Military Stores, not to be redistributed except by Washington's personal order. Two companies, about ninety men, served in 1780 and 1781 as special sharpshooters. *Ibid.*, XIX, 252, 379, 479; XX, 187, 402. A new regiment, never brought up to full strength, was organized for the Yorktown campaign, once again as a special sharpshooting unit. *Ibid.*, XXII, 257–258, 341, 426–427.

46 John W. Wright, "The Corps of Light Infantry in the Continental Army," *American Historical Review*, XXXI (1926), 454–461.

Wahab plantation.[47] Another band smashed a Loyalist force three times its size at Musgrove's Mills. Riflemen in the Deep South participated in every action from Fort Watson to Ninety-Six, to the last pitched battle at Eutaw Springs in September 1781.[48] Militia riflemen, many of them veterans of the defunct Continental rifle regiments, turned out to fight at Cowpens and Guilford Courthouse, and later marched alongside Lafayette in Virginia.[49]

Riflemen fought most successfully at King's Mountain in October 1780 and Hannah's Cowpens in January 1781. At the former, approximately 1,100 Tennesseans, North Carolinians, and Virginians, most if not all of whom carried rifles, crushed a slightly smaller but similarly armed Loyalist army in the largest single action of the war between two bodies of riflemen. The Loyalists, many of whom had modified their weapons to take bayonets, tried to decide the battle with a headlong charge that the Patriots parried by dispersing and fighting from concealment.[50] Giving way before the Loyalist onslaught, the backwoodsmen cut their opponents to pieces, winning convincingly with well-directed fire.[51] At the Cowpens, Daniel Morgan successfully mixed rifle with line tactics. His Virginia, North Carolina, and Georgia riflemen, knowing they were buttressed by Delaware and Maryland Continentals, poured a galling preliminary fire into the British before withdrawing to the rear. Nonetheless, Morgan's victory over Banastre Tarleton resulted as much from good fortune as sound tactics. If not for a sudden wheeling movement and bayonet charge by the Continentals, the steadfastness of the Virginia riflemen, the unexpected re-

---

47 Ward, The War of the Revolution, II, 738–739.

48 Jac Weller, "Irregular But Effective: Partizan Weapons Tactics in the American Revolution, Southern Theatre," Military Affairs, XXI (1957), 118–131.

49 George W. Greene, The Life of Nathanael Greene (New York, 1972), III, 189–202; Henry Lee, Memoirs of the War in the Southern Department (Washington, 1827), 170–180; Banastre Tarleton, A History of the Campaigns of 1780 and 1781 in the Southern Colonies of North America (London, 1787), 269–279, 303–312; Gaillard Hunt, ed., Fragments of Revolutionary History (Brooklyn, 1892), 29–40, 46–56.

50 According to Stedman, History, II, 220–223, many of the Loyalists at King's Mountain modified their rifles to take bayonets. See the general accounts in Commager and Morris, eds., Spirit of Seventy-Six, 1135–1145; J. Watts De Peyster, "The Affair at King's Mountain," Magazine of American History, V (1880), 401–424; Lyman C. Draper, Kings Mountain and Its Heroes (Chapel Hill, 1967), 237.

51 William Moultrie, Memoirs of the American Revolution (New York, 1968), II, 245.

turn to the field of the other militia, and a slashing cavalry charge by William Washington, the scales could have tipped to the other side.[52] Morgan's fortuitous mixture of skittish militia and dependable line troops made his gamble pay off. Yet if he had had an army capable of fighting in either irregular or line fashion, depending on the situation at hand, his battle plan would not have been so risky. Nathanael Greene's attempt at Guilford Courthouse to imitate Morgan demonstrated just how lucky the latter had been.

Greene's problem at Guilford Courthouse was indicative of basic idiosyncracies within the American military establishment. Militia and Continentals waged different types of war. This explains how Washington could phase the rifle out of the Continental Army on the one hand, and on the other advise New York to raise a regiment of militia riflemen to serve on the frontier.[53] Militia, particularly when called to fight outside their state boundaries, had a disturbing habit of coming and going as they pleased. Still, because of their predilection for hit-and-run tactics, militia fought in a way making the unmodified rifle useful to them. Continentals dressed, drilled, and fought much like their British foes. In fact, they may have become too much like them. An American officer noted that at an encounter near Green Springs, Virginia, just before Cornwallis bottled himself up in Yorktown, a British force ironically turned the tables on the American attackers. American light infantry, bayonets leveled, advanced in close order through a woods, only to be stopped and hurled back in disorder by British regulars firing individually while dodging from tree to tree.[54]

In passing it should be noted that the disparity between militiamen and Continentals was accentuated by American military organization. Continentals and militia were recruited and brigaded by states, with few exceptions. Early attempts to replace this procedure with a truly national army went nowhere. Getting all elements of this diffused organization to fight a new way would have been a monumental task.

Military conservatism played a still more important role in cur-

---

[52] Accounts in Tarleton, *Campaigns*, 214–222; Graham, *Daniel Morgan*, 289–316; Commager and Morris, eds., *Spirit of Seventy-Six*, 901–902; Stedman, *History*, II, 318–325.

[53] Fitzpatrick, ed., *Writings of Washington*, XIV, 188.

[54] Hunt, ed., *Fragments of Revolutionary History*, 50.

tailing the rifle's use during the war. To be sure, anticipating and planning for war back in 1775 was not feasible, given geographical and political divisions among colonies and the evolutionary nature of agitation for a break with the mother country. That the Patriots had to learn from experience was to be expected. Somewhere along the line, however, some farsighted strategist should have seen that the rifle was perhaps too perfect a reflection of colonial warfare, and needed to be modified to serve against an enemy of a very different nature, or else laid aside as unsuitable. Modification entailed changing the backwoodsman's aversion to training in bayonet tactics as well as physically altering the rifle, for it is erroneous to conclude that the war would have been won sooner if the entire army had been composed solely of frontier riflemen from the beginning.[55] John Simcoe, commander of the Queen's Rangers, correctly charged that riflemen, because of their limited training, "were by no means the most formidable of the rebel troops."[56]

In all fairness to Washington and his staff, it should be pointed out that they did not have a free hand at making strategy. Due to political considerations, Washington had to keep his army close to the seaboard and, as at New York, sometimes stood and fought when his instincts told him to withdraw. There is also the possibility that irregular tactics based on the rifle may have led Patriots to avoid a serious confrontation with the British, thereby reducing the Continental Army's effectiveness. That army had to be a viable deterrent to British designs for political reasons, for local and world opinion, and, on a more mundane yet no less essential level, to keep enlistments from dropping precipitately. Indeed, William Moultrie wrote after the war that Fabian tactics caused too many to "grow tired and desert."[57] Moultrie's observation could be easily tied to the disturbing "unreliability and lack of discipline" among American soldiers noted by Daniel J. Boorstin.[58]

---

55 See Sawyer, *Firearms in American History*, 33, 37, 77–79, for this type of argument.

56 John G. Simcoe, *Simcoe's Military Journal* (New York, 1844), 237. Likewise British officer George Hanger, while an admirer of the rifle as a precision weapon, criticized its limited tactical adaptability. George Hanger, *General George Hanger To All Sportsmen* (London, 1816), 122–124, 199–200.

57 Moultrie, *Memoirs*, I, 365.

58 Boorstin, *The Americans: The Colonial Experience* (New York, 1958), 368–369.

Failure to exploit the transcendant properties of the rifle, like inability to see the promise of David Bushnell's submarine the *Turtle*, exemplified a lack of appreciation for the latent powers of invention. Practically no inventive interest was taken in the rifle during the war. David Rittenhouse and Charles Willson Peale experimented with a telescopic sight for rifles in 1776, but ended their work abruptly when they almost put out their eyes. Rittenhouse later proposed to experiment with rifled cannon, but nothing came of it.[59]

At this point it would seem that American military leaders missed their chance to capitalize on the technological superiority of the rifle, albeit that chance was small. They were prone to a conservatism commonly associated with the military mind. Some had not started out that way, otherwise Washington would not have attempted to fill the army with riflemen in 1775 and early 1776. At first glance Washington's later change of heart could be viewed as a contradiction to his expressed faith in the rifle. He, along with countless others, had revered the rifle as hard evidence that the colonies had bested the mother country in at least one field of technological endeavor. Yet champions of that weapon found themselves at the edge of a void when confronted by wartime realities. Their zeal outstripped their technological knowledge; their faith was no substitute for technological awareness, and that faith ultimately faltered. The Patriots had expected great things from the rifle, but when those did not materialize they retreated to an imitative, Europeanized approach to war. When riflemen failed to produce the desired results no one really understood why. Adapting the rifle

---

[59] Maurice Babb, "David Rittenhouse," *Pennsylvania Magazine of History and Biography*, LVI (1932), 113–125; Charles Sellers, *Charles Willson Peale* (Philadelphia, 1947), I, 126–133; Force, ed., *American Archives*, 4th series, V, 729. For an analysis of this problem in the larger context of invention in colonial America in general, see my "Technology in Revolutionary America" (Ph.D. dissertation, University of California, Santa Barbara, 1978). A parallel could easily be drawn between the phasing out of the long bow in the English army and the slowness to adopt rifles centuries later. See Thomas Esper, "The Replacement of the Long Bow by Firearms in the English Army," *Technology and Culture*, VI (1965), 382–393; C. G. Cruikshank, *Elizabeth's Army* (Oxford, 1966), 102–119. Excellent discussions of the problem of technological development and slow military adaptation are in I. B. Holley, *Ideas and Weapons* (New Haven, 1953), 3–22; and Elting E. Morison, *Men, Machines and Modern Times* (Cambridge, 1966), 17–44.

to linear tactics posed one set of problems; the intellectual gymnastics of rethinking those tactics to maximize the rifle's effectiveness posed another, whose solution lay beyond the ken of the Revolutionary generation. The Pennsylvania rifle, an adaptation to one environment, did not fare as well when placed in another. It was more than a simple tool, for it reflected a certain attitude about war, an attitude not universally applicable. American military leaders, only vaguely conscious of the social nature of invention, did not really grasp this. Hence they did not successfully adapt the rifle to their tactics or their tactics to the rifle.

Before passing judgment on Washington and the rest, it must be remembered that the new nation had a restricted industrial capacity, and at no point during the war did Americans have the luxury of retooling. Congress and the states operated with marginal resources. Benjamin Franklin's atavistic proposal that pikes and bows and arrows replace firearms as standard weapons resulted as much from the constant munitions shortages as from Franklin's dislike of muskets.[60] Even if Washington and Congress had committed themselves to a new type of army equipped with rifles, they probably could not have carried it off. Pennsylvania gunsmiths would have been happy to try, since they welcomed "an excuse to lay by the Musketwork and make Rifles, which are more profitable for them," but rifles took more time to make than muskets and undoubtedly many gunsmiths assembling muskets under committee of safety and congressional contracts were unfamiliar with the art.[61] Besides, it proved impossible to keep Americans adequately supplied with muskets—much less rifles. Not only were rifles costlier and harder to make, European gunsmiths producing a large percentage of the Patriots' arms were not acquainted with rifles, or at least with American models.

Whether or not the rifle would have been used more imaginatively if the Patriots had had the industrial capacity to produce nine or ten thousand a year is a moot point. Though neither Washington nor Congress said so explicitly, the realization that they had to

60 Albert H. Smyth, ed., *The Writings of Benjamin Franklin* (New York, 1905–1907), VI, 438–439. For the munitions problems in general, see my "Clandestine Aid and the American Revolutionary War Effort: A Re-examination," *Military Affairs*, XLIII (1979), 26–30.

61 Extract from Egle, ed., *Pennsylvania in the War of the Revolution*, I, 510.

fight with whatever they could scrape together on short notice may have shaped their thinking on the rifle. Be that as it may, it can be safely stated that the "Pennsylvania rifle" may have been the product of American genius, but it was not ingeniously employed during the Revolution. What is more, given the state of American industry, the tendencies of American troops, and the incomplete technological hierarchy of the era, it is just as well that the rifle experiment was set aside.

Brigham Young University　　　　　　　　　NEIL L. YORK

Lord Howe and Lord George Germain
British Politics and the Winning of American Independence

Ira D. Gruber*

IN the past four decades many historians have tried to determine why Britain failed to win the War for American Independence. Most have agreed that the war was decided in the opening campaigns and that the failure of the British commanders could be fully explained only by considering the rebellion as both a military and a political problem. Because most reasoned that unrestricted warfare "would have defeated the real purpose of the British government, which was to make the colonies once more useful parts of the empire," they assumed that the government ruled out "mere force" and that its commanders had to combine "military pressure and persuasion."[1] These assumptions, theoretically sound and entirely plausible, are not historically correct. British politics and political con-

---

* Mr. Gruber is a Fellow at the Institute of Early American History and Culture at Williamsburg, Virginia, and a member of the Department of History, the College of William and Mary. A version of this article was presented at the Sixteenth Conference on Early American History at Williamsburg, Oct. 9, 1964.

[1] Quoting Troyer S. Anderson, *The Command of the Howe Brothers During the American Revolution* (New York, 1936), 10-13, 18. For similar interpretations see: W. M. James, *The British Navy in Adversity* . . . (London, 1926), 47, 426; Weldon A. Brown, *Empire or Independence: A Study in the Failure of Reconciliation, 1774-1783* (Baton Rouge, 1941), 6, 243 (though the narrative and his conclusion, p. 297, belie these generalizations); Eric Robson, *The American Revolution in its Political and Military Aspects, 1763-1783* (New York, 1955), 113-122; Alan Valentine, *Lord George Germain* (Oxford, 1962), 145; William B. Willcox, *Portrait of a General, Sir Henry Clinton in the War of Independence* (New York, 1964), 119; and Piers Mackesy, *The War for America, 1775-1783* (Cambridge, Eng., 1964), 33. Other historians have correctly stated the government's intentions for dealing with the rebellion but have not related them specifically to Britain's failure to win the war. See, for examples, George H. Guttridge, "Lord George Germain in Office, 1775-1782," *American Historical Review*, XXXIII (1927-28), 28; Gerald S. Brown, *The American Secretary: The Colonial Policy of Lord George Germain, 1775-1778* (Ann Arbor, 1963), 63-80; and John R. Alden, *The American Revolution, 1775-1783* (New York, 1962), 66.

189

siderations did, in fact, contribute significantly to the winning of American independence, but not in the way that historians have assumed.

By the autumn of 1775 most members of the British government thought of the rebellion in their American colonies as a military problem. Though the origins of the rebellion were political, there seemed little prospect of finding a political settlement. The colonists insisted that Parliament had no right to tax them or to regulate their domestic affairs; moreover they seemed determined to support their arguments with force. As the King and an overwhelming majority of the members of Parliament believed that they could make laws binding the colonies in all cases whatsoever, no British ministry dared accept the American claims.[2] When, therefore, the colonists had rejected Britain's meager offers of compromise and had taken up arms against the King, the North ministry was forced either to resign or to pursue a policy of military coercion. The ministers, with several exceptions, kept their places and prepared for war. Declaring the colonies in rebellion, they recruited their forces and ordered their commanders in chief to wage unlimited war on the rebels.[3]

But even amid the preparations for war, a few members of the British government remembered that the rebellion was in fact a political as well as a military problem, and these few would have an importance well out of proportion to their number. Most influential among the advocates of a political settlement was Frederick Lord North, the head of the ministry. North had no intention of attenuating Parliament's power in the colonies but was far too practical to prefer a punitive war to a negotiated peace. He favored compromises on specific problems, providing these compromises did not involve constitutional changes. He would, for example, have been willing to suspend parliamentary taxation in America if the colonial assemblies had agreed to contribute to the support of imperial defense—

[2] For examples, the King to Frederick Lord North, Sept. 11, 1774, in John W. Fortescue, ed., *The Correspondence of King George the Third from 1760 to December 1783* (London, 1927-28), III, 130-131; the King to William Legge, Earl of Dartmouth, June 10, 1775, in Great Britain, Historical Manuscripts Commission, *The Manuscripts of Rye and Hereford Corporations* . . . (London, 1892), 501-502; J. Almon, ed., *The Parliamentary Register* . . . (London, 1775-1804), I, 133-170, 468-478; Hutchinson's diary, May 12, 1775, in Peter O. Hutchinson, ed., *The Diary and Letters of* . . . *Thomas Hutchinson* . . . (London, 1883-86), I, 445.

[3] Dartmouth to General Thomas Gage, Aug. 2, 1775, separate, and Dartmouth to General William Howe, Sept. 5, 1775, secret, Dartmouth to W. Howe, Sept. 22, 1775, Colonial Office Papers, Class 5, Vol. 92, Public Record Office, London; William Eden to Lord George Germain, Sept. 27, [1775], in Hist. MSS. Com., *Report on the Manuscripts of Mrs. Stopford-Sackville* . . . (London, 1904-10), II, 9-10.

an arrangement that promised to give Britain a revenue without raising the question of Parliament's right to tax the colonists.[4]

Indeed, while in October of 1775 most British leaders were thinking of ways to crush the rebellion, North was gathering support for a peace commission. Having learned by experience that the ministry and Parliament were violently opposed to any measure that appeared concessive,[5] he described his commission as an instrument for accelerating colonial surrender, a complement to military operations.[6] In this way he soon won the support of the ministry and Parliament for a commission that would grant pardons, receive surrender, and possibly remove restrictions on colonial trade. Subsequently he even managed to have the powers of the commission enlarged, so that it might have unquestioned authority to remove the prohibition on colonial trade and to discuss grievances.[7] What Parliament did not prescribe, however, was the order in which the commission would exercise its powers. Apparently a majority of Parliament assumed that the commission would accept the surrender of a particular colony or town before doing anything else.[8] If this were to be the case, the commission would have little chance of negotiating an end to the war, as North hoped it could. But whether or not the commission would be able to fulfill his expectations depended on the commissioner and on the instructions he received.

In appointing Admiral Richard Lord Howe to the new commission, North did his best to produce a negotiated settlement. By temperament, reputation, and inclination Howe was well qualified to conciliate the rebels. A man who was adept in dealing with subordinates, who (in spite

[4] Almon, ed., *Parliamentary Register*, I, 196-214; Eden to Germain, Oct. 3, 1775, Germain Papers, William L. Clements Library, Ann Arbor, Mich.

[5] Feb. 27, 1775, in Hutchinson, ed., *Diary and Letters*, I, 399-400; Edward Gibbon to J. B. Holroyd, Feb. 25, 1775, in J. E. Norton, ed., *The Letters of Edward Gibbon* (London, 1956), II, 60-61; North to the King, [Feb. 20, 1775], in Fortescue, ed., *Correspondence of George Third*, III, 178-179.

[6] Eden to Germain, Oct. 3, 1775, Germain Papers.

[7] Almon, ed., *Parliamentary Register*, III, 1-3; 16 George III c.5, in Danby Pickering, ed., *The Statutes at Large* (Cambridge, Eng., 1762-1807), XXXI, 135-154; Germain to W. Howe, Dec. 23, 1775, Headquarters Papers of the British Army, photostats, I, no. 100, Colonial Williamsburg, Inc., Research Library, Williamsburg, Va.

[8] Augustus Henry Duke of Grafton certainly interpreted the powers of the commission in this way and on Mar. 14, 1776, proposed that they be modified to allow negotiations before the colonists had surrendered unconditionally. William R. Anson, ed., *Autobiography and Political Correspondence of Augustus Henry Third Duke of Grafton* (London, 1898), 282-283.

191

of his connections with men in high places) was not closely associated with the government or the policy of coercion, and whose name was well known in America, Howe was an ideal candidate from North's point of view.[9] But even more important, he had a strong personal interest in reconciliation, an interest born of his family's close ties with New England. His older brother had been so popular with the colonial militia while serving in America during the French and Indian War that when he was killed at Fort Ticonderoga the General Court of Massachusetts Bay voted 250 pounds to erect a monument to his memory in Westminster Abbey. Remembering this gesture and the affection it symbolized, Howe was prompt to offer his services as mediator when in late 1774 the Anglo-American quarrel threatened to become a war.[10] In so doing he did not propose alterations in the imperial constitution; he merely suggested that kind words would make British authority more palatable, whereas coercive measures would frustrate a genuine reconciliation.[11] Though the ministry was unwilling in early 1775 to sponsor a peace commission and rejected his offer, he continued to urge his friends in the administration to accept his mediation.[12] When finally, in October, North gained Parliament's approval for a commission, Howe's persistence was rewarded. North not only promised him the commission but also encouraged him to think he would have authority enough to negotiate a settlement.[13] But North's

[9] Sir John Barrow, *The Life of Richard, Earl Howe* . . . (London, 1838); Sir Lewis Namier and John Brooke, *The History of Parliament: The House of Commons, 1754-1790* (New York, 1964), II, 647-649.

[10] [J. A. Holden], "Description of the Howe Monument, Westminster Abbey," in N. Y. State Historical Association, *Proceedings*, X (Albany, 1911), 323-325; Franklin's "An Account of Negotiations in London . . . ," Mar. 22, 1775, in Albert H. Smyth, ed., *The Writings of Benjamin Franklin* (New York, 1905-7), VI, 345-354. Though there is no great collection of Lord Howe's papers, his motives may be judged from his sister's letters, several thousand of which are in the possession of the Earl of Spencer at Althorp, Northamptonshire, and from the correspondence of his political broker, Thomas Villiers, Baron Hyde, Earl of Clarendon, whose letter books are in the Bodleian Library, Oxford. Among his sister's letters, for example, are repeated expressions of the family's desire to promote a reconciliation: "we have nothing to wish but that he [General Howe] may be the means of a satisfactory peace. . . ." (Mrs. Caroline Howe to Georgiana, Lady Spencer, Aug. 11, [1775]).

[11] Richard Lord Howe to Hyde, [Feb. 9, 1775], Hyde to Howe, Feb. 10, 1775, Dartmouth Papers, William Salt Library, Stafford, England.

[12] Hyde to North, Jan. 10, 1776, Clarendon Deposit, Bodleian Library.

[13] William Knox's account of the first peace commission of 1776, in Knox Papers, Clements Lib.; Hyde to Howe, Nov. 2, 1775, and Howe to [Dartmouth], Nov. 4, 1775, Dartmouth Papers; Howe to Mark Huish, Nov. 2, 1775, Miscellaneous Manuscripts under Howe, New York Public Library, New York.

wishes did not necessarily determine what the ministry's policy would be. A better forecast of that policy was provided by the reorganization of the ministry that took place in November. The most important change came at the colonial office where the Earl of Dartmouth, who had recoiled from his responsibility for managing the war, yielded to Lord George Germain, a man with unusual enthusiasm for crushing the rebellion.[14] Germain had never been considerate of his inferiors or tolerant of insubordination. He had spoken in favor of the Declaratory Act and against the repeal of the Stamp Act in 1766, declared that leniency bred trouble both in Ireland and America, supported the Massachusetts acts in 1774, and during the first half of 1775 advocated that the colonists be forced to acknowledge Parliament's supremacy in all cases whatsoever. But Lord George's interest in the American rebellion was more than the result of his passion for upholding authority; in the American war he saw a chance to redeem a military reputation that had been ruined in 1760 when he was convicted of cowardice and found " 'unfit to serve his Majesty in any military capacity whatsoever.' "[15] Although as colonial secretary he would not serve in a military capacity, he would, as virtual minister of war, have ample opportunity to demonstrate his talent for military planning and administration. It is little wonder that he was enthusiastic over his new job. Scorning Dartmouth's moderation and saying one decisive victory, together with a blockade, would end the rebellion, he was impatient for a quick decision: "I always wished that the whole power of the state should be Exerted, that one Campaign might decide whether the American Provinces were to be subject to G. B. or free States."[16]

[14] Charles Greville to Sir William Hamilton, Oct. 31, 1775, in Hamilton-Greville Correspondence, Henry E. Huntington Library, San Marino, Calif. In addition to the changes affecting Dartmouth and Germain, Augustus Henry Duke of Grafton, who actively opposed a coercive war, and William Henry Zuylestein, Earl of Rochford, who had little liking for it, retired, while Thomas Thynne, Viscount Weymouth, who shared Germain's views, joined the government. After Nov. 10, therefore, only North and Dartmouth among the ministers favored moderation; Parliament was even more anxious than the ministry to wage a punitive war: "We have a warm Parliament but an indolent Cabinet." Gibbon to Holroyd, Oct. 31, 1775, in Norton, ed., *Letters of Gibbon*, II, 91-92. But no one was more determined than the King to drive the colonists to submission. The King to North, Dec. 15, 1774, and Aug. 18, 1775, in Fortescue, ed., *Correspondence of George Third*, III, 156, 247-248.

[15] Namier and Brooke, *House of Commons, 1754-1790*, III, 390-396; Brown, *American Secretary*, 11-26; Valentine, *Germain*, 9-100.

[16] Germain to [General Sir John Irwin], June 13, 1775, and July 20, 1775, quoting Germain to Eden, [Oct. 7, 1775], Germain Papers; Germain to [Henry Howard,

193

Before Germain had grown accustomed to the colonial office, and before the ministry had decided what the peace commission might do, chance, domestic politics, and dubious assumptions conspired to make Admiral Howe commander in chief as well as peace commissioner. In early December of 1775 a senior admiral died, vacating a lucrative sinecure North had promised to Howe. When North, forgetting his promise, awarded the sinecure to another officer, Howe threatened to resign from the navy. The ministry was, of course, anxious to avoid a breach with one of its ablest admirals and tried to find some other reward to satisfy him.[17] After more than a month of futile negotiations, it accepted his own suggestion that he be made commander in chief in America.[18] As Howe had no desire to fight against the colonists, he apparently applied for the American command to strengthen his hand as a negotiator. A majority of the ministry, for their part, were willing to appoint him commander in chief because they wanted the services of a fine professional officer and because they assumed he would not allow his hopes for peace to interfere with his conduct of the war. Germain and the King, who were the stanchest advocates of coercive measures and who saw little need for a peace commission, were delighted to employ Howe at sea;[19] in fact the King stifled the only opposition to his appointment, which came from the Earl of Sandwich and was based mainly on personal considerations.[20] Though North and Dartmouth did not share the other ministers' aversion to a

Earl of Suffolk], July 26, 1775, Miscellaneous Manuscripts, XIV, 1771-1775, Massachusetts Historical Society, Boston; Germain to Irwin, Sept. 13, 1775, in Hist. MSS. Com., *Report on the Manuscripts of Mrs. Stopford-Sackville*, I, 137.

[17] Hans Stanley to [Andrew S. Hamond], Jan. 27, 1776, Hamond Papers, Alderman Library, University of Virginia, Charlottesville; John Robinson to John Montagu, Earl of Sandwich, [Dec. 8, 1775], in G. R. Barnes and J. H. Owen, eds., *The Private Papers of John, Earl of Sandwich, First Lord of the Admiralty, 1771-1782* (London, 1932-38), II, 201.

[18] Hyde to North, Jan. 11, 1776, and Jan. 10, 1776, Clarendon Deposit; North to the King, Jan. 28, 1776 (misdated by Fortescue as Feb. 4, 1776), Fortescue, ed., *Correspondence of George Third*, III, 338.

[19] Irwin to Francis, Earl of Huntingdon, Feb. 6, 1776, in Hist. MSS. Com., *Report on the Manuscripts of the Late Reginald Rawdon Hastings . . .*, III (London, 1934), 169; Knox's account of the first peace commission of 1776, Knox Papers; Thomas Hutchinson to Thomas Oliver, Feb. 17, 1776, in Hutchinson, ed., *Diary and Letters*, II, 63.

[20] The King to North, Feb. 2, 1776, in Fortescue, ed., *Correspondence of George Third*, III, 336; the King to Sandwich, Feb. 3, 1776, in Barnes and Owen, eds., *Papers of Sandwich*, I, 112-113; Leveson Gower to William Cornwallis, Feb. 27, 1776, COR/57, 48/MS/9575, National Maritime Museum, Greenwich.

194

negotiated settlement, they fully supported Howe's candidacy,[21] thinking him well qualified to use whatever combination of force and persuasion was needed to end the war. If chance had given Howe the opportunity to ask for a dual commission, he obtained it by exploiting the dubious assumption, held by a majority of the ministry, that he would not mix politics and strategy.

The King, Germain, and many of the administration may have misunderstood Howe's intentions, but they made no mistake in drafting his orders. When he refused to share his peace commission with someone of less conciliatory views, Germain insisted that his instructions should preclude concessions. When North, Dartmouth, and Howe argued that the colonies should not be forced to acknowledge, as a prerequisite to negotiations, Parliament's right to make laws binding the colonies in all cases whatsoever, Germain at length gave in.[22] But Howe's instructions ensured that the commission would remain what Lord George and a majority of Parliament had always intended it to be: a means for accepting colonial surrender. Howe would be able to do no more than grant pardons and wait for the colonists to surrender; until they had dissolved unlawful assemblies, restored royal officials, disbanded their armies, and given up all fortifications, he could not suspend hostilities or discuss the terms of reconciliation. Although he had obtained specific terms for establishing a system of colonial contributions for imperial defense in place of taxation for revenue, a system under which the colonies would have contributed from 5 to 10 per cent of the sum voted annually by Parliament for the army, navy, and ordnance, he was unable to mention these terms until the colonies had surrendered.[23] That he was willing to serve with such a limited commission suggests both his failure to comprehend the depth of colonial dissatisfaction and the confidence he had in his own powers of persuasion.

While Howe was debating the terms of his peace commission, the government prepared his instructions for carrying on the war at sea. He was not only to impose a tight blockade on all the rebellious colonies, bringing economic pressure on the Americans and denying them military sup-

---

[21] Knox's account of the first peace commission of 1776, Knox Papers.

[22] Ibid. and Germain to Eden, Feb. 18, 1776, Auckland Papers, Additions to the Manuscripts, 34, 413, British Museum, London.

[23] Orders and Instructions for the Howe commission, May 6, 1776, C.O. 5/177; Separate instruction to the American commissioners, May 7, 1776, in Hist. MSS. Com., Sixth Report, Part I (London, 1877), 400-401.

plies from Europe and the West Indies, but also to co-operate with the British army in smashing the revolt. So that he would not mistake the meaning of his orders, the lords of the admiralty gave him specific suggestions for employing the North American squadron. His cruisers were to shelter loyal colonists and protect their property, retaliate against coastal towns where the inhabitants were in rebellion, dismantle American merchantmen that they might not be fitted for war, destroy all armed vessels, clear colonial ports of sunken obstructions and floating batteries, impress rebel seamen, and when necessary, commandeer supplies.[24] To carry out such a variety of measures he would have seventy-three warships manned by 13,000 seamen, nearly 45 per cent of all the ships and men on active service in the world's most powerful navy.[25] Although his orders authorized any deviation he thought necessary, their general tone was unmistakable. He was to use his squadron decisively.

The main British effort in 1776 was, however, to be made ashore. The plans for the summer campaign were not decreed from London but were worked out in a series of dispatches between Germain and General William Howe, brother of Admiral Howe and commander in chief of the British troops at Boston. As early as June 1775, while still second in command, General Howe had sketched his ideas for 1776. Rather than campaign from Boston, he would strangle the rebellion in New England by occupying the Hudson River valley and blockading all ports from New York to Nova Scotia. In October he expanded this plan, proposing that armies advancing from New York and Canada should meet along the Hudson and take separate routes into Massachusetts. If the campaign were to be conclusive, he would need at least 20,000 men, in addition to those in the Canadian army.[26] But Howe by no means placed his whole reliance on isolating New England and recovering territory piecemeal. He repeatedly declared that he wished to bring the Continental army to a decisive action, for only a resounding British victory would, he thought, end the rebellion.[27] Germain, who shared Howe's faith in a climactic

[24] Admiralty's instructions to Howe, May 4, 1776, and Admiralty to Admiral Samuel Graves, July 6, 1775, Admiralty Papers, Class 2, Vol. 1332, Public Record Office; Admiralty to Graves, Aug. 31, Sept. 14, Oct. 23, Oct. 15, and Sept. 14, 1775, Adm. 2/100; Admiralty to Howe, May 4, 1776, Adm. 2/101.

[25] Abstract of monthly disposition, July 1, 1776, Adm. 8/52.

[26] W. Howe to Howe, June 12, 1775, Dartmouth Papers; W. Howe to Dartmouth, separate, Oct. 9, and Nov. 26, 1775, C.O. 5/92; W. Howe to Dartmouth, Jan. 16, 1776, C.O. 5/93.

[27] W. Howe to Dartmouth, Jan. 16, 1776, and W. Howe to Germain, Apr. 25,

battle, not only approved his plans but also promised him the reinforcements he requested; indeed Lord George's principal fear during the spring of 1776 was that Howe would risk an engagement before being fully prepared.[28] On the eve of the campaign of 1776, the Colonial Secretary had every reason to be satisfied with the Commander in Chief of the army in America. Although General Howe was temporarily delayed in early July while awaiting reinforcements at Staten Island, his plans remained unchanged. He would take New York and Rhode Island before joining the Canadian army on the Hudson. If he thought his brother's commission might induce many to surrender, he was "still of Opinion that Peace will not be restored in America until the Rebel Army is defeated."[29]

But after Lord Howe joined his brother at New York, the Commanders in Chief soon deviated from the government's plans for ending the rebellion. Though his instructions were inadequate for a negotiation, though he arrived on July 12, a week after Congress had declared the colonies independent, and though his brother did not think the rebels would treat,[30] the Admiral had no intention of applying his sword until he had seen what words might do. He began by issuing a proclamation, telling the colonists that he had been appointed peace commissioner with authority to grant pardon and to end hostilties wherever royal government had been restored. Congress, realizing that he had made no substantial concession in his proclamation, ordered it published throughout the colonies "that the good people of these United States may be informed of what nature are the commissioners, and what the terms, with the expectation of which, the insidious court of Britain has endeavoured to amuse and disarm them."[31] While his proclamation was being distributed, Howe tried to open negotiations with the commander in chief of the Continental army and with Congress, but his overtures had no better reception than his proclamation. When he wrote to Washington asking for a meeting to discuss the provisions of the peace commission, Washington rejected his

---

1776, C.O. 5/93; W. Howe to Germain, Apr. 26, 1776, private, in Hist. MSS. Com., *Report on the Manuscripts of Mrs. Stopford-Sackville*, II, 30-31.

[28] Germain to W. Howe, Jan. 5, Mar. 28, and May 3, 1776, C.O. 5/93.

[29] W. Howe to Germain, July 7, 1776, C.O. 5/93.

[30] Sir Henry Strachey's journal, July 12, 1776, Hist. MSS. Com., *Sixth Report, Part 1*, 402.

[31] Howe to Germain, Aug. 11, 1776, enclosing a copy of his Declaration, C.O. 5/177; July 19, 1776, in Worthington C. Ford, ed., *Journals of the Continental Congress, 1774-1789. Volume V. 1776* (Washington, 1906), 592-593.

197

letter because it was improperly addressed; and when he applied to him again, the American commander refused to discuss an accommodation, saying he understood the Howes were "only to grant pardons [and] that those who had committed no fault wanted no pardon."[32] But even this rejoinder did not deter Howe, who soon attempted to suggest through an emissary that he could discuss a plan for replacing parliamentary taxation in the colonies with a system of fixed colonial contributions. Congress, happy with its independence, would not, however, pursue this suggestion.[33] As one of Howe's juniors remarked, "it has long been too late for Negotiation, yet it is easy to be perceived, My Lord Howe came out with a different Idea."[34]

Lord Howe's desire for a peaceful settlement also seemed to affect military operations. As his brother had neither troops nor equipment enough to attack the rebels until August 14 and as the British offensive began on the twenty-second, Lord Howe cannot be blamed for delaying the opening of the campaign. But he probably did contribute to alterations in General Howe's strategy. The General had appeared eager for a decisive action before the Admiral arrived; thereafter he concentrated on occupying territory rather than on destroying the Continental army. It is true that the American fortifications at New York were too strong to invite a frontal assault, yet the Continental army was precariously divided between Long Island and Manhattan. As British ships could move at will in either the Hudson or the East River, General Howe should have made some effort to trap his enemy.[35] His general plan for taking New York and his conduct on Long Island demonstrated, however, that he was pri-

[32] Howe to George Washington, July 13, 1776, Howe Papers, Clements Lib.; July 14, 1776, in Edward H. Tatum, Jr., ed., *The American Journal of Ambrose Serle, Secretary to Lord Howe, 1776-1778* (San Marino, 1940), 31-33; Washington to the President of Congress, July 14, 22, 1776, in John C. Fitzpatrick, ed., *The Writings of George Washington* . . . (Washington, 1931-44), V, 273-274, 321n-323n.

[33] Lord Drummond to Howe, Aug. 12, 1776, and Drummond to Washington, Aug. 17, 1776, Washington Papers, XXXII, Library of Congress, Washington; Howe to Drummond, Aug. 15, 1776, in Peter Force, ed., *American Archives* . . . 5th Ser., I (Washington, 1848), 1027; Aug. 20 and 22, 1776, in Ford, ed., *Journals of the Continental Congress*, V, 672, 696.

[34] Hamond to [Stanley], Sept. 24, 1776, Hamond Papers.

[35] Howe ignored Sir Henry Clinton's proposal for a landing at Spuyten Duyvil. Willcox, *Henry Clinton*, 103. The American generals certainly feared that they would be enveloped: John Sullivan to John Hancock, Aug. 5, 1776, in Otis G. Hammond, ed., *Letters and Papers of Major-General John Sullivan* . . . , I (Concord, N.H., 1930), 290-291; Washington to Pres. of Cong., Aug. 9, 1776, in Fitzpatrick, ed., *Writings of Washington*, V, 406.

marily interested in occupying territory. By taking possession of Brooklyn Heights, which commanded the town of New York, he planned to make lower Manhattan untenable for the rebels.[36] His strategy was, in short, to push the Continental army out of New York. The execution deviated little from the design. After landing on Long Island and driving the Americans into their lines at Red Hook and Brooklyn, General Howe made no special effort to keep them there. The rebels were caught against the East River with a superior army in their front, and yet Lord Howe never ordered his captains to block Washington's line of retreat. At least one British officer was extremely disappointed: "had our ships attackd the batteries [at Brooklyn], which we have been in constant expectation of being orderd to do, not a man could have escapd from Long Island."[37] When the Americans fled to Manhattan on the night of August 29, General Howe had accomplished part of his plan, but he had lost his finest opportunity for destroying the Continental army and for ending the rebellion.

After the battle of Long Island, the Howes' conduct of the war assumed a pattern that suggested they were trying to use no more force than they thought necessary to promote a reconciliation. Even before the rebels had fled from Brooklyn, and at a time when Lord Howe might have been devising ways to prevent their escape, he was again trying to open negotiations with Congress.[38] He apparently hoped that the British victory on August 27 would make the rebels more tractable, more willing to put down their arms and hear his terms. Congress responded to his overture by sending three delegates to meet with him on Staten Island, but he soon discovered that the Americans sought only to discredit his peace commission.[39] Frustrated once more, he joined his brother in seeing what a further application of force would do. After they had driven the Americans from New York, by threatening to trap them there, Lord

[36] W. Howe to Germain, private, Aug. 10, 1776, Germain Papers.

[37] Quoting Sir George Collier's journal kept at New York, n.d., in Louis L. Tucker, ed., " 'To My Inexpressible Astonishment' . . . ," *New-York Historical Society Quarterly*, XLVIII (1964), 304. W. Howe to Germain, Sept. 3, 1776, C.O. 5/93; Washington to Pres. of Cong., Aug. 31, 1776, in Fitzpatrick, ed., *Writings of Washington*, V, 508-509.

[38] "Journals of Captain Henry Duncan," Aug. 29-30, 1776, in John K. Laughton, ed., *The Naval Miscellany*, I (London, 1902), 125-126; Aug. 29, 30, 1776, in Tatum, ed., *Journal of Serle*, 80-83; Howe to Germain, Sept. 20, 1776, C.O. 5/177.

[39] Sir Henry Strachey's account of the meeting, Miscellaneous MSS., N.Y. Pub. Lib.; Howe to Germain, Sept. 20, 1776, C.O. 5/177.

199

Howe made still another effort at conciliation. Because he had been unsuccessful in dealing with Congress, he now appealed directly to the colonists, issuing a proclamation that invited them to discuss a reconciliation and that declared the King was disposed to allow them considerable control over their domestic affairs. So unsuccessful was this proclamation that the Howes made no new overtures for several months.[40] In the interim they rolled the Americans back from New York by a series of flanking maneuvers that won territory without forcing a full-scale engagement. Only when the American garrison at Fort Washington refused to escape or surrender did the British make a decisive attack.

The whole campaign of 1776 seemed designed to promote both a restoration of British authority in America and a genuine reconciliation. Lord Howe apparently had persuaded his brother, who shared his desire for peace,[41] to mix strategy and politics. Though the Admiral felt that each battle made conciliation more difficult, he realized that some exertion of force was necessary to make the colonists willing to negotiate. He probably reasoned, therefore, that a steady British advance and a display of overwhelming superiority would force the rebels to treat, without creating an irreparable breach. A ruthless campaign might secure a military victory, but it would never make the colonists into loyal subjects.

If ever this policy of blending strategy and politics seemed likely to succeed, it was in December of 1776, the most critical month in the War for American Independence. After Fort Washington surrendered in mid-November, the Continental army retired rapidly across New Jersey before a seemingly invincible British advance. The loss of Fort Washington, endless withdrawals, and expiring enlistments were destroying the American forces; indeed, on December 1 Washington decided to retreat across the Delaware into Pennsylvania.[42] At New York, where the British heard rumors of dissensions both in Congress and in the Continental army,[43]

[40] The Howes to Germain, Sept. 20, 1776, enclosing a copy of the Declaration, C.O. 5/177; Wilmot Vaughan, Earl of Lisburne to George Jackson, Dec. 22, 1776, Add. MSS., 34, 187.

[41] Mrs. Howe "flatters herself his [General Howe's] advice will be a little attended to, and she knows he wishes to have a peace that is creditable to both." Lady Sarah Bunbury to Lady Susan O'Brien, Aug. 21, 1775, in the Countess of Ilchester and Lord Stavordale, eds., The Life and Letters of Lady Sarah Lennox, 1745-1826 (London, 1901), I, 244.

[42] Washington to Pres. of Cong., Nov. 23, 30, Dec. 1, 1776, in Fitzpatrick, ed., Writings of Washington, VI, 303-304, 314-316, 321-322.

[43] Nov. 1, Dec. 8, 1776, in Tatum, ed., Journal of Serle, 135, 155-156; Ambrose

the Howes were preparing to exploit their belated success. The General, who could no longer expect to open the Hudson before winter, planned to capture Rhode Island and secure New Jersey by the end of the campaign. Nor did he and his brother neglect persuasion, offering a free pardon to anyone who would take an oath of allegiance to George III within sixty days of November 30. This offer, although spurned by leading rebels, was accepted by almost 5,000 colonists and was clearly the most successful of all British efforts toward peace.[44] But before half its term had expired, Washington contrived to change the course of the war. On December 26 he destroyed a detachment of Hessians quartered at Trenton and, a week later, won a second battle at Princeton. These two victories blasted the illusion of British invincibility, restored American morale, and ended the Howes' chances for a negotiated peace.[45] For the Howes the campaign of 1776 was a bitter disappointment; for Great Britain it was a disaster. The British government may not have shown great wisdom in trying to unify an empire by force; but by the summer of 1776 force alone could have restored the colonies to British rule. When the Howes failed to trap and destroy the Continental army during the campaign of 1776, they forfeited Britain's best opportunity for ending the American revolt.

Until February of 1777 most members of the British government were well pleased with the progress of the war in the colonies. If the Howes were not acting with the firmness the ministry desired, a succession of victories obscured the opportunities they had lost. London rejoiced on hearing that Long Island and New York had been captured, and General Howe was knighted for his conduct on August 27.[46] The King found the

Serle to Dartmouth, Dec. 3, 1776, in Benjamin F. Stevens, ed., *Facsimiles of Manuscripts in European Archives Relating to America, 1773-1783* . . . , XXIV (London, 1895), no. 2048.

[44] W. Howe to Germain, Nov. 30, 1776, separate, and Nov. 30, 1776, C.O. 5/93; Howes to Germain, Dec. 22, 1776, and Mar. 25, 1777, C.O. 5/177.

[45] Many British officers and officials thought the battles of Trenton and Princeton had saved the rebellion; for example: William Eddis to Eden, July 23, 1777, C.O. 5/722; Hamond's MS account of his role in the American war, Hamond Papers; Colonel William Harcourt to Simon Harcourt, Earl of Harcourt, Jan. 18, 1777, in Edward W. Harcourt, ed., *The Harcourt Papers* (Oxford, 1880-1905), XI, 203; MS journal kept by a soldier in Howe's army, 1777, MS Am 1562, Houghton Library, Harvard University; Sir George Osborn to [Sir George Pocock], May 15, 1777, Pocock Collection, Huntington Library; Dec. 27, 1776, in Tatum, ed., *Journal of Serle*, 163.

[46] George Bussy Villiers, Earl of Jersey, to Lady Spencer, Oct. 10, 1776; Mrs. Howe to Lady Spencer, Oct. 16, 1776, Spencer Papers, Althorp, Northamptonshire.

Howes' dispatches of November 30, which reached England after Christmas, "the more agreeable as they exceed the most sanguine expectations." Germain and Sandwich agreed that the capture of Fort Washington, the occupation of eastern New Jersey, and the sending of an expedition to Rhode Island put a most satisfactory end to the campaign.[47] But Germain was not entirely happy with his commanders. He was pleased with the succession of British victories, but because he had hoped "to re-conquer Germany in America"—to redeem his reputation by crushing the rebellion—he was disturbed by the Howes' proclamation of November 30, which offered pardon to rebels and loyalists alike. "This sentimental manner of making war will, I fear, not have the desired Effect."[48] Moreover, having intended that the campaign of 1776 would be decisive and not wishing to overburden the British economy, he was dismayed with General Howe's request for an additional 15,000 men for 1777.[49] He reminded the Howes that those colonists who refused pardon were to be punished and suggested that the General might manage with a reinforcement of less than 15,000 men.[50]

In late February and early March, Lord George's worst fears were realized. On February 23 the *Bristol* reached England, bringing news of Trenton and Princeton together with General Howe's first revision of his plans for 1777. Germain could be glad that the General no longer asked for a reinforcement (he now proposed leaving 9,000 men to hold Rhode Island, New York, and the lower Hudson while he took Philadelphia with an army of 10,000), but there was nothing else in the dispatches to comfort the Colonial Secretary.[51] Approving Howe's revised plan and urging him to undertake raids on the New England coasts, Lord George lectured his commanders on the importance of acting decisively: "I fear that you and Lord Howe will find it necessary to adopt such

[47] The King to Sandwich, Dec. 30, 1776, and Sandwich to Howe, Jan. 6, 1777, in Barnes and Owen, eds., *Papers of Sandwich*, I, 169, 170-172; Germain to Knox, Dec. 31, 1776, Knox Papers.
[48] Gibbon to Holroyd, Nov. 4, 1776, in Norton, ed., *Letters of Gibbon*, II, 119-120; Germain to Knox, Dec. 31, 1776, Knox Papers.
[49] Account of a conversation with Germain, Oct. 26, 1776, Lucas Collection, Bedford County Record Office, Bedford; Germain to Eden, Jan. 1, 1777, Auckland Papers, Add. MSS., 34, 413.
[50] Germain to the Howes, Jan. 14, 1777, C.O. 5/177; Germain to W. Howe, Jan. 14, 1777, C.O. 5/94.
[51] W. Howe to Germain, separate, Dec. 20, 1776, Dec. 29, 1776, and Jan. 5, 1777, C.O. 5/94; Feb. 24, 1777, in Hutchinson, ed., *Diary and Letters*, II, 139.

modes of carrying on the war, that the Rebels may be effectually distressed; so that through a lively Experience of losses and sufferings, they may be brought as soon as possible to a proper sense of their Duty."[52] Scarcely had he finished these dispatches when he received news of a more serious nature. Copies of Lord Howe's instructions for establishing a blockade reached London on March 4. The Admiral had directed his captains to be lenient with the colonists—to allow subsistence fishing, to "encourage and cultivate all amicable correspondence with the said Inhabitants, to gain their good Will and Confidence, whilst they demean themselves in a peaceable and orderly manner. And to grant them every other Indulgence which the limitations upon their Trade specified in the [Prohibitory] Act . . . will consistently admit: In order to conciliate their friendly Dispositions and to detach them from the Prejudices they have imbibed." Lest they should learn defensive warfare, he also forbade his captains to raid along the coasts.[53] If defeats at Trenton and Princeton could be charged to the misconduct of a Hessian officer, there was no way of excusing Howe's instructions to his captains, which seriously violated the spirit of the orders he had received from the ministry. Because this was the first specific example of such a violation and because he had many powerful friends in England, the government did no more than urge him to be less lenient. Both Germain and Sandwich reproved the Admiral for his indulgence to colonial fishermen, and Lord George sent a Major Nisbet Balfour to ask Sir William what he planned to do in 1777 and when he would do it.[54]

Germain clearly did not like the way the war was being managed; he was especially displeased with Lord Howe[55] and would, no doubt, have been glad to replace him with another admiral; but until he saw the results of Balfour's mission, there was little he could do. He was committed temporarily to a policy of reforming his commanders. In May he accepted their justification of a general pardon and approved Sir William's

[52] Quoting Germain to W. Howe, Mar. 3, 1777, no. 4; citing Germain to W. Howe, Mar. 3, 1777, no. 5, C.O. 5/94.
[53] Quoting Howe to Sir Peter Parker, Dec. 22, 1776, enclosed in Howe to Philip Stephens, Jan. 15, 1777, Adm. 1/487; Stephens to Howe, Mar. 4, 1777, Adm. 2/554.
[54] Sandwich to Howe, Mar. 10, 1777, in Barnes and Owen, eds., *Papers of Sandwich,* I, 288-289; Germain to Knox, June 11, 1777, Knox Papers; Howe to Germain, May 31, 1777, Germain Papers.
[55] "Lord Howe is the most disinterested man I know in permitting the Trade of Charlestown to be carryd on without interruption when he might availe himself of so many rich prizes." Germain to Knox, June 15, 1777, Knox Papers.

203

decision to go to Philadelphia by sea.[56] But when he learned in July that Balfour had failed to convert the Howes and that the British had suffered still another reverse, he began a determined campaign to replace, or at least intimidate, his commanders. Lord Howe had stubbornly defended his leniency to fishermen, arguing that by allowing them to fish he kept them from serving in the Continental army or navy. Similarly, he and his brother refused to undertake raids on New England ports, asserting that such raids would interfere with their over-all plan for the campaign. These arguments might have been convincing if they had not arrived with news of a rebel sortie from New England in which a squadron of eighteen armed vessels had put to sea, unopposed, in late May.[57] Germain now had proof of the disastrous consequences of leniency, and he intended to make the most of it. Employing irony in his reply to Lord Howe, he said he was happy that the indulgence "shewn to the Inhabitants upon the Coast, in not depriving them of the means of Subsistance has had so good an Effect"; indeed, he continued, Howe's blockade was so effective that the British Isles were teeming with American privateers. Lord George's argument was stated more bluntly by Sandwich and the lords of the admiralty who, feeling no need for indirection, censured Howe for stationing his cruisers improperly and for failing to provide intelligence of American preparations.[58] Though Germain had more confidence in General Howe than in his brother, he also encouraged Sir William to win the approval of his countrymen by retaliating against the bases of the privateers.[59] Lord George was determined to have a different war in America—with or without the help of the Howes.

Across the Atlantic the campaign of 1777 was scarcely begun. Feeling that there was little chance for ending the war, either by negotiations or by force, and that they were unreasonably harassed from Whitehall, the Howes seemed to exemplify the law of inertia. As early as April of 1777, Lord Howe expressed his sense of frustration by saying he knew not

[56] Germain to the Howes, May 18, 1777, C.O. 5/177; Germain to W. Howe, May 18, 1777, no. 11, C.O. 5/94.

[57] Stephens to Howe, Aug. 20, 1777, Adm. 2/555; Howe to Germain, May 31, 1777, private, Germain Papers; W. Howe to Germain, June 3, 1777, C.O. 5/94; Howe to Stephens, June 8, 1777, Adm. 1/487.

[58] Germain to Howe, Aug. 4, 1777, Germain Papers; Sandwich to Howe, Aug. 3, 1777, in Barnes and Owen, eds., *Papers of Sandwich*, I, 293-295; Stephens to Howe, Aug. 20, 1777, Adm. 2/555.

[59] Germain to Irwin, Aug. 29, 1777, Germain to W. Howe, Aug. 4, 1777, Germain Papers.

"what were best to be done." His brother, lamenting the weakness of his army, saw no prospect of winning the war in 1777.[60] Nor did his subsequent performance endanger the fulfillment of his prediction. Waiting until mid-June to begin the campaign, he spent two weeks trying to lure Washington away from his fortifications in New Jersey and three more in preparing to sail from New York. He did not reach the Delaware until July 30 and then decided to go to Philadelphia by way of the Chesapeake. This circuitous route combined with colonial opposition kept him from reaching Philadelphia for another eight weeks, and before he and his brother had driven the rebels from their fortifications on the Delaware, Burgoyne had surrendered at Saratoga. Indeed the Howes did not secure their hold on Philadelphia, for which they expended the Canadian army and a whole campaign, until November 23, when British shipping was at last able to reach the town. Even then, the capture of Philadelphia proved no more than an additional drain on British strength: expectations of substantial loyalist support in Pennsylvania turned out to be the private chimera of Joseph Galloway and the Allens.[61]

The Howes received Germain's dispatches of early August in October while they were struggling to open the Delaware. Lord Howe refused at first to be baited by the Colonial Secretary. When Lord George congratulated him on the success of his leniency to colonial fishermen, he paid irony with irony by thanking him for his compliment.[62] His brother was not, however, capable of such self-restraint. Though not yet sure that Burgoyne had surrendered, Sir William already knew that the Canadian army was in trouble. Feeling that he was partially responsible for whatever had happened to Burgoyne and knowing that his conquest of Philadelphia would be poor recompense for the loss of an army, he was in no mood to suffer further taunts from Germain. On October 22 he asked to be recalled, saying his recommendations had been ignored and justifying his conduct toward Burgoyne on the ground that he had warned him to expect no direct support from New York.[63] Lord Howe was more subtle.

[60] Apr. 17, 1777, in Tatum, ed., *Journal of Serle,* 212-213; W. Howe to Germain, Apr. 2, 1777, C.O. 5/94.

[61] W. Howe to Germain, Apr. 2, 1777, C.O. 5/94; W. Howe to Germain, Nov. 30, 1777, C.O. 5/95; Dec. 27, 30, and 31, 1776, in Tatum, ed., *Journal of Serle,* 163-165.

[62] Howe to Germain, Oct. 18, 1777, Germain Papers.

[63] W. Howe to Germain, Oct. 22, 1777, C.O. 5/94. As early as Oct. 16, the British heard rumors that General John Burgoyne had been defeated and lost his baggage. "Journals of Captain Henry Duncan," Oct. 16, 1777, pp. 152-153.

A month later, without referring to the ministers' dispatches, he quietly asked the admiralty to name an officer to succeed him in case poor health should force him to resign, and not until December 10 did he reply to the charges that he had neglected the blockade of New England. He had been unable to maintain an adequate blockade, he said, because most of his ships had been employed in supporting the army—his primary responsibility.[64] The government might, of course, have made effective replies to both of the Howes had any need for debating remained.

Sir William's resignation reached London on December 1, and Lord Howe's, on January 7.[65] Because the government was busy digesting Burgoyne's surrender and enjoying the Christmas holiday, no formal action was taken on their resignations until January 10, when the cabinet voted unanimously to replace General Howe. If the issue had developed slowly, it now burst forth with unusual intensity, demonstrating the dangers involved in removing any commander blessed with strong political connections. Indeed, when Lord Howe's mother poured a verbal broadside into Germain, the admiralty promptly retracted its censure of her older son and declared its complete satisfaction with his disposition of the American squadron.[66] The battle over Sir William's resignation was not, however, so quickly settled. Germain, a tougher opponent than Sandwich, was determined to replace General Howe at any cost. On January 31 the King told Lord North to decide whether he would keep the Colonial Secretary or the General. When North chose Germain,[67] he precipitated a further outburst from the Howes and their friends. Lord George's own secretary resigned in protest, as did Lord Chancellor Bathurst. Lady Howe demanded that her husband be given leave to return home with his brother, and she was supported by the Earl of Clarendon, who suggested alternatively that both of the brothers be retained.[68] The King,

[64] Howe to Stephens, Nov. 23, and Dec. 10, 1777, Adm. 1/488.

[65] W. Howe to Germain, Oct. 22, 1777, C.O. 5/94; Howe to Stephens, Nov. 23, 1777, Adm. 1/488.

[66] Germain to the King, Jan. 10, 1778, and the King to North, Jan. 13, 1778, in Fortescue, ed., Correspondence of George Third, IV, 8, 15; John Hobart, Earl of Buckinghamshire to Sir Charles Hotham Thompson, Jan. 16, 1778, Hotham Deposit, DD HO/4/19, East Riding Record Office, Beverley, Yorkshire; Stephens to Howe, Jan. 15, 1778, Adm. 2/556.

[67] The King to North, [Jan. 31], Feb. 2, 1778, in Fortescue, ed., Correspondence of George Third, IV, 13, 33.

[68] Germain to Eden, Feb. 10, 1778, Add. MSS., 34, 415; Feb. 10, 1778, in Hutchinson, ed., Diary and Letters, II, 184; Henry, Earl Bathurst to North, Feb. 15, 1778, Smith Collection, Morristown National Historical Park, Morristown, New

interceding in behalf of the Howes, who had long been his personal favorites, ordered the ministry to soften the terms of the General's recall and to give the Admiral complete freedom either to resign or to retain his command.[69] General Howe left America in May, but his brother, trapped by the arrival of a French fleet, did not sail from New York until September. Changing commanders in a war across the Atlantic was no simple matter. Even when the political battles were over, the ocean remained a formidable barrier.

At its outset the American rebellion posed what was primarily a political problem. When it became a military problem as well, a majority of the British government chose to forget politics and to seek a solution by force of arms. Ironically, those Englishmen who continued to work for a political settlement—men like North and Howe—succeeded only in hampering the majority's efforts to achieve a military victory. In persuading the ministry to approve a peace commission, North interjected imperial politics into the government's preparations for war. When subsequently Lord Howe secured the American command as well as the peace commision, strategy became hopelessly enmeshed with politics. His instructions being entirely inadequate for a successful negotiation, his attempts to promote a reconciliation did no more than forfeit Britain's best chances for a military decision. Although Germain realized as early as December of 1776 that the Howes were violating the spirit of their instructions, he could neither alter their performance nor secure their resignations before a second campaign had passed. In the interim, the Howes, shielded by the Atlantic Ocean and their friends at home, made their way dejectedly to Philadelphia, their dreams of reuniting the empire blasted by the political and military realities of the American rebellion.

Jersey; Mary Countess Howe to North, Feb. 18, 1778, in Barnes and Owen, eds., *Papers of Sandwich*, II, 292; Clarendon to North, Feb. 22, 1778, in Hist. MSS. Com., *The Manuscripts of the Marquis of Abergavenny* . . . (London, 1887), 20; Clarendon to North, Feb. 19, 1778, Clarendon Deposit.

[69] The King to North, Feb. 18, 1778, in Fortescue, ed., *Correspondence of George Third*, IV, 39; North to Sandwich, Feb. 23, 1778, in Barnes and Owen, eds., *Papers of Sandwich*, II, 292n. For examples of the King's attitude toward Lord Howe see A. M. W. Stirling, *The Hothams* . . . (London, 1918), II, 130-131; and Barrow, *Life of Earl Howe*, vii.

British Naval Failure at Long Island: A Lost Opportunity in the American Revolution

By WILLIAM L. CALDERHEAD

If the British had used their naval power to trap Washington and his army on Long Island, the American Revolution might well have foundered. William Calderhead presents a fresh analysis of British failure to prevent the American evacuation. Professor Calderhead is in the history department at the United States Naval Academy.

As the gathering darkness obscured the patriot trenches, one of the momentous nights of the American Revolution had begun. General Washington, with his defeated army of 10,000 men on the tip of Long Island, had determined to effect an escape across the murky East River to the shore of Manhattan Island. Success meant safety and a chance to fight again. Failure meant capture or destruction of most of the army. If the latter occurred, especially on the heels of the recent Declaration of Independence, the shock to the American cause would have been drastic, and the chances of England's crushing the young revolution would have been very great.[1]

It is a fact of history that the American army did escape, thus preserving hope for the patriot cause. From this critical fact, two lesser but significant points have evolved. First, the evacuation by American forces was a masterful stroke of tactics and its inception and execution reflected the generalship of Washington at its very best.[2] Secondly, the British made a serious blunder when they took

1. George O. Trevelyan, *The American Revolution* (2 vols.; London, 1914), Vol. II, Part 1, 291-92; Christopher Ward, *The War of the Revolution* (2 vols.; New York, 1952), I, 236.

2. Ward, *The War of the Revolution*, I, 235-37.

New York History   J U L Y   1976

Washington's retreat at Long Island. From Tomes, Battles of America by Sea and Land.

no steps to cut off the American line of retreat. The Royal Navy had the responsibility of preventing Washington's escape, and it was well prepared for such a task. Its total overall strength was overwhelming, and its dominance in the Long Island campaign was complete. Admiral Richard Howe, the British naval commander, had forty or more powerful warships; the Americans had none. In light of this, the success of Washington's army in extricating itself seems all the more inexplicable.

For nearly two centuries historians have pondered a rational explanation for this British failure. Some historians stressed the role of the weather. This was the theme of Henry Johnston, writing in the 1870s, and supported in more recent years by such authorities as Trevelyan, Anderson, and Billias, all of whom emphasize that "extremely unfavorable winds" prevented the navy from acting.[3] A

3. Troyer S. Anderson, *The Command of the Howe Brothers* (New York, 1936), p. 144; George Billias, *General John Glover and His Marblehead Mariners*

second group, including writers like James Flexner, stress the belief of the British high command that the East River had been effectively blockaded with the hulks of sunken ships and that in any event the British did not take seriously "the possibility of cutting Washington's line of retreat."[4] A third group of historians, including Alfred Mahan, William James, and Ira Gruber, feel that the weather problem was not insurmountable, that lack of navy and army coordination was a major consideration, and that at the very least, small vessels such as whaleboats should have patrolled the East River to prevent or warn of any impending movement for evacuation.[5]

All of these explanations are valid and do shed light on the problem as far as they go. The weather and the hazard of the sunken obstacles did restrict the movements of British ships in the narrow coastal waters. Furthermore, ships' boats were available and were not used in the key area at the critical time.[6] These are the kinds of hazards that all naval forces have to contend with in all operations. The important question is why these difficulties, of a secondary nature for such a navy, were not overcome, especially in such an important operation as this one. Until now historians have only discussed the immediate reasons for failure but not the underlying causes. The unearthing of new evidence, of a corroborative nature, and the occasion of the Bicentennial suggest a need to reexamine the Long Island campaign to ascertain an explanation for the Royal Navy's serious shortcomings.

(New York, 1960), p. 100; Henry P. Johnston, *Campaign of 1776* (Boston, 1878), p. 214; Trevelyan, *American Revolution,* II, Part I, 285.

4. James Flexner, *George Washington in the American Revolution* (Boston, 1967), p. 113. A leading authority on the British army notes that although there were hulks in the East River, Howe could still have cut off part "if not all of the American army." See John W. Fortescue, *History of the British Army,* (13 vols.; London, 1899-1930), III, 186.

5. Ira Gruber, *The Howe Brothers and the American Revolution* (New York, 1972), pp. 112-14; William James, *The British Army in Adversity* (London, 1926), p. 46; Alfred Mahan, *Major Operations of the Navies in the War of American Independence* (London, 1913), pp. 43-44.

6. The Royal Navy was noted for its skill in using ships' boats. Howe's fleet had several dozen of these and used them for special picket duty at night. See William J. Morgan, editor, *Naval Documents of the Revolution,* (6 vols.; Washington, 1972), VI, especially ships' logs of Howe's squadron for July and August of 1776.

The lower Hudson and New York-Long Island theatre of operations. From The War of American Independence *by Don Higginbotham (copyright 1971 by Don Higginbotham). Reproduced by permission of Macmillan Publishing Company.*

The key to an understanding of the Navy's position lies in an analysis of the amphibious operations that occurred in the six weeks prior to Washington's escape from Long Island. Although these operations took place on the Hudson River and in an episode completely detached from the developments on Long Island, they had a direct bearing on the outcome of that campaign.

The Hudson River action began in July of 1776 when Admiral Howe sent a force of two frigates, the *Phoenix* and the *Rose,* and three escorts on a marauding expedition under the command of Captain Hyde Parker, Jr., who would in a later war serve as Nelson's Commander-in-

Chief at Copenhagen.[7] Although Parker's reconnaissance, which took him as far north as Haverstraw Bay, was "successfully carried out," according to the British historian William James, it was met with a determined resistance which included the effective use of shore batteries, row galleys, and fireships.[8] The patriots' employment of these three weapons not only forced the British out of the Hudson but also conditioned their thinking for the next operation—trapping Washington on Long Island.

Of the three types of weapons, the first that Parker's squadron encountered were the American shore batteries. They were numerous, strategically placed in the entire harbor area, and were well-served and accurate. The enemy quickly discovered this when Parker's squadron, as it stood up the Hudson River from the Narrows, faced a gauntlet of fire from batteries at Red Hook, Governor's Island, Paulus Hook, and from a series of batteries on the east bank of the Hudson.[9] Although the rapid speed of the ships, moving under favorable wind and tide, kept the losses light, the experience convinced the British of the defensive capability of the patriot field guns.[10] A further grim reminder of this new situation was the arrival at New York at this very moment of damaged ships of the British squadron that had been repulsed by shore batteries in the recent attack at Charleston, South Carolina. The American fire had forced the grounding of three frigates, damaged the flagship, and wounded its commander, Sir Peter Parker.[11]

7. James Rolfe, *The Naval Biography of Great Britain* (London, 1825), I, 377.

8. James, *Navy in Adversity*, p. 46. There is a possibility that Howe was testing Washington's defenses on the Hudson with the thought of landing his army above New York City rather than on Long Island. If Howe did have this idea, the events on the Hudson must certainly have discouraged him.

9. "Memoirs of William Heath," July 12, 1776, in Morgan, *Naval Documents,* V, 1041.

10. General Washington, who followed the Hudson operation very closely, was a bit disappointed with the American response to the British incursion. See: GW to Pres. of Congress, Geo. Clinton, Patrick Dennis, July 12, 13, 1776 in John C. Fitzpatrick, ed., *The Writings of George Washington,* (39 vols.; Washington, 1931-1944), V, 264-269; Flexner, *Washington,* p. 98; and The Diary of Solomon Nash for July 12-13, 1776, in the Manuscript Collections of the New-York Historical Society, hereafter cited as NYHS.

11. Many British officers in New York were impressed by the damage to Parker's squadron. See: "Diary of William Bamford, Captain of British 40th Regiment,"

213

To make it more costly for Hyde Parker's squadron to withdraw, the Americans began to block the lower Hudson with hulks and chevaux-de-frise near the patriot batteries at Forts Lee and Washington. The British thereupon made plans to reinforce the squadron but dropped these plans on August 6 when it was determined that such a movement on the river would be too dangerous. Ten days later, after an effective attack by American row galleys and fireships, the British were forced to run the gauntlet of the river defenses to make their escape. They succeeded in doing so by maintaining a rapid rate of speed and by slipping through a small gap in the underwater obstructions that had not yet been filled. An American deserter who had been recently employed in positioning the sunken river obstacles piloted the ships to safety.[12]

A second major deterrent to British amphibious operations, and also revealed by Hyde Parker's experience, was the effective American employment of row galleys. To General Washington the enemy penetration of the Hudson River was a serious challenge. It not only threatened important shipping up the river but also severed vital lines of supply and communications between New England and the middle states. The Americans had no warships to counter the enemy move, but they did have another device: a row galley, propelled by oars, and mounting two cannons and a crew of from twelve to sixteen men. Within days of the threat, the American forces brought galleys from as far away as Rhode Island to the danger zone in the lower Hudson. To improve their armament, the two standard nine-pounders were removed and two eighteen-pound cannons were put in their place.[13] The tactical employment of this new weapon became Washington's personal concern, and on August 1 he informed Governor Trumbull of Connecticut (several of the galleys had been supplied by that state) that six of the vessels had been brought together, adding ". . . we propose attempting

Entry of August 1, 1776, printed in *Maryland Historical Magazine*, XXVIII (1932), 296–313.

12. Ambrose Serle, *The American Journal of Ambrose Serle* (San Marino, 1940), 56–57; "Memoirs of William Smith," August 18, 1776, in Morgan, *Naval Documents*, VI, 225–26.

13. "Captain Benjamin Trumbull's Journal of the New York Campaign," July 29, 1776, in Morgan, *Naval Documents*, V, 1273.

something against the ships above and are preparing for it."[14] On August 2 when the frigate *Phoenix* went hard aground in shallow water near Tarrytown, the Americans readied several galleys to move up the river to attack the stranded ship. But before the Americans could act, the *Phoenix* broke free.

Although the British were no longer as vulnerable, the Americans on the following day proceeded with their plans for attack. As the British lay at anchor in mid-stream, four row galleys and three schooners moved up the Hudson to engage the enemy. For nearly two hours the combatants exchanged a heavy fire at distances of up to half a mile. Although the range and the weight of metal fired favored the British (the *Phoenix* alone had forty-four guns to just eight for all the galleys combined), the Americans clearly held their own. The attackers withdrew only after sustaining heavy damage to two of the galleys and suffering sixteen casualties, including two fatalities, one of whom urged his fellow crewmen, "I am a dying man; revenge my blood my boys and carry me alongside my gun that I may die there."[15] British casualties were not recorded, but a deserter from their squadron noted a few days later that his countrymen were greatly concerned by the menace of this American weapon. Instead of smashing the smaller galleys in the battle, which would have been the normal outcome, the British frigates had barely held their own.[16] Instead of closing on the Americans the engagement had been fought at long range. Why this was done cannot be determined, but the fear of having a ship disabled in hostile waters may have led to defensive tactics. In any event, the stronger British force had lost the initiative and the Americans seized it with confidence. General Washington, who had followed the results closely, was highly

14. Fitzpatrick, *Writings of George Washington*, V, 363.

15. *Maryland Gazette*, August 15, 1776; *Virginia Gazette*, August 16, 1776; "Letter of Colonel Benjamin Tupper to Washington," August 3, 1776, Morgan, *Naval Documents*, VI, 37-38.

16. Serle, *The American Journal*, p. 53; "Journal of Capt. Henry Duncan, R.N.," August 8, 1776 in Morgan, *Naval Documents*, VI, 123. There also appears to be evidence that at least one of the galleys behaved badly in the battle. See: Robert Magaw to Colonel Wilson, August, 1776, in the Manuscript Collections of NYHS.

encouraged by the outcome. In a letter to John Hancock, President of Congress, Washington summarized the events of the battle and added that the galleys were to be repaired for "further action" and that obstacles were to be sunk "as soon as possible" near the mouth of the river to obstruct the enemy's movements. Several days later nine row galleys were on their way to Fort Washington as a reinforcement.[17]

But the weapon that gave the British their greatest concern was the fireship, and its effective use in mid-August was the third element that conditioned the Royal Navy's response to the task of closing the trap on the American army on Long Island. The first reference to this device, after New York was threatened, was made by Washington on June 3 when he urged that "fire rafts" be constructed to prevent the enemy from coming into New York harbor. The next reference, also by Washington, on July 17 speaks significantly of sloops that could be turned into fireships and of the urgency with which this should be done. The response to Washington's request was apparently positive, for within the next ten days there were "fireships and a number of fire rafts" ready to be sent against the enemy. Similar vessels of a smaller size were also being readied by an American force at Poughkeepsie, sixty miles upstream, just in case the British ventured that far. By early August the American force was ready and awaited the right opportunity.[18] Conditions during the attack by the row galleys near Tarrytown on August 3 were not favorable owing to the lack of darkness and the fact that the British ships were under way. By withholding them during this action, the Americans would later obtain the valuable element of surprise under almost ideal conditions.

In addition to the extant evidence regarding the activity

17. "Diary of Ensign Caleb Clapp," August 14, 1776, in Morgan, *Naval Documents*, VI, 182–183; GW to Pres. of Congress, Aug. 5, 1776, in Fitzpatrick, *Writings of Washington, V*, 370–72.

18. GW to Israel Putnam, June 3, 1776, and to Geo. Clinton, July 17, 1776, in Fitzpatrick, *Writings of George Washington, V*, 97, 288; "Jacob VanZandt to Captain Richard Varick," Poughkeepsie, July 31, 1776, Morgan, *Naval Documents, V*, 1307–1308. Plans for employing fireships, aside from those in the New York campaign, were being considered as early as the preceding spring. See: S. Richards, *Diary of Captain Samuel Richards* (Philadelphia, 1909), p. 93. See also: "P. Livingston to R. Livingston," August 2, 1776, and "Memoirs of General Heath," August 8, 1776, in Morgan, *Naval Documents*, VI, 20–22, 121.

of the fireships, new material has come to light that further corroborates its importance as a weapon. One of the commanders of the fireships, a Joseph Bass of Leicester, Massachusetts, survived the Revolution and years later, on the fiftieth anniversary of the New York campaign, granted a newspaper interview in which he recalled his wartime experiences against this enemy force.[19] Although he was nearly eighty, his memory was sound and the facts of his story, with only a few minor exceptions, have been confirmed by the other accounts that have already come to light.[20] In August of 1776 Bass was serving under the direction of Commodore Benjamin Tupper, a Massachusetts officer attached to the water service of Washington's army at New York.[21] Under Tupper's direction, two fireships were prepared for use against the British. The first was a sloop called the *Polly* of one hundred tons burden and nearly new.[22] Bass and a select crew of eight men formed its complement. The second vessel, of a slightly smaller size, was under Captain Thomas from New London and had a similarly selected crew. The ships were prepared in New York City and then moved under cover of darkness to Spuyten Duyvil Creek to await a propitious night for attack. The mouth of the creek marked the starting point for the attack, for although the enemy ships lay in the Hudson several miles to the north, it was necessary for the Americans to keep the fireships at a safe distance till the hour of attack in order to minimize the enemy's suspicions. The deck of each fireship was covered with specially prepared faggots of combustible wood and bundles of straw a foot in length that

19. *Worcester Journal* (Worcester, Massachusetts) of May, 1826, cited in *Frederick Town Herald* (Maryland), May 8, 1826.

20. The journals of the *Rose*, the *Phoenix*, the account of General William Heath, and of Captain Richards as well as the news accounts of the *Maryland* and the *Virginia Gazettes* confirm the validity of Bass's account.

21. Benjamin Tupper was colonel of the 21st Massachusetts Regiment and gained valuable experience in this type of operation in his amphibious victory against the British in an action at Great Barents Island, off Boston, August, 1775. See: Ward, *War of the Revolution*, p. 110.

22. Some historians, for example, Flexner, *George Washington*, p. 99, refer to these vessels as fire rafts. One was a sloop and the other a schooner. Both were very maneuverable, which made it difficult for the enemy to evade them. The *Polly* had been built in a shipyard on the Hudson River. See: Diary of Solomon Nash, entry of August 17, 1776, NYHS.

had been dipped in melted pitch. Connecting this incendiary material was a trough of fine gunpowder that extended along and under the deck from the hold into the cabin. Here a person using a match could ignite the powder train, then escape through a hole cut into the side of the vessel to a whaleboat lashed alongside. Twelve barrels of pitch were also placed in the hold and lengths of canvas strips that had been dipped in turpentine covered the yards and rigging and extended down to the deck. Only a moment was required to ignite the entire vessel.[23]

The attacks were postponed on August 8 and August 14, and the British, suspecting some kind of action, moved their forces to the west side of the river in deep water and near high cliffs along the shore. At dusk on August 16, the American forces, about eight miles away, moved silently out into the river and edged upstream under a south wind and an incoming tide. Darkness, heavy clouds, and rain created perfect conditions as the force floated noiselessly northward near the middle of the river. The Americans would have missed the enemy entirely if they had not heard a ship's bell and a sentinel on one of the vessels crying out at 11:00 P.M. that all was well.[24] As it was, it was already too late to single out the big frigates which were the targets of the fireships' attack. Captain Bass in the leading fireship was already past the major targets (all were anchored in line from south to north, beginning with the frigates *Phoenix* and *Rose*). As Bass neared the tender of the *Rose,* he was discovered, and the enemy began firing into his rigging, mast and hull. Putting his ship on a collision course, he ordered his crew off, touched his match, jumped into the whaleboat, and cast off. The fireship became interlocked with the tender's rigging and both were quickly ablaze. In moments the terrorized crew flew on deck and a number threw themselves overboard. An assortment of civilians also appeared in the flames and attempted to save themselves. The British had taken

---

23. Bass Account, *Frederick Town Herald,* May 8, 1826. None of the other accounts describe the fireships or the way in which they were readied for their mission.

24. Bass noted that the time was midnight, but the British frigates listed it as around eleven. Since the ships were keeping the watch, this was most likely the correct time of the attack.

on board a group of Loyalist families from the lower Hudson area and were planning to take them through to the British lines to safety. Ironically, this group which had escaped from one danger would perish from another.[25]

The waters were now lit by blazing ships, and the second fireship was easily spotted by the enemy. Undaunted, Captain Thomas bore down on the *Phoenix* and his vessel grappled with her. In applying a match to the combustibles, however, he "became entangled in his own fire" and had to leap into the water in an effort to save his own life. This mishap, which may have slowed his efforts to touch off the combustibles, combined with the adroit handling by the crew of the *Phoenix*, saved the frigate. Although the ship was on fire in several places, the crew cut the rigging, slipped the cables, broke lose from the clutch of the fireship, and escaped destruction.[26] Within an hour it was over, and the victorious Americans returned to their base to receive "the warmest acclamations of gratitude." Both sides had losses. Thomas and most of his crew were gone. The British lost several men on the *Phoenix*, and nearly seventy, including women and children, perished on the tender.[27]

Of far greater significance than the losses was the reaction

25. In addition to cutting American communications along the river, the ships were also giving succor to Loyalists in the area. See: GW to John Washington, July 22, 1776, in Fitzpatrick, *Writings of Washington*, V, 326; Major Hutcheson's letter on Long Island, August 8, 1776, in Morgan, *Naval Documents*, VI, 123-124.
26. This was a skillful maneuver on the part of Captain Parker that helped save his ship and was duly noted by his superiors. Serle, *American Journal*, p. 70.
27. British accounts omitted listing the casualties and American accounts noted only military losses. See: Bass account in *Frederick Town Herald*, May 8, 1826, and accounts of *Phoenix, Rose*, and General Heath as well as the newspapers, *Maryland Gazette*, August 29, 1776, and the *Virginia Gazette*, August 31, 1776. Various Revolutionary War accounts have listed four people as captains of the two fireships. They were: Sergeants Smith and Thomas Fosdick and "Commanders" Thomas and Joseph Bass. It is very likely that all four men were involved but in their own specialty. Thus the two vessels required expert ship handlers. Captains Bass and Thomas supplied these skills on the two vessels. Bass survived but Thomas drowned. The operation also required technical supervision, and Sergeants Smith and Fosdick of Nathan Hale's ranger company supplied this. Smith, on the same vessel as Thomas, died of burns. See: Billias, *General Clover*, p. 220n; *Maryland Gazette*, August 29, 1776; George Seymour, *The Documentary Life of Nathan Hale* (New Haven, 1941), p. 109; and Max Hoyt, ed., *Index of Revolutionary War Pension Applications* (Washington, 1966), under names of Bass and Fosdick. Bass had lived in Connecticut in the 1770's but later moved to Massachusetts.

on both sides to the successful use of fireships on the Hudson. Major General Heath who had observed the night battle from the high shoreline along the edge of the river wrote immediately to Washington. Praising the action, he felt that the patriots could have wreaked even greater destruction, adding, "I am confident that if an attempt should be made on the fleet below, and but one or two ships set on fire, their confusion would be beyond description."[28] Washington was also optimistic about the results of the action, noting in a message to Governor Trumbull, "I think it alarmed the enemy greatly."[29] Whether specific plans were made for further fireships at this point cannot be determined, but work was rushed on the fireships at Poughkeepsie and all units that had been readied at Spuyten Duyvil dropped down to New York City for future operations.[30]

The British reaction was critical to the next events in the campaign. The squadron quickly withdrew from the Hudson River, and Captain Wallace of the *Rose* reported to Admiral Howe the results of the recent action. The officers were then feted at a special dinner held on the flagship, and a short time later both Captains Parker and Wallace were knighted for their efforts against the American attack.[31] But it was Captain George Collier, recently arrived in port, and considered by historians to be a shrewd naval observer,[32] who spoke for many when he observed, "I must own that the present situation of this numerous fleet is extremely critical as the rebels have six fireships now in sight lying close under the cannon of the town; the first dark night when the wind blows strong down the river, they probably will send them in flames to burn us, and I foresee if they attempt it, the loss of half of our transports and merchant ships, who from terror will cut their cables, fall

---

28. "Major General Heath to General Washington," August 17, 1776, in Morgan, *Naval Documents,* VI, 217-19.

29. "George Washington to Governor Trumbull," August 18, 1776, in Morgan, *Naval Documents,* VI, 227.

30. "Major General Heath to General Washington," August 18, 1776, in Morgan, *Naval Documents,* VI, 226.

31. Serle, *American Journal,* p. 68.

32. Gruber, *The Howe Brothers,* pp. 112-14.

aboard one another, and if not burned, will be wrecked on the shore."[33]

On August 22, Admiral Howe had an opportunity to inspect the fire damage to the *Phoenix* first hand, for he hoisted his flag aboard the frigate in order to observe the troop landings on Long Island. His personal reaction is not known, but he soon took the precaution to order "ten armed boats belonging to the men-of-war to row guard about a mile above the fleet." In reference to this, Captain Collier noted, "The admiral favors me with the post of honor, lying above the shipping and nearest the enemy. I therefore never go to bed during the night nor do my officers or men as our safety (and that of the fleet) depends on our vigilence."[34] From this time and until the end of August, the fleet took special precautions and at night had fire booms out and armed boats on patrol with special officers on "row guard."[35] Still, there was uneasiness and as Collier believed, "it will prove very ineffective should the Rebels send down their fireships favored by a strong wind and tide."[36] The expected attack never materialized. Either the Americans were not yet ready, or more probably, were awaiting a direct assault on New York before using their new weapon.

In the interval, General Howe's army landed on Long Island and on August 26 outflanked and defeated the American army. The latter withdrew to its defenses on Brooklyn Heights and Washington faced one of the critical decisions of his career: Should he build up his forces to withstand a siege or attempt to escape? The fourth and final matter that affected the outcome of the campaign may now be considered; namely, the appearance that in spite of his defeat Washington was reinforcing his army. This impression in British eyes would nullify any idea that he was contemplating an evacuation. The historian Ward in analyzing this situation writes, "astonishingly enough,

33. "Journal of Admiral Sir George Collier," in Morgan, *Naval Documents,* VI, 1517-1518.

34. Ibid., pp. 1518-1520.

35. See: Logbooks and Journals of *Roebuck, Eagle, Rose,* and *Greyhound* from August 27 to August 31, 1776 in Morgan, *Naval Documents,* VI, 324-78.

36. "Journal of Admiral Collier,"August 20-28, 1776, in Morgan, *Naval Documents,* VI, 1518-1520.

not recognizing the peril of his position Washington called for reinforcements from New York."[37] Although the British observed these troop movements from their positions on Long Island and in the Narrows, their reaction is not recorded. They did *not* counter the reinforcing efforts. Instead they occupied themselves with plans to fire at the American battery at Red Hook and then in making a demonstration against New York City. The most acute observation was made by General Washington. He was aware that the British army had already made one successful flanking movement to endanger the American forces. Now the navy could match this by moving to the other flank of the patriot army on the 26th and 27th under favorable weather conditions. Such a move would not only prevent American troop reinforcements to Brooklyn Heights but, if the navy chose to remain at that spot, it would also jeopardize any American attempt at evacuation. Instead, the British navy, aside from the demonstration, did nothing. Washington had been closely observing this fleet, and "finding no danger was to be apprehended from that quarter, crossed over to Long Island."[38] The enemy obviously showed a lack of aggressiveness in the narrow waters. Perhaps a quick decision to reinforce or evacuate would, under the circumstances, not be gravely hazardous.

After Washington discovered that his forces at Brooklyn were in no condition to withstand a siege, he made a secret plan to withdraw. Historians have declared that this decision was made suddenly and on August 29 after he had discovered that a new enemy trench line had been dug dangerously close to his own.[39] Thus all reinforcements to that time were supposedly to strengthen his defenses. If the listed dates of the dispatches of two subordinates can be believed, however, Washington was forming plans to escape as soon as he had taken stock of his battle losses. There is good evidence to support this. First, Colonel Hugh Hughes, serving in a quartermaster capacity, noted that he was given verbal orders on August 27 by Washington to collect all watercraft from Spuyten Duyvil Creek on the

37. Ward, *War of the Revolution*, I, 231.
38. Johnston, *Campaign of 1776*, p. 189.
39. Flexner, *George Washington*, p. 114; Johnston, *Campaign of 1776*, p. 212.

Hudson to Hellgate on the Sound.[40] Secondly, General Heath noted, on the 28th,[41] that all boats that could be spared were to be sent down to New York "intimating that we might throw over more troops." Heath added importantly that "the *real* intention of their use was fully understood."[42]

It would seem from the above that Washington was aware of his peril—more so than were the British—that he took immediate steps to remedy it, and disguised his intentions at the same time. The Royal Navy, at the very least, must have been misled, and none of the British dispatches reveal any hint that the Americans might be readying an attempt to slip away. Admiral Howe, therefore, had no need to take any precautionary steps at least of his own volition. In fact, on August 28, the Admiral reminded his ship commanders that General Howe "had every reason to be content with the prospects before him," and added significantly, "At present we must wait upon the movements of the army."[43]

It seems clear that if the British fleet were to trap the American army on Long Island it had three alternatives. The strongest would have been the use of frigates to patrol the zone of evacuation. Unfavorable wind conditions and currents would have been a deterrent here, as historians have noted, but these would not have been insuperable. The great danger came from the enemy. First there was the risk of frigates running aground in narrow waters controlled by American shore batteries.[44] This was almost the fate of the *Phoenix* on the Hudson. Secondly there was the threat of fireships used in conjunction with obstacles and shore batteries. Thanks to the attack on Hyde Parker's force, the

40. George Washington to Colonel Hugh Hughes, August 22, 1784, Hughes Letters, Manuscript Collections of NYHS. In this letter Hughes explicitly notes that the date was August 27. Billias in *General Glover* also notes this discrepancy. See his footnote 7 on page 220.

41. Ward says this was done on "the morning of the 29th." See *American Revolution*, I, 233.

42. "Memoirs of General Heath," August 28, 1776, in Morgan *Naval Documents*, VI, 335.

43. During the war, British naval and army commanders were prone to disagreement, but the Howes were brothers and they enjoyed cordial relations. "Vice Admiral Richard Howe to Commodore Hotham," August 28, 1776, in Morgan, *Naval Documents*, VI, 337.

44. Flexner, *George Washington*, p. 113.

British captains feared the American skill with this device and would not have favored exposing big frigates merely for patrol purposes.[45]

The second alternative was to use smaller craft such as whaleboats. Again, the effective way in which the patriots had handled their row galleys would have caused the British to hesitate unless the whaleboats were protected by heavier ships, an option that has already been discounted.[46] There was still a third possibility that might have had some effect. A squadron of three ships—the *Niger* of 32 guns, the *Brune* of 28 guns, and the *Halifax* of 18—had been dispatched by Admiral Howe on August 23 to sail around Long Island, enter the Sound from the east, and harass any American efforts to reinforce the battle zone from the Connecticut area.[47] The force was a small but strong one, and its appearance greatly disturbed the patriots who at the moment had nothing in the area to counter it.[48] Most significant, these ships by coming from the opposite direction could have moved into the East River and behind Washington's lines on the same wind and tide that reportedly prevented Howe's frigates from moving up from the Narrows. The admiral, though, had given no instructions to patrol behind the American lines, and after its departure the squadron was out of communication with Howe's forces.[49] Thus on the afternoon of August 29, after nearly

45. Howe also considered himself shorthanded in ships in this campaign and obviously hesitated to risk them. Wright, *The Navy in Adversity*, p. 45.

46. In small boat operations it was always prudent to have the broadsides of the heavier guns available. Only frigates and line-of-battle ships could have supplied this. W. L. Clowes believed that whaleboats would have been practical but that "large ships were inadequate." See: his *Royal Navy* (London, 1966), III, 384.

47. *Connecticut Journal*, August 28, 1776. See also the logbooks of the *Niger* and the *Halifax* for August in Morgan, *Naval Documents*, VI, August, 1776.

48. "Journal of the New York Committee of Public Safety," August 29, 1776, in Morgan, *Naval Documents*, VI, 349.

49. There is no indication in Ambrose Serle's journal or in Lord Howe's orders to his ship commanders that this squadron should attempt to block any American escape effort. The only written orders were on August 13, when the ships were "to be stationed at the [Eastern] entrance of the Sound to prevent supplies being sent thru to the town of New York." For this citation and for August messages see: Morgan, *Naval Documents*, VI, 167, 156-293, which covers the date of arrival to departure on their mission.

circling Long Island, the British ships moved into Flushing Bay and anchored for the night.[50] This decision was a sound one from the squadron's viewpoint. It was late in the day, and major navigational hazards lay ahead in the waters between Hellgate, Welfare Island, and the East River. They were obviously not aware that Washington's army, a scant seven miles away by direct line but about ten by water, was trapped at the tip of Long Island. If the ships had continued on course for two more hours, and the Americans had little to impede them, they would have been in sight of the Brooklyn ferry crossing. In this position they would have observed the first moves at dusk for the evacuation. Most likely their presence would have forced the Americans to postpone their efforts to escape. Instead the British ships stayed at Flushing Bay just beyond range, leaving the doorway to escape wide open. Washington took advantage of this piece of good fortune and began his fateful evacuation. Little did they know it, but the small British squadron, except for the matter of two hours of daylight sailing, had come within a hair's breadth of sealing the fate of Washington's army on Long Island.

Admiral Howe has been blamed, however, for not using the forces that he had immediately at hand to prevent the American escape. What was the extent of his culpability? Two points must be noted. First, if he had suspected an evacuation, he would certainly have risked his heavy ships in the narrow waters. His daring moves under broadly similar circumstances against the French at Quiberon Bay, eighteen years before, are proof of this.[51] But secondly and most importantly, all signs pointed to no immediate American evacuation. Exposing his ships on dangerous night patrol merely to prove that the patriots were still there presented a risk that was greater than the expected returns. Playing the odds in the orthodox manner,

---

50. Washington was aware of the threat presented by this squadron and listed it as his eighth and final reason for his evacuation. Fitzpatrick, *Writings of Washington,* V, 509.

51. For an excellent summary of Howe's superb ship handling in similarly narrow waters, see: Goeffrey Marcus, *Quiberon Bay* (Barre, 1963), 152-57, and Julian Corbett, *England in the Seven Years War,* (2 vols.; London, 1918), I, 275-81, 296-304; II, 65-70. In 1776, however, Howe was nearly twenty years older and had the responsibility of an entire fleet.

the Royal Navy took no action. Admiral Howe was following a safe and, for the moment, logically justifiable approach.

Fortunately for the American cause, General Washington was not so orthodox in his own actions. Having fewer resources to work with, he was forced to be innovative and to take heavy risks. The challenge of the enemy threat in July and the near disaster in late August brought out the qualities of Washington's generalship and showed that he was capable of superb tactical efforts. Thus his response to the British naval probe up the Hudson was positive and direct. Through his personal attention to an amphibious operation in which he professed no expertise, he not only checked the enemy but he forced their withdrawal as well. In the process and in the week following, he was able to gauge the temper of the British, especially their naval arm, which would be the real arbiter of the large scale operation that General Howe had begun. Finding that his efforts (deliberate or pretended) to reinforce his army had gone unchallenged and that escape was his only ultimate recourse, his choice was clear: a secret and swift evacuation. Despite the fact that neither Washington nor his army had any proficiency or practice in this, the withdrawal was perfectly executed. Paradoxically, the landsman and novice in amphibious warfare had outwitted the professional who had spent a lifetime and had built a reputation on this type of operation. In saving his army and in preserving the American cause, Washington exhibited the breadth of ability and versatility of skills that for a half century gladdened his contemporaries and have never ceased to amaze his historical critics.

Guy Carleton versus Benedict Arnold: The Campaign of 1776 in Canada and on Lake Champlain

By PAUL DAVID NELSON

Noting the importance to the ultimate American victory of the 1776 campaign in northern New York, Paul David Nelson discusses the campaign from both British and American perspectives, and offers a new explanation for British failure. Dr. Nelson is a member of the history department at Berea College, Berea, Kentucky.

In early November, 1776, happily for the rebel party of the newly created United States, Guy Carleton withdrew his invading army from the upper reaches of Lake Champlain into Canada. Few observers doubted then, and few historians have doubted since, that America's successful defense of upstate New York in 1776 contributed much to subsequent patriot victory in the struggle for independence from Britain. Had Carleton managed to bring his legions southward and unite them with General William Howe's forces in the southern part of the state, the situation of the revolutionaries might have been grim indeed. With Britain in control of the strategic Lake Champlain-Hudson River waterway, and with the Royal navy dominating coastal sea lanes, New England would have been successfully separated from other rebelling states and all might have been conquered piecemeal.[1]

There is little agreement, however, among either contemporaries or subsequent analysts, as to why Carleton's

1. For a discussion of the importance of the Hudson River and Lake Champlain in the strategic planning of both Americans and Britons, see Hoffman Nickerson, "New York in the Strategy of the Revolution," Alexander C. Flick, ed., *History of the State of New York* (10 vols., New York, 1933), IV, 78-83, Dave R. Palmer, *The River and the Rock* (New York, 1969), and Piers Mackesy, *The War for America, 1775-1783* (Cambridge, Mass., 1964), pp. 143-44.

expedition faltered or who was responsible for that turn of events. Two major interpretations have been given. One argument, which most scholars do not accept, is that Carleton himself was to blame.[2] The more usual interpretation is that the British invasion failed because of the exertions of an American commander, Benedict Arnold, who forced Carleton into a time-consuming shipbuilding race on Lake Champlain and then fought a brilliant naval battle to impede the enemy's advance toward Fort Ticonderoga at the south end of the lake. This argument is best stated by Alfred Thayer Mahan, who declared, "That the Americans were strong enough to impose the capitulation of Saratoga, was due to the invaluable year of delay secured to them by their little navy on Lake Champlain, created by the indomitable energy, and handled with the indomitable courage, of the traitor, Benedict Arnold."[3]

Neither of these interpretations, I believe, is wholly adequate to explain the outcome of Carleton's offensive against America in 1776. Rather, the campaign was influenced by a number of factors, only one of which was military leadership, either British or American. As with all wartime situations, this one fell sway to conditions of terrain, logistics, and simple luck beyond the ability of any individual to control. Still, after giving due weight to these factors, it appears that the collapse of the English effort was due more

2. The writer most critical of Carleton's handling of the campaign of 1776 is A. L. Burt, who presented his evidence in "The Quarrel Between Germain and Carleton: An Inverted Story," *Canadian Historical Review,* XI (September, 1930), pp. 202-22, and *Guy Carleton, Lord Dorchester, 1724-1804* (Ottawa, 1960). In the same vein, see Paul H. Smith, "Sir Guy Carleton: Soldier Statesman," in George A. Billias, ed., *George Washington's Opponents: British Generals and Admirals in the American Revolution* (New York, 1969), pp. 122-25. Recent and more traditional interpretations that view Carleton in a more favorable light are Perry Eugene Leroy, "Sir Guy Carleton as a Military Leader During the American Invasion and Repulse in Canada, 1775-1776" (Ph.D. dissertation, Ohio State University, 1960), pp. 144-80, 442-99, and R. Arthur Bowler, *Logistics and the Failure of the British Army in America, 1775-1783* (Princeton, 1975), pp. 214-25.

3. Alfred Thayer Mahan, *The Major Operations of the Navies in the War of American Independence* (Boston, 1913), p. 7. Other scholars who give similar analyses of Arnold's role are Isaac N. Arnold, *The Life of Benedict Arnold: His Patriotism and His Treason* (Chicago, 1880), pp. 105-20, James T. Flexner, *The Traitor and the Spy: Benedict Arnold and John André* (New York, 1953), pp. 112-13, and Willard M. Wallace, *Traitorous Hero: The Life and Fortunes of Benedict Arnold* (New York, 1954), pp. 118-20.

to acts of omission and commission on the part of Carleton than to outstanding command decisions by Arnold. As historian Piers Mackesy has said of Carleton's activities in 1776, the evidence in his favor "is not as unequivocal as his admirers claim."[4] A reinterpretation of this exciting aspect of American Revolutionary history is warranted because previous scholars have overlooked some evidence, and no one has tried in one essay to view the campaign from both British and American angles. In addition, recent scholarship has cast new light on certain aspects of the subject.

Any discussion of the campaign of 1776 must begin by analyzing whether General Carleton could have done more to entrap the Americans in Canada at the beginning of the military season. Had he seized these rebel troops, Lake Champlain would have been his early in the summer, and he could have captured Ticonderoga before the Americans collected an army to defend it. From Ticonderoga it might have been an easy matter for him to march southward and unite his troops with those of Howe in New York City. The American army had invaded Canada the year before, with one group under Richard Montgomery moving down the Richelieu River toward Montreal, the other, led by Benedict Arnold, marching through Maine toward Quebec. In December, these detachments converged upon Quebec, and late in the month, under Montgomery's command, they assaulted Carleton's defenses, only to be repulsed with considerable losses. In the attack, Montgomery was killed, and Arnold wounded in the leg; the latter assumed leadership of patriot forces, but being too weak to mount another attack against the enemy, he besieged Carleton's army in Quebec for the rest of the winter. Both Arnold and Carleton then had awaited the spring of 1776 with the hope that their government would be first to send relief.

During the winter, Britain's prime minister, Frederick, Lord North, and his advisers determined that in the following year a major offensive would take place in America, with General Howe leading a massive army against New York

4. Mackesy, *War for America*, p. 77.

229

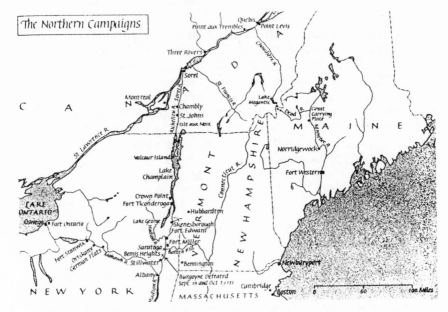

The theatre of Carleton's campaign. From The War of American Independence *by Don Higginbotham (copyright 1971 by Don Higginbotham). Reproduced by permission of Macmillan Publishing Company.*

City on the southern end of the Hudson River, and Carleton, reinforced with 10,000 men, marching southward from Canada. North and Lord George Germain, recently appointed secretary of the American Department, hoped that these troops would unite and compel the rebel opposition to submit to the crown.[5] Carleton knew nothing of these plans until the first British ship of the new year arrived at Quebec on May 6, and he apparently was surprised to learn that his major responsibilities in the coming year were to be military rather than civil. For ten years he had been a colonial governor, and in 1775 he had given little thought to suppressing the rebellion in other parts of America. Hence, the military duties suddenly handed him turned out to be more than he could handle adequately.[6] The dual

5. British planning for 1776 is admirably discussed by Ira Gruber, in *The Howe Brothers and the American Revolution* (New York, 1972), pp. 72-88.

6. Smith, "Carleton," in Billias, ed., *Washington's Opponents,* p. 121. Carleton's instructions for the campaign are in Lord George Germain to Guy Carleton, February 17, March 28, 1776, calendared in Douglas Brymner, ed., "State Papers," *Report on Canadian Archives, 1890* (Ottawa, 1891), pp. 69-70.

tasks of being civilian governor of Canada and leader of an army would prove for him irreconcilable.

In opposing the American invasion, although the British had been first to reach their army in Canada with soldiers and supplies, Carleton moved with great caution in relieving the siege of Quebec. For one thing, his intelligence reports indicated that the rebel army was much larger than it actually was.[7] For another, his reinforcements did not all arrive at once—in fact, were to dribble in until the middle of June. He did send 900 men out of the city to oppose the enemy, but the Americans had departed upriver with precipitation, and all that his army found was an empty camp. Taking the small band of troops he now had on hand, Carleton moved toward the Americans, but he continued to act with extreme care. To Germain he wrote on May 25, "The Rebels are still numerous in the Province, & talk of large reinforcements." When his ships on the St. Lawrence River ran into contrary winds near Trois-Rivières, he deposited two regiments on shore to keep an eye on the enemy and by June 2 was back in Quebec to "hasten the refitting and building of Bateaux."[8]

In the next few days, British transports continued to arrive with men and equipment, and Carleton welcomed John Burgoyne to serve as second in command of his growing army. Yet Carleton continued to exercise caution, building up his forces at Trois-Rivières in preparation for an advance instead of harassing the enemy. A new American commander, General John Sullivan, took advantage of this lull and led 2,000 men to the north side of the St. Lawrence to attack Carleton's staging base. On June 8, Sullivan's numerically inferior army was thrown back with heavy losses (especially in prisoners), and he seemed in imminent peril of being trapped by the British navy, which controlled the river between him and his only route of escape. Burgoyne had already written Germain on June 1 that the rebels could be ensnared if fifteen or twenty fast ships sailed

7. Carleton to Germain, May 14, 1776, Colonial Office Papers, class 42, vol. 35, pp. 3-11, Public Records Office, London (microfilm copy of the originals, Public Archives of Canada, Ottawa), hereafter cited as C.O. 42/ vol. number, page numbers.

8. Carleton to Germain, May 25, June 2, 1776, C.O. 42/35, pp. 45, 54.

231

quickly up the St. Lawrence; but even now Carleton refused to allow the Royal navy to be used in this way. Hence, the American general escaped with his army.[9]

At this point Carleton was conducting a policy of leniency towards the rebels, hoping to persuade them to end their opposition to British authority. He not only failed to pursue the Americans, but also released the prisoners captured at Trois-Rivières. As he later explained to Germain, his aim was "to convince all His Majesty's unhappy subjects, that the King's mercy and Benevolence were still open to them."[10] This policy may have been humane, but it was hardly designed to destroy an enemy that gave every indication of fighting tenaciously for a foothold in Canada. Carleton had let slip a real opportunity to do serious harm to the invader's army.

After June 8, Carleton did set in motion a plan which might yet entrap the rebels in Canada. He gave Brigadier General Simon Fraser command of a detachment which was to march up the north side of the St. Lawrence and besiege Arnold's garrison at Montreal. Meanwhile Burgoyne would lead a force of 4,000 troops against American lines at Sorel, while he personally sailed with the remainder of the army up the St. Lawrence to Longueuil, march overland to St. Johns, and come in behind the enemy on the Richelieu River. In order not to endanger the play by having Sullivan retreat too rapidly toward St. Johns, Carleton ordered Burgoyne not to hazard "any thing till the column on his right [from Longueuil] should be able to cooperate with him."[11]

A series of fateful accidents and a lack of vigor on his own part caused Carleton to lose this second chance to annihilate the enemy and take uncontested control of Lake Champlain. Arnold, learning of Fraser's advance, abandoned Montreal and struck out for St. Johns. Sullivan also retreated when he realized that he was about to be attacked at Sorel. By June 14 Burgoyne was pursuing the enemy up

9. John Burgoyne to Germain, June 1, 1776, Historical Manuscripts Commission, *Report on the Manuscripts of Mrs. Stopford-Sackville of Drayton House, Northamptonshire* (4 vols., Hereford, 1904–1910), II, 33.

10. Carleton to Germain, August 10, 1776, C.O. 42/35, pp. 122–23.

11. Carleton to Germain, June 20, 1776, C.O. 42/35, pp. 60–61.

the Richelieu but was holding back because of his orders not to press too hard. Meanwhile, Carleton was stranded on board his ships, the wind having failed, and Fraser was attempting to get across the St. Lawrence and into the chase. Not until June 18 did Carleton have all his columns marching from Longueuil toward St. Johns, even though he might have debarked his troops when the fleet became immobilized. By the time Carleton did get into action, the Americans had managed to destroy a number of row galleys and four schooners below the rapids at Chambly, wreck the shipyards and all useful stores at St. Johns, and burn many buildings. With all available shipping, they abandoned Canada only hours before Burgoyne's forces marched in on the eighteenth. Carleton arrived the following morning.[12]

Had Carleton succeeded in capturing Sullivan's rebel army before it escaped from Canada, the outcome of the campaign of 1776 might have been quite different. But the Canadian general had advanced from Quebec with no seeming sense of urgency, holding back on two occasions from attempting an entrapment of the enemy. Moreover, his policy of leniency towards his foes, expressed clearly by his generosity toward prisoners and perhaps by his refusal to press the Americans too hard, did not indicate that he desired to carry out an effective campaign. At least, he seemed torn between what he saw as an effective civil policy and efficient military action.[13] Of course, many of the things which slowed Carleton's pursuit of the enemy were beyond his control. If the wind blew eastward or not at all, he could not command it to change; if his reinforcements arrived in driblets instead of all at once, he must not be held responsible; if the new troops were fatigued by their ocean voyage, he could not push them beyond endurance; if his intelligence network informed him that the rebels were stronger in numbers and higher in morale than they

---

12. Carleton to Germain, June 20, 1776, C.O. 42/35, pp. 60–61; Gerald Saxon Brown, *The American Secretary: The Colonial Policy of Lord George Germain, 1775-1778* (Ann Arbor, 1963), pp. 77–78.

13. This interpretation is similar to Burt's, in "The Quarrel Between Germain and Carleton," *Canadian His. Review*, XI, esp. p. 211, and *The Old Province of Quebec* (Minneapolis and Toronto, 1933), p. 239.

actually were, perhaps he was not derelict in being wary of harassing them too vigorously[14] (but one wonders how he could not have been aware that he had under his command five times as many soldiers as the enemy and that Sullivan's men were sick and dispirited).

All these factors notwithstanding, the record of Carleton in fighting Canada's invaders was not impressive. In a letter to Germain in September, Carleton claimed that his sole purpose all along had been merely to expel the rebels from his province, and that therefore he had been successful. However, on June 20, he had written Germain, "had not the wind failed" as his part of the army sailed toward Longueuil, he might at least have entrapped Arnold's contingent in Montreal. The implication of his letter was that he intended to cut off Sullivan as well.[15] With the exception of Lieutenant Colonel Gabriel Christie, who arrived in Canada with Burgoyne, none of Carleton's subordinates criticized their commander for the Americans' escape; and Christie himself had become a bitter enemy of Carleton for other reasons. Yet on October 26, after the campaign had concluded, Christie made a telling point in a letter to Germain when he argued that had Carleton acted with vigor he could have captured the rebel army in Canada.[16] Even harsh or unfair critics at times can make cogent arguments.

So by June 20 Carleton was in possession of Canada, and the remnants of the American army were in disarray at Crown Point and Ticonderoga on the south end of Lake Champlain. But the Canadian commander did not take advantage of the situation, for he suddenly lapsed back into caution and brought his campaign to a halt. Even those scholars who have found least to criticize in his conduct against the rebels agree that at this point he was acting with more than necessary care. Yet Carleton was convinced that he had good reasons for temporarily suspending operations at St. Johns. Since he knew of no roads for marching troops

14. Leroy, "Carleton as a Military Leader," pp. 179-80; Bowler, *Logistics*, pp. 217-18.

15. Carleton to Germain, September 28, June 20, 1776, C.O. 42/35, pp. 171-75, 60-61.

16. Gabriel Christie to Germain, October 26, 1776, Germain Papers, William L. Clements Library, Ann Arbor, Michigan, hereafter cited as Clements Library.

southward, he decided it was necessary to transport them by water, and that task could be accomplished only if he constructed barges for the soldiers along with warships necessary to protect these vulnerable craft. The enemy, he was aware, possessed on Lake Champlain a sloop and three schooners, which General Philip Schuyler had captured in 1775, while the British had no warships at all.

Of course, Carleton had numerous vessels of war in the St. Lawrence River, but they could be used on Lake Champlain only if torn down, hauled around ten miles of shallow rapids in the Richelieu below Chambly, and reconstructed—a backbreaking task that would consume enormous amounts of time. He now set his army to this labor in addition to reconstructing the naval works at St. Johns in order to build barges for transporting the army. Carleton had requested of London in November, 1775, that barges be sent to him, but by late September of 1776 he had received only ten of the more than 500 needed. Besides these craft, he had gotten only fourteen small boats that mounted one bow gun each. As he pointed out to Germain in September, after receiving from the American Secretary a letter that he considered critical of his activities thus far in the campaign, he was by and large on his own in constructing a fleet to attack the Americans to the southward.[17] That he must spend months at this duty was owing solely to the fact that the Richelieu rapids existed. Perhaps these shallow waters, as much as anything else, finally determined the outcome of the campaign on Lake Champlain in 1776.

Whatever attention they gave to the lake invasion route, the British officers in Canada did not focus solely upon that alternative as a means of getting at the escaped rebels. In fact, they would have liked nothing better than to find a way to move rapidly southward by bypassing this strategic bottleneck. Thus John Burgoyne presented an alternate plan: ". . . to put myself at the head of only three British Battalions with a corps of artillery some Canadians & a large

---

17. Carleton to Germain, July 9, September 28, 1776, C.O. 42/35, pp. 96–97, 171–75. For more information on the beehive activity of the British at this time, see Burgoyne to Henry Clinton, July 7, 1776, Clinton Papers, Clements Library. The vessels Carleton had requested were diverted to William Howe's army at New York City (Mackesy, *War for America,* pp. 94–95).

Benedict Arnold. Courtesy of the American Antiquarian Society.

body of Indians which we had at command, to [take] my route by Oswego & fort Stanwix, & [establish] myself on the Mohawk River." This scheme, he believed, would divert the enemy's attention from Ticonderoga, since Burgoyne's force would pose a direct threat to the rear of that bastion of American defense. Carleton liked the plan, and approved it, but a severe shortage of provisions forced him to abandon it.[18]

This last point deserves emphasis, for as a recent scholar has argued, one of Carleton's major worries throughout his campaign was a constant shortage of provisions. The supply situation, which was "precarious in the extreme," not only affected British ability to expedite Burgoyne's diversion, but also forced Carleton to pause at St. Johns to "collect a reserve of provisions." He could not have moved forward with full force immediately, then, even had he possessed a fleet.[19] These facts, coupled with problems imposed on the British by the rapids at Chambly, cast considerable doubt on Mahan's assertion that America's subsequent triumph

18. Burgoyne to Clinton, November 17, 1776, Clinton Papers, Clements Library.
19. Bowler, *Logistics*, pp. 219–23, quotes on pp. 219, 222–23.

in the campaign was "due to the invaluable year of delay secured to them by their little navy," built by the "indomitable" Benedict Arnold. Delay for Carleton there certainly was, but whether imposed by the Americans is highly questionable.

Even given all his problems, Carleton still seems to have been too slow and careful at this stage of the campaign. If he lacked supplies, he was certainly richer in resources than his opponents, and by dragging out over three months his building of a fleet he gave the Americans a splendid opportunity—which they took advantage of—to recover after the severe trouncing they had received in Canada. Lieutenant Colonel Christie was particularly upset with Carleton's lassitude and hesitation, accusing him of ineptitude and charging that he was responsible for great delays in building the fleet. Giving due weight to Christie's enmity toward Carleton, the subordinate officer seems to have a point. Carleton's attention during the summer of 1776 continued to be divided between military and civil matters, and he may have neglected the former. In August he returned to Quebec and spent a great deal of time reorganizing the court system to conform to the provisions of the

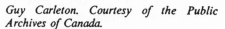

Guy Carleton. Courtesy of the Public Archives of Canada.

237

Quebec Act. And Carleton was being accurately told by his intelligence system that the rebel forces at Crown Point were tiny, decimated by smallpox, and low in morale, waiting like rotten fruit to be shaken from the tree if only the much superior British army would seize the opportunity.[20]

Yet the Canadian commander hesitated to act, not primarily because he lacked provisions but because he feared the Americans' "naval superiority" on the lake—the four small warships which the rebels commanded at Crown Point. But were these boats a threat to him? And if not should he have been aware of the fact? The truth is, on July 16, almost a month after the Americans abandoned St. Johns, the vessels were described by Major General Horatio Gates (who had replaced Sullivan as commander of the decimated army at Crown Point) as *unarmed* "Floating Waggons," which he had just then ordered to be fitted out with cannon and ammunition. It seems apparent that Carleton's excessive caution was working to the advantage of his foes while gaining nothing for himself. Had he scraped together enough transport and provisions in late June or early July to move even a part of his army against the rebels, the outcome would hardly have been in doubt. That such an effort would have required all his energy is beyond doubt; that it would have been possible to accomplish does not seem beyond reason. For on July 12 Gates was declaring that if the enemy faced him at Ticonderoga he must have 6,000 men to carry out a successful defense of that place; at that, his estimate was conservative. His effective force then consisted of hardly one-sixth that number.[21] Carleton clearly had let pass an opportunity that would not present itself again during the campaign.

Despite their own problems, the Americans in upstate New York were working feverishly to take advantage of

20. Christie to Germain, October 26, 1776, Germain Papers, Clements Library; Carleton to Germain, August 10, 1776 (from Quebec), C.O. 42/35, pp. 112–15; Horatio Gates to Congress, July 16, 1776, Letters from Major General Horatio Gates, 1775–1782, 2 vols., I, 15–18, Papers of the Continental Congress, Number 154, National Archives, Washington, D.C., hereafter cited as PCC, 154, vol. and page numbers.

21. Gates to Congress, July 16, 1776, PCC, 154, I, 15–18; Gates to Moses Hazen, July 12, 1776, Peter Force, ed., *American Archives* (9 vols., Washington, 1837–1853), Series 5, I, col. 238.

Carleton's lassitude. Philip Schuyler, as overall commander of the Northern Department, directed Horatio Gates to take charge of both the miserable army that had retreated out of Canada and of shipbuilding efforts on Lake Champlain. Gates's tasks were enormous, because he feared he might be assailed at any time by the enemy. Complicating matters, he and his military colleagues were divided as to how, or whether, to attempt a defense of the lake. Moreover, his army, as described to him on July 12 by his adjutant John Trumbull, was "a mob . . . , ruined by sickness, fatigue and desertion, and void of every idea of discipline and subordination." Already Gates had become aware of the state of the shipping on Lake Champlain. American prospects in early July were anything but encouraging.[22]

However, Gates plunged into his duties with energy. His first task was to restore his army's effectiveness as a fighting force. He imposed regulations to control marauding bands of soldiers who were plundering the countryside, worked with his officers and chaplains to convince his troops that they were not beaten, pleaded with New England governors for reinforcements, isolated soldiers who were sick with smallpox in order to curb that contagion, eased punishments for minor infractions of rules in camp, and worked to control prices that soldiers must pay sutlers for necessities. By July 26, Colonel Matthias Ogden of New Jersey declared that "General Gates . . . is putting the most disordered Army that ever bore the name into a state of regularity and defense." A month later, Gates wrote General George Washington that smallpox had been completely eradicated from the Army.[23] As his army improved, Gates decided to bring all his effective troops together to defend Fort Ticonderoga, abandoning peripheral posts such as Crown Point. Although his decision was approved

22. Philip Schuyler to Gates, July 17, 1776, Horatio Gates Papers, box 3, New-York Historical Society, New York City, hereafter cited as Gates Papers, box no., NYHS; John Trumbull to Gates, July 12, 1776, John Trumbull, *Autobiography, Reminiscences, and Letters* (New York, 1841), p. 302.

23. Matthias Ogden to Aaron Burr, July 26, 1776, Force, ed., *American Archives,* Ser. 5, I, cols. 603–04; Gates to George Washington, August 28, Gates Papers, box 19, NYHS. A discussion of Gates's efforts to reform the army is in Paul David Nelson, *General Horatio Gates: A Biography* (Baton Rouge, 1976) pp. 63–66.

by Schuyler and three other general officers, it raised a storm of protest from some New Englanders, who believed they were being abandoned to the enemy. Gates adhered to his plan, despite the controversy, and in mid-July Ticonderoga became the Americans' main post of defense.[24]

Gates also turned his attention to devising a program to counter the enemy on Lake Champlain. By July 10, he was being informed by his second in command, Benedict Arnold, that Carleton was working mightily at St. Johns to build a fleet. To oppose this threat, Schuyler, Gates, and Arnold had no choice but to attempt construction of a larger one and keep naval control of the lake.[25] It seems clear at this point that the Americans were responding to a decision Carleton had already made, rather than the Canadian commander reacting to American shipbuilding activity, as Mahan argued. Admiral Mahan may have been correct when he said that Carleton was delayed on the lake by British naval construction at St. Johns, but if so it was because of Carleton's own cautious policy and his own planning—not because Arnold forced him to do it.[26] Had Carleton been aware of American weaknesses on his front in early July—as he very likely was, or should have been— he alone must be credited with not taking advantage of it and overpowering the rebels while they were still greatly disorganized.

These observations are not meant to detract from the accomplishments of the Americans in their hectic summer of naval construction; they must be given credit for seizing the opportunity that had been handed them. On the seventeenth of July, Gates placed all shipbuilding activities at Skenesborough and Ticonderoga in the hands of Arnold, since the latter had at least some knowledge of ships acquired before the war in trading with the West Indies. Moreover, Arnold as early as June 25 had informed Washington that a fleet was needed on the lake and had called for the construction of at least twenty or thirty

24. Gates to Washington, July 29, 1776, and to Israel Putnam, August 11, 1776, Gates Papers, box 19, NYHS; "Minutes of a Council of War," July 7, 1776, Force, ed., American Archives, Ser. 5, I, col. 233.

25. Arnold to Gates, July 10, 1776, Gates Papers, box 3, NYHS.

26. Mahan, Navies in the War of Independence, p. 18.

row-galleys and gondolas. Soon a large number of ship's carpenters, armorers, blacksmiths, and sawmillers were busy under Arnold's direction at Skenesborough, putting together these small craft with the support of Schuyler and Gates, who worked mightily to keep the yards supplied with materials. By the first week of August, the American fleet consisted of the sloop and three schooners (which had been armed and refitted), and five gondolas, each carrying two 9-pound guns amidship and a 12-pound bow gun.[27]

Gates, who throughout the war was a cautious, defensive general, had no great plans for his little navy. Instead of using patriot ships to dominate the lake, he only wanted to utilize them to protect his army at Ticonderoga. Therefore, when he gave Arnold command of the flotilla on July 29, he expected the latter officer to expedite his thinking. In his written orders to Arnold a few days later, Gates directed that the patriot ships were to move down the lake no farther than Ile-aux-Tetes. Arnold was to scout the enemy's force and engage it only if it was clearly inferior in strength; but if Carleton's fleet proved superior, the American navy was to withdraw toward Ticonderoga. Under no circumstances, said Gates, was Arnold to take a "wanton risk" or show an "unnecessary display of power." General Arnold, as impetuous in his decision-making as Gates was cautious, seemingly paid little heed to his commander's admonitions. In fact, he had his own plans for fighting on the lake, and they centered not on defense but on making use of the row-galleys being built at Skenesborough to assault the enemy. By September 18 he had acquired two of these craft, and on that day he wrote Gates of his intention to take station with his fleet at Valcour Island, "where there is a good harbour, and where we shall have the advantage of attacking the enemy in the open lake, where the row-galleys, as their motion is quick, will give us a great advantage over the enemy; and if they are too many for us we can retire."[28] When he read this letter, Gates must

---

27. Gates to Arnold, July 17, 1776, Gates Papers, box 19, NYHS; Arnold to Washington, June 25, 1776, Force, ed., *American Archives*, Ser. 4, VI, col. 1108; Gates to Congress, August 5, 1776, PCC, 154, I, 27-32.

28. Gates to Congress, July 29, 1776, PCC, 154, I, 19-22; Gates to Arnold, August 7, 1776, Gates Papers, box 19, NYHS; Arnold to Gates, September 18,

have wondered if his subordinate fully understood his defensive plans for the American flotilla. But the American commander could take comfort from Arnold's closing remarks, which implied that the two generals still were in agreement not to risk patriot ships against the enemy except under the most favorable conditions.

When Arnold wrote his message on September 18, he was posted in narrow waters about twenty miles from St. Johns. On the twenty-third, however, the British placed land batteries in such a way as to drive him down to Valcour, where he anchored his fleet between the west side of the island and the mainland. At this place he awaited the enemy's advance, receiving on October 12 from Gates (who believed Arnold would retreat if faced with a superior British flotilla) approval of his disposition. Said Gates, "I am pleased to find you and your armada ride in Valcour Bay in defiance of the power of our foes in Canada." The American navy on Lake Champlain was now complete and consisted of sixteen vessels of various types. The largest ships were the sloop *Enterprise* and the schooner *Royal Savage,* each mounting twelve guns of various bores. Next in strength were two schooners, *Revenge* and *Liberty,* with eight guns apiece. Then came four row-galleys, *Lee, Trumbull, Congress* and *Washington,* all mounting eight guns, except for the *Lee,* which had only six. Finally, there were eight gondolas, all with a three-gun armament. Total personnel for the fleet numbered 856 men, almost all of them untrained in naval warfare; total gun strength was 102, ranging from three 18-pounders down to fifty-six 2-pounders.[29] The patriot flotilla was as ready as it would ever be to oppose a British advance toward Ticonderoga.

As the Americans labored at Skenesborough, unmolested by their enemies, Carleton also worked at a measured pace to build the strength of his own fleet. Although he had his problems—among which was breaking three of his ships to pieces in trying to drag them around the shallows

---

1776, Henry E. Huntington Library, San Marino, California, hereafter cited as Huntington Library.

29. Gates to Arnold, October 12, 1776, Gates Papers, box 19, NYHS; "*A List of Armed Vessels in Lake Champlain,*" reported by Richard Varick, October 12, 1776, Force, ed., *American Archives,* Ser. 5, II, col. 1039.

at Chambly—he had by September 1 considerable shipping on the Richelieu River above St. Johns. Afloat were the *Maria* and *Carleton*, one mounting fourteen 6-pounders, the other twelve; the ketch *Thunderer* and a gondola, the *Loyal Convert;* and twelve gunboats. But on September 6, the Canadian general learned of Arnold's fleet strength and realized that he had lost, temporarily, the race for naval domination of Lake Champlain. Despite his access to resources and manpower greater than the rebels had to draw upon, he had been outstripped by them. Hence, he decided that he had no choice but to strengthen his own armada by bringing up another ship from below the Chambly rapids. Immediately, he set his men to dismantling the *Inflexible*, which mounted eighteen 12-pound cannon, and reassembling it at St. Johns.[30]

A number of consequences resulted from Carleton's decision to reinforce his fleet. While he had guaranteed the British naval superiority on the lake, he had delayed his campaign for another month and given the rebels more time to strengthen their defenses. Therefore, he had for all intents and purposes precluded accomplishing anything more against the enemy in 1776. In fact, on September 28 he admitted as much when he wrote to Germain, "Unfortunately the season is so far advanced, that I dare not flatter my self we shall be able to do more, this campaign, than to draw off [the rebels'] attention, and keep back part of their Force from General Howe." The enemy, he had learned, now had a large army at Ticonderoga, a body of men which he felt he could tie down for the season; but he gave no indication of hoping or trying to do anything more at this late date. The evidence strongly suggests that even before he had launched his naval expedition against the Americans, Carleton had abandoned any idea of seizing a base at the south end of the lake, and that any "delay" imposed on him later by the naval battle with Arnold had nothing to do with his decision.[31]

Finally, on October 4 the Canadian commander had his

30. Samuel Metcalf to Jacob Bayley, July 21, 1776, Force, ed., *American Archives*, Ser. 5, I, col. 488; Carleton to Germain, September 28, 1776, with an enclosed "State of the Naval Force at and near St. Johns," C.O. 42/35, pp. 171-75, 177.

31. Carleton to Germain, September 28, 1776, C.O. 42/35, pp. 171-75.

fleet assembled at Ile-aux-Noix and began to probe southward in search of Arnold's force. With the addition to his flotilla since September 28 of the *Inflexible,* eight gunboats, and four longboats, Carleton's firepower was now twice that of the enemy. In addition, his ships were manned by almost seven hundred seasoned personnel of the Royal navy and commanded by Captain Thomas Pringle, a regular naval officer. He also possessed about six hundred barges to convey his troops southward, and Burgoyne suggested that some of these vessels be used to transport with the naval force "a Corps of the army in order to take sudden advantage of a defeat." Carleton at first agreed to, then decided against, this plan. As he wrote Germain on September 28, his purpose was "to establish a naval Force on Lake Champlain to command the navigation of that Lake, and to render the Passage for the Troops in Batteaux secure." He would hazard no soldiers on the water until Arnold's navy was effectively neutralized. Burgoyne disliked the decision, believing that the commander had made a serious mistake "by embark[ing] alone to command the fleet leaving the whole of the army" at St. Johns; but he could only fume at being left out of the upcoming fight.[32]

At Valcour Island, Arnold by now had been apprised of the British naval superiority and he fully recognized the danger he was in if he stayed put. But it was not in his nature to retreat, whatever the odds or his orders from Gates, and he decided to fight where he was. His only concession to British power was to abandon his earlier plan to engage the enemy in open water; instead he would defy Carleton's fleet from his snug harbor. For this decision he has been praised by many historians, who have seen his determination as the wisest and bravest course of action, while viewing Gates's plan as timid and unsound. From his secure anchorage, it has been argued, Arnold could concentrate his inferior firepower on his pursuers by taking advantage of prevailing southerly winds, against which the British must tack if they would come to battle with him. Or he might be

32. Carleton to Germain, September 28, 1776, C.O. 42/35, pp. 171-75; Burgoyne to Clinton, November 7, 1776, Clinton Papers, Clements Library.

overlooked entirely by the enemy, who was sailing southward toward Ticonderoga, in which case he could scamper north and wreak havoc on the barges Carleton had collected to transport his army. In any eventuality, he could more likely hinder the British by keeping his options open than by retreating to the safety of Ticonderoga's cannon. As Mahan commented, Arnold had correctly decided that "the use of the navy was to contest the control of the water; to impose delay, even if it could not secure ultimate victory," and that "the navy was useless, except as it contributed to that end; valueless, if buried in port."[33]

It is true that from the moment Carleton gained naval superiority on the lake, Arnold was faced with a choice of difficulties in trying to defend upstate New York. Perhaps at this point, neither by fighting where he was nor by withdrawing could he halt what seemed to be an inevitable thrust of the British toward Ticonderoga. Yet the question arises—was the risk he was taking by remaining at Valcour worth the gain he might achieve, or could he have secured more by retreating before a superior fleet, as Gates had ordered him to do? There are strong arguments in favor of the latter course of action. Regarding Mahan's view that Arnold's staying at Valcour might "impose delay" upon the enemy, two points can be made against this interpretation. First, Arnold himself admitted to Gates on October 11 that he would have to halt Carleton's progress for a fortnight in order to bring the campaign to a successful conclusion, and he certainly made no promise that he could slow the British for that long (in fact, after he lost two battles with Pringle's navy in the next three days, the enemy arrived at Crown Point). Second, that Carleton took from the fourth to the eleventh of October to reach the American position was the fault of the overly cautious British general rather than the result of anything Arnold did to slow his progress.[34]

---

33. Arnold to Gates, October 1, October 7, 1776, Gates Papers, NYHS; Wallace, *Traitorous Hero*, pp. 113-14; Mahan, *Navies in the War for Independence*, p. 27.

34. Arnold to Gates, October 11, 1776, Gates Papers, NYHS. Regarding Carleton's delay in coming up to Valcour Island, see Leroy, "Carleton as a Military Leader," p. 461.

Other evidence is available to argue against Arnold's decision to stay put. Any hope that he might be overlooked by Carleton seems, in retrospect at least, very remote. The British general was nothing if not methodical, and as he probed southward he was carefully checking all possible anchorages that Arnold might use. Even if Arnold were not detected, however, one wonders how he could have taken advantage of this situation and sailed his heterogeneous fleet northward—against prevailing winds—to wreak damage on Carleton's barges before being found out by the enemy and caught in a very unequal fight at the lower end of the lake. Mahan had a valid point when he argued that Arnold recognized his navy's purpose as being "to contest the control of the water," even if he "could not secure ultimate victory." Surely, however, Mahan would not maintain that a fleet should fight with such unequal odds that its fate is sealed practically before the first shot is fired. To hazard a flotilla as Arnold did under circumstances in which the enemy had twice the firepower, more maneuverability, and a position between his anchorage and the safety of Ticonderoga's cannon does not appear to be taking an acceptable risk—especially for what he might have gained. Mahan was also correct in pointing out that a fleet is "valueless, if buried in port." But was not Arnold placing himself in just such a position at Valcour? What did it matter whether he was "buried" there or at Ticonderoga, except that the latter location would have given him the protection of the fort's guns?

At the time, Arnold's decision to give battle at Valcour Island was not generally supported by Americans in upstate New York, especially those in the army. General Gates later praised Arnold's "gallant behavior, and steady good conduct" on the lake, but other patriots found fault with the American fleet commander's activities. Brigadier General John Lacey of the Pennsylvania line commented that the American fleet should have been posted closer to Crown Point from the beginning, and David Waterbury, second in command of the navy, implored Arnold to retreat in the face of such obviously superior enemy power. Another American army officer, General William Maxwell, also criticized Arnold, but his comments were so shot through with inaccuracies (such as, "Our fleet . . . was much the strongest") that he must be ignored.[35] The observations of Lacey and Waterbury, however, can not be dismissed. Unlike Maxwell, these two men had no personal enmity toward Arnold and were expressing a view that the patriot flotilla should cooperate closely with ground forces in defending Fort Ticonderoga. Gates had held this opinion at the beginning of the campaign, and in his orders of August 7 had expressly stated that if Arnold found the British fleet superior, "you will retire your squadron to Ticonderoga." There is no reason to assume that Gates had changed his mind on this matter in the intervening two months. Hence, it is possible that he later supported Arnold only because it was clear to him by then that Carleton could not take Ticonderoga and he was merely trying to keep peace in the patriot officer corps—despite his subordinate having disobeyed his explicit orders. Later on, in the campaign of 1777, General Gates would come to view Arnold as militarily impetuous and would relieve him of command. His attitude then would be based upon less evidence than he possessed after Arnold had lost practically the entire American navy to the enemy on Lake Champlain.[36]

Of the battle, itself, not a great deal need be said. As the British fleet hove into view of Arnold on October 11, it was running south under a strong breeze. When the Americans were sighted, Carleton came about with difficulty and began closing on his enemies. For a time, Arnold had the advantage, because the British ships came into the fight piecemeal. But it was only a matter of time before the firepower of Carleton began to tell against Arnold's ragged flotilla. Throughout the afternoon the

35. Gates to Governor Jonathan Trumbull of Connecticut, October 22, 1776, Waterbury's comments in a council of war, October 11, 1776, and William Maxwell to Governor Livingston of New Jersey, October 22, 1776, Force, ed., *American Archives*, Ser. 5, II, cols. 1192, 1774, 1143; John Lacey, "Memoirs of Brigadier-General John Lacey of Pennsylvania," *Pennsylvania Magazine of History and Biography*, XXV (1901), p. 504.

36. Gates to Arnold, August 7, 1776, Gates Papers, NYHS; Arnold to Gates, September 18, 1776, Huntington Library. For Gates's later views of Arnold, see Paul David Nelson, "The Gates-Arnold Quarrel, September 1777," *New-York Historical Society Quarterly*, LV (July, 1971), pp. 235–52, and Flexner, *Traitor and Spy*, p. 113.

American ships were pounded with shot; the schooner *Royal Savage* and the gondola *Philadelphia* were lost; the row-galley *Congress* was riddled below the water line; and many officers and men were killed or wounded. By nightfall, when Pringle called off his ships, the British had lost only one gunboat. The rest of the fleet was posted in a blockade line to keep the rebels entrapped. Since there was no route of escape for the Americans through the shallow northern passage behind Valcour, and since Indians surrounded them on land; their situation was grave. Compounding their problems, the American gunners had expended three-fourths of their ammunition.

Arnold, probably unnecessarily, had gotten himself into a serious dilemma, but it could never be said of him that he was not a fighter. He immediately proposed to his officers that the fleet take advantage of fog and try to slip through Carleton's blockade. Perhaps as much to their amazement as the enemy's the following morning, the plan succeeded. The patriot ships then limped about twelve miles to Schuyler's Island, where they were forced to lay to and repair damages—except on two gondolas, which were beyond salvaging and were sunk. Arnold then set out once more toward Crown Point, but his progress was slowed to a crawl by winds springing up from the south. These same breezes kept Carleton from pursuing him on the morning of the twelfth; but late that afternoon the British officer was again in motion southward. Next morning, off Split Rock, the American fleet was overtaken by the enemy and almost annihilated. Waterbury was captured, and Arnold escaped only by beaching the damaged *Congress*, which he commanded, and slipping through an Indian ambush to reach a small American garrison at Crown Point. Of the sixteen vessels that had once made up the patriot flotilla, only three escaped to Ticonderoga, there to be joined by two others that had taken no part in the battle.[37]

In arguing favorably for Arnold's decision to battle it out with the enemy on Lake Champlain, Admiral Mahan

37. Accounts of the naval battles on Lake Champlain are found in Arnold to Gates, October 12, 1776, Gates Papers, NYHS; Carleton to Germain, October 14, 1776, C.O. 42/35, pp. 198-99; Mahan, *Navies in the War for Independence*, pp. 20-25; Wallace, *Traitorous Hero*, pp. 114-18; Arnold, *Arnold*, pp. 112-17.

asked, "What was the worth of such a force as the American, such a flotilla, under the guns of Ticonderoga, the Lake being lost?" His opinion, then, was that uncontested British control of the water route to Fort Ticonderoga would spell disaster for the patriots, and must be avoided or delayed even if the American navy "should be sacrificed, as it was."[38] But was the sacrifice really worth the price? The campaign season was drawing rapidly to a close by mid-October, but had Arnold's battle delayed the enemy enough to turn the tide favorably toward the Americans? Would Carleton have reached Crown Point sooner than October 14 had his passage remained uncontested? Did his possession of Crown Point and his control of the lake lead to patriot disaster? The answer to all these questions is no, with the qualification that the British *might* have been at Crown Point one or two days earlier had Arnold not fought them; but this time factor is of insignificant consequence. Mahan's points do not bear the weight of scrutiny; the price America paid on Lake Champlain was not offset by any gain important enough to warrant the loss. The patriots by October 14 would have been in no worse a situation than they were had Arnold retreated with his fleet intact and without any loss at all. That this flotilla would have been of vital importance to the Americans a year later in their defense against Burgoyne's invasion is obvious.

The question of the consequences flowing from Carleton's possession of the lake needs to be amplified at this point. The thinking of the British general immediately after his victory over Arnold seems to be the key to understanding why Mahan was inaccurate in seeing enemy domination of the waterway as tragic for the patriots. For Carleton's mind was filled with reasons why he could not move against the Americans. On October 14 he informed Germain of his successes in the past three days, but he echoed his statement of September 28 when he closed the letter by saying, "The Season is so far advanced that I cannot yet pretend to inform your Lordship whether any thing further can be done this year." The limitations on his tactical options, as Carleton well

38. Mahan, *Navies in the War for Independence,* p. 18.

249

knew, had not been materially altered by his naval victory. Even as he transferred his troops to Crown Point (which by this time had been evacuated by the small American garrison), he became aware that Gates at Ticonderoga commanded an army of almost 15,000 men and that all approaches to the fort by land or water were dominated by patriot guns.[39] The month of grace that he had given the rebels while he brought the *Inflexible*, piece by piece, to Lake Champlain had been put to good use by them. In possession of the lake or not, he could not sail with impunity against formidable Ticonderoga.

Moreover, despite all evidence to the contrary—especially the fact that in July the Americans had declared their independence from Britain—Carleton in October continued to believe that he could use leniency to woo his errant brothers back into the fold. Hence, he paused at Crown Point, paroled American prisoners seized in the battle on the lake, including Waterbury, and sent them off to Ticonderoga in hopes that they would convert the fort's defenders into enthusiasts of the crown. If the plan ever had a chance to succeed, it was thwarted when Gates refused to allow the former prisoners to mingle with his garrison soldiers. Instead he quickly sent them home.[40]

For two weeks after Crown Point fell to him, Carleton made no effort to advance against the enemy. His hesitation about a course of action at this point appears to have been based on his decision, made perhaps weeks before, to do no more in the campaign. However, if he wanted an excuse for inaction he had one in the wind, which as Gates told Schuyler on October 26, "is now against the enemy's fleet, as it providentially has been for this week past." Finally, on the twenty-seventh Carleton bestirred himself enough to carry out a listless probe of Fort Ticonderoga's outer works, but he would not accept Burgoyne's suggestion to besiege Gates and sever American communications with the south. With winter coming on and the rebels showing

39. Carleton to Germain, October 14, 1776, C.O. 42/35, pp. 198–99; Gates, "General Return of . . . Forces," September 29, 1776, and Schuyler to Gates, October 14, 1776, Force, ed., *American Archives*, Ser. 5, II, cols. 617–18, 1039–40.
40. Trumbull, *Autobiography*, p. 33; Leroy, "Carleton as a Military Leader," pp. 471–72.

every indication of putting up a vigorous defense, Carleton pulled his men and ships back to Crown Point after less than one day's action.[41] Hence, it appears that the Canadian commander's possession of Lake Champlain was not as dangerous to the patriots as Mahan had thought.

In fact, the Americans were about to regain control of the lake, for Carleton only hesitated at Crown Point before ordering a withdrawal into Canada. His decision dismayed Burgoyne, who began to criticize the commander in his correspondence. Declared Burgoyne in a letter to Clinton on November 7, "I think this step puts us in danger . . . of losing the fruits of our summer's labor & autumn victory." Before the evacuation, said Burgoyne, he had suggested to Carleton that the British leave at least a brigade at Crown Point to tie down the rebels at Ticonderoga and keep them from reinforcing Washington's hard pressed army to the southward. But the Canadian commander listened instead to "dull, formal, methodical fat engineers," who apprised him only of the problems involved with the plan and none of its advantages.[42] Carleton, however, was well aware of the logistical problems that the scheme would entail, not the least of which was how to supply the base with provisions to last it through the winter before the lake froze over. Perhaps he could have overcome this difficulty had he begun to work on it two weeks before, but now it was too late. As for the possibility that Americans would be detached to Washington, he considered the likelihood as extremely remote. So within two weeks he was back in Quebec, once again handling civil problems.[43]

While Carleton wintered comfortably in Canada, basking in the glory of receiving a knighthood for his defense of the province, rebel troops were not sitting idly at Ticonderoga as he had planned. Instead, twelve hundred

41. Gates to Schuyler, October 26, October 31, 1776, Gates Papers, NYHS; Burgoyne to Clinton, November 7, 1776, Clinton Papers, Clements Library.

42. Burgoyne to Clinton, November 7, 1776, Clinton Papers, Clements Library.

43. Gates to Schuyler, November 5, 1776, Gates Papers, NYHS; Gates to Congress, November 5, 1776, PCC, 154, I, 113–15; Carleton to Germain, November 17, 1776, C.O. 42/35, pp. 213–14. Carleton's logistical problems are discussed in Bowler, *Logistics,* p. 224, Leroy, "Carleton as a Military Leader," pp. 542–47, and Clinton to Lord Percy, May 2, 1782, Germain Papers, Clements Library.

of them, led by Gates, were marching to join Washington. They arrived on the Delaware River above Philadelphia in time to assist in the assaults on Trenton and Princeton. At the same time, Burgoyne was in England, spreading word to Germain, North, and the king that he had opposed Carleton's withdrawal from the southern shores of Lake Champlain and making clear that he not only had a plan for the following year's campaign in upstate New York but also would not be averse to directing it.[44]

Soon it was common gossip in London, where only Burgoyne's side of the story had been heard, that "Carleton's very unaccountable conduct" (as Hans Stanley put it) in withdrawing from the lake "without any reason" had damaged Britain's war effort. Hence in March Germain wrote Carleton, "I have the Mortification to learn that, upon your repassing Lake Champlain, a very considerable number of the Insurgents . . . immediately marched from thence, and joined the Rebel Forces in . . . New York & Jersey." This detachment, said Germain, had enabled Washington to succeed in his attacks against "parts of the Winter Quarters that were taken up by . . . Howe." The American Secretary concluded his letter by informing Carleton that Burgoyne had been appointed to lead the Canadian army in the spring. This message triggered a long smoldering controversy between these two men which would have consequences for the following year's fighting. But that story is beyond the scope of this essay. The point is that the government in London found much to question in its general's handling of military affairs in the year just ended.[45]

44. Robert H. Harrison, by order of Washington, to Gates, November 26, 1776, Gates to Schuyler, November 15, 1776, and Gates to Washington, December 22, 1776, Gates Papers, boxes 4 and 19, NYHS; Burgoyne to Germain, February 28, 1777, C.O. 42/36, pp. 19-25.

45. Hans Stanley to Francis, Early of Huntington, December 18, 1776, Historical Manuscripts Commission, *Report on the Manuscripts of the Late Reginald Hastings* (4 vols., London, 1928-1947), III, 189; Germain to King George III, December 10, 1776, John W. Fortescue, ed., *Correspondence of King George the Third* (6 vols., London, 1927-1928), III, 1936; Germain to Carleton, March 26, 1777, C.O. 42/36, pp. 64-69. A thorough analysis of the historical literature on the Germain-Carleton controversy is in Leroy, "Carleton as a Military Leader," pp. 482-99. See also Burt, "The Quarrel Between Germain and Carleton," *Canadian His. Review*, XI, pp. 202-22.

In conclusion, it seems clear that British failure in the campaign of 1776 in Canada and upstate New York was due more to Carleton's mistakes than to Arnold's brilliance or heroism. This does not detract from the efforts of either Arnold or his patriot colleagues, for they certainly took advantage of the opportunites offered them. Yet, they probably could not have withstood a British assault had it been well managed and vigorously executed—as it was not under the leadership of Carleton, whose omissions and lapses were numerous. While American troops were still in Canada, Carleton hesitated to deliver two blows against them, either of which might have resulted in the entrapment of all or part of the rebel army. The Canadian commander seemed torn at this point, as throughout the campaign, between a policy of conciliation toward his enemies and harassing them mercilessly.

After the patriots had evacuated Canada, Carleton once more showed irresolution by not pushing after them. From June 19 to July 15, he was opposed by a tiny rebel army of one thousand effective soldiers which was riddled with smallpox, had no armed ships on Lake Champlain, and suffered from shattered morale. It is true that at this time Carleton had his own problems with logistics and transport, but still he might have attempted some action against his almost defenseless enemies at Crown Point. Instead, he turned his attention to building ships and transports, thereby forcing Gates and Arnold to do the same. For the next three months, Carleton did almost nothing to harass the rebels or slow their naval construction--while the campaign season drew quickly to a close. By September it was apparent that Arnold had won the race to float a superior armada on the lake, and Carleton had to delay *another* month while he brought up the *Inflexible*. Not until October 4 did the British fleet finally sail out to meet the enemy, and by then Gates had collected a large army at Ticonderoga. Thus, Carleton strongly suspected, even before he met Arnold's flotilla, that for the present season he had lost any opportunity to do more than tie down his enemies at the south end of the lake and keep them from reinforcing Washington. His conquest of the water could have no substantial bearing on the year's campaigning.

In this context, Arnold's decision to fight Carleton's fleet, which he made contrary to the orders of Gates, does not seem wise. His chances either to delay the British or to win a naval battle against superior firepower and maneuverability were very slight. He could have done more to damage the enemy by retreating than by fighting, for had he kept his fleet intact under Ticonderoga's guns, it at least could have been available for use against Burgoyne in 1777. As it was, he fought a foolhardy (if valiant) battle, lost most of his ships, and delayed the British for only two days.

After Carleton reached Crown Point in mid-October, the campaign for all practical purposes came to an end. The Canadian general could see no way short of a siege to use his domination of the lake to break the rebel army at Ticonderoga, and the season was now too advanced to carry out that kind of operation. Nor would logistics allow him to hold Crown Point through the winter, or so he thought. Hence, he withdrew his army and navy to Canada, set off in England a storm of protest against his action, and was replaced by Burgoyne as commander of British forces in the province. It is ironical that of all Carleton's decisions in 1776, the one to abandon upstate New York got him into the greatest difficulty with Germain; for under the circumstances it was perhaps the most defensible thing that he did in the campaign.

Yet the military record of Carleton for the rest of the year justified the American Secretary's determination to have someone else command the Canadian army in the following year. As Piers Mackesy correctly pointed out, the conduct of the Canadian commander in 1776—even after accounting for factors beyond his control—was hardly fraught with unequivocal success.

COWPENS: PRELUDE TO YORKTOWN

By Hugh F. Rankin

As the year 1780 drew to a close, the rebellious colonies which had dared challenge the military might of Great Britain were hanging on the ropes. The capricious gods of war, always fickle in conferring their favors, seemed to have once again switched allegiance. The hard-earned victories and near-victories by the Americans had now faded into pleasant memories. The triumph at King's Mountain was the only bright spot in an otherwise gloomy picture.

In the North, the gifted and gregarious Benedict Arnold had almost succeeded in transferring control of West Point and the Hudson River into the hands of the British, and had thrown the patriots into a frenzy of outraged dignity.

The southern states were in even more desperate straits. From the early part of 1779 the British had concentrated their chief efforts in this region because the South was considered to be the easier to reduce and, from the nature of its products, the more valuable to the mother country.[1] It was in this locale that the American generals had appeared so inept. General Benjamin Lincoln had surrendered somewhat ingloriously at Charleston and General Horatio Gates, the hero of Saratoga, had indeed exchanged "the laurels of the North for the willows of the South"[2] at Camden. Lord Cornwallis stood poised in South Carolina to strike at the rich state of Virginia. North Carolina stood between, but North Carolina was considered as only "the road to Virginia."[3] Only a few ragged remnants of Gates' defeated army stood between the British general and his goal.

The southern army was in a state of crisis. General Gates was attempting to reorganize his shattered army at Hills-

[1] Charles Stedman, *The History of the Origin, Progress and Termination of the American War*, 2 vols. (London: Printed for the Author, 1794), II, 316.

[2] Henry Lee, *Memoirs of the War in the Southern Department of the United States*, edited by Robert E. Lee (New York: University Publishing Company, 1870), 208. Hereafter cited as Lee, *Memoirs*.

[3] *The Annual Register for 1780*, 54.

[336]

256

boro in North Carolina, the place to which he had fled after the rout of his forces by Cornwallis at Camden. Members of the Continental Congress who, in the not too distant past, had sent Gates to the South with cheers and assertions that he would "Burgoyne" Cornwallis for sure, were now clamoring for his recall. The general indignation was reflected in the angry statement of one army officer, "He will be blasted in this World, and humanly judging, he ought to be in the next . . . had he behaved like a soldier himself, Cornwallis would have been ruined, and to use a common term, Cornwalladed. . . ." [4] Alexander Hamilton openly accused Gates of cowardice and emphatically stated his choice for Gates' successor:

was there ever such an instance of a general running away as Gates had done, from his whole army? And was there ever so precipitous a flight? One hundred and eighty miles in three days and a half? It does admirable credit to the activity of a man at his time of life. But it disgraces the general and the soldier. . . . But what will be done by Congress? Will he be changed or not? If he is changed, for God's sake, overcome prejudice and send GREENE. You know my opinion of him. I stake my reputation on the events, give him but fair play.[5]

Rumblings from the South added to congressional irritation as rumors indicated that Gates had lost the confidence of the people and was at odds with General William Smallwood, his second in command.[6] The cry for the removal of the unfortunate general became louder and more persistent.

Major General Nathanael Greene had been General Washington's original choice for the southern command, but he had been by-passed by Congress in favor of Gates.[7] In this

[4] Richard Varick to John Lamb, Sept. 11, 1780. Isaac Leake, *Memoir of the Life and Times of General John Lamb, An Officer of the Revolution* (Albany: Joel Munsell, 1850), 255.

[5] Alexander Hamilton to William Duane, September 6, 1780. John C. Hamilton (ed.), *The Works of Alexander Hamilton*, 7 vols. (New York: Charles S. Francis and Company, 1851), II, 124.

[6] Ezekial Cornel to William Greene, October 17, 1780. Edmund C. Burnett (ed.), *Letters of the Members of the Continental Congress*, 8 vols. (Washington: Carnegie Institution, 1931), V, 421-422. Hereafter cited as Burnett, *Letters.*

[7] Washington to Greene, n.d., quoted in George Washington Greene, *The Life of Nathanael Greene, Major-General in the Army of the Revolution*, 3 vols. (Boston: Houghton, Mifflin and Company, 1890), II, 367.

instance Congress refused to assume the responsibility of appointing the new commander, directing Washington to select a successor to Gates.[8] Greene was in disfavor with many members of Congress, but he was the choice of the delegation from the southern states, who urged Washington to designate him as the new commander.[9]

Greene, who had just finished presiding over the board of general officers which had tried and convicted Major André,[10] had his eyes on the West Point command so recently held by Arnold,[11] but Washington would only consent to a temporary appointment.[12] Despite the uncertainty of the tenure, Greene felt that he was situated for the winter; but before he could become settled, a dispatch arrived from headquarters informing him that he was the choice for the southern command, and urging him to set out without delay.[13]

Greene displayed a reluctance to make his departure, but under constant prodding from Washington, he left for the South on October 23, accompanied by his aides and Baron Steuben, who had been ordered to the South, for "there is an army to be created, the mass of which is at present without any formation at all."[14] Greene was no stranger to the desperate situation of the southern army. Nine days were

[8] Worthington C. Ford and others (eds.), *Journals of the Continental Congress*, 39 vols., Library of Congress edition (Washington: Government Printing Office, 1904-1937), XVIII, 906.

[9] John Matthews to Washington, October 6, 1780. Burnett, *Letters*, V, 408.

[10] One British observer said of him: "General Greene was originally a Quaker, a stern republican, and such was the rancor displayed throughout the whole transaction, by him and the Marquis De La Fayette that they almost literally be said to have thirsted for the blood of the unfortunate victim whom fate had put in their power." R. Lamb, *An Original and Authentic Journal of Occurrences During the Late American War, From Its Commencement to the Year 1783* (Dublin: Wilkinson and Courtney, 1809), 330.

[11] Greene to Washington, October 5, 1780. Jared Sparks (ed.), *Correspondence of the American Revolution: Being Letters of Eminent Men to General Washington, From the Time of His Taking Command of the Army to the End of His Presidency*, 4 vols. (Boston: Little, Brown, and Company, 1853), III, 106.

[12] Washington to Greene, October 6, 1780. John C. Fitzpatrick (ed.), *The Writings of Washington From the Original Manuscript Sources, 1754-1799* 39 vols., Bicentennial edition (Washington: Government Printing Office, 1931-1941), III, 370-371.

[13] Washington to Greene, October 14, 1780. Fitzpatrick, *Writings of Washington*, XX, 181-182.

[14] Washington to Steuben, October 22, 1780. Fitzpatrick, *Writings of Washington*, XX, 240-241.

spent in Philadelphia—nine days of begging and pleading for supplies. He addressed the Congress on the business of the southern department, but it was soon apparent that prospects of aid were "dismal" as that body could furnish no money, and the Board of War was devoid of clothing and "necessaries."[15] Some six weeks later he described his stay in the capital city to Alexander Hamilton:

At Philadelphia . . . I endeavored to impress those in power [with] the necessity of sending clothing and supplies of every kind, immediately to this army. But poverty was urged as a plea, in bar to every application. They all promised fair, but I fear will do little: ability is wanting with some, and inclination with others. Public credit is so totally lost, that private people will not give their aid, though they see themselves involved in common ruin.[16]

After leaving Philadelphia the new southern commander visited Annapolis and Richmond with the hope of instilling some degree of enthusiasm in the governments of Maryland and Virginia, but as one of his aides noted, "their ability is but small, their funds are empty, and their credit low."[17] Leaving Baron Steuben in Virginia to expedite the movement of supplies and assume the responsibilities of the state, Greene hastened southward.[18]

He expected to find the southern army at Hillsboro. There was no sign of them. He found that Gates had marched toward Salisbury where, according to the North Carolina Board of War, there was an adequate supply of provisions.[19] At Salisbury he discovered that General Gates had marched for Charlotte, as that village had presented better prospects

---

[15] Greene to Washington, October 31, 1780. Sparks, *Correspondence of the American Revolution*, III, 137-139.

[16] Greene to Hamilton, January 10, 1781. Hamilton, *The Works of Alexander Hamilton*, I, 204.

[17] Lewis Morris, Jr., to Jacob Morris, November 20, 1780. *Collections of the New-York Historical Society for the Year 1875* (New York: The Society, 1876), VII, 473.

[18] Greene to Steuben, November 20, 1780. Friedrich Kapp, *The Life of Frederick William Von Steuben, Major General in the Revolutionary Army* (New York: Mason Brothers, 1859), 347-349.

[19] O. H. Williams to William Smallwood, November 8, 1780. *Calendar of the General Otho Williams Papers in the Maryland Historical Society.* (Baltimore: Maryland Historical Records Survey Project, 1940), 27.

as a site for a winter quarters.[20] Hurrying to Charlotte, Greene found the army busily constructing huts against the chill of approaching winter.

In spite of the rumored ill feeling between the two, the new commander was received by his predecessor with the utmost cordiality and respect.[21] The general orders of December 3, 1780, carried the news of the transition in command. Later in the day, Greene addressed the troops and paid the retiring general the compliment of confirming all of his standing orders.[22]

Inspecting his army, Greene was appalled by his findings. His force was "but the shadow of an army in the midst of distress."[23] The army with which he was expected to drive the enemy from the South was nothing more than a ragged, undisciplined mob, using the exigencies of war as an excuse for plundering. The militia, usually considered and used as infantry, insisted upon coming out on horseback. Foraging for their mounts only added to the privations of the already depleted countryside. When the militia were not looting the holdings of the inhabitants, they were pillaging each other. Officers were openly criticised by their subordinates for their conduct of the war, for as Greene remarked, "With the militia everybody is a general."[24]

The problem of supplies was even more critical. On the day that General Greene assumed the command, Brigadier General Daniel Morgan had reported back into camp from a foraging expedition which had penetrated South Carolina

[20] Otho Williams, "Narrative of the Campaign of 1780," William Johnson, *Sketches of the Life and Correspondence of Nathanael Greene, Major General of the Armies of the United States, in the War of the Revolution,* 2 vols., (Charleston: A. E. Miller, 1822), I, 510.

[21] George Washington Greene claimed the hostility between the two generals was the result of the suffering caused both Greene and Washington as a consequence of Gates' ambition. There had also been evidence that Gates had been rude to Mrs. Greene in the past. Greene, *Life of Nathanael Greene,* III, 373. However, at every stop on the way south, Greene had defended Gates' action at Camden. Edward Carrington to Gates, November 27, 1780. Walter Clark (ed.), *The State Records of North Carolina,* 16 vols. (Winston, Goldsboro, 1895-1905), XI, 761-762.

[22] Willams, "Narrative of the Campaign of 1780," Johnson, *Sketches of the Life and Correspondence of Nathanael Greene,* I, 495.

[23] Greene to Abner Nash, December 6, 1780. "Original Letters of General Greene," *Portfolio,* 3d series, I (1813), 203.

[24] Greene to Henry Knox, December 7, 1780. "Original Letters of General Greene," *Portfolio,* 3d series, I (1813), 290-291.

almost to the limits of Camden. He reported that the cattle had been driven off, and that there was so little grain that it would hardly be worth the trouble of the troops to collect it.[25] That night Greene engaged in an all-night discussion with Colonel Thomas Polk, Gates' commissary-general, in an investigation of the military supplies and resources of the neighborhood.[26] It was found that there was a scant three days supply of provisions on hand and that ammunition was dangerously low. The country around Charlotte had been laid waste by the foraging parties of both armies and the inhabitants were concealing those cattle that had escaped the British army.[27]

Foraging parties had discovered that there were abandoned plantations to the south, with fields of corn still untouched.[28] The methodical Yankee mind of Nathanael Greene rebelled at the idea of moving into an unknown situation. Summoning Colonel Thaddeus Kosciusko, his engineer, he instructed him to locate a camp site on the Pee Dee River, near those plantations with particular reference to food, water, transportation facilities, and avenues of retreat.[29]

While awaiting Kosciusko's return, Greene became acquainted with his army and attempted to instill a degree of discipline into his ragged mob. Numerous letters were dispatched to persons of influence and authority begging for aid. His army, in spite of, or perhaps because of, Gates' attempt at reorganization, was in a ferment of inefficiency.

---

[25] Williams, "Narrative of the Campaign of 1780," Johnson, *Sketches of the Life and Correspondence of Nathanael Greene*, I, 502.

[26] Polk later made the statement that Greene had, on the following morning, better understood the situation of the country than had Gates in the entire period of his command. Winslow C. Watson (ed.), *Men and Times of the Revolution; or, Memoirs of Elkanah Watson* (New York: Dana and Company, 1856), 269.

[27] Charles Stedman, Cornwallis' commissary general states that the British army slaughtered 100 head of cattle per day while they were in Charlotte. In one day thirty-seven "cows in calf" were butchered. Stedman, *History of the . . . American War*, II, 216-217n.

[28] North Carolina Board of War to Abner Nash, December 25, 1780. Clark, *State Records of North Carolina*, XIV, 481.

[29] Greene to Kosciusko, December 8, 1780. Greene, *Life of Nathanael Greene*, III, 83-84. Kosciusko had applied for a command of light infantry troops in the South as early as August, 1780. No command being vacant, Washington had offered him the post of engineer in the southern department which he had accepted. Washington to Kosciusko, August 3, 1780. Fitzpatrick, *Writings of Washington*, XIV, 316.

261

Greene determined to mold his ragamuffins into a semblance of a fighting force. Despite the shortage of men, one troop of Virginia cavalry was sent home, Greene warning Governor Thomas Jefferson not to send them back until they were properly clothed and equipped.[30]

Ominous news came from the north. It was now definite that the British were going to make the South their main theatre of war in the approaching spring. Greene immediately called a council of war with Generals William Smallwood and Daniel Morgan, with the idea of taking the initiative and making a sudden surprise attack upon Cornwallis, then in the midst of preparations for invasion at Winnsboro, South Carolina. This burst of optimism was opposed by both generals as impracticable.[31]

Kosciusko returned from his exploration of the Pee Dee with a favorable report, and the army was straightway placed under marching orders. Before they could move the rains came. As the rain continued to fall, Greene made his first major decision as commander of the southern army—he split his army. To command the detached segment of his army he selected Daniel Morgan, who commanded a legionary force which had been created for him by Gates.[32] The stratagem was that Greene was to move the main portion of the army to the Pee Dee, while Morgan's detachment was to move to the southwest and take a position near the Broad

---

[30] Greene to Jefferson, December 14, 1780. William P. Palmer and others (eds.), *Calendar of Virginia State Papers and Other Manuscripts, 1652-1781,* 11 vols. (Richmond: The State, 1876-1893), I, 398.

[31] Greene to Thomas Sumter, December 13, 1780. *Year Book: City of Charleston, S. C., 1899* (Charleston: Lucas and Richardson, 1899), 71-72.

[32] Congress had ordered Morgan south as early as June 16, 1780. Ford, *Journals of the Continental Congress,* XVII, 519. The temperamental rifleman had refused to serve under Gates, believing that he had not been given due credit by Gates for his part in the victory at Saratoga. Morgan had sulked in his home in Virginia until after the Camden disaster. He had then thrown prejudice aside and hurried south to offer his services. Gates had welcomed the prodigal with open arms, and out of the remains of his army had created for Morgan a special corps, composed of four companies of infantry and one company of riflemen under the command of Lieutenant Colonel John Eager Howard of Maryland. The remains of two regiments of cavalry had been united under Lieutenant Colonel William Washington. George Bancroft, *History of the United States Since the Discovery of the Continent,* 10 vols. (New York: D. Appleton and Co., 1896), V, 477. Gates had been instrumental in securing Morgan's promotion to Brigadier General, October 13, 1780. Ford, *Journals of the Continental Congress,* XVIII, 921.

DANIEL MORGAN (1736-1802)

In the uniform of his Virginia rifle company which he led to Boston and Quebec in 1775.

River.[33] In his instructions Morgan was told that his mission was to give protection to that section of South Carolina and "spirit up the people." The enemy was to be annoyed wherever possible, and provisions and forage were to be collected and moved out of the path of the British Army. In the event of a move against Greene, Morgan was to harass the flank on the rear of the enemy. As he was moving into an area marked by the strife of civil war, he was to restrain his men from plundering and a receipt should be given for all supplies taken from the inhabitants.[34] This move effectively blocked the British from drawing supplies from the upper part of the state, and Greene hoped that Morgan would be able to establish a number of small magazines which would provide a haven if the American army were forced to retreat from the Pee Dee.[35] If Morgan were attacked, there was a large area in which to conduct a strategic withdrawal, and if Cornwallis attacked in force, Charleston would be open to attack by Greene. If Cornwallis attempted a conquest of North Carolina between the two forces, the militia of Mecklenburg and Rowan counties, which Cornwallis later termed "one of the most rebellious tracts in America,"[36] could possibly slow his progress, while Greene and Morgan hammered at his flanks. In the event of the failure of this scheme, and should Cornwallis successfully run the gauntlet, Greene and Morgan could confine him to a narrow corridor with Greene and the main army of the Americans keeping between the British and the seacoast and supplies separating them from their loyal adherents in the lowlands. With all factors taken into consideration, this decision to split his army was the greatest, and had the most far reaching results of any made

[33] This operation may possibly have been the result of counsel by Brigadier General William Davidson, who had advanced, before Greene's arrival, a similar plan to detach Morgan's corps to the west. Davidson to Alexander Martin, November 27, 1780. Clark, *The State Records of North Carolina*, XIV, 759.

[34] Greene to Morgan, December 16, 1780. Theodorus Bailey Myers (ed.), *Cowpens Papers, Being Correspondence of General Morgan and the Prominent Actors* (Charleston: The News and Courier Book Presses, 1881), 9-10.

[35] Greene to Washington, December 28, 1780. Sparks, *Correspondence of the American Revolution*, III, 189-191.

[36] Cornwallis to Lord George Germain, March 17, 1781. Charles Ross (ed.), *Correspondence of Charles, First Marquis Cornwallis* (London: John Murray, 1859), I, 503.

by Greene during the entire period of his command of the southern army. By this decision Nathanael Greene shaped his own destiny—and initiated a series of chain reactions which terminated in the surrender of Cornwallis at Yorktown.

The basic unit of Morgan's detachment was to be his legionary force. It was composed of about 400 of the Maryland Line and two companies of Virginians, under the command of John Eager Howard, with a cavalry support of 100 dragoons led by Lieutenant Colonel William A. Washington.[37] This force was to be augmented by militia units from North Carolina under the command of Brigadier General William Lee Davidson and other groups from South Carolina and Georgia.[38]

On Wednesday, December 20, Greene left Charlotte and marched his army to the banks of the Pee Dee and there established a "camp of repose" on the high ground across the river from the tiny village of Chatham.[39] On the following day Morgan moved out. By sunset he had reached Biggin's Ferry on the Catawba River, fifteen miles away.[40] The passage of the river was completed on December 22, and the next four days were spent marching across rough and torturous terrain. On Christmas day he had crossed the Broad River and had established his camp on the north bank of the Pacolet. The march from Charlotte had totalled fifty-seven miles.[41] Here Morgan rested.

These troop movements had not gone unnoticed by the British. Morgan's presence on their flank presented a grave problem. Lord Cornwallis' original blueprint of invasion had

[37] William Augustine Washington was the son of Bailey Washington of Stafford, Virginia, and a kinsman of George Washington. He had served in the South as a leader of cavalry under both Lincoln and Gates. He served with distinction under Greene until the battle of Eutaw Springs, September 8, 1781. In this engagement he was captured and remained a prisoner of the British until the end of the war. Myers, *Cowpens Papers*, 10.

[38] Greene to Morgan, December 16, 1780. Myers, *Cowpens Papers*, 9-10.

[39] Chatham became the present day town of Cheraw, South Carolina. As late as 1867 evidences of Greene's camp could still be distinguished. Alexander Gregg, *History of the Old Cheraws* (New York: Richardson and Co., 1867), 352.

[40] Robert Kirkwood, *The Journal and Order Book of Captain Robert Kirkwood of the Delaware Regiment of the Continental Line*, edited by Joseph Brown Turner (Wilmington: The Historical Society of Delaware, 1910), 13. Hereafter cited as Kirkwood, *Journal*.

[41] Kirkwood, *Journal*, 13.

BANASTRE TARLETON (1754-1833)
Painted by Sir Joshua Reynolds in 1782.

been to drive through North Carolina in three columns. Major James Craig was sent up the coast with a detachment of 400 men to secure Wilmington as a means of insuring the control of the Cape Fear as a supply route. The left flank, towards the mountains, was to be under the command of Major Patrick Ferguson, who was to collect loyalists as he marched. The main column under Cornwallis was to drive up the center in the avenue formed by these flanking parties.[42]

After the victory over Gates at Camden, the British army moved north to Charlotte, "an agreeable village, but in a d---d rebellious country."[43] The news that had come out of the west that Ferguson had been killed and his army routed at King's Mountain on October 7, wrecked all the carefully laid plans. Charlotte became untenable, and the British fell back to Winnsboro to regroup. A dispatch to Sir Henry Clinton requested that the troops of Major General Alexander Leslie, then in Portsmouth, Virginia, be transferred to South Carolina as reinforcements.[44] This request had been granted and the transports conveying Leslie and his men had dropped anchor in Charleston harbor on December 14. Cornwallis busied himself with last minute details as Leslie marched inland from the sea.

Among Cornwallis' subordinate officers was an arrogant young lieutenant colonel—Banastre Tarleton, a favorite of the British general.[45] The Whig inhabitants of South Carolina

[42] Cornwallis to Lord George Germain, March 17, 1781. Ross (ed.), *The Correspondence of Charles, First Marquis Cornwallis*, I, 503.

[43] *New Jersey Gazette*, January 31, 1781, quoting an aide to Cornwallis. Frank Moore (ed.), *The Diary of the American Revolution: From Newspapers and Original Documents*, 2 vols. (New York: Charles T. Evans, 1863), II, 352.

[44] Lord Rawdon to Clinton, October 29, 1781. Benjamin Franklin Stevens (ed.), *Clinton-Cornwallis Controversy Growing Out of the Campaign in Virginia, 1781*, 2 vols. (London: John Lawe, 1910), I, 63-64.

[45] Banastre Tarleton (1754-1833) had purchased a cornetcy of dragoons and, at the outbreak of hostilities, had obtained leave to come to America. He had previously served under Howe and Clinton, and had commanded the advance guard which had captured General Charles Lee in New Jersey, December, 1776. He surrendered with Cornwallis at Yorktown. Upon his return to England he was elected to the Parliament as a member from Liverpool. In 1812 he was promoted to general and created a baronet. As a member of Parliament he considered himself a military expert, which he demonstrated by criticizing the campaigns of the Duke of Wellington on the floor of the House of Commons. R. H. Vetch, "Sir Banastre Tarleton," *Dictionary of National Biography*, edited by Sidney Lee and Leslie Stephens (London: Smith Elder and Company, 1885-1900), LV, 364-369.

reserved their special hatred for this ruthless young officer. His raids through the countryside had earned him the epithets of "the Red Raider" and "Bloody Tarleton." His useless slaughter of the troops of Colonel Abraham Buford as they were begging for quarter[46] had made the term, "Tarleton's Quarters," synonymous with bloodshed and cruelty. The brutality of his corps in defeating General Huger's troops in the engagement at Biggin's Bridge, April 12, 1780, had so enraged Major Patrick Ferguson that he had to be forcibly restrained from shooting several of Tarleton's dragoons on the spot.[47] Tarleton is reported to have expressed the opinion, "that severity alone could effect the establishment of regal authority in America," and his actions certainly implied that he could have been the author of such a statement.[48] His corps, the British Legion, was one of the most disliked in the British army.[49]

On December 26 a Loyalist refugee reported from Charlotte that Greene had marched towards the Pee Dee and that Morgan had crossed the Catawba.[50] The news was confirmed on December 30.[51] This movement presented a threat to the British post at Ninety Six, the westernmost British fort in South Carolina. Ninety Six was situated in an area

[46] In the Waxhaws, May 24, 1780, as they were fleeing after the capitulation of Charleston.

[47] Sir John Fortescue, *A History of the British Army*, 13 vols. (London: Macmillan and Company, Limited, 1911), III, 309.

[48] Alexander Garden, *Anecdotes of the American Revolution, Illustrative of the Talents and Virtues of the Heroes of the Revolution, Who Acted the Most Conspicuous Parts Therein*, 3 vols. (Brooklyn: "The Union" Press, 1865), II, 269.

[49] This unit was originally raised in Philadelphia by Sir William Cathcart in 1778, and was composed of loyalists. They were first known as the Caledonian Volunteers, but this organizational title was later changed to the British Legion. The corps included both infantry and cavalry. They wore a uniform of green with light green facings. This organization surrendered at Yorktown with 24 officers and 209 enlisted men. John W. Wright, "Some Notes on the Continental Army," *William and Mary Quarterly*, 2d series, XI (July, 1931), 201. One troop of regulars from the 17th Light Dragoons was attached to the Legion, "who seemed to hold the irregulars in contempt, since they refused to wear the green uniforms of the Legion, but stuck to their own scarlet." Fortescue, *History of the British Army*, III, 309n.

[50] Cornwallis to Tarleton, December 26, 1780. Banastre Tarleton, *A History of the Campaigns of 1780 and 1781 in the Southern Provinces of North America* (London: T. Cadell, 1787), 243. Hereafter cited as Tarleton, *Campaigns*.

[51] Cornwallis to Tarleton, December 30, 1780. Tarleton, *Campaigns*, 243-244.

predominantly Tory in sentiment, and the garrison was needed for their protection. Morgan must either be eliminated or driven from the district before the campaign into North Carolina could be launched. On January first Cornwallis ordered Tarleton, with the British Legion reinforced by the First Battalion of the 71st Regiment, to cross the Broad River and push Morgan "to the utmost," and urged haste as "no time is to be lost."[52]

Morgan still rested on the Pacolet. Greene had directed militia leaders to join Morgan with their troops as soon as possible. The response had been slow. General Davidson was experiencing difficulty in raising his North Carolina militia because of Indian uprisings on the frontier, but he had written confidently that he would soon join Morgan with a thousand men.[53] On December 28, Davidson had arrived with only 120 men, but he immediately returned to North Carolina for at least 500 men who he claimed were being embodied at Salisbury. Colonel Andrew Pickens came into camp with sixty South Carolina militia.[54] Small groups also drifted in, many of whom had banded together to plunder the Tories and had come into Morgan's camp for protection.[55] On December 27, Morgan received a false report that the British were on his trail. He had speedily placed strong pickets on the perimeter and had established a defensive encampment. Officers were instructed to conduct roll

---

[52] Cornwallis to Tarleton, January 2, 1781. Tarleton, *Campaigns*, 244-245.

[53] Davidson to Morgan, December 14, 1780. James Graham, *The Life of General Daniel Morgan, of the Virginia Line of the Army of the United States, with Portions of his Correspondence: Compiled from Authentic Sources* (New York: Derby and Jackson, 1858), 263-264. Hereafter cited as Graham, *Morgan*.

[54] Andrew Pickens was risking death in the event of capture by the British. He had formerly been captured and paroled by them. He had observed the conditions of his parole until his home was plundered by a band of Tory raiders. These men had placed a noose around the neck of Pickens' son and had threatened to hang the lad unless the hiding place of valuables was divulged. Pickens had considered this a violation of his parole and had sent his family across the mountains for safekeeping, then had notified the British of his actions and rejoined the patriot forces. Edward McGrady, *The History of South Carolina in the Revolution, 1780-1781* (New York: Macmillan and Company, 1902), 18-22.

[55] James F. Collins, *Autobiography of a Revolutionary Soldier*, edited by John M. Roberts (Clinton [Louisiana]: Felicana Democrat, Print., 1869), 56. Hereafter cited as Collins, *Autobiography*.

calls every two hours and all absentees were to be reported immediately.[56]

On the same day a patrol reported that a body of about 350 Tories, under the leadership of a Colonel Waters, had advanced into the district to the vicinity of "Fair Forest," about twenty miles from Morgan, where they "were plundering and insulting the good people of the neighborhood."[57] Morgan resolved to destroy this group before they had the opportunity to make a junction with the British army. Within two days 200 mounted militia had been added to William Washington's dragoons and were sent to dispose of the invaders. As Washington's detachment advanced the Tories retreated twenty miles back to a place known as Hammond's Store.[58] There with Cornwallis on their right flank and their left protected by Ninety Six, they felt reasonably safe. After a pursuit of forty miles, Washington reached the vicinity of Hammond's around noon of December 30. Colonel Waters had drawn up his Tories in a battle line across the crest of a slope. To reach the position, Washington's troops would have to descend a long incline and then charge up a hill. As they approached the site, they captured several of the Tory pickets, who revealed the disposition of the enemy troops. Arriving opposite the enemy position, Washington deployed his forces. The mounted militia, with their rifles, were placed on the flanks to provide a covering fire, while the dragoons were located in the center. At the command, the militia fired, and the cavalry, shouting and drawing their sabres, charged across the ravine. The terrified Tories fled precipitately through the trees without firing a shot, only to be ridden down by the horses or struck down by a dragoon's sword.[59] One hundred and fifty were killed and forty taken prisoner. Washington did not lose a man. Booty collected after the skirmish included forty horses and some bag-

[56] William Seymour, *A Journal of the Southern Expedition, 1780-1781* (Wilmington: The Historical Society of Delaware, 1896), 12. Hereafter cited as Seymour, *Journal.*

[57] Morgan to Greene, December 31, 1781. Graham, *Morgan,* 267.

[58] Hammond's Store was near the present day site of "Abbeville, South Carolina.

[59] William C. Edwards (ed.), "Memoirs of Major Thomas Young," *The Orion: A Monthly Magazine of Literature and Art,* III (October, 1843), 87.

gage.[60] A small detachment was dispatched to pursue the fleeing Tories and, if practicable, to surprise the loyalist stronghold at Williams' plantation, about fifteen miles from Ninety Six. This stratagem was frustrated when the post was notified of the defeat by the fleeing refugees and the garrison joined the flight and scurried to the protection afforded by the fort at Ninety Six. The fortifications at the plantation were destroyed as were the supplies that could not be carried away. As the victorious group was returning they met a force of 200 men sent by Morgan to cover their return.[61] This foray led to cries of dismay from the loyalists of the district and influenced Cornwallis' decision that Morgan must be destroyed before any campaign could be originated.

In the short interval of Washington's absence, Morgan's little army had been increasing rapidly, but it soon developed that the sudden growth was restricting operations. The multiplying number of men and mounts were draining the area of its resources. Provisions and forage were becoming increasingly scarce. Morgan was also becoming aware of his isolated position. A communication was dispatched to Greene suggesting that the army on the Pee Dee create a diversion while Morgan's troops swung down into Georgia to harass and attack British posts in that sector.[62] While awaiting approval of this scheme, Morgan constantly shifted his troops in an attempt to make the most of the limited supplies. An effort was made to instill discipline into the new recruits by forcing them to witness the execution of malefactors. One of the Tories taken prisoner by Washington was court-martialed, convicted and hanged on the charge of desertion to the enemy and acting as a guide for Indians raiding the outposts of the American army.[63] Several days later a deserter from Washington's corps was captured, found guilty, and shot, all in the same day.[64]

---

[60] John Rutledge to the Delegates of South Carolina in Congress, January 10, 1781. John W. Barnwell (ed.), "Letters of John Rutledge," *South Carolina Historical and Genealogical Magazine*, XVIII (February, 1917), 65.

[61] Morgan to Greene, January 4, 1781. Myers, *Cowpens Papers*, 16.

[62] Morgan to Greene, January 4, 1781. Myers, *Cowpens Papers*, 16.

[63] Seymour, *Journal*, 12.

[64] Seymour, *Journal*, 13.

A message arrived from Greene, but it had been dispatched before the receipt of Morgan's request for approval of the Georgia expedition. General Morgan was advised of the recent arrival of Leslie's troops and was warned that the British would likely attempt to give him a "stroke." Greene suggested that persons who would be unsuspected by the enemy be stationed twenty or thirty miles from camp to observe and report on the movements of the British army, for "The Militia, you know, are always unsuspicious and therefore are the more easily surprized. Don't depend too much on them." Then, as if recalling Gates' scattered army after the battle of Camden, he cautioned Morgan to select and inform his officers of a rendezvous in the event that he were attacked and defeated.[65]

Another communication from Greene soon arrived in response to Morgan's proposal for a southern expedition. The message was disappointing as the suggestion was vetoed. Greene explained that the British controlled nothing of value in Georgia except their forts, to which they would retire and pay little or no attention to him. Such a move would result only in removing the services of Morgan's detachment from the southern army, which would then be vulnerable to attack by the British. It was suggested that small details be dispatched to cut the supply lines to Ninety Six and Augusta. An attack upon Ninety Six, Augusta, or even Savannah was approved if such an offensive action could be conducted with the element of surprise. As another antidote to the restlessness of Morgan, Greene recommended that small units be detached with the mission of destroying the draught horses of the enemy and waylaying British recruiting parties. A hundred expert riflemen under Colonel William Campbell had been ordered to report to the camp on the Pacolet. The action at Hammond's Store had emphasized the value of Washington's dragoons. Morgan was requested "to have Col. Washington's horse kept in as good order as possible and let the Militia do the foraging duty. We may want a body of heavy cavalry, and if they are broke down we shall have nothing to depend upon."[66]

Word was received that Tarleton was near Ninety Six and that his movements indicated a thrust at Morgan. This was followed by a warning from Greene who expressed a note of confidence in Morgan's ability to deal with the situation as he said, "Col. Tarleton is said to be on his way to pay you a visit. I doubt not he will have a decent reception and a proper dismission."[67]

Spies and deserters delivered alarming reports. Tarleton had been joined by reinforcements, had crossed the Tiger River and was pressing the pursuit. Morgan's army continued to increase as militia units supplemented his basic group, but they only accentuated the critical supply problem. The straggling militia destroyed the cohesiveness and efficiency of the detachment, and they were plundering the inhabitants when the opportunity presented itself. As the enemy approached and he surveyed his position, Morgan became uneasy and dissatisfied. He requested General Greene to recall his troops, leaving the militia in the district under the command of General Davidson and Colonel Pickens. It was his opinion that if only the militia were left in the area, Cornwallis would consider them of such little importance that Tarleton would be recalled. The militia would be just as effective in keeping the disaffected in their places as his detachment could. His troops were trained for combat, not police action.[68] Greene's answer, although it did not arrive until after the ensuing engagement, still insisted that Morgan and his troops remain in the district.[69]

The day after Morgan had dispatched this last request, the details left to guard the fords on the Pacolet came into camp. Tarleton had crossed the river and was even then close on their heels. It was now obvious that Morgan, with his straggling militia, could retreat no farther. He was, however, determined to choose the battle site. Early on the morning of

[66] Greene to Morgan, January 8, 1781. Greene Letter Book, 1781, 51-52.
[67] Greene to Morgan, January 13, 1781. Greene Letter Book, 1781, 63-64.
[68] Morgan to Greene, January 13, 1781. Graham, *Morgan*, 286.
[69] Greene to Morgan, January 19, 1781. Greene Letter Book, 1781, 92-94.

January 16, forcing many of his men to leave their food cooking, he marched his men toward the Broad River.[70]

Tarleton had been ordered in pursuit of Morgan on January first. The tidings of Hammond's Store and William's Plantation had implied an American thrust at Ninety Six. Upon Tarleton's arrival at that place, he had found the post unmolested and was under no immediate danger of assault. He had taken the opportunity to rest his troops and had issued orders "to bring up my baggage, but no women." He reported the situation to his commander and requested that he be allowed to attack and destroy Morgan. He suggested to Cornwallis that the main army move towards King's Mountain as a block to Morgan's retreat if he refused to fight and was driven back across the Broad River.[71] As Tarleton awaited approval of this plan of operation, Lieutenant Colonel Allen, commandant at Ninety Six, offered to reinforce him with troops from his garrison. Tarleton refused.[72]

Dispatches from his commanding officer contained encouragement and approval of the plan of his subordinate. Cornwallis endorsed Tarleton's strategy and commented, "You have exactly done what I wished you to do, and understood my intentions perfectly." He also informed Tarleton that his baggage was being escorted by the 7th Regiment, which was to reinforce the garrison at Ninety Six.[73] With this expression of confidence in his ability by his superior, Tarleton initiated a series of rapid marches in pursuit of Morgan. His movements for the first few days were limited, to allow the time necessary for Leslie to make a junction with Cornwallis. Reports indicated that the militia were flocking to Morgan. To counterbalance this additional strength of his opponent, Tarleton requested and received permission to attach the 7th Regiment and their three-pounder to his command.[74] On the fourteenth Cornwallis wrote, "Leslie is at

[70] Stedman, History of the . . . American War, II, 320.
[71] Tarleton to Cornwallis, January 4, 1781. Tarleton, Campaigns, 246.
[72] Roderick Mackenzie, Strictures on Lt. Col. Tarleton's "History of the Campaigns of 1780 and 1781, in the Southern Provinces of North America," (London: Printed for the author, 1787), 92. Hereafter cited as Mackenzie, Strictures. Mackenzie was a lieutenant in the 71st Regiment and was wounded at Cowpens.
[73] Cornwallis to Tarleton, January 5, 1781. Tarleton, Campaigns, 246-247.
[74] Tarleton, Campaigns, 212.

last out of the swamps," [75] and the tempo of the pursuit quickened. Morgan was now only six miles away. Tarleton planned to use log houses, previously constructed by Major Patrick Ferguson, as a base from which to observe Morgan and wait for him to make a decisive move. Before he could establish himself in this position, patrols reported that the Americans had decamped in such haste that half cooked food was still simmering over dying fires. Morgan's vacated position offered promising possibilities for provisions and forage and Tarleton accordingly marched his troops to this location.[76]

Small detachments were ordered to follow closely upon Morgan's line of march. A party of Tories brought in an American militia colonel who had been capture when he wandered too far from his troops. From interrogation of this prisoner and the reports of patrols, it was determined that the enemy was marching in the direction of the Broad River and Thicketty Mountain. There was also evidence that additional reinforcements of militia were on the march to join Morgan.[77] To insure the success of his operation, Tarleton felt that he must strike before these new troops united with his opponent. He planned an immediate action.

The following morning, January 17, the troops were awakened at three o'clock in the morning and marched toward Morgan's last reported position, with the baggage and its guard to take its position at daybreak. Tarleton planned either to surprise Morgan or force him to fight before he had the opportunity to deploy his troops properly. Approaching the American camp, two videttes were captured[78] and they revealed that Morgan had halted and had decided to make a stand at a place called the Cowpens.[79] Tarleton was jubilant

<hr>

[75] Cornwallis to Tarleton, January 14, 1781. Tarleton, *Campaigns*, 248.

[76] Tarleton, *Campaigns*, 213-214.

[77] Tarleton, *Campaigns*, 214.

[78] Mackenzie, *Strictures*, 97. Videttes were mounted pickets.

[79] Stock raisers comprised a large portion of the population of upper South Carolina. Pens were erected for the purposes of marking and salting the cattle, although at this time any grazing area was normally designated as a cowpen. The site selected for the battle had first been located on a Cherokee trading path and was known locally as "Hannah's Cowpens" from its owner. See Johnson, *Sketches of the Life and Correspondence of Nathanael Greene*, I, 377; Benjamin F. Perry, Revolutionary Incidents, No. 11, Benjamin F. Perry papers, Southern Historical Collection, Chapel Hill, North Carolina; J. B. C. Landrum, *Colonial and Revolutionary History of Upper South Carolina* (Greenville: Shannon and Co., 1897), 19.

as the prisoners and his guides described the site. Open woods offered unlimited opportunity for cavalry maneuvers. Morgan would be forced to leave his flanks exposed as there were no physical irregularities into which to tie the extremities of his battle line. The Broad River ran parallel to his rear line, eliminating any possibility of flight. Without delay Tarleton moved up within sight of the American forces and began to deploy his troops, confident that the day was as good as won.[80]

A plausible supposition is that Morgan planned to cross the Broad River and fight in the vicinity of Thicketty Mountain, where the terrain could be better adapted to his style of combat. When he had arrived on the banks of the Broad, he had found that stream swollen and deep because of the recent rains.[81] To attempt a passage would possibly have allowed Tarleton to come up while his troops were still engaged in fording the river, an event which could only result in disaster for his little army.

Military men have long made a practice of criticising Morgan's choice of a battle site and Tarleton himself stated:

> The ground which General Morgan had chosen for the engagement . . . was disadvantageous to the Americans, and convenient for the British. An open wood was certainly as good a place for action as Lieutenant Colonel Tarleton could desire; America does not produce many more suitable to the nature of the troops under his command.[82]

The position selected for the American stand was at the summit of a long, gently sloping ridge, covered with an open woods facilitating cavalry operations. The Broad River at the rear discouraged all thoughts of retreat and Morgan's exposed flanks invited encirclement. It was a situation designed to grant victory to the army with the best cavalry, and Tarleton's British Legion was generally acknowledged to be one of the

---

[80] Tarleton, *Campaigns*, 215.

[81] Robert Smith to James Iredell, January 31, 1781. Griffith J. McRee, *Life and Correspondence of James Iredell, One of the Associate Justices of the Supreme Court of the United States*, 2 vols. (New York: D. Appleton and Co., 1837), I, 483.

[82] Tarleton, *Campaigns*, 221. Henry Lee made the oft disputed statement that Morgan's decision to fight grew out of an "irritation of temper." Lee, *Memoirs*, 226.

best cavalry units in America. Morgan, in later years, defended his choice with the statement:

I would not have had a swamp in view of my militia on any consideration; they would have made for it, and nothing could have detained them from it. And as to covering my wings, I knew my adversary and was perfectly sure I should have nothing but downright fighting. As to retreat, it was the very thing that I wished to cut off all hope of. I would have thanked Tarleton had he surrounded me with his cavalry. It would have been better than placing my own men in the rear to shoot down those who broke from the ranks. When men are forced to fight, they will sell their lives dearly; and I knew the dread of Tarleton's cavalry would give due weight to the protection of my bayonets, and keep my troops from breaking up as Buford's regiment did. Had I crossed the river, one-half of the militia would immediately have abandoned me.[83]

Morgan's army had arrived at the Cowpens near sunset of January 16, and he had addressed the troops and revealed his determination to stand and fight. The men cheered. Throughout the course of the day's march he had been cursed heartily by many of the troops who had felt that the retreat had been a display of cowardice.[84] Two colonels, Brandon and Roebuck, rode in and reported that they had counted Tarleton's forces as they crossed the Pacolet and that the enemy numbered approximately 1,150 men. As soon as the men were settled, preparations for battle were initiated. Orders were issued that the militia have twenty-four rounds of ammunition ready for use before they slept.[85] The sign and countersign for the night, "Fire" and "Sword" were designed to stimulate slackening spirits.[86] The first action taken by Morgan to strengthen his forces was the addition of forty-five volunteers to Washington's corps as a measure to more nearly equal, numerically, Tarleton's cavalry. Patrols and

[83] Morgan quoted in Johnson, *Life and Correspondence of Nathanael Greene*, I, 376.

[84] Edwards, "Memoirs of Major Thomas Young," *The Orion*, III, 88.

[85] Colonel Samuel Hammond in Joseph Johnson, *Traditions and Reminiscences Chiefly of the American Revolution in the South: Including Biographical Sketches, Incidents and Anecdotes. Few of Which Have Been Published, Particularly of Residents in the Upper Country* (Charleston: Walker and James, 1851), 527.

[86] A. L. Pickens, *Skyagunsta, the Border Wizard Owl: General Andrew Pickens* (Greenville: Observer Printing Co., 1934), 68.

scouts were sent out with orders to observe the enemy's movements. Baggage was sent back to the Broad River and messengers dispatched to the bodies of militia reported to be coming in, urging them to accelerate their pace.[87] Pickens brought in a body of new recruits. Other groups hurried in, calling for ammunition, and wanting to know the state of affairs. One officer commented, "They were all in good spirits, related circumstances of Tarleton's cruelty, and expressed the strongest desire to check his progress."[88] After a council of war with the officers Morgan went among the campfires and mingled with his men, aiding his recently created cavalry to become acquainted with their newly acquired sabres. He passed from group to group, laughing with the men and "telling them that the old wagoner would crack his whip over Ben [Tarleton] in the morning as sure as they lived."[89] To the militia he said, "Just hold up your heads, boys, three fires, and you are free, and then when you return to your homes, how the old folks will bless you, and the girls kiss you, for your gallant conduct." [90]

The next morning, January 17, a scout reported that Tarleton was only five miles away and was marching light and fast.[91] Morgan's shout of "Boys, get up, Benny is coming," awakened the men.[92] The day dawned bright and bitter cold, but the troops were already being placed in position. They were all in good spirits and apparently looking forward to the approaching battle.[93]

The battle ground was slightly undulating with a thick growth of red oak, hickory and pine. Because of the grazing cattle, there was little undergrowth.[94] At the crest of the long slope Morgan placed his main line of defense, composed of

---

[87] Graham, *Morgan*, 291-292.

[88] John Eager Howard quoted in Lee, *Memoirs*, 226n.

[89] Edwards, "Memoir of Major Thomas Young," *The Orion*, III, 89. Morgan was often referred to as the "old wagoner" because of his earlier occupation. He had hauled supplies for Braddock's troops in the French and Indian War. Graham, *Morgan*, 22-28.

[90] Edwards, "Memoirs of Major Thomas Young," *The Orion*, III, 89.

[91] Morgan to Greene, January 19, 1781. Graham, *Morgan*, 468.

[92] "Memoir of Thomas McJunkin of Union," *The Magnolia: Or Southern Appalachian*, II (January, 1843), 38.

[93] Seymour, *Journal*, 13.

[94] Colonel Samuel Hammond in Johnson, *Traditions and Reminiscences*, 527.

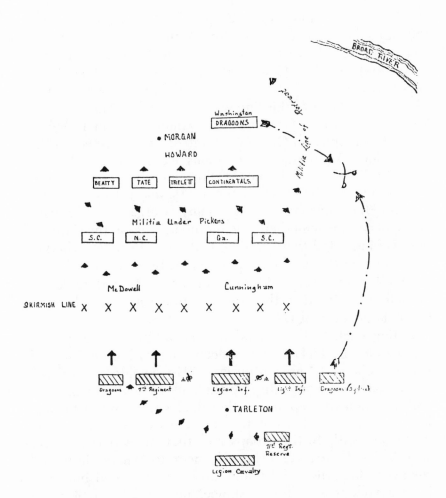

Battle of the Cowpens
January 17, 1781

the Maryland Line, a skeleton company of Delaware Continentals, and two companies of Virginia militia under Major Triplett and Captain Tate.[95] Beatty's Georgians covered the right flank. This line of 437 men was under the command of Lieutenant Colonel John Eager Howard. Approximately 150 yards down the slope were the volunteers of North Carolina, South Carolina and Georgia, about 270 men under the "brave and valuable" Colonel Pickens. A skirmish line of 150 men was posted 150 yards in front of Pickens' second line. The right segment of this line was composed of Major Joseph McDowell's North Carolina back-country riflemen, while Major Cunningham's Georgia volunteers were posted on the left. Colonel Washington's dragoons were stationed behind the main line, out of the line of fire, but still in such a position as to guard the horses of the militia and act in support.[96]

Before the appearance of the enemy, Morgan went forward and spoke to the men then placing themselves on the skirmish line. He indicated that the time had come to prove whether they were entitled to their reputation as brave men and good shots. "Let me see," said Morgan, as he turned to leave, "which are entitled to the credit of brave men, the boys of Carolina or those of Georgia."[97]

Riding back to the second line he addressed the militia commanded by Pickens. His speech rang with optimism and was calculated to fire enthusiasm. He confidently assured them that they would display their usual zeal and bravery and maintain the reputation they had gained when he had led them. He pointed out that he had experienced success in dealing with British troops and that his experience was superior to theirs. He exhorted them to remain firm and steady, to fire with careful aim, and if they would but pour in two volleys at killing distance, he would take it upon himself to insure the victory.[98] Morgan's opinion of militia was actually similar to that held by Greene, but he did recognize their value as shock troops.

As Morgan rode back to the main line, Pickens told his militia, "Ease your joints." He then told them that they could shelter themselves behind trees, but they were not to fire until the enemy was within thirty yards of their position. He cautioned them to fire low and aim at the officers.[99]

After leaving the militia Morgan addressed the main line of seasoned veterans. He spoke briefly and quietly, reminding them that he had always placed confidence in their skill and courage, and he assured them that victory was certain if they did their part. They were also warned not to become alarmed at a sudden retreat by the militia as that eventuality was included in his plan of action. At the conclusion of this short talk, he assumed his post and quietly sat his horse, awaiting the appearance of the enemy.[100]

The British troops came into view at approximately eight o'clock. Tarleton, prematurely imagining the laurels of victory upon his brow, immediately deployed his fatigued command about 300 yards in front of the American skirmish line. No time was allotted by Tarleton for a reconnaissance or a conference with his subordinates. The rank and file were ordered to discard all gear and accoutrements except their arms and ammunition. The Light Infantry, the Legion Infantry, and the 7th Regiment formed the line of battle. To protect their flanks and threaten those of the Americans, fifty dragoons under the command of a captain were placed on each extremity. The 71st Regiment, with the remaining dragoons was held in reserve 180 yards to the rear. The two cannon were placed in the center of the battle line.[101] The Americans, with no artillery to annoy the enemy could only watch with awe the precision with which the British swung into position.[102] As the attacking troops were extended they were subjected to sporadic rifle fire from small groups which had been sent out from the skirmish line. The nervous recruits of the 7th Regiment returned a scattered fire, but their uneasiness was soon calmed by British officers.[103]

[99] Pickens, *Skyagunsta, The Border Wizard Owl,* 70-71.
[100] Lee, *Memoirs,* 227-228.
[101] Tarleton, *Campaigns,* 216.
[102] Thomas Anderson, "Journal of Lieutenant Thomas Anderson of the Delaware Regiment," *Historical Magazine,* 2d series, I (April, 1867), 209.
[103] Tarleton, *Campaigns,* 216.

The impetuous Tarleton, impatient with the sluggish deployment of his weary troops, issued the order to advance before the formation was complete. As the artillery roared the infantry gave three "huzzas" and swung into a slow trot toward the American lines.[104]

Morgan, as he galloped among his men, heard the cheers and shouted, "They give us the British halloo, boys, give them the Indian halloo, by God."[105]

The British advance was met with "a heavy and galling fire" as they drew near the skirmish line of McDowell and Cunningham.[106] The green and scarlet line halted, then pushed on. The skirmish line faded back through the trees, firing as often as they could reload their rifles. One section of this first line fell back and merged with Pickens' militia. The remainder circled around and reformed in the rear of the third line. The British halted, regrouped, dressed their line, and continued their advance.[107]

Pickens ordered his command to fire by regiments, providing a covering fire for those reloading their pieces. The British assault wavered under this steady fire, but discipline overcame fear and the attack still moved forward. As the British approached within forty yards of Pickens' line, they fired a volley, few of the shots finding a mark.[108] Then, with empty muskets, and with a shout, the British rushed forward with the bayonet.[109] The courage of the untrained militia waned at the sight of the cold steel and they began to fall

[104] Anderson, "Journal of Lieutenant Thomas Anderson. . . . ," *Historical Magazine*, 2d series, I, 209.

[105] Edwards, "Memoirs of Major Thomas Young," *The Orion*, III, 101.

[106] Morgan to Greene, January 17, 1781. Myers, *Cowpens Papers*, 25.

[107] Anderson, "Journal of Lieutenant Thomas Anderson. . . . ," *Historical Magazine*, 2d series, I, 209.

[108] In 1835 a visitor to the battlefield found evidence that many shots had lodged in the trees, some as high as thirty or forty feet. Benjamin F. Perry Papers, Southern Historical Collection.

[109] At the beginning of the war the Americans had little faith in the bayonet, while the British regarded it as a special weapon for their regulars and it was their custom to charge with the bayonet whenever practicable. Steuben, apostle of shock tactics, urged that the light infantry keep bayonets continually fixed. The assault upon Redoubt No. 9 at Yorktown by the American Light Infantry was made with unloaded muskets and fixed bayonets. Wright, "Notes on the Continental Army," *William and Mary Quarterly*, 2d series, XI, 89-90. The British sergeant turned historian, R. Lamb, made the statement that the frequent rains in North America often prevented the use of the musket and made the bayonet a very important weapon. R. Lamb, *Memoir of His Own Life* (Dublin: J. Jone, 1811), 202.

back. Pickens managed to control the movement of many of his men and conducted an orderly retreat although "with haste." He led this group to the rear of the Continentals and reformed them on the right flank. The remainder, panic-stricken, fled precipitately to the spot where they had left their horses.[110]

The commander of the dragoons protecting Tarleton's right flank, a Captain Ogilvie, detected the fleeing militia and his troops were ordered to charge them.[111] As the British rode among the frightened Americans, they became scattered and disorganized. Washington, after a hurried conference with Howard, charged the British dragoons with such force that many were thrown from their horses and were unable to remount under the flashing sabres of the Americans. Those who had been able to retain their seat turned and fled with such haste that one witness later declared that "they appeared to be as hard to stop as a drove of wild Choctaw steers, going to the Pennsylvania market."[112]

Meanwhile, the British infantry had gained confidence with the flight of the militia. Their step quickened as they neared the final American line. The advance slowed as they were met with a steady and well-directed fire, and "it seemed like one sheet of flame from right to left."[113] Tarleton, having missed an excellent opportunity by failing to throw in his cavalry reserve in the pursuit of the militia, now ordered his infantry reserve into action, but still refused to commit his dragoons.[114] The British line, longer than that of the Americans, gradually began to turn the left flank of the defenders. Howard, fearing encirclement, ordered Wallace's Virginia Company to change its front. The order was mistaken and the group began to fall back. The other unit commanders, assuming that a general retreat had been ordered, also be-

[110] Lee, *Memoirs*, 228.
[111] Tarleton, *Campaigns*, 217.
[112] Collins, *Autobiography*, 57.
[113] Edwards, "Memoirs of Major Thomas Young," *The Orion*, III, 101.
[114] Major McArthur, commanding Tarleton's reserve, had urged an all-out cavalry charge as the Americans retreated. At his subsequent capture he complained bitterly that the best troops in the service had been put under "that boy" to be sacrificed. John Eager Howard quoted in Henry Lee, *The Campaign of 1781 in the Carolinas: with Remarks Historical and Critical on Johnson's Life of Greene* (Philadelphia: E. Littell, 1824), 96n.

gan a gradual withdrawal with their troops. Morgan, although the retirement was orderly, rode among the troops pleading for just one more volley and shouting, "Old Morgan was never beaten."[115] Morgan expressed apprehension to Howard, who answered by indicating the orderly line and observing that men who retreated in that good order were never beaten. This logic of his subordinate was convincing and Morgan ordered Howard to continue the retrograde movement until the infantry was under the protection of Washington's cavalry, while he rode back to fix a spot at which he wished the Americans to face about and pour a sudden volley into the face of their pursuers. Howard busied himself with straightening out his line and communicating this stratagem to his officers.[116] It was then that Washington had ridden up and told Howard that if the infantry could hold, he was going to charge Ogilvie's dragoons who were then riding down the fleeing militia in the rear.[117] Even as Howard assented, the British, thinking an American rout imminent, broke their formation and, shouting as they came, pressed forward.[118] The Americans, having retreated approximately fifty yards, reached the spot designated by Morgan, suddenly faced about and fired a volley, at a range of about ten yards, into the faces of their astonished foe. Those troops which had been, moments before, an example of British discipline and bravery, now became a milling mass of confused individuals. Howard was quick to seize the initiative. He shouted the command "charge bayonets," and "augmented their astonishment."[119] The day was won for the Americans. The British were thrown into an "unaccountable panick,"[120] and discarding their muskets and cartouche boxes, "did the prettiest

[115] Collins, *Autobiography*, 57.
[116] John Eager Howard quoted in Lee, *Campaigns of 1781 in the Carolinas*, 97-98n.
[117] William Moultrie, *Memoirs of the American Revolution, So Far as It Is Related to the States of North and South-Carolina and Georgia*, 2 vols. (New York: David Longworth, 1802), II, 255. Hereafter cited as Moultrie, *Memoirs*. William Washington is supposed to have given Moultrie his account of the battle of the Cowpens.
[118] Anderson, "Journal of Lieutenant Thomas Anderson . . . ," *Historical Magazine*, 2d series, I, 209.
[119] Tarleton, *Campaigns*, 217. Morgan to Greene, January 19, 1781. Graham, *Morgan*, 468.
[120] Tarleton, *Campaigns*, 216.

286

sort of running away."[121] This sudden flight of the infantry which coincided with Ogilvie's retreat before Washington's dragoons transformed Tarleton's crack troops into a panic-stricken mob.

The Americans pushed forward in vigorous pursuit. There was a cry of "Tarleton's quarters," but Howard counteracted this with the command of "Give them quarter." Riding among the routed troops, he called upon them to lay down their arms and they would receive good quarters. More than 500 took advantage of this promise and laid down their arms.[122] Only the artillerymen fought on, defending their cannon until they were either all killed or wounded.[123] Howard personally saved the life of one of these men, in addition to a frightened British captain who admitted that the British troops had been instructed to give no quarter and was afraid that the Americans "would use him ill." [124]

About 250 British dragoons, held in reserve, had just received orders to go into action when the critical maneuver of the Americans had thrown back the infantry, whose headlong retreat, in turn, threw the cavalry into confusion. Tarleton gave orders to reform the mounted troops approximately 400 yards to the rear while he went forward to rally the infantry and protect the artillery.[125]

The panic generated by the fleeing foot soldiers was communicated to the cavalry. The mounted troops fled through the forest, riding down such officers as dared to try to oppose their flight. Tarleton, screaming curses, attempted to rally his dragoons for a charge on the Americans, who were rushing in pursuit of the defeated enemy with a complete disregard for military formation. Tarleton's horse was killed be-

---

[121] Edwards, "Memoirs of Major Thomas Young," *The Orion*, III, 101. Although the strategy which won the battle of Cowpens developed out of a mistaken order, the maneuver of feigning retreat and then suddenly turning upon the disorganized pursuers is quite old. William the Conqueror used it to advantage in defeating Harold at the Battle of Hastings in 1066. It was also a favorite maneuver of Genghis Khan.

[122] Moultrie, *Memoirs*, II, 255-256.

[123] Cornwallis to Sir Henry Clinton, January 18, 1781. Ross, *Correspondence of Charles, First Marquis Cornwallis*, I, 82. Tarleton, *Campaigns*, 217.

[124] John Eager Howard quoted in *The Magazine of American History*, VII (October, 1881), 279.

[125] Tarleton, *Campaigns*, 216-217.

neath him. He caught another. Only fourteen officers and fifty men responded to his orders to reform.[126]

This struggle was fierce, but short and decisive. Washington personally led his men into action. His zeal almost cost him his life as he repeatedly found himself far ahead of his troops. Twice he was saved from injury, once by a stroke from his sergeant's sword and later by a lucky shot from the pistol of his bugler. Tradition states that Washington and Tarleton were engaged in personal combat and that Washington's horse had been killed by a pistol shot from Tarleton, who is reported to have received a gash on his head from a sword wielded by Washington. The British commander, finally realizing the defeat was inevitable, wheeled and fled, closely pursued by the American cavalry.[127] Respite was gained as Washington followed the wrong road for a short distance.[128] The chase continued to the Pacolet River. There the Americans were informed by a Mrs. Goudelock that Tarleton had passed some time before, although at that moment he was actually engaged in crossing the river only a few hundred yards distant. Tarleton had pressed the woman's husband into service as a guide and she feared for his safety in the event of violence. Her deception was successful. Washington turned back.[129] The British baggage train had been sent approximately fifteen miles from the scene of battle, guarded by a detachment from each unit and commanded by Lieutenant Fraser of the 71st Regiment. Fraser

[126] Tarleton, *Campaigns*, 218.

[127] Lee, *Memoirs*, 229. This flight later proved embarrassing to Tarleton, according to the following anecdote. When Cornwallis marched into Virginia from Wilmington he rested his troops in Halifax, North Carolina. In the home of Mrs. J. B. Ashe, in whose house General Leslie was quartered, Tarleton made the remark that he would be happy to see Colonel Washington as he understood he was ugly and diminutive in person. Mrs. Ashe angrily replied, "If you had looked behind you, Colonel Tarleton, at the battle of Cowpens, you would have enjoyed that pleasure." John H. Wheeler, *Historical Sketches of North Carolina, from 1584 to 1851. Compiled from Original Records, Official Documents, and Traditional Statements* (Philadelphia: Lippincott, Granbe and Co., 1851), 186.

[128] Morgan to Greene, January 19, 1781. Graham, *Morgan*, 469.

[129] Perry, Revolutionary Incidents, No. 7, Benjamin F. Perry Papers, Southern Historical Collection. One report stated that as Tarleton and his fugitives reached Hamilton's Ford the men hesitated to enter the swollen Broad River, even though they had just received word that Washington was close on their heels. Tarleton eventually drove them into the water by whipping them with the flat of his sabre. Edwards, "Memoirs of Major Thomas Young," *The Orion*, III, 102.

had early received news of the defeat from "some friendly Americans," and immediately destroyed or burned that part of the baggage which could not be carried off. The men were loaded into a wagon or mounted on spare horses and hastily made their way to the encampment of Cornwallis. This was the only body of infantry which escaped, all others being killed or taken prisoner.[130]

Cornwallis first learned of the disaster of Cowpens from this group and a detachment of dragoons who arrived at his camp on the evening of January 17. Tarleton and his fugitives did not arrive until the following morning.[131] An American prisoner of war who witnessed Tarleton's report of the battle to his superior reported that Cornwallis was leaning forward on his sword as Tarleton spoke. In his fury the British general pressed forward so hard that the weapon broke beneath his weight, and he swore loudly that he would recover the prisoners, no matter what the cost.[132]

General Leslie was now less than a day's march from making a junction with Cornwallis and further action by the British force was delayed until the arrival of these additional troops. While awaiting the scattered remnants of his dragoons to regroup, Tarleton displayed a sudden interest in the welfare of his troops which he had neglected in their somewhat injudicious employment at Cowpens. He dispatched, under the protection of a flag, a surgeon to care for, and a sum of money to be used for, his captured soldiers.[133]

When the refugees from Cowpens had been reassembled and strengthened with additional troops from other units, they were dispatched, under the command of Tarleton, upon Morgan's trail in an effort to rescue the prisoners. The chase continued for two days before it was determined that the Americans were out of reach.[134]

[130] Mackenzie, *Strictures*, 102-103. David Ramsey, *History of the American Revolution*, 2 vols. (London: John Stockdale, 1793), II, 235. Tarleton, to salve his wounded pride, and possibly to restore a minute portion of his vanquished glory, later declared that he had attacked the wagons, dispersed the enemy guard, and had burned the wagons and baggage to prevent them from falling into American hands. Tarleton, *Campaigns*, 217.

[131] Mackenzie, *Strictures*, 102-103.

[132] "Memoir of Joseph McJunkin of Union," *The Magnolia*, II, 39.

[133] Tarleton to Morgan, January 19, 1781. Myers, *Cowpens Papers*, 29.

[134] A. R. Newsome (ed.), "A British Orderly Book, 1780-1781," *The North Carolina Historical Review*, IX (July, 1932), 284-285.

The defeat at the Cowpens had been a severe and unexpected blow to British expectations, and was even more significant in its consequences than King's Mountain, for Tarleton's drubbing deprived Lord Cornwallis of the light troops which had been destined to play a major role in the invasion. Britain could not afford to lose face a second time in the South as "defensive measures would be certain ruin to the affairs of Britain in the Southern Colonies."[135] The British general made the decision to pursue Morgan with his entire command, force him to fight, and wipe out the humiliation of Cowpens. It was thus that the decision was made to launch the campaign which was to culminate in the termination of major hostilities on American soil.

Back at the Cowpens Morgan had surveyed the field of battle. He had just won an overwhelming victory over a force with which he would have been happy to fight a drawn contest. With a motley force of between 900 and 1,000 men, of whom only about 800 were actually engaged and a large number were untried militia, he had defeated a superior army of approximately 1,150 well-trained British soldiers. His casualties were amazingly light. Only twelve had been killed and sixty wounded. In contrast, British losses were staggering. Ten officers were included among the 110 killed. There had been 702 captured, 200 of them wounded. The American militia had become scattered in rounding up those of Tarleton's group who had escaped the carnage. Twenty-nine British officers were counted among the prisoners. Much valuable equipment had been taken, including two field pieces,[136] two standards,[137] 800 muskets, one travelling forge,

[135] Cornwallis to Germain, March 17, 1781. Ross, *The Correspondence of Charles, First Marquis Cornwallis*, I, 503.
[136] These cannon had an interesting background. They had been taken from Burgoyne at Saratoga by Morgan, and had been retaken from General Thomas Sumter by Tarleton in the engagement at Blackstock's, November 20, 1781. "Extracts from William's Notebook," *Calendar of the General Otho Williams Papers*, 36. These two field pieces were also probably among the four cannon captured from Greene at the battle of Guilford Court House by Cornwallis.
[137] These were the colors of the 71st Regiment and the British Legion. According to British army custom, these two units were required to henceforth wear their tunics without facings. The 71st Regiment, a Scottish Regiment, also lost their bagpipes. O. H. Williams to Dr. James McHenry, January 23, 1781, *Calendar of the General Otho Williams Papers*, 36-37.

thirty-five wagons, 100 horses and "all their music." Among the booty were seventy Negroes, who had been brought along as servants for the British officers.[138] This surprising triumph had been achieved in less than an hour.

It was apparent to the victorious Morgan that although he had won the field, he could not retain possession. Cornwallis would soon be marching with his entire army in an attempt to recover the prisoners and remove some of the tarnish from British military glory. A defeat would spoil the fruits of victory, and the decision was to move at once to the northward. Lieutenant Colonel Washington had not returned from his pursuit of Tarleton, but Morgan, after paroling the captured British officers and dispatching the news of his victory to Greene, marched north to the Catawba with his prisoners on the morning of January 18. Instructions were left for Washington to follow as soon as he returned to the field.[139]

Colonel Pickens was left behind with the local militia to bury the dead and collect the wounded of both commands. Approximately a day was spent in this operation. The wounded were placed in captured British tents and left with a guard, under a flag of truce. The militia took full advantage of their opportunities and plundered both the dead and the wounded.[140] At the completion of this task, Pickens dismissed the militia and hurried after Morgan. The race to the Dan had begun.

The battle of the Cowpens, a small engagement when considered as to the numbers engaged, was far-reaching in its results. The first reaction of Sir Henry Clinton, commandant of British forces in North America, was, "I confess I dread

---

[138] Morgan to Greene, January 19, 1781. Graham, *Morgan*, 310-311. Tarleton also claimed that the money entrusted to him for the purchase of horses and intelligence had been "lost by the unfortunate affair of the Cowpens." He also reported that similar accounts for 1781 had been lost during a forced march in North Carolina. Tarleton to the Secretary of the Board of Auditors, May 25, 1789, *Year Book: City of Charleston, S. C., 1882* (Charleston: Lucas and Richardson, 1883), 371.

[139] Morgan to Greene, January 19, 1781. Graham, *Morgan*, 469. Washington's cavalry rounded up nearly 100 additional prisoners while on their return to the battlefield. Graham, *Morgan*, 308.

[140] Collins, *Autobiography*, 58.

the Consequences."[141] For Cornwallis, it was the first link in a chain of circumstances which led to Yorktown and ultimate defeat. British critics of Tarleton have stated that the defeat at Yorktown can be traced to the loss of the light troops at Cowpens.[142]

The attention of the Continental Congress was directed towards the South at the seldom received report of a southern victory. One member of the Congress wrote to Greene:

the intelligence received was a most healing cordial to our drooping spirits . . . it was so very unexpected. It seems to have had a very sensible effect on some folks, for this is convincing proof that something is to be done, in that department.[143]

Another member felt that Maryland's acceptance of the Articles of Confederation had been a result of the news of the triumph at Cowpens.[144]

A grateful Congress voted a gold medal to Morgan, silver medals to Howard and Washington, and a sword to Pickens. Both officers and men of Morgan's army were extended "the thanks of the United States in Congress Assembled."[145] The Virginia House of Delegates voted to award Morgan a horse "with furniture," in addition to a sword.[146] John Rutledge of South Carolina, penniless and a governor without a state, could only send his "warmest and most cordial thanks."[147]

Opinion in England was, as usual, divided along political lines. The *Gentleman's Magazine* attempted to minimize the blow by declaring, "there is no great reason to believe our

[141] Clinton to Cornwallis, March 5, 1781. Clark, *State Records of North Carolina*, XVII, 989.

[142] Stedman, *History of the . . . American War*, II, 327. Mackenzie, *Strictures*, 89. *Annual Register, or a View of the History, Politics, and Literature for the Year 1781*, 56.

[143] John Matthews to Greene, February 10, 1781. Burnett, *Letters*, V, 568.

[144] Ezekiel Cornell to Governor Greene of Rhode Island, February 9, 1781. Burnett, *Letters*, V, 566n. Actually, Maryland's decision rested on the fact that she was unable to defend the Chesapeake against British sea power. The clinching argument had come when the state had applied to the French Minister for naval aid and he had, in turn, urged Maryland to ratify the articles. Edmund Cody Burnett, *The Continental Congress* (New York: The Macmillan Company, 1941), 500.

[145] Ford, *Journals of the Continental Congress*, XIX, 246-247.

[146] Graham, *Morgan*, 320.

[147] Rutledge to Morgan, January 25, 1781. Graham, *Morgan*, 332-333. Rutledge also enclosed a commission as brigadier general of the South Carolina militia for Andrew Pickens.

loss so great as the enemy would insinuate."[148] Horace Walpole, whose writings portray the extreme Whig point of view, write:

America is once more not quite ready to be conquered, although every now and then we fancy it is. Tarleton is defeated, Lord Cornwallis is checked and Arnold not sure of having betrayed his friends to much purpose.[149]

General George Washington, ever cautious, warned against overconfidence and premature victory celebrations. He feared that the southern states would regard the victory as decisive in its consequences and would tend to relax in their military exertions.[150] But his pessimism failed to dim the jubilance of the people. An aide to General Greene wrote with prophetic insight, "This is but the prelude to the aera of 1781 the close of which I hope will prove memorable in the annals of history as the happy period of peace, liberty, and independence in America."[151] William Gordon, even then collecting materials for his projected history of the Revolution, evaluated the victory thus, "Morgan's success will be more important in its distant consequences, than on the day of victory."[152]

Probably the significance of the battle was best expressed in a letter from Nathanael Greene to Henry Knox written during the siege of Yorktown. Greene said, "We have been beating the bush, and the General has come to catch the bird."[153] Cowpens was the first stroke, and "the bird" that Washington caught had been flushed.

[148] *Gentleman's Magazine and Historical Chronicle*, LI (March, 1781), 186.
[149] Walpole to Sir Horace Mann, March 30, 1781, Mrs. Paget Toynbee (ed.), *The Letters of Horace Walpole, Fourth Earl of Oxford*, 16 vols. (Oxford: The Clarendon Press, 1914), XI, 419.
[150] Washington to the President of Congress, February 17, 1781. Fitzpatrick, *Writings of Washington*, XXI, 238.
[151] Lewis Morris, Jr., to Jacob Morris, January 24, 1781. *Collections of the New-York Historical Society for the Year 1875*, VII, 477. This letter was reprinted in the *New Jersey Gazette*, February 21, 1781, as its account of the battle. Moore, *Diary of the American Revolution*, II, 375-376.
[152] William Gordon to Washington, February 28, 1781. *Proceedings of the Massachusetts Historical Society, 1929-1930* (Boston: The Society, 1931), LXIII, 452.
[153] Greene to Henry Knox, September 29, 1781, Noah Brooks, *Henry Knox, Soldier of the Revolution* (G. P. Putnam's Sons, 1900), 157.

The Second British Occupation of Augusta, 1780-1781

By HEARD ROBERTSON*

DURING the spring and summer of 1779, Sir Henry Clinton, the British commander-in-chief in North America, gradually determined upon renewed offensive operations in the southern colonies as his best hope of bringing the American Revolution to an end. Exaggerated reports of the strength and enthusiasm of the Loyalists in the south had led the ministry of Lord North at London to believe that an invasion in force, if supported by a respectable segment of the local population, would lead to the restoration of royal authority in the southern colonies and perhaps the complete defection of those areas from the revolutionary cause. Plans formulated by Clinton to translate this policy into action hinged upon use of the British enclave which had already been established around Savannah under the command of Major General Augustine Prevost as a stepping stone to the reduction, first of South Carolina, and subsequently of the entire South.

Implementation of this strategy was delayed throughout the summer of 1779 while Sir Henry awaited the arrival at New York of reinforcements from the home country. Once the expected troops arrived, plans were further disrupted during the autumn by the descent of Count d'Estaing upon the Georgia coast with a French armada and the ensuing Franco-American siege of Savannah. So long as this operation remained in progress, Clinton had no choice but to remain at New York and await the outcome, for the continued possession of a foothold in Georgia was the key to the intended southern campaign. As soon as word reached New York that Savannah had held and that d'Estaing had left the scene, plans were immediately resumed for mounting an offensive in the Carolinas, utilizing Savannah as the main British base of operations.[1]

*Lawyer of Augusta, Georgia.

Toward the end of January, 1780, a naval force under the command of Vice Admiral Marriott Arbuthnot appeared off Tybee Roads with Clinton's expeditionary force of some eight thousand men on board. While waiting for the arrival of slower vessels of the fleet Clinton conferred with Sir James Wright, restored Royal Governor of Georgia, and Major General Augustine Prevost, British troop commander at Savannah. Governor Wright, allowing the security of Georgia to override all other considerations, strongly urged Clinton to detach a portion of his force to undertake the recapture of Augusta[2] and to create a diversion in the backcountry of Georgia and South Carolina. After submitting this proposition to a council of war, Clinton reluctantly agreed to send Brigadier General James Paterson to Augusta with fourteen hundred infantry and all the cavalry at hand in order "to try the temper of the back settlements, and draw off some opposition."[3]

When the main expedition sailed northward for the attack against Charles Town, Paterson remained at Savannah to organize his foray into the interior.[4] He was spurred on by the constant urging of Wright, who argued that in addition to the strategic advantage of taking Augusta, an abundance of provisions could be found at nearby Beech Island, where "there is a great plenty of Hoggs & Indian Corn."[5]

Before the diversionary expedition was ready to march for Augusta, it became apparent to Clinton that the Americans were calling in their outlying forces, even from the backcountry, to concentrate all available troops for the defense of Charles Town. Paterson's orders were therefore countermanded. His command was diverted from its original objective and marched overland to reinforce the army under Clinton's immediate command near Charles Town. Lieutenant Colonel Thomas Brown, who was left behind with the King's Rangers and a few Indians to bolster Prevost's garrison at Savannah, remained ready at a moment's notice to invade the backcountry.[6] Meanwhile, the town of Augusta lay in undisturbed possession of the revolutionary government of Georgia—a source of constant irritation to Governor Wright who nurtured feelings of resentment over the failure of

295

the British to undertake the recovery of his entire province. Particularly galling to Sir James was the fact that a Whig assembly could sit peacefully at Augusta and elect a full rebel government almost under the shadow of his own nose.[7]

On May 12, 1780, beleaguered Charles Town was surrendered to Sir Henry Clinton by its commanding officer, General Benjamin Lincoln. More important to the British than merely taking the Carolina metropolis was the capture intact of the entire army which had been assembled to oppose the invasion of the southern colonies. The loss of Lincoln's Continentals and militia—nearly fifty-five hundred strong—momentarily shattered revolutionary resistance in the south and left the interior parts of Georgia and South Carolina defenseless.[8]

The British were quick to perceive the opportunity for a bloodless occupation of the backcountry, and in short order they proceeded to overrun most of South Carolina.[9] At the same time, British eyes again came into focus upon the town of Augusta. This time no large force was considered necessary for its recapture, for no significant bodies of revolutionary troops remained in the field in Georgia. From his post at Friday's Ferry on the Congaree River, Lieutenant Colonel Alexander Innes, commanding the South Carolina Royalists, theorized on June 8 that no more than fifty of Williamson's rebels remained at Augusta for the protection of the town. "I will pledge my life," he advised Lieutenant General Lord Cornwallis, "that three hundred men shall march to the Indian line and from thence to Augusta without firing a shot."[10] His predictions were borne out by the course of events. Brigadier General Andrew Williamson's South Carolina militia, who had formed the nucleus of the Augusta garrison since March, had evacuated the town on May 29, leaving its defense in the hands of a few Georgia militia. The civil officials of the revolutionary state regime had been advised to seek safety in the Carolinas, and there was widespread talk among the inhabitants of the nearly defenseless backcountry of submitting to the British crown.[11]

On May 20, orders were transmitted from Clinton's headquarters to Savannah, directing Lieutenant Colonel Brown to undertake the occupation of Augusta.[12] With a force of roughly three hundred men, consisting of the major portion of his own battalion, the King's Rangers, Major James Wright, Jr.'s Georgia Loyalists, and a scattering of men from other provincial units, Brown set out on his mission. Because of a lack of wheeled transport for supplies, he crossed the Savannah River at Ebenezer and proceeded up the South Carolina side of the river, where provisions were more plentiful than in Georgia. His men foraged off the countryside on their march.[13]

Brown's progress, though unopposed, was slow, and it was not until June 8 or thereabouts that he took peaceable possession of the town of Augusta. Upon his arrival, revolutionary resistance in the Georgia backcountry became momentarily non-existent. The inhabitants of Augusta immediately petitioned Governor Wright in conciliatory terms for the restoration of the King's Peace, and residents of the outlying areas followed suit. On his march from Savannah, Brown had received offers of service from various bodies of revolutionary militia, who announced themselves ready to defect to the royal cause. They were refused for obvious reasons. At Galphin's Trading Post, located at Silver Bluff about twelve miles below Augusta by river, the surrender of Hammond's South Carolina Regiment was received on its own muster field.[14] Within a matter of days after the occupation of Augusta, remnants of other Georgia and South Carolina regiments—John Dooly's, Garden's, and Middleton's—came in voluntarily to offer submission. The terms given were identical to those granted by Clinton to the Whig militia at Charles Town: upon surrendering as prisoners of war and turning in their arms, they were allowed to go to their homes on a parole conditioned upon the promise not again to take up arms against the crown.[15]

For the moment, the Whigs acknowledged the hopelessness of their situation and appeared ready to accept the return of royal government. Only a few ardent revolutionaries of the likes of Elijah Clark, William Few, and John Twiggs remained in the field. Eluding Brown's patrols, they sought safety on the frontiers of the Carolinas, while another stalwart, John Jones, was reported as having crossed the mountains to "Kaintuck."[16]

Lieutenant Colonel Brown's occupation of Augusta brought into play the dual capacity in which he was employed by the British government. He served on the one hand as military commandant at Augusta, and on the other as Superintendent of Indian Affairs in the eastern division of the Southern Indian Department. His appointment to the latter position, which included jurisdiction over Creek and Cherokee affairs, dated from June, 1779, but until his arrival at Augusta, which served as the gateway to the Indian nations, his activity in the field of Indian relations had been necessarily curtailed.[17]

As soon as he took possession of Augusta, Brown dispatched Captain Joseph Smith's company of the King's Rangers to occupy Fort Rutledge, a small post which had been thrown up and garrisoned by South Carolina revolutionary forces beyond the Cherokee boundary line. Brown expressed the hope that his men would be permitted to destroy this fort as soon as its stores and supplies could be removed. As he explained to Corwallis: "The Indians will never be satisfied whilst a fort remains in their country—they were promised that the people who have taken forcible possession of their lands should be removed." At the same time Brown gave directions to the agents of the Southern Indian Department to remove all squatters from the hunting lands of the Indians.[18] The overall effect of these measures, which were carried out during the course of the summer, was the return of the Indians to their former British allegiance, which had waned during the five years of British absence and inactivity along the frontier.[19]

As the British moved into the interior parts of South Carolina and Georgia, they took steps to secure their position by establishing a series of posts which extended in a semi-circle from Georgetown, on the coast, through Camden, Rocky Mount, and Ninety-Six to Augusta.[20] The position at Augusta was of strategic importance because it secured the western flank in this line of frontier defenses. Its location at the head of navigation on the Savannah River enhanced its value as a military post to the

British, for it served as the depot for supplying Ninety-Six as well as the Creek and Cherokee allies. The need for fortifications at Augusta was obvious, as Brown pointed out to Lieutenant Colonel Nisbet Balfour, the commanding officer at Ninety-Six, and to Cornwallis, who had succeeded Clinton in command of field operations in the southern colonies.[21] The original stockade work, "Fort Augusta," constructed of three-inch plank and completed in 1737, had last been used for military purposes in 1767, and by the time of the Revolution it was useless.[22]

Foreseeing that his request for defensive works might be delayed at headquarters, Brown brought up the matter when he went to Ninety-Six for a conference with Balfour. Balfour took up Brown's cause on this subject, though not in a way that Brown might have anticipated or appreciated. On June 24, Balfour advised Cornwallis:

> I conceive a small work [at Augusta] will be necessary, as it is so straggling a village and as there are guns and necessarys upon the spot, but particularly as there can only be Provincials in garrison, under whose care stores can be ill trusted or surprises guarded against. I should think a work for two Hundred men perfectly sufficient, with Barracks, and they have six four-pounders on the spot.[23]

Cornwallis' reply from Charles Town, dated July 3, must have been equally shocking to Balfour and Brown. Permission was granted for the construction of field works only at Augusta and Ninety-Six, and he specifically forbade the construction of any engineer's redoubts or permanent earthworks at either post.[24] Cornwallis stated no reasons for denying Brown's request, but it may be fairly assumed from his correspondence with Wright that the need for economy and the false assumption that the King's Peace had been completely restored to the backcountry caused him to act as he did. Cornwallis coldly dismissed Wright's request of further military assistance to Georgia with the comment that "so long as we are in Possession of the whole Power and Force of South Carolina, the Province of Georgia has the most ample and Satisfactory Protection by maintaining a Post at Savannah and another at Augusta, nor can I think myself justified in incurring any further expence on the Army Accounts for the Protection of Georgia."[25] As the consequence, Augusta remained unfortified throughout the summer of 1780, except for a small stockade located near the Savannah River about three-quarters of a mile northwest of St. Paul's Church. Named "Fort Grierson" in honor of Colonel James Grierson, commander of the Loyalist militia in St. Paul's Parish, it was too small to house the garrison of regular provincials and was inadequate for any serious defense of the town. By the summer's end, the errors in Cornwallis' thinking would become clear—especially to the men who wore the green and crimson of the King's Rangers.

For two months after the British reoccupation of Augusta, the backcountry was politically calm. Oaths of allegiance were accepted from Loyalists as well as former Whigs who desired to return to the King's protection, and the loyal militia was reactivated to assist Brown's royal provincials in maintaining law and order. James Grierson was restored to command of the Augusta Regiment of Militia, Matthew Lyle was entrusted with the same position in St. George's Parish, and Thomas Waters was given the command on the Ceded Lands.[26] Thomas Brown's announced intention was to maintain law and order for the benefit of friend and former foe alike—and with an iron hand. Immediately upon his arrival at Augusta, he had given public notice that he would "hang without favor or distinction any person who presumed to plunder or otherwise disturb the peaceable inoffensive planters," and for the apprehension of any such persons, he offered a reward of fifty guineas.[27] In spite of this edict, incidents of robbery and plundering of the civil population increased, particularly in the case of the Whig militiamen who had been paroled to their homes without arms and as a consequence were presumably powerless to defend themselves against marauders. Brown placed the blame for such crimes upon persons who falsely posed as Loyalists, for on June 28, he complained to Cornwallis:

> As the interior parts of this Province have been considered for some years past as a secure retreat for all the Villains and Murderers who have fled from Justice from the Southern

Provinces, the principal difficulty I have hitherto experienced has been the suppression of plunderers and horsethieves who under the specious pretext of Loyalty, have from time to time daringly assembled in defiance of all law & authority & indiscriminately ravaged the plantations of peaceable inoffensive inhabitants who have received protection as prisoners on parole.[28]

Among the more brazen of these brigands was Daniel McGirth, who passed himself off as a Loyalist partisan to disguise his activities as a cattle rustler. Operating with a band of twenty or more mounted men, he was reported by Governor Wright as having stolen and driven off to East Florida upwards of a thousand head of cattle during the summer of 1780. Another such bandit, who had Whig rather than Tory connections, was James McKay. According to Wright he was the leader of "a party Some say of 12 and others Say twenty, with which he Robs on the Highway between [Savannah] & Augusta & goes Frequently to the Banks of Savannah River and has Stop't, Robbed and Plundered Several Boats." Royal warrants for the arrest of "McGirt and his Gang" went unserved for lack of cavalry, and Wright's repeated pleas to Cornwallis for fifty mounted troops to restore order in the area between Savannah and Augusta were turned down. Capturing robbers, it was said, was a task for local authorities and not the enemy.[29]

The entire force of regulars assigned by Cornwallis for the occupation of Georgia consisted by August, 1780, of no more than eight hundred men. Roughly five hundred, composed principally of Hessian auxiliaries and Loyalists, garrisoned Savannah, while Brown's command of regular provincials at Augusta had shrunk to a strength of approximately 240 men, exclusive of convalescents and invalids. The important posts at Sunbury, on the coast, and Dartmouth, in the Ceded Lands, remained abandoned for lack of troops. To make matters worse, the spheres of civil and military authority in Georgia were not geographically coextensive. While the jurisdiction of Wright's restored government at Savannah extended theoretically over the entire province, the departmental command entrusted to Lieutenant Colonel Alured Clarke, the ranking British officer in Georgia and East Florida,

301

included only the posts at Savannah and Augusta—in addition to St. Augustine. The Ceded Lands, comprising all the settled areas lying northwest of St. Paul's Parish, were placed, because of the weakened condition of Brown's garrison, in charge of Balfour, the commanding officer at Ninety-Six.[30]

The number of effective fighting men in the Ceded Lands was estimated by Governor Wright as seven to eight hundred. This figure apparently included Loyalists as well as neutrals and Whigs. Of the latter, some had taken the British oath of allegiance, though the majority remained at large after giving their parole not to take up arms against the King. No serious effort had been made to enforce the surrender of weapons to the royal authorities, nor was any attempt made to differentiate among the paroled prisoners according to their former zeal for revolutionary service. Erstwhile officers and leaders of the rebellion remained at liberty upon the same terms as their enlisted men.[31] All the while, they were correctly suspected by Lieutenant Colonel Balfour of "plotting rebellion," engaging in surreptitious correspondence with the rebels in North Carolina, and stirring up troubles in the backcountry of South Carolina.[32]

On July 1, 1780, Sir James Wright signed into law an act of the Royal Assembly which placed severe civil restrictions upon all persons who had occupied official positions or served in the military forces of the former Whig government. Under the terms of the Disqualifying Act, 151 named leaders of the rebellion, as well as any others who might later be proven to have held civil or military office under the late regime, were disqualified from holding any office of profit or trust under the restored royal government. All such persons were denied the right to bear or possess arms. Former rebels could be required, if brought before any magistrate, to swear allegiance to the crown and to post bond and security for their continued good behavior. Penalties for non-compliance with the various sections of this act ranged from fines and imprisonment to impressment into service in the Royal Navy.[33]

During the weeks immediately following its enactment, no direct steps were taken by Wright to enforce the Disqualifying

Act in the Ceded Lands. His hesitation seems out of character, but his delay probably stemmed from a fear of employing measures that might drive the backcountry once again into open opposition. To enforce the test oath at this time might push those persons on parole, who had quietly accepted their positions as neutrals, too quickly into a choice between loyalty and rebellion. Similar provisions of Sir Henry Clinton's untimely Proclamation of June 3, 1780, which largely nullified his previous conciliatory proclamation of March 3, 1780, had produced just such unfortunate consequences in the adjacent province of South Carolina, where former Whigs were now returning to the field in small groups rather than take an oath of allegiance to George III. With such on object lesson close at hand, discretion seemed to dictate against haste.[34]

While Governor Wright moved slowly or not at all in this direction, the political and military situation in the interior parts of his province began to deteriorate. The initial calm which had followed the British reoccupation of the backcountry was succeeded first by a period of unrest, then rumors of renewed rebel activity. On July 27, Lieutenant Colonel Balfour, acting in obedience to instructions from Cornwallis, proposed sending a troop of horse to disarm the rebels and restore peace in the Ceded Lands. He requested Wright to send Lieutenant Governor Graham to accompany the troops on this mission.[35] Sir James, not replying until August 19, said that such drastic action was not necessary. He had already instructed the Georgia militia upon the enforcement of the Disqualifying Act, and he thought, moreover, that "the People on the Ceded Lands are from every information I have received, peaceable and quiet."[36]

In spite of Wright's attitude, the ranking officers in the field felt that trouble was brewing. On August 6, Brown requested advice of Lieutenant Colonel John Harris Cruger, who had succeeded Balfour in command at Ninety-Six, on the enforcement of the Disqualifying Act. Unless some of the more obnoxious of the paroled rebel leaders were removed, he thought, their Loyalist neighbors would never be able to live in peace. Five or six hundred prisoners on parole were certainly too many to remain

303

at large in one district. It would be prudent to "remove" their leaders, he recommended, by which means the lower class of people would return to a proper sense of their duty.[37]

Cruger echoed Brown's fears in a dispatch to Cornwallis which sounded upon an even more ominous note. It was said that the rebel partisan, Elijah Clark, had returned to the Ceded Lands and had recruited at least three hundred men. At the same time, Cruger "sent an express" to Savannah to hasten Lieutenant Colonel Isaac Allen to Augusta with some of his New Jersey Volunteers. He wished that upon their arrival they might see to it that "those fellows might be disarm'd positively."[38]

The fears of Balfour, Brown, and Cruger were justified. In mid-September Brown was holding talks at Augusta with the head men of the Creeks and Cherokees to cement further their alliance with the British.[39] At the time of this conference Brown's strength consisted of his own battalion, the King's Rangers, and the convalescents of Allen's New Jersey Volunteers—all in all, a force of about three hundred men.[40]

On September 14, Colonel Elijah Clark, who had recruited his irregular force of rebel partisans up to a strength of five or six hundred men, moved from the Ceded Lands and launched a three-pronged assault upon the town of Augusta. Brown was taken completely by surprise. About 9:00 A.M., he received intelligence that the camp of his Indian allies, located three miles west of his own encampment in the town, was under attack. He immediately moved to the relief of the Indians with all available Loyalist regulars and two pieces of artillery, there having been insufficient time to call out Colonel James Grierson's loyal militia. As he passed MacKay's trading post, he dropped off a detachment of men to guard the trading goods and the royal presents which were stored there for distribution to the Indians upon the conclusion of the talks. No sooner had Brown joined forces with the Indians than he learned that Clark's remaining men had swept into Augusta by the Savannah Road and were advancing upon his rear. Facing about, he returned at a quick march to give battle. When he returned within sight of the MacKay House, located upon an eminence known as Garden Hill, the rebels were attack-

304

ing the guard which he had left behind. After a brisk encounter, the Loyalists and Indians succeeded in driving off Clark's forces, though they lost their artillery in the process. Inasmuch as Garden Hill offered the best defensive position in the vicinity, they dug in around the MacKay House and its outbuildings, where they prepared to defend themselves to the last extremity. Brown was granted a respite and was able to strengthen his position and send out messengers to Cruger, when Clark's undisciplined irregulars withdrew to the town and wasted time in search of plunder.

The following day, Clark's men returned to the attack and cut off the communications of the besieged, but the time spent in looting spoiled their chances of success. For three more days, Brown and his men held out under the most appalling conditions.[41] Cut off by the rebels from any source of water, Brown's men managed to assuage their thirst by saving and drinking their own urine.[42] For rations, they had little to eat other than raw pumpkins.[43] "The greatest distress," according to a contemporary British account, "arose from being without water, every avenue which led to it being exposed to the fire of the Rebels. In other respects, the Situation was also disagreeable—dead men and horses all around the yard—wounded men and prisoners taken the first day calling out continually for a Doctor and Water, neither of which was it possible to procure for them.[44]

Brown's Indian allies, to the admiration of all, performed bravely under conditions of warfare to which they were neither accustomed nor supposedly suited. Approximately 250 of them—mostly Creeks—took part in the initial engagement with Clark's partisans and then took post alongside the regulars for the defense of the MacKay House. Their numbers were augmented during a lull in the fighting by fifty Cherokees, who swam the Savannah River and slipped into Brown's lines. The new arrivals were issued weapons from the stores on hand and served throughout the duration of the siege. The behavior of the three hundred Indians was reported by all British sources as having been admirable. During the height of the rebel rifle fire, they stuck to their assigned places in the lines like veterans, and during

305

quiet intervals they ventured on sorties which brought in five or six rebel scalps.[45]

At Ninety-Six, Cruger had already learned of the plight of the Augusta garrison from Loyalists who watched the early stages of the battle from the Carolina side of the Savannah River. By the time Brown's messengers arrived, Cruger had already called out his local militia and was making preparations to march to Brown's relief. Taking a calculated risk, he left his post at Ninety-Six in the charge of militia Colonel Moses Kirkland, and on September 16 he put his regulars in motion for Augusta.[46] At daybreak of the 18th, Cruger's column, composed of men of his own battalion of DeLancey's New York Brigade, Innes' South Carolina Royalists, and Allen's battalion of Skinner's New Jersey Volunteers, reached the banks of the river opposite the MacKay House. As soon as their arrival was detected, the rebels abandoned the siege and fled in rout order. They "were so precipitate in their flight," reported Cruger, "that we had only a few chance Shot at them on the Wing."[47] By the time the head of the relief column crossed the river, remnants of Brown's garrison had sallied out from the MacKay House and captured a number of rebel prisoners. One of these, Henry Dukes of the Ceded Lands, was instantly hanged. For the starved and exhausted regulars, no further service was possible. So few of them remained unwounded and fit for duty that pursuit of the fugitives was turned over to the Indians.[48]

When the relief expedition finally arrived in a body, Cruger sent off parties of horse to pick up "the traitorous Rebels of this Neighborhood." In his correspondence with his superiors he proposed either to send them to Charles Town as prisoners,[49] or see to it locally that they "will be roughly handled, some very probably suspended for their good deeds."[50] But when Cruger's troops returned from this mission, the full measure of frontier justice was meted out by the Loyalist commanders. "Thirteen of the Prisoners who broke their Paroles and came against Augusta have been hang'd," reported Sir James Wright, "which I hope will have a very Good Effect."[51] Lying abed with bullet wounds through both his buttocks, Thomas Brown, according to Whig traditions of the siege, vindicatively witnessed the execution of their sentences as they were dropped from a gibbet in the stair well of the MacKay House.[52]

Cruger intended, after matters at Augusta were settled, to return directly to his post at Ninety-Six. His plans were thrown off schedule when reports came in that Clark had fled only to the north bank of Little River, where he was awaiting Cruger's departure before renewing the attack upon Brown's weakened garrison. So Cruger changed his plans and marched immediately to the Ceded Lands. With his own Loyalist regulars, he proceeded up the Georgia side of the Savannah River, while about one hundred loyal militiamen were dispatched by a parallel route along the Wrightsboro Road. The two columns crossed Little River and converged upon rebel Colonel John Dooly's house, where it was learned that Clark had retreated northwesterly across the Broad River.[53] Continuing the pursuit, the British column reached and crossed the Broad River on September 25, only to discover that the elusive rebels had moved eastwardly across the Savannah River, some distance above Cherokee Ford, bound for the mountains of North Carolina. At this point, the pursuit was dropped.[54]

At Savannah, Sir James Wright had been thrown into a state of apparent shock by Clark's daring raid upon Augusta. Writing during the initial excitement of the rebel attack, he advised Lieutenant Colonel Balfour:

> . . . the most Effectual and Best Method of Crushing the Rebellion in the Back Parts of this Country, is for an Army to march without Loss of time into the Ceded Lands — and to lay Waste and Destroy the whole Territory; Mr. Waters and some very few indeed which he may mention excepted; for these People, the men have by their late conduct forfeited every claim to any favour or protection . . . [55]

To a large degree, Cruger now proceeded to follow the governor's advice. The rebel courthouse, forts, and private habitations "belonging to the most notorious Villains" in the Ceded Lands were burned, "their cattle driven off, and their property in

307

general paying the price of their treachery."[56] Wright reported that the homesteads of some one hundred of Clark's followers were devastated in this manner.[57] Mounted militiamen scoured the countryside for rebels who had aided and abetted Clark in his attack upon Augusta, and sixty-eight such fugitives were brought in—"most of them poor Wretches, who were carried down by force and threats from Clark and his adherents." Of these, forty-five were released upon taking an oath of allegiance to the crown and posting bond for their future good behavior, but twenty-three of the "worst characters" were sent to Charles Town as prisoners.[58] Among their number were John Wereat, Samuel Stirk, and Chesley Bostwick, all of whom had occupied civil offices of importance under the former state government.[59] Most of Clark's adherents, however, had gone with him as fugitives from the province. The wives and children of these men were now driven from the Ceded Lands and forced to follow their husbands and fathers in flight.[60]

Lieutenant Governor Graham was sent from Savannah to assist Cruger by officially enforcing the Disqualifying Act in the name of the provincial government.[61] Though Cruger found it necessary to return to his own post at Ninety-Six by the end of September,[62] Graham remained in the Ceded Lands for another month to complete the restoration of the King's Peace. When his work was finished, he paid Cruger a visit at Ninety-Six in order to coordinate accounts with the military.[63] While there, Graham turned in an interesting report on the results of his enforcement of the Disqualifying Act, in which he classified the inhabitants of the Ceded Lands according to loyalty or disloyalty. Out of 723 male inhabitants, 255 were counted as Loyalists, fifty-seven were probably neutrals, and the balance were rebels.[64]

At Augusta, Brown's regulars were put to work constructing fortifications with the aid of slave labor. The lack of proper defensive works had been largely responsible for the near success of Clark's raid upon the town, and the British now lost no time in guarding against similar attacks in the future. St. Paul's Church and its burial ground were chosen as the most promising site for a fort. Work progressed steadily during the fall and winter, and

308

by April, 1781, Fort Cornwallis was considered impregnable to any direct assault that might be launched by the rebels of the neighborhood. At that time it was described by the opposing commanding officer, Light Horse Harry Lee, as being "judiciously constructed, well finished and Secure from storm."[65]

During the late fall and winter of 1780-81, there were no major hostilities in the backcountry of Georgia, but there were skirmishes, incidents of plundering of the civil population, and continued harrassment of Brown's lines of supply with Savannah.[66] By early January, Alured Clarke reported serious difficulties in sending supplies upriver because of the lack of men to serve as escorts for the boats. His garrison at Savannah had been reduced to a strength of only 211 present and fit for active duty, and there was no one to spare for such service.[67] In Augusta, Brown complained that his troops were nearly destitute because of rebel plundering of his supply boats. During the assault upon the town the previous September, his men had lost all their wearing apparel except the clothes on their backs, and they were now nearly naked.

In an effort to put a stop to these depredations, Brown sent Captain Alexander C. Wylly down the Carolina side of the river with a detachment of forty Rangers and thirty Indians. When Wylly reached Matthews' Bluff, he found the rebels out in greater numbers than his party had expected, so he retreated and joined strengths with troops that Brown had brought by forced marches from Augusta. The combined elements camped for the night at Wiggin's plantation. About three hours before daybreak the revolutionaries, commanded by Colonel William Harden, launched the first of two assaults. Brown's militia fled, but his regulars held fast. When Harden's men regrouped after sunrise and dismounted for a second assault, they were overwhelmed by a counterattack and fled. Brown reported that "they were principally indebted to the speed of their horses for their escape."[68]

After the battle of Wiggin's Hill, the rebels became more daring in their forays against Brown's outposts and lines of supply. They were encouraged by the advance of Cornwallis into North Carolina, an invasion that led to the drawn debacle at Guilford

309

Courthouse on March 15, 1781. The consequences of Cornwallis' march to the northward were correctly foreseen by Sir James Wright. "I can not think this Province and So. Carolina in a State of Security," he observed, "and if Lord Cornwallis Penetrates far into No. Carolina I shall expect a Rebel Army will come in behind him and throw us into the utmost confusion and danger — For this Province is still left in a Defenceless State."[69]

In mid-February a party of rebel partisans led by "Captains Dunn and Carr" crossed over the Savannah River from the Long Cane Settlements in South Carolina and proceeded to wreak havoc in upper St. Paul's Parish and the Ceded Lands. A number of Loyalists in the Little River area were hunted down and assassinated, and the town of Wrightsboro was raided and pillaged. A small party of seven men came within five miles of Brown's post at Augusta, where they robbed and shot Major Moore of the Loyalist militia in his own house.[70] James Grierson was sent from Augusta with a detachment of his Loyalist militia to collaborate with Thomas Waters, commanding the militia in the Ceded Lands, in restoring order. By the time of Grierson's arrival there, the culprits had disappeared and he had to content himself by returning to Augusta with thirty-five prisoners, whom he charged with harbouring the enemy.[71] As Wright explained to Germain, "Two Partys of Militia immediately went out, as soon as the first Murders were known to have been Committed, but My Lord the Villains being on Horse back & the Militia on Foot, there is very little chance of their Coming up with them or taking any of them."[72]

Such forays on the part of the rebels continued throughout the spring of 1781. Brown's regulars and militia were so reduced in strength by the parties sent down river on the essential duty of protecting the supply boats that no men could be spared from the garrison to oppose such attacks from other quarters.[73] Around April 12, another body of "rebel banditti" came into St. Paul's Parish and raided Augusta and its environs with impunity. The Rev. James Seymour, Anglican rector of the parish, reported from hiding that his family had been stripped of everything of value which they possessed, down to their clothing and provisions. According to the good parson, Brown's garrison in Augusta seemed sufficiently strong for its own defense, but the enemy had taken virtual possession of the remainder of St. Paul's Parish.[74]

On May 1, Brown advised Lieutenant Colonel Friedrich von Porbeck, the Hessian officer then in command of the Savannah garrison, of the deteriorating military situation and requested reinforcements. The rebel cavalry made its appearance every day on the outskirts of Augusta, and it was his belief that the rebels intended to lay siege to the town and starve his garrison into submission.[75]

A week later Wright explained to the Royal Council that von Porbeck was unable to comply with Brown's request for reinforcements. Von Porbeck, whose garrison had been reduced in strength by sickness and the transfer of troops to St. Augustine, had scarcely more men at Savannah than the number under Brown's command at Augusta.[76] The governor immediately appealed for relief to Nisbet Balfour at Charles Town and to Alured Clarke at St. Augustine, acquainting them with the alarming state of affairs at Augusta.[77]

Meanwhile, Cornwallis had departed from the Carolinas on his fateful march to Virginia, Yorktown, and surrender. Lord Rawdon, commanding the remnants of the army which Cornwallis had left behind in South Carolina, was forced by the southward advance of General Nathanael Greene's Continentals to abandon Camden and his other backcountry posts. Orders were sent to Cruger to evacuate Ninety-Six, join forces with Brown at Augusta, and fall back upon Purysburg or Ebenezer on the lower Savannah River. These advices failed to reach Cruger, who strengthened his fortifications and prepared to defend his post.[78] Upon intercepting Cruger's dispatches, Greene ordered Lieutenant Colonel Henry Lee to move at once against Augusta, before Cruger could unite his command with Brown's. Greene then prepared to lay siege to Ninety-Six with the forces remaining under his own command.[79]

On May 21, after a remarkable march of seventy-five miles in three days, Lee captured Fort Galphin, where two companies of the King's Rangers had been stationed to serve as escorts for the supply boats and to guard the annual royal presents for the

311

Indians which were stored there. By a strategem the garrison was taken by surprise and surrendered. That evening Lee crossed the Savannah River and joined Andrew Pickens and Elijah Clark, whose militia were encamped on the heights west of Augusta. A rebel demand for surrender was scorned by Brown.[80]

The following day Lee, Clark, and Pickens surveyed the fortifications at Augusta preparatory to commencing siege operations. Midway of the straggling village, adjacent to the river bank on the site of the burying ground of St. Paul's Church, stood Fort Cornwallis, defended by Brown and his regulars. Three-quarters of a mile to the northwest and also near the river stood Fort Grierson, which was occupied by James Grierson and a body of Loyalist militia. Lee, who outranked the militia officers by virtue of his continental commission, ordered an immediate assault upon Fort Grierson, and it was quickly overpowered. The Loyalist militia suffered heavy casualties. A few of them, including Grierson, gained the safety of the river bank and made their way under its concealment to Fort Cornwallis.[81]

The attention of the revolutionary forces was now turned upon Fort Cornwallis. Because of its strength, an assault by storm was out of the question. Lee adopted regular siege tactics and commenced digging approaches and parallels from the cover of the river bank. After five days of such work, the earthworks began to assume a formidable appearance.[82]

On Friday night, May 25, one of Brown's men managed to slip through the lines and make his way to Savannah, where he reported Brown's garrison as in the greatest distress. The men were then on an allowance of one pint of corn per day and had only enough on hand to last another twenty-one days. Upon receipt of this news, Governor Wright once again sent urgent appeals for assistance to Lieutenant Colonel Alured Clarke at St. Augustine.[83] No help could again be expected from Cruger at Ninety-Six, for his own post was then under close siege. If the relief of Augusta were possible, it would have to come from St. Augustine or Charles Town.[84]

Meanwhile, Brown's position was rapidly becoming untenable. The enemy had dug approaches so close to Fort Cornwallis, a

312

rebel militiaman later recalled, that the besieging troops could touch the parapet of the fort with a hoe helve.[85] Brown, therefore, began to resort to desperate measures. Toward midnight of May 28, a party of King's Rangers sallied from Fort Cornwallis and assaulted the rebel trenches, but the attack was repulsed. The following night another such attack was driven off when Lee's men counter-attacked with bayonets.

Brown next resorted to trickery. Lee's men had constructed a Maham tower behind the shelter of an old house facing the fort. The so-called tower was simply a square pen constructed of notched logs to a height of thirty feet. The interior of its body was filled with dirt, fascines, stone, brick, and other convenient rubbish to give it strength. A floor was constructed near its summit to accommodate a six-pounder, which was the rebels' sole piece of artillery.[86] By May 31, when the construction of the tower had been pushed nearly to completion, Brown had already perceived its purpose, and his sappers had feverishly dug a mine from the fort to a location underneath the vacant house. A saboteur who posed as a deserter was sent to gain access to the tower and burn it down. Both strategems failed. The spy was made prisoner and the house was prematurely blown up without damage to the tower.[87]

Brown's position was now hopeless. The interior of his fort, raked by artillery shot from the tower, was reduced to a shambles. On June 4, Lee and Pickens made a final demand for surrender before launching an assault. Brown managed to procrastinate for another day because he disliked the idea of surrendering upon the King's birthday. At eight o'clock the following morning, the King's Rangers marched out of Fort Cornwallis and laid down their arms.[88] Three days later reinforcements from St. Augustine and Charles Town converged upon Savannah—too late to relieve Augusta.[89]

The capitulation of Fort Cornwallis, which virtually ended the war in the backcountry of Georgia, mirrored in miniature the breakdown of British strategy throughout the southern colonies. Based upon the fallacious premise that a very significant segment

313

of the population was composed of Loyalists, British policy envisioned the active and spontaneous participation of their local allies in restoring the King's Peace once the Carolinas and Georgia had been rid of rebel interference by the success of British arms. Just so favorable a military situation existed briefly during the summer of 1780, yet the southern campaign still failed. The weakness and passive nature of Loyalist support was the primary cause, though contributing factors were the failure of the British to pacify former revolutionists, and the Crown's inability to woo and win over to their side the neutrals. The divergence between British policy in South Carolina, where a military government quickly alienated neutrals and former Whigs by its Proclamation of June 3, 1780, and in Georgia, where the restored civil government refrained from any serious attempts to enforce its Disqualifying Act, produced in the end similar results. While the issue was perhaps still in doubt in Georgia, owing to the relative restraint of its provincial administration, Elijah Clark's nearly successful attack upon Augusta triggered the retaliatory measures on the part of Brown and Cruger, which drove nearly two-thirds of the entire population into the rebel camp.

When Augusta finally fell to the forces of revolution the following year, Nisbet Balfour, commiserating with Sir James Wright over its loss, placed his finger squarely upon this unification of the opposition as the ultimate cause of British failure: "With your Excellency I regret the loss of the Back Country, especially Ninety-Six and Augusta, and the more so, as the manner of it was a general revolt of the Inhabitants."[90]

NOTES

[1]Paul H. Smith, *Loyalists and Redcoats: A Study in British Revolutionary Policy* (Chapel Hill, 1964), 111-13, 124-26; William B. Willcox, *Portrait of a General: Sir Henry Clinton in the War of Independence* (New York, 1964), 292-95.

[2]Smith, *Loyalists and Redcoats*, 126-27; Sir James Wright to Sir Henry Clinton, Feb. 3, 1780, in Allen D. Candler and Lucian Lamar Knight, eds., *The Colonial Records of the State of Georgia*, 26 vols. (Atlanta, 1904-1916);

13 vols., unpublished manuscripts in Georgia Department of Archives and History, Atlanta, XXXVIII, Part 2, 269-76 (hereinafter cited respectively as *CRG* and Ms.CRG).

3Sir Henry Clinton to Lord George Germain, Mar. 9, 1780, Lord George Germain Papers, William L. Clements Library, University of Michigan (hereinafter cited as Germain Papers, WLCL).

4Wright to Germain, Feb. 18, 1780, *Collections of the Georgia Historical Society* (12 vols., *Savannah*, 1840-   ), III, 275-76 (hereinafter cited as *GHS, Collections*); Banastre Tarleton, *A History of the Campaigns of 1780 and 1781 in the Southern Provinces of North America* (London, 1787), 5 (hereinafter cited as Tarleton, *Southern Campaigns*).

5Wright to Brigadier General James Paterson, Feb. 14, 1780, Ms.CRG, XXXVIII, Part 2, 277-81.

6Clinton to Major General Augustine Prevost, Feb. 18, 1780, British Public Record Office, British Headquarters Papers, 30/55, 2584 (hereinafter cited as BPRO, Br. Hq. Papers, 30/55); Clinton to Governor Patrick Tonyn, Feb. 19, 1780, *ibid.*, 2587; Paterson to Sir Charles Hotham Thompson, May 25, 1780, Hotham Papers, DDHO 4/21, East Riding Record Office, Beverly, Yorkshire.

7Wright to Clinton, Feb. 3, 1780, Ms.CRG, XXXVIII, Part 2, 269-76; Wright to Paterson, Feb. 14, 1780, *ibid.*, 277-81; Wright to Clinton, Mar. 3, 1780, *ibid.*, 282-83; Wright to Germain, Mar. 24-25, 1780, *GHS, Collections*, III, 279-81.

8Smith, *Loyalists and Redcoats*, 128-29; Edward McCrady, *The History of South Carolina in the Revolution, 1775-1780* (New York, 1901), 538-43.

9Tarleton, *Southern Campaigns*, 26-32; William Moultrie, *Memoirs of the American Revolution* (New York, 2 vols., 1802), II, 208-09.

10Innes to Cornwallis, June 8, 1780, British Public Record Office, Cornwallis Papers, 30/11/2, 114-17 (hereinafter cited as BPRO, Cornwallis Papers, 30/11).

11Allen D. Candler, ed., *The Revolutionary Records of the State of Georgia* (3 vols., Atlanta, 1908), II, 243, 247 (hereinafter cited as *RRG*); Wright to Germain, June 9, 1780, Ms.CRG, XXXVIII, Part 2, 364-65.

12Clinton to Lt. Col. Alured Clarke, May 20, 1780, BPRO, Br. Hq. Papers, 30/55, 2754; Clinton to Wright, May 20, 1780, *ibid.*, 2756; Lt. Col. Thomas Brown to Germain, May 25, 1780, Germain Papers, WLCL.

13Clarke to Clinton, May 28, 1780, BPRO, Br. Hq. Papers, 30/55, 2772; Clarke to Cornwallis, June 23, 1780, BPRO, Cornwallis Papers, 30/11/2, 187-88; Balfour to Cornwallis, June 24, 1780, *ibid.*, 191-96.

14Brown to Cornwallis, June 18, 1780, *ibid.*, 166-68; Petition of Inhabitants of Augusta and St. Paul's Parish to Sir James Wright, June 25, 1780, Ms.CRG, XXXVIII, Part 2, 380-81.

15Brown to Cornwallis, June 28, 1780, BPRO, Cornwallis Papers, 30/11/2, 208-13; Alured Clarke to Cornwallis, June 23, 1780, *ibid.*, 187-88; Balfour to Cornwallis, June 24, 1780, *ibid.*, 191-96.

16Statement of Samuel Beckaem, June 1, 1812, Peter Force Papers, Library of Congress.

17Germain to Clinton, June 25, 1779, Clinton Papers, WLCL.

18Brown to Cornwallis, June 18, 1780, BPRO, Cornwallis Papers, 30/11/2, 166-68; Brown to Cornwallis, June 28, 1780, *ibid.*, 208-13.

19Cornwallis to Lt. Col. Nisbet Balfour, July 3, 1780, BPRO, Cornwallis Papers, 30/11/78, 3-4; List of Military Stores sent from Fort Seneca to Ninety-Six, Aug. 1, 1780, signed by Joseph Smith, Capt., King's Rangers, BPRO, Cornwallis Papers, 30/11/103, 1.

20Tarleton, *Southern Campaigns*, 86-88; Smith, *Loyalists and Redcoats*, 136.

21Brown to Cornwallis, June 28, 1780, BPRO, Cornwallis Papers, 30/11/2, 208-13.

315

22Wright to Lord Dartmouth, Sept. 20, 1773, Ms.CRG, XXXVIII, Part 1, 109.

23Balfour to Cornwallis, June 24, 1780, BPRO, Cornwallis Papers, 30/11/2, 191-96.

24Cornwallis to Balfour, July 3, 1780, BPRO, Cornwallis Papers, 30/11/78, 3-4.

25Cornwallis to Wright, July 18, 1780, Ms.CRG, XXXVIII, Part 2, 413-14.

26Claim of Matthew Lyle upon Commissioners of American Loyalist Claims, British Public Record Office, Audit Office Papers, Series 13, Bundle 36 (hereinafter cited as BPRO, AO); Claim of Thomas Waters, *ibid.*, 13/37.

27Brown to Cornwallis, June 18, 1780, BPRO, Cornwallis Papers, 30/11/2, 166-68.

28Brown to Cornwallis, June 28, 1780, *ibid.*, 30/11/2, 208-13.

29Wright to Germain, Aug. 20, 1780, Ms.CRG, XXXVIII, Part 2, 408-11; Cornwallis to Wright, July 18, 1780, *ibid.*, 413-14; Wright to Cornwallis, July 28, 1780, *ibid.*, 415-17.

30Wright to Germain, Aug. 20, 1780, *ibid.*, 408-11.

31Wright to Germain, July 19, 1780, *ibid.*, 376-79; Brown to Cruger, Aug. 6, 1780, BPRO, Cornwallis Papers, 30/11/62, 6-7.

32Balfour to Wright, July 27, 1780, Ms.CRG, XXXVIII, Part 2, 420-21.

33Disqualifying Act of July 1, 1780, printed in *RRG*, I, 348-63; Wright to Germain, July 17, 1780, GHS, Collections, III, 307-09.

34Rawdon to Cornwallis, July 7, 1780, BPRO, Cornwallis Papers, 30/11/2, 252-55; Smith, *Loyalists and Redcoats*, 131-33; McCrady, *The History of South Carolina in the Revolution, 1775-1780*, 554; Willcox, *Portrait of a General: Sir Henry Clinton in the War of Independence*, 321.

35Balfour to Wright, July 27, 1780, Ms.CRG, XXXVIII, Part 2, 420-21.

36Wright to Balfour, Aug. 19, 1780, *ibid.*, 421-23.

37Brown to Lt. Col. John Harris Cruger, Aug. 6, 1780, BPRO, Cornwallis Papers, 30/11/62, 6-7.

38Cruger to Cornwallis, Aug. 7, 1780, *ibid.*, 30/11/63, 22.

39Cornwallis to Germain, Sept. 23, 1780, BPRO, Cornwallis Papers, 30/11/76, 22-23. The Indian conference which was broken up by Elijah Clark's attack had been planned since Brown's reoccupation of Augusta the previous June. Brown to Cornwallis, June 28, 1780, BPRO, Cornwallis Papers, 30/11/2, 208-13; Brown to Cornwallis, July 16, 1780, *ibid.*, 307-12.

40Cruger to Cornwallis, Sept. 15-16, 1780, BPRO, Cornwallis Papers, 30/11/64, 67-68.

41Brown to Cruger, Sept. 15, 1780, *ibid.*, 65-66; *South Carolina and American General Gazette*, Sept. 27, 1780; Printed Account of the Siege, Sept. 23, 1780, British Public Record Office, Colonial Office Papers, 5/82, 287-88 [329-30], enclosed in Charles Shaw, Deputy Superintendent Indian Affairs, to Germain, Sept. 24, 1780, *ibid.*, 285-86 [325-28] (hereinafter cited as BPRO, CO).

42Brown to Sir George Yonge, Secretary at War, June 1, 1783, *ibid.*, 677-79 [765-68].

43Cruger to Balfour, Sept. 19, 1780, BPRO, Cornwallis Papers, 30/11/64, 75-76.

44Printed Account of the Siege, Sept. 23, 1780, BPRO, CO, 5/82, 287-88 [329-30].

45Printed Account of the Siege, Sept. 23, 1780, *ibid.*, 287-88 [329-30]; Cruger to Cornwallis, Sept. 19, 1780, BPRO, Cornwallis Papers, 30/11/64, 77-78.

46Cruger to Cornwallis, Sept. 15-16, 1780, *ibid.*, 67-68; Cruger to Cornwallis, Sept. 23, 1780, *ibid.*, 104-05.

47Cruger to Balfour, Sept. 19, 1780, *ibid.*, 75-76.

48Printed Account of the Siege, Sept. 23, 1780, BPRO, CO, 5/82, 287-88 [329-30].

316

[49]Cruger to Cornwallis, Sept. 19, 1780, BPRO, Cornwallis Papers, 30/11/64, 77-78.

[50]Cruger to Balfour, Sept. 19, 1780, ibid., 75-76.

[51]Wright to Germain, Oct. 27, 1780, GHS, Collections, III, 321-22.

[52]Hugh M'Call, The History of Georgia (2 vols., Savannah, 1816), II, 326-27; William Bacon Stevens, A History of Georgia (2 vols., Philadelphia, 1859), II, 249-50.

[53]Cruger to Cornwallis, Sept. 23, 1780, BPRO, Cornwallis Papers, 30/11/64, 104-05.

[54]Cruger to Cornwallis, Sept. 28, 1780, ibid., 116-17.

[55]Wright to Balfour, Sept. 18, 1780, Ms.CRG, XXXVIII, Part 2, 424-27.

[56]Cruger to Cornwallis, Sept. 28, 1780, BPRO, Cornwallis Papers, 30/11/64, 116-17.

[57]Wright to Germain, Oct. 27, 1780, GHS, Collections, III, 321-22.

[58]Cruger to Cornwallis, Sept. 28, 1780, BPRO, Cornwallis Papers, 30/11/64, 116-17.

[59]M'Call, History of Georgia, II, 330.

[60]Memorandum of Lt. Gov. John Graham, enclosed in Cruger to Cornwallis, Nov. 8, 1780, BPRO, Cornwallis Papers, 30/11/4, 75-77.

[61]Wright to Germain, Oct. 27, 1780, GHS, Collections, III, 321-22.

[62]Cruger to Cornwallis, Oct. 2, 1780, BPRO, Cornwallis Papers, 30/11/3, 170-71.

[63]Cruger to Cornwallis, Nov. 8, 1780, BPRO, Cornwallis Papers, 30/11/4, 76-77.

[64]Memorandum of Lt. Gov. John Graham, enclosed in Cruger to Cornwallis, Nov. 8, 1780, ibid., 75.

[65]Wright to Germain, Oct. 27, 1780, GHS, Collections, III, 321-22; CRG, XV, 265; The Rev. James Seymour to The Rev. Mr. Morice, Secretary to the Society for the Propagation of the Gospel, April 26, 1781, British Empire Church Records, S.P.G. Sup., Letters and Papers, American Colonies II (1680-1850: Georgia and Virginia), University of Texas Library; Henry Lee, Memoirs of the War in the Southern Department of the United States (New York, 1869), 356-57 (hereinafter cited as Lee, Memoirs).

[66]Letter under flag of truce, Elijah Clark to "the Honb. Lord Earl Corn Wallace," Nov. 4, 1780, BPRO, Cornwallis Papers, 30/11/4, 20.

[67]Alured Clarke to Balfour, Jan. 2, 1781, BPRO, Cornwallis Papers, 30/11/62, 14-17.

[68]Brown to Balfour, Jan. 23, 1780 (sic), ibid., 2-5. This letter is incorrectly dated. It was obviously written on Jan. 23, 1781. See: Balfour's reply to Brown, Feb. 9, 1781, BPRO, Cornwallis Papers, 30/11/109, 12-13. Cf. Brown [e] to Dr. David Ramsey, Dec. 25, 1786, printed in: George White, Historical Collections of Georgia (New York, 1855), 614-19. The site of the Battle of Wiggin's Hill is located in Allendale County, South Carolina.

[69]Wright to Germain, Jan. 26, 1781, GHS, Collections, III, 332-33.

[70]Wright to Germain, Mar. 5, 1781, GHS, Collections, III, 335-38; Address of Lt. Gov. John Graham to the Upper and Commons Houses of Assembly, Feb. 27, 1781, ibid., 338-39; Wright to Cornwallis, April 23, 1781, BPRO, Cornwallis Papers, 30/11/3, 247-48; Royal Georgia Gazette, April 26, 1781; Statement of Samuel Beckaem, June 1, 1812, Peter Force Papers, Library of Congress.

[71]Extract of letter, Grierson to Wright, March 4, 1781, quoted and summarized in: Ms.CRG, XXXVIII, Part 2, 480.

[72]Wright to Germain, Mar. 5, 1781, GHS, Collections, III, 335-38.

[73]Wright to Cornwallis, April 23, 1781, BPRO, Cornwallis Papers, 30/11/5, 247-48; Wright to Germain, April 24, 1781, GHS, Collections, III, 346-47; Royal Georgia Gazette, April 26, 1781.

[74]The Rev. James Seymour to The Rev. Mr. Morice, April 26, 1781, British Empire Church Records, University of Texas Library.

[75]Brown to Lt. Col. Friedrich von Porbeck, May 1, 1781, quoted and summarized in: Minutes of Council, May 8, 1781, Ms.CRG, XXXVIII, Part 2, 524-25. Porbeck was left in command at Savannah when Alured Clarke, commanding British troops in Georgia and East Florida, moved his headquarters to St. Augustine.

[76]Minutes of Council, May 8, 1781, ibid., 524-29.

[77]Wright to Germain, May 25, 1781, GHS, Collections, III, 351-52.

[78]Balfour to Wright, May 4, 1781, BPRO, Cornwallis Papers, 30/11/109, 31-32; Rawdon to Cornwallis, June 5, 1781, BPRO, Cornwallis Papers, 30/11/6, 174-77; Lee, Memoirs, 344.

[79]Ibid., 353.

[80]Ibid., 354-56; Wright to Germain, May 30, 1781, GHS, Collections, III, 353.

[81]Lee, Memoirs, 356-57; Pickens to Greene, May 25, 1781, Nathanael Greene Papers, Duke University Library.

[82]Lee, Memoirs, 357-58.   [83]Wright to Germain, May 30, 1781, GHS, Collections, III, 353.

[84]Rawdon to Cornwallis, June 5, 1781, BPRO, Cornwallis Papers, 30/11/6, 174-77.

[85]Tarleton Brown, Memoirs of Tarleton Brown (Barnwell, 1896), n.p.

[86]Lee Memoirs, 361-62; M'Call, History of Georgia, II, 375.

[87]Lee, Memoirs, 362-66.   [88]Ibid., 366-70; Balfour to Germain, June 27, 1781, BPRO, Cornwallis Papers, 30/11/109, 37-38.

[89]Wright to Germain, June 12, 1781, GHS, Collections, III, 354.

[90]Balfour to Wright, Aug. 1, 1781, BPRO, Cornwallis Papers, 30/11/109, 43-44.

318

"The Nature of Treason":
Revolutionary Virtue and American Reactions
to Benedict Arnold

Charles Royster

ON September 16, 1775, a detached command of more than one thousand volunteers from Continental army units arrived in Newburyport, Massachusetts. On September 19 they sailed for the mouth of the Kennebec River in Maine, from where they would march overland to attack Quebec. Before leaving Newburyport, the troops paraded in general review for the citizens on Sunday, September 17. One soldier said, "We passed the review with much honor to ourselves. We manifested great zeal and animation in the cause of liberty and went through with the manual exercise with much alacrity. The spectators, who were very numerous, appeared much affected." That same day the soldiers worshiped in the First Presbyterian Church on King Street. Citizens filled the galleries. The soldiers marched into the church with colors flying and drums beating. They formed two lines and presented arms. As the drums rolled, Chaplain Samuel Spring walked between the lines to the pulpit. The men stacked their arms in the aisles, and Spring preached extemporaneously on the words of Moses to the Lord, "If thy spirit go not with us, carry us not up hence."

Beneath them as they worshiped lay the tomb of George Whitefield, who had been the voice of the Great Awakening. More than any other man, Whitefield, with his preaching, had introduced Americans to the joys of a communal revival of piety and a sharing of the conversion experience on a continental scale. After Spring's sermon, some of the officers gathered around him, and they decided to visit Whitefield's tomb. They found the sexton and went down to the coffin. The officers got the sexton to take off the lid. After five years the body had decayed, but some of the clothes remained. The officers took Whitefield's collar and wristbands, cut them in little pieces, divided the pieces among themselves, and carried them away.

Mr. Royster is a Fellow of the Institute of Early American History and Culture and the author of a forthcoming book, *A Revolutionary People at War: The Continental Army and American Character, 1775-1783*, to be published by the Institute. An earlier version of this article was presented to the Williamsburg Seminar and at the College of Charleston, Charleston, South Carolina.

During the following weeks the expedition withstood the hardest march of the war—350 miles of wilderness in forty-five days. Some starved to death along the route; three companies turned back; but six hundred men made it. Despite the defeat and disease they suffered at Quebec, they earned great praise for themselves and their commander, Colonel Benedict Arnold.[1]

Five years and eight days after Spring's sermon, Arnold defected to the British. After months of secret negotiations, he had almost succeeded in enabling the British to seize the important American fort at West Point, New York, which he commanded. The vehemence and duration of the Revolutionaries' reaction to Arnold's treason has made him one of the most widely remembered Americans of the era. A verse published in Philadelphia soon after the treason correctly predicted that

> Masters shall still their children, and say—*Arnold!*
> Arnold shall be the bug-bear of their years
> Arnold!—vile, treacherous, and leagued with Satan.[2]

Arnold's crime excited a uniquely intense obsession among Revolutionaries. He was, in Benjamin Franklin's words, "too base to be forgot ..."[3] The widespread zeal and animation of 1775 had concealed a potential for corruption and betrayal. How could one of the principal heroes of 1775 turn from virtue to treason? How, within five years, could American strength have fallen so low that the corruption of one man could seem to threaten the survival of the Revolution? For Americans dedicated to the preservation of public virtue, these were not only historical questions but also immediate problems. If the defense of liberty relied on public virtue, signs of weakness endangered both the movement for independence and the nation's hope for survival.

[1] "Journal of Abner Stocking ...," Sept. 15, 1775, in Kenneth Roberts, ed., *March to Quebec: Journals of the Members of Arnold's Expedition* (New York, 1938), 546; J. T. Headley, *The Chaplains and Clergy of the Revolution* (New York, 1864), 92-93, 105; [Samuel Peters], "Genuine History of Gen. Arnold, by an old Acquaintance," *Political Magazine*, I (1780), 746, in Kenneth Walter Cameron, ed., *The Works of Samuel Peters of Hebron, Connecticut* ... (Hartford, 1967), 164; John J. Currier, *History of Newburyport, Mass., 1764-1905*, I (Newburyport, 1906), 272-275; [Gardiner Spring], *Personal Reminiscences of the Life and Times of Gardiner Spring* ..., I (New York, 1866), 25-26. On Arnold's march to Quebec see Christopher Ward, *The War of the Revolution*, ed. John Richard Alden, I (New York, 1952), chap. 13, and Gustave Lanctot, *Canada and the American Revolution, 1774-1783*, trans. Margaret M. Cameron (Cambridge, Mass., 1967).

[2] *A Representation of the Figures exhibited and paraded through the Streets of Philadelphia, on Saturday, the 30th of September 1780* [Philadelphia, 1780].

[3] "On General Arnold," in John Bigelow, ed., *The Complete Works of Benjamin Franklin* ..., VII (New York, 1888), 240-241.

Americans' reaction to the treason of Benedict Arnold helps us to understand how they resolved the threat to public virtue that the treason posed. The fervor of their reaction showed a bond between Arnold and his countrymen that persisted beyond his early zealous command of the volunteers who marched to liberate Canada. Consequently, to the historian, Arnold remains as useful an instrument for the study of public virtue after his treason as in his years of glory. By first examining the strength that Americans sought from virtue and then the weakness that endangered their cause during the war, we will see the origins of their concern about betrayal of Revolutionary virtue. And we will learn why this concern centered on the many crimes of Benedict Arnold.

As soldiers manifested zeal and animation in the cause of liberty, while they were striving for the Lord, they drew on two heritages, both of which placed virtue at the heart of the American Revolution. When Americans declared their independence, they agreed that it could survive only if they and their descendants maintained their virtue. They must choose voluntarily to sacrifice safety, ease, and self-interest in order to defend liberty.[4] When liberty faced armed attack, virtue called citizens to become the defending soldiers. The American who saw a British design to enslave him learned from both religious and civic teachings that the defeat of that design depended on his willingness to fight—in fact, on his eagerness to fight. The sermons of American ministers repeatedly linked the fight against Britain with the fight against sin. Engagement and zeal in both struggles offered the hope of a dual salvation: the soul of the Christian and the liberty of America. Because such engagement and zeal were voluntary—because the American chose to reject ease and sin—his service was a mark of his virtue.[5] The political ideology that American Revolutionaries adapted from English thinkers similarly stressed the citizen's responsibility to bear arms when liberty required military defense. To rely on hirelings would put the citizen in the hands of mercenaries or of the government that paid them. Worse yet, such reliance would strip a man of his title of *citizen*, because he lacked the virtue to defend himself. Without even using the guns of a standing army of merce-

---

[4] See especially Gordon S. Wood, *The Creation of the American Republic, 1776-1787* (Chapel Hill, N.C., 1969), chaps. 2, 3, and Edmund S. Morgan, "The Puritan Ethic and the American Revolution," *William and Mary Quarterly*, 3d Ser., XXIV (1967), 3-43.

[5] Perry Miller, "From the Covenant to the Revival," in his *Nature's Nation* (Cambridge, Mass., 1967), 90-120; Alan Heimert, *Religion and the American Mind from the Great Awakening to the Revolution* (Cambridge, Mass., 1966), esp. chap. 9. For a discussion of these sermons and for citations to sources see Charles William Royster, "The Continental Army in the American Mind: 1775-1783" (Ph.D. diss., University of California, Berkeley, 1977), esp. chaps. 1, 5.

321

naries, a tyrant could rule by taxing such spineless subjects and bribing favorites. Only citizens who were willing to risk their lives and property in defense of liberty could avoid such subjection—that is, only citizens who had virtue.[6]

We better understand this dual emphasis on active engagement when we see the alternative: enslavement. In describing slavery, Revolutionaries commonly used images of lethargy, sleep, and spiritual death. Enslaving the continent did not primarily mean physical bondage. It need not even have meant material hardship, because a people might surrender their independent judgment in return for corrupt riches. The worst curse was resignation to the tyrant's will. Acquiescence became habitual; then it became advantageous; finally, it became universal and permanent. One who forfeited his birthright of personal responsibility, one who lost virtue, fell into a sleep that might doom him—in this world or the one to come. One who knew the value of freedom but failed to defend it committed what General Nathanael Greene called "spiritual suicide."[7]

In 1775, Americans showed their attachment to these ideals by frequent popular military demonstrations. Citizens celebrated the prowess that they expected to show in combat, and all kinds of military exercises and uniforms, enjoyed a wide vogue.[8] A letter from Philadelphia assured the British that "the Rage Militaire, as the French call a passion for arms, has taken possession of the whole Continent."[9] Months before the Lexington and Concord skirmishes, Americans began to prepare armed resistance. Reviews and military drills attracted many spectators. Congress watched parade ground evolutions on June 8, 1775.[10] Companies drilled by moon-

[6] See esp. J. G. A. Pocock, *The Machiavellian Moment: Florentine Political Thought and the Atlantic Republican Tradition* (Princeton, N.J., 1975). On standing armies see also Lois G. Schwoerer, *"No Standing Armies!": The Antiarmy Ideology in Seventeenth-Century England* (Baltimore, 1974), and Lawrence Delbert Cress, "The Standing Army, the Militia, and the New Republic: Changing Attitudes toward the Military in American Society, 1768 to 1820" (Ph.D. diss., University of Virginia, 1976), chaps. 2, 3.

[7] Nathanael Greene to Catharine Greene, June 2, 1775, in Richard K. Showman et al., eds., *The Papers of General Nathanael Greene*, I (Chapel Hill, N.C., 1976), 83. On slavery see especially Bernard Bailyn, *The Ideological Origins of the American Revolution* (Cambridge, Mass., 1967), and the sources cited in Royster, "Continental Army," chap. 1, n. 11.

[8] Royster, "Continental Army," chap. 1; Rhys Isaac, "Dramatizing the Ideology of Revolution: Popular Mobilization in Virginia, 1774 to 1776," *WMQ*, 3d Ser., XXXIII (1976), 357-385.

[9] *Lloyd's Evening Post and British Chronicle*, in Margaret Wheeler Willard, ed., *Letters on the American Revolution, 1774-1776* (Boston, 1925), 101-102.

[10] Entry of May 27, 1775, in William Duane, ed., *Extracts from the Diary of Christopher Marshall* . . . (Albany, N.Y., 1877), 28; entry of Sept. 15, 1775, "Journal of Simeon Lyman of Sharon . . . ," Connecticut Historical Society, *Collections*, VII

light.[11] Boys between the ages of thirteen and sixteen volunteered: they were commended but were turned away. Younger boys played soldier and organized their own companies for drill.[12] Not many men had uniforms, but those who had them wore them proudly and could read descriptions of themselves in the newspapers.[13] Everywhere Revolutionaries reported rapid progress in discipline. Some observers came away from reviews and wrote that Americans were, or soon would be, equal to any troops in the world.[14]

(1899). 118; *Boston-Gazette, and Country Journal,* July 3, 1775; *Pennsylvania Ledger: or the Virginia, Maryland, Pennsylvania, and New-Jersey Weekly Advertiser* (Philadelphia), June 10, 1775; John Adams to Abigail Adams, June 10, 1775, in L. H. Butterfield *et al.,* eds., *Adams Family Correspondence,* I (Cambridge, Mass., 1963). 214; *Virginia Gazette* (Purdie), July 21, 1775, Supplement; *South-Carolina and American General Gazette* (Charleston), Aug. 11, 1775; David Ramsay, *The History of the American Revolution* (London, 1793 [orig. publ. Philadelphia, 1789]), I, 132; Samuel Richards, *Diary of Samuel Richards: Captain of Connecticut Line, War of the Revolution, 1775-1781* (Philadelphia, 1909), 10; entries of May 13, June 5, 1775. in John Rogers Williams *et al.,* eds., *Philip Vickers Fithian, Journal and Letters* ..., II (Princeton, N.J., 1934), 5, 24; entry of May 5, 1775, in Andrew Oliver, ed., *The Journal of Samuel Curwen, Loyalist,* I (Cambridge, Mass., 1972), 5.

[11]*Providence Gazette; and Country Journal* (R.I.), Feb. 18, 1775; *Va. Gaz.* (Dixon and Hunter), July 8, 1775; "Journal of Major Ennion Williams," Oct. 9, 1775, in Samuel Hazard *et al.,* eds., *Pennsylvania Archives,* 2d Ser. (Philadelphia and Harrisburg, 1852-1949), XV, 10.

[12] Joseph H. Jones, ed., *The Life of Ashbel Green*... (New York, 1849), 55-56; Willard, ed., *Letters on the American Revolution,* 102-103; Ebenezer Baldwin, *The Duty of Rejoicing under Calamities and Afflictions* ... (New York, 1776), 32; Mercy Warren, *History of the Rise, Progress and Termination of the American Revolution* ..., I (Boston, 1805), 158; *Va. Gaz.* (Dixon and Hunter), July 8, 1775; [Elkanah Watson], *Men and Times of the Revolution; Or, Memoirs of Elkanah Watson* ..., ed. Winslow C. Watson (New York, 1856), 17-18; Howard H. Peckham. ed., *Memoirs of the Life of John Adlum in the Revolutionary War* (Chicago, 1968), 3-5; *Dunlap's Pennsylvania Packet, or, the General Advertiser* (Philadelphia), Mar. 18, 1776.

[13] Entry of Nov. 13, 1775, in Williams *et al.,* eds., *Fithian, Journal and Letters,* II, 131; *Prov. Gaz.,* Apr. 15, 1775; *New-York Gazette; and the Weekly Mercury,* May 15, 1775; *Va. Gaz.* (Dixon and Hunter), June 3, 1775; *S.-C. Gaz.,* Sept. 1, 1775; *Rivington's New-York Gazetteer; or, the Connecticut, Hudson's River, New-Jersey, and Quebec Weekly Advertiser,* Nov. 9, 1775; Esther Reed to Dennis De Berdt, June 24, 1775. in [William B. Reed], *The Life of Esther De Berdt, Afterwards Esther Reed, of Pennsylvania* (Philadelphia, 1853), 217.

[14] Willard, ed., *Letters on the American Revolution,* 26, 105, 143; John Morton to Thomas Powell, June 8, 1775, in Edmund C. Burnett, ed., *Letters of Members of the Continental Congress* (Washington, D. C., 1921-1936), I, 114; Samuel Langdon, *Government corrupted by Vice, and recovered by Righteousness* ... (Watertown, Mass., 1775), 27; William Bradford to James Madison, June 2, 1775, in William T. Hutchinson *et al.,* eds., *The Papers of James Madison,* I (Chicago, 1962), 149; "A Letter sent to the Proprietor of the Gentleman's Magazine ... from Philadelphia," *Pennsylvania Magazine,* I (1775), 219; "Novanglus," III [Feb. 6, 1775], in Robert J.

Americans could believe this claim not because they matched the devices of force, pay, and rote used by the British but because they saw themselves as possessing natural or native or innate courage. [15] Revolutionaries could look at green recruits and see proficient soldiers because these men had voluntarily taken up arms to defend liberty. In February 1776 an address drafted in Congress "To the Inhabitants of the Colonies" explained that "Our Troops are animated with the Love of Freedom. . . . We confess that they have not the Advantages arising from Experience and Discipline: But Facts have shewn, that native Courage warmed with Patriotism, is sufficient to counterbalance these Advantages." [16] The Revolutionaries' military enthusiasm seemed to arise from a national virtue which would both deserve and achieve victory. After the defeat of Burgoyne's invasion in 1777, Revolutionaries drank to the toast, "May American bravery and honesty rise superior to Britannic artifice and fraud." [17]

Arnold's march on Quebec and his role in the unsuccessful assault, during which he was wounded in the right leg, won him praise as an embodiment of American zeal and animation. He proved equally ardent on later battlefields.

> By his address he so imprest,
> The views and ardour of his breast,
> On all his troops, that Arnold's soul
> Now seems t'inspire and act the whole:
> In freedom's cause, their country's right,
> They burn impatient for the fight. [18]

This poem about Arnold's battlefield leadership against Burgoyne in 1777 echoes the comparisons to Hannibal and Xenophon that first brought him to fame in 1775. [19] On January 10, 1776, Congress unanimously promoted Arnold

Taylor *et al.*, eds., *Papers of John Adams* (Cambridge, Mass., 1977-   ), II, 253; *Prov. Gaz.*, Feb. 18, Apr. 15, 1775; *N.-Y. Gaz.*, May 15, 1775; *S.-C. Gaz.*, Mar. 10, 31, 1775; Peckham, ed., *Memoirs of John Adlum*, 11-13; *Rivington's N.-Y. Gaz.* Jan. 19, 1775.

[15] See Royster, "Continental Army," 36-38, and sources cited there.

[16] Worthington Chauncey Ford *et al.*, eds., *Journals of the Continental Congress* (Washington, D.C., 1904-1937), IV, 140, hereafter cited as *Jours. Cont. Cong.*

[17] *Boston-Gaz.*, Oct. 23, 1777, in Frank Moore, comp., *Diary of the American Revolution: From Newspapers and Original Documents*, I (New York, 1860), 513.

[18] [William Wolcott], *Grateful Reflections on the Divine Goodness vouchsaf'd to the American Arms* . . . (Hartford, Conn. [1779]), 44.

[19] *The Fall of British Tyranny*, in Norman Philbrick, ed., *Trumpets Sounding: Propaganda Plays of the American Revolution* (New York, 1972), 124; Hugh Henry Brackenridge, *The Death of General Montgomery, ibid.*, 229; Thomas Jefferson to John Page [Dec. 10, 1775], in Julian P. Boyd *et al.*, eds., *The Papers of Thomas*

324

to brigadier general. Mercy Otis Warren hoped that the year 1776 would "hand down the name of Washington and Arnold to the latest posterity, with the laurel on their brow."[20] In the eyes of his countrymen Arnold had a special talent for inspiring men in the field, an inspiration that relied on the twin guarantors of American victory—obedience to God and service to the public. Besieging Quebec, Arnold wrote to Washington: "The repeated successes of our raw, undisciplined troops, over the flower of the British army; the many unexpected and remarkable occurrences in our favour, are plain proofs of the overruling hand of Providence, and justly demands [sic] our warmest gratitude to Heaven, which I make no doubt will crown our virtuous efforts with success."[21]

Yet the invasion of Canada failed, and so did the American rage militaire of 1775. By the time independence was declared, the popularity of military exercises, much less army service, had vanished. Within the next year anyone could see that comparatively few Revolutionaries would volunteer to serve in the Continental army or to stay long in the field as citizen soldiers of the militia. The Continental army became the main defense against the British— an army that had to use bounties and conscription to get soldiers and that did not receive enough support from the populace to pay or feed its men. Many Revolutionaries neither volunteered to fight for liberty nor sacrificed enough to properly sustain those who fought.[22] The central test of public virtue found Americans wanting. A year after the retreat from Canada, Chaplain Samuel Spring received a call from the North Congregational Church of Newburyport. He accepted and left the army.[23]

Need Americans have feared that the widespread lapse of virtue endan-

---

Jefferson (Princeton, N.J., 1950-   ), I, 270; John Adams to Nathanael Greene, May 9, 1777, in Bernhard Knollenberg, "The Revolutionary Correspondence of Nathanael Greene and John Adams," Rhode Island History, I (1942), 54; Jonathan Mitchell Sewall, Miscellaneous Poems ... (Portsmouth, N.H., 1801), 109; [Yale College], Two Dialogues, on Different Subjects ... (Hartford, Conn., 1776), 25; Israel Evans, A Discourse, Delivered, On the 18th Day of December, 1777, the Day of Public Thanksgiving ... (Lancaster, Pa., 1778), 12-13.

[20] Mercy Warren to Abigail Adams, Feb. 7, 1776, in Warren-Adams Letters: Being Chiefly a Correspondence among John Adams, Samuel Adams, and James Warren (Massachusetts Historical Society, Collections, LXXII-LXXIII [1917-1923]), I, 206.

[21] Benedict Arnold to George Washington, Feb. 27, 1776, in Peter Force, ed., American Archives ..., 4th Ser. (Washington, D.C., 1837-1853), IV, 1513.

[22] Royster, "Continental Army," esp. chaps. 1-3; Mark Edward Lender, "The Enlisted Line: The Continental Soldiers of New Jersey" (Ph.D. diss., Rutgers University, 1975), chap. 2. For statistics on Continental army strength see Charles H. Lesser, ed., The Sinews of Independence: Monthly Strength Reports of the Continental Army (Chicago, 1976).

[23] Dictionary of American Biography, s.v. "Spring, Samuel"; Currier, History of Newburyport, I, 272-275.

gered the survival of their liberty? We may infer that most Revolutionaries could answer, No—could even overlook the lapse—because they expected quick victory in 1777. Success would show the righteousness of their cause and end the tyrant's challenge to them to defend liberty in the field. Between the battles of Brandywine and Germantown, in September, Samuel Adams could see only two alternatives, "compleat Victory" or communal guilt: "Our troops are victorious in the North. The Enemies Troops are divided and scattered over a Country several Hundred Miles. Our Country is populous and fertile. If we do not beat them this Fall will not the faithful Historian record it as our own Fault? But let us depend, not upon the Arm of Flesh, but on the God of Armies. We shall be free if we deserve it. We must succeed in a Cause so manifestly just, if we are virtuous."[24] In October, when General Horatio Gates's forces captured Burgoyne's army, the popular celebrations confirmed this expectation. In a broadside printed within weeks of the victory, one line of a song ran, "Brave Gates will clear America before another year."[25] Most Revolutionaries would have thought that this was too slow. After the defeat of Burgoyne, people readily predicted the capture of Sir William Howe's army in Pennsylvania and an end to the war.[26] Even after Howe occupied Philadelphia, Americans hoped to hold their Delaware River forts, keep British shipping out, and force Howe to leave.[27] In

[24] Samuel Adams to James Warren, Sept. 17, 1777, *Warren-Adams Letters*, I, 369-370.
[25] *Song made on the taking of General Burgoyne* (n.p., 1777).
[26] John Penn to Arthur Middleton, Oct. 21, 1777, in Joseph W. Barnwell, ed., "Correspondence of Hon. Arthur Middleton, Signer of the Declaration of Independence," *South Carolina Historical and Genealogical Magazine*, XXVII (1926), 146; William Ellery to William Vernon, Mar. 16, 1778, in Burnett, ed., *Letters of Members of Congress*, III, 132; Elias Boudinot, *Journal or Historical Recollections of American Events during the Revolutionary War* (Philadelphia, 1894), 52-53; Roger Sherman to Jonathan Trumbull, Mar. 4, 1777, in *The Trumbull Papers*, III (Mass. Hist. Soc., *Colls.*, 7th Ser., II [1902]), 25-26, hereafter cited as *Trumbull Papers*; Jesse Root to Jonathan Trumbull, Nov. 7, 1777, *ibid.*, 188; Silas Goodell to Joshua Huntington, Nov. 5, 1777, in *Huntington Papers* (Conn. Hist. Soc., *Colls.*, XX [1923]), 74; Samuel Adams to James Warren, June 18, 1777, in Harry Alonzo Cushing, ed., *The Writings of Samuel Adams* (New York, 1904-1908), III, 374; Bernhard A. Uhlendorf, trans., *Revolution in America: Confidential Letters and Journals, 1776-1784, of Adjutant General Major Baurmeister of the Hessian Forces* (New Brunswick, N.J., 1957), 106; George Williams to Timothy Pickering, Oct. 25, Nov. 13, and Dec. 13, 1777, in "Revolutionary Letters Written to Colonel Timothy Pickering," *Essex Institute Historical Collections*, XLII (1906), 320, 322, 325; Henry Laurens to Robert Howe, Oct. 25, 1777, in Frank Moore, ed., *Materials for History, Printed from Original Manuscripts: Correspondence of Henry Laurens, of South Carolina* (New York, 1861), 58; see also John Brooks to [?], Jan. 5, 1778, Mass. Hist. Soc., *Proceedings*, XIII (1874), 243.
[27] Ebenezer David to Henry Bliss, Nov. 7, 1777, in Jeannette D. Black and William Greene Roelker, eds., *A Rhode Island Chaplain in the Revolution: Letters*

326

November 1777, Chaplain Ebenezer David heard "the people . . . cry fight fight and make an end of it."[28]

The army's winter at Valley Forge did not daunt this demand for quick victory. On the contrary, the survival of the army, the British withdrawal from Philadelphia to New York in June 1778, and the announcement of the American alliance with France in May of that year, convinced most Revolutionaries that the war was almost over. In Lancaster, Pennsylvania's capital in exile, people danced the Burgoyne's Surrender, and bettors who thought the war would last longer than six more months could get five-to-one odds.[29] Even after such bettors won at the beginning of 1779, they probably could have gotten favorable odds if they had been foolish enough to lay a new bet that the war would last much longer. In October 1778, Lieutenant William Thompson reported to his regimental commander that the Pennsylvania Executive Council refused to appropriate money for recruiting the state's undermanned Continental line: "they again hinted that the war would be shortly finished, and there was no need for throwing the State to farther Expences."[30] For two years, from spring 1778 to spring 1780, most Revolutionaries tried to disregard the armed conflict in the belief that British withdrawal from the continent and recognition of American independence were imminent.[31] From American officers, British officers, loyalists, foreign

of Ebenezer David to Nicholas Brown, 1775-1778 (Providence, 1949), 60; entry of Nov. 21, 1777, "Diary of James Allen, Esq., of Philadelphia, Counsellor-at-Law, 1770-1778," Pennsylvania Magazine of History and Biography, IX (1885), 425-426; Henry Laurens to Benjamin Huger, Nov. 15, 1777, in Moore, ed., Correspondence of Laurens, 62-63; Joseph Ward to James Bowdoin, Nov. 12, 1777, The Bowdoin and Temple Papers (Mass. Hist. Soc., Colls., 6th Ser., IX [1897]), 412-413; "Thoughts of a Freeman," Jan. 17, 1778, in Jared Sparks, ed., The Writings of George Washington . . . , V (New York, 1834), 498; Richard Henry Lee to Arthur Lee, Oct. 13, 1777, in James Curtis Ballagh, ed., The Letters of Richard Henry Lee (New York, 1911-1914), I, 328; Richard Henry Lee to Patrick Henry, Oct. 16, 1777, ibid., 331; Committee of Foreign Affairs to Commissioners at Paris, Oct. 6, 1777, in Francis Wharton, ed., The Revolutionary Diplomatic Correspondence of the United States (Washington, D.C., 1889), II, 399.

[28] Ebenezer David to Nicholas Brown, Nov. 23-25, 1777, in Black and Roelker, eds., Rhode Island Chaplain in the Revolution, 69.

[29] Letters from Lancaster, Apr. 27, 1778, Royal Gazette (New York), May 19, 1778; Alfred Hoyt Bill, Valley Forge: The Making of an Army (New York, 1952), 127. See also Marquis de Chastellux, Travels in North America in the Years 1780, 1781, and 1782, rev. trans., Howard C. Rice, Jr. (Chapel Hill, N.C., 1963), I, 176-177, and Elizabeth Cometti, "Morals and the American Revolution," South Atlantic Quarterly, XLVI (1947), 62-71.

[30] William Thompson to Richard Butler, Oct. 5, 1778, in Hazard et al., eds., Pa. Archives, 1st Ser., VII, 65. See also John Robert Sellers, "The Virginia Continental Line, 1775-1780" (Ph.D. diss., Tulane University, 1968), 319-321.

[31] Henry Knox to William Knox, Sept. 14, 1778, quoted in Francis S. Drake, Life and Correspondence of Henry Knox . . . (Boston, 1873), 59; Washington to

observers, and Revolutionaries at home we hear that Americans were "tired of the war."[32] In 1780 the Continental army reached one of its lowest points

George Mason, Mar. 27, 1779, in John C. Fitzpatrick, ed., *The Writings of George Washington from the Original Manuscript Sources, 1745-1799* (Washington, D.C., 1931-1944), XIV, 299-300; Washington to John Augustine Washington, May 12, 1779, *ibid.*, XV, 60; July 6, 1780, *ibid.*, XIX, 136; Washington to the States, May 22, 1779, *ibid.*, XV, 122-123; Washington to Elbridge Gerry, Jan. 29, 1780, *ibid.*, XVII, 462-463; Washington to Fielding Lewis, July 6, 1780, *ibid.*, XIX, 130-133; William Ellery to William Vernon, Mar. 16, 1778, in Burnett, ed., *Letters of Continental Congress*, III, 132; entry of Nov. 28, 1778, in Henry D. Biddle, ed., *Extracts from the Journal of Elizabeth Drinker* ... (Philadelphia, 1889), 112; John Dickinson to Caesar Rodney, June 1779, in George Herbert Ryden, ed., *Letters to and from Caesar Rodney, 1756-1784* (Philadelphia, 1933), 305; William Livingston to Jonathan Trumbull, Aug. 23, 1779, *Trumbull Papers*, III, 424-425; Richard Henry Lee to [Thomas Jefferson], Mar. 15, 1779, in Ballagh, ed., *Letters of Richard Henry Lee*, II, 39; *Boston-Gaz.*, July 6, Sept. 21, Nov. 30, 1778; *Connecticut Courant, and the Weekly Intelligencer* (Hartford), July 14, 1778; *New-Jersey Journal* (Chatham), Mar. 29, 1780; *Pa. Packet*, July 4, 1780; Thomas Clark to James Hogg, Sept. 6, 1778, in Walter Clark, William L. Saunders, and Stephen B. Weeks, eds., *Colonial and State Records of North Carolina* (Raleigh, Winston, Goldsboro, and Charlotte, 1886-1914), XIII, 478, hereafter cited as *N.C. Col. Rec.*; William Livingston to Baron van der Capellen, Nov. 30, 1778, quoted in Theodore Sedgwick, Jr., *A Memoir of the Life of William Livingston* ... (New York, 1833), 311-312; Lewis Morris, Jr., to Lewis Morris, May 1778, "Letters to General Lewis Morris," New-York Historical Society, *Collections*, VIII (1875), 455; Nathanael Greene to Lewis Morris, Sept. 14, 1780, *ibid.*, 469; Patrick Henry to George Mason, Mar. 27, 1779, in H. R. McIlwaine, ed., *Official Letters of the Governors of the State of Virginia: The Letters of Patrick Henry*, I (Richmond, 1926), 362; entry of Sept. 13, 1777, in William H. W. Sabine, ed., *Historical Memoirs from 12 July 1776 to 25 July 1778 of William Smith* ... (New York, 1958), 205; entry of Jan. 19, 1779, in Sabine, ed., *Historical Memoirs from 26 August 1778 to 12 November 1783 of William Smith* ... (New York, 1971), 66; Charles Inglis to Joseph Galloway, Dec. 12, 1778, "Letters to Joseph Galloway, from Leading Tories in America," *Historical Magazine*, 1st Ser., V (1861), 299; Daniel Coxe to Joseph Galloway, Dec. 17, 1778, *ibid.*, 358; John Armstrong, *Life of Anthony Wayne*, in Jared Sparks, ed., *Library of American Biography*, 1st Ser. (Boston, 1834-1848), IV, 43; William Weeks to Clement Weeks, Apr. 30, 1778, in Hiram Bingham, Jr., *Five Straws Gathered from Revolutionary Fields* (Cambridge, Mass., 1901), 27; entry of Sept. 14, 1778, in John Berkenhout, "Journal of an Excursion from New York to Philadelphia in the Year 1778," *PMHB*, LXV (1941), 89-90; John McDonald, Intelligence, Dec. 16, 1778, in B. F. Stevens, ed., *Facsimiles of Manuscripts in European Archives Relating to America, 1773-1783* ... (London, 1889-1895), I, no. 107; Andrew Elliot to earl of Carlisle, Dec. 12-16, 1778, *ibid.*, V, no. 543; "Salem Diary," May 30, 1778, in Adelaide L. Fries, ed., *Records of the Moravians in North Carolina*, III (North Carolina Historical Commission, *Publications*, [1926]), 1234; Joseph Reed to Nathanael Greene, Sept. 2, 1780, in [Reed], *Life of Esther Reed*, 327-328; Benjamin Rush to Anthony Wayne, Aug. 6, 1779, quoted in Henry B. Dawson, *The Assault on Stony Point, by General Anthony Wayne* ... (Morrisania, N.Y., 1863), 124.

[32] Entries of Jan 23, Apr. 8, July 19, 1778, in Sabine, ed., *Historical Memoirs*.

of public support—not only suffering a worse winter than at Valley Forge but coming close to starvation after the autumn harvests. General Washington could not undertake a fall campaign.

We may suspect that the Revolutionaries' persistent expectation of victory arose partly from a fear that the failure of public virtue might doom their cause if the war went on much longer. We find many grounds for such fear in Americans' conduct from 1778 to 1780. People were weary of the war, but they were still lively. In these years the United States enjoyed what one historian calls "an enormous economic boom."[33] As long as Continental currency had value, the American army supplied itself by spending money— an ever-accelerating flow of paper dollars that swelled in volume until they became worthless. The steady depreciation not only encouraged people to spend the money fast before it sank further, but also encouraged them to charge more for goods and services in order to hedge against losses, a practice that hastened the depreciation. During 1779 the Quartermaster General's and Commissary General's departments spent a total of $109,169,000 currency.[34] E. James Ferguson estimates that during the whole war the Continental and state governments, the British army, and—after 1780—the French army spent the equivalent of $214-$215 million specie in America.[35] In his journal a French army commissary officer wrote of the Americans, "They love money."[36] Most of the money went first to the farmers who supplied the armies, the towns, and the cities with food. People complained that the

---

1776-1778 of William Smith, 290, 343, 420; entries of Jan. 14, Feb. 15, 1779, in Sabine, ed., Historical Memoirs, 1778-1783, of William Smith, 64, 74; William Heron's Information, Sept. 4, 1780, in Stevens, ed., Facsimiles of Manuscripts in European Archives, VII, no. 733; entry of Oct. 24, 1779, in E. A. Benians, ed., A Journal by Thos: Hughes (Cambridge, 1947), 74; Washington to Henry Laurens, Nov. 11, 1778, in Fitzpatrick, ed., Writings of Washington, XIII, 227-228; Uhlendorf, trans., Revolution in America, 150; Charles Stedman, The History of the Origin, Progress, and Termination of the American War, I (London, 1794), 310; Cornelius Stagge, Intelligence, Feb. 18, 1780, in E. B. O'Callahan, ed., Documents Relative to the Colonial History of the State of New-York, VIII (Albany, 1857), 786-787; Mathieu Dumas, Memoirs of His Own Time . . . , I (London, 1839), 89; Baron Steuben to Congress, Jan. 28, 1780, quoted in John McAuley Palmer, General Von Steuben (New Haven, Conn., 1937), 222; Charles Inglis to Joseph Galloway, Feb. 25, 1779, "Letters to Galloway," Hist. Mag., 1st Ser., VI (1862), 238; Whitmel Hill to Thomas Burke (n.d.), in N.C. Col. Recs., XIV, 3.

[33] E. James Ferguson, The American Revolution: A General History, 1763-1790 (Homewood, Ill., 1974), 145.

[34] Jours. Cont. Cong., XV, 1432-1433.

[35] Ferguson, American Revolution, 145.

[36] Entry of Oct. 17-20, 1780, in Thomas Balch, ed., The Journal of Claude Blanchard, Commissary of the French Auxiliary Army Sent to the United States during the American Revolution, 1780-1783, trans. William Duane (Albany, N.Y., 1876), 71.

government's purchases drove up all prices and further depreciated the -money; meanwhile, those with something to sell profited from the expenditures. The Deputy Quartermaster General in New Jersey reported in November 1779, "Our People cry out against the Q. M. for raising the prices and none more willing to get the highest than themselves." His report in June contained the best brief summary of the career of Continental dollars: "bad as the money is its wanted."[37]

So as not to get stuck with bad money while it got worse, people spent it. Despite the rise of necessary expenditures, many Americans had money left for luxuries, primarily imported ones, obtained by privateering, risky trade with Europe, and traffic with the enemy.[38] A European laughed at an advertisement in Philadelphia: "Tobacco, as good as the best imported."[39] The fashions and manners were homegrown imitations of English style, aided by clothing and other goods that were the genuine imported articles. Americans wanted British goods so much that a merchant who imported clothing from France relabeled it British.[40] From Paris, Benjamin Franklin complained in 1779, "When the difficulties are so great to find remittances to pay for the arms and ammunition necessary for our defense, I am astonished and vexed to find, upon inquiry, that much the greatest part of the Congress interest bills come to pay for tea, and a great part of the remainder is ordered to be laid out in gewgaws and superfluities."[41] The Americans had credit in France and in the Netherlands, where they could buy not only Continental products but British goods through the Dutch. European subsidies and loans helped Americans to spend money on European manufactured goods.[42]

[37] Moore Furman to [Nathanel Greene?], Nov. 15, 1779, in Anne deB. MacIlvaine *et al.*, eds., *The Letters of Moore Furman, Deputy Quarter-master General of New Jersey in the Revolution* (New York, 1912), 39: Furman to Greene, June 9, 1779, *ibid.*, 8.

[38] Ferguson, *American Revolution*, 116, 145-147, 173-174; Curtis P. Nettels, *The Emergence of a National Economy: 1775-1815*, The Economic History of the United States, II (New York, 1962), 12, 14-22; Robert A. East, *Business Enterprise in the American Revolutionary Era* (New York, 1938), 31-32, 35-36, 51-53, 62, 74-77, 149-150; Clarence L. Ver Steeg, *Robert Morris: Revolutionary Financier* (Philadelphia, 1954), 50-51; Lee Nathaniel Newcomer, *The Embattled Farmers: A Massachusetts Countryside in the American Revolution* (New York, 1953), 131-132; Anne Bezanson, *Prices and Inflation during the American Revolution: Pennsylvania, 1770-1790* (Philadelphia, 1951), 296-297; Charles Christopher Crittenden, *The Commerce of North Carolina, 1763-1789* (New Haven, Conn., 1936), 133-149. See also Royster, "Continental Army," chap. 9 and sources cited there.

[39] Edward J. Lowell, *The Hessians and the other German Auxiliaries of Great Britain in the Revolutionary War* (New York, 1884), 210.

[40] East, *Business Enterprise in the Revolutionary Era*, 52-53.

[41] Benjamin Franklin to John Jay, Oct. 4, 1779, in Wharton, ed., *Revolutionary Diplomatic Correspondence*, III, 365.

[42] Nettels, *Emergence of a National Economy*, 14, 17, 20.

Edmund Pendleton believed that some of the dealers in America were British agents, but his countrymen seemed oblivious to the danger of subversion: "such is the Spirit to trade, that *if Belzebub was to appear with a Cargoe— the people would deal with him.*"[43]

We cannot know with precision how widely these imports were shared. There can be little doubt that they spread rapidly during these years and that the few Americans who made fortunes from privateering or importing or trading across British lines could not have done so if many less wealthy Revolutionaries had not been able and anxious to buy. In "a nearly universal black market" profits on imported goods ran up to 600 percent.[44] Before the war, nonimportation, the call to wear homespun, and the rejection of tea had mobilized resistance to British tyranny.[45] Such repudiation of luxuries had not only applied economic pressure to Britain but also demonstrated Americans' commitment to virtuous frugality. No tyrant could exploit a dependence on luxuries in order to enslave them. Now, as Americans told themselves that the struggle with Britain would soon end, they seemed to be losing the virtue on which independence was supposed to rest. In the summer of 1780, Joseph Reed, the chief executive of Pennsylvania, deplored the importation of "sugar, wines, spirits, and gewgaws of every kind, only calculated to gratify pride, intemperance and folly; and for these the men and provisions of the country are sent forth in quantities and numbers that would give us great relief, if applied to the service of the country."[46] New Hampshire's delegate in Congress, Josiah Bartlett, knowing that the Americans' cause was as just as the Israelites', regretted that "we are a crooked and perverse generation, longing for the fineries and follies of those Egyptian task masters from whom we have so lately freed ourselves."[47] Perhaps thinking of such warnings, one of Washington's aides said, "All cry out that nothing but Oeconomy can save us, and yet no one allows that he or she is extravagant."[48]

[43] Edmund Pendleton to William Woodford, Nov. 1, 1779, quoted in Mrs. Catesby Willis Stewart, *The Life of Brigadier General William Woodford of the American Revolution*, II (Richmond, Va., 1973), 1111.

[44] Ferguson, *American Revolution*, 145-147.

[45] See especially Morgan, "Puritan Ethic," *WMQ*, 3d Ser., XXIV (1967), 3-18; J. E. Crowley, *This Sheba, Self: The Conceptualization of Economic Life in Eighteenth-Century America* (Baltimore, 1974), chap. 5.

[46] Joseph Reed to Washington, July 15, 1780, in Jared Sparks, ed., *Correspondence of the American Revolution; Being Letters of Eminent Men to George Washington, from the Time of His Taking Command of the Army to the End of his Presidency*, III (Boston, 1853), 19.

[47] Josiah Bartlett to William Whipple, Apr. 24 and May 29, 1779, quoted in H. James Henderson, *Party Politics in the Continental Congress* (New York, 1974), 239.

[48] Tench Tilghman to James McHenry, Jan. 25, 1779, in Bernard C. Steiner, *The Life and Correspondence of James McHenry* ... (Cleveland, Ohio, 1907), 26.

An extensive trade with the enemy in New York City grew in all three directions—New Jersey, New York, and Connecticut. During the Valley Forge winter, Pennsylvanians took food to Philadelphia for hard money. But the trade through British lines around New York was for manufactured goods.[49] By 1780, importation at New York City had reached its prewar volume,[50] thus serving a much larger market than the region controlled by the British army. State authorities and the Continental army tried to block this trade, but after the American victory at Yorktown, nothing could stop its rapid growth. According to an article in the New-Jersey Journal, people in New Jersey objected to paying taxes for the support of the war in 1782 because "our hard money is continually going in great quantities to our enemies: the country is drained of its cash"; if the army and the government could not prevent the people from sending money to the enemy to buy British goods, then the people ought not to support the army and the government with taxes.[51] In 1778 Governor William Livingston had said that good wine would remain rare in America until the United States declared war on Portugal.[52]

Some Americans' determination to profit from the war went beyond the opportunities provided by supply and demand. Much evidence suggests that graft and fraud pervaded the supply of the army throughout the war.[53] In 1778, when holding recruiting officers accountable for the expenditure of bounty money had failed to end graft, Congress resolved that "it is essential to the liberties of the United States that due attention should be paid to the expenditure of their public monies, to enable them to support the war, and avoid that system of corruption and tyranny which prevails in the government of their unnatural enemies."[54] Yet a popular saying current during the

[49] East, Business Enterprise in the Revolutionary Era, 49-50, 180; Oscar Theodore Barck, Jr., New York City during the War for Independence ... (New York, 1931), 133-135; Thomas Jefferson Wertenbaker, Father Knickerbocker Rebels: New York City during the Revolution (New York, 1948), 211-212; Robert McCluer Calhoon, The Loyalists in Revolutionary America, 1760-1781 (New York, 1973), 326-329; Adrian C. Leiby, The Revolutionary War in the Hackensack Valley: The Jersey Dutch and the Neutral Ground, 1775-1783 (New Brunswick, N.J., 1962), 107-109; R. Arthur Bowler, Logistics and the Failure of the British Army in America, 1775-1783 (Princeton, N.J., 1975), 72-73, 159-160; Richard Buel, Jr., "Time: Friend or Foe of the Revolution?" in Don Higginbotham, ed., Reconsiderations on the Revolutionary War: Selected Essays, Contributions in Military History, No. 14 (Westport, Conn., 1978), 139-143; See also Royster, "Continental Army," chap. 9 and sources cited there.
[50] Ver Steeg, Robert Morris, 53.
[51] N.-J. Jour., June 19, 1782.
[52] William Livingston to Henry Laurens, June 18, 1778, quoted in Sedgwick, Life of William Livingston, 294.
[53] Royster, "Continental Army," esp. chap. 9.
[54] Jours. Cont. Cong., X, 132.

war advised, "Grease well and speed well."[55] Line officers and staff officers exploited their positions for personal profit, but soldiers probably suffered more from the frauds of contractors or suppliers, though these men were sometimes government officials too. Americans repeatedly sold defective food, clothing, gunpowder, and other supplies to their own army. Wagoners drained the brine from barrels of pickled meat to lighten their loads, then charged at the full weight for shipping spoiled meat; meat packers drained the brine and replaced it with water, which kept up the weight but ruined the meat; barrels of flour arrived at camp with the flour in the middle scooped out; cobblers used old scraps to make shoes that looked good but quickly fell apart; the army received bundles of blankets that, when opened, revealed that each blanket was only a fraction of the proper size; gunsmiths cheated the government when hired to repair arms; large quantities of gunpowder were "bad and not to be depended on."[56] Looking back on Americans'

[55] Entry of Apr. 9, 1778, in Theodore G. Tappert and John W. Doberstein, eds., *The Journals of Henry Melchior Muhlenberg*, III (Philadelphia, 1958), 141.

[56] Roger Sherman to Jonathan Trumbull, Apr. 23, 1777, *Trumbull Papers*, III, 46; Peter Colt to Jonathan Trumbull, Dec. 16, 1779, *ibid.*, 461; Samuel B. Webb to Jeremiah Wadsworth, Dec. 9, 1779, in Worthington Chauncey Ford, ed., *Correspondence and Journals of Samuel Blachley Webb*, II (New York, 1893), 225-226; Jean De Kalb to comte de Broglie, Dec. 25, 1777, quoted in Friedrich Kapp, *The Life of John Kalb, Major-General in the Revolutionary Army* (New York, 1884 [orig. publ. 1870]), 143; Washington to Philip Schuyler, June 9, 1776, in Fitzpatrick, ed., *Writings of Washington*, V, 118; Washington, General Orders, June 16, 1776, *ibid.*, 140; Washington to Board of War, Dec. 6, 1779, *ibid.*, XVII, 222; Washington to Robert Morris, Oct. 31, 1782, *ibid.*, XXV, 314-315; Furman to Stephen Lowrey, Aug. 29, 1779, in MacIlvaine et al., eds., *Letters of Moore Furman*, 15; Nathanael Greene to Nicholas Cooke, July 4, 1775, in George Washington Greene, *The Life of Nathanael Greene, Major-General in the Army of the Revolution* (New York, 1867-1871), I, 96-98; Nicholas Cooke to Committee of Safety, July 7, 1775, *Revolutionary Correspondence from 1775 to 1782* ... (Rhode Island Historical Society, *Collections*, VI [1867]), 112; William Heath to George Washington, May 10, 1782, *The Heath Papers*, III (Mass. Hist. Soc., *Colls.*, 7th Ser., V [1905]), 376; Lewis Morgan to Nathanael Greene, Oct. 6, 1779, in American Philosophical Society, *Calendar of the Correspondence, Relating to the American Revolution* ... (Philadelphia, 1900), 108; John Russell Bartlett, ed., *Records of the State of Rhode Island and Providence Plantations in New England*, VIII (Providence, 1863), 436; Williams to Pickering, July 12, 1778, "Letters to Pickering," *Essex Inst. Hist. Colls.*, XLIII (1907), 15; David Brooks to David Humphreys, Aug. 22, 1782, quoted in Frank Landon Humphreys, *Life and Times of David Humphreys* ..., I (New York, 1917), 249; Christian Febiger to William Davies, Dec. 3, 1781, Jan. 23, 1782, in William P. Palmer, ed., *Calendar of Virginia State Papers and Other Manuscripts* ... (Richmond, 1875-1893), II, 636, III, 44-45; Henry Harrison Metcalf, ed., *Laws of New Hampshire* ..., IV (Bristol, N.H., 1916), 390-391; [Joseph Plumb Martin], *Private Yankee Doodle; Being a Narrative of Some of the Adventures, Dangers and Sufferings of a Revolutionary Soldier*, ed. George F. Scheer (Boston, 1962 [orig. publ. Hallowell, Me., 1830]), 150; Richards, *Diary of Samuel Richards*, 77.

response to the advance of Burgoyne's army, former Chaplain Spring complained from his new pulpit in Newburyport that "the wheels of publick interest did but just move, while those of private interest were rattling all over the country."[57]

We should not picture the army and its suppliers as devoted mainly to fraud and theft any more than we should picture Revolutionary society as living in idle luxury. Rather, we see that inextricably involved in the winning of the Revolution were the practices which the Revolution sought to expel from American society. A vivid and precise vocabulary described these practices: "*smart money*" was a recruiter's illegal take; "horse-beef" was soldiers' rations of dubious origin; "CUSTOMHOUSE OATHS" were perjury; "*mushroom* gentlemen" were the newly prosperous Revolutionaries; "jocke[y]ing" was getting rid of paper money before it lost value.[58] As Washington's aide Tench Tilghman wrote in 1779, "We Americans are a sharp people."[59] This sharpness, which was so clearly evident in common speech, found its way into Revolutionary ideology only as an implacable enemy—primarily alien but potentially native—and hardly found its way into the Revolutionary vision of the future at all. If American independence depended on public virtue, how could one resolve the conflict between the demanding ideals and the sharp practice that betrayed them? Revolutionaries could denounce engrossers and extortioners—both rich farmers and rich merchants—but the rich were not the only ones who indulged fraud and greed. Selfishness itself, apart from the volume of its proceeds, drove out virtue and left a man unable to defend himself. Speaking of the builders of defective boats in 1775, Private George Morison described a dilemma that persisted for many Revolutionaries when self-seeking later grew more widespread and more successful: "Did they not know that their doings were crimes—that they were cheating their country, and exposing its defenders to additional sufferings and to death?... These men could enjoy the sweets of domestic ease, talk about liberty and the rights of mankind, possibly without

[57] Samuel Spring, *A Sermon Delivered at the North Congregational Church in Newbury-port* ... (Newbury-port, Mass., 1778), 18-19.

[58] Robert Munford, *The Patriots,* in Philbrick, ed., *Trumpets Sounding,* 290; [Benjamin Gale], *Brief, Decent, But Free Remarks, and Observations* ... (Hartford, Conn., 1782), 7; [Martin], *Private Yankee Doodle,* ed. Scheer, 150; Nathanael Greene to Nicholas Cooke, July 4, 1775, in Greene, *Life of Nathanael Greene,* I, 96-98; John Murray, *Jerubbaal, Or Tyranny's Grove Destroyed, and the Altar of Liberty Finished* ... (Newbury-port, Mass., 1784), 49; *Boston Gaz.,* Nov. 29, 1779; Williams to Pickering, Feb. 28, 1779, "Letters to Pickering," *Essex Inst. Hist. Colls.,* XLIII (1907), 202.

[59] Tilghman to McHenry, Jan. 25, 1779, quoted in Steiner, *Life and Correspondence of McHenry,* 25-26.

even a recollection of their parricidal guilt, which in minds subject to any reflection, would excite the most poignant remorse."[60]

Perhaps the widespread failure to enlist, to stay in the army, to supply the army, and to avoid corrupting vices could seem less "parricidal" because the war was believed to be almost over. But the British did not leave in 1778, or in 1779, or in 1780. Instead, in 1780 they returned to the offensive. What hope could American independence and virtue rely on when they faced not imminent victory but the danger of defeat? If surrender to the British on the battlefield should complete the ruin of the public virtue, how could American minds escape "the most poignant remorse"?

Between May and October of 1780 the popular expectation of imminent victory received three sharp blows: the surrender of Charleston to the British on May 12; the rout of Horatio Gates's southern army at Camden on August 16; and the defection of General Benedict Arnold to the British on September 25. The loss of Charleston sent more Americans into captivity than any other defeat of the war—2,571 Continental soldiers and about 800 militia and citizens. Three months later, Americans suffered their bloodiest defeat of the war, when 1,050 men were killed or wounded at Camden.[61] Gates had arrived with 3,050 Continentals and militia. After the battle, only about 700 reported for duty at the rendezvous.

Congress had given Gates the southern command against the wishes of Washington, partly because of Gates's reputation for inspiring the populace to support the Continentals, as he had done in capturing Burgoyne. On the day of battle at Camden, Gates put his North Carolina and Virginia militia in the center and on the left. They alone outnumbered the whole British force. But they ran without firing a shot, and that night Gates found himself sixty miles from the battlefield.[62] Three months later, some Virginia militiamen explained their conduct. After describing their lack of training and their fatigue, they concluded, "Panic-struck by the Noise and Terror of a Battle which was entirely New to most of us; We . . . were so unhappy as to abandon the Field of Battle . . ."[63]

[60] George Morison, "Journal of the Expedition to Quebec," Sept. 28, 1775, in Roberts, ed., *March to Quebec*, 512.

[61] Howard H. Peckham, ed., *The Toll of Independence: Engagements and Battle Casualties of the American Revolution* (Chicago, 1974), 70, 74.

[62] Ward, *War of the Revolution*, ed. Alden, II, chaps. 64-65; Paul David Nelson, *General Horatio Gates: A Biography* (Baton Rouge, La., 1976), chap. 8; Franklin and Mary Wickwire, *Cornwallis: The American Adventure* (Boston, 1970), chap. 7.

[63] Petition and Memorial of Sundry Militiamen of the tenth Division of Amherst County to the Virginia House of Delegates, Nov. 9, 1780, Virginia State Library, Richmond. I owe this reference to the work of John D. McBride.

Similarly, although General Benjamin Lincoln probably could not have taken his force out of Charleston before the siege without being defeated in the field, his decision to defend the city also relied on South Carolinians' promises to fight to the end. The civilians of Charleston were among the first to favor surrender.[64] Mercy Otis Warren later explained that "the conduct of the citizens of Charleston cannot be accounted for, but from the momentary panic to which the human mind is liable, when sudden danger presses, before it has time to collect its own fortitude, and to act with decision and dignity, consistent with previous principles."[65] Soon many South Carolinians swore loyalty to the king and took British documents of "protection," expecting to be left alone in return for not opposing occupation.[66] Thus the two defeats not only wiped out a large part of the Continental army but also showed how little the populace could count on its own firmness in battle in the face of a British offensive. Were Americans losing the ability to defend themselves? What influence could so undermine native courage? The premises of the Revolution told its adherents that public virtue was lost through surrender to corruption.

Finally, Benedict Arnold had almost succeeded in selling the most important fort in America—West Point—to the British by betraying his own command there and, Americans thought, by helping the British to capture George Washington. The Revolutionaries, despite their pride in defeating the enemy in the woods or controlling all the territory outside British lines, still reacted most strongly to the loss of set battles and fixed posts, such as Fort Washington, Fort Ticonderoga, and Philadelphia.[67] West Point had long seemed to be the impregnable security for communication between New England and the rest of the continent. We can hardly

[64] George Smith McCowen, Jr., *The British Occupation of Charleston, 1780-82*, Tricentennial Studies, No. 5 (Columbia, S.C., 1972), 5-6, 11; John Richard Alden, *The South in the Revolution, 1763-1789*, in Wendell H. Stephenson and E. Merton Coulter, eds., *A History of the South*, III (Baton Rouge, La., 1957), 240; Don Higginbotham, *The War of American Independence: Military Attitudes, Policies, and Practice, 1763-1789* (New York, 1971), 356-357; Marvin R. Zahniser, *Charles Cotesworth Pinckney: Founding Father* (Chapel Hill, N.C., 1967), 62-64; David Ramsay, *The History of the Revolution of South-Carolina, from a British Province to an Independent State*, II (Trenton, N.J., 1785), 59-60; Royster, "Continental Army," chap. 10, n. 49.

[65] Warren, *History of the American Revolution*, II, 173-174.

[66] McCowen, *Occupation of Charleston*, 11, 52-53, 55; John Rutledge to South Carolina Delegates in Congress, May 24, 1780, "Letters of John Rutledge," *S.C. Hist. Gen. Mag.*, XVII (1916), 133-134; Sir Henry Clinton to William Eden, May 30, 1780, quoted in William B. Willcox, ed., *The American Rebellion: Sir Henry Clinton's Narrative of His Campaigns, 1775-1782* . . . (New Haven, Conn., 1954), 175, n. 3; Paul H. Smith, *Loyalists and Redcoats: A Study in British Revolutionary Policy* (Chapel Hill, N.C., 1964), 128-130.

[67] Royster, "Continental Army," 175-188, 209-211, 282-283.

appreciate the depth of their shock when Americans realized how close they had come to losing the fort and the commander-in-chief by betrayal. The losses and near-loss challenged the expectation of imminent victory and called into question the assumptions about American strength on which such expectation had partly rested.

The newspapers of the war years contain comparatively little discussion of the war through much of 1778, all of 1779, and the early months of 1780. Then, in June 1780 and in the following months, an outpouring of articles fills the columns, calling Revolutionaries to renew their lapsed effort to support the army and expel the British. Both in newspapers and in private correspondence people said that the loss of Charleston might do more good than harm if it awoke Americans to win their independence, which remained far from secure.[68] The idea of awakening recurred often because many writers described the public spirit of the previous two years as sunk in a long sleep.[69] Seeing through their mistaken security and selfishness, Americans would regenerate their army with new recruits and reenlistments, as well as pay and supplies and the help of militia. These could best come from a popular willingness to place the war effort ahead of personal security for life and property—that is, from public virtue.

These appeals did not revive the *rage militaire* of 1775, but they did represent a widespread wish for such a revival. The Revolutionaries knew that the most common and most important decisions of the later war years dealt not with allegiance to independence but with the character of independence. They did not so much fear losing the war as losing the virtue that gave the war its purpose. They expressed this fear in a recurrent nostalgia for the spirit of 1775. Almost everyone who talked about the beginning of the war contrasted Americans' early ardor and unselfishness with the meanness of later years.[70] General Jedidiah Huntington, in May 1780, anticipated the French army's disgust at the Americans' ill-supplied army and greedy populace: "is it not a possible Thing to revive the feelings which pervaded every Breast in the Commencement of the War, when every Man considered the Fate of his Country as depending on his own Exertions."[71]

The call for a revival of public support for the war in 1780 and the later celebrations of Yorktown and of peace tried to reclaim the conviction that the Revolution owed its success to Americans' unified virtuous efforts. But these attempts first to overcome, then to forget, the weaknesses and divisions during the war—even if successful—could not recover the spirit of 1775

---

[68] *Ibid.*, chap. 10, n. 51.
[69] *Ibid.*, chap. 10, n. 52.
[70] Wood, *Creation of the American Republic*, 102; Royster, "Continental Army," chap. 10, n. 46.
[71] J[edidiah] Huntington to Jeremiah Wadsworth, May 5, 1780, *Huntington Papers*, 150.

because that spirit had assumed that Americans were fighting to escape or defeat such wartime selfishness. The spirit of 1775 was not just supposed to revive from time to time or to do battle in the American character with vices that might sometimes prevail. Rather, the spirit of 1775 was supposed to be the American character. From Chester County, Pennsylvania, "I.C." wrote in April 1779, denouncing the pride, greed, and luxury that had arisen in the last four years:

> O ye heroes of America, was it to obtain an unlimited restraint to such licentiousness that ye drew your swords, and rushed to victory with such military prowess! ... Or have we bid farewell to common sense itself, as well as the character under that name, that we are willing to sacrifice all that is precious ... only to have it in our power to gratify a few moments of the most precarious pleasures of sense; or at best to hoard up a heap of yellow dust. ... O that God would raise up, and send on the American stage, some Addison, Tillotson, or Whitefield; or rather, someone in the spirit and power of an Elijah, to turn the hearts of the children to the fathers, and the disobedient to the righteousness of the just, and thus prepare us a people for the Lord our God.[72]

The true spirit of 1775 was one of anticipation rather than accomplishment. The Revolutionaries had believed that they were passionately united in willingness to sacrifice, in innate strength, in aspiration to achieve permanent continental happiness. When they looked back to 1775, they could remember not so much what they had done as how they had felt. They rightly believed that this feeling of anticipation gave the crucial impetus to Revolutionary effort throughout the war. They did not want to stop seeing this spirit as a constant source of American success and instead see it as an unattainable ideal or as a set of values that needed the corrupt aid of worldly devices in order to survive. Consequently, while the Revolutionaries were seeking their independence and enjoying its fruits with many departures from their ideal of public virtue, they cherished their original picture of themselves. In the revival of newspaper appeals after the fall of Charleston, one writer warned, "In times of public danger like the present, I hold every species of inaction of the nature of treason."[73]

During the war, Doctor Benjamin Rush observed a variant of the mental illness known as hypochondriac madness or "tristimania." The popular names for this variant were "tory rot" and "protection fever." But the names were misleading. Rush called the special disorder "Revolutiana." It did not affect active loyalists; rather, it was "confined exclusively to those friends of Great Britain, and to those timid Americans, who took no public part in the war." The sufferer's derangement was induced "by the real or supposed

---

[72] Pennsylvania Gazette, and Weekly Advertiser (Philadelphia), Apr. 7, 1779.
[73] Pa. Packet, June 20, 1780.

distresses of his country." The characteristic mental symptom of tristimania was "*distress*," manifested in delusions such as these: the victim believed that he had "consumption, cancer, stone, and above all . . . impotence, and the venereal disease"; he believed that he was an animal, that he had an animal in his body, or that he had inherited the soul of an animal; he believed that he had no soul; he believed that he would drown the world with his urine; he believed that he was made of glass; he believed that he was dead. Rush observed that "all the erroneous opinions persons affected with this form of derangement entertain of themselves are of a degrading nature. . . . But the most awful symptom of this disease remains yet to be mentioned, and that is DESPAIR." According to Rush, "many of them died" of protection fever— in some cases during exile or confinement, in some cases by "seeking relief from spirituous liquors"—but "the disease. . . passed away with the events of the American revolution."[74]

Rush knew only two remedies for protection fever. The first was "to avoid reading news-papers, and conversing upon political subjects, and thereby to acquire a total ignorance of public events." If the sufferer objected to that remedy, "he should be advised to take a part in the disputes which divide his fellow citizens." The Revolution, Rush said, was like the breath of garlic eaters. Anyone who did not want to be offended by it had to eat and stink with the rest. By "imbibing a portion of party spirit, we become insensible of the vices and follies of our associates in politics, and thus diminish . . . this source of hypochondriacal derangement."[75]

Of course, Rush's observations of mental illness did not describe all Revolutionaries, since most took some active part in the contest and worked to convince themselves that they had done even more. However, the expressions of reawakened zeal in 1780, which denounced the preceding two years of sleep and climaxed in the public's reaction to the treason of Arnold, revealed the disquiet caused by the corruption within the Revolution. This zeal also demonstrated the Revolutionaries' desire to believe that corruption did not exist or that it could be extirpated. In their choice of words and rituals for the denunciation of the worst American traitor, Americans drew on their concern about their own betrayal of their highest Revolutionary ideals. If we can liken their distress over the widespread shortcomings among Revolutionaries to suffering from protection fever, we can say that in the revival of war rhetoric in 1780 and especially in the reaction to Arnold's treason, the Revolutionaries tried Rush's second remedy on themselves.

[74] Benjamin Rush, *Medical Inquiries And Observations, Upon the Diseases of the Mind* (New York, 1962 [orig. publ. Philadelphia, 1812]), 78-83, 95, 114-115; Rush, "Influence of the American Revolution," in Dagobert D. Runes, ed., *The Selected Writings of Benjamin Rush* (New York, 1947), 332.
[75] Rush, *Medical Inquiries*, 75, 114-115.

339

The victims of protection fever were not neutrals; they had clear sympathies, but they did not want to be linked with the wartime distresses which the active people on their side were helping to cause. So they tried to remain detached, but their illness gave them the delusion that, in spite of their detachment from the evils of war, their bodies or their souls harbored some malignancy or fragility which became an obsession. In a similar way, active Revolutionaries wanted to believe that they were escaping the selfishness that would have enslaved them if they had collaborated with British corruption. When widespread self-seeking began to look irreversible—capped by unprecedented military defeats and the treason of the most successful battlefield general on the American side—the Revolutionaries turned to the corruption of one man whose ruin would signify the defeat of corruption within the Revolution. These accusations palliated, for a while, the awareness that some of Arnold's traits ran deep in the American Revolution.

The reaction to Arnold's treason revealed that in his crimes, as in his achievements, he shared many attributes with his countrymen. Even while they tried to disavow him by denunciation, his selfish guilt continued to rankle in their minds. "I stand confounded and shocked at the thoughts of such a viper even being brought into the world," a newspaper correspondent wrote.[76] If the hero Arnold could betray the cause and come so near to ruining it, what security did America have? Light-Horse Harry Lee told Anthony Wayne, "I cannot rid my soul of the curses. . . . Have any other detection, have more conspirators come out[?]"[77] To study Arnold's character was to see the frightening ease with which virtue could be perverted.

Arnold's character—which thousands thought they knew so well when they heard him called a hero, and again when they heard him called a viper—remains hard to grasp.[78] He sought extremes: the highest rank, the hardest march, the hottest combat, the most luxurious social display, the coolest secret calculation, the most decisive act of the war, the highest possible price. But whatever satisfaction those extremes seemed to promise always eluded him. Arnold received high praise for his energetic command at Fort Ticonderoga, in Canada, on Lake Champlain, and at the battles of

[76] Pa. Packet, Sept. 25, 1781.

[77] Henry Lee to Anthony Wayne, Sept. 27, 1780, in Henry B. Dawson, ed., Papers Concerning the Capture and Detention of Major John André (Yonkers, N.Y., 1866), 71.

[78] The most valuable studies of Arnold are Willard M. Wallace, Traitorous Hero: The Life and Fortunes of Benedict Arnold (New York, 1954); Willard M. Wallace, "Benedict Arnold: Traitorous Patriot," in George Athan Billias, ed., George Washington's Generals (New York, 1964), 163-192; Carl Van Doren, Secret History of the American Revolution (New York, 1941); and James Thomas Flexner, The Traitor and the Spy: Benedict Arnold and John André (New York, 1953). See also Richard J. Koke, Accomplice in Treason: Joshua Hett Smith and the Arnold Conspiracy (New York, 1973).

Saratoga. Washington singled him out for a personal gift of epaulettes and sword knots as tokens of esteem and offered him command of a wing of the army in 1780. Newspaper articles written under the pen name of "Monsieur De Lisle" late in 1777 and early in 1778 told Americans that Arnold "is said to possess what we call, in our country, the 'rage militair[e].' "[79]

But two problems dogged Arnold: money and promotion. Charges of plunder and graft followed him from Canada and reached a peak after his command of liberated Philadelphia in 1778. At the instigation of Pennsylvania state authorities, he was court-martialled in 1779 on several charges and convicted of using wagons in public service to transport his own merchandise. He was sentenced to a reprimand, which Washington made as close to a compliment for Arnold's other services as he could. In fact, Arnold had used his authority over city commerce to profit from his own secret investments in British manufactured goods. Contemporaries suspected as much because of his lavish expenditures, but they could not prove it. He earned the enmity of Pennsylvanians by his arrogant exercise of military authority, his aristocratic social display, and his preference for the company of rich Philadelphians who had collaborated with the enemy during the British occupation of the city. He married one of them. His wartime extravagance mirrored his career as a merchant before the war, when he had built one of the biggest houses in New Haven, Connecticut. Now, as ever, Arnold's tastes outran his graft, and he needed more money. He pursued military status with comparable ardor. He had begun his wartime career in a dispute over rank with Ethan Allen. At Saratoga, he quarrelled with Gates, who gave him no command. He then went into battle on his own and was shot in the same leg that had been wounded at Quebec. Owing partly to the apportionment of general officer appointments among the states and partly to some congressmen's aversion to Arnold's ambition, Congress, in February 1777, had promoted five junior brigadier generals over his head to major general. Only after his service against a British raid on Danbury, Connecticut, was Arnold promoted to major general, and only after Saratoga was his seniority over the other five generals restored. As the British learned when they got him, no rank or income could match Arnold's claims.

One kind of phrase recurred in Arnold's vocabulary: "Conscious of the rectitude of my intentions"; "conscious of my own innocency and integrity."[80] He gave himself his head in everything he undertook and treated all

---

[79] *Boston Gaz.*, Feb. 16, 1778.

[80] Wallace, *Traitorous Hero*, 198, 253; Benedict Arnold to Horatio Gates, Oct. 1, 1777, quoted in James Wilkinson, *Memoirs of My Own Times*, I (Philadelphia, 1816), 259; [United States], *Proceedings of a General Court Martial . . . For the Trial of Major General Arnold . . .* (Philadelphia, 1780), 40, 51; Benedict Arnold to George Washington, Sept. 25, 1780, in Dawson, ed., *Papers Concerning . . . André*, 26-27.

opposition—whether an overdue challenge to his graft or a snub of his military prowess—as an attack on his integrity. In practice, his integrity amounted to nothing more than his indulgence of his will. After defecting to the British, he did not deign to pretend that he had changed his mind about the political ideas at stake in the war. He promptly endorsed the British constitution and deplored the Americans' French alliance, as he had formerly praised the liberty for which he had fought against Britain: the righteous side was the side he favored. However, such favor had a price. Arnold secretly negotiated with Sir Henry Clinton over a sixteen-month period before he got the right price and the right command to betray. In the meantime, he sent pieces of intelligence as gestures of good faith. Finally, he agreed to surrender West Point for £20,000. After the Americans captured Clinton's emissary, Major John André, and Arnold fled to New York City, the British still paid him £6,000, plus £525 expenses and pensions for himself and his family. Carl Van Doren summarizes the deal: "No other American officer made as much money out of the war as Arnold did."[81]

By any standard—moral, political, psychological—Arnold's behavior was selfish and destructive. Understandably, shock, denunciation, and the desire to punish followed this treason. The American Revolution had disclosed other turncoats, beginning with Benjamin Church in the first year of the war.[82] But none attracted anything like the obsessive attention devoted to Arnold's treason. Americans saw more than a criminal in Arnold—they saw a freak. He was not just a deserter or an assassin on a grand scale; he was an aberration in nature. Yet they did not find ready consolation in his uniqueness. "Somehow or other," General Henry Knox's aide wrote, "I cannot get Arnold out of my head."[83] Arnold's rotten heart made him all the more vivid and harder to dismiss. Nathanael Greene said of him, "How black, how despised, loved by none, and hated by all. Once his Country's Idol, now her horror."[84] There were many simple explanations of the man: Arnold was greedy; Arnold was ambitious; Arnold had been vicious since birth; Arnold had sold himself to Satan; Arnold was mad. But the clarity of these explanations did not lead Americans from horror to insight and then to fuller reliance on their own refusal to sell out. Instead, when they spoke of Arnold, such certainty only intensified their horror. Addressing Arnold, a letter in the *Pennsylvania Packet* gave up trying to show him as he was: "I took up my pen with an intent to shew a reflective glass, wherein you might at one view behold your actions; but soon found such a horrid ugly deformity in the out

---

[81] Van Doren, *Secret History*, 387.

[82] *Ibid.*, chaps. 1-5.

[83] Samuel Shaw to John Eliot, Oct. 1, 1780, in Josiah Quincy, *The Journals of Major Samuel Shaw . . . with a Life of the Author* (Boston, 1847), 81.

[84] Nathanael Greene to [?], Oct. 15, 1780, *Hist. Mag.*, 2d Ser., I (1867), 204.

lines of your picture, that I was frightned at the sight, so the mirrour dropped and broke to pieces! each of which discovered you to be a gigantick overgrown monster, of such a variety of shapes, all over ulcerated, that it is in vain to attempt to describe them."[85] People seldom proposed specific plans to capture Arnold or kill him, nor did they write him off as only a pitiful homeless malcontent. They did not try hard to devise new ways to thwart potential traitors. There could be only one Arnold, and when his countrymen talked about him, that is what they said—over and over, in exhaustive detail and fervent imagery: there could be only one Arnold.

Eight days after Arnold's flight, the adjutant general of the Continental army, Colonel Alexander Scammell, wrote, "Treason! Treason! Treason! black as hell! That a man so high on the list of fame should be guilty as Arnold, must be attributed not only to original sin, but actual transgressions. . . . we were all astonishment, each peeping at his next neighbor to see if any treason was hanging about him: nay, we even descended to a critical examination of ourselves. This surprise soon settled down into a fixed detestation and abhorrence of Arnold, which can receive no addition."[86] The next day, a British intelligence report said that the Americans' reaction to the treason revealed "their distrust of themselves."[87] Among his countrymen, Arnold reached the limits of ignominy in 1783 when Silas Deane cut him dead socially in London.[88] To be cast out by an outcast was the just fate of a fallen American. Europeans reacted differently. When Lafayette heard that the British had made Arnold a brigadier general, he remarked that "there is no accounting for taste."[89]

Washington and Jefferson each approved an attempt to capture Arnold—once while he was in New York City and once while he was leading an invasion of Virginia. Jefferson drafted an authorization to kill Arnold as a

[85] *Pa. Packet*, Sept. 25, 1781.

[86] Alexander Scammell to Col. Peabody, Oct. 3, 1780, in Dawson, ed., *Papers Concerning . . . André*, 66.

[87] Andrew Elliot to William Eden, Oct. 4-5, 1780, in Stevens, ed., *Facsimiles of Manuscripts in European Archives*, VII, no. 739.

[88] On Deane see Flexner, *Traitor and Spy*, 237-238; Van Doren, *Secret History*, 170-171; Silas Deane to Barnabas Deane, Jan. 31, 1782, in Charles Isham, ed., *The Deane Papers*, V (N.-Y. Hist. Soc., *Colls.*, XXIII [1890]), 31; Silas Deane to Benjamin Franklin, Oct. 19, 1783, *ibid.*, 213-214; Joshua Hett Smith, *An Authentic Narrative of the Causes Which Led to the Death of Major André* . . . (London, 1808), 290; and Benjamin Franklin to Robert Morris, Mar. 30, 1782, in Wharton, ed., *Revolutionary Diplomatic Corrspondence*, V, 279. On the origins and significance of Deane's exile see especially Morgan, "Puritan Ethic," *WMQ*, 3d Ser., XXIV (1967), 25-34; E. James Ferguson, *The Power of the Purse: A History of American Public Finance, 1776-1790* (Chapel Hill, N.C., 1961), 90-94, 102-104, 110; and Henderson, *Party Politics*, chap. 8.

[89] Marquis de Lafayette to Madame de Lafayette, Feb. 2, 1781, in *Memoirs, Correspondence and Manuscripts of General Lafayette*, I (New York, 1837), 386.

last resort but then changed his mind.[90] Americans said that if they caught Arnold, they would hang him, then cut off the leg that had been wounded in the service of America, bury the leg with full military honors, and hang the rest of the body on a gibbet.[91] A public demonstration acted out this division of merit with Arnold's effigy.[92] The Revolutionaries frequently said that the failure of Arnold's plot showed God's providential protection of General Washington and the United States; Americans seemed to hope that the defeat of Arnold's conspiracy would enable them to amputate from the righteous cause all that he stood for.

A year after the treason, the New-Jersey Journal recalled that "the streets of every city and village in the United States, for many months, rung with the crimes of General Arnold."[93] In New Milford, Connecticut, hundreds of inhabitants paraded figures of Arnold and Satan through the illuminated town to the sound of firecrackers. The effigy was hanged, cut down, and buried. In Norwich, Connecticut, a crowd destroyed the tombstone of Arnold's father. To celebrate the victory at Yorktown, people in Newburgh, New York, burned Arnold in effigy. Within days of his flight to the British, Philadelphians paraded a two-faced effigy of Arnold, on which the head constantly turned, while behind him stood the devil, offering a bag of gold and holding a pitchfork to prod him into hell. At the end of the route, the effigy was burned—though, as a Quaker woman noticed, the newspapers said that the fire had consumed Arnold himself.[94] A five-year-old boy in Philadelphia—a refugee from Charleston—knew and remembered

[90] Washington to Henry Lee, Oct. 20, 1780, in Fitzpatrick, ed., Writings of Washington, XX, 223-224; Thomas Jefferson to Peter Muhlenberg, Jan. 31, 1781, in Boyd et al., eds., Papers of Jefferson, IV, 487-488; Aaron Ogden, "Autobiography of Col. Aaron Ogden, of Elizabethtown," New Jersey Historical Society, Proceedings, 2d Ser., XII (1892), 23-24; James Robertson to Henry Clinton, Oct. 1, 1780, quoted in Winthrop Sargent, The Life and Career of Major John André ... (Boston, 1861), 379.

[91] N.-J. Jour., Aug. 1, 1781; Providence Gaz., Aug. 11, 1781; New-Jersey Gazette (Trenton), July 25, 1781.

[92] William Abbatt, ed., Memoirs of Major-General William Heath (New York, 1901), 297.

[93] N.-J. Jour., Nov. 21, 1781.

[94] James Thacher, A Military Journal during the American Revolutionary War ... (Boston, 1823), 579-580; Pa. Packet, Oct. 3, 1780, Jan. 16, 1781; Representation of the Figures ... paraded through ... Philadelphia; Samuel Adams to Elizabeth Wells Adams, Oct. 10, 1780, in Cushing, ed., Writings of Samuel Adams, IV, 210; James Madison to Thomas Jefferson [Oct. 5, 1780], in Hutchinson et al., eds., Papers of Madison, II, 112; Boston Gaz., Oct. 23, 1780, Nov. 12, 1781; Conn. Courant, Dec. 12, 1780, Nov. 6, 1781; Va. Gaz. (Clarkson and Davis), Oct. 21, 1780; entry of Oct. 4, 1780, in Biddle, ed., Journal of Elizabeth Drinker, 129; Wallace, Traitorous Hero, 269; entries of Sept. 29-30, 1780, "Journal of Samuel Rowland Fisher, of Philadelphia, 1779-1781," PMHB, XLI (1917), 311, 314-315.

Arnold's crime by seeing on the cover of an almanac the picture of a double-faced Arnold shadowed by the devil with tempting gold and threatening dart.[95]

Arnold represented the worst crimes against virtue. Revolutionaries who had held him high among patriots now decided that his entire career showed a fixed, desperate hunger for riches. Even while undertaking large crimes of extortion and treason for huge sums, he would also embezzle petty amounts of army stores and cheat soldiers of their pay. Now Americans could see the truth and tell Arnold that

> Thy public life was but a specious show
> A cloke to secret wickedness and shame. . . .
> Hence thou hast lurk'd beneath the fair disguise
> Of *freedom's* champion, *mammon's* sordid slave.[96]

A newspaper published Beelzebub's letter of instruction to Arnold. His "INFERNAL MAJESTY" commanded, "We expect that you will . . . put an end, by a capital stroke, to all the pretensions of that people, and we flatter ourselves that after their subjection they will be in a few years as corrupted, as wicked, as cruel as their mother country."[97] How else but by his double face could so many of Arnold's countrymen have spoken him so fair while he was so systematically corrupt? Fortunately, America was too virtuous to satisfy his lust for opulence. His was a greed which Britain and Satan had created and which only they could reward.

Nor had Arnold's combat services shown him to be a virtuous leader. One version said that he had always been a coward at heart; another said that Americans could allow him bravery because even bandits and assassins had a sort of bravery; another said that he had bravery but not courage—that is, animal spirits but not moral character. The valor of General Richard Montgomery, who had been killed at Quebec, would live eternally, while Arnold's weakness would make him infamous to posterity. Revolutionaries agreed that Arnold's supposed valor in the field had really been an unreliable giddiness, brought on by drunkenness or mental unbalance. Such violence revealed innate depravity, not native courage.

Beginning within days of his flight to the British, Arnold's countrymen began to make their most frequent and most eloquent comment about him: he must be feeling an agonized remorse. He would, they prayed, despair and

[95] Joseph Johnson, *Traditions and Reminiscences Chiefly of the American Revolution in the South* . . . (Charleston, S.C., 1851), 255.
[96] *The Fall of Lucifer. An Elegiac Poem on the Infamous Defection of the Late General Arnold* [Hartford, Conn., 1781], 7-8.
[97] *Pa. Packet*, Oct. 7, 1780.

die. Like Judas, he would hang himself.[98] Or he would bear the mark of Cain—and an American mark of Cain on Arnold, unlike God's mark on Cain, meant that the first person who saw the traitor would kill him.[99] The Revolutionaries gave their evil effigy of Arnold the capacity for remorse. In this quality it differed most from the man himself. There is no evidence that Arnold felt repentance for his treason, and much evidence that he felt none. He was, in Van Doren's words, "the Iago of traitors."[100] Yet the surest and worst punishment that Revolutionaries could imagine for Arnold—the torture they knew he could not escape—was a life of guilt. After a career of pretending to be uniquely courageous while he was weak, of professing virtuous patriotism while he cheated his countrymen, of proclaiming innocence and integrity while he negotiated surrender to mammon, what fate could await him but the lifelong horror of realizing that he had betrayed God's cause?[101]

Private Samuel Downing was in the 2nd New Hampshire Regiment at Tappan, New York, when Arnold defected. In 1863, when Downing was one hundred years old, an interviewer asked him about Arnold. The old man's memory had changed the facts, but the Revolutionaries in 1780 would have approved of the reaction to Arnold's treason which Downing gave to posterity: "he ought to have been true. We had true men then; 'twasn't as it is now. Everybody was true: the tories we'd killed or driven to Canada."[102]

Downing reflected the Revolutionaries' determination to achieve unanimity in virtue, a determination which they had also demonstrated earlier in the Revolutionary movement. The treatment of Arnold's effigy resembled in many ways Americans' earlier rejections of Governor Thomas Hutchinson and King George III.[103] As we see in the rituals of repudiation, the

[98] *Fall of Lucifer*, 12, 12n; [David Rittenhouse], *Weatherwise's Town and Country Almanack, for the Year of our Lord, 1782* . . . (Boston, Mass. [1781]), frontispiece; *Boston Gaz.*, Aug. 13, Nov. 26, 1781.

[99] Eleazer Oswald to John Lamb, Dec. 11, 1780, quoted in Isaac Q. Leake, *Memoir of the Life and Times of General John Lamb* . . . (Albany, N.Y., 1857), 266-267.

[100] Van Doren, *Secret History*, preface.

[101] In addition to the sources cited above, many other sources illustrating the themes in my analysis of the reaction to Arnold's treason may be found in Royster, "Continental Army," chap. 10, n. 79.

[102] E. B. Hillard, *The Last Men of the Revolution*, ed. Wendell D. Garrett (Barre, Mass., 1968 [orig. publ. Hartford, Conn., 1864]), 34-35.

[103] Bernard Bailyn, *The Ordeal of Thomas Hutchinson* (Cambridge, Mass., 1974), esp. chap. 7; Peter Shaw, "Their Kinsman, Thomas Hutchinson: Hawthorne, The Boston Patriots, and His Majesty's Royal Governor," *Early American Literature*, XI (1976), 183-190; Winthrop D. Jordan, "Familial Politics: Thomas Paine and the Killing of the King, 1776," *Journal of American History*, LX (1973), 294-308; Robert Middlekauff, "The Ritualization of the American Revolution," in

Revolutionaries' resolve to maintain public virtue relied not only on inherited ideas but also on a strong current of emotion. A widespread aspiration to permanent national righteousness gave them the hope that liberty would survive, that they need not despair. Signs of internal corruption were interpreted as the workings of alien conspiracy. This interpretation implied that public virtue was not so weak as to betray the cause if only the conspirators could be eliminated. Some historians have used the word "paranoiac" to describe the Revolutionaries' fear of a conspiracy against their liberties.[104] One scholar has even concluded that the American Revolution was "the product of a delusion."[105] But unlike the supposed conspiracies by loyalists or by the king and his ministers, Arnold's plot was a real conspiracy. Americans' reaction to it—more violent and long-lasting than the treatment of Hutchinson and the king—was not a paranoid fear of a nonexistent enemy plot. Yet as in the earlier denunciations, Revolutionaries went beyond the facts of Arnold's treason to create an effigy whose ruin could prove the virtuous strength of its destroyers. They revealed the bond between this effigy and themselves when they endowed their Arnold with remorse. They could not fully believe that Arnold was vicious enough to be free from guilt for his treason—perhaps because they, not he, repented betraying the ideals of the Revolution for selfish gain. Americans could acknowledge lapses of zeal from which virtue could still revive. But to accept the full measure of their failure between 1778 and 1780—to admit their points of resemblance to Arnold—would have left future perseverance in the public virtue of 1775 open to doubt, if not certainly doomed. From the fear of this fate came the legacy that ran through the denunciation of Arnold—not a delusion of conspiracy, but the desperate claim that the public virtue of 1775 could survive as the basis for American independence.

Some Revolutionaries, however, were no longer willing to entrust America's future to the voluntary patriotism of their countrymen. The rise to power of the advocates of strong central government in 1781 owed much to the failure of virtuous effort by the public.[106] Continental and state govern-

---

Stanley Coben and Lorman Ratner, eds., *The Development of an American Culture* (Englewood Cliffs, N.J., 1970), 31-43.

[104] James H. Hutson, "The American Revolution: The Triumph of a Delusion?" in Erich Angermann et al., eds., *New Wine in Old Skins: A Comparative View of Socio-Political Structures and Values Affecting the American Revolution* (Stuttgart, 1976), 177-194, esp. 179; Philip Greven, *The Protestant Temperament: Patterns of Child-Rearing, Religious Experience, and the Self in Early America* (New York, 1977), 348-354; Nathan O. Hatch, *The Sacred Cause of Liberty: Republican Thought and the Millennium in Revolutionary New England* (New Haven, Conn., 1977), 119-120, 131-132.

[105] Hutson, "American Revolution," in Angermann et al., eds., *New Wine in Old Skins*, 190.

[106] On the wartime nationalists see especially Merrill Jensen, "The Idea of a

ments' authority seemed especially inadequate when the test of their effectiveness became their capacity to coerce rather than their capacity to mobilize voluntary efforts. Robert Morris won unprecedented powers and unanimous appointment as Superintendent of Finance not because most Revolutionaries admired him or agreed with him but because they needed him. Morris understood the basis of his authority; he announced his intention to replace "the convulsive Labors of Enthusiasm" and "the empty Bubbles of Hope" with "the Solid Foundations of Revenue" and "the sound and regular Operations of Order and Government."[107] However, Morris and some of his fellow nationalists, especially Gouverneur Morris and Alexander Hamilton, erred when they hoped to found a permanently strengthened government on the public's need for able leaders. Such men, they believed, could maintain a national responsibility and solvency which the public would not voluntarily sustain. To succeed as a basis for governmental authority, this reasoning had to assume that the Revolutionaries would tacitly or openly give up their pretensions to public virtue and acknowledge their dependence on the superior men in their midst.[108]

These leading nationalists were convinced that the war years had shown the irremediable failure of public virtue. However, we can infer from the reaction to Arnold's treason that most Revolutionaries did not agree with the nationalists. Pillorying Arnold's effigy revealed a strong need to show how much Arnold differed from his countrymen.[109] The qualities they attributed to him—weakness, madness, vice, and greed—made him a traitor. Their own qualities—native courage and public virtue—made them patriots. His treason threatened American independence and liberty. Their patriotism sustained American independence and liberty. Victory over conspirators was

National Government during the American Revolution," *Political Science Quarterly*, LVIII (1943), 356-379; Jensen, *The New Nation: A History of the United States during the Confederation, 1781-1789* (New York, 1950), pt. 1; Ferguson, *Power of the Purse*, pt. 2; Henderson, *Party Politics*, chaps. 10-12; Wood, *Creation of the American Republic*, pts. 4-5; Richard H. Kohn, *Eagle and Sword: The Federalists and the Creation of the Military Establishment in America, 1783-1802* (New York, 1975), chap. 2; Richard H. Kohn, "American Generals of the Revolution: Subordination and Restraint," in Higginbotham, ed., *Reconsiderations on the War*, 104-123.

[107] Robert Morris to Benjamin Franklin, Nov. 27, 1781, and Morris to the Governors of the States, Oct. 19, 1781, in E. James Ferguson *et al.*, eds., *The Papers of Robert Morris, 1781-1784*, III (Pittsburgh, Pa., 1977), 85, 282.

[108] See especially Gerald Stourzh, *Alexander Hamilton and the Idea of Republican Government* (Stanford, Calif., 1970), and Max M. Mintz, *Gouverneur Morris and the American Revolution* (Norman, Okla., 1970).

[109] Catherine L. Albanese, *Sons of the Fathers: The Civil Religion of the American Revolution* (Philadelphia, 1976), 94-95; David R. Johnson, "Benedict Arnold: The Traitor as Hero in American Literature" (Ph.D. diss., Pennsylvania State University, 1975), chaps. 2, 7.

not enough: the victory had to be won by virtue. Arnold would not be the last conspirator pilloried by a righteous people. As the wartime nationalists and later the Federalists learned, no leaders or institutions could long succeed by basing their claim to allegiance on the public's betrayal of the ideals of 1775. The future of American political ideology lay not only in appealing to a Union, a Constitution, a group of proven leaders, or other visible tokens of victory. That future would also depend on the appeal to public virtue. The Revolutionary War's legacy claimed such virtue for Americans but left them open to doubt that they were still achieving it.[110]

[110] On the continuing importance of public virtue in American political thought see, for example, Lance G. Banning, *The Jeffersonian Persuasion: Evolution of a Party Ideology* (Ithaca, N.Y., 1978); Drew R. McCoy, "The Republican Revolution: Political Economy in Jeffersonian America, 1776 to 1817" (Ph.D. diss., University of Virginia, 1976); and Fred Somkin, *Unquiet Eagle: Memory and Desire in the Idea of American Freedom, 1815-1860* (Ithaca, N.Y., 1967).

THE
Pennsylvania Magazine
OF HISTORY AND BIOGRAPHY

Treason and its Punishment in Revolutionary Pennsylvania

"PENNSYLVANIA," said Chief Justice Thomas McKean, "was not a nation at war with another nation, but a country in a state of *civil war;* and there is no precedent in the books to show what might be done in that case. . . ."[1] In these words he explained in 1781 Pennsylvania's status during the Revolutionary period. Actually, until February 11, 1777, when the Whig legislature passed an act defining treason, and defined it in prospective terms, every man residing in Pennsylvania had a legal right to choose his party, Whig or Tory. By all Whig standards that was a generous decision, but the historian may justifiably extend the characterization of civil war to the whole period that lasted from the suspension of all law in May, 1776, until the expulsion of the Doan band of guerrillas in June, 1784. In these years, the revolutionists faced as a major problem the fact that many inhabitants were adherents of the British and ready to oppose the new government with violence. If revolution was justified, this sort of adherence to the Crown, as distinguished from the passive resistance of the nonassociators and nonjurors, had to be regarded as a high crime. To meet the active

[1] As reported in *Respublica v. Chapman,* 1 Dallas 53, page 58.

287

threat, the Whigs used, in the first place, prosecution in the courts; and whenever this procedure seemed inadequate, they resorted to bills of attainder, that is, procedures which led to an official judgment without trial. In either event, the principal penalties were forfeiture and death. The seizure of loyalist estates was intended to be a punitive measure (and, of course, a financial provision for the state). The hanging of perhaps a score of men, on the other hand, was carried out less to punish than to warn. There exists no way to measure the effectiveness of the warning.

It is paradoxical that, during the Revolution, neither prosecutions for treasonable offenses, nor acts of attainder, were initiated against Pennsylvanians by the British government, while in the same period headstrong Pennsylvania Whigs proscribed, or prosecuted as traitors, hundreds of citizens who had never deviated from the allegiance in which they were born. The policy of prosecution developed as the armed resistance directed by the Continental Congress grew more serious. As resistance gradually became revolution, so the concept of treason to America matured.

Though a few men in America might in spirit side with the British, it was not anticipated, at the start, that many would render physical aid to the redcoats. It was in the autumn of 1775 that this calm and trusting attitude began to change in Pennsylvania, for on August 23 of that year the King had issued a proclamation calling upon his officers and loyal subjects in America for aid in suppressing rebellion and sedition. When the proclamation was received in Philadelphia, certain men, chiefly natives of England, undertook to transmit intelligence to the British cabinet. The intercepting of their report on October 6 caused a tremendous stir. Pennsylvania leaders felt that the letter constituted an invitation to the British to invade the province, and Congress immediately recommended that the provincial assemblies and committees of safety arrest and secure all persons "whose going at large may endanger the safety of the colony, or the liberties of America."[2]

2 Worthington C. Ford, ed., *Journals of the Continental Congress, 1774–1789* (Washington, 1904–1937), III, 280, hereinafter *Journals of Congress*. For details on the Kearsley group see William Duane, ed., *Extracts from the Diary of Christopher Marshall . . .* (Albany, 1877), 45–46; *Pennsylvania Archives, Second Series*, XIII, 295–296, 298, 503–504; Peter Force, *American Archives* (Washington, 1837–1853), *Fourth Series*, III, 240–241; *Second Report of the*

In effect, the resolution of Congress vested in the extralegal Whig committees the power of imprisoning citizens at will. As for the immediate situation, Dr. John Kearsley, Leonard Snowden, and other leaders of this Philadelphia group of loyalists were ordered held in various county jails as the prisoners of Congress itself, during pleasure.

The situation in which these prisoners found themselves involved was deplorable. For most political prisoners, physical suffering was great. While they were in prison, Kearsley died and Snowden is said to have lost his reason, but these misfortunes resulted from the inefficiency of the infant government rather than from intentional cruelty. Colonial jails were unwholesome places, never designed nor intended for long-term incarcerations. Congress was far too busy to devote time to penal reform, and it was impossible to turn over these prisoners to local authorities, even after the formation of new governments; an inherent barrier to transfer lay in the circumstance that no legal basis existed at any time for holding these men.

In the months that followed the exposure of Kearsley's activities at Philadelphia, other incidents made evident the certainty that loyalist individuals and groups would generate further interference. Notably, John Connolly, a former Pennsylvanian, was captured in Maryland with commissions for a regiment of "Loyal Foresters" and a plan to bring about an uprising in the vicinity of Fort Pitt. Like the Philadelphians, Connolly and his close associates became congressional prisoners.[3]

Becoming increasingly aroused, Congress moved gradually into a firmer policy in treating loyalism. On January 2, 1776, there was passed a second resolution urging assemblies and committees of safety "by the most speedy and effectual measures" to counteract

---

Bureau of Archives of the Province of Ontario (Toronto, 1904), 1219–1223; George Stevenson to Council of Safety, Nov. 12, 1776, Records of the (1st) Council of Safety, Division of Public Records, Harrisburg; Loyalist Transcript, IV, 310–311; V, 470–471; XLIX, 417–445; L, 42–57; LI, 5–11, 513–517, New York Public Library.

3 On the Connolly group see Elizabeth H. Buck, "John Connolly," *Dictionary of American Biography* (New York, 1928–1944), XXI, 188–189; H. M. Stephens, "Sir Alan Cameron," *Dictionary of National Biography* (London, 1885–1900), VIII, 285–286; E. Irving Carlyle, "John Ferdinand Smyth Stuart," *ibid.*, LV, 102–103; *The Royal Commission on the Losses and Services of the American Loyalists, 1783 to 1785, Being the Notes of Daniel Parker Coke . . .* (Oxford, 1915), xviii.

353

inveterate toryism.[4] True, this resolution called for no more than what the committees had in mind already, and it appears to have been aimed chiefly at those persons who were accusing Congress of secretly plotting a declaration of independence. Five months later, in the middle of May, another recommendation of Congress cleared the legal atmosphere by putting an end to the civil authority of the Crown. A stiffened attitude toward aggressive loyalists followed inevitably. On June 24, Congress decided on capital punishment for such spies as were not subjects of any of the United Colonies, at the same time recommending that the various legislatures enact punishments for inhabitants and residents guilty of offering aid or comfort to the King of Great Britain or other enemies of America. All this demanded a commitment from the government of Pennsylvania, which had hitherto ignored these matters; "treason to America" had been punished only by public indignities and irregular imprisonment, following hints or suggestions given by Congress.

The Pennsylvania convention to frame a new constitution, which met during the assembly's recess, enacted, on September 5, 1776, an ordinance on treason. McKean's discussion of treason law seems to have ignored this legislation. The committee that drafted the ordinance was dominated by moderates, and, considering the extremism of the other delegates, the precedents in English law, and the tendency of treason statutes passed in subsequent years, the provisions of the ordinance were not harsh. High treason was defined as the offense of any person owing allegiance to Pennsylvania (that is, of any inhabitant or voluntary resident) who should "levy war against this state or be adherent to the King of Great Britain or others of the enemies of this state or the enemies of the United States of America by giving him or them aid or assistance." Forfeiture of all real and personal estate, and imprisonment for any term not exceeding the duration of the war, was the penalty set. Persons who knew of such treason and concealed it, or who knowingly received or assisted a traitor, were to be adjudged guilty of misprision of treason. Such were to forfeit one-third of their estates, and to be imprisoned for any term not exceeding the duration of the war.[5] This humane

---

4 *Journals of Congress*, IV, 18–20.

5 *The Statutes at Large of Pennsylvania from 1682 to 1801*, IX, 18, hereinafter *Statutes at Large*.

ordinance was nominally in force until the following January, but, because courts of oyer and terminer did not exist in that period, it was not invoked. The sole person formally charged with high treason in 1776 was never brought to trial.[6] At that time a trial would have been fraught with legal difficulties, brought about by the effective suspension of the whole body of law previously practiced in Pennsylvania.

A second ordinance, that of September 12, against seditious utterances, was drawn less liberally. The offense was defined as speaking or writing in an attempt to "obstruct or oppose . . . the measures carrying on by the United States of America for the defense and support of the freedom and independence of the said states." Anyone accused was to be tried by the nearest justice of the peace, and persons convicted were to be imprisoned, or bound over to keep the peace, at the justice's discretion. If the justice thought the prisoner too dangerous to be allowed bail, two other justices of the peace were to be consulted, and two of the three were empowered to imprison for a term not exceeding the duration of the war. Although appeal to the council of safety was permitted, no provision was made for keeping a record or for impaneling a jury.[7] The principal attack on the new measure came from the remnant of the old provincial assembly. On September 26, the last day of its corporate existence, this group nullified the ordinance, charging that it was a dangerous attack on the people's liberties, and a violation of their most sacred rights.[8] No prosecutions under the ordinance are known to have occurred.

Pennsylvania's Whig leaders were unable to gain respect for their own laws. This circumstance, in combination with the imminent danger of invasion, brought about in November, 1776, an unusual outburst of hysteria in Philadelphia. A group of Whig extremists suddenly began to break into houses, seize suspects, and commit them to prison. On November 25, these Whigs held hearings at the Indian Queen tavern. Thomas McKean, the only revolutionist of prominence who was present, acted as chairman; probably he pre-

[6] *Colonial Records of Pennsylvania*, XI, 12, hereinafter *Colonial Records;* Peter Force, *American Archives, Fifth Series*, III, 194; J. Thomas Scharf and Thompson Westcott, *History of Philadelphia, 1609–1884* (Philadelphia, 1884), I, 326.

[7] *Statutes at Large*, IX, 19.

[8] *Pennsylvania Archives, Eighth Series*, VIII, 7586.

sided unwillingly, as the proceedings were not consistent with the stand he later professed. A witness repeated testimony he had given three months before, concerning men who made boasts of their loyalty, or who joined in the chorus of "God Save the King" at private social gatherings. The meeting was inconclusive, for the vigilantist movement was poorly supported and was already petering out. At least one other meeting was held to examine the culprits, but this time McKean did not attend.

The total number of persons arrested in this drive late in 1776 is unknown. Seven prominent citizens, none of them dangerous at the time, were held in prison until December 13, when the council of safety released them on terms similar to those of a military parole. An eighth victim was still in prison in January.[9] Though further information is lacking, it can be assumed that the movement subsided very quickly, partly because alarm over the military situation increased, but also because there were no sensational discoveries to feed and fire the antiloyalist drive.

Before the transitory character of the wave of persecution was evident, however, panic seized the peaceful conservatives of Philadelphia. What happened is not altogether clear and definite, but it appears that a young lawyer, Christian Huck, learned that the leaders of the drive had listed two hundred persons, whom they intended to imprison or to banish to North Carolina, and that the list included not only his own name but also those of many kinsmen of the Allen connection, the group of families which ranked highest in provincial society. Huck passed this information to others. John, Andrew, and William Allen, brothers-in-law of Governor Penn, and their young cousins, Tench Coxe and Edward Shippen, joined Huck in flight to New Jersey, seeking the protection of the British army. Whether Joseph Galloway was aware of Huck's story is unknown, but his flight to British headquarters was another result of the same outburst of hysteria. Still others, frightened by the extremists, hid in the countryside for a time and returned to Philadelphia only when a

9 Draft minutes of the meeting of Nov. 25, 1776; Joseph Stansbury to Council of Safety, Dec. 6, 10, 12, 1776; parole of Stansbury and five others, Dec. 13, 1776; Joel Arpin to Council of Safety, Jan. 3, 1777, all in Records of (1st) Council of Safety. It is possible that this vigilantism was officially inspired, as Galloway believed. Thomas Mifflin to Washington, Nov. 26, 1776, William B. Reed, *Life and Correspondence of Joseph Reed* (Philadelphia, 1847), I, 266–267.

degree of stability had been restored. Eventually, Shippen and Coxe were forgiven and permitted to return.[10] The significant result of this flare-up, brought on by an irresponsible minority, was that some of the ablest men in the state were alienated, driven to the British permanently. What they had claimed was only the right of neutrality, and by more tolerant treatment they might in time have been won over by the revolutionists. The later behavior of the elder Jared Ingersoll,[11] of Chief Justice Benjamin Chew, and of many others illustrates this probability. The Allens, and Galloway, and their kind had not been spies or traitors; much as they disliked separation from the British Empire, until persecution embittered them they were more than reluctant to take up arms against Americans.

Two measures of the first assembly to meet under the new constitution are of vital significance, inasmuch as they established judicial safeguards for civil rights and provided a lasting statute for the prosecution of treasonable offenses. The first of these achievements was the revival of the laws. An act passed January 28 and effective February 11, 1777, declared binding the common law of England and, so far as they were not in conflict with the political revolution, all British and provincial statutes hitherto in force in Pennsylvania.[12] This act brought an end to committee government and cleared the way for the re-establishment of courts. As a second accomplishment, the assembly enacted a new law to displace the treason and sedition ordinances passed in September, 1776. The treason act of 1777, though long in force, was not necessarily an improvement over the ordinances mentioned, but it was milder than the treason laws of most governments of the time. A committee of six assemblymen, extremists without legal training or political experience, had been appointed on January 13 to draft a treason bill. They reported a bill which, after some amendment, was adopted on February 11, and,

[10] Alexander Graydon, *Memoirs of a Life, Chiefly Passed in Pennsylvania within the Last Sixty years* . . . (Harrisburg, 1811), 108–109, 261; Thomas Balch, *Letters and Papers Relating Chiefly to the Provincial History of Pennsylvania* . . . (Philadelphia, 1855), 255–256; "Diary of James Allen," *Pennsylvania Magazine of History and Biography (PMHB)*, IX (1885), 193; Loyalist Transcript, XLIX, 77.

[11] Lawrence H. Gipson, *Jared Ingersoll: A Study of American Loyalism* (New Haven, 1920), 374.

[12] *Statutes at Large*, IX, 29.

except for changes in the penalties, remained the fundamental treason law of the state until 1860. It seems certain that the bill was actually drawn for the committee by a trained lawyer. Three other states passed, at about the same time, treason acts similarly worded, and it is therefore conceivable that the bill was discussed with, and perhaps written by, one or more of the delegates to Congress.

The act identified seven specific offenses, each of them constituting high treason when committed by Pennsylvanians and directed against Pennsylvania or the United States: accepting a commission from the enemy; levying war; enlisting, or persuading others to enlist, in an enemy army; furnishing arms or supplies to the enemy; carrying on a traitorous correspondence with the enemy; being concerned in a treasonable combination; and furnishing intelligence to the enemy. The penalty for treason was disinheritance and death, with forfeiture of all property, including the dower of the traitor's wife, but excepting such income as the supreme court might appropriate to the offender's wife and child, or to the child only. Section III of the new act replaced the sedition ordinance of September 12, 1776, and defined misprision of treason to include, specifically, these offenses: speaking or writing in opposition to the public defense; attempting to convey intelligence to the enemy; attempting to incite resistance to the government or a return to British rule; discouraging enlistment; stirring up tumults, or disposing the people to favor the enemy; and opposing, and endeavoring to prevent, the revolutionary measures. Anyone convicted of misprision of treason was to be imprisoned for the duration of the war, and to forfeit half of his estate.[13]

Despite the increased severity of the penalties provided, the effect of this law was unpredictable, though usually liberal towards loyalists. Some lawyers have held that the list of categories recited was intended to limit the scope of treason prosecutions.[14] This interpretation is disputed, but it gains support from the fact that every prosecution on which we have adequate information falls into one or another of the categories specifically enumerated. Whether or not the view of the intention is correct, under the existing political conditions the very severity of punishment operated in favor of narrow

13 *Ibid.*, 45.
14 *Anthony Cramer, Petitioner v. U. S. A., Appendices to Brief for the U. S. on Reargument*, U. S. Supreme Court, No. 13 Oct. Term, 1944, 234-235.

application of the law. The humane treason ordinance of 1776 was appropriate for the punishment of all the guilty, while the act of 1777 was practicable only to punish a few *in terrorem*. The legislators had turned away from an enlightened, but as yet unenforceable, penology, to embrace once more the prevailing Anglo-American system, which was becoming to weak governments. The records of the court of oyer and terminer show that, exclusive of proceedings initiated by conditional bills of attainder, which we will later consider as a special class, the prosecution of 118 persons for high treason was begun during the war. Of these, twenty-three were acquitted at trial, and but four were convicted. Furthermore, three of the four found guilty were pardoned, and only one man, Ralph Morden, was hanged.[15] The record of punishments for misprision of treason under this act is also unimpressive. For the state, two counties excepted, the total of men charged was eighty-one; the result was one case abated by death, twenty-five acquitted, and fifteen convicted, of whom not more than three suffered the full penalty of imprisonment and partial forfeiture.[16]

In practice the act was too liberal and uncertain for the loyalists' own good. In enumerating rather definite classes of treason, in requiring two witnesses, and in its purely prospective outlook, it was well within the liberal tradition established by the treason statute of 25 Edward III, on which Coke had written:

Therefore, and for other excellent laws made at this Parliament, this was called *Benedictum Parliamentum*, as it well deserved. For except it be *Magna Charta*, no other Act of Parliament hath had more honour given unto it. . . . And all this was done in severall ages, that the faire Lillies and Roses of the Crown might flourish, and not be stained by severe and sanguinary Statutes.[17]

But like the mother statute, the Pennsylvania act proved so restrictive in its application that subsequent legislatures could not let it

[15] Oyer and Terminer Docket, 1778–1786, Philadelphia Office of the Prothonotary of the Supreme Court; Conviction and Clemency Papers, Return of the Special Commission of Oyer and Terminer for Bedford County, Sept. 28—Oct. 2, 1778, Division of Public Records.

[16] Oyer and Terminer Docket, 1778–1786; dockets of the courts of Quarter Sessions in the courthouses at Philadelphia, Doylestown, West Chester, Lancaster, York, Carlisle, Bedford, and Greensburg; estreats of all the fines imposed in the State, 1780–1783, Supreme Court Notes, XLV, Historical Society of Pennsylvania.

[17] Quoted in *Cramer* v. *U. S., Appendices*, 56.

stand alone. For one thing, two witnesses were required to prove either treason or misprision of treason. In default of two, it was doubted whether any appropriate punishment could be imposed.[18] An act of March 8, 1780, resolved this uncertainty, declaring that an offense containing elements of treason could be prosecuted and punished as a misdemeanor.[19] Many prosecutions for "misdemeanor" are recorded, and, although few of the available records contain specifications, it is to be supposed that a substantial number of such cases were political. In York County, for example, prosecutions for treasonable misdemeanor had certainly begun before the act of 1780 was passed, but the cases we know about were dismissed after its passage, perhaps to escape any argument that the new enactment proves the earlier rule.[20] In the same county, at least four men were convicted of political misdemeanor in 1780 and 1781; the heaviest sentence was a fine of twenty-five pounds specie, along with imprisonment from October until the following Independence Day.[21]

The small number of executions for treason was also attributable to the circumstances that some persons indictable for treason were technically guilty of other heinous offenses as well. Loyalists helped the British cause whenever they found a clear opportunity, fusing their politics with their personal advantage to the extent that other men did and still do. Moreover, they were freed from normal inhibition by the consideration that they need respect neither the new laws nor the would-be government. In a number of places they operated as uninstructed guerrillas, rendering themselves liable to prosecution for nearly every felony.

The range and variety of felonies was great, and most of the crimes so classified were, according to the basic statutes and rules of penal law, punishable by death. Yet the degree of inhumanity suggested by this circumstance had been greatly mitigated in Pennsylvania by importing, in 1718, "benefit of clergy." Originally, in the

18 Jonathan Dickinson Sergeant to George Bryan, May 12, 1779, *Pennsylvania Archives*, VII, 396.

19 *Statutes at Large*, X, 110.

20 E.g., *Respublica* v. *Casper Spahr* and *Respublica* v. *Daniel and John Lamot*, indictments, Historical Society of York County, York.

21 *Respublica* v. *Nicholas Yost*, v. *Samuel Worley*, v. *James Brittain*, v. *John Ham*, Quarter Sessions Docket No. XII, 139–140, 144, 224, 234, 265, No. XIII, 5, Office of the Clerk of Quarter Sessions, York; and the indictments for those cases at the Historical Society of York County.

Middle Ages, this privilege was reserved for felons who possessed clerical status; in the following centuries, it became democratized to affect finally all persons convicted of certain felonies for the first time, as a statutory commutation of the death penalty to a branding of the hand and brief imprisonment. In Pennsylvania, benefit of clergy proved by no means a dead letter; although nominally abolished in 1794, it actually continued in force until 1860, with the difference that after 1794 branding was omitted and judges were required to grant the benefit without awaiting the prisoner's request.[22]

At first, early in 1777, when counterfeiting the currency and uttering counterfeit bills were made capital offenses, benefit of clergy was allowed for those offenses. There followed numerous complaints of the part played by loyalists in depreciating the currency. Therefore, by four acts passed in the years 1779–1781, both offenses were "ousted of clergy"; the death sentence became mandatory upon even a first conviction.[23]

Definition of the capital crime of robbery, unchanged since 1718, was broadened in 1780, and at the same time the barbarous penalties for horse stealing were increased.[24] Collectors who had been robbed of public moneys began flooding the legislature with requests for exonerations. To meet the situation in eastern counties, where loyalist communities were obviously in connivance with the plunderers, an unsuccessful attempt was made in the assembly to extend to Pennsylvania in modified form the Statute of Winchester, so as to make the township in which the crime was committed liable to the collector for his loss, for damages, and for all the costs of litigation in case the offenders were not caught within thirty days.[25]

In a six-year period, 1778 through 1783, the civil authorities of the state hanged forty-eight men for crimes other than treason.[26] It is notable in this connection that the executions between the coming of

22 Leonard Manyon, "Benefit of Clergy," *Encyclopaedia of the Social Sciences* (New York, 1930–1934); Sections XI and XIV, act of May 31, 1718, *Statutes at Large*, III, 204, 206–207; Section IX, act of Sept. 22, 1794, *ibid.*, XV, 177, repealed by act of Mar. 31, 1860, P. L. 452.

23 Two acts of Mar. 20, 1777, *Statutes at Large*, IX, 100, 104; acts of Nov. 26, 1779, Mar. 25 and June 1, 1780, Apr. 7, 1781, *ibid.*, X, 12–16, 189, 212, 307.

24 Acts of Mar. 8 and 10, 1780, *ibid.*, X, 110–112.

25 *Minutes of the First Session of the Sixth General Assembly of the Commonwealth of Pennsylvania* (Philadelphia, 1781), 556.

26 *Colonial Records*, XI–XIII, *passim*, for death warrants; *cf. Journal of the Senate . . . of Pennsylvania*, III, 61 (Jan. 5, 1793).

William Penn and the outbreak of the war had not exceeded eighty-four.[27] Just how many of the forty-eight hanged were actually loyalists cannot be ascertained, since few records of the cases are available; it is evident, however, that a substantial number of the men convicted had acted with some political motivation. For example, when it was made clear that Abijah Wright, a captured loyalist, had entered a man's house by night to kidnap him for the British, the charge against him was changed from treason to burglary, and he was quickly convicted and hanged.[28] Similarly, after James Sutton led a mutiny on the Whig privateer *Chevalier de la Luzerne*, and induced the crew to deliver the vessel to the British as a prize, he was convicted of piracy and hanged.[29] A third Pennsylvania loyalist, Thomas Wilkinson, sentenced to be hanged in chains on a similar specification of piracy, was allowed to live because of a serious technical error in his trial.[30] In four years, 1779–1782, twenty-two men were tried for counterfeiting, of whom eleven were acquitted and eleven convicted, and five of those convicted were hanged.[31] The captured members of the Nugent and Shockey gang, who were apparently part of Colonel William Rankin's Associated Loyalists, were prosecuted chiefly as counterfeiters and robbers; at least two were hanged for uttering counterfeit bills, and two for robbing someone of a bottle of yeast worth three pence.[32] James Roberts, who risked his life by carrying Rankin's messages to Sir Henry Clinton, was upon his return tried and executed for offering counterfeit currency.[33] The noted Fitzpatrick, guerrilla and plunderer of Whigs, was

27 Lawrence H. Gipson, "Crime and Its Punishment in Provincial Pennsylvania," *Pennsylvania History*, II (1935), 12–14.

28 *Pennsylvania Packet*, Dec. 8, 1778.

29 *Ibid.*, Oct. 24 and Dec. 2, 1780; "Journal of Samuel Rowland Fisher," *PMHB*, XLI (1917), 310; *Colonial Records*, XII, 535; transcript of the record of Sutton's conviction, Sept. 25, 1780, Conviction and Clemency Papers.

30 Case of Thomas Wilkinson, convicted in U. S. Admiralty Sessions, *ibid.*; *Colonial Records*, XII, 730, 732, 751, and XIII, 135; "Journal of Samuel Rowland Fisher," *PMHB*, XLI (1917), 427.

31 William Bradford, "Statement of Facts and Observations Respecting the Penal Laws," Dec. 3, 1792, entered on *Journal of the Senate . . . of Pennsylvania*, III, 61 (Jan. 5, 1793).

32 Cases of Benjamin and James Nugent, of Henry Trout, and of Christopher Shockey, Conviction and Clemency Papers; *Colonial Records*, XII, 179, 375, 386.

33 Case of James Roberts, *ibid.*, 375; Christopher Sower, Jr., to John André, Oct. 5, 1779, and Nov. 5, 1779, page 4 of an eight-page résumé of the correspondence between Rankin and Clinton, 1780, Sir Henry Clinton Papers, William L. Clements Library.

convicted of burglary and larceny, and was the first Pennsylvania loyalist to die at the hands of the civil authorities.[34] The fabulous Doan gang—loyalist guerrillas, guides to escaping prisoners of war, harborers of British emissaries—committed at least thirty robberies of collectors of taxes and militia fines, or of county treasurers. It was the practice of the Doans to seize the collectors' tax warrants and duplicates, and to warn collectors to desist from performing their official functions. In the opinion of Whig officials, it was simplest to treat these men as burglars or robbers; as such the state tried and convicted eighteen of the Doan gang, of whom seven received benefit of clergy and eight were hanged.[35]

One of the more difficult problems facing the Whigs was how to treat loyalists captured while serving under British enlistment, commission, or letters of marque. Congress ordered on December 30, 1777, that henceforth such persons should be turned over to their respective states for punishment. Washington, whose forces would have to bear the brunt of retaliation for any drastic action, chose in general to let the resolution "sleep."[36] Presumably, then, any provincial troops taken were either held or exchanged as prisoners of war. By exception, Frederick Verner, a Pennsylvania officer in the British service, was held prisoner by Congress to await trial for treason in the state courts, and apparently state officials were greatly relieved when an opportunity arose to exchange him for an American civilian then in the hands of the British.[37] Not until July, 1779, did the state actually face the important question. The decision came following the transfer to state custody of a number of naval prisoners, seamen and marines from Pennsylvania who had been captured on the loyalist privateers *Patsy* and *Impertinent*. It became necessary to

[34] Case of James Fitzpatrick, Conviction and Clemency Papers; *Pennsylvania Packet*, Aug. 29, Sept. 26, Oct. 10 and 29, 1778.

[35] These statistics do not include those Doan associates who were outlawed by the courts; their case is discussed later.

[36] Washington to President of Congress, Apr. 4, 1778, J. C. Fitzpatrick, ed., *The Writings of George Washington* (Washington, 1931–1944), XI, 217. Congress repeated the order on Aug. 28, 1778, *Journals of Congress*, XI, 848.

[37] *Colonial Records*, XI, 561, 720–721, 752; Historical Manuscript Commission, *Report on American Manuscripts in the Royal Institution of Great Britain* (London, 1904–1909), I, 418–419; *Journals of Congress*, XI, 797–798, 848; XII, 1198; XIII, 315. Verner had been attainted of high treason conditionally, as described later, and was apparently the only person *captured* during the forty days of grace allowed by act of Mar. 6, 1778.

determine whether these captives were traitors, pirates, or prisoners of war. President Reed, always attentive to the interests of Washington's army, asked McKean for an advisory opinion regarding the prisoners, and in asking presented an important lead, for he asked the Chief Justice to distinguish, if necessary, "between the predicament of such as Joined the Enemy before the Declaration of Independence, the New Establishment of Civil Government, or any other Era he may judge material."[38] Thus he threw the way open for a very striking decision.

McKean proved co-operative; in a few days he produced an opinion to the effect that all prisoners who did not owe allegiance to Pennsylvania on February 11, 1777, or any subsequent date, were to be regarded as prisoners of war, while the others might be prosecuted for treason upon the sea at a specially constituted court of oyer and terminer. It is evident, then, that McKean and Reed deserve credit for establishing a liberal policy for such cases. McKean was under no obligation to distinguish a civil from a foreign war, as he did in this instance; in fact, to do so was contrary to the tone of all the rhetoric and legislation of the revolutionists. And to recognize, as he did, the existence of an anarchic interregnum, with a consequent season of free choice of sides, was an enormous theoretical concession. Of the several dates that he might have set for the terminus of the period of choice, McKean generously chose the last, "the safer course in so unprecedented and doubtful a case," because treason was not accurately defined or declared by the legislature until the time mentioned.[39] It is doubtful that this opinion would have been politically possible a year earlier, and perhaps its acceptance can best be explained as a matter of military expediency. Evidently, the opinion introduced into the revolutionary government a broadened sense of military responsibility. Under the rule set forth, most of the loyalist prisoners in detention at the moment could be held for trial, since they had not joined the British until the latter part of 1777. Never-

38 Capt. James Montgomery to Reed, June 9, 1779, *Pennsylvania Archives*, VII, 476–477; *Colonial Records*, XII, 49, 71.

39 *Ibid.*, XII, 74–75; McKean's opinion, Aug. 13, 1779, *Pennsylvania Archives*, VII, 644–646. For the method of prosecuting sea traitors see act of Sept. 9, 1778, *Statutes at Large*, IX, 281–282. Despite the language of the congressional resolution of May 14, 1776, and of the act of Jan. 28, 1777, McKean could not conceive that the common law had been inoperative during the interregnum.

theless, early in 1780 the council authorized their exchange as prisoners of war.[40]

It is therefore surprising to learn that Reed attempted, a few months later, to punish as a traitor a man who, as he knew, had joined the British in 1776. This was Lieutenant Samuel Chapman of the British Legion, who had been captured at sea and taken to Massachusetts, where at first he was treated as a prisoner of war. Reed requested that Chapman be extradited to Pennsylvania, and Massachusetts acceded. The explanation given at the time by the prisoner's family and friends is the only one that has come down to us: Reed took this action, so they said, to oblige General John Lacey, at that time the councillor from Bucks. A native of that county, and in fact a cousin of Lacey, Chapman had taken a prominent part in the engagement at the Crooked Billet near Philadelphia, on April 30, 1778. In that fight a small party of provincial and British troops surprised and put to flight a brigade commanded by Lacey, causing heavy American losses. The consequent indignation of Lacey, it was said, was the mainspring of the action against Chapman. This explanation is supported by circumstance; Lacey was one of the few men sitting at the council table at the time the request was sent to Massachusetts.[41] In view of the earlier interchange between Reed and McKean, Reed must have written the letter against his better judgment.

McKean, who showed great deference to the legislature, could nevertheless be depended upon to hold judicial ground against any challenge from the executive branch. Chapman, who was brought into his court in April, 1781,[42] pleaded that he had always been a British subject, had never been a "subject or inhabitant" of the commonwealth, and was now a prisoner of war. McKean, in giving his decision on these points, merely confirmed and elaborated the ad-

[40] McKean to Reed, Sept. 20, 1779, *Pennsylvania Archives*, VII, 703–705; *Colonial Records*, XII, 246.

[41] Reed to Jeremiah Powell, May 19, 1780, *Pennsylvania Archives*, VIII, 254; G. P. [George Playter] and Christopher Sower, Jr., to Oliver Delancey, Memorandum concerning Lt. Samuel Chapman, September, 1780, Sir Henry Clinton Papers; *Royal Pennsylvania Gazette*, May 5, 1778.

[42] Chapman had been attainted *nisi* by a proclamation of the Council, which he had ignored; he was therefore not tried, but was brought before the Supreme Court to give reasons in arrest of judgment.

visory opinion he had given in 1779, that until February 11, 1777, a choice of sides was legal. In saying so, he laid less emphasis than before on the fact that the treason act passed on that date, and gave more attention to the act of January 28, 1777, which revived the laws as of February 11, following. The wording of the latter act, he said, indicated a belief of the legislature that no laws were in force between, as a beginning point, either May 14 or July 4, 1776, and February 11, 1777. This belief he held to be sufficient to establish legally the existence of an interregnum. If no laws were in force, there was no protection; then allegiance (the reciprocal of protection) could not be required; then treason (the betrayal of allegiance) could not exist, and Chapman was a prisoner of war. Accordingly, he was exchanged a few weeks later.[43] Thus the first and perhaps the most important Pennsylvania ruling on the citizenship of loyalists was made.

Doubtless the hangman's harvest would have been larger had the courts and lawyers relaxed their vigilance. In the legal defense of Tory causes, James Wilson was most prominent. So galling was his success to the extreme Whigs that some of them sought to make him the scapegoat for the economic derangement of 1779. Scarcely less active than Wilson was the Philadelphia attorney William Lewis (1748–1819). These two were assisted for a short time, at the height of the treason trials, by George Ross (1730–1779) of Lancaster. Either Wilson, or Lewis, or both, appeared for the defense in nearly every treason case that was docketed in Pennsylvania down to that of John Fries in 1799.[44] Both were men of highly conservative background, Wilson a Scottish Seceder turned Episcopalian, and Lewis a nominal Quaker. Later both became extreme Federalists. These facts suggest that their effective defense of the loyalists may have been due in part to a special and sympathetic understanding of the predicament of their clients, and also in part to a conviction that such persons could again become useful citizens.

43 *Respublica* v. *Samuel Chapman*, 1 Dallas 53–60; Supreme Court Appearance Docket (April 1780–September 1781), 330, Philadelphia Office of the Prothonotary of the Supreme Court; "Journal of Samuel Rowland Fisher," *PMHB*, XLI (1917), 325, 419, 424, 427; intelligence memorandum of Lt. Samuel Chapman, May 11, 1781, Sir Henry Clinton Papers.

44 Robert L. Brunhouse, *The Counter-Revolution in Pennsylvania 1776-1790* (Harrisburg, 1942), 75–76; J. S. Futhey and Gilbert Cope, *History of Chester County* (Philadelphia, 1881), 635–636; Supreme Court Appearance Docket, and Oyer and Terminer Docket, for the war years.

It became evident before the end of 1777 that the general treason act could not cope with widespread, notorious, and successful treason. When British forces entered the state that autumn, thousands of loyalists flocked to the protection of the royal standard. Many of these men left property within the American lines and therefore could be punished, whether captured or at large, merely by abridging their right to a day in court. Before the end of this civil war, attainders or outlawries had been enacted by the assembly, and independently, under statutory authority, by the executive branch, and under the common law by the judges.

On September 17, 1777, a few days after the battle of Brandywine, the assembly appointed a committee to draft a bill for confiscating the estates of those who had joined the enemy. This committee never reported, for its function was absorbed by a second committee appointed but a few weeks later "to digest some Plan for preventing Supplies and Intelligence going to the Enemy." The latter group proposed "a Degree of Military Power" until the new assembly should convene, and following this proposal a council of safety was created—the second board of that name—and was vested with dictatorial powers, especially with regard to the lives and property of loyalists. The new council of safety passed an ordinance on October 21, which called for sequestrating the estates of all inhabitants who "have, or hereafter shall, abandon their families, or habitations," to join the British. Transactions made by loyalists after such abandonment were declared null and void, and loyalists were denied any appeal from the decisions of the commissioners appointed in each county to enforce the decree. However, it appears that only five confiscations took place, four in Northampton County and one in York County; the gross revenue realized under this ordinance was £142 14s 10d specie.[45]

It seemed obvious to the Whig extremists that the policy of confiscation must be continued and must be provided with a firmer basis in law. In December the council of safety was dissolved, although its ordinance of October 21 was continued by specific action of the

---

[45] *Journals of the House of Representatives of the Commonwealth of Pennsylvania* (Philadelphia, 1782), I, 91, 93, 95 (Sept. 17, Oct. 6, 8, 1777); *Colonial Records*, XI, 325–331; *Pennsylvania Archives, Sixth Series*, XIII, 231–238; Attainder Papers at Division of Public Records. The personal property of James Rankin was seized under this ordinance; since he was later attainted of high treason, it is accounted for under the Attainder Act.

367

assembly. Even before that time, on November 27, Congress intervened to urge that each state seize and sell the estates of such of its citizens as had forfeited their right to protection, and recommended that the proceeds be invested in the continental loan office. This last suggestion was ignored, but on the same day the assembly appointed a committee of three to draft a confiscation bill.[46]

The bill was drawn without delay and was reported on December 23, but not passed until March 6 following. Robert Whitehill, the common factor of personality in all the other confiscation committees, also headed this committee, and the trained mind of Thomas McKean worded the bill. In its complete acceptance of the policy of conditional attainder, the first and final draft mirrors clearly the bitterness and frustration built up in Whig circles during the winter of Valley Forge. The terms were harsh.

Harking back to a procedure developed to deal with the Jacobites during the uprising of 1745, the new act to combat loyalism named thirteen of the most prominent persons who had joined the British, gave them until April 21 following to surrender and stand trial under the general treason act, and provided that any of the thirteen failing to surrender before the set limit should stand attainted of high treason. To be so attainted would mean, of course, the forfeiture of all property to the commonwealth, the loss of all right to inherit or have heirs, and, in case of capture, hanging.[47]

Furthermore, the act affected not alone the thirteen named, but provided for other and similar attainders by the executive. To the supreme executive council the House delegated authority to proclaim at its discretion additional attainders, which became absolute forty days after the date of proclamation. Agents for forfeited estates were appointed for each county, with authority to seize the property of the supposed traitors and to sell it after the forty-day period set.

Acts of attainder had long been unpopular. Even Henry VIII had expressed doubt as to the legality of condemning a man unheard. Absolute acts of attainder, such as those passed in New York and in

[46] *Journals of the House of Representatives* (Philadelphia, 1782), I, 12, 18 (Nov. 27, Dec. 8, 1777); *Journals of Congress*, IX, 971.

[47] Act of Mar. 6, 1778, *Statutes at Large*, IX, 201–215, based upon 19 Geo. II cap. 26, an act of Parliament. Joseph Galloway, the Allen brothers, and perhaps others named in the Pennsylvania act, could have been cleared under the decision in the Chapman case, 1 Dallas 53–60, had McKean not held that the legislature was entitled to pass *ex post facto* laws.

Delaware, forbade trial, and the conditional attainder procedure of 1745, now borrowed by Pennsylvania, was dangerous only to a slightly lesser degree. In either form, attainder embodied the notion that the legislature, or even the executive, could with safety assume the guilt of an untried individual, even when the offense involved was in its nature highly technical and, moreover, political.[48]

At the bottom, there was slight difference between absolute and conditional attainder; to labor the distinction is to ignore the significant, even though imponderable, effect upon its victim of the attainder proclamation itself. However innocent he might be in a technical sense, it was a rare defendant who could demonstrate that he had provided to the cause of independence such support as would encourage him to risk his life before a partisan judge and an antagonistic jury. The loyalists knew that in 1777 anarchy had prevailed in Pennsylvania, and they suspected that anarchy would prevail there again, as indeed it did in 1779. For most loyalists, then, the condition imposed was unacceptable, and their return for trial was scarcely to be anticipated. There was also the regrettable and inevitable circumstance that damage done to reputations by the publication of names was not to be repaired by surrender, however prompt, even in case a *nolle prosequi* or a rapid acquittal resulted.[49]

The carelessness with which the council prepared attainder proclamations increased the damage to reputations, as the record clearly shows. The names of persons supposed to have joined the enemy were sent to the council by the agents for forfeited estates. These agents, who profited by receiving a percentage on sales of estates, all too often based their reports on hearsay and assumption, since not even sworn information was required before a proclamation was posted. In a few cases, an influential Whig may have saved a Tory friend from proscription, as we know that Major Solomon Bush saved the elder Thomas Coombe·and a few others, but it is certain that there was no systematic screening of names before they ap-

48 C. H. McIlwain, *The High Court of Parliament and Its Supremacy: An Historical Essay on the Boundaries Between Legislation and Adjudication in England* (New Haven, 1910), 225–229; Julian P. Boyd, ed., *The Papers of Thomas Jefferson* (Princeton, 1950), II, 189–193.

49 E.g., the case of Tench Coxe, discussed by his political enemy Graydon in *Memoirs*, 109, and the case of Benjamin Gibbs, a passive loyalist, reported in *Respublica* v. *Gibbs*, 4 Dallas 253–255 and 3 Yeates 429–438; both had surrendered on conditional attainder, and had been discharged by the court without trial.

369

peared on the proclamations. Embarrassing mistakes were made, families were broken up, and innocent persons found their lives ruined.[50] On the other hand, inefficiency of operation not infrequently left untouched the lives and property of other persons, of the sort for whom the penalties had been intended.

Despite omissions, the number of persons attainted was considerable. The basic statute named thirteen, and the council added many more: the four proclamations issued in 1778 included 396 persons; the two of 1779 named thirty-two persons; the two of 1780 listed forty-three persons; and the two of 1781, the two last, added sixteen more. Repetitions caused by misnomer introduce a slight uncertainty into statistics, but the total of attainders *nisi* announced by the legislative and executive branches was certainly close to 500.[51] That nearly four-fifths of these attainders came in 1778, following the winter of Valley Forge, is not surprising. During that winter loyalist hopes rose highest, and British sympathizers in Pennsylvania enjoyed their best opportunity for flight.

The fate of the five hundred persons conditionally attainted in Pennsylvania can be readily traced in the records. One died with the British during his forty-day period of grace, and two others, after surrendering, died before trial; 113 avoided absolute attainder by surrendering within the time limit set, and, of these, less than a score came to trial, for the evidence was in most cases too flimsy for prosecution. One man was exchanged as a prisoner of war without trial, thirteen were tried and acquitted, and three were tried and convicted. One of the three convicted, being insane, was pardoned, and the other two, John Roberts and Abraham Carlisle, were hanged.

The conditional attainders of some 386 persons became absolute when they failed to surrender. Aside from Chapman, who was released as a British subject, six of these attainted traitors fell into the hands of the Whigs during the war, and the supreme court awarded execution against them. Five of the six, however, were

---

50 Attainder Papers, Circular from Council to the Agents, broadside, May 6, 1778; Loyalist Transcript, LI, 529; advertisements of Samuel Garrigues, Jr., and of John Taylor, *Pennsylvania Packet*, Aug. 29, 1778, and Jan. 14, 1779; *in re* Dennis Crockson, *Colonial Records*, XII, 58, 65.

51 The text of the ten proclamations is given in *Colonial Records*, XI, 482–485, 493–495, 513–518, 610–612, 768, XII, 27–29, 496–497, 665–666, 710–711, and *Pennsylvania Archives*, *Fourth Series*, III, 774–777. The reports of agents and other documents concerning confiscated estates are given in *Pennsylvania Archives*, *Sixth Series*, XII–XIII.

subsequently pardoned, with the end result that of the 386 only one, David Dawson, was hanged.[52] He was probably the first American ever legally executed untried, under the provision of a bill of attainder. It were well had he been the only one.

In desperate effort to check the activities of the Doan gang, special varieties of attainder were invoked. The assembly passed a law naming seventeen members of the band, for each of whom a reward of £300 would be given, dead or alive.[53] But the heaviest artillery was outlawry, a sort of judicial attainder brought to bear on the guerrillas by Chief Justice McKean.

Outlawry was a process of the common law used very rarely in America, even in the eighteenth century. Although in 1718 an act of assembly had been passed to implement this procedure in Pennsylvania, it had never been invoked. Since it was based on indictment, and was administered under many safeguards, outlawry was more regardful of human dignity than were the legislative or executive types of attainder, but it did deny the ultimate right to a trial. In four proclamations during the years 1782 to 1784, the judges cited seventeen of the Doan gang, on sixty-one counts, calling on them to surrender and be tried for their lives, or in default of surrender, to be adjudged outlaws sentenced to death.[54] By calling their offense robbery or burglary, and by disregarding the large degree of political motivation present, it was possible to ignore the effect of the Treaty of Paris, which terminated the prosecution of loyalists for political offenses; therefore pursuit of the Doans continued to the end of the decade. The supreme executive council even applied to Sir Guy Carleton, during the last days of the British occupation of New York, for extradition of some of the outlaws then in that city. The council did not inform the British commander, of course, that the men wanted were loyalists. Carleton agreed to the request in principle, but he could not find the outlaws.[55]

52 Supreme Court Appearance Docket, and Oyer and Terminer Docket, for the war years; *Colonial Records*, XI–XIII; *Pennsylvania Archives*, VII–VIII.

53 Act of Sept. 8, 1783, *Statutes at Large*, XI, 109.

54 Supreme Court Appearance Docket (1782–1783), 226–230, (1783–1786), 215; Oyer and Terminer Docket (1778–1786), 142, 146–147, 193, 239; *Respublica v. Aaron Doan*, 1 Dallas 86.

55 *Colonial Records*, XIII, 680; *Pennsylvania Archives*, X, 101–103, 131; Alfred J. Morrison, tr., Johann David Schoepf, *Travels in the Confederation, 1783–1784* (Philadelphia, 1911), I, 126–127. The literature on the Doans is extensive; much accurate information, and some that is wildly inaccurate or imaginative, appears in George MacReynolds, ed., *The New Doane Book* (Doylestown, 1952).

371

None of the band responded to the spider's invitation. They remained in the countryside, carrying on their bitter campaign against collectors until the militia were mustered against them in June, 1784. Thereafter they seem to have been entirely law-abiding, and a number of the associates drifted to New Brunswick and Lower Canada.[56] Individual members were captured from time to time, at least eight of them in 1783 and 1784. One outlaw, an accessory, was allowed benefit of clergy. A number of the standing outlawries against the Doans were argued in court and were set aside because of error in the proceedings, though that step did not preclude trial and conviction. In Whig circles no noteworthy objection to the principle of outlawry was raised until October, 1784, after the supreme court handed down its first award of execution under this process, following argument but without trial.

Then, in view of the novelty of the procedure, and in order to seek a special opinion from the court, President Dickinson and the council delayed issuing the death warrant against Aaron Doan. The precedent, they felt, would be illiberal and dangerous. On March 28, 1785, a majority of the council, to justify their vote that they could not legally issue a death warrant in this case, alleged a number of technical errors in the proceedings, and suggested that the assembly reverse the outlawry.

This assumption of a right of the executive to review court decisions was not well received. The chief justice could find no error in his work, and the assembly was unsympathetic. After nearly three years of waiting, confined in irons and expecting death, Aaron Doan was finally pardoned on condition that he leave the United States forever.[57] In October, 1785, the supreme court awarded execution

[56] Commissioners of Washington County to Dickinson, June 28, 1784, *Pennsylvania Archives*, X, 584–585; certified copy (1875) of the official List of United Empire ("U.E. List") Loyalists in Upper Canada, Public Archives of Canada; index and abstracts of loyalist petitions, New Brunswick Provincial Archives, 1785, Nos. 81, 86, and 1786, Nos. 100, 122–124, 126, Public Archives of Canada; Henry C. Mercer, "The Doans and Their Times," *Collection of Papers Read Before the Bucks County Historical Society*, I (1908), 271–282. Robberies of collectors were numerous after 1784, but were not necessarily the work of the Doan gang. Henry Wynkoop to McKean, Mar. 16, 1786, *Pennsylvania Archives*, XII, 298–299; Wynkoop to Council, May 6, 1786, *ibid.*, XII, 302.

[57] *Respublica* v. *Aaron Doan*, 1 Dallas 86; *Colonial Records*, XIV, 388, XV, 214; George Bryan to James Irwin, Oct. 20, 1784, *Pennsylvania Archives*, X, 609; petitions of Aaron Doan, Oct. 17, 1784, Nov. 8, 1785, and memorial of seven refugees in Halifax, N. S., Dec. 30, 1785,

against a second member of the band, but the council pardoned him also.[58]

Again, in 1788, the issue of hanging a man without trial arose. In March of that year George Sinclair was apprehended. Earlier, he had been attainted of high treason, for which he could no longer be punished, but the court had also outlawed him as one of the Doan bandits, and there they had him. On argument his outlawry was set aside, but he was tried and convicted of burglary—no longer a capital offense—and was sentenced to ten years' imprisonment at hard labor.[59] In the same year, two others of the gang, Abraham and Levi Doan, were arrested, and were duly reminded in court that their lives were forfeited.

Aware that the Doans had been initially the victims of persecution and were now harmless, many citizens would have been glad to let them go, but their old enemies, the Scotch-Irish minority in Bucks, demanded that the outlawry take its course. Moreover, the two prisoners, like the exiles to Virginia and certain other loyalists, were in reality victims of intra-governmental jealousies. The assembly, dominated by Republicans, took an interest in this case and without due tact urged the council, dominated by Constitutionalists, to exercise clemency. The executive thereupon took the attitude that its constitutional monopoly of pardon was at stake, and refused to yield. After months of delay, the council voted down a renewed request of the assembly for a reprieve, and on September 24, 1788,

---

ibid., X, 348, 716–718; *Minutes of the Second Session of the Ninth General Assembly* (Philadelphia, 1785), 295–297 (Apr. 7, 1785). A year after his departure from Pennsylvania, Aaron Doan was tried in New Jersey and convicted of robbery of a tax collector; again he was sentenced to be hanged. Being reprieved, not pardoned, he evidently escaped, and subsequently he received a grant of land in Upper Canada. Minutes of Oyer and Terminer, July sessions, 1788, Essex County, N. J., and minutes of the New Jersey House of Representatives, Sept. 3, 1788, both in New Jersey State Library, Trenton; certified copy of the "U. E. List," Public Archives of Canada.

58 *Respublica* v. *Robert Johnston Steele*, 1 Dallas 92; *Colonial Records*, XIV, 558. At an unknown date Thomas Bulla, Jr., attainted of high treason and outlawed as a bandit, returned to the state; in some way he escaped the death penalty, but he was sued by a collector whom he had robbed. Loose slip, *ca.* 1800, lying between pages 231 and 232 of the Oyer and Terminer Docket for 1778–1786.

59 *Respublica* v. *St. Clair*, 2 Dallas 101, act of Oct. 4, 1788, *Statutes at Large*, XIII, 163; *Colonial Records*, XVI, 209.

373

Abraham and Levi Doan were hanged.[60] They were the last loyalists of Pennsylvania to suffer that punishment, and perhaps the only persons ever executed on outlawry in this country.

There remains for consideration the effect of attainder on the wives of traitors. Of necessity they continued within the American lines after their husbands fled. At least three marriages were abandoned because of political differences, differences in which attainder was an added factor.[61] Flight was seldom possible for an entire family, and except at the evacuation of Philadelphia, it was rare for a wife to accompany her husband. Even when it was possible, clandestine travel was risky, and New York, the usual refuge, was a crowded garrison town, expensive and unsuitable for rearing a family. Therefore, attainder brought about an increase of travel on pass from Pennsylvania through the American lines to New York. Such travel became so heavy that it aroused serious fears of betrayal in American headquarters.

On April 24, 1779, the supreme executive council took note of Washington's objections to the excessive number of recommendations for passes. Agreeing that the security of the army was at stake, the council decided that passes should be recommended only "in cases of a particular and extraordinary nature," and that the person passed must give two sureties that, lacking special permission, he or she would not return to Pennsylvania. Nevertheless, before the end of the year no less than forty-four "cases of a particular and extraordinary nature" were recognized.[62]

In June, a grand jury made the following presentment:

the wives of so many of the British emissaries remain amongst us, keeping up a most injurious correspondence with the enemies of this country, by sending all the intelligence in their power, and receiving and propagating their poisonous, erroneous and wicked falsehoods here, which pernicious practice, in our judgement, ought immediately to be inquired of and remedied.[63]

[60] *Autobiography of Charles Biddle* . . . (Philadelphia, 1883), 232–234; *Colonial Records*, XV, 497, 500–501, 515, 535, 544; case of Abraham and Levi Doan, 1788, Conviction and Clemency Papers.

[61] Loyalist Transcript, XXV, 146–162, 214–225, XLIX, 323–356.

[62] *Colonial Records*, XI, 757, and *passim*.

[63] Reed, II, 147.

But as no action was taken, frustrated Whigs presently began to lay plans for a vigilantist expulsion of the wives and children of the exiles. A mob, gathered for that purpose, became deflected into the famous siege of James Wilson's house, where many Republican leaders had gathered.[64]

Rumors of incidents of the kind so subjectively described by the grand jury are not hard to find. In December, 1779, Jane, wife of Robert White, an attainted traitor, was accused of trading with the enemy. Again, in March, 1780, Rebecca, wife of the attainted traitor Samuel Shoemaker had, it was alleged, aided prisoners and others in their escape to the British lines. It happened that Mrs. Shoemaker had earlier petitioned for a passport, which the council refused as inconsistent with the interest of the state. Stirred to new action, the council reversed its stand, and resolved to give notice to wives of traitors that they *must* apply for passes and proceed to the enemy lines before April 15 next; their failure to do so would "make it necessary to take farther measures for this purpose, as the public security shall require." It is doubtful, however, that such notice was ever published, as no passes were granted during the time allotted. Moreover, with feminine persistence, Mrs. Shoemaker applied again in May for a permit to go to New York *and return*.[65]

No definite banishment of loyalist dependents occurred until June, 1780, when a military crisis was thought imminent. Martial law was authorized by the assembly on the first of June, and was proclaimed on the ninth. On the sixth, without legal basis, solely on the ground of danger to the state, President Reed and the council gave public notice "to wives & children of those persons who have Joined the enemy" to leave the state within ten days. Any remaining after that time were to be considered entitled to no further protection, and liable to treatment as enemies of the state. Clearly, this was an executive bill of pains and penalties, an extension of the attainder act of 1778; worse than that, it punished a group for the alleged offenses of a few.

The time limit of ten days was rather poorly observed. In June and July warrants were issued to commit five wives to the workhouse until they should give security to leave Pennsylvania, not to return,

---

64 Brunhouse, 75.

65 *Colonial Records*, XII, 198–199, 203–204, 206–207, 224, 270–271, 352.

and at the end of October passes to New York had been given to twenty-four additional wives under the June 6 proclamation and other supplemental orders of banishment. Two other wives were indulged for a time because of ill health, and one, Elizabeth Graeme Ferguson, was permitted to remain in the state, in essence pardoned of her husband's offense.[66] Mrs. Ferguson's own activities, in conveying to President Reed the offer of a British bribe, had made her in the eyes of the Constitutionalists more dangerous to the American cause than any other woman, except possibly Susanna Adams and Margaret Arnold. Susanna Adams was the only woman attainted of high treason, and, of course, Margaret Shippen Arnold was the wife of Benedict Arnold.

The enumeration here presented probably falls short of complete documentation for the story of banishment; there is no way of telling how many women and children were silently indulged by sympathetic officials, or how many of them actually suffered banishment by the decisions of others.

We find, then, that the revolutionary state prosecuted offenses that it considered subversive under a variety of charges: high treason, misprision of treason (which embraced sedition), piracy, burglary, robbery, misdemeanor, counterfeiting, uttering counterfeit currency, and larceny. The procedures that the state invoked, besides infrequent connivance in vigilantist action, were prosecution on indictment, outlawry, acts of attainder, and executive proscription. The penalties imposed were fines, imprisonment, forfeiture, disherison, banishment, and death by hanging.

In general, men at the upper level of the new government—army officers, the supreme executive council, and the higher courts—dealt with the more militant loyalists. On this level, sympathy was rarely evident, but legal experience and respect for precedent helped to shape decisions. Here the treatment of aggressive loyalists, though unpredictable, was usually mild. Fortunately for most offenders, in Anglo-American law the enforcement of penalties was still controlled by the broadly merciful policy of punishment *in terrorem*. Imprison-

---

[66] *Ibid.*, XII, 377, 386–387, 390–391, 397, 425, 494, 503, 509, 518, 522; *Pennsylvania Archives, Second Series*, III, 358–360; act of Apr. 2, 1781, *Statutes at Large*, X, 281; memorial of Daniel Coxe to Clinton, June 28, 1780, memorial of Coxe, Samuel Shoemaker, and John Potts to Clinton, July 4, 1780, Coxe to John André, Aug. 27, 1780, Sir Henry Clinton Papers.

ment was impracticable, extreme penalties were barbarous and likely to invite reprisals; the tendency therefore was to find some excuse for clemency.

In some respects Pennsylvania's loyalists were better off than those of other states. For example, Pennsylvania passed fewer acts of attainder or confiscation than either New York or New Jersey. Moreover, the New York legislature proclaimed judgment of death without trial, whereas the acts of attainder passed in Pennsylvania took effect only if the accused failed to surrender. Yet in certain respects Pennsylvania was comparatively severe. Pennsylvania executed four men for treason, Connecticut but one. The wives of traitors may have fared worse in Pennsylvania, where their dower was forfeited, and where they were banished, than in Virginia or most other states. The acts of attainder passed in Massachusetts and in some other states applied only to property and rights of residence, but those of Pennsylvania applied ultimately to property and life.

Dickinson College   HENRY J. YOUNG

THOMAS WHARTON, EXILE IN VIRGINIA, 1777-1778

by James Donald Anderson*

In September 1777, upon instructions from the Second Continental Congress, the Commonwealth of Pennsylvania exiled twenty dissident men, the majority of whom were prominent Quakers, to Winchester, Virginia. The incident formed one of the gravest violations of individual rights and English common law by the patriots during the course of the War of American Independence.

One of the Friends involved was Thomas Wharton (1730/31-1784), often designated as "Senior" to differentiate him from his cousin of the same name (1735-1778) who adopted the identification "Junior." A member of a wealthy mercantile family, Wharton associated with the influential politicians and merchants of Philadelphia and its environs. A moderate, he had supported changes in the relationship of the colonies with the mother country, having proposed a commonwealth system remarkably similar to that adopted a century and a half later. He had accepted, albeit reluctantly, final independence. He enthusiastically supported charitable activities and for seventeen years participated in the affairs of the Pennsylvania Hospital. With his father and brothers, and such men as Benjamin and William Franklin, Joseph Galloway, Sir William Johnson, and George Croghan, he speculated in frontier lands as well as investing in such organizations as the Illinois, Indiana, and Grand Ohio (Vandalia) land companies. Hard-nosed but scrupulously honest in business affairs, he had made many enemies in local commercial circles, and his support of Galloway's and Franklin's efforts to rid the province of the Penns engendered hostility among political foes now gaining power.[1]

The sequence of events leading to Wharton's banishment to Virginia began with a letter from General John Sullivan to Congress. On August 25, 1777, Sullivan reported that in some baggage abandoned on Staten Island he had discovered some papers reputedly originating from the Spanktown Yearly Meeting. These documents indicated that the Quakers worshipping there collected intelligence about American forces and relayed

---

* Dr. Anderson, of Kane, Pennsylvania, a retired military officer, has taught history at the University of Akron and Virginia Polytechnic Institute and State University.

[1] The most recent study of the Whartons is James Donald Anderson, "Thomas Wharton, 1730/31-1784; Merchant in Philadelphia," unpublished Ph.D. dissertation, University of Akron, 1977. See also Anderson, "Vandalia: The First West Virginia?" *West Virginia History*, XL (Summer 1979), 375-392.

the information to the British. This letter created an immediate sensation in Congress. The delegates took little time to test the validity of Sullivan's evidence. Inquiries would have confirmed that the Spanktown Yearly Meeting did not exist, and that there were marked inconsistencies about the stated dates of troop movements.[2]

Sullivan's letter accusing the Quakers of treason arrived at a critical time, because the delegates momentarily expected a clash between Sir William Howe's advancing army and George Washington's defending forces. On August 26 Congress had ordered Delaware and Pennsylvania to insure that the "notoriously disaffected . . . be apprehended, disarmed, and secured." Specifically, Pennsylvania was to seize "fire-arms, swords, and bayonets" in the hands of those "who have not manifested their attachment to the American cause," the non-associators. By the patriots' definition, this included virtually all Quakers, whose large numbers in the state's southeastern counties made them particularly visible.[3]

John Hancock referred the letter to a three-man committee composed of John Adams, William Duer, and Richard Henry Lee. Adams and Lee had never concealed their dislike for Quakers collectively and as individuals. In October 1774, while the First Congress sat, Israel Pemberton and other Friends had confronted an indignant Adams and vigorously protested New Englanders' treatment of Quakers. Further, the lifestyle and attitude of rich Philadelphia merchants irritated Adams, who found pleasure in "humbl[ing] the pride of Jesuits, who call themselves Quakers, but love Money and Land better than Liberty or Religion." He attacked speculators such as Wharton, viewing them as "actuated by a land jobbing Spirit like that of William Penn." Lee also referred to "the universal ill fame of some capital persons" whom he dreaded would use "their mischevous interposition in favor of the enemy."[4] The committee's deliberations were short and perfunctory.

The three men presented their findings to the main body of Congress on

[2] Sullivan to John Hancock, August 25, 1777, *Papers of the Continental Congress* (microfilm edition, Washington, D.C., 1961), reel 178; Thomas Gilpin, *Exiles in Virginia* (Philadelphia, 1848), pp. 37, 61-63.

[3] *Pennsylvania Archives*, 1st series (Philadelphia, 1852-1860), V, 551-552; Wilbert H. Siebert, "The Loyalists of Pennsylvania," *The Ohio State University Bulletin*, XXIV, no. 23 (April 1, 1920), chapter III.

[4] Worthington Chauncey Ford et al., editors, *Journals of the Continental Congress, 1774-1789* (Washington, D.C., 1904-1937), VIII, 688-689 (hereafter JCC); John Adams, *Diary and Autobiography of John Adams*, edited by L. H. Butterfield (Cambridge, Mass., 1961), II, 152-153, III, 311-313; Adams to Abigail Adams, September 8, 1777, *Adams Family Correspondence*, edited by L. H. Butterfield (New York, 1965), II, 337-338; Lee to Patrick Henry, September 8, 1777, Edmund G. Burnett, editor, *Letters of Members of the Continental Congress* (Washington, D.C., 1921-1936), II, 486-487.

the evening of August 28. In addition to considering Sullivan's letter, the committee also researched some Quaker writings, particularly a publication of the Philadelphia Meeting of Sufferings dated December 20, 1776, which allegedly confirmed the Friends' disloyalty to the independence movement. Acting on the report, Congress recommended to the Supreme Executive Council of Pennsylvania that specific Friends be arrested, as well as other Quakers who "evidenced a disposition inimical to the cause of America." The designated Philadelphians included Israel, James, and John Pemberton, Abel James, Henry Drinker, Joshua Fisher and his sons Thomas and Samuel, and Thomas Wharton, Sr. Congress additionally ordered Council to commandeer all papers of a "political nature," which at that time and place could have been all-inclusive, and the records of the Philadelphia Meeting of Sufferings. Former Governor John Penn and former Chief Justice Benjamin Chew, whose presence embarrassed both Congress and the state government, were also to be apprehended and immediately moved out of the city.[5]

On Sunday, August 31, the Supreme Executive Council, Thomas Wharton, Jr., presiding, acted on Congress's resolution, which it considered a direct order. Council instructed David Rittenhouse, Colonel William Bradford, and two other officers to "seize & Secure" a total of forty-one individuals, including all those named by Congress (see table). It directed that the accused be offered a parole which included a promise not to give information to the British. If they refused, they were to be arrested and held at the Free Masons' Lodge. In an attempt to demonstrate their understanding of the social and economic positions of the potential prisoners, the councilmen noted that they "would not without necessity commit many of the persons in the Common Goal, nor even to the State Prison."[6]

On September second and third Vice-President George Bryan supervised the roundup of the accused. All contacted complied with the pronouncement except Israel Pemberton, John Hunt, and Samuel Pleasants, who refused to recognize the order's validity. The searchers found few papers of any consequence, and the arrests created unpleasant scenes at several of the prisoners' homes. John Pemberton, for example, a haughty member of his family but a devoted minister of the Meeting, repulsed the first attempt to arrest him. The angered officials then summoned a guard of ten men, and, when Pemberton declined to leave his chair, they removed him bodily from the house and took him forcibly into custody. Other men arrested Wharton, not

---

[5] JCC, VIII, 694-695.
[6] *Pennsylvania Colonial Records* (Philadelphia, 1852-1860), XI, 283-284.

PERSONS ORDERED ARRESTED AUGUST 31, 1777

Thomas Afflick (X) (Y)
Elijah Brown (Y)
Phineas Bond, M.D. (X) (paroled)
Rev. Thomas Coombe (X) (paroled)
Henry Drinker (X) (Y)
Charles Eddy (Y)
Caleb Emlen (X) (discharged)
Samuel Emlen, Jr. (X) (Z)
Joshua Fisher (X) (Z)
Myers (Miers) Fisher (X) (Y)
Samuel Fisher (X) (Y)
Thomas Fisher (X) (Y)
Joseph Fox
Thomas Gilpin (X) (Y)
John Hunt (X) (Y)
William Imley (paroled)
Samuel Jackson (X) (not located)
Abel James (X) (Y)
John James (not located)
Charles Jarvis (X) (Y)

Owen Jones, Jr. (X) (Y)
Adam Kuhn, M.D. (X) (took oath)
William Lenott
Thomas Ashelton Mech (X)
Samuel Murdoch (X) (paroled)
Israel Pemberton (X) (Y)
James Pemberton (X) (Y)
John Pemberton (X) (Y)
Edward Penington (X) (Y)
Thomas Pike (X) (Y)
Samuel Pleasants (X) (Y)
George Roberts (X) (Z)
Hugh Roberts (X) (Z)
Samuel Shoemaker (X) (paroled)
William Smith (Y)
William Smith, D.D. (X)
William Drewett Smith (Y)
Alexander Stedman (to state prison)
Charles Stedman, Jr. (to state prison)
Jeremiah Warder (X) (Z)

Thomas Wharton, Sr. (X) (Y)

NOTES:
X = to be released on their own recognizance if they met requirements to remain at home, on call, and gave no information to the enemy.
Y = Exiled to Virginia.
Z = Released due to illness of self or family, for age, or for other personal reasons.

SOURCES: *Pa. Col. Records*, XI, 287-288, 296, 309; John F. Watson, *Annals of Philadelphia and Pennsylvania in the Olden Days* . . . (enlarged, revised edition by Willis F. Hazard, Philadelphia, 1909), III, 201. The formal disposition of other cases is unknown. Additional Quakers were arrested and held at the Lodge; there is no evidence explaining these other arrests or their disposition.

without some loud protests, but their search of his home revealed nothing. After he refused the proffered parole, they led him off to join the others at the Free Masons' Lodge.[7]

The men assembled at the Lodge formed a mixed group. The reasons behind Council's selections will, unfortunately, remain a mystery. The grounds surely involved some personal animosity, although the disposition of each case was treated individually and privately. A few choices, such as the Pembertons, the Fishers, and Wharton, derived from previous conflicts with the radicals. William Smith, provost of the local college, later became

[7] *Ibid.*, XI, 286, 287-289; John Pemberton, "The Life and Travels of John Pemberton, A Minister of the Gospel of Christ," *The Friends Library*, VI (1842), 291.

a noted Tory. Other choices are less obvious, as in the cases of fencing master Thomas Pike, joiner Thomas Afflick, hatter Charles Jarvis, and druggist or doctor William Drewett Smith. Council even approved at least one substitution, Owen Jones, Jr., for his more famous father. Of those exiled, all were Quakers except Pike and W. D. Smith.[8]

One can only hazard a guess as to the rationale behind Wharton's arrest, but several possibilities emerge with a recounting of his relationship with the new politicians controlling Pennsylvania. Although he had protested against the Stamp Act, he had refused to sign the nonintercourse agreements against the Townshend Acts. He had gained many enemies as a result of his commission as a tea agent and by his continued support of the East India Company despite his cooperation with the local committee in 1773. He openly opposed a break with Britain over the Coercive Acts. He recoiled from the colonies' resorting to arms, and only hesitantly accepted independence. His relative standing in the leadership of the Quakers, his compliance with the Meeting's policy of noninvolvement, and his known association with the now discredited Joseph Galloway contributed to his opponents' suspicion. Finally, his pressing for congressional approval of the new colony of Vandalia and removal of Connecticut settlers from the Wyoming Valley alienated many delegates, particularly those from New England. Combining all these actions, one can see that Wharton had become vulnerable to some sort of repression even though, from virtually any viewpoint, the proceedings against him were drastic.[9]

The step taken by Council puzzled outsiders as well as those affected. James Allen, a member of one of Pennsylvania's most illustrious families, commented that the government "seems determined to make this country intolerable to all who are not actually its friends." He joined the prisoners in wondering why "the most discreet, passive, & respectable characters are dragged forth . . . tho' no charge can be made." He further noted, striking at the heart of the matter, "Men's former characters for integrity & virtue instead of availing them only expose them as it is supposed their influence must be greater."[10]

---

[8] Siebert, "Loyalists," *Ohio State University Bulletin*, XXIV, no. 23, 36; Robert F. Oaks, "Philadelphians in Exile: The Problem of Loyalty During the American Revolution," *Pennsylvania Magazine of History and Biography* (hereafter *PMHB*), XCVI (1972), 304; Robert Proud to William Proud, Anno 10, 1778, *ibid.*, XXIX (1905), 230; Alexander Graydon, *Memoirs of a Life Chiefly Passed in Pennsylvania Within the Last Sixty Years* (Harrisburg, 1811), p. 304; A. M. Stackhouse, *Col. Timothy Matlack, Patriot and Soldier* (n.p., 1910), p. 22.

[9] See Anderson, "Thomas Wharton," chapter V.

[10] "Diary of James Allen, Esq., of Philadelphia, Counsellor-at-Law, 1770-1778," *PMHB*, IX (1885), 288 (entry for September 5, 1777).

Confusion reigned at the Lodge on September 2. The guards at first refused admission to the many visitors who flocked to see the prisoners, but by nightfall some relatives managed to get inside. The question of visitors remained unsettled the next day when one sentinel threatened to shoot a man who talked to the Friends through a window. Both Philadelphia Town Major Lewis Nicola and Bradford created additional turmoil by denying any responsibility either for the inmates or the guards. A city magistrate, Benjamin Paschall, attempted to obtain information about the arrests in order to secure a judicial hearing for the internees, but he learned from Bryan that no official investigation would be forthcoming. The captives protested such "a stretch of arbitrary power," and Paschall vowed "to avert a blow so fatal to the liberties of Pennsylvania." [11] His efforts, however, failed to win support from his fellow justices and officials in the executive department.

On the third, officers apprehended and then delivered Hunt, Pleasants, and Israel Pemberton to the Lodge. Their arrival triggered numerous protests, which lasted until the exiles returned from Winchester. They remonstrated to the president and Council of their state and to Congress. They also appealed for public support. With some difficulty, they located a printer who courageously reproduced their "addresses" and distributed the broadsides widely through the area. Emphasizing the righteousness of their cause and their characters, they demanded their release if not presented with valid accusations. They stood on solid ground legally because the recently adopted state constitution specifically forbade arrests, searches, and seizures of private property without duly sworn warrants.[12]

Council in the meantime had decided the prisoners' fate. The members even at this early stage anticipated some embarrassment resulting from their impulsive actions and wanted to get the prisoners out of the sight and hearing of the populace. Bryan asked Congress's advice on their disposition, suggesting that either Augusta County or Winchester, Virginia, might be "suitable places ... to secure these persons." On the third, Congress agreed that Staunton would be a "most proper place ... for their residence and se-

---

[11] "Journal and Transactions of the Exiles" (hereafter "Exiles' Journal"), 9th Month (September) 2, 3, 1777, in Gilpin, *Exiles*, pp. 67-69. Quaker month designations will hereafter be converted to regular usage.

[12] *Ibid.*, pp. 92-95; Prisoners in the Free Masons' Lodge, "To the President and Council of Pennsylvania," broadsides (Philadelphia, September 4, 5, 1777); Declaration of Pennsylvanians' Rights, Sections IX, X, Constitution of 1776, in Theodore Thayer, *Pennsylvania Politics and the Growth of Democracy, 1740-1776* (Harrisburg, 1953), appendix II.

curity," though some delegates wondered if the proof of their alleged treason sufficed to justify the decision.[13]

News that they were to be sent to the Virginia frontier further distressed the prisoners. Their compatriots appointed Wharton and five others a committee to survey their situation and draft additional protestations. They prepared a message to Congress which John Reynell and Owen Jones, leaders of the sympathetic group still at liberty, delivered. Since the state Council had rejected their demand for a fair hearing, they now appealed to Congress, for that body had originated their difficulties. The prisoners reiterated their innocence and true affection for America, pleading for an opportunity to defend their pacifistic reactions to the war. Imprisonment, though, had little affected their characters; their use of such adjectives as "arbitrary, unjust, and cruel" to describe their harassers harmed rather than helped their cause.[14] The congressional delegates by this time had graver problems on their hands and refused to give the prisoners' request any consideration.

Congress's approval of Council's recommendation sent officialdom into motion. The latter instructed Bradford to arrange transportation to move selected prisoners to Staunton beginning September 6. It cautioned him, however, to treat them in a "manner...consistent with their respective characters and the Security of their persons."[15] The security involved not only prevention of escape but also protection of the prisoners from bodily harm by overly zealous patriots. The tone of these instructions reveals Council's continuing need for good public relations and uncertainty about its position on the prisoners. The next day's Council action reinforced this hesitation; the members modified the standard oath of allegiance to the state and offered it to the prisoners:

I .... do swear (or affirm) that I will be faithful and bear true allegiance to the Commonwealth of Pennsylvania as a free and independent state.

Acceptance of the oath became the sole criteria for discharge from imprisonment. The officials hoped that the prisoners would take the oath and be promptly and quietly released. The problem would then disappear. Congress, also desiring to resolve a developing dilemma, concurred with Council's decision. Henry Laurens of South Carolina, possibly recalling previous contacts

---

[13] *Pa. Archives*, 1st ser., V, 574; JCC, VIII, 707-708; New Hampshire delegates to the President of New Hampshire, September 2, 1777, Burnett, *Letters*, II, 471.

[14] "Exiles' Journal," Gilpin, *Exiles*, pp. 77, 82; Prisoners in the Free Masons' Lodge, "To the Congress," broadside (Philadelphia, September 4, 1777).

[15] Supreme Executive Council to Colonel William Bradford, September 4, 1777, RG 27, Secretary to the Supreme Executive Council, Pennsylvania State Archives; *Pa. Archives*, 1st ser., V, 582; *Pa. Col. Records*, XI, 290.

with Wharton and his brothers, considered the whole affair "silly" and predicted "that Congress and council will eventually make rediculous figures." [16] One complication existed; the persistent prisoners refused to take the easy and safe step of cooperation. Probably they believed that if Council had willingly lowered their requirements now, it could in the future erase all conditions for release. Regardless, the prisoners would accept only a complete and unqualified discharge, for they maintained that they had committed no crimes.

Complications delayed the prisoners' departure from the city; for one thing, state officials could not locate sufficient wagons. The prisoners continued to remonstrate for their liberty, and, by so doing, violated their sect's instructions to be resigned to their fate. They ascertained that their presence had become a political football to be kicked from Council to Congress and back. They had hoped to play one legislature against the other, but the tactic had turned to their disadvantage. Both bodies agreed that the solution rested on the prisoners' acceptance of the oath. On the sixth Council recommended that Congress decide the matter since the Pennsylvanians did not have "time to attend to this business." Congress replied that Council was in the best position to act in the manner "most conducive to the public safety." Moreover, some delegates retained their dislike and distrust of the prisoners. James Lowell took pride in Congress's "due Vigor" in ordering the Quakers' arrests, stating that "Israel and the Tribe" had armed themselves against the Paxton boys, and now the "wretches" hypocritically hid behind a constiution they refused to support.[17]

On Sunday, September 7, the prisoners rested and remained calm. They received no visitors, "wishing to have the day more particularly to themselves in stillness." They built moral courage for the ordeal they now knew lay ahead. On Monday Congress abandoned any responsibility for the prisoners and urged that they be immediately sent to Virginia. Council concurred and issued orders for the departure.[18] The internees did not receive

---

[16] Supreme Executive Council to Bradford, September 5, 1777, RG 27, Pennsylvania State Archives; Supreme Executive Council Minutes, September 5, 1777, *Pa. Col. Records*, XI, 291-292; Laurens to John Lewis Gervais, September 5, 1777, Burnett, *Letters*, II, 476-477.

[17] Isaac Melcher to T. Wharton, Jr., September 5, 1777, and Supreme Executive Council to Congress, September 6, 1777, *Pa. Archives*, 1st ser., V, 584, 593; Supreme Executive Council Minutes, September 6, 1777, *Pa. Col. Records*, XI, 293; JCC, VIII, 718-719; Lovell to Joseph Trumbull, September 7, 1777, Burnett, *Letters*, II, 484-485.

[18] Henry D. Biddle, editor, *Extracts from the Journal of Elizabeth Drinker from 1759-1807, A.D.* (Philadelphia, 1889), p. 46 (entry for September 7, 1777); Supreme Executive Council Minutes, September 9, 1777, *Pa. Col. Records*, XI, 295-296. Dr. Phineas Bond, Reverend Thomas Coombe, and William Imlay were included in the order but were not exiled. Bond was incensed that he was not permitted to go.

the news from Bradford quietly; they issued another remonstrance to Council. Moreover, they assembled all their appeals into a pamphlet which, upon its issuance by Robert Bell, received mixed notices. Richard Henry Lee declared the addresses "indecent"; James Allen described them as "spirited" and noted that "many of the warmest Whigs think this an instance of unjustifiable oppression." [19] Later a London printer reissued the document as a demonstration of the discrepancies between what the American patriots said and their actual deeds.

Once the decision became irrevocable, practical measures consumed the prisoners' time. On the tenth they requested from Nicola and the Council information concerning their mode and means of travel, the amount of baggage they could take, the means of payment of expenses, and permission to maintain communications with their families. Nicola could answer only a small portion of their questions because he was as ignorant of future conditions as were the prisoners. There would be sufficient wagons and carriages to carry them "in such a manner as not to be crowded," but baggage space would be limited. Council allocated £100 (Pennsylvania currency) for the prisoners' and escorts' expenses to Reading and instructed Nicola to turn the prisoners over to Jacob Morgan, lieutenant of Berks County, who would then supervise their journey to Virginia. [20]

That same day the officials permitted Wharton and most of the prisoners to visit their families, obtain clothing and other necessities, and settle their affairs. Adding to the sadness of the occasion, another old friend deserted Wharton; Benjamin Towne refused to print the prisoners' remonstrance but did agree to publish Congress's versions of their pleas. Perhaps William Goddard had been correct in his negative evaluation of Towne's character, especially considering that Wharton's old competitor Bradford promised to publish the protest in the next edition of the *Pennsylvania Journal.* Nine of the prisoners applied to judges Thomas McKean and John Evans for writs of *habeas corpus,* but, judging from his past actions, Wharton unaccountably did not join them. [21] These appeals, however, could not delay the outcome.

---

[19] *Pa. Archives,* 1st ser., VI, 509-510; [Israel Pemberton] *An Address to the Inhabitants of Pennsylvania*... (Philadelphia, 1777); Lee to Patrick Henry, September 8, 1777, Burnett, *Letters,* II, 487; "Diary of James Allen," *PMHB,* IX, 293 (entry for October 1, 1777).

[20] Prisoners in Masonic Lodge to Nicola, September 10, 1777, and Supreme Executive Council to Nicola, same date, RG 27, Pennsylvania State Archives. Only two wagons were alloted for 20 men's baggage (Nicola to Timothy Matlack, September 11, 1777, *ibid.*).

[21] "Exiles' Journal," September 10, 11, 1777, Gilpin, *Exiles,* pp. 130-131. Towne had been associated with Wharton and Goddard in publishing *The Pennsylvania Chronicle* (see Anderson, "Thomas Wharton," chapter VI).

By the eleventh the prisoners' removal from Philadelphia could no longer be postponed. Not that the internees did not try. A tempestuous scene greeted their escorts upon their arrival at the Lodge. A group of the prisoners and some sympathetic Friends angrily met them with a demand that they show their authority in writing. The escorts refused. Thereupon the prisoners presented a final ultimatum for their release. Describing their punishment as "illegal [,] unjust [,] arbritary [,] and contrary to the Rights of Mankind," they declined to budge from the Lodge.[22] Their jailers ignored this demand; they forcibly drove the Quakers out of the building and into the waiting wagons. An eyewitness described the action as they dragged Wharton out:

> One impudent Jack in an officer insulted our neighbor Wharton as they were forcing him into the wagon and called him a D——d Tory, but he was soon intimidated by Murdoc Taylor (tho' only one of the gazers) whose compassion was so raised that he flew at the miscreant and swore he would thrust his hands down his throat and pull out his heart if he dared abuse a Prisoner.[23]

The large crowd watching this event became much distressed; reportedly, some of the male witnesses openly wept. Others, including some blacks, reached up and grasped John Pemberton's hand as the wagons moved out.[24] It was a deeply emotional, unpleasant occasion for all concerned.

Not until five o'clock in the afternoon did matters calm sufficiently for the small convoy of wagons and carriages, guarded by two cavalrymen of the city's Light Horse Troop, to leave. The prisoners, still not formally charged, passed by large numbers of silent citizens who lined the streets to the outskirts of the city. Moving past the falls on the Schuylkill, the party plodded on until darkness, reaching Palmer's Tavern. After resting overnight in some neighboring houses, they departed in the morning and traveled to Pottsgrove, following a circuitous route to avoid the advancing British army. There the Potts family refused to permit further travel and extended their hospitality to the exiles. Already the lack of baggage space (and prior planning) hurt; several of the Quakers could not change their linen and the escorts agreed to linger until additional baggage arrived from Philadelphia.[25]

---

[22] *PMHB*, XV (1891), 122.

[23] "Excitement in Philadelphia on Hearing of the Defeat at Brandywine," *ibid.*, XIV (1890), 66.

[24] *Ibid.*, p. 65; "Life of John Pemberton," *Friends Library*, VI, 292.

[25] "Exiles' Journal," September 11-13, 1777, Gilpin, *Exiles*, pp. 133-135; William Duane, editor, *Extracts from the Diary of Christopher Marshall* ... (Albany, 1877), p. 127 (entry for September 15, 1777). The baggage finally was delivered at Reading.

Writs of *habeas corpus* approved by Judge McKean arrived at Pottsgrove by messenger on the fourteenth and were served on the escorts, who refused to honor them. Having witnessed the success of the first legal efforts, Wharton and the other ten exiles now applied for release from custody. No additional actions were possible, however, before militiamen from Berks County arrived and drove them back onto the road. A five-hour journey took them to Reading, where a hostile audience greeted them with rocks and jeers. John Pemberton observed, "The people's spirits [were] greatly enraged and many appeared to be in a wicked disposition." The local citizenry protested the presence of another group of unsavory prisoners to overtax their limited facilities. Both state and Continental governments used the town as a convenient place to locate English, Hessian, and Tory prisoners of war and continued to do so, over strong objections from the local council of safety, for the remainder of the war. Deeply concerned, the exiles settled down behind the staunch walls of Widow Eve Withington's tavern, grateful for the safety of a close guard but unhappy to be forbidden visitors at first.[26]

The prisoners remained at Reading for five days, one reason being John Pemberton's illness. Alexander Graydon, a paroled Philadelphian who had been captured by the British on Manhattan, found them generally contented. Wharton received some good news on the evening of the fifteenth: Judge McKean had approved his application and those of the others for release on the writs of *habeas corpus*. His joy, however, was short-lived.[27]

Upon hearing of the writs, the Supreme Executive Council acted immediately to prevent the prisoners' release. Ignoring McKean's instructions, Council commanded the escorts to implement their orders and have the Quakers taken to Virginia. That Thomas Wharton, Jr., presided at this meeting must have divided the family even further. Moreover, on the sixteenth, the Assembly had passed a law aimed specifically at repressing the exiles' civil rights. The act legalized the arrests earlier in the month on a basis of an "imminent danger to the state" created by the British invasion. It suspended the issuance of writs of *habeas corpus* for all individuals arrested as "suspected persons" by Council until the next regular session of the legislature. This clearly established an *ex post facto* law which, while not expressly forbidden by the constitution, did, as James Allen noted, "trample

---

[26] "Exiles' Journal," September 14, 1777, Gilpin, *Exiles*, pp. 135-136; Duane, *Diary of Christopher Marshall*, p. 127 (entry for September 15, 1777); "Life of John Pemberton," *Friends Library*, VI, 292; Morton L. Montgomery, *History of Berks County, Pennsylvania, in the Revolution, from 1774-1783* (Reading, 1894), pp. 151-167, esp. pp. 153-154.

[27] Graydon, *Memoirs*, pp. 269-270; "Exiles' Journal," September 15, 1777, Gilpin, *Exiles*, pp. 136-137.

389

on the ... laws ... of natural Justice & humanity" and was "the very extreme of Tyranny." The exiles concurred with his opinion that "the civil war has rendered the minds of our Governors desperate & savage."[28]

On the eighteenth, finally resigned but still defiant, the exiles participated in a ceremony formally placing them in the custody of Jacob Morgan. They requested additional wagons from Morgan, but he did not respond. Their destination had now been changed from Staunton to Winchester. Despite John Pemberton's persistent sickness, plus continued confusion between the prisoners and their custodians, on the twentieth they were loaded into their wagons and moved on to Lebanon, arriving just after five o'clock to a "Civil Reception." The next day they traveled on, stopping for lunch at Hummel. This gave them an opportunity to view and explore a limestone cave on Swartara Creek. After being impressed by nature's wonders, they pressed onward to John Harris's ferry. The lodging there depressed them, as James Pemberton commented, "for want of good housekeeping."[29]

Thus, they did not mind leaving Harris behind the next morning. They paddled across the Susquehanna River in relays using "two little tottering canoes," apprehensively watching their baggage and carriages being floated over the water. They also disliked the ride to Carlisle, which Wharton described as "disagreeable." Some mounted militia met them on the way, a few of whom hurled such insults as "Tories [and] other indiscreate tokens of prejudice" at the Quakers. They stayed that night and two more days in "pretty good quarters." Wharton met "Many Tradesmen" with whom he was acquainted, but one encounter particularly touched him. He talked through a cell's bars to Dr. John Kearsley, who had been deported from Philadelphia for his anti-patriot activities. Loneliness was catching up with him; he missed his "poor Children" and longed for his wife. His trust in God and in an "easy" conscience, however, consoled him. The "great Civility" with which the people of Carlisle treated the prisoners relieved his ap-

---

[28] Supreme Executive Council Minutes, September 16, 1777, *Pa. Col. Records*, XI, 308-309; "An Act to empower the Supreme Executive Council ..." from *Pennsylvania Evening Post*, September 18, 1777, in "Exiles' Journal," Gilpin, *Exiles*, pp. 137-139; *Laws of the Commonwealth of Pennsylvania*, I (Philadelphia, 1810), xlv, 137; "Diary of James Allen," *PMHB*, IX, 293 (entry for October 1, 1777). For McKean's negative reaction, see "Diary of Robert Morton," *PMHB*, I (1877), 6 (entry for September 22, 1777).

[29] T. Wharton to Rachel Wharton, September 20, 1777, Wharton-Willing Collection (hereafter WWC), Historical Society of Pennsylvania (hereafter HSP); "Life of John Pemberton," *Friends Library*, VI, 292; "Exiles' Journal," September 20-23, 1777, Gilpin, *Exiles*, pp. 143-144; James Pemberton Diary, 1777-1778, HSP, entries for September 21-23, 1777. Quotations from the Society's manuscript collections are used with the permission of the Historical Society of Pennsylvania.

prehensions, since insults, as James Pemberton noted, were "indeed fewer than could be expected considering how we have been misrepresented." [30] Handbills degrading Quakers in general and the prisoners in particular had been circulated, reputedly by Bradford and his cohorts, along the route traveled by the exiles.

After two days' rest and the adjustment of their baggage, the group leisurely rolled southward to Shippensburg on the twenty-sixth and on to a tavern near Chambersburg the next day. Lack of available space forced Wharton, Hunt, and two Fishers to continue three or four miles further down the road. They began having trouble locating food in the countryside, finding several taverns with bare larders. They also handed out copies of the broadsides printed before they left Philadelphia in an attempt to justify their position. John and Israel Pemberton and a few other stalwarts held a meeting and then spoke "for this once highly favoured land" to a crowd near their lodgings, but the latter step did not sit well with some of their companions. James, the most politically minded of the Pemberton trio, noted, "Most of us thought [it] unnecessary." [31]

On Monday, the twenty-eighth, they left Pennsylvania, traversed a narrow strip of Maryland, and crossed into Virginia at Watkin's Ferry. Wharton and some others preceded and waited on the south bank for the main body. This was their last day on the road; they reached Winchester about six o'clock that evening. At Philip Bush's inn they met John Smith, lieutenant of Frederick County, who accepted their custody from the sheriff of Berks County; this act severed their connection with their home state. Although each side eyed the other with suspicion and uncertainty, Smith attempted to put the prisoners at ease by authorizing a walk around the town and permitting them to explain their situation. Wharton stayed at Bush's, but others had to find shelter elsewhere. [32]

The exiles' presence complicated life for Smith, and the next two days' events did not ease his concern. He knew how to handle the Hessian prisoners of war who arrived from Lebanon on the thirtieth; their status was clear-cut. On the contrary, the disposition of and the method of treating the Quakers "confused" him. Pennsylvania's orders were imprecise.

---

[30] T. Wharton to Rachel Wharton, September 24, 1777, WWC, HSP; James Pemberton Diary, HSP, entry for September 23, 1777; Edward Penington to Benjamin Lightfoot, September 24, 1777, Penington Section, Gardner Collection, HSP.

[31] James Pemberton Diary, HSP, entries for September 26-28, 1777; "Life of John Pemberton," *Friends Library*, VI, 293; "Exiles' Journal," September 27, 1777, Gilpin, *Exiles*, p. 155.

[32] "Life of John Pemberton," *Friends Library*, VI, 293; "Exiles' Journal," September 30, 1777, Gilpin, *Exiles*, p. 157.

He did not come under that state's jurisdiction, but he promised the Philadelphians he would obtain instructions from his own government. The immediate hatred manifested by the local townsfolk did not simplify his task. "About noon some terbulent persons" assembled outside the inn, screaming "very peremptorily" that the prisoners be run out of town, violently if necessary. Smith, fearing for the exiles' safety, prohibited them from leaving the inn and placed armed guards to seal all its exits. This compelled all the Quakers to crowd into the tavern; some had to furnish their own bedding. This swift action, however, "moderated" the gathering and, after a time, quiet returned.[33]

Smith asked Virginia Governor Patrick Henry for guidance. Henry had known Wharton and several other prisoners while a delegate to the First Continental Congress, but he had recent information from Richard Henry Lee. Before the exiles' departure, Lee had warned the governor that the Quakers intended "to make disturbance and raise discontent" in Virginia, recommending that they be "well secured there, for they are a mischievous people." Wharton, with his companions' approval, wrote to Henry to take advantage of "our former Acquaintance." He reviewed the circumstances and events which took the prisoners to Winchester, and asked Henry for a legal hearing, reasonable liberty of movement, and the "comfortable subsistence" promised by Pennsylvania authorities. He also contacted some Virginia Friends, requesting that they visit Williamsburg and support the exiles. After carefully reviewing the situation, Henry and the Virginia Council instructed Smith "to continue Protection" of the prisoners, "to exert himself to afford humane Treatment," and to allow liberty and exercise "for the benefit of their health." In addition, they told Smith to caution the people that renewal of their threats against the Quakers would be "highly Derogotory & Dishonourable" to their state.[34] Overall, Virginia's executives had acted as fairly as possible as conditions merited, and their orders generally satisfied the Quakers.

The Pennsylvanians, in the meantime, remained confined to Bush's inn and its courtyard. Smith, however, gradually relaxed his requirements

---

[33] "Life of John Pemberton," *Friends Library*, VI, 293; "Exiles' Journal," September 30, 1777, Gilpin, *Exiles*, pp. 159-160; James Pemberton Diary, HSP, entry for September 30, 1777. The Hessians had been captured at Trenton.

[34] Lee to Henry, September 8, 1777, Burnett, *Letters*, II, 487; T. Wharton to Rachel Wharton, October 6. 1777, WWC, HSP; T. Wharton and Samuel Pleasants to Governor and Council of Virginia, October 2, 1777, "Exiles' Journal," Gilpin, *Exiles*, pp. 167-171; T. Wharton, Israel and John Pemberton to Robert Pleasants and Edward Stabler, October 3, 1777, *Bulletin of the Friends' Historical Society*, II (1908), 25-26; H. R. McIlwaine, editor, *Journals of the Council of the State of Virginia*, II (Richmond, 1932), 9.

as the local populace accepted the exiles' presence. On October 11 he permitted Wharton, Penington, and Gilpin, accompanied by a guard, to walk about three miles in the countryside, an event which "proved refreshing and much to our satisfaction."[35] Religious meetings held daily at the inn helped convince the Virginians of the Quakers' sincerity. Although curiosity attracted the people, including Smith and some guards, once that was satisfied, spiritual sympathy brought all together. Others journeyed to Winchester to converse with these sophisticated visitors. Lord Fairfax discussed agriculture with Wharton for several hours on November 4, and both found the experience "agreeable." About October 12 the guards vanished, but they later reappeared at intervals. William Drewett Smith made an even more favorable impression among the populace when he obtained permission to move about the vicinity and render medical services.[36]

The exiles were not completely self-centered. Their thoughts often dwelled on their families. Loneliness particularly affected men like Wharton, whose previous travel experience had been limited to the immediate area of Philadelphia. He wondered about such domestic matters as sufficient firewood for the winter, the cutting of a tree in the meadow, and the obtaining of adequate food, especially after September 26, when the British occupied the city.[37] Officially, correspondence to and from the exiles and their families passed through the hands of Timothy Matlack, secretary to the Supreme Executive Council. Since the letters were subject to censorship by the Council and by the British, the writers carefully avoided controversy, particularly political matters.[38] An amazing number of travelers carried private letters and oral communications to Winchester and back to Philadelphia. By this means the exiles kept informed of events elsewhere even though politics remained a forbidden subject of conversation with local citizens.

Wharton had given supervision of his business affairs—what he had left considering the effects of the war—and his property to his brother Isaac who, with brother William's assistance, also watched over Rachel and the children. Care of the warehouses along the Delaware and rental houses

---

[35] T. Wharton, Israel and John Pemberton to Pleasants and Stabler, October 3, 1777, *Bulletin of the Friends' Historical Society*, II, 25; T. Wharton to Rachel Wharton, October 12, 1777, WWC, HSP.

[36] "Life of John Pemberton," *Friends Library*, VI, 293-294; T. Wharton to Rachel Wharton, October 6, November 6, 1777, WWC, HSP; "Exiles' Journal," October 13, 1777, Gilpin, *Exiles*, p. 174.

[37] For example, T. Wharton to Rachel Wharton, October 6, December 14, 1777, WWC, HSP.

[38] See notation on T. Wharton to Rachel Wharton, January 20, 1778, *ibid.*; "Examined and Sealed. W. Smallwood," notation on Isaac Wharton to T. Wharton, March 6, 1778, *ibid.*

occupied Isaac's time. He confessed, however, in February 1778, "I continue in the same inactive Condition as when thou was forced from Us."[39] Wharton could not separate himself from his lifetime occupation, but he did not discover the true, deplorable condition of his business until he returned home. Whether by necessity or by choice, Isaac in his letters touched only lightly on commercial circumstances, limiting his discussions to family news, especially emphasizing the state of everyone's health.

The crowded conditions at Bush's inn bothered the exiles. As security was relaxed, many hunted for new places to live. Wharton also considered Bush's demands for "four & Five Thousand pounds [per] year for only a part of our Support" outrageous. Costs mattered to each of the prisoners since they paid all expenses out-of-pocket; neither Pennsylvania nor Virginia contributed to their upkeep. Wharton, though, appeared to have surplus funds to loan to a needy Hessian officer and to buy a pair of black horses, although this latter extravagance almost broke him. Ever the businessman, he asked Robert Pleasants to invest "at interest" or in real estate some money the Annapolis merchant Richard Sprigg promised him. With John Hunt, he located a room at the home of Widow Elizabeth Jolliffe six miles north of town, but miserable weather, a condition which plagued them throughout their stay, prevented their moving until the end of November.[40] Others also found suitable quarters in the vicinity.

Cold, rain, and snow characterized the autumn and winter the Friends endured at Winchester. "Snow about a foot deep and continuous falling" and "dull morning with rain & hail" are typical entries in James Pemberton's diary. The almost constant cold and dampness affected the health of all, and Wharton suffered a continual battle with his gout. The affliction struck within a week of his arrival and remained with him until his return to Philadelphia. At times a doctor bled him, but that did little to relieve the pain in his head. He asked Rachel to send tea, chocolate, and other scarce items to supplement his diet, and the arrival of a pair of "Flannel Drawers" particularly pleased him.[41]

[39] Isaac Wharton to T. Wharton, December 19, 1777, February 2, 1778, *ibid.*

[40] T. Wharton to Rachel Wharton, November 6, December 14, 1777; Wharton to Robert Pleasants & Co., February 2, 1778; Richard Sprigg to T. Wharton, February 12, 1778, all *ibid.*; Lieutenant De Terry to David Franks, November 14, 1777, *PMHB*, XXIV (1900), 373; map of Winchester in Oaks, "Philadelphians in Exile," *ibid.*, XCVI, 319-320. The stay at Bush's cost him £11.14.0, Virginia currency (receipt, Bush to T. Wharton, November 26, 1777, Correspondence, Wharton Papers [hereafter WP], HSP). There may have been a connection between the Jolliffes, Owen Jones, and Wharton since her husband had advertised in the early issues of *The Pennsylvania Chronicle* (see edition of November 23, 1767, in which Jolliffe advertised a tavern and surrounding grounds in Winchester for sale).

[41] T. Wharton to Rachel Wharton, October 12, December 28, 1777, January 20, 28, 1778, WWC, HSP; James Pemberton Diary, HSP, entries for November 29, 1777, January 17, 1778.

The weather, sickness, and loneliness depressed him, and he sought moral sustenance to escape his material world. Religion had always influenced his life, but now, with few other distractions, only thoughts of release to freedom competed with spirituality in his mind. His close association with John Hunt reinforced his devotion. "The more I am with Him the more I love Him," he confided to Rachel; "He is a truly Great Man." Together, he and Hunt conducted meetings at their lodgings. "Its with Inexpressibly satisfaction I can say," he told his wife, "that My Mind enjoy[s] a tranquility superiour to that, I was before to witness." Hunt's death on March 31, 1778, from complications arising from the amputation of his left leg, greatly saddened him. Hunt had gone "from works to rewards," Wharton later noted, praising the minister's preaching "as his lamp was burning out." He blamed Hunt's demise on the officials who condoned their "unjustly suffering" such "banishment." [42]

Relations among and between the exiles generally stayed cordial throughout the period, but, understandably, some personality conflicts created friction and misunderstandings. Dissension split the consensus when two of the prisoners escaped and returned to Philadelphia. On December 8, without a word to the others, William Drewett Smith took what appeared to be a routine ride; he did not return. His action shocked Wharton not only because Smith had violated the exiles' agreement to confide all moves to each other, but that he thus willed "repurcussions" on those left behind. "Indeed," Wharton informed Owen Jones, "it may subject us to many Difficulties." He judged correctly; the authorities took immediate steps to secure the exiles. Two months later, on February 16, Thomas Pike quietly slipped away. Now more resigned, the exiles philosophically accepted his departure even though both he and Smith were not Quakers. James Pemberton thought Pike had acted "dishonourably, ... but we considered him not to be under the same restraint of principle as we did." Wharton particularly regretted Pike's leaving; he had loaned him £4.10.0 in November. [43]

Reaction to Smith's defection meshed with the almost simultaneous accusation that Owen Jones, Jr., had speculated in the conversion of gold to Con-

---

[42] T. Wharton to Rachel Wharton, October 6, 12, 1777, WWC, HSP; Wharton to James Corbyn and James Talwin, May 11, 1778, T. Wharton Letterbook, 1773-1784, WP, HSP; James Pemberton Diary, HSP, entries for November 6, 1777, April 1, 1778.

[43] T. Wharton to Owen Jones, December 10, 1777, and to Rachel Wharton, December 14, 1777, WWC, HSP; Henry Drinker to Elizabeth Drinker, December 3, 1777, *PMHB*, XV (1891), 235-236; James Pemberton Diary, HSP, entries for February 16, 17, 1778; indebiture, Pike to T. Wharton, November 5, 1777, Correspondence, WP, HSP. Smith had been exiled even after he had signed the required oath. Pike apparently fled onward to New York.

tinental currency to the debasement of the bills. Acting on information in intercepted letters, the Continental Board of War ordered Jones to be placed under close custody and that all the exiles be moved to Staunton, a more isolated frontier town than Winchester. All were denied writing materials except in the presence of the county lieutenant until they affirmed that they would not act "against the Independency of the United States of America." This restriction upset the prisoners, who immediately composed appeals to Congress and to the Supreme Executive Council and dispatched them with Alexander White, a local attorney who promised to plead their case before each body at York and Lancaster respectively.[44]

The petitioners argued that the decisions were as unjust as the orders which had sent them to Virginia. They stated that they had corresponded solely about personal affairs with their families and friends. Further, County Lieutenant Smith had disdained to censor their messages. They had used only the already discounted Continental currency to deal with local tradesmen, employing gold in but one transaction. Regardless, as a wartime measure, the British had smuggled specie into the interior to undermine the Americans' paper money. As to Staunton, winter weather and horrible road conditions made the trip virtually impossible. In addition, the health and age of several of the exiles made such a venture hazardous, particularly since the facilities available there were unknown. Congress postponed any decision on the matter on January 5. The Supreme Executive Council, to the contrary, placed the affair entirely in the delegates' hands because the state now considered the exiles to be "Prisoners of the United States," and therefore thought it not "pertinent or proper" to decide their disposition. Council did suggest, however, that Congress could either restrain or release the Quakers. The exiles had found an unexpected ally in Timothy Matlack, who supported Jones and the other prisoners' position in Council.[45] Ultimately, Winchester remained the exiles' domicile, but it is difficult to determine if this resulted from decision or apathy on the authorities' part. The delay,

---

[44] Resolution, Board of War, December 8, 1777, *Pa. Archives*, 1st ser., VI, 74-75; Duane, *Diary of Christopher Marshall*, p. 149 (entry for December 11, 1777); T. Wharton to Rachel Wharton, December 28, 1777, WWC, HSP. The extent of Jones's involvement may never be known, but some speculation did occur (see Theodore Thayer, *Israel Pemberton, King of the Quakers* [Philadelphia, 1943], pp. 226-227).

[45] To the Congress and Executive Council of Pennsylvania, December 19, 1777, *Papers of the Continental Congress*, reel 51; Meirs Fisher to Alexander White, December 20, 1777, "Exiles' Journal," Gilpin, *Exiles*, pp. 194-196; JCC, X, 8; *Pa. Col. Records*, XI, 395; Council to Congress, January 5, 1778, RG 27, Pennsylvania State Archives; Timothy Matlack to Owen Jones, Jr., January 5, 1778, *Pennsylvania Archives*, 2nd series (Harrisburg, 1874-1890), III, 160.

moreover, exerted heavy emotional pressure on the prisoners and their families.[46]

Wharton took advantage of this opportunity to write to Thomas Wharton, Jr., his first contact with his cousin since the incident began the previous August. He described the hardships endured by the prisoners and asked that they not be sent to Staunton. Despite basing his appeals on kinship, he could not restrain his rage; subtlety was not a part of his nature. "Thou gave thy consent to this Unheard of Cruelty, without so much of a single Proof being taken to justify the same," he ranted. "I beg thee Seriously to consider, that, it was by virtue of your Warrant We were seized and made Prisoners, and therefore all the Hardships and Distresses which we may Suffer lays at your door," he continued. He knew that Thomas, Jr., would rest easier if he convinced Congress of the righteousness of their case and obtained their release. To reinforce his statement, he enclosed a letter from Penington, who addressed the council president in a similar vein.[47] Apparently his cousin ignored this missive, and with justification; it surely broadened instead of closing the breach between the two men. Wharton would have done well to have cooled his anger before setting pen to paper.

Two months or so later, President Wharton did inform prisoner Wharton of the steps which the state planned to take against those declared to be traitors, particularly those who cooperated with the British in their occupation of Philadelphia. Wharton sent an extract from the letter to Rachel, and the proposed penalties, including estate confiscation, deeply worried the prisoners' families in the city. She discussed the contents with Elizabeth Drinker and with William Smith's wife, and all looked apprehensively to future developments.[48]

Wharton also wrote to Nathaniel Folsom, a delegate from New Hampshire whom he had met during the sitting of the First Congress. Emphasizing his own innocence and circumstances, he argued that an open hearing "could have Exempted myself from the Charge Exhibited" as "by my Principles [I am] witheld & restrained from doing anything that shall tend to shed Human blood." He appealed to Folsom's compassion, "to the humane feelings of thy Mind," requesting him to relieve the sufferings of the families left behind "without the Assistance of that Connection who heretofore provided for their substinence." Cancellation of the move to

---

[46] T. Wharton to Rachel Wharton, December 28, 1777, January 20, 26, 1778; Isaac Wharton to T. Wharton, February 2, 1778, all WWC, HSP.

[47] T. Wharton to T. Wharton, Jr., January 20, 1778, *ibid.*

[48] Biddle, *Journal of Elizabeth Drinker*, p. 89 (entry for March 28, 1778).

Staunton would be appropriate because of sickness among the exiles and reports of a serious shortage of "bread Corn" there. How Folsom reacted to Wharton's letter is unknown, but the Quaker gleefully reported to Rachel that on January 25 they had been informed that Congress had suspended their move southward.[49]

Support for the exiles came from many sources, but mainly from Quaker Meetings throughout Pennsylvania. Information reached Winchester that "Six or Seven Friends" had arrived at Lancaster "Either to Obtain Our Liberty or a Trade," the first mention of a possible exchange of prisoners. The rumors did not specify for whom the exiles might be substituted. Quaker leaders in Philadelphia sent a long comment to Council explaining with common sense that the prisoners could not harm America regardless of their location. In February and March a veritable stream of Quakers and prisoners' wives visited Lancaster and York to plead their case. Mary Pemberton, Israel's wife, saw George Washington, who interceded with Council on her behalf to permit travel to Winchester. Congress's vacillation disturbed Wharton, and he concluded, "I see but little prospect of a return to My Dear Connections while this Civil War continues." With expectations of an indefinite stay well in mind, he asked Rachel to send him some summer clothing, writing materials, tea, coffee, alcoholic beverages of various kinds, food, and money. He also wanted "A Small tooth Ivory Comb" because he intended "to Let my Hair grow, if I can bear it."[50] Experts in the care of wigs were scarce in Winchester.

On March 7, 1778, Council notified Congress that existing conditions permitted the exiles to return home "without danger to the commonwealth or the common cause of America." The many visitors had convinced the councilmen that continuing to hold the prisoners in Virginia damaged the ideological basis of the patriots' cause. Congress agreed, and on March 16 ordered the Board of War to effect their release. Not until April 8, however, was that decision transmitted to the exiles. Apparently the Board had expected additional information from Council before it acted. That same day Council instructed Francis Bailey and Captain James Lang to go to Winchester, escort the prisoners to Shippensburg, and "set them at liberty."

[49] T. Wharton to Folsom, January 20, 1778, and to Rachel Wharton, January 26, 1778, WWC, HSP.

[50] T. Wharton to Robert Pleasants, February 2, 1778, and to Rachel Wharton, February 8, 1778, *ibid.*; "Observations Concerning the Memorial of Israel Pemberton and Others," January 31, 1778, *Pa. Archives*, 2nd ser., III, 144-146; *Pa. Col. Records*, XI, 426-427; Council to George Washington, April 6, 1778, *Pa. Archives*, 1st ser., VI, 401. Other wives involved were Phoebe (James) Pemberton, Susannah (Owen) Jones, Mary (Samuel) Pleasants, and Elizabeth (Henry) Drinker.

Two days later, after listening to further appeals to the interests of the exiles, Council changed their destination to Lancaster. The government stressed one requirement for their freedom; the exiles would not be reimbursed for their expenses by the state, which held them accountable for all the costs of "arresting & confining..., their journey, & all other incidental charges."[51] In a rather belated gesture to appease those he and Council had wronged, Thomas Wharton, Jr., instructed Bailey and Lang to handle

them on the road with that polite attention and care which is due from men who act upon the highest motives to Gentlemen whose station in life entitles them to respect, however they may differ in political sentiments from those in whose power they are.[52]

His orders contrasted strongly with the manner in which the prisoners had been treated the previous September. The reconciliation came too late for Thomas Gilpin; he had died on March 2.[53]

News of their pending release arrived at Winchester on April 16 in the form of a letter from Matlack to James Pemberton. Matlack warned the exiles not to violate existing laws in their haste to return to their homes. They had to obtain permission in writing from Council (or Congress, or General Washington) before they could traverse the American lines and enter British-held Philadelphia. Bailey and Lang reached Winchester on the seventeenth. Since the trip had tired their horses, the escorts recommended that the Quakers precede them on their way and both officials would join them later at Frederick, Maryland. The exiles began their journey in small groups from their scattered lodgings. Wharton and Charles Eddy moved out on the eighteenth; others followed their example the next day. For the exiles' protection, the escorts gave them each a pass authorizing their travel to Lancaster. On the morning of the twenty-first, Wharton, together with Eddy, Penington, and the three Fishers, linked up with the main body at John Hough's house in Loudoun County east of South Mountain. This provided an opportunity for Wharton to meet a man with whom he had completed several deals for Virginia lands. From there they traveled at a leisurely pace to Lancaster, arriving at the state's temporary seat-of-power on the twenty-fourth.[54]

[51] *JCC*, X, 238; Horatio Gates to President and Council of Pennsylvania, April 8, 1778, *Pa. Archives*, 1st ser., VI, 402; Supreme Executive Council Minutes, April 8, 1778, Committee of Safety Collection, Miscellaneous Collection, HSP; *Pa. Col. Records*, XI, 406-462.

[52] T. Wharton, Jr., to Bailey and Lang, April 10, 1778, Committee of Safety Collection, HSP.

[53] James Pemberton Diary, HSP, entry for March 2, 1778.

[54] *Ibid.*, entries for April 16, 18, 21, 24, 1778; receipt, Elizabeth Jolliffe to T. Wharton, April 18, 1778, and pass, Bailey and Lang to T. Wharton, same date, Correspondence, WP, HSP. The

The next day, Drinker and James Pemberton called on Thomas Wharton, Jr , who received them with "civility." Since they wanted to speak to Council as a body, the president suggested that they submit a written statement. Their petition demanded simply that Pennsylvania restore "the full enjoyment of liberty we have been so long deprived." Council, either from discomfort, reluctance to face its accusers, or lingering distaste, refused an audience. The members did, though, issue an order "which shall be deemed a discharge," a copy of which they gave each prisoner. Although this satisfied no one, Matlack urged that they pursue the matter no further.[55] The debate between the exiles and Council involved a definition of the term "discharge." Council assumed it meant an exoneration of their conduct; the exiles believed it less satisfactory than the appropriate "pardon" or even "parole." The future decided the dispute. Although the Quakers later suffered personal harassment from patriots in groups or individually, neither the state nor Congress accused them of treasonous behavior again.

The exiles departed from Lancaster after the unsatisfactory confrontation with Council. Two days later, on April 30, after an overnight stop at Pottsgrove, Wharton and his comrades happily reentered Philadelphia, which they had not seen for eight long months. Their joy, however, was "considerably abated" at the "sorrowful appearance" of the countryside, mute evidence of the ravages of occupation by a hostile army.[56]

Thus ended a most traumatic experience for the sixteen survivors. Their friends and relatives greeted them with great affection. Sympathy for the exiles was widespread, particularly among those who shared their beliefs. Wharton received a message of hope from George Churchman, who, after informing him that the mare entrusted to his care had foaled, described his deep emotions concerning the exiles and the future:

I have heard that all your Company that survived, have got to Phil[a] again, after your Virginian Pilgrimage, & have a Desire which seems fixed in a Measure of Brotherly Love, that Instruction may be gained by you & all of us, from the Difficulties which attend us in the present Situation of our altered Country, Whereby the Necessity of more deeply attending to the Fear of him who ruleth in Heaven & can dispose of the Inhabitants of the Earth as he sees meet, may be imposed on each of our minds to lasting Benefit.[57]

---

widow charged Wharton £24.12.7, Virginia currency, for "his board & keeping his horse." On Wharton's purchases of Virginia land, see Anderson, "Thomas Wharton," pp. 141-143.

[55] "Life of John Pemberton," *Friends Library*, VI, 297; James Pemberton Diary, HSP, entries for April 25-27, 1778; Supreme Executive Council Minutes, April 27, 1778, *Pa. Col. Records*, XI, 472-473.

[56] "Life of John Pemberton," *Friends Library*, VI, 297; James Pemberton Diary, HSP, entries for April 28-30, 1778.

[57] Churchman to T. Wharton, May 11, 1778, WWC, HSP.

Wharton returned to Philadelphia a tired and sick man. Although the war had virtually destroyed his business and the high taxes he had to pay as a non-associator ruined him financially, he attempted to resume his customary activities. Less than a year later, however, he suffered what apparently were two severe strokes. He never recovered his health. He adhered to the orders of the Meeting House and did not sign an oath of allegiance to Pennsylvania, although his brothers in the city did, followed by Samuel and Joseph Wharton, Jr., upon their escape from England and France. He did witness the marriage of daughter Mary to fellow exile Owen Jones, Jr., in 1780. He died, still embittered at his misfortunes, on December 1, 1784.

Tench Coxe: Tory Merchant

THE outbreak of the American Revolution confronted Tench Coxe, then barely twenty years of age, with the most difficult problem of his long life—whether to side with his countrymen or to remain loyal to the monarchy which in decades past had lavishly bestowed lands, including most of West Jersey and a vast western estate, on his forebears. At the outset of the imperial crisis, Coxe supported the American cause. Like Joseph Galloway, John Dickinson, Andrew Allen and a goodly number of his close relatives, Tench favored a policy of remonstrance and petition, protest up to but not including the use of force. His was the middle ground which, as he failed to realize, is so often untenable in an era of revolutionary upheaval.

This fact was brought home to him by the battle on Lexington Green, by the organization of a Continental Army, and, above all, by the Declaration of Independence. This he could not accept— home rule within the Empire, yes; separation from Great Britain, no. For a few months after the famous Declaration he held his tongue and continued in business. Then, a sudden intensification of patriot ardor in Philadelphia led to a witch hunt which forced many Tories, silent and avowed, to flee the city. On December 2, 1776, Coxe joined the exodus, driven away, he recalled years later, "by the violence and threats of a body of armed men to the British army."[1] He went first to New Jersey and, after only a brief stay, to British-occupied New York City, where he spent the next eight or nine months at the house of Edward Goold, a long-time family friend and a member of the prominent merchant firm of Ludlow & Goold. During these months of involuntary leisure, Coxe eagerly awaited a victory of the Redcoats which would open the way for British occupation of his native city and his return home. He did not have long to wait.

1 *Federal Gazette*, Nov. 22, 1788.

48

402

On the morning of September 26 some 3,000 British troops commanded by Lord Cornwallis marched into Philadelphia accompanied by a number of the city's prominent Tory exiles, among them Joseph Galloway, Andrew Allen, William Allen and Tench Coxe.[2] Whether or not (as later charged) "with a British officer locked in his arm,"[3] Coxe entered a quiet and sparsely populated city, its stores left empty by departing Whig merchants, its population consisting largely of women, children, and Quaker pacifists. "Philadelphia is rather a lovely city of considerable size . . . and . . . the public squares are beautiful . . . the City is very charmingly situated in level fertile country," a Hessian commander wrote on the day of the occupation.[4] To Coxe, happy to be "safely home after so many fatigues and perils,"[5] it doubtless appeared even more beautiful than to its invaders, his return a symbolic vindication of the wisdom of his commitment to the English.

The half-deserted city which the British occupied on September 26 was quickly transformed. Other Tory exiles returned, English and Scotch merchants arrived aboard British transports, business resumed, and Philadelphia became again the busy commercial hub and lively social center with which Coxe was familiar.[6] The presence of British nobles and British officers dazzled the local Tories; the circulation of British gold appeased the neutrals; and the superior power of the British army silenced the secret patriots. The winter social season of 1777–1778 was one of the liveliest in memory, so convivial, indeed, that Benjamin Franklin was led to deny that Howe had taken Philadelphia by commenting that Philadelphia had taken Howe. More likely, the General and his staff beguiled the city's elite who recklessly abandoned themselves to a season of gaiety, attempting to blot from consciousness the dim realization that the glittering new social order might not last. For the moment,

2 "Diary of Robert Morton," *The Pennsylvania Magazine of History and Biography* (*PMHB*), I (1877), 7.

3 *Aurora*, Aug. 23, 1804.

4 Bernhard A. Uhlendorf and Edna Vosper, eds., "Letters of Major Baurmeister during the Philadelphia Campaign, 1777–1778," *PMHB*, LIX (1935), 413–414.

5 Colburn Barrell to Tench Coxe (TC), Nov. 8, 1777, quoting TC to Barrell, Oct. 22, 1777. All manuscripts cited are in the Tench Coxe Papers at The Historical Society of Pennsylvania.

6 See Willard O. Mishoff, "Business in Philadelphia During the British Occupation 1777–1778," *PMHB*, LXI (1937), 166–167.

"Assemblies, Concerts, Comedies, Clubs and the like," made them, like the Hessian officer who so commented in January, 1778, "forget there is any war, save that it is a capital joke."[7] In short, weekly balls at the City Tavern, performances by British officers of farces, comedies, and tragedies at the Southwark Theater on South Street,[8] official receptions, public spectacles, and private parties[9] (many of which Coxe doubtless attended) overshadowed a war whose outcome was by no means certain.

A week after Howe's triumphant conquest of Philadelphia, the Americans challenged him at Germantown, a few miles outside the city where most of the British troops were quartered. Washington's audacity was no match for British numerical superiority, and in the confused battle that ensued Washington lost a thousand men, twice as many as his adversary. Repulsed but undaunted, Washington continued to harass Howe's forces as they sought to clear the Delaware for the British fleet, commanded by Lord Howe the British general's brother who impatiently waited to sail up the Bay and join forces with the army in Philadelphia. American resistance proved futile, however, and by December the British were in secure control of the Delaware forts. Cast down by the defeats of Brandywine and Germantown, Washington now went into winter quarters on a bleak plateau at Valley Forge, scarcely twenty miles from Philadelphia, where it was assignment enough merely to keep his wretched, starving, and freezing army intact. Howe, snug and secure in Philadelphia, did not even bother to attack. But to those Philadelphia Tories not blinded by self-interest, the seemingly impregnable British position in Philadelphia was offset by the most important American victory of the war—the stunning defeat inflicted on the British at Saratoga, where, on October 17, 1777, General Burgoyne, deprived of the support of an auxiliary force under Lieutenant Colonel Barry St. Leger and anticipated aid from New York City, surrendered his entire army, some 5,000 strong, to General Horatio Gates. That Coxe's own correspondence contains

7 "Extracts from the Letter-Book of Captain Johann Heinrichs of the Hessian Jäger Corps, 1778-1780," *PMHB*, XXII (1898), 139.

8 Fred L. Pattee, "The British Theater in Philadelphia in 1778," *American Literature*, VI (1935), 381-383.

9 Ellis Paxson Oberholtzer, *Philadelphia, A History of the City and its People* (Philadelphia, n. d.), I, 268.

only laconic comments on what must have been to him a disquieting development[10] was owing to his agreement with the viewpoint expressed in a letter from his friend Goold: "I shall make no reflections upon this melancholy affair," the New Yorker said. "I expect our Turn will come next."[11]

The dispatch with which Coxe and Goold took advantage of the opening of the Philadelphia market suggests how eager they were to store up profits during the British occupation. As Coxe put it: "If we must suffer misfortunes, we ought to drain all the good from them possible."[12] During his months of idleness in New York he had discussed with Goold his plans to resume business in Philadelphia, and the two had agreed on an informal partnership, including "a recommendation of each other to our respective friends."[13] In a gesture that revealed both his respect for the reputation Coxe & Furman (the now defunct merchant firm of Tench's father, William Coxe) still enjoyed in the Caribbean and his fondness for Tench, Goold persuaded his partner, Gerard Beekman, to recommend himself and Coxe "mutually throughout all the islands," averring that "it was equally the same whether the cargoes were shipped to one or the other."[14] Once his friend was safely back in Philadelphia, Goold seized the first opportunity to ship goods the two had purchased jointly the previous summer.[15] "I hope you have got our things," he wrote on October 26. "If Philadelphia is to be headquarters I think they will be safest there. . . . Turn them into Cash as soon as possible and remit the nt proceeds in good Bills. . . ."[16]

Coxe, having already "embarked in Business" on his own account,[17] "it not being proper to use as heretofore the names of our

[10] Rumors of Burgoyne's surrender reached Philadelphia on October 25. It was confirmed by general orders dated November 4. "Diary of Robert Morton," *PMHB*, I (1877), 24, 26.

[11] Edward Goold to TC, Oct. 26, 1777.

[12] TC to Goold, Mar. 1, 1778.

[13] TC to Goold, Mar. 17, 1778.

[14] Goold to TC, May 6, 1778.

[15] The first ships from New York carrying supplies and provisions arrived in Philadelphia about four weeks after the British occupation. Mishoff, "Business in Philadelphia . . . ," *PMHB*, LXI (1937), 167. By Nov. 11, 1777, young Robert Morton reported that "2 brigs and 2 sloops came from the fleet with the provisions for the Army and went up Schuylkill." "Diary of Robert Morton," *PMHB*, I (1877), 27.

[16] Goold to TC, Oct. 26, 1777.

[17] The first letter in Coxe's revised business letter book was Oct. 6, 1777.

late W[illiam] C[oxe] & M. Furman,"[18] ran an advertisement immediately, offering for sale the merchandise shipped by Goold: "Tench Coxe has for sale at the house of Mrs. Ford in Walnut Street, next door to the corner of Second Street," read an ad of October 25, "cotton counterpanes . . . pearl necklaces . . . brocades, satin . . . silk-knee garters . . ." and a "few boxes of Keyser's pills" for venereal disorders, rheumatism, asthma, dropsy, and apoplexy.[19] During subsequent weeks, Goold not only shipped additional consignments but persuaded many other prosperous New York merchants—among them, Stephen Skinner, Richard Yates, Robert Watts, Daniel Ludlow, Gerard Beekman, Isaac Low and Abraham Cuyler—to make Coxe their agent. No other merchant in Philadelphia enjoyed such profitable connections, and to the extent that trade with New York flourished so too would Coxe. Since he sold on a commission basis—usually receiving five per cent on all goods sold—his profits were exactly proportional to the size and value of the cargoes consigned him. And his New York associates, gratifyingly for him, were in a position to ship largely. In early November, for instance, Goold procured for him "a very large consignment from Mr. Isaac Low and Mr. Abraham Cuyler to the Amount of . . . near £3,000."[20]

By the same conveyance Coxe also received a rich cargo from Colburn Barrell, to whom he needed no introduction from Goold. A Bostonian who had affirmed his allegiance to the Crown by sailing for England at the onset of the Revolution, Barrell soon returned home, establishing himself as a merchant in New York City where, in 1777, he and Coxe became close friends. They also made plans for an informal business association once British arms should clear the way for Coxe's return to Philadelphia. Upon hearing that his friend was "got safely home," Barrell promptly prepared to send "as good an assortment as I can make out, which I believe will be from two to four thousand."[21] This was only the beginning. Over

---

18 TC to William Ballyn, Mar. 14, 1778. Coxe was extremely cautious about involving his father or Moore Furman, even by name, in any of his business transactions. To Isaac Hartman he explained that "it might be dangerous to my father & Mr. Furman to have their names appearing in any Business done in this Town, while Gen'l Howe's Army is here. . . ." TC to Hartman, Oct. 30, 1777.

19 *The Pennsylvania Evening Post*, where the ad was repeated on subsequent days.

20 Goold to TC, Nov. 10, 1777.

21 Barrell to TC, Nov. 8, 1777.

the next seven months, he consigned Coxe numerous and valuable cargoes, and as their profits mutually grew so did their affection, if the tone of their letters is a reliable gauge. But the bands of gold which united them in friendship were fragile, readily snapping with the departure of British troops from Philadelphia in June, 1778.

To Coxe, the smooth and successful resumption of trade was as pleasing for what it promised as for what it immediately secured him. His first consignments were received by the third week in October, a month or so before the American abandonment, on November 20, of the last of their Delaware River forts.[22] Five days later, Philadelphia's Tory newspaper reported that "the Delaware River never had near the number of ships in it as are at present, there being supposed to be upwards of four hundred," and that a large number of "well-laden" merchant vessels were daily expected from the West Indies and New York.[23] Goold had seen to it that some of the latter were assigned to Coxe—"a considerable cargo of dry goods" and other merchandise worth "upward of £5000 Stg" aboard the ship *Richtie;* assorted provisions from Skinner & Yates—loaf sugar, coffee, lemons, rice, porter, and wine aboard their armed schooner *Reed;* as well as consignments from other New York merchants, including Barrell, who shipped among other goods aboard his brig *Bella* "100 pipes choicest madeira."[24] Some days later, Coxe expressed his gratitude to Barrell and "my other good friends in New York from whose consignments, and some speculations of my own I find I am likely to have a very comfortable Assortment of Dry & wet goods, well adapted to the present demands here."[25] And the

---

22 Oberholtzer, I, 267. Although the voyage was hazardous, vessels had arrived via the Delaware during the weeks before the fall of the last of the Patriot river forts, among them vessels carrying goods, as described above, consigned to Coxe. With the abandonment of the American forts, the British fleet began to arrive. On November 24, Robert Morton noted that "Twenty or thirty sail of vessels came up this morning from the fleet"; on succeeding days additional ships arrived, especially from November 27-30, when the fleet was "coming up in great numbers." "Diary of Robert Morton," *PMHB*, I (1877), 31.

23 *The Pennsylvania Evening Post*, Nov. 25, 1777.

24 Goold to TC, Nov. 15, 1777; Barrell to TC, Dec. 13, 1777; TC to Skinner & Yates, Dec. 20, 1777. Both the *Bella* and the *Richtie* sailed regularly from New York to Philadelphia carrying cargoes consigned to Coxe. Like other vessels belonging to New York merchants, they usually sailed with the British fleet. See TC to Barrell, March, 1778. Custom house clearances were announced in *The Pennsylvania Evening Post*. See, for example, the issue of Dec. 20, 1777.

25 TC to Barrell, Dec. 15, 1777.

demand, owing to the needs both of the British Army and Philadelphia's steadily growing population, was brisk, producing soaring prices[26] and speculative wind-falls.[27]

Despite his awareness that the onset of winter meant that "our Navigation must stop before long,"[28] Coxe began looking for larger quarters and in mid-December moved to a new store, "one of the best" in Philadelphia, "it being within call of the Coffee House."[29] To a more cautious businessman, expansion of any kind might have appeared ill-advised, for the trade between New York and Philadelphia was subject not only to the vagaries of winter weather but to the control of British officials. That regulation might go so far as outright prohibition had been demonstrated only a week earlier. The avidity with which New York merchants took advantage of higher prices in Philadelphia[30] ("Some people will burn their fingers, thro their rage for shipping hither," Coxe commented) prompted General Howe to take swift action to obviate both possible shortages in New York and an overstocked market in Philadelphia. On December 5 he issued orders that "no more vessels than those already cleared should be permitted to go to Philadelphia."[31] Coxe's confidence in the continued expansion of his business activities was not altogether misguided, however. Just as British officials could regulate and even prohibit trade so they also could lighten restrictions or lift bans. Much depended on one's influence with British officialdom, and few merchants were in a better position to secure favors than he.

Coxe's emphatic affirmation, many years later, that "I never was in any employment whatever under Great Britain or her Governors, Generals, Admirals,"[32] was indisputably correct, and he scarcely can

---

26 TC to Skinner & Yates, Dec. 20, 1777.

27 TC to Watts & Kearney, Dec. 20, 1777.

28 TC to Barrell, Dec. 15, 1777.

29 *Ibid.* The store was rented from the administrator of the estate of Colburn Barrell's brother, who had lived in Philadelphia. *Ibid.* It was on Front Street, "the third door above Market-Street." *The Pennsylvania Evening Post,* Dec. 20, 1777.

30 TC to Goold, Dec. 19, 1777.

31 Goold to TC, Dec. 6, 1777. "The intention," Goold explained, "is to prevent our provisions being all sent off which were going fast."

32 *Aurora,* Oct. 8, 1800. William Duane of the *Aurora* also charged some years later that Coxe "took an oath of allegiance to the British," an allegation which Coxe denied. *Aurora,* Aug. 24, 1804.

be blamed for failing to add the proverbial "but." Yet he was (as his own correspondence clearly reveals, despite the many statements on the subject he subsequently excised) on close terms with high-ranking British officials whose cooperation he solicited and on whose patronage and support his prosperity was based.

Trade with New York City and the West Indies, the mainstays of his business, could not be conducted at all, much less thrive, save by the permission of the commanding general or his subordinates. With British soldiers quartered over his own store,[33] Coxe scarcely could have been unaware either of the extent of British power or the advantages of a cordial relationship with influential officials. His assiduous cultivation of them, moreover, was totally in character, revealing a trait which time was to enhance.[34] Nor was his success lost on his New York correspondents. Soliciting his agent's help in recovering some £200 imprudently advanced to a British army officer, Edward Goold reflected their viewpoint when he alluded to the confidence reposed in Coxe by the commanding general.[35]

Concessions to favored merchants were merely an incidental aspect of the regulation of the commerce of British-occupied America. Such control was rather dictated by the exigencies of the war effort as a whole; the prosperity or failure of merchants, Tory or English, was subordinate to the needs of an army of occupation. Regulation was accordingly strict.[36] By the terms of a proclamation issued by

33 Joseph Sherwell to TC, May 15, 1779.

34 From Goold, Feb. 7, 1778. Not that Coxe's New York associates were laggardly in successfully cultivating British officials. Goold himself was gratified by the "genteel" behavior of "Mr. Elliot," superintendent general in New York, who, he informed Coxe "is a good man and a good friend to me." Goold to TC, Nov. 10, 1777; May 29, 1778. He was equally proud of his relationship with "Mr. Gordon," the paymaster general, who, he boasted, "will readily do anything . . . to serve me." Goold to TC, Feb. 7, 1778. For his part, Barrell could report that "I am on very good terms with the Ordinance office here & Commissary Grant [of the artillery] is very obliging to me." Barrell to TC, April 22, 1778.

35 In 1778, as he would in the 1790's, Coxe curried the favor not only of major officials but minor ones as well. A representative letter reads: "During Capt Waddy's stay here he called upon me for some small assistance in the Cash way, with which I did myself the pleasure of supplying him." TC to John Ferrers, Jan. 20, 1778.

36 Theoretically the water-borne trade of Philadelphia, as well as that of New York, remained subject to the various acts of Parliament passed before the war and to the Prohibitory Act of November, 1775, which became effective on Jan. 1, 1776. Passed in retaliation for an act of the Continental Congress which forbade American trade with Great Britain and her colonies, the Prohibitory Act forbade all American trade until peace should be re-

Howe on December 4, 1777, all merchants' ships were required to make entry of vessels and submit accurate manifests of their cargoes.[37] Any goods not so declared, or landed without a license, were subject to seizure and forfeiture. Even after acquiring the requisite licenses, importers of rum, spirits, molasses and salt were subject to close surveillance and regulation. These products were to be stored in the owner's or importer's warehouses available for inspection by British officials and sold only with their permission.[38] Similar regulations were imposed on vessels leaving Philadelphia; ship masters were required, under penalty of forfeiture of goods and imprisonment, to submit sworn manifests "specifying the quantity and quality of the goods, and by whom shipped, together with the permission granted for the loading of the vessel." Nor could vessels in ballast depart without permission. Initially, ships in the royal service were specifically excepted from these restrictions, but within days it became apparent that British naval officers, in collusion with New York and Philadelphia merchants, were evading the law. Accord-

---

stored. It included a proviso, however, allowing the commander in chief or the commissioners for restoring peace to grant special export licenses. 16 George III, Cap. 5, as cited in Oscar T. Barck, *New York City During the War for Independence* (New York, 1931), 120–121.

[37] An earlier proclamation, dated Nov. 24, 1777, stated that in view of the "evil consequences" of an "unrestrained trade in spiritous liquors," all masters of merchant ships must report to British officials the amount on board and be granted a permit before landing it. *The Pennsylvania Evening Post*, Nov. 25, 1777.

[38] *Ibid.*, Dec. 4, 1777. A proclamation of December 9 imposed additional regulations specifying the conditions under which the city's citizens might purchase certain enumerated articles. "No Rum or Spirits of inferiour quality" in excess of one hogshead or less than ten gallons were to be sold at one time to any individual and none without a permit. The proclamation also limited the quantity of molasses and salt that could be sold without special permission, and required special licenses for the sale of all drugs. *Ibid.*, Dec. 9, 1777.

Coxe described the specific procedures as follows: "All Salts, Medicines, molasses & every kind of spirits, viz Brandy, Rum, geneva, &c. are bonded on landing & if sold even by an importer in any Quantity whatever, they are liable to seizure & occasion a forfeiture of the truck or dray on which they are carried, unless there be a special permit from the Inspector of prohibited Articles, for the very parcel in question. So that every quantity of Geneva from one case to one hundred which I sell to a retailer must have a Special permit." A major purpose of such minute regulation, he explained, was to prevent trade in contraband goods. "They cannot be so publickly vended, nor can they be sold in such small quantities as those that are reported." TC to Tennant, Ross, Kennedy, & Morrice, Apr. 30, 1778.

These regulations were roughly the same as those General Howe imposed on the trade of New York City by a proclamation dated July 17, 1777. For an account of the latter, see Barck, 123–124.

410

ingly, a proclamation of December 18 ordered that vessels in His Majesty's service be subject to the same regulations as were previously imposed on merchant ships.[39] Such regulations applied, of course, to all shipping, domestic and foreign, out of Philadelphia,[40] but the West Indian trade—the prop on which the fortunes of American merchants so long had stood—was subjected, some four months after the British occupation, to even more rigorous control. Before March, 1778, all ships from the British islands were required to have licenses from their governors, a requirement that did not severely curtail trade with the mainland colonies. In that month, however, the governors were instructed not to grant licenses to merchant ships sailing to Philadelphia and New York. Henceforth, permissions for importation were, in Coxe's words, "procurable" only from "the General or Admiral" who required that "the ships be well-armed, the owners well known."[41]

For New York and Philadelphia merchants who chose to remain safely within the law such regulation was particularly burdensome. For one thing, the necessity of returning their ships from one city to the other in ballast cut deeply into profits. Far preferable was the traditional practice of transporting a cargo from New York to Philadelphia, taking on there another cargo for the West Indies where, in turn, goods would be put aboard for the return trip to New York. Such profitable three-legged voyages still were possible,

---

39 *The Pennsylvania Evening Post*, Dec. 20, 1777. In mid-January, 1778, British authorities imposed still stricter rules on the activities of merchants. A proclamation issued by Joseph Galloway, Superintendent General, on January 17 forbade the sale of any goods by public vendue save by license from the city police and under strict regulations, including payment of a fee to be appropriated "for the public uses of the city of Philadelphia and its environs." *Ibid.*, Jan. 17, 1778.

40 Trade with all ports not held by the British was, of course, also prohibited. *Pennsylvania Ledger*, Apr. 15, 1778.

41 TC to Goold, Feb. 7, 1778. This, as Coxe said, was Howe's intention. He delayed issuing the requisite orders for at least a month, however. On this point Coxe's letters so confuse rumor with fact that it is not possible to determine the precise date of the regulation which was imposed not by a public proclamation but on orders from the commanding general to Superintendent General Joseph Galloway. It definitely was in effect before the end of March, at which time Howe's orders were reinforced by a circular letter from the British Ministry to the governors of the West Indian islands. See TC to Barrell, Mar. 6, 1778; to Thompson, Apr. 1, 1778. Howe's motive in imposing stricter regulation, so a highly-placed British officer told Coxe, was owing to the fact that "the Enemy receive large supplies by taking Vessels unarmed or whose Masters make no defence." TC to Richard Yates, Mar. 7, 1778.

but to accomplish them one must enjoy the confidence of highly-placed British officials, preferably the commanding general himself. It was here that Coxe's services proved invaluable to his New York correspondents. As early as December 8, 1777, for example, Richard Yates consigned Coxe a cargo aboard his "armed schooner Reed," requesting him to secure a permit "either from Lord or General Howe" to send the ship to Granada for a cargo to be shipped to New York.[42] "It being a point of the last consequence," Coxe reported, "I waited on Captain McKenzie," secretary to Lord Howe: "He informed me that Capt. Hammond was the Admiral's chief Agent here and that he would make it a point to do anything with him to obtain the necessary permit . . . I . . . shall leave nothing neglected which may tend to the accomplishment of this important point. . . ."[43] Nor did he. Five days later he had "the very great pleasure" of informing Yates that "I have this Inst. a note from Head Quarters" granting the *Reed* a license "to go to Granada."[44] As if to prove that one good turn from Hammond deserved another, Coxe at the same time was soliciting the Captain's aid in securing compensation for Abraham Cuyler whose vessel "the Snow Sir William Johnson" was lost near Cape Henlopen, en route from New York to Philadelphia with a consignment for Coxe. "I will endeavor to make it appear that the Snow was plundered and destroyed . . . which must really have been the case," Cuyler's efficient agent reported. He was successful. By order of Captain Hammond, who willingly came to Coxe's aid, the commander of his majesty's ship *Lizard* gave the requisite certificate.[45]

Not every Philadelphia merchant, however exalted his social position, had ready access to the close advisers of both the commanding general and Admiral Howe, to men like McKenzie and Hammond,[46]

---

[42] Yates to TC, Dec. 8, 1778; TC to Skinner & Yates, Dec. 30, 1777.

[43] TC to Skinner & Yates, Dec. 15, 1777.

[44] TC to Skinner & Yates, Dec. 20, 1777. Specifically, Yates had instructed Coxe to secure a cargo in Philadelphia to the value of £1,500, and if unsuccessful to deliver that sum in gold to the captain of the *Reed* who was "to purchase the goods we have directed him to procure" in Granada "& ship us agreeable to the directions we have given him." Yates to TC, Dec. 8, 1777. Even the patronage of the Howes was no guarantee of success. As described below, the *Reed* was captured by an American privateer.

[45] TC to Cuyler, Dec. 16, 23, 1777; to Capt. McKenzie, Dec. 19, 1777.

[46] Coxe also successfully cultivated other members of General Howe's staff, as attested by the following statement: "Mr. Goold in one of his late letters mentioned that Mr. Low

nor, like Coxe, to Commissary General Daniel Wier and other officers with lucrative contracts to award.[47] The major reason for his preferred position is suggested by the impressive roster of Coxe's family connections who held prominent positions during the British occupation. Clearly the most influential was Joseph Galloway, the most powerful civilian official in Philadelphia. Although their kinship was distant,[48] standards of a society which continued to count as relatives cousins three or four times removed dictated that it be acknowledged and, in view of the authority invested in Galloway by Lord Howe, it could not fail to be important. Howe's confidence in the former advocate of American rights was singular, whatever its basis. Perhaps Sir William warmly appreciated one whose ideas on reconciliation were similar to his own; perhaps he was convinced of the Philadelphian's ability; perhaps he perceived that to compensate for his own slack administration he needed the services of a more efficient and sterner man. In any event, on December 4, 1777, the commanding general issued two proclamations granting Galloway virtually the full extent of authority it was within his power to confer. The first designated him Superintendent General of police and invested him with powers as sweeping as the authority of government itself—"the suppression of vice and licentiousness, preservation of the peace . . . the regulation of the markets and ferries" and supervisor of "other matters in which the economy, peace, and good order of the City of Philadelphia and its environs are concerned."[49] As if such authority were not enough for one man, even under a military regime, Howe issued a second proclamation on the same day appointing Galloway "Superintendent of all imports and exports to and from Philadelphia," and conferring powers so broad that the Superintendent exercised virtually absolute control of the

---

was desirous of having a Box returned which went for Col. Cuyler from N. York. I have spoken to Mr. Hill, the General's steward, who tells me that the Box is on board one of the Vessels, which is not yet discharged, but he assures me, that it shall be sent [to] my house as soon as he can get it out." TC to Low & Cuyler, Dec. 16, 1777.

47 Coxe and Weir were on intimate terms. See TC to Barrell, May 10, 1778.

48 Jane Galloway Shippen, Coxe's aunt, was Galloway's niece.

49 *The Pennsylvania Evening Post*, Dec. 4, 1777.

city's commerce.[50] To a merchant as dependent on water-borne trade as was Coxe, official favors, easily within the power of his distant relative to grant, might make the difference between flush profits and economic disaster. In short, he scarcely needed to be told, as Colburn Barrell, in an oblique reference to Galloway, reminded him that "*you have acquaintance, influence, and credit with the public officers* . . . who can recommend you to the Captains &ca. by which means [*measures*] of great importance may be set on foot."[51]

Galloway was only the most prominent of Coxe's many relatives and acquaintances who occupied important offices or enjoyed the confidence of the Howe brothers. His friend, David Franks, was "agent for the contractors for vitualling His Majesty's troops at Philadelphia," and also, for a time, Commissary of Prisoners.[52] Andrew Allen, Tench's brother-in-law who had returned to Philadelphia with the British Army, was on intimate terms with its commander who had expressed his mutual esteem by appointing Allen some months before the occupation lieutenant governor of Pennsylvania during Governor John Penn's exile.[53] Though in seclusion at his rural retreat in Northampton County, James Allen, Andrew's brother, occasionally returned to his native city where he "met with great civility from many military Gentlemen, & dined with Sr. William Howe . . . an affable, easy, humane gentleman."[54] Coxe's brother-in-law George McCall was married to the daughter of Daniel Chamier, British commissary general in North America.[55] Having successfully raised the West Jersey volunteers for Royal Service, Daniel Coxe, Tench's uncle, came to British-occupied Phila-

[50] *Ibid.* Two "wardens of the port . . . to whom all persons were to pay due obedience" assisted Galloway as did an "Inspector of Prohibited goods." TC to Skinner & Yates, Dec. 20, 1777; to Thomas Attwood, Mar. 3, 1778.

[51] Barrell to TC, Apr. 9, 1778. Italics in original.

[52] Daniel Chamier to David Franks, Feb. 8, 1776. David's brother, Moses Franks of London, had entered into a contract (along with Arnold Nesbitt and Adam Drummond) to supply the British army with provisions. See Edward E. Curtis, *The Organization of the British Army in the American Revolution* (New Haven, 1926), 173–175, where the contract is printed.

[53] "Diary of James Allen, Esq. of Philadelphia, Counsellor-at-Law, 1770–1778," *PMHB*, IX (1885), 425; William A. Benton, *Whig-Loyalism* (Rutherford, N. J., 1969), 201.

[54] "Diary of James Allen," *PMHB*, IX (1885), 434.

[55] TC to Goold, Mar. 17, 1778. McCall "goes to New York," Coxe wrote, "at the particular request of Mr. Chamier whose daughter he married, & who means to put him in office there. . . ."

delphia where Howe promptly appointed him "one of the magistrates to Govern the civil affairs within the lines."[56]

Even such powerful connections could not prevent the sharp decline Coxe's commissions underwent in January, 1778. Both nature and man were responsible: the former for the "uncommonly severe winter"[57] which, early in January, "froze the Schuylkill over solidly and the Delaware from the banks nearly to the middle;"[58] the latter for General Howe's decision to forestall severe shortages of goods by imposing an embargo on all shipping in the city's port. According to "positive instructions" issued on December 23 to Galloway,[59] no goods whatever were to be shipped to Great Britain, Ireland, or the West Indies, and no goods to any part of the American continent occupied by the King's troops "but by a special permit to be obtained from the General himself."[60] Howe was not particularly lavish with permits, and for a time it appeared, as Coxe remarked, that "the Embargo and the Ice together might have stop'd the Navigation."[61] That the embargo did not was owing to the ingenuity of Coxe's New York consignors,[62] notably Goold. Royal transports and the British packet still sailed, weather permitting, between New York and Philadelphia and Goold had discovered, even before the embargo, that clandestine shipments might easily be arranged through compliant officials. Thus, in mid-November, he persuaded Captain Waddy of His Majesty's ship *Adventure* to secret in the latter's cabin some chests of tea, a scarce and expensive commodity in Philadelphia. Informing Coxe that the Captain would find a way

56 TC to William Ballyn, Mar. 14, 1778.

57 Goold to TC, Mar. 13, 1778.

58 "Letters of Major Baurmeister . . . ," *PMHB*, LX (1936), 51.

59 TC to Goold, Dec. 19, 1777; to Wigram, Jan. 24, 1778; to Gerard G. Beekman, Dec. 23, 1777.

60 TC to Wigram, Jan. 24, 1778. The embargo upset conditional contracts Coxe had made for goods to be sent to these places, especially a tentative purchase agreement for tobacco and staves to be shipped to England. TC to Wigram, Mar. 23, 1778. Other merchants too, Coxe lamented to Wigram, "have involved themselves in difficulties by vesting considerable sums in Articles which cannot be shipt." *Ibid.*

61 TC to Terrill & Kearney, Jan. 23, 1778.

62 Coxe's trade during the winter months of 1778, however, was not exclusively confined to New York. Late in January, for example, he reported to Goold that "I have got a freight for the Richtie amounting [to] about £800 Stg from the Bay of Hond[ura]s to London." TC to Goold, Jan. 21, 1778.

415

of evading diligent customs officers, Goold cautioned his agent not to mention the shipment "where it might prejudice him."[63] What was so promisingly commenced in November continued during succeeding months: in February Goold sent "sundry goods . . . which through the interest of Mr. Dashwood I have got by the packet— the captain knows nothing more than that it is a box of value. . . . Keep your own counsell."[64] A month or so later, Isaac Low sent Coxe "a trunk of goods by one of the transports" which he was "in some apprehension for, lest it should be seized."[65] Goold had no such apprehensions about "my things" shipped at the same time "by the packet," which he was certain would "run no risk from the manner they were taken on board."[66]

Friendly British officials not only cooperated with Tory merchants in shipping and entering contraband goods but, according to Coxe, themselves engaged in illegal profiteering. "The commissaries," he told his London banker, "I really believe shipt cargoes on their own account, under the appearance of Government business."[67] They were, he might have added, set a fine example by their superior, Daniel Chamier, the commissary general, who made handsome profits in illegal trade.[68] Nor were the commissaries unique. They were joined, according to the definitive study of British supply services during the Revolution, by quartermaster generals and other British officers, many of whom "came home with more gold in their pockets than they had when they went out or than their slender salaries in America would warrant."[69]

For Tory merchants, trade, legal or illegal, suffered handicaps other than British regulations and seizures. One problem was securing an adequate medium of exchange, a difficulty that had beset Americans for well over a century. To a commission merchant like

---

[63] Goold to TC, Nov. 15, 1777.

[64] Goold to TC, Feb. 15, 1777.

[65] Goold to TC, Mar. 25, 1779. Such apprehensions were obviously justified. "The transports," Coxe wrote a week later, "have brought around some goods which have been seized in many instances wherever they could find them." TC to Goold, Mar. 13, 1778. See also TC to Skinner & Yates, Mar. 23–25, 1778.

[66] TC to Goold, Mar. 13, 1778.

[67] TC to Wigram, Mar. 23, 1778.

[68] Curtis, 100.

[69] *Ibid.*, 145–146.

Coxe the issue was crucial, for the confidence reposed in him by his correspondents measurably depended on his success in securing acceptable modes of remitting the large balances in their favor. The most controversial currency media was Pennsylvania's colonial paper money, whose continued circulation and acceptance seemed to many, merchants and consumers alike, the best solution to the acute shortage of specie. But not even the united effort of the city's more responsible businessmen was sufficient to arrest its constant depreciation.[70] "On our arrival," Coxe observed, "our paper money passed equal with gold and silver," but by mid-December, as another Philadelphian noted, it was "entirely dropt, and not passable."[71] Nor were other varieties of money in circulation of certain value. "One of the most difficult points to manage here is our cash," Coxe complained, "of which we have some of almost every Species under heaven,"[72] including Spanish pistoles and "the old light Gold."[73] Coxe managed it by making remittances in "public bills" or bills of exchange drawn by British officials. The most desirable of these were paymaster's bills, but commissary bills as well as those drawn by officials of the Royal hospital, naval officials, the commissary of prisoners and others were acceptable.[74] Coxe explained his procedure: I take "the utmost pains to rest my Cash as soon as received in good Bills. . . . From D. Franks & other good residents here, I get bills and pay them at my leisure in all kinds of money,"[75] remitting the

70 Coxe was among those merchants who sought to arrest its decline by signing an agreement to accept it at par with specie. See J. Thomas Scharf and Thompson Westcott, *History of Philadelphia, 1609-1884* (Philadelphia, 1884), I, 366; Mishoff, "Business in Philadelphia," *PMHB*, LXI (1937), 176; "Diary of Robert Morton," *PMHB*, I (1877), 12. Because not all merchants agreed to do so and because of the problem of foreign exchange, the attempt failed. By December, 1777, Coxe along with other merchants who had signed the agreement reluctantly concluded that to continue to adhere to it would be to court bankruptcy and so refused any longer to accept the paper money save under necessity and, even then, at a high discount.

71 TC to Gerard G. Beekman, Dec. 23, 1777; "Diary of Robert Morton," *PMHB*, I (1877), 37.

72 TC to Barrell, Mar. 23, 1778.

73 TC to Isaac Low & Abraham Cuyler, Jan. 24, 1778. Other money in circulation included the Spanish milled dollars and the real, Portuguese half-johannes and moidores, and the New York pound (worth about half the pound sterling).

74 Barrell to TC, Nov. 28, 1777; TC to Welles & Grovenor, Dec. 1777; TC to Cuyler, May 7, 1778; TC to Barrell, May 10, 1778.

75 TC to Low & Cuyler, Jan. 24, 1778. Coxe was forced to pay for bills in "all kinds of money" because of General Howe's remissness in regulating the exchange value of English

public bills, in turn, either directly to his New York correspondents or to their London bankers.[76]

The former were gratified, both by Coxe's successful sales and the manner of his payments. "I wish every one of your correspondents were as well pleased with you as I am, & I have the pleasure to tell you the generality of them are very well satisfied," Goold wrote on March 25.[77] They should have been. The "prevalence of the partiality"[78] in favor of Coxe made him the ideal agent, binding to him by hoops of gold those New York merchants whose pockets he was lining. Nevertheless, Tory merchants, Coxe included, continually deplored, "this vicious rebellion" which occasioned such burdensome restrictions on trade. Peace, whether the result of a British or an American victory, would, in their view, bring stable trading conditions and surer, if smaller, profits.[79] Indeed, the swiftness and willingness with which many of them—Goold, Thomas Attwood, Richard Yates, Daniel Ludlow—later switched to the American side suggests that their first loyalty may, all along, have been to the pocketbook rather than to the King. As one of Coxe's business partners remarked with unconscious mockery, "War or Peace, all serves the purpose of some."[80] In their defense, on the other hand, it should be observed that they doubtless sincerely subscribed to Adam Smith's comment that he had "never known much good done by those who effected to trade for the public good. It is an affectation,

---

and foreign money. Coxe complained to Barrell on March 23 that "a proclamation was hourly expected to be issued from the General's Office, fixing Guineas . . . & excluding cob'd pistoles, doubloons, french Guineas & much other foreign coin, of which a good deal was passing among Us. Tho I am well assured this proclamation was written out, it never was published, as that all these kinds of moneys continued to be rec'd by one half the merchants. Finding that it would affect my Sales if I refused these Coins, I continued to take them making it a rule to lay out every farthing of them as fast as rec'd in good Bills—as long as this could be done with't giving a premium on Exchange."

[76] TC to Goold, Jan. 21, 1778; Barrell to TC, Nov. 28, 1777. Coxe's own profits were, for the most part, sent in the form of bills of exchange drawn by British officials to Wigram in London for safe keeping. See TC to Goold, June 13, 1778.

[77] Goold to TC, Mar. 25, 1778.

[78] Barrell to TC, Apr. 9, 1778. The phrase, quoted by Barrell, was Coxe's.

[79] Barrell to TC, Nov. 28, 1777.

[80] Goold to TC, Apr. 2, 1783.

indeed, not very common among merchants, and very few words need be employed in dissuading them from it."[81]

Tory merchants, the cream of British officialdom, as well as many of Coxe's socially prominent relatives and friends—Allens, Chews, Francises,[82] Shippens, Frankses, among them—doubtless attended Tench's wedding on January 14, 1778,[83] making it one of the highlights of the city's social season. The bride was Catherine McCall, daughter of Samuel McCall, Philadelphia merchant, and Anne Searle, both of whom were deceased.[84] Like Coxe, she was a member in good standing of the tightly knit Philadelphia elite—her sister, for instance, was married to Thomas Willing.[85] Tench's own happiness, however, must have been tinctured by anxiety about her health, which was perhaps affected by tuberculosis.[86] But, for the moment, he doubtless shared the view of a relation that "every thing is gay, & happy & it is likely to prove a frolicking winter."[87]

A happy marriage and a flourishing business led him to close his eyes both to the implications of his wife's illness and the possibility not only of Britain's abandonment of Philadelphia but her eventual defeat by the Americans. To a less complacent man the latter possibility clearly would have been rendered the more likely by news of the Franco-American treaties of February, 1778, an "unnatural alliance" which joined "French Royalty and American Liberty,"[88] and which bolstered the latter by providing the military assistance essential to its success. Not that this was the design of the French king, who rather sought revenge for his nation's defeat by England

81 Adam Smith, *An Inquiry into . . . the Wealth of Nations* (New York, 1937), 423.

82 Coxe's aunt, Mrs. Sarah Francis (widow of Turbett Francis), was in Philadelphia during the occupation. TC to James Meyrick, Jan. 27, 1778.

83 TC to Thomas Attwood, Mar. 3, 1778.

84 After the death of his first wife in 1757, McCall, on Jan. 31, 1759, married Mary Cox. He died in Philadelphia in September, 1762. Gregory B. Keen, "The Descendents of Jöran Kyn, The Founder of Upland," *PMHB*, V (1881), 452–453.

85 Margaret L. Brown, "Mr. and Mrs. William Bingham of Philadelphia," *PMHB*, LXI (1937), 287.

86 "Mr. McCall tells me Mrs. Coxe has frequent returns of her old disorder," Goold wrote on Apr. 2, 1778. "Had you not better let her try Long Island during the hot months."

87 "Diary of James Allen," *PMHB*, IX (1885), 432. Coxe apparently suspended business for some weeks before and after his wedding. There are no entries in his letter book between Dec. 23, 1777, and Jan. 20, 1778.

88 Alfred J. Beveridge, *The Life of John Marshall* (Boston, 1916), II, 2.

in the Seven Years War, less than two decades earlier. The revolt of England's colonies offered an opportunity to humble a powerful rival and to redress the balance of power in favor of France. Following the news of Burgoyne's surrender at Saratoga, the Comte de Vergennes, Louis XVI's foreign minister, moved cautiously toward open intervention on the side of the Americans, whom France had been secretly aiding since the war began. The final decision to do so was prompted by the well-based fear that England, having suffered a major defeat, would now seek to reunite the Empire by granting the Americans liberal concessions. On February 6, 1778, France and America signed treaties of commerce and alliance, pledging themselves to fight together until Britain recognized American independence. Although Vergennes' motive, as was said, may have been to abort reconciliation of England and her rebellious colonies while promoting French monopolization of the latter's trade, the generous terms of the alliance remain even today a rare exception to the history of western diplomacy. In exchange for the aid of France's mighty army and navy, the Americans were required only to promise to defend the West Indian possessions of her new ally. Coxe did not record his reaction to what, in retrospect, was surely the single most important and decisive event of the war. But the irony of an alliance between Washington's depleted, ragged, and hungry army and the military forces of a great world power scarcely could have escaped his notice.

More promising to him, however, was the conciliatory bill passed by Parliament on February 17, eleven days after the conclusion of the French alliance. Introduced by Lord North some three months earlier, this measure authorized the appointment of a peace commission empowered to renounce parliamentary taxation of the Americans, as well as the right to station military forces in the colonies without their consent, and all acts of Parliament to which the Continental Congress objected. For all this, in turn, the colonies had only to acknowledge the sovereignty of the King. To Coxe, such "ample terms" not only conceded all the Americans could expect or even wish but were a gratifying vindication of his own wisdom. "I am particularly happy on the Country's acct and on my own, because it shews that I had some Reason for the hope I entertained, that this would be the footing" on which "England would put this Country," he wrote to a friend in St. Croix. "I now look for a speedy & happy peace, in which America will have a fixt constitution, not to be infringed by either side."[89] His misplaced optimism was doubtless wishful thinking,[90] dictated by his unhappiness with "the Melancholly Continuance of this ruinous war" and a longing for an answer to his prayer: "May heaven in its Mercy give us a Speedy end to it."[91] In any event, he refused to believe that the Americans would spurn such generous concessions, a refusal that was positively obtuse in view of the joy with which the patriots greeted news of the French alliance and their deep distrust of British sincerity. Even the English envoys themselves realized upon their arrival in Philadelphia early in June (as perhaps Coxe also may have done by that time) the futility of concessions short of independence.[92] But at least Coxe was consistent—in the spring of 1778 as in 1775–1776 his deepest wish was for peace and autonomy within the British Empire.

That expectation governed the conduct of his substantial share of Philadelphia's wartime trade during the spring of 1778. Coxe's comment that "my sales have been as good as any merchant in this place"[93] is supported by the large payments he made either to his

89 TC to Isaac Hartman, Apr. 26, 1778. News of the conciliatory act reached Philadelphia in mid-April. Not until that time did the envoys appointed under that act sail for America.

90 This is the more evident in view of Coxe's own contradiction of the optimistic view he characteristically expressed. In a letter of April 19, he wrote: "I am clear in my own judgement that the Congress . . . will reject these ample propositions being incompatible with their [about four words crossed out of MS] of independency." But he added that he would take "no important step till I see the issue." TC to Summers & Cliburn, Apr. 19, 1778.

91 TC to Barrell, Dec. 20, 1777.

92 The British emissaries—the Earl of Carlisle, William Eden, George Johnstone—left England on April 16. They were accompanied by Sir John Temple and John Berkenhart, who as special agents were instructed to flatter and if necessary bribe the Americans into acceptance. The Carlisle Commission arrived in Philadelphia on June 6, 1778. A month before, the Continental Congress, sitting at York, Pa., had ratified the Franco-American treaties unanimously and whatever slim chance of success the emissaries might have had was gone. Instead of a warm reception from the Americans, they were greeted by the depressing sight of British preparations to evacuate Philadelphia. How could they threaten the Congress with an attack by Redcoats who were retreating to New York? They thus scarcely could have been surprised when the Americans, on June 17, announced that they would not negotiate with Carlisle and his colleagues unless American independence were recognized and British military forces withdrawn. The members of the Commission thereupon departed for New York, where they continued their futile efforts until the following winter.

93 TC to Watts & Kearney, Mar. 1, 1778.

New York correspondents or to their London bankers. Early in March, for example, he remitted "£4500 & upward" to the accounts of several New Yorkers by two homebound British fleets, as well as a "handsome remittance" of more than £3,500 to Colburn Barrell. Continuing consignments from New York and elsewhere over succeeding weeks netted Coxe even more substantial profits. "I have had several West India & dry goods Consignments of very Capital Value, & have made some few Speculations which have not turned out amiss," he boasted in mid-March.[94] By this time he was eager to enlarge his trading activities, even in the face of its almost total dependence on an army of occupation which, according to rumors already circulating, might soon leave.

He perhaps hoped that if the Americans regained control of Philadelphia his Toryism would be forgiven as merely a youthful indiscretion and that he would be allowed to carry on business as usual; perhaps he genuinely believed that an amicable settlement of the war, including a general amnesty, would take place; perhaps he was among those a cynical British officer had in mind when he remarked "that the inhabitants of Philadelphia 'are very stout-hearted—for money!';"[95] more likely, he was merely bowing to parental pressure. In any event, on March 19, 1778, he sent out a circular letter, offering the former clients of Coxe, Furman & Coxe his own services in conducting their business affairs in America during "this confused time," as well as after "this unhappy contest is settled."[96] Its purpose, so he told Goold, was "to secure all the old friends of our house & give them an opportunity of introducing me to New Ones."[97] The true motive behind the circular was revealed in its statement of assurance that if Tench Coxe should discontinue his mercantile

---

[94] TC to Benjamin Yard, Mar. 14, 1778.

[95] Quoted in Mishoff, "Business in Philadelphia . . . ," *PMHB*, LXI (1937), 177.

[96] Mar. 19, 1778. As to the future, Coxe observed that "when peace shall be restored to this country I shall still be happy in paying them every attention, either in Conjunction with my former Copartners or by myself." His circular letter concluded with this recommendation of his friend Goold: "As the course of your mercantile affairs may make a friend of Character & Abilities in Business necessary in other parts, I will make use of the freedom of mentioning Edward Goold Esquire of New York as a Gentleman from whom you may expect every Justice & security in Business."

[97] TC to Goold, Mar. 17, 1778. Coxe's ambition did not outrun his prudence, however. "From the political sentiments of some of our St. Croix friends," he confided, "I do not think it will be quite proper to send one to any of them yet."

activities then the old firm of Coxe & Furman or its successor—Coxe, Furman & Coxe—would resume business. With Tench a Tory, William Coxe, Sr., a neutral, and Moore Furman an active patriot, the former partners apparently were playing a clever game of heads I win, tails you lose. The rules were perhaps prescribed by the firm's senior partner, William Coxe. "My father," Tench wrote a St. Croix friend, "is desirous of making a final settlement of all our late Concerns that we may be ready either to begin together or separately as may be hereafter agreed on among Us."[98] To Tench himself, as to most young men of twenty, present prospects were more important than plans for the future.

During the weeks immediately following, his optimism appeared justified. "The number of Inhabitants, Refugees, and Military being great,"[99] he explained, the opportunities afforded by the Philadelphia market were virtually limitless.[100] Coxe, as before, was in a position to meet the demand. His various correspondents "having shipt largely to this port," he observed on March 25, "I have had my hands extremely full;"[101] a month later, he estimated that he had received over recent weeks "consignments from New York,

98 TC to Benjamin Yard, Mar. 14, 1778.

99 TC to Terrill & Kearney, Apr. 10, 1778. The population of the city increased from around 22,000 or 24,000 at the time of the British occupation to approximately 60,000 by the spring of 1778. Mishoff, "Business in Philadelphia . . . ," *PMHB*, LXI (1937), 170.

100 "A cargo from Ireland in the provision way would certainly yield a very great profit at this Market," Coxe wrote. "There are no quantities of Beef, pork, Butter, or Tongues in my hand here, and the price of our fresh provisions is so high from the amazing number of Inhabitants, that there can be no doubt of a pretty ready sale. . . ." TC to Isaac Low, Apr. 1, 1778.

Coxe was not certain that the state of the Philadelphia market would remain so favorable and cautioned his correspondents to exercise prudence in consigning goods to him. "It seems to me very probable," he explained to Barrell on Mar. 23, 1778, that "if the Rage for shipping hither should be as great as it was last fall that many kinds of goods will be as dull here as with you & some of them as low. We have at present a very considerable quantity of goods in Town, & our quantities will be made as great as yours by two or three such fleets as came in Nov. & Dec'r. This being the case it appears to me that your best plan will be as I have constantly advised to keep as tolerable an assortment in both places, as your Invoice will admit of and make the best of your Cargo at both Markets. I would not advise you to let the present price or demand for any Article here, tempt you to send more than ½ or ⅔ of what you may have of it, provided you have a tolerable sale for it [in] New York."

101 TC to Pennington & Biggs, Mar. 25, 1778. Barrell continued to assign large shipments to Coxe. On April 9, the latter acknowledged a consignment of "fashionable suits, coats, and breeches." Two days later the brig *Bella* arrived in Philadelphia with another consignment. TC to Barrell, Apr. 12, 1778.

Maderia, Britain, & the West Indies to the amount of £30,000."[102] A ready market for such large shipments of goods may have been assured, but fluctuating prices rendered profits somewhat more chancy.[103] To such merchants as were lucky they also offered the possibility of speculative windfalls.[104] Coxe was among the lucky ones, though, it should be added, that chance was hedged by his knowledge of the market. This was the case in his speculations (often undertaken in partnership with Goold and James Thompson) in tobacco whose profitability he attributed to his ability to judge the quality of that staple.[105] Since other merchants were less skillful, the "few that do understand it have in their power to make too much Advantage of their knowledge."[106] The success of other speculations hinged on advance or "inside" information, as when Coxe hinted to a West Indian correspondent that a profitable shipment of staves from Philadelphia might be made "if it were practicable to know of the ports being opened some little time before it takes place."[107] The surest way of all to assure success was to control one's source of supply, a possibility Coxe explored in mid-April when he was

[102] TC to Isaac Hartman, Apr. 26, 1778. In April Coxe sold merchandise valued at £2,100 for Barrell alone. TC to Barrell, May 20, 1778.

The cargoes consigned Coxe included virtually every type of article for which there was a demand by either the army or the city's civilian population. They included, at one time or another, such items as woolens, linens, haberdashery, satin, silks, blankets, buttons, teas, provisions of all kinds, looking glasses, medicine, wines and spirits. On some goods, foreign linens, drillings, dowglasses, for instance, his profits were enhanced by drawbacks.

[103] The prices at which Coxe sold were largely dependent on the quantity and nature of shipments from England which by the spring of 1778 were arriving "in abundance." TC to Low, Mar. 29, 1778.

[104] Given the fluctuating value of money (including the depreciation of paper currency) and the uncertainty of the supply of goods, commodity prices sharply rose and fell, making speculation inevitable. See Mishoff, "Business in Philadelphia . . . ," *PMHB*, LXI (1937), 166.

[105] See Goold to TC, Mar. 13, 1778; TC to James Thompson, March, and Apr. 1, 1778. Since the Americans controlled the tobacco producing states, that commodity was not easy to procure. One method was suggested by Goold: "I am told the best Tobacco with you has been purchased at 50/per Ct. by a Mr. Faran from this place. What think you of Speculating in about 10 or 12 Hhds. If very good it might be got off among some Privateers. These things are done here. If you approve of it I have no objection to be half Concerned in that Quantity." Goold to TC, Apr. 11, 1778.

[106] TC to Low, Apr. 1, 1778.

[107] *Ibid.* "Staves of different kinds are not scarce here," Coxe explained, "and as many people are much disappointed about shipping some quantities of them, they also I am of opinion might be tempted to sell low. The difficulty with us, as with them is the shipping them off."

424

asked by two New York merchants "about a concern in a privateer."[108] His most grandiose speculative projects were planned in cooperation with Colburn Barrell who, in reply to Coxe's suggestion of a joint venture, replied: "I fear I have no capacity for it but what think you of sending some proper person in whose integrity and capacity you can put the firmest reliance to St. Augustine with a commission to speculate in Prizes and prize goods. . . . He might purchase a prize with a rich Cargo & bring it to Philadelphia or New York. . . . I am but hinting . . . but something capital may be done —if you engage, I crave the favour of being concerned." Coxe, who in any event preferred employing his capital in Philadelphia "in little occasional strokes," decided, as Barrell thought he might, that this scheme was "chimerical."[109] That he prospered more than most other speculators was doubtless owing to his ability to consign such grand designs to the realm of fantasy. Even so, he occasionally suffered reverses; given the hazards of transportation it could not have been otherwise. The most severe loss was the capture of the *Reed*, owned by Skinner & Yates of New York but addressed to their Philadelphia agent, by American privateers on the schooner's return voyage from the West Indies "upon a special permission obtained from the commander in chief"[110] by Coxe who anticipated a "handsome commission"[111] through the sale of her cargo of sugar, limes,

108 TC to Summers & Cliburn, Apr. 19, 1778. Coxe wrote: "You will agree with me that it will be best to defer doing anything of that kind. . . . The fitting of a privateer is expensive, and it would be mortifying to have a Vessel thus fitted rendered useless. I doubt not that some *lawful* Voyages or other commercial plans may be executed in the course of this summer, in which it would give me pleasure to be concerned with you & our good friend Mr. Goold." *Ibid.* The fitting out of privateers had only recently been permitted. In March, 1777, Parliament had authorized the Lords of the Admiralty "to grant letters of marque to private ships to make reprisals against ships of the rebellious colonies." Barck, 131.

One of the most profitable of Coxe's activities was the sale of ships for his correspondents. In January, 1778, for example, Richard Yates requested him to dispose of the former's *Mariners*, a "sound" brig that "carries about 240 Tons." Unable to sell the brig at the price Yates wanted, Coxe reported that "The only thing that I am of opinion can be done with her is to get her again into the Service of the Government." Yates to TC, Jan. 5, 1778; TC to Yates, Mar. 17, 1778.

109 Barrell to TC, Apr. 9, 1778; TC to Barrell, May 10, 1778.

110 TC to Lindsay, Apr. 11, 1778.

111 TC to Yates, Mar. 7, 1778; to Skinner & Yates, Mar. 23–25, Apr. 14, 1778; Yates to TC, Mar. 17, 25, 1778. TC described the capture to Skinner & Yates in a letter of Mar. 23–25, 1778: "I am extremely Sorry indeed to be able to inform you positively that the Reed is gone. A Gentleman of the name of Dubois, who is acquainted with Mr. Yates says he saw

cocoa, and coffee, worth on the Philadelphia market about £4,000. Aware that the risks of trade must be accepted if its emoluments were to be enjoyed, Coxe was not particularly downcast. "I am sorry for it," he told Goold, "but must think myself well off with my present fortune. Very few indeed of my fellow citizens have been as much favored."[112]

He was indeed favored, not only in fortune but by those whose patronage made it possible. In the spring of 1778, as during previous months, British trade regulations were not so stringent as to obviate large profits for such merchants as enjoyed the confidence of port officers and contractors or who were familiar with the law's loopholes. The trade with the British West Indies is a case in point. Shipments to and from the former, as was mentioned previously, were rigorously regulated, and in March Coxe learned from his friend Commodore Hammond that General Howe "is determined to knock up all speculations from that way." In passing on this information to a New York correspondent, Coxe explained a significant exception: "He wishes to see the Army, Navy & inhabitants supplied nevertheless, & intends to grant special licences for that purpose to persons in whom he can confide. . . ."[113] The result was that the few merchants who, like Coxe, had ready access to the commanding general's deputies enjoyed a virtual monopoly. So long as they received some permissions, the precise number granted was of no great consequence; if only a few licenses were issued, as Coxe explained, "the quantities imported will be small . . . ," and "there will be no difficulty in making the prices anything that the holders of the Commodities may choose."[114] Not only was Coxe awarded a goodly num-

---

her in the hands of the Americans. He came passenger in the Thames Frigate. He informs when he came into the Bay the Schooner was in Sight and a signal given by the Thames. She hove up along side, there being some Gallies in Sight. The Capt. of the Thames put some refugees and an officer or two aboard the Reed, and sent her against the Gallies. She had an engagement with them and behaved extremely well. But after they returned as . . . [there was a] Gale coming on, the Capt. of the Thames advised the Schooner to put to Sea, which she did and the day after came in again when she went ashore and was taken by the Americans. . . ."

112 TC to Goold, Mar. 31, 1778.

113 TC to Low, March, 1778. The frequency with which Coxe in letters describing the West Indian trade used the terms "confide" and "confidential men" suggests the importance that he attached to his own favored position with the General and his aides.

114 TC to Low, March, 1778.

ber of the special licenses issued[115] but he willingly offered "my little influence" to obtain them for some of his New York correspondents.[116] For royal favorites like Coxe, moreover, the risks of such trading ventures were sometimes minimal, for they were, in effect, quasi-public projects. Not only did the British government provide ships but it afforded armed protection. For example, the schooner *Lovely Nancy*, in which Coxe owned a one-third interest, sailed early in April for the Bahama Islands, "with a permission from Sir William Howe for ye purpose of importing provisions & refreshments," protected by a convoy consisting of an "armed schooner" and "a Stout armed ship" and "provided herself with four Swivels, powder Ball & men sufficient."[117]

In Coxe's case, such successful transactions seemed only to sharpen the acquisitive instinct; the emoluments of government-sponsored ventures might be supplemented by profits from illegal trade.[118] The precise extent of his participation in the clandestine operations that were carried on during the British occupation—just as they previously had been during British rule—cannot be known, if only because they necessarily were kept as secret as possible. But Coxe's correspondence reveals enough concrete examples of his participation to suggest that it was not exceptional, though perhaps it may not have been extensive. The most conspicuous incident occurred toward the end of April. From Alexander Kennedy & Co., a partnership of St. Croix merchants, Coxe received a consignment aboard the sloop *Lord Howe* by way of the British island of Tortola.[119]

---

115 TC to Barrell, Mar. 23, 1778; Samuel Herv & Co. (St. Christopher) to TC, Feb. 19, 1778; TC to Goold, Apr. 11, 1778; TC to Thompson, March, 1778.

116 TC to Skinner & Yates, Apr. 4, 1778. A number of permissions "have been given lately to people who have suffered in the cause," Coxe explained, "and who have had some interest." See also Goold to TC, Mar. 25, Apr. 24, 1778; TC to Barrell, Stoughton & Davis, Apr. 12, 1778.

117 TC to Wigram, Apr. 7, 1778. Coxe's own interest in the schooner was further protected by insurance which he secured from Wigram, his London correspondent.

118 The same was true of his close business associate Goold, who handled contraband goods smuggled into New York City. Goold to TC, Mar. 25, 1778.

119 The vessel's custom house and other papers stated that she was destined for Halifax and the Captain carried a number of letters addressed to Coxe. This subterfuge was employed to guard against a mishap in Philadelphia. Should British officials there challenge the master, he could pull out the letters to Coxe stating that he had only put into that port on his way to Halifax. See TC to Tennant, Ross, Kennedy & Morrice, Apr. 30, 1778.

427

In addition to a quantity of sugar, the cargo included articles (muskets, rum, and gin, among other items) whose importation, save under the strictest regulations, was forbidden. Since he preferred not to handle some of the contraband goods (especially the guns) which his associates had included in the cargo, Coxe was annoyed and apprehensive.[120] "The severity of the new regulations here, together with the vigilance of the officers, & [a] Great number of King's ships . . . renders the landing of any prohibited articles extremely difficult," he wrote his temporary partners, cautioning them not "to hazard a cargo of this nature" again. But either loyalty to his associates or his own avarice outran discretion, and he assured them "you will learn from Capt. Price," the master of the vessel, "that these things are managed in some Instances. . . . It will be most prudent to defer the sale till the Vessel is gone, as the discovery . . . might lead to dangerous enquiries."[121] Once having yielded, Coxe recklessly abandoned himself to yet grander projects,[122] proposing to Kennedy & Co. that he use his influence to secure "permission to import from St. Croix "a cargo of Rum, Sugars, Geneva" and other products "as provisions & refreshments for his Majesty's Army, Navy & loyal inhabitants." He would attempt to persuade influential customs officials, Coxe said, "that as the court of Denmark is in perfect unity with the King . . . the objections of its being a foreign Island will be overlooked." What could not be done legally, however, might be done clandestinely, and should his influence prove of no avail he was ready with an alternative plan: Send a cargo, "regularly cleared" from an English island, to Philadelphia, but let the vessel's custom house and other papers "shew that she was bound for Halifax." If Coxe could not manage an entry in Philadelphia, he was confident he could arrange for the ship to proceed to Halifax or

120 He could not have been surprised, however, for Goold had warned him of Kennedy's efforts to ship and land contraband goods. Goold to TC, Mar. 25, 1778.

121 TC to Tennant, Ross, Kennedy & Morrice, Apr. 30, 1778.

122 Coxe's acquiescence and his proposal of a similar project appear particularly reckless in view of his cautiousness when Goold first mentioned Kennedy's plans. "I am at a loss to guess who Mr. Kennedy is & wish you had let me into his character," he wrote. Afraid that "his Vessel coming in . . . will get both herself and me into a difficult Situation," Coxe affirmed that "I do not wish to do any business where Oaths must be trifled with, or which will make me liable to the general suspicion. However I will do all for him that in honor & Conscience I can. But will not act against either of them for any man breathing be his Connexion ever so valuable. . . ." TC to Goold, Mar. 31, 1778.

"for England with the first Convoy."[123] Such shrewd, if illegal, projects were abandoned almost as soon as they were hatched. Not only did the commanding general firmly refuse a permit for the St. Croix voyage but Coxe was compelled to order the captain of the *Lord Howe* to pull up anchor with all possible speed and "to direct him to proceed without loss of time on account of the information which had been most cruelly lodged against the sloop for importing Arms."[124] The worst was yet to come. A day later, on a Sunday evening, Galloway "ordered the arms seized . . . in my store; my clerk sleeps there, and [I] being out at the time he had the key; this being mentioned Mr. G. directed his Deputy to Break open the door. . . ."[125] Coxe's indignation was mirrored in the reaction of his alter ego, Goold: "*Some people* in office with you are more severe than is really necessary. . . . Why this severity? I am as much prejudiced against smuggling as any Man can be—but—I cannot at present look upon this thing in that light."[126]

123 TC to Tennant, Ross, Kennedy & Morrice, Apr. 30, 1778. Although such shipments were contrary to acts of Parliament, Coxe also "pressed" English officials for permission to send out on the return voyage of the *Lord Howe* "a parcel of lumber which I have now in store." When Galloway, the Superintendent General, refused to grant him the indulgence, Coxe turned to his friend O'Beirne, presumably an influential customs house officer, to "do the needful." Not only was O'Beirne unable to do so, but he also failed to secure the permission Coxe had requested for the St. Croix voyage. On May 2, Coxe wrote his correspondents: "Mr. O'Beirne has just called upon me, and acquainted me that the Admiral & General say they have no power to permit the exportation of lumber to the West Indies or indeed any other goods. . . . They do not choose to give a license to import from St. Croix, on account of its being a foreign Island. . . . As to a permission to bring in goods from Tortola, they say it is unnecessary, as the Governors have power to grant this for every thing but spirits of every quality & Molasses. If your Governor should not give you permission, they said that you should have a free entry here. . . . But that you must be regularly cleared, & bring up no Rum or Molasses." TC to Tennant, Ross, Kennedy & Morrice, May 2, 1778.

124 TC to James Bruely, May 3, 1778. Coxe's explanation of the affairs appears disingenuous (or maybe he merely had overestimated the immunity conveyed by his close relationship with British officials). "You may remember," he wrote Bruely, "that the owners were desirous of procuring a letter of Marque for this Vessel, & in order to her being completely fitted for that purpose, had put on board of her 40 or 50 stands of arms. Finding that this Paper could not be obtained, I ordered the Musquets on shore, & considering them as supernumerary implements of the Vessel did not think of entering them at the Custom House any more than if they had been a Couple of spare Sails. . . . I offered them for Sale at the King's Armory before I would suffer anybody else to purchase them, thinking government was entitled to the preference. They did not want them, and I then proposed selling them to any transport that might have Occasion for them. . . ."

125 TC to Skinner, Yates & Van Dam, May 5, 1778.

126 Goold to TC, May 6, 1778.

Coxe attributed such setbacks to Lord Howe's withdrawal of his favor, a withdrawal reflected in the sudden coolness of subordinates, like Galloway, previously so obliging. It was not only Coxe upon whom the commanding general suddenly ceased to smile, however, but upon other formerly favored merchants. This was owing, as Coxe correctly perceived, to Howe's replacement by Sir Henry Clinton, whose arrival in Philadelphia was expected momentarily, and to the former's firm resolve not "to do anything but absolutely necessary business."[127] What Coxe did not know was that the new commanding general was bringing with him the King's orders to abandon Philadelphia.[128] Having concluded that the former American capital did not have the military importance attributed to it by Howe, and uncertain of where France would throw her weight, the British high command decided to play it safe by ordering Clinton to withdraw to New York, there to plan a major campaign in the South. From the beginning of the British occupation Coxe's business associates in New York had been apprehensive about its permanence. As early as November, for instance, Goold had reminded his partner that "wherever Head Quarters is" their goods would be "safest," and cautioned him that "if you have any reason to apprehend that the army will quit your place then send them here as soon as you can."[129] During succeeding months, Goold and other New York merchants continued to admonish their Philadelphia agent to be prepared for the city's evacuation.[130] But Coxe was confident that their fears were groundless. "I find that many of my friends at New York are apprehensive that the Army thinks of removing from this place," he wrote on March 25. "There is not the

127 TC to Tennant, Ross, Kennedy & Morrice, May 2, 1778.

128 On March 7 Lord Germain appointed Clinton to replace Howe, leaving it to the new commander's discretion whether to hold or abandon Philadelphia. Some two weeks later, however, Clinton was instructed by the King to evacuate Philadelphia.

129 Goold to TC, Nov. 5, 1777.

130 See, for example, Barrell to TC, Feb. 14, 1778, and Goold to TC, Feb. 15, 1778. Goold was so certain of eventual British evacuation of Philadelphia that he not only urged Coxe so to arrange his business affairs as to be prepared for that event but insisted that he be ready to flee the city himself. In reply to Goold's invitation, extended early in March, that should Philadelphia be evacuated Tench and his wife would be welcome guests at the Goold's New York home, Coxe insisted that such arrangements were needless. TC to Goold, Mar. 8, 1778.

least reason for their concern."[131] He could not have known, of course, that the British Ministry already had ordered the city's evacuation. He assuredly was justified in believing that "it is impossible for General Washington to do anything,"[132] and he understandably was preoccupied by the condition of his wife, who during the last week of April became critically ill, so ill indeed that he "once thought her lost."[133] Nevertheless, only a determination to suspend belief could have led him to ignore the possibility. Even after Sir Henry Clinton's arrival in Philadelphia on May 8, Coxe, refusing to credit rumors that the new commander planned to leave the city, remained certain that the British were in Philadelphia for a long stay.[134]

On May 18, General Howe's staff officers honored the retiring commander by inviting some 750 guests to a fête which climaxed a season of lavish entertainment. Designated the "meschianza," it opened at four o'clock on a bright and sunny afternoon with a "grand regata" along the Delaware.[135] English officers and their wives, along with their more socially prominent Philadelphia sympathizers, were transported in brightly decorated boats, gaily responding to the cheers of the thousands who lined the docks. Disembarking at Walnut Street wharf, the guests walked between columns of grenadiers standing rigidly at attention to the elegant Wharton mansion in the center of whose "great lawn, which extended down to the Delaware" a triumphal arch had been erected. Here there was a "tilt or tournament," sprightly band music, a grand ball, rockets and fireworks, all climaxed by a midnight banquet in an elegant saloon where tables "were loaded with 1,040 plates, dishes, etc." and served by a host of servants who "satisfied every desire before one could express it." There were many toasts, "no lack of huzzas, and the dance, resumed after the banquet, lasted until six o'clock in the

---

131 TC to Low, Mar. 24, 1778. See also TC to Goold, March 31, in which Coxe observed that there was "not the least symptom" of British withdrawal and "many powerful Reasons which render it impossible."

132 TC to Goold, Mar. 31, 1778.

133 TC to Skinner, Yates & Van Dam, May 5, 1778.

134 TC to Barrell, May 10, 1778.

135 Oberholtzer, I, 274.

morning."[136] The guest list included a good number of Coxe's relatives and friends—the Chews, the Redmans, the Bonds, the Shippens, the Frankses[137]—and perhaps Tench himself.

Although blithely unaware that the extravaganza symbolized the end of an era, Coxe was disturbed by the "confused state of affairs" occasioned by the change of command. By the second week of May official permissions for the clearance of ships, without which trade ground to a halt, were as scarce as they had been plentiful only a few weeks earlier. Philadelphia's harbor was crowded with idle ships which could neither be loaded nor sold.[138] The revival of trade depended on Sir Henry Clinton, the new commanding general, who having arrived on May 8 was, as Coxe commented, so "totally engaged in receiving the returns and making the new arrangements" that the prospect appeared poor.[139] Nor was the frosty reception Coxe suddenly met from British officials encouraging.[140] Not that his relationship with them over previous months had been uniformly cordial. Certain buildings belonging to his friend John Coxe, and

[136] The quotations are from "Letters of Major Baurmeister," *PMHB*, LX (1936), 179–180. See also *Royal Pennsylvania Gazette*, May 26, 1778. An excellent account is in Oberholtzer, I, 275.

[137] The list is taken from Oberholtzer, I, 275–276.

[138] Commenting on his inability to sell their brig *Bella*, Coxe wrote Barrell, Stoughton & Davis on May 9, 1778, that "so great a number of vessels of all kinds are for sale, that it is not possible to do anything with the Brig . . . ," despite the fact that "her guns are good and extremely valuable." He could only recommend that "if privateer commissions should be granted in America she would do well for that business."

[139] The more so in view of an embargo which was imposed on May 9, 1778. TC to Goold, May 9, 1778; TC to Barrell, May 10, 1778. "Our business is on the same uncertain footing as with you," Coxe complained to Goold on May 9. "Four West India men have been entered here & a fifth under the same circumstance was seized. . . . These are strange doings." TC to Goold, May 9, 1778. Early the following week he informed Barrell that no ships were allowed to sail, a ban for which he could not "well guess the Reason." TC to Barrell, Stoughton & Davis, May 12, 1778.

[140] Commenting on the baffling uncooperativeness of Galloway and his subordinates Coxe plaintively remarked to Goold that "you are very happy in having as good a man as Mr. Elliot for your Superintendent General." TC to Goold, May 9, 1778. In a similar vein Coxe complained to Barrell and associates that although Admiral Howe had "preferred" Coxe's memorial praying permission for Barrell's brig to sail with the British fleet "then preparing," Tench could "hear nothing of its being handed to headquarters. The General's secretary informed me that it had never been sent to that office." TC to Barrell, Stoughton & Davis, May 9, 1778.

entrusted to Tench's care, had been taken over in the face of his angry protest for use as an armory;[141] other property belonging to John Coxe was subject to vandalism and thievery by British soldiers[142] against which Tench's remonstrances were of no avail; moreover, soon after John Coxe's departure for England in December, 1777,[143] the Barrack Master of the city, Captain Paine, demanded that Tench turn over the key to his friend's residence. Not only that, Paine also "plagued" Coxe "in my personal affairs" and, in general, "has behaved in ye most un-Genteel Manner to many of ye citizens with some of whom he was intimate before his Escalation" to Barracks Master, "among others, Billy Allen & myself."[144] Now, in May, what had been atypical, if bothersome, high-handedness became, so Coxe believed, systematic harassment. The behavior of Joseph Galloway he viewed as "uncommonly malevolent,"[145] particularly the incident already described in which the Superintendent General, searching for contraband goods, ordered his deputies to break open the door of Coxe's warehouse. "A step so indecent & cruel you may be sure gave me no little shock," Coxe angrily reported. "If I ever forget, it must be because my senses & feelings are impaired by Time & I hope to remember it in the day when I can punish him for it without any fear of his Patron."[146] Although not going to the extreme of search and seizure, other British officials were also (and to Coxe inexplicably) uncooperative.[147] But he could at least console himself that a few influential British officers continued to promote his interests. One steadfast ally was Commodore Hammond who interceded with both Admiral and General Howe in an effort to secure Coxe a license to import a cargo from Madeira.[148]

---

141 TC to Goold, June 16, 1778. The buildings were taken over by a Major Farmington of the Artillery who used them as an armory until the British evacuation of the City.

142 TC to John Coxe, Mar. 18, 1778.

143 TC to John Dennie, Dec. 17, 1777.

144 TC to John Coxe, May 21, 1778.

145 TC to Bruely, May 2, 1778.

146 TC to Skinner, Yates & Van Dam, May 5, 1778. The contraband for which Galloway was searching consisted of the arms Coxe had received aboard the *Lord Howe*, whose cargo had been consigned to Coxe by a group of St. Croix merchants.

147 TC to Thompson, May 17, 1778.

148 TC to Barrell, Stoughton & Davis, May 9, 1778.

Another was Daniel Wier, the Commissary General, who, Coxe wrote on May 21, was exercising "all the influence" he could exert to win approval of his solicitation of "permission to export a quantity of goods as agent for the contractors."[149]

Such efforts were exercises in futility, for the British commanders, as both the Commodore and the Commissary General doubtless knew, surely would not issue licenses to supply a city they planned to turn over to the enemy. Coxe, however, mistook the stirring of military activity of the British, preparatory to leaving Philadelphia,[150] as preparations for a campaign to crush the American army. The British were preparing to take the offensive, he wrote on May 22, and "are throwing out everything that can induce the people out of the lines to believe they are going to evacuate ye City. Their view is probably to bring General Washington as near ye city as possible & so push into his rear & force him to a General Action."[151] Within a few days the illusion was shattered, the blow the more stunning because so unexpected. By early June, orders came from Headquarters instructing the city's merchants to ship out all goods on hand.[152] Coxe was not entirely unprepared. The repeated warnings of his New York associates had been a constant reminder that should Philadelphia be evacuated speedy action must be taken to assure the safety of their goods, a step he quickly proceeded to follow. He also hurried about in a frantic effort to collect outstanding debts (amounting to at least £9,000 as of May 24)[153] and to dispose of goods on hand, whether by sale or immediate shipment to New York. For the latter expedient, Coxe, at the insistence of his New York correspondents, had made plans months before. Reassuring Goold on March 31 that "I ought to omit nothing which will conduce to the safety and interest of my friends," he reported that he had two vessels in readiness to transport the property of his consignors back to New York.[154] On May 28, two idle vessels belonging to his

---

149 TC to Summers & Cliburn, May 21, 1778.

150 It began as early as May 21 when the British began "loading the heavy baggage, all the heavy artillery, and the greater part of the train on board the Ships." "Letters of Major Baurmeister," *PMHB*, LX (1936), 175.

151 TC to Wigram, May 22, 1778.

152 TC to Barrell, June 8, 1778.

153 TC to Aduljo & Maitland, Sept. 24, 1785.

154 TC to Goold, Mar. 31, 1778. Some twenty years later a copy of this letter was acquired in some way by the editor of the *Gazette of the United States* as documentary proof of Coxe's

New York friends (though not the same as those to which Coxe had referred two months earlier) were anchored in Philadelphia harbor —the brig *Bella*, property of Colburn Barrell, and the brig *Expedition*, owned by Yates & Skinner. Hastily, not even taking time to prepare bills of lading or separate invoices, Coxe, with the assistance of his four clerks,[155] had them loaded with all the goods in his well-stocked warehouse.[156] Within five days, a scene "the most confused I ever was in,"[157] the job was done and on June 4, 1778, from his store facing the river Coxe could see the two brigs, sails billowing, as they dropped down the river, carrying away the rich cargo.[158] Though gratified by his success, Coxe was exhausted. "O God My dear friend," he confided to Goold, "what with hurry, Business & Anxiety, I am almost jaded to Death. Such another week as the last would have put an End to my Existence. To increase my Distress Mrs. Coxe is extremely ill."[159]

During the following days, as the British completed preparations for evacuating the city, apprehension about his wife's health rose steadily.[160] He stifled it as best he could in order to concentrate his attention and energy on what, for the moment, was "the most important point,"[161] collecting the large sums of money owing to his correspondents and himself. Since many of his creditors were hastily packing up for departure with the British from a city which, in the

---

Toryism during the Revolution. *Gazette of the United States*, Oct. 5, 1799. A week or so before his letter to Goold, Coxe similarly had assured Barrell that he had "two Vessels here at my command, whose sole employment should be carrying the effects of my friends & myself." TC to Barrell, Mar. 23, 1778.

155 TC to Aduljo & Maitland, Sept. 24, 1785.

156 TC to Barrell, June 8, 1778. See also TC to Goold, June 4, 1778. They were loaded under the watchful eye of British officials who were overseeing the order to Philadelphia merchants to reship all their goods. *Ibid.*

157 TC to Yates, June 3, 1778.

158 Aboard the *Bella* were goods belonging to Colborn Barrell, Benjamin Davis, John Houghton, Edward Goold, Isaac Low, Abraham C. Cuyler, Beekman, Son & Goold, Gerard and George Beekman, Thomas B. Attwood, Hamilton Young, Alexander Kennedy & Co., Christopher Miller, Philip Kearney and Robert Watts; aboard the *Expedition* was a shipment of wine belonging to Skinner & Yates.

159 TC to Goold, June 3, 1778.

160 Sometime in May, Coxe apparently sent her to his father's retreat at Sunbury. How long she remained there is not revealed in his correspondence.

161 TC to Barrell, June 3, 1778.

words of a Hessian officer, resembled "a fair during the last week of business,"[162] it was apparent that what he did not immediately garner might be lost irretrievably. Although forced in some instances to take goods in payment,[163] he generally insisted on taking "securities from all persons that owe me here, except really good men, payable in bills of Exc^e in London,"[164] preferably paymaster's bills.[165] Simultaneously, he was attempting to sell such goods as had not been shipped to New York on June 4, a task made the more difficult because of "a great glut on the market."[166] Nevertheless, during the week or so preceding the evacuation, he sold "sundry merchandize" belonging to Abraham Cuyler for the sum of £2,600,[167] and such goods of Barrell's as remained in his hands for about £8,000.[168] In view of the estimated indebtedness of some £10,000 sterling with which the British evacuation left other merchants saddled,[169] Coxe was remarkably successful in collecting the money outstanding on his books.[170]

Nevertheless, it was, as Coxe repeatedly said, a time of "distress and trial,"[171] the more poignant because of his wife's illness. "Mrs. Coxe continues extremely ill," he lamented. "Heaven only knows what will be the Event—I dare not begin to fear for her."[172] To add to his burden, the departing British Army treated him no more kindly than had the patriot vigilantes some eighteen months earlier —muskets stored in his warehouse were seized on orders of the commander in chief;[173] lumber on hand was confiscated for the use of the

---

162 "Letters of Major Baurmeister," *PMHB*, LX (1936), 175.
163 TC to Barrell, June 3, 1778.
164 TC to Barrell, Goold & Attwood, June 16, 1778.
165 TC to John Coxe, June 10, 1778.
166 TC to Thomas Attwood, June 3, 1778.
167 "Account with Abraham C. Cuyler," June, 1778.
168 TC to Barrell, June 17, 1778.
169 *Pennsylvania Packet*, July 18, 1778.
170 Some merchants hurriedly left Philadelphia, however, without settling their accounts with Coxe, among them Samuel Kerr, formerly of Virginia, Henry Johns, "a tolerably honest man" who carried away "goods to a good amount," James Stuart, who was "wealthy and well able to pay," and Michael Jacobs, who "has behaved in a very dishonest way." TC to Barrell, Goold & Attwood, June 16, 1778.
171 TC to Barrell, June 17, 1778; to Goold and others, June 17, 1778; to Skinner, Yates & Van Dam, June 16, 1778.
172 TC to Goold, June 4, 1778.
173 John Smith to TC, May 22, 1778.

British armory;[174] a departing British officer stole valuable furniture from John Coxe's house on Front Street of which Tench was custodian.[175] "The British Army here have used me in such a way that I must not trust myself to speak of their conduct," he angrily complained on June 10.[176] The worst was yet to come. On the eve of the evacuation, British soldiers quartered above Coxe's store broke open a first-story window, wrecked and plundered the store, making off with a hundred cases of gin, among other things.[177]

By this time it was clear that whatever his wishes Coxe could not join the 3,000-odd fellow-Loyalists (including his brother-in-law, Andrew Allen)[178] who were preparing to leave the city with the King's troops. His wife was obviously too ill to withstand the trip to New York and his devotion to her far outweighed fears for his personal safety.[179]

The evacuation began on June 17 when British troops, heavily encumbered by provisions and equipment, moved across the river into New Jersey, and Royal transports, carrying heavy guns, auxiliary troops, and a large retinue of Tories, sailed out of the harbor. Just after dawn on the 18th the rear guard departed, encountering on their way an American patrol entering the city. Some shots were exchanged, but the Redcoats marched on,[180] leaving behind them a city in ruins—houses wrecked, "trees destroyed . . . churches and public buildings defiled . . . Camp litter and filth everywhere; fences broken; . . . gardens and orchards trampled up and ruined."[181] It

---

174 TC to Mrs. Wood, June, 1778.

175 TC to John Coxe, June 10, 1778. The officer was "Capt. Bulkely, now of the 43d," who "lived in a house of mine" and to whom Tench "lent" furniture belonging to John Coxe. Upon learning of the theft, Tench pursued the captain who relinquished some of the furniture but "still secreted more." Coxe complained to General Clinton's aide-de-camp, Lord Rawdon, who would have made Bulkely pay had not the Captain "got away in his vessel too soon." TC to Goold, June 16, 1778.

176 TC to John Coxe, June 10, 1778.

177 Joseph Sherwell to TC, May 15, 1779.

178 Andrew Allen has "gone with the British Army to New York," his brother James said, "from whence he intends going to England." "Diary of James Allen," *PMHB*, IX (1885), 440.

179 Even if his wife had not been critically ill he presumably would have remained in Philadelphia for what he elliptically described as "other reasons." TC to Yates, June 3, 1778; to John Coxe, June 10, 1778.

180 "Letters of Major Baurmeister," *PMHB*, LX (1936), 181. For a brief account of the evacuation see *The Pennsylvania Evening Post*, June 20, 1778.

181 Oberholtzer, I, 281. An investigation by the Pennsylvania Assembly estimated that the damage to property in and around the city was almost £200,000. *Ibid.*

was the most desolate day of Coxe's life. His world was in shambles, his wife slowly dying, his well-calculated plans destroyed, his property, repute, and safety in jeopardy. His last letter before the British left mirrored his despair: "And now my dearest best Friend," he wrote to Goold, "I am to bid a long adieu. I ask Mrs. Goold to receive my tender love. . . . Shall I ever sufficiently thank you for your innumerable unparalleled acts of Kindness, Friendship & Generosity towards me. This American World will not afford you happiness sufficient for ye goodness of your excellent heart. . . . I bid you a long & tender farewell earnestly beseeching the God of all mercies to preserve protect & defend you. . . . Kiss your dear little Children for me."[182] Whatever his fears and perhaps his plans for departing "this American World," such melodramatic phrases accurately portrayed his belief that his happiness and security were now at an end. "Farewell" he hastily scrawled in his letter book as he closed it on the evening of June 17th, and, then, in large letters merely "Fare!"

On the morning following the evacuation, Major General Benedict Arnold, accompanied by "Col. Jackson's Massachusetts regiment," took possession of Philadelphia.[183] The American commander, who was invested by Washington with authority to establish military law in the city and to prevent the removal or sale of any goods in possession of the inhabitants until it could be determined "any or what thereof may belong to the king of Great Britain, or any of his subjects"[184] promptly directed that all persons having certain goods in excess of the needs of their own families make an immediate "return of the same to the town major" by noon on June 20.[185] Whatever his personal plight, Coxe could take satisfaction in having shipped off and sold the sizeable quantity of goods belonging to his Tory correspondents. He also could take some comfort in the knowledge that, just as influential friends and relatives had smoothed the road to his business success during the British occupation, so now highly-placed Whig acquaintances and connections might rescue him from the lash of patriot retaliation. The assistance of his cousin Colonel Tench Tilghman, who as Washington's aide-de-camp had

[182] TC to Goold, June 17, 1778.
[183] *The Pennsylvania Evening Post*, June 20, 1778.
[184] *Ibid.* Washington issued the latter instruction in pursuance of a resolution of the Continental Congress, dated June 4, 1778.
[185] *Ibid.*

earned the unqualified confidence of the General, was already assured, Tilghman having agreed to forward letters addressed to Coxe by Edward Goold in New York;[186] the strong support of his close friend David S. Franks, aide-de-camp to General Arnold was certain. As Tench sadly realized, however, the threat to his security and property came not from the American army but from the Pennsylvania civil authorities.

On May 21, 1778, Coxe's name had appeared on a "Proclamation of Attainder" issued by the Supreme Executive Council of Pennsylvania "against certain persons adjudged guilty of High Treason."[187] Two days later,[188] acting quickly to forestall conviction, he had taken the oath of allegiance prescribed by an act of the Pennsylvania legislature enacted in June of the previous year.[189] Whether such a simple act of repentance revealed an absence of commitment to either side, a flexible conscience, or a desperate effort to salvage his fortune, and perhaps his neck, cannot be known. But if Coxe believed that this alone would avert his conviction he was being uncharacteristically fanciful. Something more than an oath was needed, as the fate of other prominent Tories attested. Joseph Galloway, members of the Allen family, David Sproat, and Samuel Kirk, business associates during the occupation, among other acquaintances and relatives, also were attainted of treason and their property subsequently confiscated.[190] A symbolic reminder of the threat he faced was the

---

186 TC to Goold, June 17, 1778.

187 *Pennsylvania Archives*, Fourth Series, III, 676. The proclamation was printed in the *Pennsylvania Packet* on June 3, 1778.

188 Although the manner in which he either secured a pass or arranged to travel outside British lines without one is not clear, Coxe presumably left Philadelphia on May 22 to seek out a Pennsylvania notary before whom he could take an oath of allegiance to the United States (see the note below). This may account for a five-day gap—May 22-28, 1778—in his letter book.

189 Coxe preserved a copy of the oath in his papers. It read as follows: "I HEREBY CERTIFY, THAT [Tench] Cox of the City of Philadelpa. Merchant [hath] voluntarily taken and subscribed the OATH [of alle]giance and Fidelity, as directed by an ACT [of Gen]eral Assembly of Pennsylvania, passed the 13th [day of] June, A.D. 1777. Witness my hand [and seal the] 23 day of May A.D. 1778. ([s]) John Knowles" (brackets indicate missing words due to damage to the MS). There is another copy of this document in the HSP from which the bracketed material is taken.

190 See Lorenzo Sabine, *Biographical Sketches of Loyalists of the American Revolution* (Boston, 1864), I, 158, 453-457; II, 324-325, 541. Coxe's friend, David Franks, to give one more example, was arrested in 1778 for having provided the British with information. *Ibid.*, I, 444.

439

civilian tenant of Joseph Galloway's splendid mansion at the corner of 6th and Market Streets, George Bryan, Acting-President of the State's Supreme Executive Council. Even more ominous was the popular wrath which soon erupted against those who had collaborated in the alleged barbarities of the British invaders, a situation which to Coxe must have been a chilling reminder of his experience in November, 1776, when angry patriots drove him from the city. Now, again, Tories were being mobbed and some even executed (though, interestingly enough, they were craftsmen and artisans, rather than well-to-do merchants).[191] "The consternation occasioned" by the British evacuation, one of Coxe's relatives and associates commented, "was terrible, as every man obnoxious to the American rulers was offered up a Victim to their resentment."[192] The popular mood was mirrored by a writer in *The Pennsylvania Evening Post* who asked if those "villanous [sic] paricides who have aided, abetted, and comforted our most unnatural foes in the commission of every murder, theft, and rapine" should be left "in peace and safety, to enjoy . . . the blessings of that freedom for which we have been contending at the price of everything that is dear?" Reject the "death-bed repentances" of the Tories, it was urged, remembering that "even the ark of the Lord should be no sanctuary for crimes so heinous."[193]

These were weeks of frustration, humiliation, and anguish. The proclamation of attainder and treason was distressing enough; anxiety over his wife's fatal illness would have been painful at any time. Combined, they rendered this a period of unrelieved despair, and perhaps of regret. His seemingly inexorable fate, however, was averted not by repentance but by the influence of his father, William Coxe, Sr. Assurances "from my father soon put the danger of personal confinement or injury out of the question," he wrote to his cousin William Tilghman in mid-July.[194] The danger presumably

---

[191] Two old men, Abraham Carlisle and John Roberts, one a carpenter, the other a miller, were accused of collaboration and "of harsh treatment of Whigs." They "were convicted, sentenced to death and hanged on the commons." Oberholtzer, I, 283.

[192] "Diary of James Allen," *PMHB*, IX (1885), 438.

[193] *Pennsylvania Evening Post*, July 18, 1778.

[194] July 13, 1778. According to Tench this statement was made to his wife, but Tench himself obviously received the same assurances.

was removed by one or several of William Coxe's influential friends or relatives[195] who had farsightedly embraced the American cause and could command the ear of Pennsylvania's Chief Justice, Thomas McKean,[196] who along with Congress and the State government had returned to Philadelphia. "The chief justice has been sitting at the city court-house for several days past, the *Evening Post* announced on July 9, in order "to hear the charges against Tories accused of joining & assisting the British Army."[197] On one of those hot days Coxe appeared before him. "His behaviour," Tench reported to William Tilghman, "was much more friendly than I could have expected & genteel." Although Coxe was required to give bond for his impending trial, he came away from the conference convinced that "no proofs" would "be laid" against himself or other prominent Loyalists before the Grand Jury, and that "we shall in general be dismissed."[198] Such confidence could only have been based on Mc-Kean's assurances. One of Coxe's partisan critics, writing some twenty years later, declared that, though "proscribed . . . as a traitor," Coxe escaped severe punishment "only from compassion to his youth and the worth of some of his relatives."[199] The "man who saved him, whose influence protected him," another political enemy correctly pointed out, was McKean.[200] Certainly his conversation with the Chief Justice transformed Coxe. Momentarily forgotten were the preceding harrowing days, gone the despair of the man who had scribbled "Farewell" in his letter book. "I should prefer," he complacently wrote his cousin, "a general dismissal of the charges rather than an act of oblivion because I see no necessity for an oblivion of a man's conduct whose intentions at least were not criminal and who can only be rendered offensive by an ex post facto law."[201]

195 Coxe was pleasurably shocked by the attention paid him by influential patriots who were family friends. As he commented to Tilghman, "I have received many extraordinary visits considering all circumstances." TC to Tilghman, July 13, 1778.

196 McKean, who had been appointed Chief Justice of Pennsylvania on July 28, 1777, was distantly related to Coxe by marriage.

197 *The Pennsylvania Evening Post*, July 9, 1778.

198 TC to Tilghman, July 13, 1799.

199 *Gazette of the United States*, Sept. 4, 1799.

200 *Aurora*, Aug. 29, 1804.

201 TC to Tilghman, July 13, 1799.

Soon after his interview with the Chief Justice, Coxe escaped the heat of the city and the "filth, stench and flies" which, according to one observer, were "scarcely credible,"[202] by renting "a little retirement . . . for the summer at the Falls of Schuylkill."[203] The change would not only make his wife more comfortable but, he ardently wished, perhaps restore her health. This, he soon painfully learned, neither climate nor medicine could do. Some two weeks later, on July 22, she died.[204] Coxe was again cast into deep gloom. Two months of anguish ensued, relieved only by the dismissal "by proclamation" of the charge of high treason.[205] Coxe explained, many years later, that "he submitted himself to legal investigation, and was informed that there were enough of witnesses in his favor, but none against him."[206] Youth has its own amazing resilience and before long, following a visit with his parents some time in September,[207] Coxe, displaying once again his characteristic optimism, was ready to resume mercantile business. It was now his job to pick and choose from his past in order to master his future. "I am (if permitted)" he wrote, "likely to become a good American."[208]

Lafayette College JACOB E. COOKE

[202] Christopher Marshall, who returned to Philadelphia on June 24, 1778. Oberholtzer, I, 281.

[203] TC to Tilghman, July 13, 1778.

[204] Keen, "The Descendants of Jöran Kyn," *PMHB*, V (1881), 458.

[205] *Pennsylvania Archives*, Fourth Series, III, 938; *ibid.*, Sixth Series, XIII, 475.

[206] *Aurora*, Aug. 25, 1804. The absence of adverse witnesses was explained by a writer in *The Pennsylvania Evening Post* on July 18, 1778, who commented that many Philadelphia Whigs were indebted to some of the accused Tories, men of former "office and power," for previous favors. Moreover, "those Whigs who left the City, could not possibly be acquainted with facts but by information," and were reluctant to offer hearsay evidence acquired from an "informer," a species of person who "heretofore has been held in high obloquy and reproach."

[207] TC to Goold, Oct. 20, 1778.

[208] TC to John Coxe, June 10, 1778.

The Associated Loyalists: An Aspect of Militant Loyalism

By EDWARD H. TEBBENHOFF*

THE Associated Loyalists are generally dismissed by historians of the American Revolution as a band of thieves and murderers. Described as licensed outlaws, they ranged from the gentle hills of Connecticut to the sand dunes along the Jersey coast, purportedly looting homes and churches, burning crops, carrying off prisoners and livestock, and generally leaving death and destruction in their wake.[1] Although armed by the British and ostensibly fighting for the king, neither whig nor tory remained safe from their depredations. The historian Thomas Jones, himself a loyalist, maintained that profit became the sole basis of their allegiance. They operated, Jones argued, in collusion with whig marauders—both sides giving notice "of the persons most proper to make prisoners of, the situation of their houses, and where the most plunder was likely to be obtained." Lorenzo Sabine, the mid nineteenth century author of one of the first objective studies of loyalism, echoed Jones' view, pronouncing the conduct of the organization "disgraceful." Had it not been for the Associated Loyalists, Sabine stated flatly, "the warfare in the region of Long Island and in New Jersey would have been far different; and horrors, at which humanity revolts, would not have stained the records of the Revolutionary era." Unfortunately, more recent historians have accepted this analysis with little further investigation.[2]

---

*The author is currently pursuing doctoral studies at the University of Minnesota, Minneapolis, where he is a teaching assistant in the history department. This article is the product of a graduate seminar at Duquesne University, Pittsburgh. The author would like to thank James G. Lydon and Joseph R. Morice of Duquesne, and Arthur Acton of Marietta College, Marietta, Ohio, for their help and encouragement.

[1] Justin Winsor, ed., *The American Revolution: A Narrative, Critical and Bibliographical History* (New York, 1972), 198.

[2] Thomas Jones, *History of New York During the Revolutionary War*, 2 v. (New York,

[115]

443

In this scene, titled "The Tory's Day of Judgment," patriots gather on the village green to punish the loyalists in their midst. One loyalist is run up a pole while another waits to be tarred and feathered. This picture illustrated John Trumbull's book McFingal: A Modern Epic Poem *(New York, 1795).*
THE NEW-YORK HISTORICAL SOCIETY

The interpretation presented here aims more at understanding the Associated Loyalists than judging them. Made bitter and vindictive by their hardships, the organizers of the Associated Loyalists demanded to be "unleashed against rebellion," to lay waste the seacoasts of the enemy, employing a policy of destruction and terrorism, thus forcing each American to choose one side or the other.[3] Other more moderate men favored a strictly limited, tightly controlled use of armed loyalists. They realized that a war of destruction such as the militants proposed would completely poison the American political climate and cast grave doubts on the possibility of reconciliation. The moderates retained a tight control of the Associated Loyalists and carefully monitored their activities. As a result, the raids conducted by the organization seldom exhibited the extremes of violence desired by the organizers and chronicled by historians. A fuller understanding of the Associated Loyalists may shed some light on a misunderstood aspect of loyalism. Furthermore, examining how and why the militant loyalists were restrained may provide insights into why the American Revolution lacked many of the violent intolerances found in other similar upheavals.

In a suggestive article on armed loyalism, John Shy points out that "during 1778, Loyalists moved from the periphery toward the center of the war, and as they did so the lower Hudson valley became especially important as the place where first-hand British impressions of American Loyalism were most readily and influentially formed."[4] Two

---

1968), I, 302; Lorenzo Sabine, *Biographical Sketches of Loyalists of the American Revolution,* 2 v. (Port Washington, 1966), II, 21. For recent studies that accept the view of Jones and Sabine, see Oscar Theodore Barck, *New York City During the War of Independence, 1776–1783* (Port Washington, 1966), 203–06; William A. Benton, *Whig-Loyalism: An Aspect of Political Ideology in the American Revolution* (Cranbury, N.J., 1969), 196–97; and Thomas Jefferson Wertenbaker, *Father Knickerbocker Rebels: New York City During the American Revolution* (New York, 1948), 229–31. In this study, the terms "whig" and "rebel" are used interchangeably throughout this article. "Whig," while not completely accurate as a description of the American revolutionaries, is used here simply as a convenience, and in preference to the words "American" and "patriot," which carry even greater connotative meanings. The term "rebel," of course, was used by the loyalists themselves to describe the revolutionary side.

3 John Shy, "Armed Loyalism: The Case of the Lower Hudson Valley," in Shy, *A People Numerous and Armed: Reflections on the Miiltary Struggle for American Independence* (New York, 1976), 188.

4 *Ibid.,* 185.

distinct views on the nature and conduct of the war emerged. Certain loyalists, British officials, and military men saw the traditional loyalist claim of widespread allegiance as illusory. They urged that Britain should place no great reliance on the allegiance of much of the population, for their loyalty all too frequently shifted with military fortune. The Earl of Carlisle, who headed the unsuccessful peace commission of 1778, lamented, "in our present condition the only friends we have, or are likely to have, are those who are absolutely ruined for us."[5]

Chief among the latter were those militant loyalists, known collectively as the Refugees, whose hatred, fear, or desperation attached them irrevocably to the British cause. Occupied New York became the haven for such men from throughout the colonies—old colonial governors, wealthy landowners, merchants deprived of their estates, and simple ordinary citizens fleeing physical abuse and persecution. They had become convinced, in the words of one, "that they must be miserable—perhaps lose everything unless the King prevails."[6] Like many loyalists, the Refugees favored a policy of actively prosecuting the war, continually applying pressure until the revolution collapsed. The Refugees also desired something more: they wanted not only victory but vengeance. "They frowned on all talk of concessions, pardons and moderation, and demanded a war *à outrance* and a Carthaginian peace."[7] Noted one Refugee, "I shall suffer much in my property but will bear it cheerfully, provided the day of retribution is not passed."[8]

Campaigns of terrorism and retaliation proved central to the militants' solution for victory. Besides gratifying the Refugees' thirst for vengeance, such a war of destruction would exhibit the invincibility of British power and inflict psychological as well as physical damage. Lord Rawdon, a Briton who later in the war commanded a loyalist regiment, noted as early as 1776, "I think we should (whenever we get

[5] Frederick Howard, fifth Earl of Carlisle to Lady Carlisle, July 21, 1778, quoted in *ibid.*, 186.

[6] Charles Inglis to Joseph Galloway, December 12, 1778, Thomas Balch Papers, New York Public Library. Hereafter cited as Balch Papers. The term "Refugees" seems to have been applied by contemporaries—British, loyalist, and whig—as a general name for those more militant loyalists who advocated a hard-line stance on the conduct of the war. The term is not confined to a particular period but was used throughout the war.

[7] Arthur Acton, "The Diary of William Smith, August 26, 1978 to December 31, 1779," (Ph.D. diss., University of Michigan at Ann Arbor, 1970), xlviii.

[8] Charles Stewart to Joseph Galloway, December 1, 1778, Balch Papers.

further into their country) give free liberty to the soldiers to ravage it at will, that these infatuated creatures may feel what a calamity war is."[9] William Franklin, the last royal governor of New Jersey, continually urged the ministry to adopt more stringent measures. In a letter to Lord George Germain, Secretary of State for the Colonies, he wrote that a majority of Americans "ardently wish to see a respectable Army of the King's Forces sent into their Country, and say they would far rather see the whole Country laid waste, though their property would be destroyed with others, rather than live under such Tyranny as they are compell'd to at present."[10] Those in rebellion, the Refugees argued, should be made aware that the British could strike virtually anywhere along the coastline and that the Congress could do little to protect its adherents. Governor William Tryon of New York, immediately prior to his raids on Fairfield and New Haven in 1779, issued a threatening proclamation to the inhabitants of Connecticut. He warned them of the dangers of supporting the rebellion:

The existence of a single habitation on your defenseless coast ought to be a constant reproof to your ingratitude. Can the strength of your whole Province cope with the force which might at any time be poured through every district in your country? You are conscious it cannot. Why then will you persist in a ruinous and ill-judged resistance?[11]

By openly advocating a war of depredation and revenge the Refugees willingly burned their bridges behind them. They could never again accommodate themselves with their countrymen should Britain fail to achieve anything but complete victory. William Smith, a loyalist vehemently opposed to the Refugees' proposals, movingly described their pitiable dilemma:

They can be safe by Nothing but a Conquest of their own Country. If America prevails by the Sword or obtains Concessions to her Contentment, the Tories are ruined. In either Case they must finally abandon the Continent.[12]

[9] Francis, Lord Rawdon to the Earl of Hastings, September 25, 1776, quoted in Shy, *People Numerous and Armed*, 286.

[10] William Franklin to Lord George Germain, November 12, 1778, quoted in Mary Beth Norton, *The British Americans: The Loyalist Exiles in England, 1774–1789* (New York, 1972), 166.

[11] "An Address to the Inhabitants of Connecticut. . . ," New York *Royal Gazette*, July 7, 1779.

[12] William H. Sabine, ed., *Historical Memoirs . . . of William Smith*, 3 v. (New York, 1958–71), II, 39. Hereafter cited as Smith, *Memoirs*.

The ideas promoted by the Refugees reflected only a portion of loyalist sentiment. Other more moderate loyalists and British officials sought a different means of conducting the war. Their attitudes stemmed from different experiences and perspectives. Having generally suffered less for their loyalty, the moderates could better afford the luxury of open-mindedness toward the whigs.[13] Not blinded by a spirit of revenge, they were better able to detect the subtleties of political allegiance. Under what conditions, for example, would a New Jersey farmer become disgusted with the machinations of Congress and permanently resume his faith and trust in, and support of, the English government? The moderates perceived a shallow commitment among many supporters of the rebellion. In January 1778, Peter DuBois, a New Jersey loyalist, reported to Sir Henry Clinton that "General discontent [with Congress] prevails amongst the most disloyal and disaffected." If this demoralization—evidenced by recruiting problems, rising desertion rates, sky-rocketing prices coupled with a steady devaluation of continental money, plus simple weariness of years of indecisive warfare—could be exploited, the rebellion would collapse from lack of support. The moderates urged that "the great middle ground between active rebellion and active Loyalism should be broadened and strengthened, not cut away" by acts of terrorism and retaliation.[14] They proposed to treat those not actively engaged in fighting the British with leniency. Peter DuBois noted:

I would have the leading men secured and treated with humanity, but reserved for justice; but the aged and decrepid [sic]—the women and children—the industrious peasant—and the man unarmed and unarrayed for hostile purpose, should rest in quiet in his own cottage, and pursue the labours of his fields, without interruption; to him the horrors of war should

---

[13] Acton, "Diary of William Smith," xlvii–xlix, lxxiii–lxxiv; Shy, *People Numerous and Armed*, 189, 191–92. Of the two leading moderates, for example, neither William Smith nor Andrew Elliot suffered unduly. Smith remained on fairly good terms with Governor George Clinton of New York and other leading revolutionaries even after he entered the British lines. Smith was also one of the very few leading loyalists whose property escaped confiscation; see Benton, *Whig-Loyalism*, 198. Andrew Elliot actually advanced himself politically and financially during the British occupation of New York; see Robert Ernst, "Andrew Elliot, Forgotten Loyalist of Occupied New York," *New York History*, LVII (July 1976), 285–320.

[14] Memorandum, January 24, 1778, Clinton Papers, William L. Clements Library, Ann Arbor, Michigan. Hereafter cited as Clinton Papers. Shy, *People Numerous and Armed*, 187–88.

be unknown, whatever might be his speculative opinions, provided those were not accompanied with open acts of persecution and violence against those who differed in sentiments with him.[15]

Such beliefs did not mean, of course, that victory on the field of battle should be ignored. The armed loyalists could be used to good effect, but only if they were tightly controlled. Their mobility and intimate knowledge of the countryside, to cite only two of their attributes, would prove extremely useful to the British.[16] William Smith, a foremost advocate of moderation, urged that continual raids upon the seacoasts would keep whig militia in perpetual mobilization and "bring the Rebels to despair of Safety under their Republican Leaders!" He emphasized, however, that the objects of these raids must be military targets, not civilian ones, for continuous and indiscriminate plundering would turn friends into enemies and strengthen the hand of Congress.[17]

The dilemma embedded in the debate between the Refugees and the moderates centered on the control of the armed loyalists. Andrew Elliot, another leading proponent of moderation, neatly summed up the tension between these two disparate views in a letter to the Earl of Carlisle:

They [the Refugees] wish much to be embodied under a Commander of their own to make excursions; this plan if well conducted under the Commander in Chief of His Majesty's forces may be useful if a destructive war is to be carried on, as in that case they might in armed vessels annoy all the Coast on the Sound, destroy shipping, boats, warehouses, etc etc, the burning of dwelling houses can answer no purpose and excursions to Jersey a Country already destroyed by both sides would only distress. . . . Country people and fill our Jails with Prisoners that Congress would never pay any attention to, as private revenge would often direct the seizing of Prisoners; It will therefore be dangerous to use Refugees but as the Commander in Chief directs and to him alone they should look up, a separate command given to any other person will produce disagreeable consequences in times

[15] Peter DuBois to Mrs. DuBois, May 28, 1779, quoted in William Nelson, ed., *Documents Relating to the Revolutionary History of the State of New Jersey*, 5 v. (Trenton, 1901–17), III, 427–28.

[16] Bernard Uhlendorf, ed., *Revolution in America: Confidential Letters and Journals, 1776–1783, of Adjutant General Major Baurmeister of the Hessian Forces* (New Brunswick, N.J., 1957), 361.

[17] Smith, *Memoirs*, III, 240; Acton, "Diary of William Smith," xxxvii.

when revenge and necessity go hand in hand and England aims more at conciliating than conquering.[18]

Prior to 1779, militant loyalists in New York had no unified or effective organization to promote their views. While various provincial regiments existed, many loyalists seemed reluctant to bear the long-term enlistments, harsh discipline, and the possibility of being sent "to Provinces far distant from that in which they formerly resided, and where they have Friends and Connections, and might be employed to the most Advantage."[19] Furthermore, British commanders had hitherto shown little interest or confidence in these levies. As a result the militants gathered in the taverns of the city, lamenting in equal measure British neglect and the whigs' ill-treatment of them.[20]

The arrival in New York of William Franklin, in October 1778, significantly altered this situation. The natural son of Benjamin Franklin, and until 1776 the royal governor of New Jersey, Franklin had been imprisoned for two years in Connecticut. Embittered by the "extraordinary rigor and severity" of his treatment and the death of his wife (he blamed her death on "the difficulties she had to encounter, and the uneasiness of mind she labored under, on account of his long absence and the treatment he received"), Franklin harbored a deep resentment toward the whigs.[21]

Once released from prison, Franklin had planned to emigrate to England, but "an unwillingness to quit the scene of action, where I might be of some service, if anything is intended to be done" convinced him to remain in New York. He quickly became aware of the dissatisfaction among the loyalists concerning their role in the war. He noted in 1778 that "many of the Loyalists in America think they have Reason to complain not only of Slights and Inattentions, but of Ill-usage, from

[18] Andrew Elliot to the Earl of Carlisle, February 1, 1779, quoted in Benjamin F. Stevens, comp., *B. F. Stevens' Facsimiles of Manuscripts in European Archives Relating to America, 1773–1783*, 25 v. (London, 1889–1898), I, no. 115.

[19] Draft of a Plan for the Regulation of Refugees . . . , June 23, 1779, Colonial Office Papers, Public Record Office, London, 5/80, 45, as found in the microfilm edition. Hereafter cited as PROCO ____.

[20] Several indications of the Refugees' bitter feelings concerning the conduct of the war appear in the *Royal Gazette*, June 16 and July 14, 1779.

[21] Memorial of William Franklin, March 24, 1784, *Transcripts . . . of the Commission of Enquiry into the Losses and Services of the American Loyalists*, 60 v., New York Public Library, XL, 330–33. Hereafter cited as Loyalist Transcripts.

William Franklin, the natural son of Benjamin Franklin, was the last royal governor of New Jersey and a militant loyalist. Following his involvement as a major leader in the Associated Loyalist movement, he went to England in 1782 and remained there until his death in 1813. PENNSYLVANIA MAGAZINE OF HISTORY AND BIOGRAPHY

those who ought to have favoured and encouraged them. Good Policy, if there was no other Motive would certainly have dictated a quite different Conduct."[22]

The governor's expulsion from office, his imprisonment, and his anger at Britain's treatment of the loyalists combined to make him an advocate of militancy. He became convinced the loyalists should retaliate for acts committed against them by whig committees. By embodying themselves into associations, he argued, the loyalists could harass the militia while simultaneously providing the British with provisions, firewood, and other essentials.[23]

An incident arose in late 1778 which allowed Franklin to exhibit his leadership. Eight loyalists, captured on Long Island while gathering wood for the British army, were tried by Connecticut authorities, convicted for treason, and sentenced to death. When word of this reached New York, the loyalists were outraged because the captives had not been treated as prisoners of war. Franklin insisted that eight whig prisoners, all from Connecticut, be released from British jails in New York and placed in his custody. He proposed to hold the men hostage, demanding that Connecticut officials exchange the convicted loyalists. If the captured loyalists were harmed in any way, Franklin promised that the prisoners he held would receive the same punishment. Sir Henry Clinton initially opposed the idea, fearing reprisals against the captive officers of Burgoyne's army (taken at Saratoga). Eventually, however, Clinton relented and the exchange took place. The episode is significant for several reasons. It immediately increased the morale of the loyalists, demonstrating that some attention was at last being paid to their plight. Issac Ogden, a New York loyalist, related that Franklin's action evinced "a certain *spirit* that has been wanting," and would convince the loyalists "throughout the Continent" that "Government will no longer tamely see some of the King's best Subjects sacrificed with Impunity."[24] The action also demonstrated Franklin's lead-

22 William Franklin to Joseph Galloway, November 16, 1778, quoted in William Herbert Mariboe, "The Life of William Franklin, 1730(1)–1813, *Pro Rege Et Patria*" (Ph.D diss., University of Pennsylvania, Philadelphia, 1962), 485; Papers of the Society for the Propagation of the Gospel, Library of Congress, quoted in *ibid.*, 487.

23 *Ibid.*, 487–88.

24 The incident is related in a letter from Isaac Ogden to Joseph Galloway, November 22, 1778, Balch Papers.

ership; he became a figure the militant loyalists could rally around. Finally, and most importantly, the Refugees' success strengthened their confidence in their own proposals. They became further convinced of the efficacy of a war of retaliation.

Encouraged by their success, the militants formed a "Refugee Club" in New York during the winter of 1778–79. The club served to build morale by uniting loyalists from throughout the colonies into a single organization. With William Franklin as chairman, the club met every fortnight to discuss politics and the conduct of the war.[25] Its organizers conceived the club's purpose as both military and civilian. On behalf of the club, Franklin produced a number of plans for action. One proposal called for the formation of an intelligence board to acquire information from outside the British lines and convey it directly to Clinton's headquarters. The club also wished to take the offensive by conducting raids into Connecticut and Rhode Island. This would have created a third loyalist force, in addition to the provincial regiments, serving mainly with the British army, and the New York loyalist militia, an organization maintained primarily for the defense of the city. The commander-in-chief ignored the plan for an intelligence board. He also objected to an independent military organization, arguing that it would create difficulties in command procedure. He felt that loyalist raiding parties would alarm the whigs at a time when he hoped to lull them into a sense of security. Lastly, Clinton argued that the expense of such measures would create too great a drain on his war chest.[26]

Clinton's seeming reluctance to actively prosecute the war angered both the Refugees and the more moderate loyalists. Relations between Sir Henry Clinton and the leading loyalists had rarely been good. He proved too indecisive, too hesitant; he constantly offered excuses for not moving at the right moment. In part this stemmed from Clinton's belief (for the most part correct) that effective loyalist support would appear only in those areas the British forces occupied on a permanent

---

[25] Isaac Ogden to Joseph Galloway, December 15, 1778; David Sproal to Joseph Galloway, January 11, 1779; and William Franklin to Joseph Galloway, February 6, 1779, Balch Papers.

[26] Plan of a Board of Intelligence, PROCO, 5/82, 53; William Franklin to Joseph Galloway, February 6, 1779, Balch Papers; Mariboe, "Franklin," 493; John André to _____ Barre, November 13, 1779, quoted in Wertenbaker, *Father Knickerbocker Rebels*, 229.

basis. Quick darting thrusts into the hinterland or expeditions not designed to occupy and hold territory would prove senseless. The citizenry, quite understandably, he believed, would never come forward and declare their allegiance if they felt the king's troops would be gone the next week or the next month.[27] Clinton also opposed on humanitarian grounds the predatory war advocated by the Refugees. He believed that type of war "unworthy of a great nation" and doubted it would have any positive effect.[28]

The loyalists seethed with frustration under Clinton's command. "Having determined against a predatory war," complained William Smith, "and conceiving that the Want of Reinforcements would justify his not attacking the Highland Forts and penetrating the Country, he had resolved to do Nothing, and yet hope for Approbation."[29] Clinton's task was difficult. Although he acted as commander-in-chief, he could not afford to offend his American allies and usually tried to evade the issue of arming the loyalists. They, of course, realized this and openly mocked him for his ambivalence. A loyalist wag characterized Clinton as sitting at headquarters and boasting:

> For forage and house
> I care not a louse;
> For revenge let the loyalists bellow.
> I swear I'll not *do* more
> To keep them in humour,
> Than play on my violencello.[30]

The commander-in-chief's almost complete disregard of the club's proposals failed to deter William Franklin from his objective. In June 1779, he collaborated with Governor William Tryon of New York on a comprehensive plan for the "Regulation of Refugees." Tryon, in the

[27] William B. Wilcox, ed., *The American Rebellion: Sir Henry Clinton's Narrative of His Campaigns, 1775–1782* (New Haven, 1954), xlvi. Hereafter cited as Clinton, *American Rebellion*. See also Sir Henry Clinton to Lord Percy, May 1776, quoted in Wilcox, *Portrait of a General: Sir Henry Clinton in the War of Independence* (New York, 1964), 83–84.

[28] Clinton Memorandum, September 4, 1778, Clinton Papers; quoted in Wilcox, "British Strategy in America in 1778," *Journal of Modern History*, XIX (June 1947), 119.

[29] Smith, *Memoirs*, III, 151.

[30] Joseph Stansbury, "A Pasquinade Struck Up at New York on the 25th of August, 1780," quoted in Winthrop Sargent, *The Loyalist Poetry of Joseph Stansbury and Dr. Jonathan Odell* (Albany, 1860), 67.

words of one loyalist, "was too much guided by personal Resentment" of the whigs, and had once boasted of his intention to "fire every Committee-man's House" throughout the country.[31] The plan he and Franklin submitted reflected their militancy. They proposed that the loyalists within the British lines place themselves under "the immediate Command of Governor Franklin with the Rank of_____ of Provincials and the Title of Director General and Commandant of the Associated Loyalists." Franklin would have the power to appoint officers, and issue any regulations or orders "subject to the Approbation of the Commander-in-Chief." Operating from bases in Rhode Island and on Long Island, Staten Island, and Sandy Hook, and furnished with arms, ammunition, camp equipage, and small armed vessels, these "associators" intended to carry out "Enterprises for distressing the Enemy, in any Quarter not expressly forbidden by the Commander-in-Chief." The associators would be "entitled to the Plunder they take, which is only from Rebels." No "Excuses, Barbarities, or Irregularities" against the rules of war were to be permitted, although punishment for such abuses was vague. Finally, the associators would keep and exchange their own prisoners of war.[32]

Franklin and Tryon submitted their plan in July 1779, but heard nothing from headquarters until October. At that time Major John André, Clinton's aide-de-camp, returned a list of "Regulations for the Associated Refugees" to Franklin, desiring his comments. André's list incorporated many of the elements of the Franklin-Tryon plan but demanded strict accountability of all supplies and money issued by the government. Most importantly, André's list demanded full control, by Clinton, of all campaigns undertaken by the Refugees. The associators would retain their own prisoners subject to the approval of a board of officers at headquarters who would decide "the Propriety of Capture at their first Sitting after the Prisoners are brought in." The regulations also hinted that the Refugees did not always discriminate among those whom they plundered. "No Refugees," the list states, are "on any Pre-

[31] John Vardill to William Eden, April 11, 1778, quoted in *Stevens' Facsimiles*, IV, no. 438.

[32] Copy of a Plan delivered by Major General Tryon to Sir Henry Clinton, K.B., in July 1779, PROCO, 5/82, 48–49. The term "associators," although not an official title, referred strictly to those loyalists under the direction of Franklin and Tryon and thus included under their plan.

In 1778, Sir Henry Clinton became the supreme commander of British forces in America, with his headquarters in New York. Judged as a cautious general and uneasy in his command, he failed to aid Cornwallis in the Yorktown campaign in 1781 and thereafter resigned. This portrait is from an engraving by A. H. Ritchie.
THE NEW-YORK HISTORICAL SOCIETY

tense to take Persons from their Houses within the King's Posts, much less plunder them as being Rebels, excepting when in Acts of Absolute Rebellion, yet then their Effects are not to be seized, as Trial must preceed any Act of Rigor." To further discourage indiscriminate terrorism, "Any Persons of whatsoever denomination" passing through the British lines without observing the regulations would receive punishment "as disaffected Persons or Robbers."[33]

Franklin returned André's plan early in November. He agreed to accept the command and render an accounting of all government disbursements, but he was plainly disenchanted by the tight regulations. He urged that the Refugee's plan "or something similar" be adopted. He stressed that the lack of faith the Refugees exhibited toward Clinton would nullify any effective command relationship the general might exercise. "Unless the Refugees and other Loyalists are regularly embodied, and put under the Command of a Person in whom they confide, and to whom they have an Attachment . . . they can answer no valuable purpose."[34]

Clinton embarked on Christmas Day for a campaign in the South without acting on any of the proposals.[35] It seemed he would do nothing to organize any type of loyalist association until forced to do so by a higher authority. Realizing this, the Refugees decided to appeal directly to their allies in Lord North's ministry.

In the late winter of 1780, George Leonard sailed to London bearing a memorial to Lord George Germain, the colonial secretary. Selected for his vigorous efforts in directing a party of New England loyalists in forays against Connecticut, Leonard presented his petition on behalf of "those who left their all to follow the Royal standard." He described the success of his operations in bringing supplies to New York and in harassing outposts and commerce to such an extent that Massachusetts voted 50,000 dollars to suppress the raiders. Leonard had originally funded these activities from his own pocket. Now financially exhausted, and left without a base of operations when British troops evacuated Newport, he proposed that the ministry create and supply an organization to continue these activities. Leonard's memorial, endorsed by the Refugee Club, suggested a proposal based on the Franklin-Tryon plan of the previous June. A major difference in the two proposals, however, was the substitution of a board of directors to replace the single commander originally called for.[36]

---

[33] Copy of a Plan delivered by Major André to Governor Franklin, October 1779, PROCO, 5/82, 50–51.

[34] William Franklin to André, November 10, 1781 [*sic.*, 1779], PROCO, 5/82, 52.

[35] Mariboe, "Franklin," 499.

[36] Memorial of George Leonard, Clinton Papers; Mariboe, "Franklin," 499–500.

In order to better insure a favorable reception of their memorial, the club sought the help of influential Americans living in England. These men—Sir William Pepperell, Joseph Galloway, Daniel Leonard, Thomas Bradbury Chandler, and Israel Mauduit—had previously advocated the increased utilization of loyalists. With their aid, Leonard's memorial gained the attention of Germain.[37] Eager to unite the loyalists in America into a strong and cohesive front, the colonial Secretary willingly endorsed the project.

Germain issued Sir Henry Clinton a broad set of instructions based upon Leonard's memorial. He appointed William Franklin, Josiah Martin, Timothy Ruggles, Joseph Wanton, Daniel Coxe, George Duncan Ludlow, and George Leonard as a "Board of Directors for the Conduct and Management" of the organization. Each of these men had been active in the Refugee Club and had signed Leonard's petition. The directors served without pay or rank in the army. Germain charged the organization with "Annoying the Sea Coasts of the revolted Provinces and distressing their Trade." Arms, ammunition, vessels, and supplies would be furnished at British expense as the commander-in-chief "shall judge proper for the Service, and can spare." Germain further stipulated that the associators could "undertake no Enterprise" without making Clinton "acquainted with their Intentions." To encourage enlistments, all captured material would be divided equally among the men by a formula set by the board. In addition, each man who served under the directors for the length of the rebellion would receive a grant of two hundred acres of land.[38]

The latitude of Germain's instructions is highly significant to an understanding of subsequent events. The colonial secretary noted that the creation of a loyalist association had the approval of himself and George III. All other matters, particularly the regulation and control of the Associated Loyalists, would be determined by Clinton, who could, if he wished, delegate all power to the board of directors. If

[37] Sabine, *Biographical Sketches of Loyalists in America*, II, 174; Minutes of the Proceedings of the Honorable Board of Directors of Associated Loyalists, November 29, 1781. Hereafter cited as Board Minutes. The Minutes from September 14, 1780, to January 26, 1781, are in PROCO, 5/82, 149–74. The Minutes from January 4, 1781, to February 26, 1782, are in the Clinton Papers. Minutes from April 3, 1782, to June 29, 1782, are available on microfilm at the Princeton University Library.

[38] Lord George Germain to Sir Henry Clinton, April 21, 1780, PROCO, 5/82, 135–36.

something went wrong, however, if the Refugees misbehaved, the commander-in-chief would ultimately be held answerable for their actions. Clinton—a man afraid of responsibility, a general who as a subordinate proved capable and active but who as commander-in-chief proved overly cautious and sluggish and who continually pestered Whitehall for permission to resign—faced a difficult situation. He must govern an embittered set of men, bent on a war of destruction and retaliation, a kind of war Clinton himself preferred not to condone and believed would bring few good results.[39]

The Refugees, on the other hand, believed they had at last achieved their goal of a separate command to conduct a predatory war. In mid autumn the board of directors met with Clinton. He asked them to draw up a proposed set of regulations to govern their association. The Refugees' draft listed the members of the board and appointed them with full power "for associating, embodying, ordering, governing, and employing the Loyalists in North America for carrying on Operations against His Majesty's revolted Provinces." The proposed regulations conformed to Germain's instructions but contained additional amendments the board of directors believed "would answer the expectations of His Majesty from such an institution."[40]

The commander-in-chief examined the board's proposals and found them too liberal. He secretly contacted Chief Justice William Smith of New York and the province's lieutenant-governor, Andrew Elliot. He wished them to point out the dichotomy between Germain's instructions and the regulations set down by the directors. Clinton asked the two loyalists if they would "offer another Instrument for this Establishment."[41] It seems that Clinton's action was calculated to ease his responsibilities in governing the Associated Loyalists. Well known for their opposition to predatory warfare, both Smith and Elliot could be relied upon to draw up regulations keeping the Refugees tightly in check. In sanctioning small expeditions and raids along the coast, Clinton utilized the virtues of the armed loyalists. By using moderate loyalists to regulate the actions of their more radical brethren, Clinton

[39] Clinton, *American Rebellion*, xlix–l; Wilcox, *Portrait of a General*, 70.

[40] Copy of a Draft of Instructions for the Board of Associated Loyalists, Proposed to Sir Henry Clinton, October 28, 1780, PROCO, 5/82, 121. Hereafter cited as Proposed Instructions.

[41] Smith, *Memoirs*, III, 345.

459

eased the fears of the two most moderate spokesmen that a war of terrorism would ensue. Finally, by not disclosing to the militant loyalists the aid of Smith and Elliot in formulating the regulations, Clinton prevented an open fissure in loyalist ranks.

The proposed regulations of the board of directors interpreted their powers broadly. In contrast, the regulations submitted by Smith and Elliot reflected a structured, highly legalistic approach that circumscribed the powers of the board. An examination of the two sets of proposed regulations makes the differences in approach readily evident.[42]

1. The directors desired to frame "Articles of Association" subjecting the associators to all orders and regulations the board judged "necessary and proper." Smith and Elliot maintained that Clinton must have final approval of the articles and exercise "a Control on all the orders the Board is to make."

2. The board wanted the commander-in-chief to furnish all arms, ammunition, equipment, provisions, and armed vessels necessary to conduct raiding activities. All captures made by the Associated Loyalists would become their property and be evenly distributed by the board. If the loyalists operated in conjunction with the king's army, they were to receive the same pay as regular soldiers. The board would have charge of all prisoners captured by the organization and could exchange them only for captured associators, "except in Special Cases either assented to" by Clinton or the board. Mariners employed in the service of the Associated Loyalists could not be impressed by the Royal Navy. Sick and wounded associators would be received into the king's hospitals. Finally, each man serving "during the Continuance of the Rebellion" would receive a grant of two hundred acres of land "clear of all Fees and Expenses of Office." The moderates objected that the second article of the board's regulations contained too many specific promises that "may have been asked in England and refused." This objection centered particularly around the exchange of prisoners. Smith and Elliot maintained that "the very Power they ask" includes "the Right to correspond on that Subject." Such a trust in a subordinate body, they argued, deserved deep consideration.

[42] See Proposed Instructions, 121–24; and Smith, *Memoirs*, III, 345–46.

Andrew Elliot was one of the leading loyalists in New York. At one time Collector of the Port of New York, he also served on the governor's council prior to the Revolution. The British appointed him lieutenant-governor of New York Province in 1780, a post he held until 1783. After the war, he returned to his native Scotland.
PENNSYLVANIA MAGAZINE OF HISTORY AND BIOGRAPHY

3. The board promised that no expeditions would take place without acquainting the commander-in-chief of their intention and gaining his approval. The moderate loyalists complained that this article did not subject "the Conduct of the Enterprise while the Party is out and the Continuance of it to the General's Pleasure."

4. The directors hoped that "all Refugees and other Loyalists" within the British lines (excepting privateers and those in provincial regi-

ments) would be forbidden to make excursions into enemy country unless under the direction and control of the board. The moderates believed this article to be unnecessary unless all the Refugees were to be directed by the board "whether they associate or not." Smith and Elliot pointed out that the Refugees in New York were "already under the General's Command by being within his Power," and noted that it might make these Refugees uneasy "if they thought they had other Masters."

5. With the approbation of Clinton, the directors proposed to form "conjunct Expeditions" against the enemy "with such private Vessels of War, as may, tho not owned by Associators, be willing to act with them." Smith and Elliot saw no need of this article. If the Refugees formed an association, nothing would hinder them from acting with other of the British forces as long as Clinton concurred with the decision.

6. The board stressed that the officers of all expeditions had orders "to be particularly careful" that their men not hurt or molest innocent or inoffensive persons. If through "Mistake or Necessity" an incident occurred, the Associated Loyalists would restore the property or compensate for it. The moderates felt that this article, as stated, was only advice. It had no sanction by not providing against "vindictive Rage and lawless Fury." They urged that the directors ought not to be the judges between the offended persons and the associators.

7. The board of directors promised to examine any letters, papers, or other intelligence obtained on their expeditions and communicate the information to Clinton. Smith and Elliot insisted that intelligence should come "instantly" to headquarters and "not wait till a Board is formed to speculate upon it."

8. The directors of the Associated Loyalists wished to appoint a secretary to keep minutes of their meetings. The secretary would receive pay and all the necessary supplies for his work. Elliot and Smith urged that this article be carefully worded or considerable expense to the government might ensue.

Concluding its regulations, the board desired to appoint the member first named in the commission, William Franklin, as its president. A majority of the board would form a quorum for all regular business. In

William Smith, a leading loyalist, was a jurist and a historian. In 1777, he refused to take the oath of allegiance to New York State and withdrew to New York City. After the war he went to England and then to Canada, where he became a chief justice. This portrait is from a miniature by Henry Stubble, ca. 1785.
THE NEW-YORK HISTORICAL SOCIETY

times of "extraordinary Emergency," however, any three members would constitute a quorum "when more Members cannot be collected in Time."

Soon after they completed their alterations, Smith and Elliot met with Clinton to explain their views. The commander-in-chief approved the document, stating that the ideas contained therein concurred with his own. The two loyalists charged Clinton and even his secretary (who took notes on the meeting) with secrecy, stating that "the restraints upon the Board" would disgust the militants and make them jealous of the trust Clinton placed in the more moderate loyalists.[43]

The "restraints" imposed by Clinton's commission both surprised and angered the Refugees. On December 1, 1780, the directors sent Clinton a letter of protest. They concluded that the restrictions the commission contained "would militate against if not entirely frustrate the good purposes intended by such an establishment."[44] The nature of the directors' complaints give a good indication of their intentions for the organization. They outlined their principal objections to the commission as follows:[45]

1. The confidence of the king in establishing the board "is rendered in a manner fruitless" by subjecting the board of directors to the "Regulations, Limitations, and Restrictions" imposed by Clinton in his commission. The board complained that "the Directors are made merely ministerial," and that nothing "of Consequence" was left to their discretion.

2. They complained that prisoners taken by the associators were neither confined nor treated as the board proposed, that is, "neither better nor worse than they treat the Loyalists." The board complained that the rebels refused to consider captured loyalists as prisoners of war. This practice "cannot be Stop'd or prevented but by *Retaliation*." They also believed the board should control or at least be consulted on the treatment of nonmilitary prisoners.

3. The board objected that Clinton's commission allowed loyalists not under the board's direction to make excursions on their own. Confusion and disorder would result from the excesses of others and defeat the purpose of the organization—"to bring the Exertions of the Body of Loyalists under one general Direction."

4. The directors believed that the fifth and seventh articles of Clinton's commission contained too many restraints upon the board. "We conceive it indeed absolutely essential," the directors concluded, "to that predatory kind of War proposed . . . that a Latitude of Command . . . be allowed to their Officers, when on Excursions, to conduct

[43] Smith, *Memoirs*, III, 349.

[44] Board Minutes, November 30, 1780.

[45] See Board of Directors to Sir Henry Clinton, December 1, 1780, PROCO, 5/82, 137–42.

themselves as Circumstances may seem to them to require." The associators' own knowledge of the country and of the enemy permitted them to "act much more advantagiously than can possibly be directed by any Orders given at New York."

5. The board proposed that only the parties directly involved rather than the whole association be liable for damages against loyal or inoffensive persons.

The directors concluded their objections by expressing their firm desire to aid in supressing the rebellion. They informed Clinton that their only motive was "to answer the Expectations His Majesty has been pleased to place in us. . . ."

Clinton refused to heed the protests of the Refugees. He knew they would have to accept his commission or give up their project. He wrote them expressing his surprise at their objections and noted that his commission had been formulated only after "the maturest Deliberation." He urged them to re-examine the commission and hoped it would "answer every necessary purpose. . . ."[46]

The board of directors, on its part, swallowed its pride and "unanimously determined to make the Experiment and if possible, to carry on the Commission into full Execution, and omit nothing which may be in the Power of the Board for obtaining the beneficial Purposes proposed by it."[47] As Franklin later reported to Joseph Galloway, the directors had come to realize it was *"Either this or none."* The board then worked quickly to draw up articles of association and a public declaration that conformed to Clinton's commission. The commander-in-chief approved them, and on December 30, 1780, "A Declaration by the Honourable Board of Directors of Associated Loyalists" appeared in Rivington's *Royal Gazette* to officially announce the formation of the organization.[48]

In January 1781, the board of directors began to mobilize its forces. While no regular enlistment rolls of associators is available, Frank-

[46] Sir Henry Clinton to Board of Directors, December 10, 1780, Clinton Papers, quoted in Mariboe, "Franklin," 511–12.

[47] Board Minutes, December 8, 1780.

[48] William Franklin to Joseph Galloway, January 28, 1781, PROCO, 5/82, 38: Board Minutes, December 18–25, 1780; *Royal Gazette*, December 30, 1780.

465

lin estimated by the end of the first month that "there cannot be less than 4 or 500 who have already associated."[49] The associators organized themselves in three "societies" in order to strike more effectively at the enemy. One group maintained a base at Kingsbridge, New York, to operate against rebel forces in the Hudson Highlands. Another society, based at Lloyd's Neck on Long Island, used whaleboats to attack the coast of Connecticut. A third force harrassed the coastline of New Jersey from havens at Bergen Point and Paulus Hook.[50]

An examination of the minutes of the board of directors reveals some interesting facts and calls into question many prevailing assumptions concerning the character of the organization. Appointment to the board meant acceptance of rigorous, time-consuming, and not always satisfying work. The board received no pay for its services.[51] This refutes Thomas Jones' statement that the board received £200 per year in salary and undermines his contention that the board acted primarily for self-gain.[52] The board gave serious attention to its duties and maintained a heavy work agenda. During much of 1781 the board met on an average of every other day.[53] It determined the places to be attacked, usually supply centers, blockhouses, the bases of rebel privateers, and small encampments and outposts. Since these are traditional military targets, the generalization that the Associated Loyalists destroyed homes and churches, and looted and murdered people indiscriminately, becomes highly questionable.

What may be described as a typical expedition of the Associated Loyalists took place on April 18, 1781. Six boatloads of Associated Loyalists, led by Captain Nathan Hubbel, set out for the coast of Connecticut. At sunset the men spied an enemy schooner lying near

[49] William Franklin to Joseph Galloway, January 28, 1781, PROCO, 5/82, 39.

[50] Mariboe, "Franklin," 515.

[51] Loyalist Transcripts, XL, 335. In his memorial to the claims commission in London, Franklin testified that while president of the board of Associated Loyalists, he "went through much fatiguing business, and continued exerting himself without any pay or emolument whatsoever for that Service. . . ." Similar testimonies appear in the memorials of Robert Alexander (Loyalist Transcripts, XXXVI, 157), and Anthony Stewart (Anthony Stewart Papers, Maryland Historical Society, Baltimore).

[52] Jones, History of New York, I, 303. Jones erroneously states that the board of directors consisted of twenty-five members.

[53] Board Minutes, January to December, 1781.

shore. They "pursued her with all possible Dispatch," but the schooner, with "a heavy Southerly Wind favoring her," escaped safely into New-field harbor. Shots exchanged between the loyalists and the town's militia had little effect except to discourage Hubbel's men from pursuing the schooner any further. The associators sailed eastward toward New Haven and "with perfect Silence landed about a Quarter of a Mile from the Fort." They quickly seized the interior and surrounded the barracks, challenged only by a sentry who fired and then ran off. The loyalists stormed the barracks, killed one man who opposed them, and captured eleven prisoners and eighteen stands of arms. After spiking the cannon, setting fire to the barracks and other wooden structures, and loading their boats with prisoners and booty, the victors "having effected the Business returned without loss to Lloyd's Neck. . . ."[54]

Division of prizes captured on a raid adhered to a carefully regulated system set by the board. From the net proceeds of all captured goods, ten percent was immediately allocated to a retribution fund to indemnify persons wrongfully molested. Another ten percent went to a charity fund to aid injured associators or their families. Five percent of the prize money was reserved for the three officers accompanying every expedition. The captain received one half; the rest being equally divided between a lieutenant and an ensign. Other members of the expedition shared equally in the remainder.[55]

The board of directors chafed under the restraints placed upon it. Franklin complained to Germain of the constant applications the board was forced to make to the commander-in-chief for "every trivial matter necessary for the equipment of our parties."[56] On another occasion he objected that even after proper application was made, frequently nothing was done about the requests.

The General . . . tells us in the politest terms he is desirous of affording us every Assistance—that he expects great Matters from the Associators and that they ought to be and must be encouraged. But as he cannot think of letting us have a separate Establishment, or of making us independent of

[54] Nathan Hubbel to the Board of Directors, April 21, 1781, PROCO, 5/82, 399.
[55] Articles of the Associated Loyalists, PROCO, 5/175, 449–50.
[56] William Franklin to Lord George Germain, February 20, 1781, PROCO, 5/175, 449–50.

any Military Department, we are referr'd from one to another for every trifling Want, and sometimes after going the Rounds we find ourselves again at Headquarters Quarters where we first set off, without having obtained our Errand.[57]

Franklin asked Joseph Galloway, Sir William Peppernell, Thomas Bradbury Chandler, Israel Mauduit, and other loyalist agents in London to appeal to Germain to ease the restrictions upon the Associated Loyalists.[58] Nothing seems to have come of this request, however, and the organization remained under Clinton's control.

Relations between the militant loyalists and the commander-in-chief further deteriorated in October 1781 when the loyalists learned of Lord Cornwallis' surrender. Article Ten of the articles of capitulation stated that "natives or inhabitants of different parts of this country at present in York or Gloucester are not to be punished on account of having joined the British army." Washington refused to accept the article, arguing that the captured loyalists failed to retain any status as prisoners of war but rather were subject to the civil laws of their respective states. Several states had passed legislation declaring citizens who supported Great Britain guilty of treason.[59] The loyalists believed that the British, in assenting to the article, had simply disregarded them and had effectively signed the death warrants of many of their brethren.

The board of directors reacted to the surrender with horror and disbelief. Franklin angrily informed Germain: "It is scarcely possible to give your Lordship an adequate Idea of the Surprize and Distress which the Perusal of the 10th Article of the Capitulation has occasioned in the Minds of every American Loyalist. They are in fact considered . . . in no better Light than as Runaway Slaves restored to their former Masters. . . ."[60] Franklin seemingly did not overstate the situation. The board's commander at Lloyd's Neck reported that Article Ten "reaches the Hearts of the unfortunate Loyalists of this Place . . .

[57]William Franklin to Joseph Galloway, January 28, 1781, PROCO, 5/82, 42.

[58]Ibid. See also Board Minutes, November 8 and 29, 1781.

[59]Mariboe, "Franklin," 527–28. See also James Westfall Thompson, "Anti-Loyalist Legislation During the American Revolution," Illinois Law Review, III (June/October 1907), 81–90, 147–71.

[60]William Franklin to Lord George Germain, November 6, 1781, PROCO, 5/175, 462.

I wish to know whether we too are to be sacrificed."[61] The British commander at Savannah reported higher desertion rates among loyalist regiments as a result of Article Ten. Clinton himself wrote Germain: "It is impossible to describe the indignation, horror, and dismay with which the American refugees who had either taken up arms in our cause or flown to us for protection read the *tenth article* of that convention."[62] Franklin urged Clinton to issue a proclamation promising retaliation if any loyalists were put to death. The commander-in-chief demurred but attempted to allay the fears of the loyalists by declaring that "it should be given out in Public Orders that no Distinction would ever be made in any situation of Public Affairs, between the loyalists and the King's Troops, but the one be equally the object of his Care and Concern with the other."[63] Apparently, Clinton's efforts did not totally calm the loyalists' bitter feelings over the incident. Circulating in New York at this time, the following bit of doggerel indicates the bitter irony of the loyalists' situation:

> 'Tis an honor to serve the bravest of nations
> And be left to be hanged in their capitulations.[64]

The Associated Loyalists continued their operations throughout the summer, but following the surrender of Cornwallis in October 1781, the heart seemed to go out of the organization. During the month of December 1781, the board met only six times and the five pages of minutes are devoted to routine affairs. Yet by March the advent of the spring campaign stirred the board to action. Plans were laid to establish a new base at Sag Harbor, Long Island, and to conduct more ambitious programs, which included raids into Pennsylvania and Maryland.[65] In April, however, an event occurred which brought about the dissolution of the Associated Loyalists and blackened the reputation of the organization from that day to this.

On April 12, 1782, a party of associators led by Captain Richard Lippincot received permission from the board to exchange some pris-

---

[61] Joshua Upham to William Franklin, November 3, 1781, PROCO, 5/175, 468.

[62] Clinton, *American Rebellion*, 352, 591.

[63] Board Minutes, November 8, 1781.

[64] Claude Halstead Van Tyne, *The Loyalists in the American Revolution* (Gloucester, Mass., 1959), 288.

[65] Board Minutes, December 4, 18, 19, 24, 26, and 27, 1781; Mariboe, "Franklin," 534.

oners for loyalists held by the rebels. Lippincot, however, took one of the prisoners, Lieutenant Joshua Huddy, to New Jersey and hanged him in reprisal for the killing of a loyalist prisoner a few weeks earlier. The incident immediately became a *cause célèbre*.[66] Washington demanded the surrender of the persons responsible. He threatened to hang a British captain in retaliation. Clinton refused to relinquish Lippincot, but he did bring him before a court-martial to investigate the incident. In an inquiry that lasted much of the summer, Lippincot testified that he acted under verbal orders from the board of directors. The board maintained that this was untrue, but they approved of Lippincot's action. The directors argued that the hanging did not represent a crime but an act of just retaliation. Lippincot eventually received an acquittal on the grounds that he believed he followed the instructions of the board.[67]

Of greatest significance, however, were the repercussions the incident had for the Associated Loyalists. In May 1782, Sir Guy Carleton replaced Clinton as commander-in-chief. In one of his last official acts, however, Clinton directed that "no Expedition or Excursion against the Enemy shall take place from the Posts under their [the board's] Charge, without His Excellency's particular Order."[68] The board continued to meet and draw up plans for continued raids, sending them to headquarters for the approval of Carleton, who consistently refused them permission to undertake any operation. The board suspected Carleton would never consent to any future operations; it also expressed disgust that Lippincot had been brought to trial for the murder of Huddy. The directors continued to regard Lippincot's action as legitimate and were incensed that the British prosecuted loyalists for

[66] A note pinned to Huddy's coat contained the following warning: "We, the Refugees, have with grief long beheld the cruel murders of our brethren, and finding nothing but such measures daily carrying into execution, we, therefore, determine not to suffer without taking vengence for the numerous cruelties, and thus begin, having made use of Captain Huddy as the first object to present to your view, and further determine to hang man for man, as long as a refugee is left existing. UP GOES HUDDY FOR PHILIP WHITE." Quoted from Larry Bowman, "The Court-Martial of Captain Richard Lippincot," *New Jersey History*, LXXXIX (Spring 1971), 27.

[67] The fullest treatments of the Huddy affair are in Bowman, "Court-Martial of Captain Richard Lippincot," 23–26; Katherine Mayo, *General Washington's Dilemma* (New York, 1938), 69–84; and Frederick Bernays Wiener, *Civilians Under Military Justice: The British Practice Since 1689, Especially in North America* (Chicago, 1967), 113–22.

[68] Board Minutes, May 2, 1782.

This is the will of Joshua Huddy. It was dictated and then signed by him just before he was hanged on April 12, 1782, by a band of associators. In his will, he commits his soul to the Almighty, his body to the earth, and his "substance" to his two children. THE NEW JERSEY HISTORICAL SOCIETY

the killing of rebels. In August, the board disbanded the organization, firing a parting shot at Clinton and Carleton. The loyalists would "not serve in future," they declared, "under persons in whom they can place no reliance."[69]

The Huddy affair remains *the* event by which historians have judged the Associated Loyalists. While the execution of Huddy should

[69] Unsigned paper, June 15, 1782, Clinton Papers, quoted in Wertenbaker, *Father Knickerbocker Rebels*, 232.

not be condoned, the atmosphere that gave rise to it must be understood. The action directly reflects the willingness of the Refugees to employ retaliatory warfare. Although it cannot be proved, the execution of Huddy probably indicates the desperation of the radical loyalists when confronted with the winding down of the war and Britain's willingness to negotiate a peace.[70] The Huddy affair, however, is atypical of the activities of the Associated Loyalists. It is the only deliberate execution conducted by the organization on record. How many other Huddys might there have been had not the moderates controlled the actions of the Refugees? The Huddy affair must be considered in any discussion of the Associated Loyalists, but it should not obscure the rest of their history nor be used as the sole basis for judging their actions.

The role of the Associated Loyalists in the American Revolution needs re-evaluation. Heretofore vilified by historians as outlaws interested mainly in profit and self-gain, they have not been viewed as victims of the civil war that raged around them. Imprisoned, driven from their homes, made refugees, the Associated Loyalists demanded revenge on their enemies. Had they been allowed to retaliate as they wished, the war surrounding New York City might have been an even more bitter and desperate struggle than it was. But the instincts of the Refugees were tempered and controlled by an alliance of moderate loyalists and British officials who tightly regulated the organization. While they chafed under the moderates' control, the Associated Loyalists had little choice but to obey the former's regulations or cease operations altogether. In the one noteworthy instance in which the Associated Loyalists transgressed their authority, the commander-in-chief suspended the organization's activities and ultimately forced its disbandment.

---

[70]This was the opinion of Clinton, who wrote: "There were many circumstances accompanying this transaction which would almost warrent a suspicion that it was done with a view to precluding all future reconciliation between Great Britain and the revolted colonies. Having, therefore, most probably long thirsted after indiscriminate retaliation, and finding that I was disinclined to sanction it by my having refused to issue a threatening proclamation in consequence of the tenth article of the capitulation of Yorktown, these gentlemen appear to have taken this bold step for the purpose of forcing that measure." Clinton, *The American Rebellion*, 361. For a similar view, see Piers Mackesy, *The War for America, 1775–1783* (Cambridge, 1964), 490–91.

Lord Cornwallis surrendered his British army to Gen. George Washington at Yorktown, Virginia, on October 19, 1781. In this engraving, Washington gestures toward Gen. Benjamin Lincoln, who is about to receive Cornwallis's sword from Gen. Charles O'Hara. [*NJHS*]

Elizabethtown 1782: The Prisoner-of-War Negotiations and the Pawns of War

JOSEPH J. CASINO

THE MILITARY CLIMAX of the American Revolution came when the British surrendered at Yorktown in October 1781. Major military operations on land all but ceased in North America; except for those who lived in and around New York City and Charleston, South Carolina, the war could now seem comfortably remote. Although the war continued to rage at sea and on the diplomatic and economic fronts for more than a year after Yorktown, for most Americans the war was over.

Unfortunately, that was not the case for American and British prisoners of war. If Yorktown had ended the major fighting, there was still no treaty of peace, and the thousands of prisoners of war held by both sides continued to languish in confinement or, if they were lucky, to live under parole. Many of them had been imprisoned for years; in fact, the financial and security demands of maintaining the large number of prisoners became a serious burden to the combatants. As a new campaign between the main armies of George Washington and his British counterpart, Sir Henry Clinton, became less likely, however, the rival governments and commanders turned to the question of a prisoner-of-war release. To this end, a series of important negotiations took place between the British and the Americans at Elizabethtown (now Elizabeth), New Jersey, in early 1782. This essay examines the course of those meetings, on which hung the fate of so many men, and considers the motives that guided the discussions on both sides. Further, it suggests that those motives frequently did little credit to either side—that humanitarian concerns often counted for little, and that the prisoners of war ultimately became pawns in a much wider military and diplomatic game.

On August 3, 1781, the Continental Congress received a report on the status of captured American merchant and privateer seamen (known collectively as "marine prisoners") held by the British. While restricted to the condition of a single type of prisoner, for the

ELIZABETHTOWN 1782 / 1

475

Crown also held American soldiers and civilians, the document proved of wider significance, for it set in motion a train of events leading to a general conference on prisoner exchange. The report, however, began grimly: Many of the marine prisoners were being confined on board overcrowded and disease-ridden prison ships in New York harbor. The report alleged that the British capitalized on these savage conditions to force the Americans to enlist in the royal navy. As was the custom, each side was expected to provide maintenance for their own marine prisoners in enemy hands. Congress, however, was running out of money for this purpose, and the British continually refused to release or exchange them until the charges were paid. But since British merchant seamen captured by American vessels were held by the individual states, instead of by Continental authority, Congress had no British seamen to offer in exchange. So there was very little prospect that American marine prisoners would be freed unless they were included in a general cartel, and unless in the future, British marine prisoners were delivered to Continental commissaries of prisoners and not to the states. This the states were not likely to agree to, since they used British prisoners of war to fill their military quotas and to staff their own fleets of ships. The best that could be hoped for in the meantime was an alleviation of the prisoners' misery.[1]

On August 21, Gen. George Washington, at the direction of Congress, issued a formal complaint to the commanding officer of the British fleet regarding the conditions on the New York prison ships. He requested that an American military officer be allowed to investigate the situation personally. The British reply, though polite, insisted that every effort was being made to thin the population on the ships and that conditions there were up to European standards, statements ill-designed to heighten American optimism. An invitation was extended for an American visit to the ships, but only if the British were allowed to investigate conditions in the "Jails and Dungeons," as well as the mines, where British prisoners-of-war were incarcerated.[2]

Congress had in its hands at this time several depositions from former marine prisoners testifying that the British used cruelty to force them into British service. The British regarded captured American seamen as rebels and pirates without belligerents' rights, actually indicting them for treason. Moreover, Benjamin Franklin, who had in 1779 successfully arranged the exchange of some American marine prisoners held in England, but whose efforts were curtailed by 1780 because of his inability to supply British marine prisoners in exchange, reported that the British had begun "thinning" the New York prison ships by transferring American marine prisoners from there to prisons in England. According to Franklin's calculations, British and Irish jails held five hundred Americans in September 1781, eight hundred in November, and more than a thousand by April 1782.[3]

All of Franklin's efforts to provide relief for the prisoners in England were nullified by the swelling numbers in those jails. Therefore, he recommended in November 1781 that Congress take drastic action. A certain number of British prisoners in American hands, he said, should be treated in the same manner as their American counterparts abroad, who received from the British government fewer rations than Spanish and French prisoners. He also argued that no exchanges should be acquiesced in until the Americans in Europe had been set at liberty.[4] Two months earlier, Congress already had agreed to set apart five hundred British prisoners who would be refused exchange until the American prisoners in England should be returned, and had made plans for transforming Symsbury Mines in Connecticut into a state prison for the purpose of retaliation.[5]

There was no doubt that marine prisoners in Europe and New York were being treated worse than nonmarine prisoners; yet it was equally clear that, short of a general cartel, little could be done for them. On December 27, Washington submitted to Congress two letters from the commissary general of prisoners showing the amount due for the maintenance of marine prisoners, the number remaining in captivity, the misery of their confinement, and the improbability of their release or exchange. Washington repeated that since most of them were not in Continental service, he had no authority to exchange them. Even if he had authority, he lacked equivalent British marine prisoners to enter into an exchange. Had the states adopted a congressional plan obliging captains of privateers to deliver their prisoners to Continental authorities, this would not have been the case. Bringing all classes of prisoners under one regulation by a general cartel, he maintained, would put a stop to the mutual complaints of ill-treatment, for it was true that in the previous two years neither side had seen any reason to complain of the treatment accorded nonmarine prisoners.[6]

Questions of finance were added to humanitarian interests in making a general cartel imperative, especially after the large influx of new British prisoners from Yorktown.[7] The fifth of the articles of capitulation signed on October 19, 1781, stipulated that the British prisoners were to be supplied the same rations allowed to soldiers in the Continental army.[8] A committee of Congress thereupon reported that the provisions furnished to Cornwallis's defeated army were to be paid for by the British at a general settlement.

ELIZABETHTOWN 1782 / 3

477

Since the American superintendent of finance, Robert Morris, assumed that the United States would eventually be called upon to reimburse the British for rations issued to American captives at Charleston, South Carolina, he gave it as his opinion that those rations should be deducted from the allowance granted by Congress to American officers.[9]

A November 21 report of the board of war outlined other burdensome items of expense to America. Great amounts of money, the report noted, were being paid out for the support of the numerous men and women belonging to the Saratoga Convention troops. At that time, for example, there were three hundred women and children attached to an equal number of prisoners at York, Pennsylvania. The board advocated sending in on parole all prisoners so encumbered and counting the children capable of bearing arms as full-fledged prisoners of war to be counted as such in any exchange. Hessian and other German prisoners and their children, unlike the British, could be let out to work for their keep; if they refused, they could be coerced to work by withholding their rations. Presumably, the long-term effect of such a policy would be an increase in the American population, and the short-term advantage would be a double savings to the Continent. In any event, the board concluded, the question of expense was so pressing that a specific date should be fixed for settling past accounts and for compelling the British to support their own prisoners.[10] Two days later, Congress resolved that Robert Morris and the board of war should quickly take measures "for the safe keeping and support of the prisoners of war in the possession of the United States, so as to ensure their safety as much as may be, and to render their support less burthensome to the finances of these states."[11]

Negotiations Begin

It was the British, however, who made the first overtures. On November 24, Sir Henry Clinton, the British commander in chief, proposed a meeting of Joshua Loring, his commissary general of prisoners, with Abraham Skinner, the American commissary general of prisoners, at Elizabethtown, New Jersey, or Staten Island, New York. The conferees, Clinton suggested, would arrange for the exchange of officers including John Burgoyne and Lord Cornwallis, who, although free on parole, were still considered to be prisoners under American control.[12] Washington, thinking to expand the possibilities of this minimal gesture, directed Skinner to go to Elizabethtown and authorized him to use the mode of

4 / ELIZABETHTOWN 1782

478

composition when similarity of rank would not suffice. Skinner was to attempt to have American prisoners in Canada included in the exchange, as well as to trade American civilian and marine prisoners for British civilians taken at Yorktown. Cornwallis was not to be included, and if Loring refused to negotiate because of that reservation, Skinner was to report back to Washington immediately.[13]

The Elizabethtown meetings opened in December, with Skinner pressing for the exchange of Gov. Thomas Burke of North Carolina for some of the nonmilitary Yorktown prisoners. The American negotiator threatened to have all of the British civilian prisoners recalled from their paroles if Loring failed to meet his terms on Burke. He also called for an exchange of officers taken by both sides in the fighting in Canada in 1776 (and who had since been on parole).[14] But the British refused to proceed in any exchange unless Cornwallis were included. With negotiations temporarily suspended, Skinner reported back to Washington and Congress for further instructions.[15]

Optimism was rekindled in January 1782, when Skinner offered to exchange Burgoyne for prisoners taken in 1776 at the Cedars during the Canadian campaign, provided that some allowance be made for the French officers sent in on parole by the British. All other prisoners, except Cornwallis, were to be exchanged also. This time Clinton quickly agreed, directing Loring to ratify the proposal.[16] On February 9, agreement was signed by Skinner and Loring to exchange Burgoyne for an equivalent of 1,047 officers and soldiers, and other officers for their equivalent in rank on the other side.[17]

It was a beginning; but what of the stumbling block regarding Cornwallis? Apparently, Clinton was under the mistaken impression that Washington at Yorktown had insisted on the exchange of Cornwallis only for American diplomat Henry Laurens of South Carolina, then imprisoned in England. After the February 9 agreement, Clinton pressed for the exchange of Cornwallis for either Laurens or for one brigadier general, seven colonels, and two lieutenant colonels.[18] When he reported to Congress on February 18, Washington denied he had ever promised the exchange of Cornwallis for Laurens, since he never had posssesed the authority to do so. But, he added, prohibiting the exchange of Cornwallis was destructive to the morale of those captive American officers who could be exchanged only by composition (that is, for a number of lesser-ranking Americans).[19]

Washington's report also injected a new consideration into the discussions. David Sproat, the British commissary of naval prisoners, had suggested that perhaps American marine prisoners could be exchanged for captured British soldiers. Washington considered this unwise because it would have provided the British with a considerable reinforcement and would cause a constant depletion of prisoners in American hands available for exchange, while providing no benefits to the Continental war effort, since few or none of the naval prisoners in New York were in Continental service. Humanitarianism here had to give way to Washington's centralist prejudices. Only when the states no longer held captured British seamen separately could Congress have a sufficient supply of naval prisoners with which to bargain with the British on equal terms for the release of American marine prisoners.[20]

Meanwhile, Superintendent of Finance Robert Morris, Gen. George Washington, and Secretary at War Benjamin Lincoln had conferred on the issues of safe-keeping and inexpensive feeding of the Yorktown prisoners; and they decided on December 5, 1781, that the British prisoners should be sent to Lancaster, Pennsylvania, there to be rationed under contract, and the Anspach and Hessian prisoners sent to Frederick, Maryland, there to be rationed at Morris's direction until a contract could be obtained. Henry Knox and Gouverneur Morris were delegated to negotiate with the British for the settlement of past accounts and for the establishment of regular provisioning for the future. Washington approached Clinton on the subject in a letter of December 6.[21]

From Clinton's reply of January 2, 1782, it was apparent there was some misunderstanding as to the functions of the American commissioners. As Washington subsequently explained, they were principally to settle past and future expenses, not to facilitate an exchange of prisoners.[22] On January 23, Clinton announced he was ready "to send Commissioners . . . to meet those named in yours, either at Elizabethtown, or at Amboy . . . who shall be fully prepared . . . to liquidate the Expences of maintaining Prisoners, and to make solid arrangements for providing for them in future, as well as to facilitate their Exchange."[23]

The slight difference of opinion as to the purpose of the meeting was cancelled when, on February 18, Congress authorized Washington to negotiate "a cartel or cartels, either general or special," for the "subsistence, safe keeping, exchanging, liberating, and better treating of all prisoners of war, whether of land or sea," and "to take such measures for the liberation of citizens who have been captured not in arms" or "to negotiate any separate treaty concerning such citizens, for the mutual prevention of any future captures: provided such cartel, cartels and agreements, establish rules for the similar treatment of prisoners of war and citizens captured by either power in all cases whatsoever." He was also empowered to take

6 / ELIZABETHTOWN 1782

480

measures for settling all past accounts respecting prisoners. A secret resolve at the end of the resolution forbade Washington to negotiate a cartel for the exchange of Lord Cornwallis by composition.[24]

Both Washington and the commissioners objected to the secret resolve. In a letter to Congress of February 20, Washington recounted how, on his return from the Yorktown victory, Robert Morris had informed him that the subsistence of British prisoners had become such a serious expense that it was absolutely necessary to obtain payment of the money already due to the United States, and to establish some regular mode of payment in the future. Now that the objective was finally attainable, the secret resolve of Congress presented a serious obstacle. The exchange of General Cornwallis, Washington argued, would certainly be one of the first demands of the British commissioners, and if not granted, it would sabotage a settlement of the maintenance question. That would prove to be a greater burden to the United States than to the British since the Americans held more British prisoners than the British held Americans.[25]

Debate in Congress over Washington's charges was heated but short. Accusing Cornwallis of barbarism in the South, Arthur Middleton of South Carolina moved that not only should Cornwallis not be exchanged, but that unless Henry Laurens were immediately enlarged on parole, Cornwallis should be recalled from his parole. Middleton also argued that unless the British settled past and future accounts, their prisoners should be forced to work for their livelihood or otherwise disposed of for the public benefit. In the end, however, a motion of Abraham Clark, delegate from New Jersey, was accepted, authorizing Washington to exchange Cornwallis by composition provided Henry Laurens were liberated and all accounts for the support of prisoners were speedily settled.[26]

On March 11, 1782, Henry Knox and Gouverneur Morris were formally appointed to meet with the British commissioners at Elizabethtown on March 15 to negotiate the items outlined in the February 18 resolution of Congress.[27] In his detailed instructions to them, Washington identified their principal objectives as the settlement of accounts for the subsistence of prisoners of all descriptions, obtaining payment or security for the payment of the large balance that was presumed due to the United States, and establishing certain arrangements for the regular payment of subsistence in the future. It was likely, Washington added, that neither side would have adequate vouchers to prove their claims. In that event, the American commissioners were to accept a sum of money in full and final discharge for past expenses. Then, in order to prevent future disputes, they were to determine what constituted a ration,

ELIZABETHTOWN 1782 / 7

481

The American prisoner-exchange negotiators at Elizabethtown were Henry Knox (*left*) and Gouverneur Morris (*right*). [*NJHS*]

to agree on what vouchers would be considered mutually valid, and to obtain and give assurances for the regular monthly and quarterly payment of the balances when they became due. Before proceeding to the negotiation of exchanges, the commissioners were to give due regard to the February 23 resolution regarding the exchange of Cornwallis. However, if the exchange of Cornwallis proved impracticable, they could proceed to the exchange of other officers. The commissioners, in accordance with the resolution of December 20, 1781, were also to inquire into the status and operation of the board of directors of Associated Loyalists in order to devise means for the prevention of future depredations by that body; and should the commissioners enter into either a general or special cartel, they were to insist that in the future "citizens not in arms" were not to be considered as subjects of capture unless they were acting as guides or spies.[28]

The American commissioners were also authorized, should Rear Admiral Robert Digby choose to send representatives, to discuss the treatment and exchange of marine prisoners. Washington urged them to remonstrate warmly on the conditions under which marine prisoners were confined, and he supplied them with documents collected by Congress testifying to British cruelty. In negotiating on the support and mode of payment for the subsistence of seamen, the commissioners were to be guided by the instructions

8 / ELIZABETHTOWN 1782

relating to the rations allowed to soldiers. However, because of the scarcity of British marine prisoners held by Congress, Washington was not optimistic that anything significant could be accomplished in this regard.[29]

In informing Sir Henry Clinton that Henry Knox and Gouverneur Morris had been duly appointed to meet British commissioners at Elizabethtown on March 15, Washington emphasized that they were fully empowered to negotiate the exchanges of Lord Cornwallis and Henry Laurens, but not of Cornwallis for Laurens. Clinton appointed Brig. Gen. Charles O'Hara and Col. Robert Abercrombie as his commissioners, and both commanders made preparations for the cessation of hostilities in the meeting area and for the accommodation of the representatives.[30] In response to Washington's invitation, Digby also agreed to enter into the negotiations with regard to marine prisoners through the same commissioners, O'Hara and Abercrombie, but only on the issue of exchange.[31] Thus, the negotiators on both sides approached the meeting hampered by various conflicting priorities and reservations through which cynicism and pessimism could easily becloud humanitarian concern for the prisoners themselves.

Toward a Cartel

The American commissioners set out for Elizabethtown on March 12; but at that point, Clinton had begun to stall for time. Two days later Washington received a letter written by the British commander on March 7, claiming that because of the long delay between the initial overtures and the final agreement for the meeting, he had been obliged to nominate new commissioners to replace O'Hara and Abercrombie. In order to afford the new appointees sufficient time to become acquainted with the issues to be discussed, Clinton requested a postponement of the meeting until April 10.[32]

Clinton's real motives for the postponement are obscure. Perhaps the delay was occasioned by military plans then being discussed at a board of general officers in New York. On March 8, Clinton had suggested an expedition up the Delaware River, with the object of capturing or destroying the American shipping and stores collected there, and seizing the Bank of North America in order to destroy American public credit and create general confusion. He hoped also to retrieve those prisoners of Cornwallis's army who might be fortunate enough to escape during the attack.[33] At a council of war on March 10, opinions among the officers on the proposed expedition were divided. At another meeting on March

ELIZABETHTOWN 1782 / 9

483

28, opinion was still divided: four in favor, two against.[34] Yet nothing resulted from these plans, and it may be true, as Clinton professed, that the delay was occasioned by his expectation of dispatches from England informing him of a cartel settled between Britain and France, which he wanted to use as the basis for the Elizabethtown negotiations.[35]

Henry Knox and Gouverneur Morris arrived at Elizabethtown on March 15 and only then received word of Clinton's desire for a postponement. Both they and General Washington sent urgent requests for a meeting earlier than April 10, claiming inconveniences to the American commissioners. They left Elizabethtown and waited for a reply in Morris County, New Jersey.[36] Clinton could have devised no better method than this delay in hostile territory to unnerve the American commissioners, and perhaps that also was his intention.

Clinton protested that his request for a delay had been sent sufficiently early to prevent the American commissioners from setting out; but even though the reasons for the postponement still existed, he agreed, in a spirit of accommodation, to appoint March 28 as the new meeting date.[37] Clinton and Digby informed their new commissioners, Maj. Gen. William Dalrymple and Andrew Elliot, of their powers and the new schedule.[38] Knox and Morris thanked Clinton for his action and returned to Elizabethtown on March 28. Clinton's commissioners did not arrive until two days later, which is understandable since Dalrymple had to attend the council of war on March 28.[39]

Mutual exchange of powers took place on March 31. Already irritated from two weeks of delays in New Jersey, the American commissioners immediately expressed their disappointment with the limits of Admiral Digby's authorization, which extended only to the exchange of marine prisoners, and said nothing regarding the settlement of past accounts and provisioning in the future. Morris and Knox were convinced that the objective of the British was solely to regain their captives, with no concern for the sums of money due or to become due in the future. But since Washington had not objected to Digby's limitation, neither did the American commissioners.[40]

On April 1 both sides ascertained the limits within which hostilities would cease during the meetings, and they agreed to meet every morning at 10:30 A.M. The *modus agendi* decided on stated that the questions to be discussed should be taken up in the order in which they appeared in Washington's March 11 authorization to his commissioners: that is, first, a cartel for care, exchange, liberation and better treatment of prisoners; second, liberation of civilians; third, liquidation of past accounts. Propositions were to be made in writing, and answers were to be submitted in writing the following day. Any separate article of a proposition was not to be considered as binding to the general article agreed upon.[41]

Sir Henry Clinton later noted that his expectations from the conferences were raised from this first meeting since the liquidation of accounts was listed as the last of the subjects to be discussed. This, in his mind, implied an earnestness on the part of the Americans to expedite the other two objectives, since if the lengthy question of accounts were discussed first, humanitarian interests would have been jeopardized. As the meetings progressed, however, Clinton charged the Americans with not "shewing the same ardent desire to shorten and alleviate the miseries of Captivity" that the British commissioners did. Clinton saw the Americans as "governed altogether by principles of interested policy, which ought not to have taken place in deliberations wherein the rights and feelings of humanity were mutually declared to be so deeply interested."[42]

From the outset, the meetings went badly. At the first major conference on April 2, the American commissioners proposed a classification of prisoners: military, naval, offenders against the laws of war, and citizens. Procedures were suggested for the exchange of the first two categories and for the speedy trial of the third. Citizens, the Americans claimed, should not be considered as liable to capture, and those already imprisoned should be released. The British response on April 3 insisted on a clarification of the categories and protested that the American definition of citizen would have exempted from captivity nearly all American militiamen. The British also wanted a revision in the description of offenders against the laws of war, which would identify those criminals as acting under their own authority. Discussion of the other issues of exchange and imprisonment of citizens were deferred until Dalrymple and Elliot had consulted with their superiors.[43]

Already, the American commissioners concluded that the British intended to treat all captive Americans as military prisoners while exempting from punishment Loyalist irregulars who committed brutalities under British commissions. Morris and Knox accordingly dropped all considerations of classification, arguing that their object was simply to liberate all captive Americans everywhere in the world. Then, ignoring their own agenda, but adhering to the principal objectives emphasized in Washington's March 11 instructions, the Americans turned directly to the questions of subsistence.[44] They insisted that some general principle be adopted concerning the liquidation of accounts when vouchers were missing or defective, even though they expressed confidence that the existing

ELIZABETHTOWN 1782 / 11

485

evidence would favor the United States. The Americans pressed for a comparison of prisoners held by each side beginning with March 1, 1778, since before that time the expenses had been small and probably weighted on neither side. After that time, however, Knox and Morris claimed, the United States held a surplus of five thousand British prisoners over the number of Americans held by the British.[45]

On the other side, Dalrymple and Elliot, in their response of April 5, were flabbergasted at what they considered American sabotage of the negotiations. The Americans' demand for settlement of accounts was entirely out of order since the agreed-upon agenda placed that issue as the last to be negotiatied. The British, on account of their different interpretation of what constituted a prisoner of war, also denied that America enjoyed a balance of five thousand prisoners; and they expressed surprise that the American commissioners insisted on the liberation of all American captives everywhere in the world, since they had known from the start that the powers of Clinton and Digby extended only to America. Making this demand indispensible would, they explained, bring the conference to an abrupt and unsuccessful end.[46]

Impasse

Thus, only five days into the proceedings, a crisis had developed. Both sides agreed that this impasse put an end to the general cartel proposed by Washington. Dalrymple and Elliot suggested that exchanges be conducted as usual by the commanders-in-chief within their respective precincts, with the British paying a ransom for any balance of soldiers left in American hands, and the Americans giving British soldiers in exchange for any balance of sailors left in British hands. But in their report to Clinton, the British commissioners sadly confided that the Americans would probably veto any exchange since what they apparently really wanted was for the British to pay them periodically a certain sum of money for the maintenance of British prisoners in American jails.[47]

That is exactly what the Americans did on April 8. Claiming insurmountable obstacles to any exchange of prisoners, Morris and Knox demanded that the commissioners proceed to the other items on the agenda—specifically, the settlement of accounts. Then, in a shrewd gesture of avoiding long delays in the compilation of those accounts, the Americans offered to accept for the United States the

12 / ELIZABETHTOWN 1782

Gen. Henry Clinton (*left*) commanded the British forces in New York. Andrew Elliot (*right*) represented the British at the Elizabethtown negotiations. [*NJHS*]

sum of £200,000 for the balance of all accounts from the commencement of the war.[48]

At this point Dalrymple and Elliot wrote to Clinton, wondering whether any useful purpose would attend the continuation of the meetings.[49] Similarly, Gouverneur Morris wrote to Superintendent of Finance Robert Morris on the latter's proposal to accept clothing and rum instead of money from the British but was not very optimistic about the British response. He wrote that he was drafting the superintendent's proposal "hessitatingly," and lamented that "we make Haste slowly here for I can with truth say that we are as yet but at the threshold of the Business and I am heartily tired."[50]

The American demand for £200,000 seemed so extraordinary to the British commissioners that they deferred giving an answer until they had consulted with Clinton. After receiving the dispatches, Clinton requested that Elliot return to headquarters and explain his absence to the Americans as necessitated by some business relative to the port of New York.[51] Not until April 13 did Elliot return with Clinton's response, which labelled as preposterous the American proposal of a cash settlement. Certainly, he alleged,

ELIZABETHTOWN 1782 / 13

487

the balance of the expense of maintaining prisoners from the commencement of the war would be in the British favor. Clinton proposed, however, to remove the other major obstacle to a cartel by promising to obtain the liberation of all American prisoners of war in his or Digby's hands in return for those prisoners in American hands. If, after that, British prisoners remained in Washington's possession, then Clinton would strive to have released sufficient prisoners from all parts of the realm to make up the balance. Then, if there still remained a surplus in American captivity, Clinton proposed to ransom them according to the terms of the cartel just concluded between Great Britain and France—that is, at the rate of about two dollars for every private soldier.[52] With regard to subsisting prisoners in the future, Clinton suggested that each side should be permitted either to purchase provisions for them at the market price within the other's lines or have them sent to them from the opposite lines, whichever would be most expedient for the suppliers.[53]

The American commissioners answered on April 14. They could not accept either naval prisoners or ransom money in exchange for British soldiers and insisted that their demand for £200,000 was not unreasonable. Indeed, they were sure that an even greater sum was due. Since this difference of opinion had now made the liquidation of past accounts more imperative, the Americans announced they would not enter into any exchange of prisoners until that matter had been settled. They adamantly rejected allowing British commissaries to purchase provisions within American lines but insisted that each party should cause provisions to be sent to their captive countrymen from within their own lines. Disheartened, the British commissioners forwarded the proceedings to Clinton, requesting his orders for the dissolution of the conference.[54]

The next day, Dalrymple and Elliot appealed to the Americans' humanity. If, as the American commissioners had insisted, British commissaries would be allowed only to send out provisions from within their own circumscribed lines, British prisoners of war would inevitably suffer from shortages because of their dispersed situation and problems of transportation in the American countryside. Unless the British were allowed to purchase in America, the subject would have to be dropped altogether and prisoners would be maintained, as in the past, at the expense of the capturing nation.[55]

Unruffled, Morris and Knox not only again refused to permit the British to purchase provisions in America but even claimed that they could not agree to the suggestion of maintaining prisoners as in the past until the quantities, prices, and mode of payment of

14 / ELIZABETHTOWN 1782

rations were settled.[56] Dalrymple and Elliot protested that the proposal of maintenance as usual was merely based on the fifth of the articles of capitulation at Yorktown, to which Washington has already agreed, and they consequently avoided fixing the value of a ration.[57]

On the morning of April 17 the American commissioners presented a paper which listed their values for various rations which would be provided to British prisoners of war on the condition that American prisoners be furnished with the same articles at the same rate, with the condition that accounts be settled every three months and balances paid. The Americans knew that it would cost the British more to provide equal rations, not having the vast areas of American agricultural lands under their control. But a fixed rate, as well as the American denial that certain categories of Americans were legal prisoners of war, meant that a balance would always be due to the United States and not to Great Britain. In addition, since the Americans maintained that they already held many more British prisoners than the British held American, they demanded an immediate payment of £50,000 for the provisions and fuel issued between January 1 and June 1, 1782.[58]

Both sides refused to compromise, concluding that nothing worthwhile could be accomplished by a continuance of the meetings. All disputed matters were consequently referred back to Washington and Clinton, and the fate of prisoners on both sides was once again in doubt. Both sets of commissioners protested that they had made "every humane and consistent offer" and regretted the consequences for the prisoners of war.[59] The cease-fire was extended for twenty-four hours after the commissioners had left Elizabethtown, and on April 20, they parted.[60]

Breakdown and Recriminations

In a lengthy letter of April 22, Sir Henry Clinton reported to Washington his interpretation of the reasons for the failure of the conference. The early demand made by the Americans for the liberation of all American prisoners throughout the world, when they most certainly were aware of Clinton's limited powers, indicated to him "a premeditated design of objecting to the extent of my Commissioners powers, that they [the Americans] might have a pretext for declaring that a general Cartel would not be agreed to." This point was proven to him by the American persistence in this demand even after he had engaged to procure the liberation of all prisoners in the British realm. The Americans' refusal to exchange seamen for soldiers or to enter into partial exchanges as usual, as well as their rejection of a ransom for the balance, as was customary in all wars, evidently demonstrated "that humanity towards American Prisoners did not in the least influence their councils, but that they were determined at all events to retain our Prisoners as long as they could for interested purposes." Clinton hoped at least that Washington would allow exchanges by commissaries of prisoners to proceed as usual, and that he would assent to the British proposals of April 13. Rejection of this would of course mean that British prisoners continue to be supplied according to the terms of the capitulations under which they had been captured.[61]

In their reports of April 21 and 22, the American commissioners argued that the deficiency of real powers vested in Dalrymple and Elliot was the chief cause of bringing the discussions to an unsuccessful termination. Every important proposition, they explained, was referred to Clinton, and some of the papers delivered were actually dictated by Clinton, who, unacquainted with the informal discussions carried on by the commissioners, did so without considering the immediate objections that would naturally arise. Not only was this process time-consuming, but it also destroyed any freedom of discussion on the part of the British commissioners. Consequently, many important details did not receive sufficient attention. Had the British agreed to their general propositions, the American commissioners explained, the exchange of Henry Laurens, for instance, would necessarily have followed. Even had they acceded to terms that would have justified partial exchanges, the Laurens case would certainly have been settled. In their discussions, Dalrymple and Elliot had consistently pressed the question of whether the American commissioners were empowered to give Laurens in exchange for Cornwallis. Of course, any proposition on that subject would have had to be transmitted to the British ministry, which alone had the power to dispose of a state prisoner. Just as consistently the Americans had answered that their powers extended to every aspect of exchanges.[62]

Henry Knox and Gouverneur Morris came away with the impression that the British planned to object to pay anything for the support of the Saratoga Convention prisoners, and meant also to dispute payment for the Yorktown prisoners. In addition, the British commissioners had repeatedly hinted that they considered the Elizabethtown meeting as introductory to a larger one in which the business would be completed. They had asked, for example, whether Washington would write to Clinton to resolve the differences. The American response had been stern: Washington would not write, and since the "methods of reason and argument" had

16 / ELIZABETHTOWN 1782

490

failed, "nothing was left but coercion, the exercise of which would probably induce an application from General Clinton."[63]

In reading the minutes of the meetings, one comes away with the impression that, notwithstanding the pious blusterings on both sides regarding humanitarianism, the welfare of the prisoners was definitely a secondary priority. For some prisoners, the almost intentional failure to resolve outstanding issues at Elizabethtown may actually have worsened the conditions of their confinement. Washington again complained in June 1782 to Digby of the barbarous conditions aboard the New York prison ships.[64] Three months later, Congress condemned the British for attempting to destroy the morale of the American marine prisoners by pointing to the failure of negotiation as evidence that they had been abandoned by their government.[65]

In the same month as Washington's complaint to Digby, the Americans themselves began employing similar psychological pressures against the Hessians and other German prisoners in their possession.[66] In one reported case, German Convention prisoners at Reading, Pennsylvania, were separated from their officers and shut up in rooms so crowded that they could neither sit nor lie down. They were allowed only ten ounces of bread and ten ounces of meat daily, generally rotten and unfit to eat, and they were compelled to pay their jail keeper for both water and fuel. On July 30, they were visited by an American clergyman who announced: "The King of Great Britain refused to pay for their maintenance, their Tyrant princes also had abandoned and sold them, the Congress did therefore leave it to their choice, either to enlist in the American Service, or pay 30/ currency of Pennsylvania for their past maintenance in hard money, which sum, if they could not afford to pay, the farmers would advance for them, on binding themselves to serve them for three years, in both of which cases they must take the Oath of Allegiance to the United States."[67]

Generals Benjamin Lincoln and Moses Hazen told them on August 8 that "provisions could no longer be allowed to them as their army was in want thereof," and that they must therefore accept one or the other of the above-mentioned propositions.[68] Throughout the remainder of 1782, and as late as July 1783, there were frequent complaints from Hessians and other German prisoners that they had been forced to work for the inhabitants of Pennsylvania as slaves and coerced into enlisting in American service by close confinement, whippings, and withholding of provisions.[69]

These charges came in spite of the official American policy after Elizabethtown of making a distinction in favor of the Hessians. In fact, the failure of the negotiations was used as a pretext for enlisting them in United States service, since recruiting in America was going so badly in 1782. Washington anxiously hoped in April that these enlistees could join his army before the commencement of active campaigning, and he insisted that they be recruited for Continental service and not credited to the states in whose lines they would serve.[70] Thus, the unsuccessful meetings served the purposes of military men and centralists alike.

Thoughout May, June, and July 1782, Congress, the commander-in-chief, and the superintendent of finance discussed methods of retaliation and solutions to the subsistence question with Washington's request in mind. It was finally decided to allow Hessians and other prisoners to enlist in American service and indenture themselves out to the inhabitants with the promise of land bounties and American citizenship at the end of their service.[71] British prisoners, however, were consistently refused these options and after July 11 were close confined, with all provisions stopped for the women and children attached to the captives.[72] Despite the official favoritism paradoxically linked with some actual cases of coercion, so few Germans enlisted in American service or applied for American citizenship that by December 11, 1782, Congress softened its longstanding policy by allowing British prisoners to hire themselves out.[73]

Why Failure?

The American insistence at Elizabethtown and in subsequent, equally unsuccessful, conversations that no partial exchanges be concluded and that American seamen not be exchanged for British soldiers was grounded in the hard realities of the last years of the war.[74] The Americans were forced to contend that American seamen, not being in public service, were civilians, and therefore subject neither to capture nor exchange. Such a policy ignored the distress of those prisoners, and may have bothered the consciences of American leaders less because of eighteenth-century disregard for that class. Also, to have released British veterans for service in America in order to free those "civilian" seamen would, it seemed, have jeopardized one of the supposed military advantages of the United States at the same time that it mocked American claims of independent nationhood.[75] While Britain still held an advantage in wealth and naval strength—and that advantage increased daily—she was hard-pressed to provide enough trained foot-soldiers for service in America. Britain's superiority at sea guaranteed that she could always hold large numbers of American seamen prisoner, but the

18 / ELIZABETHTOWN 1782

The British prison ship *Jersey*, moored in Wallabout Bay on the East River, was one of at least thirteen vessels that held American prisoners in New York City during the revolutionary war. More than a thousand Americans were imprisoned within the *Jersey*'s hull. This nineteenth-century engraving identifies by number the various parts of the vessel, including (2) guards' tent; (8) sutler's room, where goods were sold to prisoners; (9) upper and spar decks, where prisoners exercised; (10) prisoners' ladder; (12) prisoners' galley; (13) gun room, housing imprisoned officers; (14, 15) hatchways to prisoners' quarters; and (17, 18) between-decks prisoners' quarters. [*NJHS*]

Confederation was hampered by the diminishing size of the Continental navy, the increasing pressure of the British naval blockade, and the distribution of what British marine prisoners there were among the states and America's allies.[76]

Partial exchanges of any sort of prisoner, especially officers, was also considered harmful to American interests because by that means Britain would be able to set free her most important and influential military leaders, thus removing the principal weapons the Americans had to force the British to accede to American terms.[77] An unexchanged Cornwallis, for example, made good political propaganda at home, especially in the South, and stirred up political controversy in England, where Cornwallis traded accusations with Sir Henry Clinton over the Yorktown debacle. In addition, by forcing the British to supply American prisoners at great expense, and by denying them the privilege of purchasing provisions in the countryside, the Americans hoped to increase the economic burden that had already made the war unpopular in England while accentuating the failure of British forces to pacify permanently any significant territory outside New York and Charleston.

The last two years of the war on the American side were characterized by general war-weariness, growing hostility between the military and an ineffectual Confederation government, officers' resignations, and poor enlistments. The Elizabethtown meetings occurred in a period bounded at one end by the mutinies of the Pennsylvania and New Jersey lines in January 1781 and at the other by the Newburgh conspiracy in March 1783. Bombarded by insinuations of a military coup, George Washington desperately wanted to keep his army active, but he did not have sufficient forces or supplies for offensive operations against New York or Charleston. For the commander-in-chief this was the critical moment of the war. Cornwallis's surrender was merely "an interesting event that may be productive of much good if properly improved." But, he warned, "if it should be the means of relaxation and sink us into supineness and [false] security, it had better not have happened."[78] Certainly, this was not the most opportune moment to release thousands of British foot-soldiers, no matter what the consequences for American prisoners.

Even after the British commanders on their own initiative had begun to release American prisoners, and American marine prisoners in England and Ireland were being sent home through the auspices of Benjamin Franklin, American leaders balked at reciprocating.[79] Not until April 15, 1783, did Congress agree to release all prisoners in accordance with article eight of the provisional treaty of peace.[80]

20 / ELIZABETHTOWN 1782

494

Since the question of accounts was never settled, and since prisoners of all descriptions were ultimately released, American intransigence in the face of what appears to have been British liberality and humanitarianism might seem misguided and cruel. This is especially true when it is recalled that after Yorktown, British strategy almost entirely gave up using land forces in North America, relying instead on naval attacks on American commerce, attacks on the French in the West Indies, and coastal raids by Loyalist commandos. On March 4, 1782, Parliament had voted to discontinue offensive warfare in America. Two months later, Sir Guy Carleton, appointed to succeed Clinton, arrived in New York with orders from the new Rockingham ministry to evacuate British troops from America.[81] The veteran foot-soldiers refused exchange by the Americans were therefore not wanted anyway, and in the meantime the British navy made a shambles of American commerce. Yet Washington distrusted Carleton's pacific and conciliatory pronouncements as a subterfuge under which the British were attempting to win the war at another level.

The "relaxation," and false "security," and "supineness" that Washington railed against really had to do with a disastrous decline in the Whig zeal that had characterized the early years of the war. Republican virtue was being eroded by the soothing manipulations of the British and by horrendous economic problems. By 1780, American currency had collapsed, exchange had been reduced to barter, and Congress could no longer procure supplies for Washington's troops by consent in the market place. As the British naval blockade strangled American commerce, the enormous cost of provisioning British and German prisoners became unbearable. It seemed senseless to allocate hard-to-procure provisions to prisoners when Washington's troops were mutinying because of shortages; hence, the American insistence at Elizabethtown on settlement of past accounts and agreement on regular payments by the British in the future. It may have been inhumane to leave Americans rotting in British prisons; but the threat of a military coup at home, combined with the embarrassment of having to force the states to contribute to the war effort, made the solution of the economic question imperative.[82] What the Americans wanted and needed was British money or release from the obligation of provisioning British prisoners, not seamen to staff a merchant marine bottled up in port by a much superior British navy, and not additional foot-soldiers who could neither be paid nor supplied to join the ranks of Washington's disgruntled army.

In a very real sense, the British in 1782 were winning the economic war. "Every Body," wrote Robert Morris on July 18, is "in extreme Want of Money as well as myself owing to the terrible

495

Many American prisoners-of-war were incarcerated in the Rhinelander Sugar House, located on the corner of William and Duane streets in New York City. [NJHS]

Blows which our Commerce has sustained."[83] The British blockade and rumors of peace reduced the flow of hard money, since tax money coming from the states was drying up and few merchants were willing to buy French goods at inflated wartime prices, only to have to sell them at a loss in the event of a treaty.[84] Reduced trade with France made it increasingly difficult to sell bills of exchange on that country, and for that reason the superintendent of finance had difficulty meeting the specie obligations of the United States government that fell due during the summer of 1782. He was forced to adopt any expedient at hand, such as extracting specie from New York by selling Virginia tobacco to British merchants under an agreement with George Eddy, or by forcing the British to pay for the subsistence of their prisoners in American hands.[85]

The British could use the military stalemate and talk of peace to their advantage by undermining the economic situation in America. The exploitable weakness of the Confederation was its shortage of specie and the American desire for British dry goods. The illicit trade between Americans hungry for glass, earthenware, wrought silk, and printed cotton and the British in New York who stockpiled these goods and happily extracted scarce specie from the American economy in payment, had reached alarming proportions by 1782.[86] Washington's poorly supplied and low-morale army

22 / ELIZABETHTOWN 1782

496

could do nothing to stop the illicit trading, and the states refused to enact or enforce legislation making it a capital crime.[87]

The specie drain prevented Robert Morris's reestablishment of a credible American currency and guaranteed that Washington's army would lack the means to launch an offensive against the British. Without a currency that American farmers and manufacturers would willingly receive in exchange for their goods, there was no realistic way of extracting those goods to satisfy the grumbling army. The volume of the illicit trade with the British also put a damper on American-French relations at a time when the British were working hard to destroy the alliance. The trade showed the French that they could never supplant the American demand for British manufactures. American revolutionary regimes were further demoralized by having to wage war, albeit ineffectively, on their own citizens in order to control the illicit trade and were embarrassed by the decline in republican virtue that the volume of that trade signified.[88]

Having failed to defeat the Americans on the battlefield, the British had found a way, they thought, to corrupt the revolution by internal subversion and ensure a demoralized, economically weak, and politically divided nation in the postwar period. Returning American prisoners, ostensibly out of the goodness of their hearts, was, in a sense, as much another way the British had of guaranteeing the instability of the republic. Unacquainted with the real economic problems of their nation during the period of their captivity and indoctrinated in the lack of concern of their government for their plight, the prisoners would return, the British hoped, to swell the ranks of disgruntled military men still in active and neglected servitude.

American leaders realized the futility of attempts to curtail illicit trade with the British. Robert Morris wrote on May 10, 1782, "the history of human affairs demonstrates the inefficacy of penal laws to prevent such a commerce, when the temptation is great."[89] John Taylor Gilman of New Hampshire argued, "the Number of Persons who feel the (private) benefit of this Trade is so great that it is the Opinion of some any further Attempts to prevent the same would be idle."[90] Of course, George Washington could not indulge in such public fatalism, commissioned as he was to do everything in his power to apprehend those engaged in the trade. In his instructions to Knox and Morris before the Elizabethtown meetings, he warned them to be careful to prevent "abuses of flags of truce during the cessation of hostilities which could lead to illicit commerce with civilians and improper transferences of property." But, he immediately added, "if, however, winking at such abuses proved advantageous for gathering intelligence of enemy intentions, then it was justifiable."[91]

That addition is illuminating. Washington sensed that the war had to be carried on vigorously regardless of his enforced inactivity, the economic woes of his countrymen, and the decline in republican virtue in America. He realized that the British must also have an exploitable weakness, and if the illicit trade in New York provided the vehicle through which that weakness could be discovered, so be it. Perhaps that is why Washington approached the Elizabethtown negotiations less sanguine about their direct outcome than did financier Morris. He was looking for another way of waging war against the enemy—a way equivalent in its force to the British corruption of American unity through materialism, and a way consistent with the practical realities of a military stalemate and an approaching peace.

Washington discovered more than one exploitable weakness. The American commissioners learned, for example, of the deep antipathy between the regular army and the Loyalist forces. The board of directors of the Associated Loyalists, they reported, "are more odious and more disagreeable to the British Army than to us. The disgust against them among the military is general, but they have numerous adherents among the disaffected. "Mutual jealousy," they concluded, "and sincere hatred have arisen and are likely to continue and increase."[92] Here was a weakness the Americans could exploit, especially after the selection of Capt. Charles Asgill, a British officer, for execution in retaliation for the hanging of Capt. Joshua Huddy, a New Jersey militia officer, by Loyalists.[93] Henry Knox and Gouverneur Morris noted that the situation provided Washington with the "opportunity of adding much Fuel to the fire kindled between" the Loyalists and the regulars, since "should the Perpetrators of the Deed be delivered up (even if pardoned afterwards) the lesser agents will no longer confide in the greater who will in their turn foster the most rancourous animosity—and should a British Officer be executed in consequence of a Refusal to deliver up or punish the guilty the resentments of the Army will be proportionately inflamed."[94] Washington probably had no intention of actually executing the unlucky Asgill, but he prolonged the period of uncertainty into late 1782 in order to undermine British-Loyalist relations.

By turning a blind eye to the illicit traffic with the British, the American commissioners were able to construct a picture for General Washington of an occupied New York disillusioned and on the brink of unrest in the waning days of the war. "The several Provincial Corps," they reported, "are apprehensive of being drafted into

In 1782 the Americans threatened to execute Capt. Charles Asgill (*left*), a British prisoner-of-war, in retaliation for the Loyalist hanging of Joshua Huddy, a New Jersey militia officer, whose home (*right*) was located in Colts Neck, Monmouth County. [*NJHS*]

other Regiments and sent into the West Indies." The overall picture was one of dissension and low morale. "The Army and Navy in New York are upon very bad terms together," they observed, "the Army blame the Navy, the Navy the Army, the Board of Directors and their Disciples blame both."[95]

Without a viable army capable of conducting offensive operations, there was little Washington could do to extirpate the crumbling British military edifice in New York. Of far greater potential, however, was the disillusionment of the loyal civilian population with the British war effort. "The Inhabitants are pretty generally disgusted with the manner of conducting the War," Washington learned from his commissioners, "and have formed an opinion that notwithstanding assurances to the contrary they will be deserted by the British upon the first unfavourable turn of their affairs." Here was an exploitable weakness which, if handled properly, could effectually nullify the specie-draining and morale-sapping problem of the illicit trade. Knox and Morris gathered information that the inhabitants "feel a disposition to desert the Royal cause entirely and prepare for a change by converting their property into money and sending [it] out of the Lines. This disposition we have encouraged as by that means while we derive strength and resources the Enemy will.lose them tho' imperceptibly yet effectually, and the Commerce which has hitherto been carried on to such extent corrupting the People on the Borders will be greatly diminished."[96]

In this war of corruption and counter-corruption, the action of Congress was necessary. There was clearly no purely military solution. In the opinion of the American commissioners, the loyal

ELIZABETHTOWN 1782 / 25

499

civilians were "in a state of despondency arising in a great degree from doubts of the Treatment they will receive from us." The American commissioners were convinced "that their apprehensions from us form the only Bond by which most of them are now connected with the Enemy." Force would not do; only seduction would suffice. "It is unnecessary to add," they concluded, "that if hopes of pardon could be extended to this class of People they would seize the earliest opportunity of abandoning the cause they have espoused."[97]

Washington did recommend a pardon, but Congress procrastinated.[98] The terms of the preliminary treaty of peace, signed in Paris on November 30, were known in New York shortly after the start of the new year. Articles five and six provided Loyalists with protection of their persons, liberty, and property. But Congress failed to approve these articles until May 30, 1783, and once it did, its resolution had little effect as states and local committees disregarded the recommendation and began a persecution of the Loyalists.[99] The peace treaty and Congress's lack of authority had made Washington's subtle strategy irrelevant.

The Prisoners of War in Perspective

Thus, in the twilight war after Yorktown, the welfare of the prisoners of war took second place to larger and more sophisticated issues. Somewhat ironically, in the last years of the war soldiers and sailors mattered less and less, and the arts of diplomatic cunning, economic manipulation, and internal subversion mattered more and more. The nature of the war had changed and so had its weapons. Despite passionate claims on both sides of their interest in humanitarian concerns, military prisoners were viewed more as expense items or propaganda weapons with which to discredit the enemy or cause economic difficulty. Negotiators at Elizabethtown seemingly were more concerned with costs and international image, and with using the meetings to cover surprise commando raids, to boost morale at home, or to gather information about the enemy's exploitable weaknesses, than they were about the liberty of their countrymen.

Notes

[1]Worthington C. Ford, ed., *Journals of the Continental Congress, 1774–1789* (Washington, D.C., 1904–37), 21:815, 829–30 (hereafter, *JCC*); Diary, August 1, 1781, and E. James Ferguson and John Catanzariti, eds., *The Papers of Robert*

Morris, 1781–1784 (Pittsburgh, Pa., 1975–), 2:3–4 and note 2 (hereafter, *Morris Papers*).

The literature on prisoners of war in the Revolution is voluminous. Unless cited otherwise, descriptions of P.O.W. life in captivity in this essay are based on the following: Henry R. Stiles, ed., *Letters From the Prisons and Prison-Ships of the Revolution* (New York, 1865); William R. Cutter, ed., "A Yankee Privateersman in Prison in England, 1777–1779," *The New England Historical and Genealogical Register* 30 (1876):174–77, 343–52; "Journal of Samuel Cutler," ibid. 32 (1878):42–44, 184–88, 305–8, 395–98; Worthington C. Ford, ed., "British and American Prisoners of War, 1778," *Pennsylvania Magazine of History and Biography* 17 (1893): 159–74, 316–24; Hiram Stone, ed., "The Experiences of a Prisoner in the American Revolution," *Journal of American History* 2 (1908):527–29; James Lenox Banks, *David Sproat and Naval Prisoners in the War of the Revolution* (New York, 1909); Charles E. West, "Prison Ships in the American Revolution," *Journal of American History* 5 (1911):121–28; Eugene L. Armbruster, *The Wallabout Prison Ships* (New York, 1920); William Hammond Bowden, ed., "Diary of William Widger of Marblehead, Kept at Mill Prison, England, 1781," *The Essex Institute Historical Collections* 73 (October 1937): 311–47; ibid. 74 (January 1938): 22–48; ibid. (April 1938): 142–58; Olive Anderson, "The Treatment of Prisoners of War in Britain during the American War of Independence," *Bulletin of the Institute of Historical Research* 28 (1955):68–83, and "The Establishment of British Supremacy at Sea and the Exchange of Naval Prisoners of War, 1689–1783," *English Historical Review* 75 (1960):77–89; David L. Sterling, ed., "American Prisoners of War in New York: A Report by Elias Boudinot," *William and Mary Quarterly*, 3d ser., 13 (1956):376–93; Richard H. Amerman, "Treatment of American Prisoners during the Revolution," *Proceedings of the New Jersey Historical Society* 78 (1960):257–75; Howard Lewis Applegate, "American Privateersmen in the Mill Prison during 1777–1782," *The Essex Institute Historical Collections* 97 (October 1961):303–20; Ernest J. Moyne, "The Reverend William Hazlitt: A Friend of Liberty in Ireland during the American Revolution," *William and Mary Quarterly*, 3d ser., 21 (April 1964):288–97; John K. Alexander, "American Privateersmen in the Mill Prison during 1777–1782: An Evaluation," *The Essex Institute Historical Collections* 102 (1966):318–40; "Forton Prison during the American Revolution: A Case Study of the British Prisoner of War Policy and the American Prisoner Response to That Policy," ibid., 103 (1967):365–89, and "Jonathan Haskins' Mill Prison 'Diary': Can It Be Accepted at Face Value?" *New England Quarterly* 40 (1967):561–64; Jesse Lemisch, "Jack Tar in the Streets: Merchant Seamen in the Politics of Revolutionary America," *William and Mary Quarterly*, 3d ser., 25 (July 1968):402–4; William R. Lindsey, "Treatment of American Prisoners of War during the American Revolution," *The Emporia State Research Studies*, 22 (1973):5–32; and Catherine M. Prelinger, "Benjamin Franklin and the American Prisoners of War in England during the American Revolution," *William and Mary Quarterly*, 3d ser., 32 (1975):261–94. General works, including Danske Dandridge, *American Prisoners of the Revolution* (Charlottesville, Va., 1911), Charles Metzger, S.J., *The Prisoner in the American Revolution* (Chicago, 1971), and Larry G. Bowman, *Captive-Americans: Prisoners during the American Revolution* (Athens, Oh., 1976), are inadequate for the period after Yorktown. References to the Elizabethtown negotiations in 1782 are scant, and the most recent work does not even mention them.

[2]George Washington to the Officer Commanding his Britannic Majesty's Ships of War, August 21, 1781, John C. Fitzpatrick, ed., *The Writings of George Washington from the Original Manuscript Sources, 1745–1799* (Washington, D.C., 1931–44), 23:24–25 (hereafter, *Writings of Washington*); Edmund Affleck to George Washington, August 30, 1781, Washington Papers, Library of Congress, Washing-

ELIZABETHTOWN 1782 / 27

501

ton, D.C. This reply was submitted to Congress, which instructed Washington to act upon it as he saw fit. Washington to the President of Congress, September 4, 1781, *Writings of Washington*, 23:83–84; *JCC*, 21:930.

[3]John Green to Robert Morris, November 20, 1781, and notes, *Morris Papers*, 3:215–17. See also Prelinger, "Benjamin Franklin and the American Prisoners of War in England during the American Revolution," 261–94.

[4]Ibid.

[5]Resolution of September 18, 1781, *JCC*, 21: 973–74.

[6]Washington to the President of Congress, December 27, 1781, *Writings of Washington*, 23:407–8.

[7]Washington to Nathanael Greene, October 31, 1781, ibid., 23:311.

[8]Articles of Capitulation, October 19, 1781, Papers of the Continental Congress, National Archives, Washington, D.C., no. 152, 10:299–307 (hereafter, PCC). The capitulation agreement, along with Washington's letter of October 19, was submitted to a committee of Congress on October 24. *JCC*, 21:1071; Washington to the President of Congress, October 19, 1781, *Writings of Washington*, 23:243.

[9]Robert Morris to the Paymaster General, November 21, 1781, and notes, *Morris Papers*, 3:223–25; *JCC*, 21:1082n, 1083n.

[10]*JCC*, 21:1132–34. For the number of women and children at York, see Secretary at War to the President of Congress, July 10, 1782, PCC, no. 149, 1:497.

[11]*JCC*, 21:1134.

[12]Gen. Sir Henry Clinton to General Washington, November 24, 1781, Great Britain, Historical Manuscripts Commission, *Report on American Manuscripts in the Royal Institution of Great Britain* (London, 1904–9), 2:354 (hereafter, *Report on American MSS*); Washington to the President of Congress, December 3, 1781, *Writings of Washington*, 23:369.

[13]Washington to Abraham Skinner, December 5, 1781, *Writings of Washington*, 23:372. The civilians taken at Yorktown were British and Loyalist merchants.

[14]*JCC*, 21:1181; Washington to Abraham Skinner, December 20, 1781, and to Gov. George Clinton, January 30, 1782, *Writings of Washington*, 23:401, 472. The Canadians who had surrendered at St. Johns on November 2, 1775, had been permitted to return home on parole. The American garrison at the Cedars, thirty miles north of Montreal, had surrendered in the spring of 1776 without a fight. Benedict Arnold, then in the American service, was able to obtain the release of the captives by promising an exchange. Christopher Ward, *The War of the Revolution* (New York, 1952), 1:160–61, 198.

[15]Exchange of prisoners, December 17, 1781, *Report on American MSS*, 2:365; Washington to the President of Congress, December 24, 1781, *Writings of Washington*, 23:403–4.

[16]Abraham Skinner to Joshua Loring, January 14, 1782, and General Sir Henry Clinton to Joshua Loring, January 21, 1782, *Report on American MSS*, 2:382, 384.

[17]Prisoners, February 9, 1782, ibid., 2:397.

[18]Clinton to Joshua Loring, January 21, 1782, and to Washington, February 11, 1782, and Joshua Loring to Abraham Skinner, February 12, 1782, ibid., 2:384, 398.

[19]Washington to the President of Congress, February 18, 1782, *Writings of Washington*, 24:4–6.

[20]Ibid. Washington had expressed similar sentiments earlier in a letter to the secretary at war, in which he proposed bringing all British prisoners under Continental control. "I know of no method," he explained, "so likely to put an end to the mutual complaints of both sides as that of having all Prisoners given up to the Comy. General to be by him exchanged," Washington to the Secretary at War, December 29, 1781, ibid., 23:413.

28 / ELIZABETHTOWN 1782

[21]Diary, December 5, 1781, *Morris Papers*, 3:332–33; Washington to Clinton, December 6, 1781, *Writings of Washington*, 23:373. Possibly Washington's first letter was lost, for he repeated his invitation on December 31. Washington to Clinton, December 31, 1781, ibid., 418–19.

[22]Washington to Clinton, January 11, 1782, ibid., 23:440–41; Clinton to Washington, January 2, 1782, Washington Papers.

[23]Clinton to Washington, January 23, 1782, ibid. While waiting for a reply, Washington asked Robert Morris to begin compiling the necessary accounts regarding the maintenance of prisoners. Washington to Robert Morris, January 25, 1782, *Morris Papers*, 4:115. When Clinton's response arrived on February 7, Henry Knox and Gouverneur Morris were duly informed. Diary, February 7, 1782, ibid., 4:178.

[24]*JCC*, 22:76–77.

[25]Washington to the President of Congress, February 20, 1782, *Writings of Washington*, 22:9–12.

[26]*JCC*, 22:93–95.

[27]Washington to Henry Knox and Gouverneur Morris, March 11, 1782, *Writings of Washington*, 24:53–55. American strategy was formulated during conferences at Robert Morris's office on February 25, and March 9, 10, and 11. Diary, February 25, March 9, 10, and 11, 1782, *Morris Papers*, 4:300, 375, 385, 387.

[28]Washington's Instructions to Henry Knox and Gouverneur Morris, March 11, 1782, *Writings of Washington*, 24:55–57. Advised in 1780 to employ "the zeal of his [the King's] faithful refugee subjects within the British lines in annoying the seacoasts of the revolted provinces and distressing their trade," Clinton in January 1781 had established a board of Associated Loyalists to organize raids along the coast. Germain to Clinton, April 21, 1780, *Report on American MSS*, 2:237. Although technically under Clinton's authority, the board, headed by William Franklin of New Jersey, acted independently. They corresponded directly with the British ministry, which appointed its members, and had their own commissary of prisoners, and possessed the right to exchange prisoners taken by their forces. They bridled at any interference from Clinton, and their overzealous activities proved an embarrassment to the commander-in-chief. Knox and Morris to Washington, April 21, 1782, PCC, no. 169, 7:389–95. In the spring of 1782, for example, they retaliated for one of their number being shot while a captive by taking Capt. Joseph Huddy, a New Jersey militia officer, from a British prison ship and hanging him from a tree on the heights of Middletown, Monmouth County, New Jersey. Washington, in turn, selected by lot a British prisoner, Capt. Charles Asgill, to be executed unless the perpetrator of Huddy's murder were delivered up for trial or otherwise punished. James Thomas Flexner, *George Washington in the American Revolution, 1775–1783* (Boston, 1967), 479. General accounts of the Huddy-Lippincott-Asgill affair include Katherine Mayo, *General Washington's Dilemma* (New York, 1938), and Larry Bowman, "The Court-Martial of Captain Richard Lippincott," *New Jersey History* 89 (1971): 23–36.

[29]Washington's Instructions to Knox and Morris, March 11, 1782, *Writings of Washington*, 24:55–59. Certainly, Digby's proposal to exchange British soldiers for American seamen was inadmissible. Washington hoped for some alleviation of seamen's miseries through private endeavors, such as the application of money for Philadelphia mariners raised by subscription among Philadelphia merchants. Washington to Knox and Morris, March 13, 1782, ibid., 24:64–65.

[30]Washington to Clinton, February 26, 1782, to Elias Dayton, February 26, 1782, and to Abraham Skiner, February 26, 1782, ibid., 24:21–23.

[31]Washington to Digby, February 26, 1782, ibid., 24:22; Digby to Washington, March 5, 1782, *Report on American MSS*, 2:411.

[32]Diary, March 12, 1782, *Morris Papers*, 4:393; Clinton to Washington, March

ELIZABETHTOWN 1782 / 29

503

7, 1782, *Report on American MSS*, 2:414; Washington to Knox and Morris, March 14, 1782, *Writings of Washington*, 24:66–67.

[33]Minutes of the board of general officers, March 8, 1782, *Report on American MSS*, 2:414

[34]Minutes of the board of general officers, March 10, 1782, and March 28, 1782, ibid., 2:416, 434.

[35]Clinton to Commissioners Dalrymple and Elliott, April 2, 1782, ibid., 2:439–40.

[36]Gouverneur Morris to Robert Morris, March 22, 1782, and notes, *Morris Papers*, 4:438–41; Washington to Knox and Morris, March 14, 1782, and to Clinton, March 14, 1782, *Writings of Washington*, 24:66–68; Gouverneur Morris and Henry Knox to Washington, April 22, 1782, and to Clinton, March 16, 1782, PCC, no. 169, 8:365–69. It was during this delay that Parliament, on March 25, passed an act legally defining American captives as prisoners of war. Benjamin Franklin to Robert R. Livingston, March 30, 1782, Francis Wharton, ed., *Revolutionary Diplomatic Correspondence* (Washington, D.C., 1889), 5:277, and to John Jay, April 24, 1782, Henry P. Johnston, ed., *The Correspondence and Public Papers of John Jay* (New York, 1890–93), 2:194.

[37]Clinton to Washington, March 18, 1782, *Report on American MSS*, 2:424; Clinton to Morris and Knox, March 18, 1782, PCC, no. 169, 8:367–68.

[38]Clinton to Dalrymple and Elliot, March 18, 1782, *Report on American MSS*, 2:424; Digby to Dalrymple and Elliot, March 18, 1782, and Clinton to Dalrymple and Elliot, March 25, 1782, PCC, no. 169, 8:324–36.

[39]Morris and Knox to Clinton, March 21, 1782, and to Washington, April 22, 1782, PCC, no. 169, 8:368–69.

[40]Gouverneur Morris to Robert Morris, March 31, 1782, *Morris Papers*, 4:490–91; Minutes of the proceedings of the commissioners, March 31, 1782, PCC, no. 169, 8:320–21; Morris and Knox to Washington, April 22, 1782, PCC, no. 169, 8:369–70.

[41]Minutes of the proceedings of the commissioners, April 1, 1782, PCC, no. 169, 8:326–27.

[42]Clinton to Washington, April 22, 1782, PCC, no. 169, 8:396.

[43]Minutes of the proceedings of the commissioners, April 2, 1782, PCC, no. 169, 8:327–36. Robert Morris had high expectations from the meetings. At a conference at headquarters on March 16, to discuss the disposition of Hessian and other German prisoners, he persuaded Washington and a committee of Congress to take no action until they had heard from the commissioners at Elizabethtown. He also wrote to Congress on March 21 that as soon as the commissioners had returned, he would submit a plan of relief for American marine prisoners, which involved granting passports to export Virginia tobacco to some of the British "merchants-capitulant" of Yorktown in return for the application of part of the proceeds to the relief of marine prisoners in New York. Diary, March 16, 1782, Morris to the President of Congress, March 21, 1782, and to the Governor of Virginia, April 10, 1782, *Morris Papers*, 4:404–7, 413, 433, 558. Confident the accounts would be settled, Morris directed the commissioners to inform the British that "from one End of this Continent to the other" he could "obtain Whatever is wanted for the public Service, by a *Scrip* of the Pen." Estimating the cost of maintaining the British and Hessian and other German prisoners at more than $1,000 a day, Morris insisted that the British commander "must provide for this Expence or my Measures will be such as to bring eternal Disgrace on them and justifiable Relief to our Treasury." Robert Morris to Gouverneur Morris, April 3, 1782, ibid., 4:510. See also Clinton to Washington, April 22, 1782, PCC, no. 169, 8:397–99.

30 / ELIZABETHTOWN 1782

[44]Minutes of the proceedings of the commissioners, April 4, 1782, Morris and Knox to Washington, April 22, 1782, and Clinton to Washington, April 22, 1782, PCC, no. 169, 8:338–41, 370–73, 399–400. Throughout the meetings, the American commissioners were receiving further instructions and advice from Washington and Robert Morris. Knox was especially enjoined to be careful of what was said in secrecy, since one of his attendants was a British spy. With regard to the exchange of Henry Laurens, Washington did not think that any revision in his instructions to the commissioners was in order, since, although Laurens's limits had been extended, he was still not free to leave England. Washington to Knox and Morris, March 19, 28, and 30, and to Henry Knox, March 30, 1782, *Writings of Washington*, 24:79, 89–91, 95–96. Special cases and additional information were forwarded to the commissioners by Robert Morris. Reports of conditions in English prisons were sent, and Morris entreated the commissioners to press for their relief and exchange. He also urged that something be done for the seven to eight hundred Continental prisoners and about twelve hundred American citizens reported to be harshly treated in Canada. On April 16, he sent the commissioners a copy of the same cartel agreement between France and England, which Clinton had wanted his commissioners to use as the basis for their negotiations. Diary, March 16, and April 15, 1782, Robert Morris to Gouverneur Morris, March 24, 1782, *Morris Papers*, 4:412, 447, 575; Robert Morris to Henry Knox and Gouverneur Morris, April 16, 1782, Official Letterbook Copy of the Office of Finance, Robert Morris Papers, Library of Congress, Washington, D.C.; Clinton to Dalrymple and Elliot, April 2, 1782, *Report on American MSS*, 2:439–40.

[45]Minutes of the proceedings of the commissioners, April 3, 1782, PCC, no. 169, 8:336–38.

[46]Minutes of the proceedings of the commissioners, April 5, 1782, and Clinton to Washington, April 22, 1782, PCC, no. 169, 8:341–44, 400–401.

[47]Minutes of the proceedings of the commissioners, April 6 and 7, 1782, Morris and Knox to Washington, April 22, 1782, and Clinton to Washington, April 22, 1782, PCC, no. 169, 8:344–47, 374, 401–2; Dalrymple and Elliot to Clinton, April 6, and Clinton to Dalrymple and Elliot, April 7, 1782, and Peter Russell to Captain Smith, April 7, 1782, *Report on American MSS*, 2:441–43.

[48]Minutes of the proceedings of the commissioners, April 8, 1782, Morris and Knox to Washington, and Clinton to Washington, April 22, 1782, PCC, no. 169, 8:348–50, 374–77, 402–3; Dalrymple and Elliot to Clinton, April 8, 1782, *Report on American MSS*, 2:443.

[49]Dalrymple to Clinton, April 8, 1782, *Report on American MSS*, 2:444.

[50]Gouverneur Morris to Robert Morris, April 8, 1782, *Morris Papers*, 4:549–550. Robert Morris had suggested that the British deliver to the lines at Charleston one or two hundred hogsheads of rum and three to five hundred bushels of salt along with some summer clothing, and at New York summer clothing, provided that American agents be permitted to purchase at current prices or to contract with Gouverneur Morris for delivery at prices to be fixed by him. Robert Morris to Gouverneur Morris, April 3, 1782, *Morris Papers*, 4:510.

[51]Elliot was superintendent of the port of New York.

[52]Minutes of the proceedings of the commissioners, April 13, 1782, and Clinton to Washington, April 22, 1782, PCC, no. 169, 8:350–53, 377–79; Dalrymple and Elliot to Clinton, and Clinton to Dalrymple and Elliott, April 8, 1782, and Clinton to Dalrymple and Elliot, April 9, and April 12, 1782, *Report on American MSS*, 2:443–44, 446–47, 448.

[53]Minutes of the proceedings of the commissioners, April 13, 1782, and Morris and Knox to Washington, April 22, 1782, PCC, no. 169, 8:350–53, 371–72, 379–80.

[54]Minutes of the proceedings of the commissioners, April 14, 1782, Clinton to Washington, April 22, 1782, and Morris and Knox to Washington, April 22, 1782, PCC, no. 169, 8:353–54, 378–80, 404–5; Dalrymple and Elliot to Clinton, April 14, 1782, *Report on American MSS*, 2:450.

[55]Minutes of the proceedings of the commissioners, April 16, 1782, Clinton to Washington, April 22, 1782, Morris and Knox to Washington, April 22, 1782, PCC, no. 169, 8:354–55, 380, 405. Clinton to Dalrymple and Elliot, April 15, 1782, *Report on American MSS*, 2:451.

[56]Minutes of the proceedings of the commissioners, April 16, 1782, PCC, no. 169, 8:355–57.

[57]Minutes of the proceedings of the commissioners, April 16, 1782, PCC, no. 169, 8:357–58.

[58]Minutes of the proceedings of the commissioners, April 17, 1782, PCC, no. 169, 8:358–60.

[59]Dalrymple and Elliot to Clinton, April 17, 1782, and Clinton to Dalrymple and Elliot, April 18, 1782, *Report on American MSS*, 2:456, 457; Minutes of the proceedings of the commissioners, April 19, 1782, PCC, no. 169, 8:360–64.

[60]Knox and Morris to Dalrymple and Elliot, April 19, 1782, and to Washington, April 22, 1782, PCC, no. 169, 8:364, 382; Dalrymple to Knox and Morris, April 19, 1782, *Report on American MSS*, 2:459.

[61]Clinton to Washington, April 22, 1782, PCC, no. 169, 8:409–11.

[62]Morris and Knox to Washington, April 21 and 22, 1782, PCC, no. 169, 8:372, 389–90, 394–95.

[63]Ibid.

[64]Washington to Digby, June 5, 1782, *Writings of Washington*, 24:315–16.

[65]Resolve of September 9, 1782, *JCC*, 23:555–59.

[66]Instructions of Robert Morris and Benjamin Lincoln, July 11, 1782, Shelburne Papers, William L. Clements Library, University of Michigan, Ann Arbor, Michigan. See also *Report on American MSS*, 3:41–42.

[67]German Troops, January 1–4, 1783, *Report on American MSS*, 3:314–15.

[68]Ibid.

[69]Lt. Carl Reinking to Carleton, December 10, 1782, Washington Papers. See also *Report on American MSS*, 3:372, 407–8, 4:101, 103, 106, 107, 109, 131–32, 153, 160, 167, 172–73, 186, 187, 189–90, 230.

[70]Washington to the Secretary at War, April 27, 1782, *Writings of Washington*, 24:175–77.

[71]Ibid.; Diary, May 1, 6, 7, 10 and June 10, 1782, Robert Morris Papers; *JCC*, 22:274–76, 316–18, 321, 323–24, 335–36, 343–44, 372–73; PCC, no. 149, 1:395–96, 481, 485, 497.

[72]Resolution of July 11, 1782, *JCC*, 22: 382.

[73]Secretary at War to the President of Congress, September 13, 1782, PCC, no. 149, 2:171–73; *JCC*, 23:785.

[74]On these negotiations and the abortive meeting at Tappan, New York, on September 25–28, 1782, see *JCC*, 22:421–22, 460n, 23:462–63, 551, 555–59, 563–64, 581–83, 606–7, 608, 660–61; PCC, no. 149, 1:611–12, 2:1–2, 7–9, 11–12, 15, 17–19, 21–23, 25–26, 29, 31, 35, 41, 43, 45, 47, no. 169, 9:54–55, 65–67. *Report on American MSS*, 3:119, 123, 129–30, 131, 133, 134–36, *Writings of Washington*, 24:405–6, 25:38, 71–72, 111–112, 134, 136–38, 146, 161–62, 169, 185–86, 191–92, 195–97, 201–2, 221–22, 231–32; Gouverneur Morris to Henry Knox, September 13, 1782, Knox Papers, New York Public Library, New York City (hereafter NYPL); Carleton to Washington, July 7, 1782, Washington Papers; Diary, June 18 and September 14, 1782, Robert Morris Papers; Washington to Robert Morris, September 2, 4, 16, and October 3, 1782, *Writings*

32 / ELIZABETHTOWN 1782

of Washington, 25:108–9, 122–23, 163, 235–36; James Madison to Edmund Pendleton, July 16, 1782, Edmund C. Burnett, ed., *Letters of Members of the Continental Congress* (Washington, D.C., 1933), 6:385, (hereafter, *Letters of Congress*); Schedule of Proceedings at Tappan, British Army Headquarters Papers, reel 15, no. 5688, NYPL.

[75]On American opinion of merchant seamen, see Jesse Lemisch, "Jack Tar in the Streets," 371–407.

[76]Washington to the President of Congress, July 9, 1782, and to Robert Morris, December 11, 1782, *Writings of Washington*, 24:405–6, 25:418. British sailors captured in European waters were turned over to the French, who, contrary to American expectations, used them in exchange for French, rather than American, marine prisoners, *JCC*, 22:245–46. Secretary at War to Washington, June 12, 1782, Washington Papers. Partial exchanges of marine prisoners did occur contrary to American policy, principally through Benjamin Franklin and the governors of several states. The Americans, however, delayed as long as possible the release of British marine prisoners. *JCC*, 22:413–14; *Report on American MSS*, 2:496, 3:74, 80, 117; Carleton and Digby to Washington, August 2, 1782, Washington Papers; Washington to the President of Congress, August 5, 1782, and to the Agent of Marine, January 6, 1783, *Writings of Washington*, 24:466–67, 26:12–13; PCC, no. 169, 9:78–80; Diary, August 13, 15–17, 20–23, 27 and September 10, 1782, Robert Morris Papers.

[77]Washington to the Secretary at War, October 7, 1782, *Writings of Washington*, 25:240.

[78]Flexner, *George Washington in the American Revolution (1775–1783)*, 405–9, 421–22, 468–69, 477, 483–508.

[79]The North Carolina delegates in Congress wrote to their governor on August 19, 1782, "the sending our prisoners to America at this Juncture is not by any means a clear proof of benevolence, it may with equal probability be passed to the Acct. of cunning: for the enemy wish and expect to get regular Soldiers in exchange for those people, many of whom are neither Soldiers nor Sailors. There is certainly a disposition in the present English Ministry to excite among the people of America some desire of a Separate peace." *Letters of Congress*, 6:447. See also note 77 above and various letters to Carleton in British Army Headquarters Papers, reel 15, nos. 5342, 5350, 5355, 5449, NYPL.

[80]*JCC*, 24:242–43; *Writings of Washington*, 25:340–41, 342–43, 345–48, 350–52, 370; Carleton to Washington, April 24, 1783, Washington Papers; *Report on American MSS*, 4:63, 70, 76–77, 80, 101, 103, 106, 107, 109, 131–32, 153, 154–55, 160, 167, 172–73, 186, 187, 189–90, 201, 222–23, 230.

[81]William B. Willcox, *Portrait of a General: Sir Henry Clinton in the War of Independence* (New York, 1962), 462; Howard H. Peckham, *The War for Independence* (Chicago, 1958), 188–89.

[82]James Madison wrote to Edmund Randolph on September 24, 1782: "The arrears to the army in January next will be upwards of six million dollars. Taxes cannot be relied on. Without money there is some reason to surmise that it may be as difficult to disband an army as it has been to raise an army." *Letters of Congress*, 6:492.

[83]Robert Morris to Richard Butler, July 18, 1782, Robert Morris Papers, NYPL. William C. Houston, receiver of continental taxes for New Jersey, wrote to Morris on June 21, 1783, "no money has come into the receipt since my last . . . . Such an inundation of Goods has poured into the Country from abroad and such a rage of buying has infected the People that not a Shilling can be obtained for the Publick. And the Effect of this Evil increases, because Cash goes out much faster than Trade replaces it." William C. Houston Collection, Princeton University

ELIZABETHTOWN 1782 / 33

507

Library, Princeton, New Jersey.

[84]Robert Morris to Comte de Grasse, May 16, 1782, U.S. Naval Academy Library, Annapolis, Maryland.

[85]See note 43 above. "France did not hold themselves obliged to pay any more Bills for Interest due on the Loan Office Certificates and that they would be protested if drawn. . . ." John Taylor Gilman to Josiah Bartlett, July 9, 1782, *Letters of Congress*, 6:380. See also Benjamin Huntington to Andrew Huntington, July 13, 1782, ibid., 6:382.

[86]Robert Morris, "State of American Commerce and Plan for Protecting It," May 10, 1782, U.S. Naval Academy Library. Gouverneur Morris to Thomas Willing, June 18, 1782, Gouverneur Morris Papers, Columbia University Library, New York City; Richard Buel, Jr., "Time: Friend or Foe of the Revolution?" Paper presented at U.S. Military Academy Symposium on the American Revolutionary War, April 23, 1976, 24. "British goods are issued from the Enemy's lines," James Madison wrote to Edmund Randolph on June 4, 1782, "with greater industry than they have ever been, and as is universally believed, with the knowledge, if not at the instigation of those in power." *Letters of Congress*, 6:368. "The trade with N. York," he wrote again on the 18th, "threatens a loss of all of our hard money. . . . I have little expectation that any adequate cure can be applied, whilst our foreign-trade is annihilated and the enemy in New York make it an object to keep open this illicit channel." Ibid., 6:373. Allowing the British to travel out of their lines with provisions for their prisoners contributed to the specie drain since it also led to illicit trade between American civilians and British commissaries of prisoners. *Report on American MSS*, 2:338, 408, 470, 475, 3:13, 51, 94, 127, 145, 359, 388, 402–3, 405, 415, 419.

[87]Buel, "Time," 25.

[88]Ibid., 26.

[89]Robert Morris, "State of American Commerce and Plan for Protecting It," May 10, 1782, U.S. Naval Academy Library.

[90]Gilman to the President of New Hampshire, June 19, 1782, *Letters of Congress*, 6:374. The Virginia Delegates in Congress wrote to their governor on June 25, 1782 that: "It is . . . discovered that supplies of British goods are imported under collusive captures concerted between Vessels from N. York and Vessels fitted out on the neighbouring coasts." Ibid., 6:375. Washington was apprised of the seriousness of the situation by Lt. Col. William Stephens Smith who wrote on February 24, 1783, that "the people of Connecticut are falling into their [the British] Plans, and I am sorry to say are supported by the Govr. and Executive of the State. . . ." Washington Papers. Washington responded on March 3 that he had little doubt "that the intercourse with New York by way of the Sound is in a manner without restriction" and that he knew that "the very Boats which are Armed and Commissioned for the purpose of cutting off the Communication, are employed in facilitating the Trade. . . ." *Writings of Washington*, 26:179.

[91]Washington to Knox and Morris, March 28 and 30, 1782, ibid., 24:89–91, 95–96.

[92]Knox and Morris to Washington, April 22, 1782, PCC, no. 169, 7:389–95.

[93]See note 23 above and *Letters of Congress*, 6:366, 455, 528, 533–34, 535–36, 540; *JCC*, 23:690–91, 715, 719–20, 845, 847; *Writings of Washington*, 24:146–47, 217–18, 319–20, 25:359; Wharton, ed., *Revolutionary Diplomatic Correspondence*, 5:635–37; Elias Boudinot, *Journal or Historical Recollections of American Events during the Revolutionary War* (Philadelphia, 1894), 60–61,; PCC, roll 200, item 194, 23–24; British Army Headquarters papers, reel 12, no. 4443.

[94]Knox and Morris to Washington, April 22, 1782, PCC, no. 169, 7:389–95.

[95]Ibid.,

[96]Ibid.

[97]Ibid. The Loyalists may have had reason to be apprehensive. In December 1782, according to historian Thomas Jones, the rebels took revenge on those Loyalists who had decided not to leave Charleston, South Carolina, with the evacuating British. He wrote that, "The Loyalists were seized, hove into dungeons, prisons and provosts. Some were tied up and whipped, others were tarred and feathered; some were dragged to horse-ponds and drenched till near dead, others were carried about the town in carts with labels upon their breasts and backs with the word 'Tory' in capitals written thereon. All the Loyalists were turned out of their houses and obliged to sleep in the streets and fields, their covering the canopy of heaven. A universal plunder of the friends of government took place and, to complete the scene, a gallows was erected upon the quay facing the harbour, and twenty-four reputable Loyalists hanged in sight of the British fleet, with the army and refugees on board." Catherine S. Crary, ed., *The Price of Loyalty: Tory Writings from the Revolutionary Era* (New York, 1973), 358–59.

[98]Washington to Knox and Morris, April 30, 1782, and to the President of Congress, April 30, 1782, *Writings of Washington*, 24:186–87, 190–91. For the discussion of the pardon in Congress, see *JCC*, 22:334–35, 378.

[99]*JCC*, 24:370–71; Crary, ed., *The Price of Loyalty*, 354–79.

ELIZABETHTOWN 1782 / 35

This cartoon, "Shelb—ns Sacrifice," presents loyalist reaction to the terms of the Treaty of Paris and to Shelburne, the British prime minister. Courtesy of the Library of Congress.

A Tory-eye View of the Evacuation of New York

By ROBERT ERNST

The vanquished British army could simply go home after the war. The vanquished loyalists already were home, but dare not stay. The final days of British rule were, for them, days of despair and desolation. Robert Ernst is Professor Emeritus of History at Adelphi University.

E VACUATION DAY "was held in grateful remembrance by the inhabitants of New York, and was, till a few years since, annually celebrated with fireworks and with military display." So wrote the historian John B. McMaster a century after the last remnant of British troops on the eastern seacoast had sailed down the Narrows on November 25, 1783.[1] But not every New Yorker shared this grateful remembrance; neither did the thousands of out-of-state refugees who had clustered in the port city during the British occupation. To those participants, the evacuation only mitigated the ungrateful betrayal of loyal subjects by their own government.

During the seven years since the British captured New York City, more and more loyalists had made their way, singly or in groups, to this haven of security. But safety did not mean comfort. The destruction of much of the town by fire in 1776 and 1778, the presence of thousands of soldiers and sailors, and the arrival of new refugees created an acute housing shortage. Buildings deserted by rebellious New Yorkers were soon occupied, and new houses were erected on vacant lots, but newcomers without money were lucky to find shelter in a

This essay was originally presented at a conference, "The End of the Revolution in New York State," sponsored by Sleepy Hollow Restorations and the Division of Historical and Anthropological Services of the State Education Department, in November 1983, at North Tarrytown.

1. *A History of the People of the United States from the Revolution to the Civil War* (8 vols.; New York, 1883–1913), 1:103.

New York History OCTOBER 1983

511

"canvas town" of nondescript shacks built onto the ruins in the burnt-out section.[2]

The first group of refugees arrived from Virginia in August 1776. Several thousand more came when Philadelphia was evacuated in June 1778, and by 1781 some 25,000 refugees from various colonies and from upstate counties were in New York City. After abandoning Savannah in July 1782 the British brought most of their officers and some civilians to New York. In January 1783 more tories arrived from Charleston.[3] As the war drew to a close, New York became the sole American haven for tory refugees.

For many of these loyalists life in the city was full of hardship. The authorities doled out inadequate rations and firewood until Sir Guy Carleton's board of refugee claims voted annuities of £20 to successful applicants. However, despite price-fixing, the black market was such that a pensioner could scarcely afford necessities.[4]

In contrast to the life-style of most refugees, some loyalists lived in comparative ease. Officers and their wives, successful merchants, owners of privateers, and well-connected individuals gave lavish dinners and attended fancy dances and theater parties. Shopkeepers, with well-stocked stores, managed to do good business, craftsmen found their skills in demand, and tavernkeepers catered to servicemen and free-spending officers.[5]

A year and a half before the final evacuation, anxious loyalists were still relying on George III to resist American independence. On November 27, 1781, six weeks after Cornwallis's defeat at Yorktown, the king had urged a vigorous prosecution of the war.[6] Loyalist spirits were bolstered by the news of Admiral Rodney's virtual destruction of a French fleet in the Caribbean.[7] Their fighting mood was captured by William

2. Thomas J. Wertenbaker, *Father Knickerbocker Rebels* (New York, 1948), pp. 213–14; Henry P. Johnston, "Evacuation of New York by the British," *Harper's Magazine* LXVII (June-November 1883), 912.

3. Alexander C. Flick, ed., *History of the State of New York* (10 vols.; New York, 1933–1937), III:346; Beverley Robinson to Sir Henry Clinton, August 8, 1782, Clinton Papers, William L. Clements Library, University of Michigan, Ann Arbor; Wertenbaker, *Father Knickerbocker Rebels*, p. 215.

4. Wertenbaker, *Father Knickerbocker Rebels*, p. 215. Carleton arrived at New York on May 9, 1782.

5. *Ibid.*, pp. 216–18.

6. In a speech to Parliament. *Royal Gazette*, February 13, 1782.

Smith in his diary on May 13, 1782: "I find hourly Evidences of the Reluctance of the High Tories as they are called to a generous Conciliation. . . . What this class of men hope for is a Triumph by the Sword."[8]

But then came the unexpected news that George III had acceded to American independence. Alarmed loyalists were enraged at the Ministry, and some were ready to defend themselves to the very end.[9] A meeting of tories at Roubalet's City Tavern unanimously approved addresses to the king and to Sir Guy Carleton and Admiral Robert Digby lamenting the proposed recognition of American independence and asking that the loyal inhabitants and refugees at New York "be enabled to seek refuge elsewhere."[10]

The most conspicuous loyalists sensed that their careers were at an end, that their personal fortunes would never be restored, and that their lives would be permanently disrupted. Beverley Robinson is a case in point. Born into a well-known Virginia family, he had married the wealthy Susanna Philipse and by the outbreak of the Revolution had become one of the richest property owners in the province of New York. In 1777 he had refused to take an oath of allegiance to the patriot cause and fled from his mansion opposite West Point to the safety of British-occupied New York City. He recruited volunteers, served as an officer of loyalist units, and was particularly effective as a director of British intelligence. In October 1779 the legislature of New York State attainted him—as also his wife and eldest son— banished him and confiscated his property.[11]

"Oh my dear Sir," Robinson wrote to Sir Henry Clinton, "what dreadful and distressing Tidings . . . —the Independence of America given up by the King without any condition whatsoever, the Loyalist[s] of America to depend on the mercey of their Enemies for the restoration of their possessions, which we are well assured they will never grant, the Greatest part of the

---

7. *Ibid.*, May 29, 1782.

8. William Smith Diary, VII, New York Public Library. See *Royal Gazette*, June 1, 1782, for an address of "loyal refugees" to Sir Guy Carleton.

9. Ewald Gustav Schaukirk, *Occupation of New York City by the British* (New York, 1969), p. 25, entry of August 4, 1782.

10. K. G. Davies, ed., *Documents of the American Revolution* (21 vols.; Shannon and Dublin, 1972–1981), XIX, 318; *Royal Gazette*, August 10, 1782.

11. *Dictionary of American Biography*, XVI:34; Mark M. Boatner III, *Encyclopedia of the American Revolution* (New York, c.1966), pp. 937–38.

Beverley Robinson. From Harper's New Monthly Magazine, *September 1851.*

Estates that have been confiscated by them are already sold."[12]

Early in 1782, months before the despairing Robinson embarked for England, groups of loyalists had been leaving New York. Sailing vessels advertised for emigrants while owners offered houses and stores for sale. "Genteel furniture," china and glassware were available at huge discounts.[13] The tory sense of total abandonment is well expressed in a loyalist lament to a friend in England: "the door is shut against their return, and they have no hopes from Britain, where men, they think, are more inclined to their enemies than to them. The panic that we had on the first news occasioned alarming desertions in some of the provincial corps, but it is getting over, as those who deserted did not find the reception they expected. ... an evacuation of New York is expected, and many are preparing accordingly."[14]

Although by mid-October 1782 prominent and active tories engaged passage for England, they were by no means the

12. Beverley Robinson to Sir Henry Clinton, August 8, 1782, Clinton Papers.

13. Claude H. Van Tyne, *The Loyalists in the American Revolution* (c.1902; repr. Gloucester, Mass., 1959), p. 289.

14. Extract from a letter from a "Gentleman of Character in New York," October 2, 1782, in *London Chronicle*, November 16–19, 1782.

earliest to leave the city. A few had departed early in the war, and some of the poorer ones got permission to sail in government transports.[15] Others, doubtless discouraged by the Franco-American alliance of 1778 and the appearance of a French fleet in American waters, headed for England with the British fleet in October 1778. More embarked with another fleet in December 1779, and after Yorktown, some New Yorkers accompanied Cornwallis on his return home.[16] These early departures, however, were insignificant when compared with the exodus of 1782–83.

The Crown offered asylum in Canada. As early as 1777 General Howe had promised land there to 200 officers and 50 privates in the provincial corps at the end of the war, and early in 1782 civilian loyalists were allotted land—500 acres to heads of families and 300 to single men. By September many were preparing to leave, and the first convoy of loyalists sailed for Halifax on October 6 with 460 persons. Most were farmers who had petitioned for permission to settle in Nova Scotia. They were given an allowance of twenty-one days' rations for their passage,

15. John Watts and Roger Morris, members of the provincial council, sailed from New York on May 4, 1775. See *Letterbook of John Watts of New York* (New York, 1928), p. xiv; Wilbur H. Siebert, *The Flight of the American Loyalists to the British Isles* (Columbus, Ohio, 1911), p. 14.

16. Siebert, *Flight of American Loyalists*, p. 208; *Journal of Lieutenant John Charles Philip von Krafft*, New-York Historical Society *Collections* XV (1882), 155.

Robinson's house, opposite West Point, was confiscated at the end of the Revolution. From Magazine of American History, *February 1880.*

515

provisions for one year, clothing, medicine, land grants, farming tools, and arms and ammunition for hunting and defense. Those who were receiving monetary allowances also obtained a full year's pay in advance.[17]

By 1783 anxiety increased among the tories in New York. A sympathetic observer commented, "It is surprising what England gives up; it is shameful how the Loyalists are abandoned! To the hundreds who proposed to go to Nova Scotia, there is also a stoppage, for they hear that they can get no more than six months provisions, (those who went in the Fall received twelve months.) Proceedings at home give but little encouragement to put any trust in such a government!"[18]

The royal proclamation of February 14, 1783 declaring the cessation of hostilities was read to a large assemblage at the city hall on April 8. According to one account, it was greeted with "groans and hisses . . . attended by bitter reproaches and curses upon their king, for having deserted them in the midst of their calamities. The greatest despair is depicted in every countenance."[19] Some who had served in loyalist militia units tore the lapels from their coats and trampled upon them, wailing that they were ruined; others complained that they had to shift for themselves without hope from king or country.[20] As a wealthy New Yorker concluded, "the Loyalists, for the present, must bow under the yoke—there is no prospect of deliverance." Another observer alleged that, in their hopeless situation many tories went mad and, in his words, "some have put a period to their miserable existence by drowning, shooting, and hanging themselves."[21]

It was not merely the sense of betrayal and abandonment by the British government that dismayed and angered the tories, but also the manifest antagonism of those they continued to call rebels. "All accounts from the country bespeak the utmost violence," wrote one New Yorker in April. "Threats are thrown out, and vengeance denounced against all here. The town now swarms with Americans, whose insolence is scarce to be

17. Oscar T. Barck, *New York City During the War for Independence* (New York, 1931), p. 209, citing Extracts from Lord Dorchester Papers; *Royal Gazette*, October 19, 1782.

18. Schaukirk, *Occupation of New York City*, pp. 27–28, entry for March 22, 1783.

19. *Pennsylvania Packet*, April 17, 1783.

20. James Riker, *"Evacuation Day," 1783* (New York, 1883), p. 4.

21. April 6 and 13, 1783, in *London Chronicle*, June 5–7, 7–10, 1783.

516

borne." If the British troops were too hastily withdrawn, he predicted, there would be an indescribable "scene of confusion and distress."[22] A contrary view was expressed by a patriot who declared that the delayed departure of the British "only served to encrease the spirit and resentment of the people against the loyalists, which, instead of subsiding, seems every day to rise and be more determined against their re-admission among us." Some, unwilling to risk the consequences, decided to emigrate, "which indeed [as he put it] is the most prudent step they can take."[23]

Fear of reprisals may well have been heightened by a letter, signed "An American," which appeared in at least two newspapers (and perhaps more), asserting that during the war 1,644 American prisoners had died from "inhumane, cruel, savage and barbarous usage" on the British prison ship *Jersey* anchored at New York. "Britons, tremble," the writer warned, "lest the vengeance of Heaven fall on your Isle, for the blood of these unfortunate victims!"[24] If the number of deaths was wildly inflated, the vindictive tone of the letter was symptomatic.

General Carleton was keenly aware of the anti-tory fury of the revolutionaries, whom he described as "greatly elated and intoxicated by the peace" and without even the appearance of desiring a reconciliation with their antagonists. They were actively organizing to prevent loyalist property from being restored and even to stop loyalists from returning. "Almost all of those who have attempted to return to their homes," Carleton wrote in May, "have been exceedingly ill treated, many beaten, robbed of their money and clothing, and sent back." Ten days later he observed that "the violent and interested associations for the exclusion of the loyalists are daily extending and with circumstances of additional rage. It would be endless to transmit the resolves and publications of the different meetings."[25]

Tories responded with contempt or with their own insults and threats. Unconciliatory and disdainful of American conduct,

22. April 13, 1783, in *London Chronicle*, May 17–20, 1783.

23. *Pennsylvania Packet*, July 22, 1782.

24. *Connecticut Gazette* (New London), April 25, 1783; *Pennsylvania Packet*, April 29, 1783.

25. Carleton to Thomas Townshend (No. 76), May 27, 1783, Carleton to Lord North (No. 82), June 6, 1783, British Headquarters Papers, Public Record Office, photostat in New York Public Library.

one tory declared: "This country is all confusion[;] the very Government Said to be established is tottering[,] Committees forming in every state and declarations and Resolves from those Committees & that no restoration shall be made. The present Government will comply with what the Giddy multitude please to dictate[;] in short all at present Anarchy and confusion. ... "[26] On August 8, 1783 William Bayard was still referring to "the wicked Infamous, and unprovoked Rebellion" and to the rebels—"for I shall never call them anything else."[27] Mayor David Mathews was said to have treated very roughly an American officer who complained of misconduct and who, on leaving the city, barely escaped a barrage of stones. An overwrought tory who allegedly had spent years burning patriot grist mills and meeting houses now walked the streets with a pointed cane, talking only of rebels and sedition.[28] In New York harbor a mob boarded a ship flying the United States flag, tore it down and carried it through the streets, accompanied, it was snidely remarked, "by a chosen band of band-itti of negroes, sailors and loyal leather apron'd statesmen."[29] General Carleton and Admiral Digby promptly denounced this breach of the peace as having a "mischievous tendency to prolong the Animosities."[30]

During the spring and summer, as irrevocable decisions were reached, throngs of royalists made hurried preparations to leave. In view of the scarcity of shipping, they sold their household goods for what they would bring. Whatever was portable was offered for sale, and auctions were commonplace. In some instances furniture was repainted or otherwise disguised in fraudulent sales so that true owners could never reclaim it. Until the authorities prohibited demolition of houses without proper proof of ownership, even buildings were dismantled for saleable brick or lumber. Plunder and pilferage were widespread.[31]

26. Stephen Skinner to Effingham Lawrence, June 11, 1783. MS. Letterbook of Stephen Skinner, New-York Historical Society. Skinner noted that New York City was crowded with refugees who were well treated but if a loyalist made his appearance elsewhere he was certain to be insulted.

27. Bayard to General Frederick Haldimand, August 8, 1783, quoted in Johnston, "Evacuation of New York," p. 913.

28. *Pennsylvania Packet*, September 18, 1783.

29. *Manual of the Common Council of the Corporation of New York*, 1870, p. 817. The incident occurred on October 20, 1783.

30. October 27, 1783, British Headquarters Papers, photostat, New York Public Library. The proclamation was drafted by William Smith. Smith, Diary, VII, October 28, 1783.

Many of the tories attainted of treason by the New York legislature were creditors to whom considerable amounts were due upon bonds, mortgages and other contracts. Since the police courts had no jurisdiction over debts contracted before May 1777, these loyalists applied to Carleton for relief. Sir Guy appointed a commission to examine their claims and adjust or settle debts of at least £10 incurred by the city's residents. Thomas Jones, though sympathetic to Carleton, considered the commission "idle, frivolous, and inefficacious" because it had no power to compel payment of debt. Since the commission had no power to consider debts contracted before November 1, 1776, those who had loaned money before that date begged Carleton to require payment, but in vain.[32]

Sir Guy has been justly praised for his evenhandedness and humanity in dealing with the loyalists. He was concerned that houses and other property be restored to their rightful owners, and he deliberately cultivated loyalist friendship.[33] On April 15, 1783 he gave orders to carry out the terms of the provisional peace treaty and announced that a board of three British officers and two Americans had been appointed to supervise all embarkations. The board was instructed to look into the validity of claims to property being loaded onto vessels, and to prevent evasion the transports themselves were to be inspected before leaving port. Nobody was to embark as a refugee who had not lived for twelve months within the British lines unless he had a special passport from the commandant. As a sort of afterthought, Carleton ordered that the refugees "take Care [that] no Person of bad Character is suffered to embark with them."[34]

Carleton's decision to hold on to New York City until the tories were evacuated reflected a shrewd policy of gaining time for the promotion of settlements elsewhere in the Empire, particularly the uninviting and sparsely populated Nova Scotia. Fundamentally, however, Sir Guy acted out of a sense of responsibility for a just and humane treatment of the loyalists. As late

31. *Pennsylvania Packet*, September 18, 1783; Riker, "*Evacuation Day*," p. 7; Barck, *New York City During the War*, p. 214; Schaukirk, *Occupation of New York City*, p. 28, August 25, 1783.

32. Thomas Jones, *History of New York During the Revolutionary War*, E. F. DeLancey, ed. (2 vols.; New York, 1879), II, 264–67.

33. Smith, Diary, VII, February 15, 1783. On several occasions Smith mentions loyalist dejection, anxiety, and despair. See entries of February 13, 20, 25, and April 20, 1783.

34. *New-York Gazette and Weekly Mercury*, April 21, 1783.

as August 1783 he was unwilling to set a date for completion of the evacuation of New York. "The violence in the Americans which broke out soon after the cessation of hostilities," he wrote to the President of Congress, "encreased the number of their Countrymen who looked to me for escape from threat[e]ned destruction, but these terrors have of late been so considerably augmented that almost all within these lines conceive the safety, both of their property and of their lives, depend upon their being removed by me." If loyalist fears continued unabated, and refugees continued to pour into the city, he asserted, "I shall hold myself acquitted from every delay in the fulfilling my orders. . . . "[35]

Sir Guy's policy on evacuating Negroes was similarly motivated, as he claimed, by a sense of responsibility for them, but he may also have believed, as Benjamin Quarles observes, that if Great Britain reneged on its wartime promises to them of freedom, similar promises in future wars would not be trusted.[36] He ordered that no slaves be carried off but carefully excluded those blacks who had become free before his arrival at New York. As he wrote, "I had no right to deprive them of that liberty I found them possessed of," so he had a record made of each such individual's history, including the name of the original owner, should there be a claim for compensation. By this means he hoped to prevent fraud and to provide data in case of future controversy. "Had these Negroes been denied permission to embark," he explained, "they would in spite of every means to prevent it have found various methods of quitting this place, so that the former owner would no longer have been able to trace them and of course would have lost in every way all chance of compensation."[37]

Since the preliminary articles of peace included an agreement that the British forces should not carry away any Negroes or other American property, Congress instructed General Washington to arrange for their transfer into American hands. Accordingly, at Washington's invitation, Carleton conferred with

---

35. Carleton to Elias Boudinot, August 17, 1783, British Headquarters Papers, photostat, New York Public Library. William Smith drafted Carleton's letter. Smith, Diary, VII, September 13, 1783.

36. Benjamin Quarles, *The Negro in the American Revolution* (Chapel Hill, 1961), p. 171.

37. Carleton to Governor John Parr of Nova Scotia, April 26, 1783, in Davies, ed., *Documents*, XXI, 166. See also Smith, Diary, VII, May 9, 1783.

Sir Guy Carleton. Engraving by A. H. Ritchie. Courtesy of the Public Archives of Canada.

him on May 6, 1783. The British commander remarked that among the 6,000 civilians already evacuated were some Negroes. When Washington protested that this violated the provisional treaty, Sir Guy defended his policy of registering blacks. If their transportation was later declared to be an infraction of the treaty, he remarked, the owners would be compensated by the Crown. When Washington declared that the real value of a slave depended upon his industry and sobriety and could not be ascertained from a mere register, Carleton responded that if no record of blacks were kept, their former owners would inevitably lose them. At least the registry kept open the possibility of compensation.[38]

To say that Sir Guy sought to promote emancipation would,

38. For a good treatment see Quarles. *The Negro in the American Revolution*, pp. 167–72.

521

of course, be absurd. Many blacks were transported regardless of their wishes, particularly if they were the property of departing loyalists. For example, at least two blacks sailed with several prominent tory families on the *Christiana* in November. Indeed, hundreds of unregistered Negroes managed to embark on private vessels. Nor were all blacks within the British lines evacuated. A few were reclaimed by Washington's commissioners. Sick, aged and helpless Negroes were deliberately stranded in New York by departing loyalists.[39]

The mass exodus of loyalists began on April 27, when 7,000 civilians and troops, including 660 blacks, sailed in a large fleet for Nova Scotia. How long the evacuation process would take could not then be predicted because nobody knew how many loyalists would take passage or how much shipping would be available.[40] In mid-June, 3,000 persons, including at least 130 blacks, embarked on fourteen transports bound for Nova Scotia. The next day Carleton encouraged other loyalists to settle on the island of Abaco in the Bahamas, and he had earlier countenanced a group planning a fur trading community at Fort Frontenac at the head of the St. Lawrence River in Canada. Prominent or wealthy individuals obtained passage for England, but the vast majority of emigrants went to Nova Scotia. Port Roseway, later known as Shelburne, was founded by several thousand of them in the summer of 1783.[41]

The exodus was already in full swing when Carleton received final orders for the evacuation of New York. Because shipping was not immediately available, it was not until four months later that the evacuation was completed.[42] In the middle of August,

39. Diary of Samuel Shoemaker of Philadelphia, pp. 4–5, typed copy in the New-York Historical Society of the original ms. in the Historical Society of Pennsylvania; Quarles suggests that perhaps 4,000 Negroes departed from the city during the evacuation. These were in addition to the 3,000 whose names were on the register of blacks by November 30 at the end of the evacuation *The Negro in the American Revolution*, pp. 171–72. Harry P. Yoshpe, *The Disposition of Loyalist Estates in the Southern District of the State of New York* (New York, 1939), p. 91.

40. Carleton to Governor John Parr, April 26, 1783, in Davies, ed., *Documents*, XXI, 165. For blacks see Ellen G. Wilson, *The Loyal Blacks* (New York, c. 1976). p. 53.

41. Correspondence published in *Daily Advertiser*, January 1794, quoted in I.N.P. Stokes, *Iconography of Manhattan Island, 1498–1928* (6 vols.; New York, 1915–1928), V, 1163–64; *New-York Gazette and Weekly Mercury*, June 16, 1783; *Pennsylvania Packet*, July 1, 1783; Notice to Loyalists, May 26, 1783, *Manual of the Common Council*, p. 788. A thousand are said to have emigrated to the Bahamas. Barck, *New York City During the War*, p. 213; Siebert, *Flight of American Loyalists*, pp. 17–18.

all potential emigrants were required to report their names to the adjutant general and be ready to embark before the end of the month. This caused general distress among the already frantic tories.[43]

Some who intended to settle in Nova Scotia were angered by a rumor that British land policy discriminated in favor of the rich. More than 600 irate tories, meeting at Roubalet's tavern, protested against the best lands being granted to fifty-five individuals who had applied for 275,000 acres and sent agents to survey the land and choose the most fertile and desirable locations. These fifty-five were said to be mostly "in easy circumstances, and with some exceptions, more distinguished by the repeated favours of government, than by either the greatness of their sufferings, or the importance of their services."[44].

Greed was not rewarded. Carleton responded to the petitioners that proposed grants of 5,000 acres to a single individual would not be permitted. Although Governor Parr offered thousand-acre tracts to the "fifty five," their agents refused to consider the reduction, and so the proposed land grant was denied. As Oscar Barck points out, this case and others like it showed that some tories sought advantages not available to others.[45]

The prospect of resettling in Nova Scotia evoked varying emotions. "Some look smiling, others melancholy, a third class mad," wrote a contemporary. "Some there are who represent the cold regions of Nova-Scotia as a new-created Paradise, others as a country unfit for any human being to inhabit."[46] Many tories could not make up their minds to leave. As William Smith expressed it, "the flight of the loyalists is also painful, not only to the wiser Sort, who see the evils of it in General Policy, but to private Friendship, and what is more to private Interests. Partners in Trade—Fellow commoners in Lands—Debtors—Ex[ecuto]rs and Adm[inistrato]rs &c &c to go away to the confusion of all that have Settlements to be made with them."[47]

---

42. July 21 was the date designated by Britain for the evacuation. That same day the definitive peace treaty reached New York.

43. *Royal Gazette*, August 16, 1783; Smith, Diary, VII, August 18, 1783.

44. *Royal Gazette*, August 9, 16, 1783; *New-York Gazette and Weekly Mercury*, August 25, 1783; *Manual of the Common Council* (1870), pp. 806–07.

45. Barck, *New York City During the War*, pp. 213–14.

46. *Pennsylvania Packet*, September 23, 1783.

47. Diary, VII, September 13, 1783.

Because so many procrastinated, the British officials ordered persons bound for Nova Scotia to embark by 3 PM, September 20, or the government would not pay their passage.[48]

Beginning on September 15, a large fleet transported 8,000 people from New York to Port Roseway, where there was great congestion. Despite government assistance, they had neither adequate shelter nor sufficient arable farmland. Timber and fish were abundant, but felling trees and fishing were not attractive to merchants and military men. Discouragement produced a new exodus before 1785 and by the winter of 1787, when the government ended food distributions, people were streaming out of Port Roseway to other parts of the Empire.[49]

By the end of October 1783, after most of the loyalists had left New York, Carleton reported that he only awaited the return of the transports so that the remaining persons and equipment could be evacuated.[50] The former customs collector, Andrew Elliot, who had become the Acting Governor of British New York on April 17, wound up his official duties.

As Elliot wrote to Lord North, the city was a scene of hurry, gloom and distress. The acting governor was troubled by the continuing hostility to tories, specifically a New York State law permitting New Yorkers to sue tory occupants of their houses and lands, offers of depreciated military certificates in exchange

48. *Royal Gazette*, September 20, 1783; Barck, *New York City During the War*, p. 214.

49. *Royal Gazette*, September 17, 1783; Siebert, *Flight of American Loyalists*, p. 18.

50. Carleton to Lord North, October 26, 1783, British Headquarters Papers, photostat, New York Public Library.

Loyalists encamped at Johnston (Cornwall) on the St. Lawrence in 1784. Watercolor by James Peachey. Courtesy of the Public Archives of Canada.

for loyalists' property, and organized attempts to oust all loyalists from the United States.[51]

Months before the evacuation was completed, New York had begun to lose its tory complexion. Houses which had been occupied by British officers, commissaries, army doctors, or soldiers' families, or used as warehouses or hospitals were restored gradually to their owners. New Yorkers who had fled in 1776 filtered back into the city. Shipping was reopened on the Hudson, and trade resumed with the other American states.

As the evacuation neared its end, Carleton arranged for the British withdrawal from the city. He notified Washington on November 19 that on the twenty-first his forces would retire from Kingsbridge, McGowan's Pass (at what is now the northeast corner of Central Park), Hempstead and all of eastern Long Island, and that he expected to withdraw from Brooklyn and New York City at noon on the twenty-fifth, or "as soon after as wind and weather" allowed.[52] Before that date Governor George Clinton and General Washington met at Tarrytown and rode south through Yonkers and Harlem to just beyond the "barrier," a fortified line across Manhattan.

At eight o'clock on the cold, clear morning of November 25, American troops at McGowan's Pass marched to the barrier, on the Bowery, near Grand Street. There, sitting on the grass, they waited for the British to withdraw. At one o'clock the British troops began their march down the Bowery, along Chatham and Queen streets toward the East River wharves, whence they were rowed to the fleet in the harbor. As crowds gathered, American troops started down the Bowery on the heels of the redcoats but turned to march from Queen Street (now Pearl) west along Wall to Broadway, halting opposite Cape's Tavern. An infantry and artillery detail then moved down Broadway to raise the American flag at Fort George.[53]

Flying over the fort was the royal ensign, nailed to the flagstaff. The halyards had been cut away, the cleats removed, and the pole itself greased. A sailor tried three times to scale the

51. Elliot to Lord North, November 18, 1783, calendered in Davies, *Documents*, XIX, 449; Robert Ernst, "Andrew Elliot, Forgotten Loyalist of Occupied New York," *New York History* LVII (July 1976), 316–17.

52. Wertenbaker, *Father Knickerbocker Rebels*, pp. 266–67; *Manual of the Common Council* (1870), pp. 822–23.

53. Wertenbaker, *Father Knickerbocker Rebels*, p. 268; *Pennsylvania Packet*, December 2, 1783; Johnston, "Evacuation of New York," pp. 918–19.

In this 1883 illustration, a well-groomed John Van Arsdale prepares to unfurl the American flag at Fort George in New York City, November 25, 1783. From Frank Leslie's Illustrated Newspaper, *November 24, 1883.*

flagstaff but failed; on his fourth attempt he succeeded with the help of a ladder and cleats newly nailed onto the pole. The British banner was torn off and, with new halyards, the Stars and Stripes were raised to the cheers of a huge crowd of bystanders and the firing of guns.[54]

General Carleton was unaware of the mischief at the flagpole. His last despatch, written on November 28 aboard the H.M.S. *Ceres*, went as follows: "His Majesty's Troops, and such of the Loyalists as chose to emigrate, were, on the 25th Inst., withdrawn from the City of New York in good order, and embarked

---

54. *Pennsylvania Packet,* December 2, 1783; Wertenbaker, *Father Knickerbocker Rebels,* p. 268; Riker, *"Evacuation Day,"* pp. 15–16; Johnston, "Evacuation of New York," p. 920, citing letter of an eyewitness, Captain Van Dyke, published in *Manual of the Common Council* (1870).

without the smallest circumstance of irregularity or misbehaviour of any kind."[55]

The British lingered for several days as their ships made ready to leave the harbor, Carleton's and Admiral Digby's being among the last to depart. Weighing anchor on December 4, the *Ceres* and the frigate *Cyclops* carried to England numerous "gentlemen tories"; Admiral Digby followed on the fifth.[56] Thus ended the evacuation of New York.

It would be a mistake to assume that no tories remained in New York City when it was handed over to the Americans. Whether for reasons of family ties, business connections or simple expediency, an indeterminate number decided to stay.[57] They were neither happy nor hopeful. When James DeLancey departed from West Farms in April 1783, an old friend who remained behind told him: "I am now a poor man with a large family to provide for. My cattle have all been stolen, my negroes have run away, my fences are burnt up, and my house and barns in ruin. Of all my property nothing now remains but naked fields. I don't know *how* I shall get along."[58]

Altogether more than 29,000 loyalists sailed from New York in 1783, and more than 28,000 of these went to Canada, New Brunswick and Nova Scotia. Possibly 11,000 had departed before 1783, and of these probably 6,000 went to the British Isles and the rest to Canada. Possibly a total of 40,000 left New York State during and after the Revolution, four-fifths of them civilians and the majority New Yorkers.[59]

Disillusioned, disappointed, and dismayed in varying de-

---

55. Carleton to Lord North, November 28, 1783 in Johnston, "Evacuation of New York," p. 923.

56. Siebert, *Flight of American Loyalists*, p. 17; Johnston, "Evacuation of New York," pp. 922–23.

57. The population of the city immediately after the final evacuation has been estimated at about 15,000. There is no way of knowing how many of the inhabitants were tories. Johnston, "Evacuation of New York," p. 913. An order of the Sons of Liberty that all loyalists leave the city by May 1, 1784 proved impossible to enforce. Flick, *History of the State of New York*, III, 356–57.

58. Quoted in Catherine S. Crary, ed., *The Price of Glory: Tory Writings from the Revolutionary Era* (New York, 1973), p. 395.

59. The MS. report of Brook Watson, British Commissary General at New York, November 24, 1783, gives 29,244 as the total number of men, women and children who departed. 28,347 settled in Canada, chiefly around St. John in New Brunswick and Shelburne (the former Port Roseway) in Nova Scotia. Of these, 12,383 were men, 5,486 women, 9,246 children, and 1,232 servants. Johnston, "Evacuation of New York," p. 913; Barck, *New York City During the War*, 216n.

527

grees, the tories who abandoned New York City made the best of their bad situation. They effected their own personal safety, though at considerable psychological cost. Some hoped for at least partial compensation for financial and property losses, although Britain eventually reimbursed only a fortunate few for a fraction of their claims.

The evacuation of New York was complicated and prolonged, but as such, it was successful. It was carried out as humanely as possible under the circumstances. With respect to the fulfillment of obligation to those who had loyally served the Crown in moving them to Nova Scotia, to the sheer number of evacuees, and to the magnitude and the safety of the operation itself, probably no other evacuation of civilians has ever quite matched the evacuation of New York in 1783.